THE

ERIK
ERIKSON

READER

By Erik H. Erikson

Childhood and Society (1950, 1963)

Young Man Luther (1958)

Insight and Responsibility (1964)

Identity: Youth and Crisis (1968)

Gandhi's Truth (1969)

Dimensions of a New Identity (1974)

Life History and the Historical Moment (1975)

Toys and Reasons (1977)

Identity and the Life Cycle (1959, 1980)

The Life Cycle Completed (1982)

Vital Involvement in Old Age (with Joan M. Erikson and Helen Q. Kivnick) (1986)

A Way of Looking at Things: Selected Papers from 1930 to 1980 (edited by Stephen Schlein, Ph.D.) (1987)

Edited by Erik H. Erikson

Adulthood (1978)

THE

ERIK

ERIKSON

READER

Selected and Edited by Robert Coles

W. W. NORTON & COMPANY

NEW YORK   LONDON

For information about permission to reproduce selections from this book, write
to Permissions, W. W. Norton & Company, Inc., 500 Fifth Avenue, New York,
NY 10110

The text of this book is composed in Bembo
with the display set in Trajan
Composition by Allentown Digital Services Division
of R. R. Donnelley & Sons Company
Manufacturing by The Haddon Craftsmen, Inc.
Book design by Chris Welch

Library of Congress Cataloging-in-Publication Data
Erikson, Erik H. (Erik Homburger), 1902–
[Selections. 2000]
The Erik Erikson reader / selected and edited by Robert Coles.
p.   cm.
Includes bibliographical references and index.
ISBN 0-393-04845-4
1. Psychoanalysis.   2. Erikson, Erik H. (Erik Homburger), 1902–
I. Coles, Robert.   II. Title.
BF173.E652   2000
150.19'5—dc21   99-41168
CIP

W. W. Norton & Company, Inc., 500 Fifth Avenue, New York, N.Y. 10110
www.wwnorton.com

W. W. Norton & Company Ltd., 10 Coptic Street, London WC1A 1PU

1   2   3   4   5   6   7   8   9   0

Gratefully remembering Erik and Joan

CONTENTS

THE

ERIK
ERIKSON

READER

INTRODUCTION

Well over a century before a reader like this could even be imagined in America, an obscure neurologist and psychiatrist was doing his best to understand how the mind works, and with what clinical consequences. That physician, Sigmund Freud, dared learn from his patients, and indeed, from himself, in a most unusual way—he attended carefully the dreams he heard described in his office, and he paid a lot of attention to his own dreams, to his mind's action during the night, to the events and incidents he woke up remembering, the stories that had unfolded while he lay sleeping, and that now, upon occasion, held fast to his memory—as if he had actually been someplace, met certain individuals, and so doing, experienced pleasure or apprehension or outright fear.

To be sure, Freud was hardly the first of history's writers to understand the importance of dreams, the revelations they offer us when light summons us from rest, and an enlightenment of sorts thereupon persists, so that what we have dreamed gives us later pause as we go about our day's activities. Shakespeare, of course, realized how much our dreams tell and signal, and before him, the Greek playwright of an older civilization. But Freud was a physician rather than a playwright; he was a psychiatrist in

his forties during the late 1890s when he was taking dreams seriously, trying to let them be, collectively, his teacher, and writing about the lessons
he had learned, which became available for others at the very onset of this
twentieth century when, in 1900, *The Interpretation of Dreams* was published. By no means did that book, for all its knowing brilliance, for all
the light it cast on our awareness of ourselves as its readers, meet with the
quick and widespread approval of Freud's Viennese colleagues. In a sense,
this most ambitious and searching and far-reaching of his efforts, a volume now considered a landmark in this century's cultural and intellectual life, stirred for years suspicion and disdain among those who mattered
in Vienna's educational world. As a matter of fact, that book's appearance
cost its author, for a while, the approval he wanted, and nudged him toward an outsider's situation. He craved what we call "tenure," a profes-
sorship that indicated academic acceptance, and instead he was dismissed,
even reviled, by many of his fellow doctors, and others, as he continued
his research, wrote it up, during the early years of this century—though,
as with rejection and notoriety in other lives, there were favoring moments: the one whom many denounce becomes known by others as a
person who dared speak his mind, speak the unspeakable, hence someone to be taken seriously, even sought out, approached through his
printed words, or on the occasion of any lecture he gives, and even in
person for a conversation, an exchange of ideas.

So it was that Dr. Freud gradually became well known to some, a
doctor and a writer to be read, heard, watched in the capital city of the
Austrian-Hungarian empire or, later, in the much smaller nation of Austria that emerged from the ruins of the Second World War—hardly countries rife with progressive thinking. Nevertheless, the writer of a book
that relentlessly and insistently explored the meaning of dreams, their
overall significance in our waking hours, no matter their fleeting occurrence at sleep time, now persisted in pursuing the leads that dreams had
provided. Freud had himself become a kind of dreamer, a psychological
visionary who was undeterred by the critical opposition that came his
way and was, rather, firmly set on his investigative and narrative projects.
He had discovered a lot, had figured out how to convey through words
his observations, thoughts, to others—and not least, he had decided to
persuade others not merely through his books, but also through a persuasive connection to them. The institutional life of psychoanalysis (the
Vienna Psychoanalytic Society) thereby became a further destiny for his

body of ideas: now they informed meetings, discussions, the manner through which membership in an organization was granted.

Of Freud's children, his youngest, Anna (born in 1895, just as he was developing his views on dreams, on the unconscious as a harbinger of their expression), was the only one to follow her father's steps and become a psychoanalyst. She witnessed firsthand those first decades of a profession's emergence—the years in which her father risked professional isolation and the scorn of various others, including those in universities and churches. And she saw how he methodically, tenaciously built a world around him, with patients and students and colleagues informally gathered, some from nearby, but more and more, as word of his work spread, some from afar. In 1972, herself a figure, the world over, of great distinction and accomplishment (she had carried her father's comprehension of grown-up life to that of the young, and so founded the discipline of child psychoanalysis), she knew there was much to remember, and not much time left for her own stated witness to go fully on the record. Though she had, now and then, been quite willing to speak in public about what had transpired as she saw it, she now offered me the following cautionary advice, even remonstrance during an interview with her: "It is always hard to go back in time: we know that in our work with patients (they have to fight to remember!), but we often forget what happened in earlier times, in history; we know some of the facts, but we can't appreciate what it was like 'back then,' because we weren't there, and so we have no way of knowing what it meant for my father to try to get his ideas across, and win people to them—and for those he convinced, or persuaded, what it meant for them to be associated with him.

"Today, he is known as 'a great man,'—to many, I should be careful to add, and many others would disagree [with that designation]—but he was not highly esteemed from the start [of his career]. Even after he'd written one book after another, offered all his conclusions to his friends and associates in Vienna, or his more distant friends elsewhere (how does the expression go, 'interested parties'?), he was still struggling hard, on behalf of his ideas. And in order to be 'respectable' then, and be sure you were going to make an adequate living (a 'good living,' to switch into a moral vein!) and be sure of your future (in a school or in a hospital) you had to think twice before coming to Dr. Freud and his colleagues in Vienna— for sure!"

She stopped, smiled wanly, mused about the shifts history makes, the ironies it provides—even as she emphasized the difference between now (psychoanalysis as an accepted, even celebrated body of knowledge) and back then (her father as an intellectual and psychiatric pioneer, whose formulations opened door after door of consideration, speculation). Suddenly she stiffened in her body, in her manner of speech: "It is hard to talk at this time about a time long ago. But if you want to know about those of us who worked in the first days of psychoanalysis [I had asked as much in a letter to her], then I can refer you to my written statements [she thereupon mentioned them, giving special attention to her essay 'Difficulties in the Way of Psychoanalysis,' an address she gave to the New York Psychoanalytic Institute in the late 1960s], but I'd rather speak offhand."

In no time she was allowing her preference full sway—and soon I was hearing about August Aichhorn, whose *Wayward Youth* she had always admired, and about Helen Ross, who had come to Vienna from the American Midwest and whose brother Charlie became President Truman's press secretary—and, too, about the person whose writing this book means to enable readers to ponder, Erik Erikson. In fact, I well knew, Erikson had once been an analysand of Anna Freud's. I knew, too, that because of what Anna and her father were trying to do in Vienna during the 1920s, when young Erik Homburger (Homburger was his stepfather's name) arrived, his life would most decidedly and dramatically change—he would find his future occupation, and he would find a love that culminated in marriage. It was a privilege, an eye-opening visit for me, to hear Anna Freud talk about a fellow child psychoanalyst of hers who had once been her analysand. Erikson had been her student in the courses she gave at the Vienna Psychoanalytic Institute—and by then (the early 1970s) this distinguished, even renowned writer and teacher, whose books had greatly influenced thousands of Americans, had become a professor at Harvard University, where (I well knew) the students took to him with great enthusiasm. (And we should keep in mind that his writing forged unprecedented insights into growing up in America, even if he came here when he was just over thirty, and not as a fluently speaking visitor.)

Yet again, though, Miss Freud was worried about perspective—mine, of course, and maybe that of others: "I know that here in the States [she spoke as the Englishwoman she had become] you all know Erik Erikson (how do you say it—he has become a 'household name'!). I'm not sure that many realize how his life became what it is, and that's his main interest (isn't it!): 'identity,' how we become the individuals, the men or women we know ourselves to be, and others recognize—well, as *us*. I remember him as a man in his twenties. He came to us through his childhood friend, Peter Blos [who also became a child psychoanalyst]. We had begun a school for the children of those who had come to Vienna to see my father—many were Americans. By then my father and his books were widely known, especially in America—and it was a riddle to him (perhaps 'irony' is the correct word here), because he was no 'fan,' as Americans would put it, of the States. I recall him saying: 'I don't understand that country,' and then he smiled, and added: 'I don't understand why they have turned toward us [his theories] faster than anywhere!' He had come here [in 1916], and your foremost psychologist, William James, had greeted him warmly, but he never sensed any overwhelming enthusiasm, and I think he had misread a country then—maybe still—hard for many of us in Europe to figure out. You need to know history—for a long while, I know, people came to America to settle it, but among the professional classes in Europe, there was no interest in going to America, whereas Americans who were doctors or professors or writers came to Europe.

"Maybe I'm above my neck here, and am in trouble, but when the Nazis seized power in Germany, it wasn't as easy for some of us to think of quickly leaving Austria or Germany [where some psychoanalysts lived, especially in Berlin] for North America. In fact, Erik was the first in our Vienna world to want to leave for America [in the early 1930s, after Hitler's ascension as chancellor, in 1933] and we did wonder why—but his wife was from Canada, and had gone to college in New York City, I recall [at Barnard]. They were wise to leave, and lucky to be able to go there, we now readily say, but I wondered when they left what they'd do. He had become a talented teacher, first, and then he learned to be a psychoanalyst with us, but he had not gone to college, or any professional [graduate] school, and I do recall wondering whether he'd be able to find a job, make a living—[he had] no 'credentials,' as you say, and child psychoanalysis had yet to become an established (or 'regular') profession.

"I remember asking Erik, 'What will you do, and where will you go to do it?' I had in mind that maybe he'd find a job as a teacher, and get to work psychoanalytically with some children—what he'd begun doing here with us. He put his hand through his hair (a frequent gesture of his,

I used to think, to admit some anxiety, or better, uncertainty) and then he said: 'We'll find our way, we just will.' He spoke in German, but he was beginning to speak in English with the help of Joan, and that was what did happen: he found his way and he became an American, 'with all his might' is how I put it when I think about the new life he started here, becoming one of this country's writers—who explained what he'd learned from us in his very own way, I think it fair to say."

She was, with those last words, getting close to a designation or approximation of her former analysand's "new life," its nature and purpose. Erik and Joan Erikson did, indeed, leave Vienna for America in 1933, and soon enough he was living in Massachusetts, then Connecticut, then California, and back East, in Massachusetts—a child psychoanalyst who knew well how to work with children and young people so commonly called adolescents or teenagers. He taught his newly acquired discipline in colleges, took part in seminars, took on patients. He carried a substantial clinical load at the Austen Riggs Center in Stockbridge, Massachusetts, and right away impressed academic psychologists such as Henry A. Murray, at Harvard, and the doctors who worked at Yale's Child Study Center. In California, he became a noteworthy part of the San Francisco Psychoanalytic Institute, and gloried, I think it fair to say, in the invitations of America's West, an open vitality that he found engaging, even as he couldn't help being drawn to a landscape of great and often surprising beauty. In New England, of course, he was a bit closer to Europe and its proud intellectuality, though a wry sense of humor and the part of him that had never experienced the routines and rituals of academic life gave him a certain immunity from the professorial self-assurance he encountered in well-known universities. In Vienna he had been a layman rather than a physician-psychiatrist among the Freud circle—like Anna Freud herself, who had also managed to avoid the educational hurdles that for young Erik Erikson were distinctly uninviting. "He was a loner, and his very own person, not easily fitted into the usual classification," Miss Freud observed, and then her shrewd attempt at the evaluation of national character—a version, really, of Erikson's interest in that subject: "I think he found a home in America that he'd not had in Europe—once in 'the States' he could be welcomed as a person who wasn't attached to 'the old country,' and was very anxious to turn this 'new land' into the home he'd been seeking, and at last had found."

She went on to speak of Erikson's "*Wanderjahr*," which he had mentioned often, even worked into the last introduction he wrote to *Child-hood and Society* (1985). Even then, perhaps, as he wandered through fields and forests, he was learning intuitively about the word "identity," the phrase "identity crisis." He would later use these words again and again as a writing psychoanalyst, ever determined to explain the complexities, psychological and social, that come the way of young people in their attempts (sometimes their painful struggles) to "grow up," meaning find their place in a particular town, nation, and time. What I have just stated may seem unexceptional, even obvious to some readers—yet that was often Erikson's purpose: to connect the depths of psychoanalytic inquiry and awareness to the surface, even homespun knowledge we all acquire as we enter, then go through our lives. No question, for instance, many youths have to contend with their wishes and desires as they pass the muster of their consciences, seek expression, fulfillment, in human connections of one kind or the other. Still, such a time in a young man's, a young woman's life occurs in one place, in one decade of one century; hence the mooring a youth feels as one tied, deep down, to a family, a religion, a neighborhood, a contemporary world with its demands, requests, requirements, values, assertions and, too, the bearings a youth finds as he or she decides to head here or there in an effort to find direction—to get some realized sense of meaning with respect to human existence, its purpose and significance.

No wonder, then, a psychoanalyst whose ancestry was Danish, but who lived in Germany, then learned a profession in Austria, only to come to the United States with a Canadian-born wife, and see his three children, two sons and a daughter, become Americans, would develop a strong interest in the way psychology intersects with sociology, culture and nationalism, history. No wonder, too, a man who had in his background Judaism and Protestantism, and who was a child during the First World War, a parent during the Second World War, and saw the continent that was home to his ancestors, immediate as well as distant, turn into a region of fear and hate, even murder, despite the so-called "advancement," the richness of tradition, to be found there—it is truly no surprise that such a person would give great thought to the effect events in the world at large have on many of us, no matter the private or personal aspects of our particular lifetime. When Freud titled one of his most broadly and philosophically searching books *Civilization and Its Discontents,* he was sending an implicit signal to his colleagues that Erikson,

more than any of them, maybe, was prepared by his fate to receive, reflect upon, how our worries and times of unrest tell us a lot about who
we are, where we live, and, very important, what we have learned to up-
hold, regard as decisively valuable. We fall short, quiver with "phobias,"
"anxieties" (those oft-used clinical words!) that have their origins not only
in our family life (all those "complexes" which psychoanalysis has sub-
mitted to this century!), but in the town, the time that is our own to
claim but that, not rarely, exerts its authority upon us.

Those of us fortunate enough to know and work with Erikson the
teacher, and share with him as would-be or about-to-be clinical observers, often heard him talk quite directly about the personal interests
and theoretical claims that characterize his writing. I well recall, in that
regard, a seminar in which Erikson, as leader, talked at great length of
Freud—the story, as it were, that prompted and informed books such as
Group Psychology and the Analysis of the Ego and *Moses and Monotheism*. Yes,
the former book summoned Freud's interest in the mind and its workings; the latter book similarly explored the complicated and extensive origins of the "Super-Ego," of religiously transmitted oughts and naughts
that become for so many of us lifelong mandates, sources of alarm and
foreboding and regret or remorse. But for Erikson such an occasion was
not only one for psychoanalytic rumination, speculation, but rather for
a broad discussion, as he was wont to put it, of "the relationship between
ideas and historical actuality as it influences them." (I have pages of notes
with those foregoing words on them.) Freud was intent, always, on tracing the sources of our troubles, and he did so as a psychological archae-
ologist, ever ready to go back across the years, ascertain what happened
when, and why, and with which consequences. His main cast of characters for any patient's drama were the parents, the siblings: the family
counts in our continuing effort to make do with life—our memories of
early family years and our later arrangements with others as a repetition
of that past, an echo faint or loud. As he grew older, Freud held to his
original concepts, paradigms, but he also lived to see himself and his
family put in great possible danger: Hitler's rise to power and all that it
would mean for millions, certainly including the entire Freud family.
When his daughter Anna was taken into custody by the Gestapo, he
knew he had best depart Austria immediately, if at all possible. And lucky
for him, he and his wife and children were let out, though not his sisters,
who eventually perished in a concentration camp. But he already knew

what was ahead, well before the Nazis entered Vienna, and so in the book on group psychology he was trying to comprehend what comes over presumably well-educated and reasonable people when they became part of a crowd (a group), if not a racist or political mob—and when he contemplated Moses, his fate, he was seeking to know what it means to be a proud people, singled out by God in their own estimate of their history, and so resented by others.

Here is Anna Freud looking back—and referring to her father in a way Erikson would, were he then present to make the case: "My father was horrified by what was happening in Germany [in the 1920s and 1930s], and he began to wonder why people give way to craziness that goes beyond psychiatric—even psychoanalytic—conceptualization: the madness of mobs, and the scapegoating that can get going when social violence runs through a society. That is what Erik Erikson helped us all realize— as he put it: 'childhood,' even that, is connected to 'society'; and all of us adults, supposedly 'mature,' can fall prey to an irrationality that belongs to the mob, but the mob, as Erikson would remind us, is set in motion by the 'society,' and by 'history'—there you have his important contribution to our [psychoanalytic] thinking."

I could imagine Erikson's grateful ears tingling were he to hear such a compliment from his analyst and teacher. But he knew, anyway, what he had striven hard to recognize as he roamed America, and he realized that he had developed his own take on Freud and his work, on psychoanalysis and its possibilities, its occasional limits, as a mode of introspection and human connectedness. He became, by 1950, when *Childhood and Society* was published, and thereafter, as his essays and books appeared, a giant figure both within his profession and in the American academic and cultural world to which he belonged, no matter his lack of formal education, an irony he himself sometimes mentioned. Indeed, when he became, finally, a professor at Harvard he was often ready to leave—claiming an "inability" to adjust to the academic life. He was, in a way, ever the rebel, quick to distance himself from perceived "stuffiness" or proclaimed (and institutionalized) "certainties" (I well recall his use of both words!), which he regarded with skepticism, even alarm.

No wonder, then, he sought human understanding through not only psychoanalysis but the study of history, and of individuals (Luther and Gandhi) who made a difference in history. All his writing reveals that search, essentially an unashamedly moral one. He searched for "insight," yes, but also for the "responsibility" that such psychological awareness places on us who study and practice psychoanalysis and on the patients who receive its gifts: those who have been given so much must respond to others far less privileged with respect to what they can perceive within themselves and others. All his writing, as well, reveals an urgent effort to sustain psychoanalysis by extending its wisdom to other terrains of reflection. He was an artist as a young man who later became an artist as a psychoanalyst—he called upon religious traditions and historical learning in such a way that he could contemplate ambiguities and paradoxes and contradictions, rather than try to banish them in the name of theoretical absolutism. Not least, he was a marvelously interesting and compelling storyteller, who made the English language his own, savored its evocative and dramatic invitations, and thereby drew to his wise words countless interested (and needy) students, readers, fans: a master of clinical observation who avoided the reductive mannerisms of the clinic, and so doing, became a spirited emissary of the Dr. Freud whose ideas helped Erik H. Erikson become, in turn, a spokesman for, an interpreter of, those ideas, and maybe, in his own vigorous, knowing manner, a lifesaver of them, one who ensured their continued and meaningful presence among so many of us.

I

ON CHILDREN

Nearby and Far Away

Not all of us who work with children (as teachers, as would-be healers) venture much beyond our usual bounds; inevitably, we go to schools, to hospitals and clinics—there to learn about the young, to assist them in learning about themselves (or in a classroom, about a subject matter), and there sometimes even to learn from them, to hear their questions, the thoughts and concerns on their minds. What we are told offers clues, but also reminders: we are brought back in time to our earlier lives, to the curiosities we once harbored, the wonder about the world—brought back to, in the poet William Blake's words (become Erikson's in *Childhood and Society*), the "toys and reasons" we once found so compelling, distracting, and, so often, instructive not only for the present, but for the lifetime that followed those first years.

When young Erikson started teaching school children in Vienna, he often asked the children to draw, even as he himself loved to draw—and he often tried to stir them to imagine how others their age lived. The Eskimos in distant America's Alaska had captured his attention, interest, and he labored hard to connect the boys and girls in his classroom with those far away. There were books about those youngsters who lived amid abundant snow and ice, and a determined teacher succeeded in bringing an

Arctic world into that of Central Europe—as he once recalled with some pride. "I knew of my own desire to study the Eskimos by reading about them, and I knew I had thoughts, or better, hope, that one day I'd go see people whose life I'd been exploring second-hand, through the interest in them of others [his students]. I remember being surprised by the attention the children paid—more so than [to] our 'routine' work: maybe that was it, we were taking a break, [taking] a long trip across European land and the ocean and American land and Canadian land (I was teaching geography with the help of Eskimos!) and they [the schoolchildren] became 'absorbed,' that's the word! Besides geography, they were learning to spell (the strange names of people and places!), and they were learning history and current events—what had happened to the Eskimos, and what was happening in the world that could affect them.

"We were studying 'art,' too, of course—looking at pictures, and trying to sketch our own versions. I kept saying: an artist finds something interesting with his eyes (*her* eyes—I said back then!) and then tries to show himself, or someone else looking over his shoulder, what there is to see and keep in mind. I once told Anna Freud, during an analytic hour, that I was trying to encourage the children to be *sovereigns,* to stake out their personal claim to what their eyes had noticed in books. She laughed; she said that the children would welcome what I was doing, but they might be frightened, put off, because they'd already learned the big lesson in school—to follow the teacher's lead, not be their own guide. That was a big discussion, for sure, and it had psychoanalytic echoes to it: individuality as against conformity! I still remember that hour! Maybe my whole career was beginning then: I wanted to stay within the conventional and the established, but I wanted to—well, go see for myself, [which was] what I was encouraging the children to do."

He most certainly did go see for himself. By the time he was in his early thirties he had, at last, a diploma in hand, one from the Vienna Psychoanalytic Institute, and he had learned a great deal about children, as a psychoanalyst who worked with them, but also as a teacher who tried to help them do the intellectual and emotional work that takes place in a school. In fact, upon his arrival in the United States, those Eskimos would still be in his thinking, even as he went out of his way to get to meet and know children not unlike them in certain respects—Native American boys and girls growing up under the authority of a nation, yet with attachments to customs, loyalties to the received messages of tribal elders, who by no means had the same preoccupations, values, aspirations that were to be found in, say, Cambridge, Massachusetts, or New York City, where newly arrived psychoanalysts like himself were fast beginning to catch a foothold. The result was "field-work," extended visits to the Sioux Indians in the Dakotas, to the Yurok in California, and eventually, the lively, even entrancing writing such people prompted from their wide-eyed, quite attentive visitor, who had by then not only mastered psychoanalytic observation, but the distinct lyrical possibilities of the English language.

So it would begin: a fine writer's career, with wonderfully suggestive phrases like "hunters across the prairie," and "fishermen along a river"—descriptions of the far away that helped illuminate what was going on nearby in various children as they learned their "toys and reasons." The child psychoanalyst who wrote with such engaging eloquence had begun to know his new nation (of which he'd be a citizen for the rest of his life) with a thoroughness, with a willingness to look wide across a great land, to learn from its children in such a way that their various circumstances got realized as the persuasive forces in their young lives; hence his eventual assertion that "childhood" is much shaped by the "society" in which a boy or girl lives—a discovery that was, for Erikson, and later, for the rest of us, important and helpful to contemplate, even as Freud had asked us to think of certain other aspects of the lives of our sons and daughters, our schoolchildren.

HUNTERS ACROSS THE
PRAIRIE

from *Childhood and Society*

1. THE HISTORICAL BACKGROUND

At the time of our trip to South Dakota, Scudder Mekeel was field representative of the Commissioner of Indian Affairs. Our investigation had the immediate and most urgent purpose of trying to find out whence came the tragic apathy with which Sioux Indian children quietly accepted and then quietly discarded many of the values taught them in the immensely thoughtful and costly experiment of federal Indian education. What was wrong with these children was obvious enough: there were two rights for them, one white and one Indian. But only by investigating this discrepancy did we find the remnants of what was once right for children on the prairie.

To be true to the clinical nature of our investigation, I must introduce the material on ancient child training to be presented here with a great deal of circumstantial description. In order to arrive at a clearing where we may see the matter of infancy and society in better light, I must take the reader through the thorny underbrush of contemporary race relations.

The Pine Ridge Indian Reservation lies along the Nebraska state line in the southwest corner of South Dakota. It shares the fate of the rolling high plains:

The slow hot wind of summer and its withering
or again the crimp of the driving white blizzard
and neither of them to be stopped
neither saying anything else than:
"I'm not arguing. I'm telling you."[1]

Here 8,000 members of the Oglala subtribe of the Sioux, or Dakota, live
on land allotted to them by the government. When the Indians settled on
this reservation, they turned their political and economic independence
over to the United States government on condition that the government keep all whites from hunting and settling in their territory.

Only the most stubborn of romantics will expect to find on a reservation of today anything resembling the image of the old Dakotas who
were once the embodiment of the "real Indian"—a warring and hunting man, endowed with fortitude, cunning, and cruelty. His image until
recently adorned the American nickel, a strange tribute to a strange relationship, for this defeated predecessor thus occupies a place reserved for
monarchs and presidents. But his historical reality stems from the far
past.

> Life was good on the high plains of the Dakotas before the white man
> came. . . . Buffalo moved in dark masses on the grasslands; the Black
> Hills and Rockies were populous with deer, beaver, bear and other
> game. . . . Starvation was usually far from their tepees.[2]

Organized in a flexible system of "bands," the Dakota once followed
the buffalo over the vast plains in long queues on horses and with travois.
Periodically they gathered in well-organized camps of light tepees. Whatever they did together—camping, big buffalo hunting, and dancing—was
strictly regulated. But constantly small groups, colorful and noisy, followed
the impulse to radiate from the main body, to hunt small game, to steal
horses, and to surprise enemies. The cruelty of the Sioux was proverbial
among the early settlers. It extended unsparingly to themselves when in
solitary self-torture they sought a guiding vision from the Great Spirit.

But this once proud people has been beset by an apocalyptic sequence
of catastrophes, as if nature and history had united for a total war on their
too manly offspring. It must be remembered that it had been only a few
centuries before the whites settled among them that the Sioux had come

to the high plains from the upper Missouri and Mississippi and had organized their lives around the hunt of the buffalo. The relative youth of this adjustment may well be the explanation of the fact that, as Wissler put it, "When the buffalo died, the Sioux died, ethnically and spiritually. The buffalo's body had provided not only food and material for clothing, covering and shelter, but such utilities as bags and boats, strings for bows and for sewing, cups and spoons. Medicine and ornaments were made of buffalo parts; his droppings, sundried, served as fuel in winter. Societies and seasons, ceremonies and dances, mythology and children's play extolled his name and image."[3]

First, then, the buffalo was vanishing. The whites, eager for trade routes to the greener pastures of the West, upset the hunting grounds and playfully, stupidly, slaughtered buffalo by the hundred thousands. In search for gold they stampeded into the Black Hills, the Sioux' holy mountains, game reservoir, and winter refuge. The Sioux tried to discuss this violation of their early treaties with United States generals, warrior to warrior, but found that the frontier knew neither federal nor Indian law.

The ensuing wild and sporadic warfare did not come to a definite end until 1890, when the Seventh Cavalry revenged the death—many years earlier—of their highly exhibitionistic comrade, General Custer. In the massacre at Wounded Knee, hundreds of Sioux, outnumbered four to one, were killed by well-armed soldiers, although the majority had already surrendered. "The bodies of some of the women and children were found two or three miles away where they had been pursued and killed."[4] In 1937, photographs picturing these bodies were still tacked to the walls of Pine Ridge's only drugstore and soda fountain.

During this historical period of a search for a new economy, the Sioux encountered in successive waves many kinds of new Americans who typified the white man's restless search for space, power, and new ethnic identity. The roaming trappers and fur traders seemed acceptable enough to the nomadic Sioux. They shared the Indians' determination to keep the game intact; they brought knives and guns, beads and kettles; and they married Indian women and became devoted to them. Some American generals too, were entirely acceptable, and in fact were almost deified for the very reason that they had fought well. Even the Negro cavalry fitted into Sioux values. Because of their impressive charges on horseback, they were given the precious name of "Black Buffaloes." Neither did the consecrated belief in man demonstrated by the Quakers and early missionaries fail to impress the dignified and religious leaders of the Sioux. But as they looked for fitting images to connect the past with the future, the Sioux found least acceptable the class of white man who was destined to teach them the blessings of civilization—namely, the government employee.

The young and seething American democracy lost the peace with the Indian when it failed to arrive at a clear design of either conquering or colonizing, converting or liberating, and instead left the making of history to an arbitrary succession of representatives who had one or another of these objectives in mind—thus demonstrating an inconsistency which the Indians interpreted as insecurity and bad conscience. Red tape is no substitute for policy; and nowhere is the discrepancy between democratic ideology and practice more obvious than in the hierarchy of a centralized bureaucracy. For this the older Indian who had been reared in the spirit of a hunter democracy, leveling every potential dictator and every potential capitalist, had a good, not to say malicious, eye. It is hard to imagine the exposed and yet responsible role in which the agents of the government found themselves in the early days. Yet some managed well by sheer humanity.

But then followed the guerrilla war over the children which makes the beginning of federal education, as remembered by the older Sioux, anything but appealing. In some places "children were virtually kidnaped to force them into government schools, their hair was cut and their Indian clothes thrown away. They were forbidden to speak in their own language. Life in the school was under military discipline and rules were enforced by corporal punishment. Those who persisted in clinging to their old ways and those who ran away and were recaptured were thrown into jail. Parents who objected were also jailed. Where possible, children were kept in school year after year to avoid the influence of their families."[5] This general attitude was not completely abandoned until 1920.

During all this time, only one white type stirred the Indian's imagination to the point of influencing his dress, his bearing, his customs, and his children's play: the cowboy. From 1900 to 1917, the Sioux made a determined attempt to develop and to enjoy a cattle economy. But Washington, aware of the higher power both of the erosion of the soil and of Midwestern cattle interests, was forced to decree that the Sioux could not be cowboys on the land allotted to them. The loss of their herds, which had rapidly increased, and the later land boom which made petty capitalist spendthrifts out of the unprepared Sioux, were modern catastrophes which, psychologically, equaled the loss of the buffalo. No wonder, then, that some missionaries convinced the aquiline-nosed Sioux that they were the lost tribe of Israel—and under God's lasting curse.

There followed the most recent period, when the Sioux were supposed to turn into farmers on allotted land which was already eroded and just about to become subject to the great drought. Even today only a fraction of this land is suitable for wheat, corn, and grain crops.

It is understandable, then, that the Sioux have consistently and fruitlessly blamed the United States government for the breaches of promise and for the administrative mistakes of former regimes. As for the whites, instances of error and faithlessness have never been denied even by those who unwittingly or helplessly perpetrated them. There are accounts of American generals reporting to the government and of Indian commissioners reporting to Congress which speak of the deep shame felt by these men as they listened to the dignified reproaches of the old Indians. In fact, the conscience of the American people was at times so readily awakened that sentimentalists and politicians could exploit it for purposes entirely detrimental to a realistic approach to Indian problems.

The government has withdrawn the soldier and has created an imposing and humane organization for the American Indian. The administrator has been superseded by the teacher, the physician, and the social anthropologist. But the years of disappointment and dependence have left the Plains Indians unable to trust where they can hardly afford to distrust. Where once the Indian was a man wronged, he is now comparable to what in psychiatry is called a "compensation neurotic"; he receives all his sense of security and identity out of the status of one to whom something is owed. Yet it must be suspected that even if the millions of buffaloes and the gold taken from the Black Hills could be returned, the Sioux would not be able to forget the habits of dependence or manage to create a community adapted to the present-day world, which, after all, dictates to the conquerors as well as to the conquered.

No wonder, then, that the visitor on the reservation after a short while feels as if he were a part of a slow-motion picture, as if a historical burden arrested the life around him. True, the town of Pine Ridge looks much like a rural county seat anywhere in a poorer section of the Middle West. The government buildings and schools are clean, roomy, and well appointed. The teachers and employees, Indian and white, are well shaven and friendly. But the longer one stays on the reservation, the wider one roams and the closer one looks, the more it becomes apparent that the Indians themselves own little and maintain it badly. Seemingly calm, usually friendly, but generally slow and apathetic, the Indians show surprising signs of undernourishment and disease. Only at an occasional ritual dance and at the drunken brawls in bootleg cafés off the reservation can some of the immense energy be seen which is smoldering beneath the idle surface. At the time of our visit to Pine Ridge, the Indian problem seemed to be caught somewhere between the majestic turn of the wet and dry cycles, the divine wastefulness of the democratic process, and the cheerful ruthlessness of the free-enterprise system: and we know that for those who are caught unprepared in these wheels, the mills of proletarization grind fast and fine. Here the Indian problem loses its ancient patina and joins the problems of colored minorities, rural and urban, which are waiting for busy democratic processes to find time for them.

2. JIM

One day at the trader's, Mekeel and I had met Jim, a lean and sincere young Sioux, obviously one of the more assimilated high school graduates and therefore, as we had learned to expect, troubled in mind. Jim had left the reservation years before to marry a girl belonging to another closely related Plains Indian tribe and to live among her people. After a conversation during which it was explained to him what my vocation was, he said that he was not satisfied with the way things were going with the education of his children, and that he wished we had come to his reservation instead of to Pine Ridge so that his wife and he could talk things over with me. We promised to make an early excursion to his town.

When we neared the simple, clean homestead, the little sons were playing the small Indian boy's favorite game, roping a tree stump, while a little girl was lazily sitting on her father's knees, playing with his patient hands. Jim's wife was working in the house. We had brought some additional supplies, knowing that with Indians nothing can be settled in a few hours; our conversation would have to proceed in the slow, thoughtful, shy manner of the hosts. Jim's wife had asked some women relatives to attend our session. From time to time she went to the door to look out over the prairie which rolled away on every side, merging in the distance with the white processions of slow-moving clouds. As we sat and said little, I had time to consider what Jim's place among the living generations of his people might be.

The few long-haired old men among the present inhabitants of these reservations remember the days when their fathers were the masters of the prairie who met the representatives of the United States government as equals. Once the actual fighting had ceased, these Indians had learned to know the older generation of Americans whose God was a not-too-distant relative of the Indian's Great Spirit and whose ideas of an aggressive but dignified and charitable human life were not so very different from the brave and generous characteristics of the Indian's "good man."

The second generation of Indians knew hunting and fur trading only from hearsay. They had begun to consider a parasitic life based on government rations their inalienable right by treaty, and thus a "natural" way of life.

Jim obviously belonged to the third generation, who have had the full benefit of government boarding-school education and who believe that they, with their superior education, are better equipped for dealing with the white man. They cannot point to any basic accomplishment, however, beyond a certain superficial adaptation, for the majority of them have as little concept of the future as they are beginning to have of the past. This youngest generation, then, finds itself between the impressive dignity of its grandparents, who honestly refuse to believe that the white man is here to stay, and the white man himself, who feels that the Indian persists in being a rather impractical relic of a dead past.

After a period of pensive waiting, Jim's wife announced that her women relatives were coming. It was some minutes before we also were able to see the two figures approaching in the distance.

When they finally arrived, there was a round of bashful, yet amused, greetings, and we sat down in a circle under the shade of pine boughs. By chance I was sitting on the highest fruit crate (chairs are scarce on the prairie). Saying jokingly that it was uncomfortable to be elevated like a preacher, I turned the box so that it would be lower. But it was weaker in this position and I had to turn it back again. Jim then silently turned his seat so that he was sitting as high as I was. I remember this as but one incident typical of a quiet tact which Indians are apt to show.

While Jim looked plainly worried, his wife had the expression of one who is preparing for a very serious conversation about which she has already made up her mind.

Mekeel and I had decided that in our conversation we would not aim directly at Jim's domestic difficulties, whatever they might be, but would ask the group for comments on what we had heard at Pine Ridge about the various phases of child life on the Plains. So we talked about the customs concerning childbirth and child rearing, securing fragmentary accounts of what was once done and of present changes. The women showed a humorous frankness throughout, though their bashful smiles indicated that they would not have dared to bring up certain subjects in the presence of men had Mekeel not been able to throw details into the conversation which surprised them and set their memories and critical powers to work. They had obviously never thought that such details could be of any interest to white people or had anything to do with the world reflected in the English language.

Jim did not add much to this conversation, which lasted for several hours. When the middle of the first decade of life was being considered, the contrast between his grim silence and the women's amused acceptance of the various ways in which children anticipate the activities of adulthood became more marked.

Finally it was time for lunch, and the women went into the house to prepare it. It was now Jim's turn, and he went right to his problem. His children used sexual words in their play, and he could not tolerate it. His wife laughed about them and at him, claiming that all children use these words and that it did not make any difference. He was sensitive to the white men's insinuations that Indians were obscene and had undesirable sexual habits. We agreed that white men did secretly accuse Indians of being sexually indulgent, but then all peoples do accuse their neighbors of the perversions which they themselves are most ashamed of; in fact, they like to give foreign names to their own perversions. But Jim did not wish to make this matter relative. He held that in reality the Sioux were "strong" men who mastered their sexual urges and did not allow their children to use obscene language; and that there was no reason why his children should do what Sioux children were not allowed to do. He thus demonstrated that he had always held with the belief that the Sioux were essentially "stronger" than his wife's very closely related tribe and that, in fact, he held against his wife's tribe the identical prejudices which the whites held against his tribe, the Sioux. Such reflection of the prejudices of the dominant group in the mutual discrimination of subgroups is, of course, universal. Thus it happens that Sioux with considerable admixture of white blood call their full-blooded fellows "niggers" and are, in turn, called "white trash."

As patients do in therapeutic interviews, Jim then contradicted himself so openly that it amounted to a confession. He related that on his last visit to his childhood home in Pine Ridge, he had been disturbed by the language which his relatives' children were using. Such a state of affairs could not have existed when he was a child, he said. We asked him who would have been the person to suppress it. "My father," he answered.

Further questioning revealed that Jim's father had spent most of his childhood in foreign countries. As Jim enlarged on this it became more and more obvious that foreign conditioning had induced his father, after returning to his own people, to hold up standards for his children which were different from those of the other Sioux children. In so doing he had built a wall between his children and those of his tribesmen: the wall which now isolated Jim from his children—and from himself. Unhappy as he had become in consequence of this inner blocking, Jim found himself helplessly creating conflicts in his own family by insisting that his warm-hearted wife interfere, by the use of outright parental prohibition, with habits which the Sioux as well as her own tribe let pass as a matter to be taken care of eventually by shaming or, if necessary, by the grand-parents' calm admonishment.

We tried to explain to Jim the power of ambivalence conflicts. He must have secretly rebelled against his father's wish to estrange him from his playmates. He had suppressed open rebellion only at the price of doing to his children now what his father had done to him. But because he had never really made his father's foreign cause his own, his actions only caused anger in his wife, vexation in his children, and paralyzing doubt in himself.

He thought about this for a few minutes and then said, "I guess you have told me something"—high and wordy praise from an Indian. Lunch was prepared. The rebellious wife and her women auxiliaries waited ceremoniously outside the door until the master of the house and his guests had finished.

Such, then, were the intimate conversations with heavy-hearted Indians in their homes on the high prairie. These conversations were one of the main sources of our material concerning Sioux childhood as it once was. It is obvious that in this field there are no facts free of the most far-reaching connotation. Jim's desperate attempt at regaining a sense of rightness by means inimical to himself and those close to him may give us a first glimpse into a strange mechanism—namely, the compulsive identification of the man whose tribal integrity has been destroyed, with the very destroyer himself. People's feelings have, it seems, always been aware of what we have learned to conceptualize only recently—that small differences in child training are of lasting and sometimes fatal significance in differentiating a people's image of the world, their sense of decency, and their sense of identity.

3. AN INTERRACIAL SEMINAR

Our second major source of data was a small seminar in which Mekeel and I were joined by educators and social workers of both white and Indian origin, and in which we discussed the various opinions voiced by the teachers in the Indian Service. Here it was necessary to realize first the fact that the same childhood data which in neurotic conflicts are subject to repression and falsification, in biracial dispute underlie a nearly impenetrable mutual defensiveness. Every group, of whatever nature, seems to demand sacrifices of its children which they later can bear only in the firm belief or in the determined pretense that they were based on unquestionable absolutes of conduct: to question one of these implicit absolutes means to endanger all. Thus it comes about that peaceful neighbors, in the defense of some little item of child training, will rear up on their hind legs like angry bears who have come to believe that their cubs are in mortal danger.

On the surface, the complaints brought to our seminar had a professional and reasonable ring. Truancy was the most outstanding complaint: when in doubt Indian children simply ran home. The second complaint was stealing, or at any rate gross disregard of property rights as we understand them. This was followed by apathy, which included everything from lack of ambition and interest to a kind of bland passive resistance in the face of a question or of a request. Finally, there was too much sexual activity, a term used for a variety of suggestive situations ranging from excursions into the dark after dances to the mere huddling together of homesick girls in boarding-school beds.

The least frequent complaint was impertinence, and yet one felt that the very absence of overt resistance was feared by the teachers as if it were the Indians' secret weapon. The discussion was pervaded by the mystified complaint that no matter what you do to these children, they do not talk back. They are stoical and non-committal. They make you feel that maybe they understand, until they suddenly prove to have acted otherwise. You "cannot get at them."

The deep and often unconscious fury which this fact had gradually aroused in the most well-meaning and best-disciplined educators really came to expression only in "personal" opinions which teachers here and there added to their official opinions. One time-bitten old educator's ire was aroused by the quiet reference made by some teachers of Indian origin to the Indians' love of children. He exclaimed that Indians did not know what it meant to love a child. Challenged, he based his opinion on the observation of the simple fact that Indian parents who had not seen their children for as long as three years neither kissed them nor cried when they finally came to call for them. He was unable to accept the suggestion, corroborated by the oldest observers, that such reserve governed, from the earliest times, the meeting between Indian relatives, especially in the presence of non-relatives. For him such book knowledge was contradicted by two decades of personal and indignant observation. Indian parents, he insisted, felt less for their children than animals do for their young.

Granted that cultural disintegration and inability to care for children economically or spiritually may bring with it apathy in personal relations, it was, of course, appalling to be confronted with such a radical misunderstanding which could by no means be considered a relic of a less understanding period. Colonel Wheeler, who knew the Sioux as conqueror, not as educator, did "not believe that any race of people exists on earth who are more fond of their families than are the American Indians." Who was right? Had the conquering general turned too sentimental or the worn-out educator too cynical?

A number of the strongest opinions were volunteered only privately. "Enuresis is really the worst difficulty," a male teacher, part Indian, said, adding, "but we Indians could not discuss enuresis in a group including women." He felt that the lack of proper toilet training was the cause of most of the trouble in Indian education. A white employee volunteered to point to another problem as being "really the worst." Quoting confidential remarks of medical authorities in the Indian Service, he said, "Indian parents not only let their children masturbate, they teach them to masturbate." He thought this was the cause of all trouble, but was unwilling to discuss the subject in the presence of Indians. As far as facts could be determined, neither enuresis nor masturbation was more frequent in Indian schools than in boarding schools or foster homes anywhere. Masturbation was, actually, a mere assumption, nobody having remembered seeing any but small children touch themselves. It was interesting, then, to note that the "real," the most indignant, and the most unofficial complaints concerned areas of early conditioning which have aroused the attention of psychoanalysts in Western culture (and which were discussed in the section on pregenitality [this section appears in *Childhood and Society,* Chapter 2]).

The whites, activists in educational matters, proved to consider every omission in child training, such as the complete lack of attention paid by Indian parents to anal, urethral, and genital matters in small children, a most flagrant commission with most definite malicious intent. The Indians, on the other hand, being permissive toward smaller children and only verbally cruel toward older ones, considered the white man's active approach to matters of child care a destructive and most deliberate attempt to discourage children. Whites, they thought, want to estrange their children from this world so as to make them pass through to the next world with the utmost dispatch. "They teach their children to cry!" was the indignant remark of an Indian woman when confronted with the sanitary separation of mother and child in the government hospital, and especially with the edict of government nurses and doctors that it was good for babies to cry until blue in the face. Older Indian women expecting the birth of a grandchild would quietly wail like the Jews before their sacred Wall, becrying the destruction of their nation. But even educated Indians could not suppress the feeling that all the expensive care given their children was essentially a diabolic system of national castration. Beyond that there was on the Indian side the strange assumption that the whites wanted to destroy their own children too. Since the earliest contacts between the two races the Indians have considered most repugnant the white habit of slapping or beating children into compliance. Indians would only scare the child by saying the owl might come and get him—or the white man. What conflicts they were thus causing and perpetuating in their children, the Indians, in turn, could not see.

The unofficial complaints, then, assume (with our most advanced theoretical assumptions) that even seemingly arbitrary items of child training have a definite function, although in secret complaints this insight is used for the most part as a vehicle of mutual prejudice and as a cover-up for individual motivations and unconscious intentions. Here is truly a field for "group therapy" of a kind which would not aim at psychiatric improvement for the individual participant but at an improvement of the cultural relations of those assembled.

Of items significant in cultural prejudice, I shall briefly illustrate three: respect for property, cleanliness, efficiency.

One day a schoolteacher brought with him a list of his pupils. There was nothing very remarkable about any of these children except, perhaps, the poetic flavor of their names (equivalents: Star-Comes-Out, Chase-in-the-Morning, Afraid-of-Horses). They were all well-behaved, yielding to the white teacher that which is the teacher's and to the Indian home that which belongs to the home. "They have two sets of truths," the teacher explained, putting it more politely than did some of his colleagues, who are convinced that Indians are "born liars." He was satisfied, on the whole, with their scholastic achievements. The only problem he wished to discuss was one presented by a certain little boy who lived a relatively isolated existence among the other children as if he were, somehow, an outcast.

We inquired into the status of the boy's family among the Indians and the whites. Both groups characterized the father of the boy with the same three fateful words, "He has money." The father's regular visits to the bank in the nearest town gave him, it appeared, that "foreign smell" which an ant acquires when crossing over the territory of another "tribe," so that it is killed on return. Here the traitor apparently becomes dead socially, after he and his family, once and for all, have acquired the evil identity of "he-who-keeps-his-money-to-himself." This offends one of the oldest principles of Sioux economy—generosity.

The idea of storage over a prolonged period of time is foreign. If a man has enough to keep starvation at least around the corner, has sufficient time for meditation, and something to give away now and then, he is relatively content. . . . When a man's food is low, or all gone, he may hitch up his team and take his family for a visit. Food is shared equally until none is left. The most despised man is he who is rich but does not give out his riches to those about him. He it is who is really "poor."[6]

In the Sioux system, the crowning expression of the principle of leveling wealth was the "give-away," the offering of all the host's possessions to his guests at a feast in honor of a friend or relative. To perceive by contrast the ideal antithesis to the evil image of the miser, one must see, even today, an Indian child on some ceremonial occasion give away what meager pennies or possessions his parents have saved for just such an occasion. He radiates what we shall later formulate as a sense of ideal identity: "The way you see me now is the way I really am, and it is the way of my forefathers."

The economic principle of the give-away and the high prestige of generosity was, of course, once allied with necessity. Nomads need a safe minimum of household property which they can carry with them. People who live by hunting depend on the generosity of the luckiest and most able hunters. But necessities change more rapidly than true virtues, and it is one of the most paradoxical problems of human evolution that virtues which were originally designed to safeguard an individual's or a group's self-preservation become rigid under the pressure of anachronistic fears of extinction and thus can render a people unable to adapt to changed necessities. In fact, such relics of old virtues become stubborn and yet elusive obstacles to re-education. For, once deprived of their over-all economic meaning and universal observance, they fall apart. They combine with other character traits, of which some individuals have more, others less, and fuse with surrounding group traits, such as poor-white prodigality and carelessness. In the end the administrator and teacher cannot possibly know when they are dealing with an old virtue, when with a new vice. Take the relief checks and the supplies of food and machinery due individual families on the basis of old treaties and officially distributed according to need and desert: one could always know when a man had received such "gifts," for all over the prairie little wagons would bring his temporarily less lucky relatives toward their rightful participation in a feast of primitive communism. Thus, after all the decades of educational efforts toward Indian participation in our monetary civilization, the ancient attitudes prevail.

The first insight which emerged from the discussion of these items was that nothing is more fruitless in the relationships between individuals or groups than to attempt to question the ideals of the adversary by demonstrating that, according to the logic of one's own conscience, he is inconsistent in his preaching. For every conscience, whether in an individual or a group, has not only specific contents but also its own peculiar logic which safeguards its coherence.

"They are without initiative," the exasperated white teachers would say; and indeed the wish of an Indian boy to excel and to compete, while fully developed under certain circumstances, may disappear completely under others. The members of a running team, for example, may hesitate at the start of a race. "Why should we run?" they say. "It is already certain who is going to win." In the back of their minds there may be the reflection that he who wins will not have too good a time afterwards. For the story of the little Boy-Whose-Father-Has-Money has its parallels in the fate of all those Indian boys and girls who show signs of actually accepting the demands of their educators and of finding delight and satisfaction in excelling in school activities. They are drawn back to the average level by the intangible ridicule of the other children.

Mekeel illustrated the Indian girl's special problems by pointing to a particularly tragic detail. The first impression the little Indian girl must get on entering a white school is that she is "dirty." Some teachers confess that they cannot possibly hide their disgust at the Indian child's home smell. The movable tepee, of course, was freer of accumulated smell than the frame houses are now. During school time the child is taught cleanliness, personal hygiene, and the standardized vanity of cosmetics. While having by no means fully assimilated other aspects of white female freedom of motion and of ambition which are presented to her with historically disastrous abruptness, the adolescent girl returns home prettily dressed and clean. But the day soon comes when she is called a "dirty girl" by mothers and grandmothers. For a clean girl in the Indian sense is one who has learned to practice certain avoidances during menstruation; for example, she is not supposed to handle certain foods, which are said to spoil under her touch. Most girls are unable to accept again the status of a leper while menstruating. Yet they are by no means comfortably emancipated. They are almost never given the opportunity, nor are they indeed prepared or willing, to live the life of an American woman; but they are only rarely able to be happy again in the spatial restrictions, the unhygienic intimacies, and the poverty of their surroundings.

Ingrained world-images cannot be weakened by the evidence of discrepancies nor reconciled by arguments. In spite of the ideological chasm demonstrated in these examples, many Indian parents were reported to make honest and successful attempts to induce obedience to the white teacher in their children. However, the children seemed to accept this pressure as a form of compliance not backed up by a sense of deeper obligation. They often responded to it with unbelievable stoicism. This, it seemed to us, was the most astonishing single fact to be investigated: that Indian children could live for years without open rebellion or any signs of inner conflict between two standards which were incomparably further apart than are those of any two generations or two classes in our culture. We found among the Sioux little evidence of individual conflicts, inner tensions, or of what we call neuroses—anything which would have permitted us to apply our knowledge of mental hygiene, such as it was, to a solution of the Indian problem. What we found was cultural pathology, sometimes in the form of alcoholic delinquency or of mild thievery, but for the most part in the form of a general apathy and an intangible passive resistance against any further and more final impact of white standards on the Indian conscience. Only in a few "white man's Indians," usually successfully employed by the government, did we find neurotic tension, expressed in compulsions, overconscientiousness, and general rigidity. The average Indian child, however, did not seem to have what we call a "bad conscience" when, in passive defiance of the white teacher, he retreated into himself; nor was he met by unsympathetic relatives when he chose to become truant. On the whole, then, no true inner conflict reflected the conflict of the two worlds in both of which the individual child existed.

But the tonus and tempo of life seemed to recover some of its old vitality only in those rare but vivid moments when his elders extolled the old life; when the larger family or the remnant of the old band packed their horse carts and converged somewhere on the prairie for a ceremony or a festival to exchange gifts and memories, to gossip and to calumniate, to joke and—now on rarer occasions—to dance the old dances. For it was then that his parents and especially his grandparents came closest to a sense of identity which again connected them with the boundless past wherein there had been no one but the Indian, the game, and the enemy. The space in which the Indian could feel at home was still without borders and allowed for voluntary gatherings and, at the same time, for sudden expansion and dispersion. He had been glad to accept centrifugal items of white culture such as the horse and the gun and, later, motorcars and the dream of trailers. Otherwise there could be only passive resistance to the senseless present and dreams of restoration: when the future would lead back into the past, time would again become ahistoric, space unlimited, activity boundlessly centrifugal, and the buffalo supply inexhaustible. The Sioux tribe as a whole is still waiting for the Supreme Court to give the Black Hills back to them and to restore the lost buffalo.

Their federal educators, on the other hand, continued to preach a life plan with centripetal and localized goals: homestead, fireplace, bank account—all of which receive their meaning from a space-time in which the past is overcome and in which the full measure of fulfillment in the present is sacrificed to an ever higher standard of living in the ever distant future. The road to this future is not outer restoration but inner reform and economic "betterment."

Thus we learned that geographic-historic perspectives and economic goals and means contain all that a group has learned from its history, and therefore characterize concepts of reality and ideals of conduct which cannot be questioned or partially exchanged without a threat to existence itself. Items of child training, as we shall now demonstrate, are part and parcel of such concepts of reality. They persist when possible in their original form, but if necessary in distorted facsimiles as stubborn indications that the new way of life imposed by the conquerors has not yet been able to awaken images of a new cultural identity.

4. SIOUX CHILD TRAINING

A. Birth

The Dakota women who gave us information on the old methods of child training were at first reticent. To begin with, they were Indians. Then also, Mekeel, whom they had known as anthropologist and friend, was now a government man. And then, it was not quite decent to talk to men about things concerning the human body. Especially the subject of the unavoidable beginning, namely pregnancy, always caused some giggling. Although vomiting and other physiological disorders of pregnancy are said to be a rare occurrence among them, Indian women seem conscious of a radical change of character during this time which in retrospect appears embarrassing. It is said that only when pregnant do the usually gentle Indian women abuse their husbands and even, upon occasion, strike their children. Thus different cultural systems have different outlets for the expression of the deep ambivalence which pervades the woman who, much as she may have welcomed the first signs of pregnancy and much as she may be looking forward to the completed baby, finds herself inhabited for nine long months by a small and unknown, but utterly dictatorial, being.

Customs in regard to delivery have, of course, changed completely. White women usually speak with scorn about the "unhygienic" custom of the older Indian woman, who made herself a bed of sand in or near her home on which she lay or knelt to have her baby, pressing her feet against two pegs driven into the ground and grasping two other pegs with her hands. However, this bed, called "a pile of dirt" by the whites, seems to have been an important feature of the specific Plains hygiene system, according to which every bodily waste is given over to sand, wind, and sun. The manifestations of this system must have puzzled white people: menstrual pads and even placentas were hung in trees; the bodies of the dead were placed on high scaffolds; and defecation took place in specified dry places. On the other hand, it is hard for the Indians to see the hygienic superiority of the outhouse, which, though admittedly more modest, prevents sun and wind, but not flies, from reaching the bodily waste.

White and Indian women regularly remark that "no moaning or groaning" was heard from Indian women of the older generation during childbirth. There are stories which tell of Indian women who followed their people a few hours after being left behind to give birth to a baby. It seems that the old wandering life, which necessitated adapting to the change of seasons and to the sudden movement of buffalo and enemy, often left little or no time for aftercare and recuperation. Older women see in the changes which modern hygiene and hospitals are bringing about in the younger generation's custom of childbearing not only a danger to the tradition of fortitude, but also an injustice to the baby, who thus learns to cry "like a white baby."

B. Getting and Taking

As we now present a list of data significant in the Sioux system of child-rearing, the single datum owes its significance largely to the women's wish to convey a point dear to their traditional ethos, and yet sometimes also to our wish to check a point dear to our theoretical anticipations. Such a list, then, can neither be exhaustive nor entirely conclusive. Yet we thought we detected a surprising convergence between the rationale given by the Indians for their ancient methods, and the psychoanalytic reasoning by which we would come to consider the same data relevant.

The colostrum (the first watery secretion from the milk glands) was generally considered to be poison for the baby; thus the breast was not offered to him until there seemed to be a good stream of perfect milk. The Indian women maintained that it was not right to let a baby do all the initial work only to be rewarded with a thin, watery substance. The implication was clear: how could he trust a world which greeted him thus? Instead, as a welcome from the whole community, the baby's first meal was prepared by relatives and friends. They gathered the best berries and herbs the prairie affords and put their juice into a buffalo bladder, which was fashioned to serve as a breastlike nursing bottle. A woman who was considered by all to be a "good woman" stimulated the baby's mouth with her finger and then fed him the juice. In the meantime, the watery milk was sucked out of the breast and the breast stimulated to do efficient work by certain older women who had been commanded in their dreams to perform this office.

Once the Indian baby began to enjoy the mother's breast he was nursed whenever he whimpered, day or night, and he also was allowed to play freely with the breast. A small child was not supposed to cry in helpless frustration, although later to cry in rage could "make him strong." It is generally assumed that Indian mothers return to their old "spoiling" customs as soon as they can be sure they will not be bothered by the health authorities.

In the old order the baby's nursing was so important that, in principle at least, not even the father's sexual privileges were allowed to interfere with the mother's libidinal concentration on the nursing. A baby's diarrhea was said to be the result of a watery condition of the mother's milk brought about by intercourse with the father. The husband was urged to keep away from the wife for the nursing period, which, it is said, lasted from three to five years.

It is said that the oldest boy was nursed longest and that the average nursing period was three years. Today it is much shorter, although instances of prolonged nursing persist, to the dismay of those whose job it is to foster health and morals. One teacher told us that an Indian mother quite recently had come to school during recess to nurse her eight-year-old boy, who had a bad cold. She nursed him with the same worried devotion with which we ply our sniffling children with vitamins.

Among the old Sioux there was no systematic weaning at all. Some mothers, of course, had to stop nursing for reasons beyond their control. Otherwise the children weaned the mother by gradually getting interested in other foods. Before finally abandoning the breast altogether, however, the infant may have fed himself for many months on other food, allowing time for his mother to give birth to the next child and to restore her milk supply.

In this connection I remember an amusing scene. An Indian child of about three was sitting on his mother's lap eating dry crackers. He frequently became thirsty. With a dictatorial gesture and an experienced motion he reached into his mother's blouse (which, as of old, had openings on the sides from the armpits down), in an attempt to reach a breast. Because of our presence she prevented him bashfully, but by no means indignantly, with the cautious movement of a big animal pushing aside a little one. But he clearly indicated that he was in the habit of getting a sip now and then while eating. The attitude of the two was more telling than statistical data in indicating when such little fellows, once they can pursue other adventures, definitely stop reaching into their mother's blouse—or, for that matter, into the blouse of any woman who happens to have milk. For such milk, where it exceeds the immediate needs of her suckling baby, is communal property.

This paradise of the practically unlimited privilege of the mother's breast also had a forbidden fruit. To be permitted to suckle, the infant had to learn not to bite the breast. Sioux grandmothers recount what trouble they had with their indulged babies when they began to use nipples for the first vigorous biting. They tell with amusement how they would "thump" the baby's head and how he would fly into a wild rage. It is at this point that Sioux mothers used to say what our mothers say so much earlier in their babies' lives: let him cry, it will make him strong. Good future hunters, especially, could be recognized by the strength of their infantile fury.

The Sioux baby, when thus filled with rage, was strapped up to his neck in the cradleboard. He could not express his rage by the usual violent motion of the limbs. I do not mean to imply that the cradleboard or tight swaddling clothes are cruel restrictions. On the contrary, at first they are undoubtedly comfortably firm and womblike things to be wrapped and rocked in and a handy bundle for the mother to carry around while working. But I do wish to suggest that the particular construction of the board, its customary placement in the household, and the duration of its use, are variable elements used by different cultures as amplifiers of the basic experiences and the principal traits which they develop in their young.

What convergence can we see between the Sioux child's orality and the tribe's ethical ideals? We have mentioned generosity as an outstanding virtue required in Sioux life. A first impression suggests that the cultural demand for generosity received its early foundation from the privilege of enjoying the nourishment and the reassurance emanating from unlimited breast feeding. The companion virtue of generosity was fortitude, in Indians a quality both more ferocious and more stoical than mere bravery. It included an easily aroused quantity of quickly available hunting and fighting spirit, the inclination to do sadistic harm to the enemy, and the ability to stand extreme hardship and pain under torture and self-torture. Did the necessity of suppressing early biting wishes contribute to the tribe's always ready ferocity? If so, it cannot be without significance that the generous mothers themselves aroused a "hunter's ferocity" in their teething infants, encouraging an eventual transfer of the infant's provoked rage to ideal images of hunting, encircling, catching, killing, and stealing.

We are not saying here that their treatment in babyhood *causes* a group of adults to have certain traits—as if you turned a few knobs in your child-training system and you fabricated this or that kind of tribal or national character. In fact, we are not discussing traits in the sense of irreversible aspects of character. We are speaking of goals and values and of the energy put at their disposal by child-training systems. Such values persist because the cultural ethos continues to consider them "natural" and does not admit of alternatives. They persist because they have become an essential part of an individual's sense of identity, which he must preserve

as a core of sanity and efficiency. But values do not persist unless they
work, economically, psychologically, and spiritually; and I argue that to
this end they must continue to be anchored, generation after generation,
in early child training; while child training, to remain consistent, must be
embedded in a system of continued economic and cultural synthesis.
For it is the synthesis operating within a culture which increasingly tends
to bring into close-knit thematic relationship and mutual amplification
such matters as climate and anatomy, economy and psychology, society
and child training.

How can we show this? Our proof must lie in the coherent meaning
which we may be able to give to seemingly irrational data within one
culture and to analogous problems in comparable cultures. We shall,
therefore, indicate in what way various items of our material on Sioux
culture seem to derive meaning from our assumptions, and then proceed
from this hunter tribe to a comparison with a tribe of fishermen.

As we watched Sioux children sitting in the dark corners of their
tents, walking along the trails, or gathered in great numbers around the
Fourth of July dance, we noticed that they often had their fingers in
their mouths. They (and some adults, usually women) were not sucking
their fingers, but playing with their teeth, clicking or hitting something
against them, snapping chewing gum or indulging in some play which
involves teeth and fingernails on one or both hands. The lips, even if the
hand was as far inside the mouth as is at all possible, did not participate.
Questioning brought the astonished answer: yes, of course, they had always done this, didn't everybody? As clinicians we could not avoid the
deduction that this habit was the heir of the biting wishes which were
so ruthlessly interrupted in early childhood—just as we assume in our
culture that thumb-sucking and other sucking habits of our children
(and adults) compensate for sucking pleasures which have been frustrated or made uncertain by inconsistent handling.

This led to an interesting further question: Why were women more apt
to display this habit than the equally frustrated men? We found a twofold
answer to this: women, in the olden days, used and abused their teeth to
chew leather and flatten the porcupine quills which they needed for
their embroidery. They thus could apply the teething urges to a toothy
activity of high practicality. And indeed, I saw a very aged woman sitting
in her tent, dreamily pulling a strip of moving picture film between her
few remaining teeth, just as she may have flattened the porcupine quills

long ago. It seems then, that tooth habits persisted in women because for them they were considered "normal," even when no longer specifically useful.

Generosity in the Sioux child's later life was sustained not by prohibition, but by the example set by his elders in the attitude which they took toward property in general and to his property in particular. Sioux parents were ready at any time to let go of utensils and treasures, if a visitor so much as admired them, although there were, of course, conventions curbing a visitor's expression of enthusiasm. It was very bad form to point out objects obviously constituting a minimum of equipment. The expectation, however, that an adult should and would dispose of his surplus caused much consternation in the early days, when the "Indian giver" offered to a white friend not what the friend needed, but what the Indian could spare, only to walk off with what he decided the white man could spare. But all of this concerned only the parents' property. A parent with a claim to good character and integrity would not touch a child's possessions, because the value of possessions lay in the owner's right to let go of them when *he* was moved to do so—i.e., when it added prestige to himself and to the person in whose name he might decide to give it away. Thus a child's property was sacrosanct until the child had enough of a will of his own to decide on its disposition.

C. Holding and Letting Go

Generosity, we are interested to note, was not inculcated by calling stinginess bad and "money" dirty but by calling the give-away good. Property as such, with the exception of the aforementioned minimum equipment for hunting, sewing, and cooking, had no inherent goodness. The traders never tire of repeating stories of Indian parents who come to town to buy long-needed supplies with long-expected money, only to smilingly grant their children their every whim, including their wish to take new gadgets apart, and then to return home without supplies.

In the chapter on pregenitality we enlarged upon the clinical impression that there is an intrinsic relationship between the holding on to and letting go of property and the infantile disposition of excrement as the body's property. [See *Childhood and Society,* Chapter 2.]

And, indeed, it seems that the Sioux child was allowed to reach by himself a gradual compliance with whatever rules of modesty or cleanliness existed. Although the trader complained that even five-year-olds would in no way control their excretory needs while at the store with their shopping parents, teachers say that as soon as the very young Indian child knows what is expected of him—and, most important, sees the older children comply—accidents of soiling or wetting at day school are extremely rare. The complaint that they, like children of other cultures, wet their beds in boarding schools is another matter. For some reason enuresis seems to be the "normal" symptom of the homesick, the billeted child. Therefore, one may say that these children, far from not having learned any control, seem able to adapt to two standards without compulsive tendencies to retention or elimination. The bowels become regulated because of the example set by other children, rather than by measures reflecting the vagaries of the parent-child relationship. Thus the small child, as soon as he can walk, is taken by the hand by older children and is led to places designated by convention for purposes of defecation. It is probably in this connection that the small child first learns to be guided by that coercion to imitate and by that avoidance of "shaming" which characterizes so much of primitive morality. For these apparently "unprincipled savages" often prove to be timidly concerned about gossip which indicates that they have not done the proper thing or have done a thing improperly. The Sioux child undoubtedly becomes aware of the changing wave lengths of didactic gossip before he quite understands its detailed contents, until gradually, inexorably, this gossip includes him, encouraging his autonomous pride in being somebody who is looked upon with approval; making him mortally afraid of standing exposed and isolated; and diverting whatever rebellion may have been thus aroused in him by permitting him to participate in gossip against others.

It can be said that the Sioux attitude toward anal training in childhood does not contradict that concerning property. In regard to both, the emphasis is on free release rather than on rigid retention, and in both, the final regulation is postponed to a stage of ego development when the child can come to an autonomous decision which will give him immediate tangible status in the community of his peers.

D. "Making" and Making

In Sioux childhood, the first strict taboos expressed verbally and made inescapable by a tight net of ridiculing gossip did not concern the body and its modes, but rather patterns of social intimacy. When a certain stage, soon after the fifth year, was reached, brother and sister had to learn neither to look at nor to address one another directly. The girl would be urged to confine herself to female play and to stay near the mother and tepee, while the boy was encouraged to join the older boys, first in games and then in the practice of hunting.

A word about play. I had been most curious to see the Indian children's toys and to observe their games. When for the first time I approached the Indian camp near the agency, proceeding carefully and as if uninterested, so that at least a few of the children might not be disturbed in their play, the little girls ran into the tents to sit beside their mothers with their knees covered and their eyes lowered. It took me some time to realize that they were not really afraid but just acting "proper." (The test: they were immediately ready to play peek-a-boo from behind their mothers' backs.) One of them, however, who was about six years old, sat behind a large tree and obviously was too intent on solitary play to notice me or to comply with the rules of feminine shyness. As I eagerly stalked this child of the prairie, I found her bent over a toy typewriter. And her lips as well as her fingernails were painted red.

Even the youngest of the girls are thus influenced in their play by the radical change taking place in their older sisters, the pupils of the boarding school. This became obvious when the women of the camp made small tepees, wagons, and dolls for me in order to demonstrate what they had played with as children. These toys were clearly intended to lead little girls along the path to Indian motherhood. One little girl, playing with one of these old-fashioned toy wagons, however, unhesitatingly put two doll women in the front seat, threw the babies in the rear compartment, and had the ladies "drive to the movies in Chadron." However, all of this is still feminine play: a girl would be ridiculed mercilessly should she try to indulge in a "boyish" game, or dare to become a tomboy.

The aspirations developed in the boys' play and games have changed less than those of the girls, although cowboy activities have largely displaced those of the buffalo hunter. Thus while I was observing the little dolls "going off to town," a tree stump near which I was sitting was roped by the girl's little brother with gleeful satisfaction. Psychologically, such a game is obviously still considered serious training by the older children and adults, although it is "useless" in reality. Upon one occasion I laughed, as I thought, with and not at a little boy who told his mother and me that he could catch a wild rabbit on foot and with his bare hands. I was made to feel that I had made a social blunder. Such daydreams are not "play." They are the preparations for skills which, in turn, assure the development of the hunter or cowboy identity.

In this respect one very old custom is of special interest, namely, the play with "bone horses," small bones three or four inches long which the boys gather at places where cattle (formerly buffalo) have been killed. According to their shape, they are called horses, cows, or bulls, and are either fingered continuously in the boys' pockets or are used by them when playing together at games of horse racing and buffalo hunting. These bones are for the Sioux boys what small toy cars are in the lives of our boys. The phallic shape of these bones suggests that they may be the medium which allows little boys in the phallic and locomotor stage, while fingering "horses," "buffaloes," "cows," and "bulls," to cultivate competitive and aggressive daydreams common to all males of the tribe. It fell to the older brothers, at this stage, to introduce the small boy to the ethos of the hunter and to make loyalty between brothers the cement of Dakota society. Because of their exclusive association with the boasting older boys, the smaller ones must have become aware early enough of the fact that direct phallic aggressiveness remained equated with the ferocity of the hunter. It was considered proper for a youth to rape any maiden whom he caught outside the areas defined for decent girls: a girl who did not know "her place" was his legitimate prey, and he could boast of the deed.

Every educational device was used to develop in the boy a maximum of self-confidence, first by maternal generosity and assurance, then by fraternal training. He was to become a hunter after game, woman, and spirit. The emancipation of the boy from his mother, and the diffusion of any regressive fixation on her, was accomplished by an extreme emphasis on his right to autonomy and on his duty of initiative. Given boundless trust, and gradually learning (through the impact of shaming rather than through that of inner inhibition) to treat his mother with reticence and extreme respect, the boy apparently directed all sense of frustration and rage into the chase after game, enemy, and loose women—and against himself, in his search for spiritual power. Of such deeds he was permitted to boast openly, loudly, and publicly, obliging his father to display pride in his superior offspring. It is only too obvious that such a sweeping initial invitation to be male and master would necessitate the

establishment of balancing safeguards in the girls. While the arrangement of these safeguards is ingenious, one cannot help feeling that the
woman was exploited for the sake of the hunter's unbroken "spirit"; and,
indeed, it is said that suicides were not uncommon among Sioux women,
although unknown among men.

The Sioux girl was educated to be a hunter's helper and a future
hunter's mother. She was taught to sew, to cook and conserve food, and
to put up tents. At the same time she was subjected to a rigorous training toward bashfulness and outright fear of men. She was trained to walk
with measured steps, never to cross certain boundaries set around the
camp, and—with approaching maturity—to sleep at night with her
thighs tied together to prevent rape.

She knew that if a man could claim to have touched a woman's vulva,
he was considered to have triumphed over her virginity. This victory by
mere touch was analogous to his right to "count coup"—i.e., to claim
a new feather in his bonnet when he had succeeded in touching a dangerous enemy in battle. How similar these two victories are could still
be seen in the gossip column of an Indian Reservation school paper put
out by the children: it specified the number of times certain boys had
"counted coup" against certain girls—i.e., had kissed them. In the old
days, however, any public bragging on the part of the boys was insult-
ing to the girl concerned. The girl learned that she might be called on
during the Virgin Feast to defend her claim to virginity against any accusation. The ceremony of this feast consisted of symbolic acts apparently compelling the admission of the truth. Any man who, under these
ceremonial conditions, would and could claim that he had so much as
touched a girl's genitals could have that girl removed from the elite
group.

It would be wrong to assume, however, that such ritual warfare precluded affectionate love between the sexes. In reality the seemingly paradoxical result of such education was a doubly deep affection in individuals
who were ready to sacrifice prestige points for love; in the boy, whose
tenderness tamed his pride to the extent that he would court a girl by
calling her with the love flute and by enveloping her and himself in the
courting blanket in order to ask her to marry him—and in the girl, who
responded without suspecting him of other than honorable intentions
and without making use of the hunting knife which she carried with her
always, just in case.

The girl, then, was educated to serve the hunter and to be on her guard against him—but also to become a mother who would surely not destroy in her boys the characteristics necessary to a hunter. By means of ridiculing gossip—"people who did such and such an unheard-of thing"—she would, as she had seen her mother do, gradually teach her children the hierarchy of major and minor avoidances and duties in the relations between man and man, between woman and woman, and especially between man and woman. Brother and sister, or parent-in-law and child-in-law of the opposite sex, were not permitted to sit with one another or to have face-to-face conversations. A brother-in-law and sister-in-law, and a girl and her maternal uncle, were allowed to speak only in a joking tone to one another.

These prohibitions and regulations, however, were made part of highly significant relationships. The little girl old enough to avoid her brother knew that she would ultimately use her skill in sewing and embroidery, on which she was to concentrate henceforth, for the fabrication and ornamentation of beautiful things for his future wife—and for his children, cradles and layettes. "He has a good sister" would be high praise for the warrior and hunter. The brother knew that he would give her the best of all he would win by hunting or stealing. The fattest prey would be offered his sister for butchering, and the corpses of his worst enemies left to her for mutilation. Thus she too would, via her brother's fortitude and generosity, find an opportunity to participate actively and aggressively in at least some aspects of the high moments of hunt and war. Above all, in the Sun Dance, she would, if proven virtuous, bathe the brother's self-inflicted wounds, thus sharing the spiritual triumph of his most sublime masochism. The first and basic avoidance—that between brother and sister—thus became a model of all respect relationships and of helpfulness and generosity among all the "brothers" and "sisters" of the extended kinship; while the loyalty between brothers became the model of all comradeship.

I think it would be too simple to say that such avoidances served to forestall "natural" incestuous tension. The extreme to which some of these avoidances go, and the outright suggestions that the joking between brothers-in-law and sisters-in-law *should* be sexual, rather point to an ingenious provocation as well as diversion of potential incestuous tension. Such tension was utilized within the universal task of creating a social atmosphere of respect in the ingroup (to each according to his family status); and of diverting safely to the prey, to the enemy, and to the outcast all the need for manipulative control and general aggressiveness provoked and frustrated at the biting stage. There was, then, a highly standardized system of "proper" relationships which assured kindness, friendliness, and considerateness within the extended family. All sense of belonging depended on the ability to acquire a reputation as somebody who deserves praise for being proper. But he who, after the gradual increase of the pressure of shaming, should persist in improper behavior, would become the victim of ruthlessly biting gossip and deadly calumniation: as if, by refusing to help in the diversion of the concerted aggressiveness, he himself had become an enemy.

Today the Sioux boy will catch a glimpse of the life for which his play rituals still prepare him only by observing and (if he can) joining in the dances of his elders. These dances have often been described as "wild" by whites who obviously felt in them a twofold danger growing out of the gradually rising group spirit and the "animalistic" rhythm. However, when we observed older Sioux dancers in one of the isolated dance houses, they seemed, as the hours of the night passed, to express with their glowing faces a deepening concentration on a rhythm which possessed their bodies with increasing exactness. Lawfulness kept step with wildness. In comparison, it was almost embarrassing to observe the late arrival of a group of young men, who obviously had learned to dance jazz also. Their dance was completely "out of joint," and their gaze wandered around in a conceited way, which by comparison made the spiritual concentration of their elders only the more impressive. Old Indians tried to hide pitying smiles behind their hands at this display.

Thus on occasion the dances and ceremonies still proclaim the existence of the man with the "strong heart" who has learned to use the tools of his material culture to expand his hunting powers beyond his body's limitations. Mastering the horse, he has gained a swiftness of which his legs were incapable in order to approach animal and enemy with paralyzing suddenness. With bow and arrow and tomahawk, he has extended the skill and strength of his arm. The breath of the sacred pipe has won him the good will of men; the voice of the love flute, the woman's favor. Charms have brought him all kinds of luck with a power stronger than naked breath, word, or wish. But the Great Spirit, he has learned, must be approached only with the searching concentration of the man who, naked, alone, and unarmed, goes into the wilderness to fast and to pray.

5. THE SUPERNATURAL

A. The Sun Dance

The paradise of orality and its loss during the rages of the biting stage, as we suggested in the preceding chapter [see *Childhood and Society,* Chapter 2], may be the ontogenetic origin of that deep sense of badness which religion transforms into a conviction of primal sin on a universal scale. Prayer and atonement, therefore, must renounce the all too avaricious desire for "the world" and must demonstrate, in reduced posture and in the inflection of urgent appeal, a return to bodily smallness, to technical helplessness, and to voluntary suffering.

The religious ceremony of highest significance in the life of the Dakota was the Sun Dance, which took place during two four-day periods in summer, "when the buffalo were fat, the wild berries ripe, the grass tall and green." It started with ritual feasting, the expression of gratitude to the Buffalo Spirit, and the demonstrations of fellowship among fellow men. Fertility rites followed, and acts of sexual license such as characterize similar rites in many parts of the world. Then there were war and hunting games which glorified competition among men. Men boisterously recounted their feats in war; women and maidens stepped forward to proclaim their chastity. Finally, the mutual dependence of all the people would be glorified in give-aways and in acts of fraternization.

The climax of the festival was reached with the consummation of self-tortures in fulfillment of vows made at critical times during the year. On the last day the "candidates of the fourth dance" engaged in the highest form of self-torture by putting through the muscles of their chest and back skewers which were attached to the sun pole by long thongs. Gazing directly into the sun and slowly dancing backwards, the men could tear themselves loose by ripping the flesh of their chests open. Thus they became the year's spiritual elite, who through their suffering assured the continued benevolence of the sun and the Buffalo Spirit, the providers of fecundity and fertility. This particular feat of having one's chest ripped open *ad majorem gloriam* constitutes, of course, only one variation of the countless ways in which, all over the world, a sense of evil is atoned for and the continued generosity of the universe assured, and this often after an appropriately riotous farewell to all flesh *(carne vale).*

The meaning of an institutionalized form of atonement must be approached both ontogenetically, as a fitting part of the majority's typical sequence of experiences, and phylogenetically, as part of a religious style. In the particular tribal variation here under discussion I find it suggestive that there should be a relationship between the earliest infantile trauma suffered (the ontogenetic yet culturewide loss of paradise) and the crowning feature of religious atonement. The ceremony would then be the climax to the vicissitudes of that deliberately cultivated (yet, of course, long forgotten) rage at the mother's breast during a biting stage which interferes with the long sucking license. Here the faithful would turn the consequently awakened sadistic wishes which the mothers assigned to the future hunter's ferocity, back against themselves by making their own chests the particular focus of their self-torture. The ceremony, then, would fulfil the old principle of "an eye for an eye"—only that the baby, of course, would have been incapable of perpetrating the destruction for which the man now voluntarily atones. It is hard for our rational minds to comprehend—unless we are schooled in the ways of irrationality—that frustrated wishes, and especially early, preverbal, and quite vague wishes, can leave a residue of sin which goes deeper than any guilt over deeds actually committed and remembered. In our world only the magic sayings of Jesus convey a conviction of these dark matters. We take His word for it, that a wish secretly harbored is as good—or rather, as bad—as a deed committed; and that whatever organ offends us with its persistent desires should be radically extirpated. It is, of course, not necessary that a whole tribe or congregation should follow such a precept to the letter. Rather, the culture must provide for a convention of magic belief and a consistent system of ritual which will permit a few exceptional individuals who feel their culture's particular brand of inner damnation especially deeply (and, maybe, are histrionic enough to want to make a grand spectacle of it) to dramatize, for all to see, the fact that there is a salvation. (In our times, logical doubters and disbelievers often have to take refuge in disease, seemingly accidental mutilation, or unavoidable misfortune in order to express the unconscious idea that they had wanted too much in this world—and had gotten away with it.)

B. Vision Quest

We begin slowly to comprehend that homogeneous cultures have a systematic way of giving rewards in the currency of higher inspiration and exalted prestige for the very sacrifices and frustrations which the child must endure in the process of becoming good and strong in the traditional sense. But how about those who feel that they are "different," and that the prestige possibilities offered do not answer their personal needs? How about those men who do not care to be heroes and those women who do not easily agree to be heroes' mates and helpers?

In our own culture Freud has taught us to study the dreams of neurotic individuals in order to determine what undone deed they could not afford to leave undone, what thought unthought, what memory unremembered in the course of their all too rigid adaptation. We use such knowledge to teach the suffering individual to find a place in his cultural milieu or to criticize an educational system for endangering too many individuals by demanding excessive compliance—and thus endangering itself.

The Sioux, like other primitives, used the dream for the guidance of the strong as well as for the prevention of anarchic deviation. But they did not wait for adult dreams to take care of faulty developments; the adolescent Sioux would go out and seek dreams, or rather visions, while there was still time to decide on a life plan. Unarmed, and naked, except for loincloth and moccasins, he would go out into the prairie, exposing himself to sun, danger, and hunger, and tell the deity of his essential humility and need of guidance. This would come, on the fourth day, in the form of a vision which, as afterwards interpreted by a special committee of dream experts, would encourage him to do especially well the ordinary things such as hunting, warring, or stealing horses; or to bring slight innovations into the institutions of his tribe, inventing a song, a dance, or a prayer; or to become something special such as a doctor or a priest; or finally, to turn to one of those few roles available to confirmed deviants.

For example: A person who was convinced he saw the Thunderbird reported this to his advisers, and from then on at all public occasions was a *"heyoka."* He was obliged to behave as absurdly and clownishly as possible until his advisers thought he had cured himself of the curse. Wissler reports the following instructive *heyoka* experience of an adolescent:

One time when I was about thirteen years old, in the spring of the year, the sun was low and it threatened rain and thunder, while my people were in a camp of four tepees. I had a dream that my father and our family were sitting together in a tepee when lightning struck into their midst. All were stunned. I was the first to become conscious. A neighbor was shouting out around the camp. I was doubled up when first becoming conscious. It was time to take out the horses, so I took them.

As I was coming to my full senses I began to realize what had oc-curred and that I should go through the *heyoka* ceremony when fully recovered. I heard a herald shouting this about, but am not sure it was real. I knew I was destined to go through the *heyoka*. I cried some to myself. I told my father I had seen the Thunder-Bird: "Well, son," he said, "you must go through with it." I was told that I must be a *heyoka*. If I did not go through with the ceremony, I would be killed by light-ning. After this I realized that I must formally tell in the ceremony ex-actly what I experienced.[7]

As can be seen, it was important that the dreamer should succeed in conveying to his listeners the feeling of an experience which complied with a recognized form of manifest dream and in which he was the overwhelmed recipient, in which case the higher powers were assumed to have given him a convincing sign that they wished him to plan or change his life's course in a certain way.

The expiation could consist of anti-natural behavior during a given period, or for life, depending on the interpretation of the advisers. The absurd activities demanded of the unlucky dreamer were either simply silly and absurd or terrifying. Sometimes he was even condemned to kill somebody. His friends would urge compliance, for defense against evil spirits was more important than the preservation of individual life.

One conversant with the ego's tricky methods of overcoming feelings of anxiety and guilt will not fail to recognize in the *heyoka's* antics the ac-tivities of children playing the clown or debasing and otherwise harm-ing themselves when they are frightened or pursued by a bad conscience. One method of avoiding offense to the gods is to humiliate oneself or put oneself in the wrong light before the public. As everybody is induced to permit himself to be fooled and to laugh, the spirits forget and forgive and may even applaud. The clown with his proverbial secret melancholy and the radio comedian who makes capital of his own inferiorities seem to be professional elaborations in our culture of this defense mechanism. Among the Sioux too, the much-despised *heyoka* could prove to be so artful in his antics that he could finally become a headman.

Others might dream of the moon, a hermaphrodite buffalo, or the double-woman and thus learn that they were not to follow the life plan designed for their sex. Thus a girl may encounter the double-woman who leads her to a lone tepee.

> As the woman comes up to the door and looks in she beholds the two deer-women sitting at the rear. By them she is directed to choose which side she shall enter. Along the wall of one side is a row of skin-dressing tools, on the other, a row of parfleche headdress bags. If the former is chosen, they will say, "You have chosen wrong, but you will become very rich." If she chooses the other side, they will say, "You are on the right track, all you shall have shall be an empty bag."[8]

Such a girl would have to leave the traditional road of Sioux femininity and be active in her quest after men. She would be called *witko* (crazy) and be considered a whore. Yet she too could gain fame in recognition of her artfulness, and achieve the status of a hetaira.

A boy may see:

> ... the moon having two hands, one holds a bow and arrows, the other the burden strap of a woman. The moon bids the dreamer take his choice; when the man reaches to take the bow, the hands suddenly cross and try to force the strap upon the man who struggles to waken before he takes it, and he also tries to succeed in capturing the bow. In either event he escapes the penalty of the dream. Should he fail and become possessed of the strap he is doomed to be like a woman.[9]

If such a boy does not prefer to commit suicide he must give up the career of warrior and hunter and become a *berdache,* a man-woman who dresses like a woman and does woman's work. The *berdaches* were not necessarily homosexuals, though some are said to have been married to other men, some to have been visited by warriors before war parties. Most *berdaches,* however, were like eunuchs, simply considered not dangerous to women, and therefore good companions and even teachers for them, because they often excelled in the arts of cooking and embroidery.

A homogeneous culture such as that of the Sioux, then, deals with its deviants by giving them a secondary role, as clown, prostitute, or artist, without, however, freeing them entirely from the ridicule and horror which the vast majority must maintain in order to suppress in themselves what the deviant represents. However, the horror remains directed against the power of the spirits which have intruded themselves upon the deviant individual's dreams. It does not turn against the stricken individual himself. In this way, primitive cultures accept the power of the unconscious. If the deviant can only claim to have dreamed convincingly, his deviation is considered to be based on supernatural visitation rather than on individual motivation. As psychopathologists, we must admire the way in which these "primitive" systems undertook to maintain elastic mastery in a matter where more sophisticated systems often fail.

6. SUMMARY

The Sioux, under traumatic conditions, has lost the reality for which the last historical form of his communal integrity was fitted. Before the white man came, he was a fighting nomad and a buffalo hunter. The buffalo disappeared, slaughtered by invaders. The Sioux then became a warrior on the defense, and was defeated. He almost cheerfully learned to round up cattle instead of encircling buffalo: his cattle were taken from him. He could become a sedentary farmer, only at the price of being a sick man, on bad land.

Thus, step for step, the Sioux has been denied the bases for a collective identity formation and with it that reservoir of collective integrity from which the individual must derive his stature as a social being.

Fear of famine has led the Sioux to surrender communal functions to the feeding conqueror. Far from remaining a transitional matter of treaty obligation, federal help has continued to be necessary, and this more and more in the form of relief. At the same time, the government has not succeeded in reconciling old and new images, nor indeed in laying the nucleus for a conscience new in both form and content. Child training, so we claim, remains the sensitive instrument of one cultural synthesis until a new one proves convincing and inescapable.

The problem of Indian education is, in reality, one of culture contact between a group of employees representative of the middle-class values of a free-enterprise system on the one hand, and on the other, the remnants of a tribe which, wherever it leaves the shadow of government sustenance, must find itself among the underprivileged of that system.

In fact, the ancient principles of child training still operating in the remnants of the tribe undermine the establishment of a white conscience. The developmental principle in this system holds that a child should be permitted to be an individualist while young. The parents do not show any hostility toward the body as such nor do they, especially in boys, decry self-will. There is no condemnation of infantile habits while the child is developing that system of communication between self and body and self and kin on which the infantile ego is based. Only when strong in body and sure in self is he asked to bow to a tradition of unrelenting shaming by public opinion which focuses on his actual social behavior rather than on his bodily functions or his fantasies. He is incorporated into an elastic tradition which in a strictly institutionalized way takes care of his social needs, diverting dangerous instinctual tendencies toward outer enemies, and always allowing him to project the source of possible guilt into the supernatural. We have seen how stubborn this conscience has remained even in the face of the glaring reality of historical change.

In contrast, the dominating classes in Western civilization, represented here in their bureaucracy, have been guided by the conviction that a systematic regulation of functions and impulses in earliest childhood is the surest safeguard for later effective functioning in society. They implant the never-silent metronome of routine into the impressionable baby and young child to regulate his first experiences with his body and with his immediate physical surroundings. Only after such mechanical socialization is he encouraged to proceed to develop into a rugged individualist. He pursues ambitious strivings, but compulsively remains within standardized careers which, as the economy becomes more and more complicated, tend to replace more general responsibilities. The specialization thus developed has led this Western civilization to the mastery of machinery, but also to an undercurrent of boundless discontent and of individual disorientation.

Naturally the rewards of one educational system mean little to members of another system, while the costs are only too obvious to them. The undisturbed Sioux cannot understand how anything except *restoration* is worth striving for, his racial as well as his individual history having provided him with the memory of abundance. The white man's conscience, on the other hand, asks for continuous *reform* of himself in the pursuit of careers leading to ever higher standards. This reform demands an increasingly internalized conscience, one that will act against temptation automatically and unconsciously, without the presence of critical observers. The Indian conscience, more preoccupied with the necessity of avoiding embarrassing situations within a system of clearly defined honors and shames, is without orientation in conflicting situations which depend for their solution on an "inner voice."

The system underlying Sioux education is a primitive one—i.e., it is based on the adaptation of a highly ethnocentric, relatively small group of people, who consider only themselves to be relevant mankind, to one segment of nature. The primitive cultural system limits itself:

In specializing the individual child for one main career, here the buffalo hunter;

In perfecting a narrow range of the tool world which extends the reach of the human body over the prey;

In the use of magic as the only means of coercing nature.

Such self-restriction makes for homogeneity. There is a strong synthesis of geographic, economic, and anatomic patterns which in Sioux life find their common denominator in *centrifugality*, as expressed in a number of items discussed, such as:

The social organization in bands, which makes for easy dispersion and migration;

The dispersion of tension in the extended family system;

Nomadic technology and the ready use of horse and gun;

The distribution of property by the give-away;

The diversion of aggression toward prey and outgroup.

Sioux child training forms a firm basis for this system of centrifugality by establishing a lasting center of trust, namely the nursing mother, and then by handling the matter of teething, of infantile rage, and of muscular aggression in such a way that the greatest possible degree of ferocity is provoked, channelized socially, and finally released against prey and enemy. We believe that we are dealing here, not with simply causality, but with a mutual assimilation of somatic, mental, and social patterns which amplify one another and make the cultural design for living economical and effective. Only such integration provides a sense of being at home in this world. Transplanted into our system, however, the very expression of what was once considered to be efficient and aristocratic behavior—such as the disregard for property and the refusal to compete—only leads to an alignment with the lowest strata of our society.

7. A SUBSEQUENT STUDY

In 1942, five years after my fieldtrip with Mekeel, a companion of our 1937 reservation days, Gordon MacGregor, directed an intensive and extensive study of 200 Pine Ridge children. This was part of a larger Indian Education Research Project which undertook to gather detailed material on childhood and tribal personality in five American Indian tribes. The study was jointly sponsored and staffed by the University of Chicago and by the Indian Service. MacGregor and his group had the opportunity, as we had not, of having Indian children observed in school and home throughout a year, and this by a team of observers who had had experience with other Indian tribes as well as with white children, and who mastered a variety of specially adapted tests. His study, therefore, can serve as an example of the verification of clinical impressions—and as a progress report.

I shall first abstract here a few of the items of old child training which—according to MacGregor's account[10]—seem to have persisted in one form or another, especially among the full-blood or less mixed-blood Indians of the reservation population.

Babies, so MacGregor reports, are pinned into a tight bundle. While held, they are lightly rocked without interruption. Some children are weaned as early as nine months, some as late as thirty-six months; most of them somewhere between eleven and eighteen months. There is little thumbsucking. Pacifiers were observed in three cases: one was of rubber, one was of pork, and one was a wiener. The habit of "snapping the thumbnail against the front teeth" is a common Dakota habit. Tooth-clicking occurs predominately among women and girls.

The early development of the child is watched by adults with amusement and patience. There is no hurrying along the path of walking or talking. On the other hand, there is no baby talk. The language usually taught first is the old Indian one: English is still a problem to many children when they enter school.

Toilet training is accomplished primarily by example. When no white people are around, the infant perambulates without diapers or underpants. However, there is a tendency to hasten bowel control and to specify localities for excretion.

Modern Dakota children are carefully trained to be generous. They still receive valuable gifts such as horses. Children of five, six, and seven give freely—and pleasantly. "At one funeral where there was much giving, a small boy of the bereaved family spent his only dime to buy artificial orange powder in order to give a bucket of orangeade ceremonially to the visiting youngsters." Property is sometimes removed but otherwise not protected against children, a fact watched by white people "in bewilderment and utter frustration."

The main means of education are warning and shaming. The children are allowed to scream in rage; it "will make them strong." Spanking, while more frequent, is still rare. Shaming is intensified, especially if the child continues to misbehave, and adults at home single out as misbehavior primarily selfishness and competitiveness, the seeking after gains based on the disadvantage of others. Tense home situations are evaded by visiting homes at some distance.

Little boys (instead of playing with bow and arrow, and buffalo-foot bones) are given ropes and slingshots and, for the glory of the hunter's spirit, are encouraged to chase roosters and other small animals. Girls play with dolls and at keeping house.

By the time he is five or six, the Dakota child has acquired a feeling of security and affection in the family. Some separation of sexes is initiated, but the institution of avoidance has been abandoned: this, in fact, is noted by all observers as the most outstanding change. It is only in paired dances that brothers and sisters will avoid one another.

In school those of more mixed blood are learning to enjoy competition, and school in general is enjoyed as a get-together when family ties are outgrown. Yet many withdraw from competitive activities, and some refuse to respond at all. "To be asked to compete in class goes against the grain with the Dakota child, and he criticizes the competitive ones among his fellows." This difficulty, paired with the inability to speak English and fear of the white teacher, leads to frequent instances of embarrassed withdrawal or running away. The child is not punished when he runs home: his parents themselves are used to quitting work or community when embarrassed or angered.

Younger boys hit girls more than is usual in white schools. In older boys, competitive games such as baseball may on occasion lead to embarrassment because of the necessary display of competitiveness. However, there is an increased tendency among boys to fight in anger both at home and in school.

The older girls still act afraid of boys and men, always travel with other girls, refuse to ride horseback, and keep completely apart from boys.

The boarding school, which (compared to the homes) is a place of physical luxury and of rich opportunities for varied interests, affords the pleasantest years in the child's life—and yet the great majority of students who enter high school do not graduate; they sooner or later play truant and finally quit for good. Causes are, again and again, embarrassment over situations in which the problem of shame and competition, of full blood and mixed blood, and of male and female have become insoluble because of the change in mores. Moreover, long training does not seem to promise a better-defined identity—or a more secure income.

Except in boom years, grown boys and girls tend to stay in the reservation or to return to it. Because of their early training, their home seems to be the most secure place, although the school years have made both home and youngster less acceptable to one another. Having learned that poverty can be avoided, the youngsters mind seeing their fathers idle, or shiftless; now more ambitious, they deplore the persistent trend toward dependence upon the government; now more accustomed to white ways, they find the continuous pressure of critical gossip destructive, especially where it undermines what little they themselves have assimilated of white ways. As for themselves, what they have learned in school has prepared them for a homogeneous development of tribal rehabilitation which is kept from jelling by the inducements of the armed services, of migratory labor, and of industrial work. The latter trends expose them to the problems of the poorest white rural and colored urban populations. Only to be a soldier gives new luster to an ancient role—when there happens to be a war on.

Those who follow their teachers' example and go to college or prepare for civil-service positions, as a rule seek employment on other reservations to escape the double standard, which recognizes them as better trained, yet expects them to be silent when their more experienced elders speak. Thus potential leaders are lost to the community. Young men and women of integrity and stamina still emerge; but they are the exceptions. Reliable new models for Dakota children have not yet crystallized.

We have outlined what, according to MacGregor's study, has remained constant in Indian child rearing. Let us now see what is changing.

The greatest change in Dakota life has probably been in the status of the family as a whole: instead of being a reinforcement of self-sufficiency it has become the refuge of those who feel isolated and inefficient. The strongest remaining tie seems to be that between brothers: a healthy tie, easily transferable and usable for the establishment of new communal pursuits. The weakest relationship, however, seems to be that between the children and their fathers, who cannot teach them anything and who, in fact, have become models to be avoided. Instead, boys seek praise from their age mates. Among girls, almost all of the old avoidances have been abandoned or weakened to the point where they are little more than empty acts of compliance. A strange mixture of sadness, anger, and, again and again, shame and embarrassment seems to have stepped into the breach of these old respect relationships. Getting an education and getting a job are new and strong ambitions, which, however, are apparently soon exhausted because they cannot attach themselves to any particular roles and functions. The children feel what their elders know—namely, that (and these are my words) "Washington," the climate, and the market make all prediction impossible.

MacGregor's study employed an extensive "battery" of interviews and tests in order to arrive at a formulation of the "Dakota personality," a composite picture which, he says, represents neither the "personality of any one child nor the personalities of a majority of the children: it could not be said to exist in all its elements in any one child, let alone in a majority." I shall not question or discuss the methodology used in the study, but shall merely abstract some of the data which throw light on these children's inner life.

To settle one question which, I am sure, many a reader has been wanting to ask: The intelligence of the Dakota children is slightly above that of white children. Their health, however, corresponds to that of the underprivileged rural whites. Chronic hunger, no doubt, causes apathy, and much of the slowness, the lack of ambition, and also the grinding bitterness of reservation life is simply due to hunger. Yet MacGregor's group, after exhaustive study, feels that the general apathy is as much the cause as it is the result of the hunger; for it has hindered initiative and industry in situations which offered chances of improvement.

Tests of thematic imagination among the Dakota children and spontaneous stories told by them reflect their image of the world. In the following, it must be kept in mind that such tests do not ask: how do you see the world and how do you look at things?—since few adults, fewer children, and no Indian children would know what to say. The testers therefore present a picture, or a story, or pages with vague inkblots on them, and say: what do you see in *this?*—a procedure which makes the child forget his reality, and yet unconsciously give away his disappointments, his wishes, and, above all, his basic attitude toward human existence.

Dakota children, so their testers say after careful quantitative analysis of the themes produced and the apperceptions revealed, describe the world as dangerous and hostile. Affectionate relationships in early home life are remembered with nostalgia. Otherwise the world for them seems to have little definiteness and little purpose. In their stories the characters are not named, there is no clear-cut action and no definite outcome. Correspondingly, caution and negativism become the major characteristics of the utterances of the group as a whole. Their guilt and their anger are expressed in stories of petty and trivial criticism, of aimless slapping or of impulsive stealing, just for vengeance. Like all children, they like stories in which to escape from the present, but the Dakota child's imaginativeness returns to the time before the coming of the white man. Fantasies of the old life "are not recounted as past glories but as satisfactions that may return to make up for the hardships and fears of the present." In the children's stories, action is mostly initiated by others, and it is mostly inconsiderate, untrustworthy, and hostile action, leading to fights and to the destruction of toys and property, and causing in the narrator sadness, fear, and anger. The narrator's action leads almost always to fighting, damaging of property, breaking of rules, and stealing. Animals, too, are represented as frightening, and this not only in the traditional cases of rattlesnakes, roaming dogs, and vicious bulls, but also in that of horses, which these children, in actuality, learn to handle early and with pleasure. In the frequency of themes, worry about the death of other people, their sickness, or their departure, is second only to descriptions of hostility emanating from people or from animals. On the positive side there is the universal wish to go to movies, fairs, and rodeos, where (as the testers interpret it) children can be with many without being with anybody in particular.

The study concludes that the children in the earliest age group tested (6 to 8) promise better-organized personalities than they will later have; that the group from 9 to 12 seem relatively the freest, the most at ease with themselves, although already behind white children in exuberance and vivacity; and that with the advent of puberty, the children begin to retire more completely within themselves and to lose interest in the world around them. They resign themselves and become apathetic and passive. The boys, however, show more expression and ambition, though in a somewhat unbalanced way; while the girls, as they enter pubescence, are prone to display agitation, followed by a kind of paralysis of action. In adolescence, stealing triples and the fear of the ill will of society seems to include elders and institutions, white and Indian.

In view of all of these observations it is hard to see how MacGregor's group can have come to their main conclusion, namely, that the "crippled and negative" state of Dakota child personality, and its rejection of life, emotion, and spontaneity, are due to "repressive forces set in action early in the child's life." My conclusion would be, as before, that early childhood among the Dakota, within the limits of poverty and general listlessness, is a relatively rich and spontaneous existence which permits the school child to emerge from the family with a relative integration— i.e., with much trust, a little autonomy, and some initiative. This initiative between the ages of nine and twelve is still naïvely and not too successfully applied to play and work; while it becomes inescapably clear only in puberty that what initiative has been salvaged will not find an identity. Emotional withdrawal and general absenteeism are the results.

MacGregor's material makes it particularly clear and significant that the breakdown of the respect relationships, together with the absence of goals for initiative, leaves unused and undiverted the infantile rage which is still provoked in early child training. The result is apathy and depression. Similarly, without the balance of attainable rewards, shaming becomes a mere sadistic habit, done for vengeance rather than for guidance.

The view of the adult world as hostile, understandable as it is on grounds of social reality, seems to have received a powerful reinforcement from the projection of the child's inner rage—which is why the environment is pictured not only as forbidding but also as destructive, while loved ones are in danger of departing or dying. Here I feel strongly that the Dakota child now *projects* where in his old system he *diverted*. A striking example would be the horse, once a friendly animal, which here becomes the object of projection. But at the same time it seems to me to be the now hopelessly misplaced and distorted original image of an inimical beast of prey. In the buffalo days, as we saw, there was an animal on whom all the early provoked affective imagery of hunting and killing could be concentrated, there is now no goal for such initiative. Thus the individual becomes afraid of his own unused power of aggression, and such fear expresses itself in his seeing, outside of himself, dangers which do not exist, or which are exaggerated in fantasy. In social reality impulsive and vengeful stealing finally becomes the lone expression of that "grasping and biting" ferocity which once was the well-guided force behind hunting and warring. The fear of the relatives' death or departure is probably a sign of the fact that the home, with all its poverty, represents the remnant of a once integrated culture; even as a mere dream of restoration it has more reality—than reality. It is, then, not this system of training as such and its "repressive forces" which stunt the child, but the fact that for the last hundred years the integrative mechanisms of child training have not been encouraged to sustain a new promising system of significant social roles, as they had done once before when the Dakota became buffalo hunters.

The cattle economy, we are happy to hear from MacGregor, is making consistent progress, together with the rehabilitation of the soil and the return of the high grass. However, the establishment of a healthy cattle economy again called for government rations, which, with the forgetful advance of history, are losing their original character of a right acquired by treaty and are becoming common dole. Industrial opportunities still call the Indian away from a consistent concentration on his communal rehabilitation, while they offer the shiftless Indian only the lower identities in the American success system. But at least they pay well, and they pay for work rendered, not for battles lost in the last century. In the end, with all respect and understanding for the Indian's special situation and nature, and with fervent wishes for the success of his rehabilitation, the conclusion remains inevitable that he can in the long run benefit only from a cultural and political advance of the rural poor and of the non-white population of the whole nation. Child-training systems change to advantage only where the universal trend toward larger cultural entities is sustained.

FISHERMEN ALONG A SALMON RIVER

from *Childhood and Society*

1. THE WORLD OF THE YUROK

For comparison and counterpoint, let us turn from the melancholy "warriors without weapons" to a tribe of fishermen and acorn gatherers on the Pacific coast: the Yurok.[1]

The Sioux and the Yurok seem to have been diametrically opposite in the basic configurations of existence. The Sioux roamed the plains and cultivated spatial concepts of centrifugal mobility; their horizons were the roaming herds of buffalo and the shifting enemy bands. The York lived in a narrow, mountainous, densely forested river valley and along the coast of its outlet into the Pacific. Moreover, they limited themselves within the arbitrary borders of a circumscribed universe.[2] They considered a disk of about 150 miles in diameter, cut in half by the course of their Klamath River, to include all there was to this world. They ignored the rest and ostracized as "crazy" or "of ignoble birth" anyone who showed a marked tendency to venture into territories beyond. They prayed to their horizons, which they thought contained the supernatural "homes" from which generous spirits sent the stuff of life to them: the (actually non-existent) lake upriver whence the Klamath flows; the land across the ocean which is the salmon's home; the region of the sky which sends the deer; and the place up the coast where the shell money comes from. There was no centrifugal east and west, south and north. There was an "upstream" and a "downstream," a "toward the river," and an "away from the river," and then, at the borders of the world (i.e., where the next tribes live), an elliptical "in back and around": as centripetal a world as could be designed.

Within this restricted radius of existence, extreme localization took place. An old Yurok asked me to drive him to his ancestors' home. When we arrived, he proudly pointed to a hardly noticeable pit in the ground and said: "This is where I come from." Such pits retain the family name forever. In fact, Yurok localities exist by name only in so far as human history or mythology has dignified them. These myths do not mention mountain peaks or the gigantic redwoods which impress white travelers so much; yet the Yurok will point to certain insignificant-looking rocks and trees as being the "origin" of the most far-reaching events. The acquisition and retention of possessions is and was what the Yurok thinks about, talks about, and prays for. Every person, every relationship, and every act can be exactly valued and becomes the object of pride or ceaseless bickering. The Yurok had money before they ever saw a white man. They used a currency of shells of different sizes which they carried in oblong purses. These shells were traded from inland tribes; the Yurok, of course, never "strayed" near the places on the northern coast where they could have found these shells in inflationary numbers.

This little, well-defined Yurok world, cut in two by the Klamath, has, as it were, its "mouth open" toward the ocean and the yearly mysterious appearance of tremendous numbers of powerful salmon which enter the estuary of the Klamath, climb its turbulent rapids, and disappear upriver, where they spawn and die. Some months later their diminutive progeny descend the river and disappear out in the ocean, in order that two years later, as mature salmon, they may return to their birthplace to fulfill their life cycles.

The Yurok speak of "clean" living, not of "strong" living, as do the Sioux. Purity consists of continuous avoidance of impure contacts and contaminations, and of constant purification from possible contaminations. Having had intercourse with a woman, or having slept in the same house with women, the fisherman must pass the "test" of the sweat house. He enters through the normal-sized door; normal meaning an oval hole through which even a fat person could enter. However, the man can leave the sweat house only through a very small opening which will permit only a man moderate in his eating habits and supple with the perspiration caused by the sacred fire to slip through. He is required to conclude the purification by swimming in the river. The conscientious fisherman passes this test every morning.

This is only one example of a series of performances which express a world image in which the various channels of nature and anatomy must be kept apart. For that which flows in one channel of life is said to abhor contaminating contact with the objects of other channels. Salmon and the river dislike it if anything is eaten on a boat. Urine must not enter the river. Deer will stay away from the snare if deer meat has been brought in contact with water. Salmon demands that women on their trip up or down river keep special observances, for they may be menstruating.

Only once a year, during the salmon run, are these avoidances set aside. At that time, following complicated ceremonies, a strong dam is built which obstructs the ascent of the salmon and permits the Yurok to catch a rich winter supply. The dam building is "the largest mechanical enterprise undertaken by the Yurok, or, for that matter, by any California Indians, and the most communal attempt" (Kroeber). After ten days of collective fishing, orgies of ridicule and of sexual freedom take place along the sides of the river, reminiscent of the ancient pagan spring ceremonials in Europe, and of Sioux license before the Sun Dance.

The supreme ceremony of the fish dam is thus the counterpart of the Sioux's Sun Dance; it begins with a grandiose mass dramatization of the creation of the world, and it contains pageants which repeat the progress of Yurok ethos from centrifugal license to the circumscribed centripetality which finally became its law and its reassurance of continued supply from the Supernatural Providers.

To these ceremonials we shall return when we can relate them to Yurok babyhood. What has been said will be sufficient to indicate that in size and structure the Yurok world was very different from—if not in almost systematic opposition to—that of the Sioux.

And what different people they are, even today! After having seen the apathetic erstwhile masters of the prairie, it was almost a relief, albeit a relief paired with shock, on arrival at a then nearly inaccessible all-Yurok village, to be treated as a member of an unwelcome white minority and to be told to go and room with the pigs—"they are the white man's dog."

There are several all-Yurok villages along the lower Klamath, the

largest representing a late integration, in the Gold Rush days, of a number of very old villages. Situated on a sunny clearing, it is accessible only
by motorboat from the coast, or over foggy, hazardous roads. When I undertook to spend a few weeks there in order to collect and check my data
concerning Yurok childhood, I met immediately with the "resistive and
suspicious temperament" which the Yurok as a group are supposed to
have. Luckily I had met and had worked with some Yurok individuals living near the estuary of the Klamath; and Kroeber had prepared me for
folkways of stinginess, suspicion, and anger. I could therefore refrain from
holding their behavior against them—or, indeed, from being discouraged
by it. So I settled down in an abandoned camp by the river and waited
to find out what might in this case be specifically the matter. It appeared
that, at the coast, I had visited and had eaten meals with deadly enemies
of an influential upriver family. The feud dated back to the eighties of the
last century. Furthermore, it seemed that this isolated community was unable to accept my declaration of scientific intention. Instead, they suspected me of being an agent come to investigate such matters as the
property feuds brought about by the discussion of the Howard-Wheeler
Act. According to ancient maps, existing only in people's minds, Yurok
territory is a jigsaw puzzle of community land, land with common ownership, and individual family property. Opposition to the Howard-
Wheeler Act, which forbids the Indians to sell their land except to one
another, had taken the form of disputing what the single Yurok could
claim and sell if and when the act should be repealed, and one of my suspected secret missions apparently was that of trying under false pretenses
to delineate property rights which the officials had been unable to establish. In addition, the fatal illness of a young Shaker and the visit of high
Shaker clergy from the north had precipitated religious issues. Noisy
praying and dancing filled the night air. Shakerism was opposed at the
time not only by the government doctor, with whom I had been seen
downriver, and by the few survivors of the ancient craft of Yurok medicine, but also by a newly arrived missionary. He was a Seventh-Day Ad-
ventist, the only other white man in the community, who by greeting me
kindly, although with undisguised disapproval of the cigarette in my
hand, compromised me further in the eyes of the natives. It took days of
solitary waiting before I could discuss their suspicions with some of the
Indians, and before I found informants who further clarified the outlines
of traditional Yurok childhood. Once he knows you are a friend, how-

ever, the individual Yurok loses his prescribed suspicion and becomes a dignified informant.

The unsubdued and overtly cynical attitude of most Yurok toward the white man must, I think, be attributed to the fact that the inner distance between Yurok and whites is not as great as that between whites and Sioux. There was much in the centripetal A B C of Yurok life that did not have to be relearned when the whites came. The Yurok lived in solid frame houses which were half sunk in the ground. The present frame houses are next to pits in the ground which once contained the subterranean dwellings of ancestors. Unlike the Sioux, who suddenly lost the focus of his economic and spiritual life with the disappearance of the buffalo, the Yurok still sees and catches, eats and talks salmon. When the Yurok man today steers a raft of logs, or the Yurok woman grows vegetables, their occupations are not far removed from the original manufacture of dugouts (a onetime export industry), the gathering of acorns, and the planting of tobacco. Above all, the Yurok has been concerned all his life with property. He knows how to discuss a matter in dollars and cents, and he does so with deep ritual conviction. The Yurok need not abandon this "primitive" tendency in the money-minded white world. His grievances against the United States thus find other than the inarticulate, smoldering expression of the prairie man's passive resistance.

On the Fourth of July, when "the mourners of the year" were paid off in an all-night dance ritual, I had the opportunity to see many children assembled to watch a dance, the climax of which was not scheduled until dawn. They were vigorous and yet graceful, even-tempered, and well-behaved throughout the long night.

2. YUROK CHILD PSYCHIATRY

Fanny, one of Alfred Kroeber's oldest informants, called herself, and was called by others, a "doctor." So far as she treated somatic disorders or used the Yurok brand of physiological treatment, I could not claim to be her professional equal. However, she also did psychotherapy with children, and in this field it was possible to exchange notes. She laughed heartily about psychoanalysis, the main therapeutic principles of which, as will be shown presently, can easily be expressed in her terms. There was a radiant friendliness and warmth in this very old woman. When melancholy made her glance and her smile withdraw behind the stone-carved pattern of her wrinkles, it was a dramatic melancholy, a positive withdrawal, not the immovable sadness sometimes seen in the faces of other Indian women.

As a matter of fact, Fanny was in an acute state of gloom when we arrived. Some days before, on stepping out into her vegetable garden and glancing over the scene, a hundred feet below, where the Klamath enters the Pacific, she had seen a small whale enter the river, play about a little, and disappear again. This shocked her deeply. Had not the creator decreed that only salmon, sturgeon, and similar fish should cross the fresh-water barrier? This breakdown of a barrier could only mean that the world disk was slowly losing its horizontal position, that salt water was entering the river, and that a flood was approaching comparable to the one which once before had destroyed mankind. However, she told only a few intimates about it, indicating that perhaps the event could still become untrue if not talked about too much.

It was easy to converse with this old Indian woman because usually she was merry and quite direct, except when questions came up bordering on taboo subjects. During our first interviews Kroeber had sat behind us, listening and now and again interrupting. On the second day, I suddenly noticed that he was absent from the room for some time, and I asked where he had gone. The old woman laughed merrily and said, "He give you chance to ask alone. You big man now."

What are the causes of child neuroses (bad temper, lack of appetite, nightmares, delinquency, etc.) in Yurok culture? If a child, after dark, sees one of the "wise people," a race of small beings which preceded the human race on earth, he develops a neurosis, and if he is not cured he eventually dies.

The "wise people" are described as not taller than a small child. They are always "in spirit," because they do not know sexual intercourse. They are adult at six months of age, and they are immortal. They procreate orally, the female eating the male's lice. The orifice of birth is unclear; however, it is certain that the "wise" female has not a "woman's inside"— that is, vagina and uterus, with the existence of which, as will be shown later, sin and social disorder entered the world.

We observe that the "wise people" are akin to infants. They are small, oral, and magic, and they do not know genitality, guilt, and death. They are visible and dangerous only for children because children are still fixated on earlier stages and may regress when the stimulation of the daylight is waning—then, becoming dreamy, they may be attracted by the "wise people's" childishness and by their intuitive and yet anarchic ways. For the "wise people" are without social organization. They are creative, but they know no genitality and, consequently, what it means to be "clean." Thus the "wise" men could well serve the projection of the pregenital state of childhood into phylogeny and prehistory.

If a child shows disturbances or complains of pain indicating that he may have seen "wise people," his grandmother goes out in the garden or to the creek, or wherever she has been informed that the child has played after dark, cries aloud, and speaks to the spirits: "This is our child; do not harm it." If this is of no avail, the grandmother next door is asked to "sing her song" to the child. Every grandmother has her own song. American Indian cultures seem to have an amazing understanding of ambivalence, which dictates that in certain crises near relatives are of no educational or therapeutic use. If the neighbor grandmother does not avail, Fanny is finally appealed to and a price is set for the cure.

Fanny says she often feels that a patient is coming:

Sometimes I can't sleep; somebody is after me to go and doctor. I not drink water, and sure somebody come. "Fanny, I come after you, I give you ten dollars." I say, "I go for fifteen dollars." "All right."

The child is brought by his whole family and put on the floor of Fanny's living room. She smokes her pipe to "get into her power." Then, if necessary, the child is held down by mother and father while Fanny sucks the first "pain" from above the child's navel. These "pains," the somatic "causes" of illness (although they, in turn, can be caused by bad wishes), are visualized as a kind of slimy, bloody materialization. To prepare herself for this task Fanny must abstain from water for a given period. "As she sucks, it is as if her chin were going through to your spine, but it doesn't hurt," one informant reports. However, every "pain" has a "mate"; a thread of slime leads Fanny to the place of the "mate," which is sucked out also.

We see that to the Yurok disease is bisexual. One sex is represented as being near the center of the body, which is most susceptible to sorcery, while the other has wandered to the afflicted part, like the floating uterus

in the Greek theory of hysteria or the displaced organ cathexis in the psychoanalytic system.

Having swallowed two or three "pains," Fanny goes to a corner and sits
down with her face to the wall. She puts four fingers, omitting the
thumb, into her throat and vomits slime into a basket. Then, when she
feels that the "pains" she has swallowed are coming up, she holds her
hands in front of her mouth, "like two shells," and with spitting noises,
spits the child's "pain" into her hands. Then she dances, making the
"pains" disappear. This she repeats until she feels that all the "pains" have
been taken out of the child.

Then comes the Yurok version of an interpretation. She smokes again,
dances again, and goes into a trance. She sees a fire, a cloud, a mist, then
sits down, fills her pipe anew, takes a big mouthful of smoke, and then has
a more substantial vision, which makes her say to the assembled family
something like this: "I see an old woman sitting in the Bald Hills and
wishing something bad to another woman. That is why this child is sick."
She has hardly spoken when the grandmother of the child rises and confesses that it was she who on a certain day sat in the Bald Hills and tried
to practice sorcery upon another woman. Or Fanny says, "I see a man and
a woman doing business [having intercourse], although the man has
prayed for good luck and should not touch a woman." At this, the father
or the uncle gets up and confesses to his guilt. Sometimes Fanny has to
accuse a dead person of sorcery or perversion, in which event the son or
the daughter of the deceased tearfully confesses to his misdeeds.

It seems that Fanny has a certain inventory of sins (comparable to the
"typical events" of our psychotherapeutic schools), which she attaches,
under ritualistic circumstances, to a certain disturbance. She thus makes
people confess as facts tendencies which, in view of the structure of the
culture, can be predicted, and the confession of which is profitable for
anybody's inner peace. Having an exalted position in a primitive community, Fanny is, of course, in possession of enough gossip to know her
patients' weaknesses even before she sees them and is experienced enough
to read her patients' faces while she goes about her magic business. If she,
then, connects a feeling of guilt derived from secret aggression or perversion with the child's symptoms, she is on good psychopathological
grounds, and we are not surprised to hear that neurotic symptoms usually disappear after Fanny has put her finger on the main source of ambivalence in the family and has provoked a confession in public.

3. YUROK CHILD TRAINING

Here are the data on childhood in the Yurok world.

The birth of a baby is safeguarded with *oral* prohibitions, in addition to the genital ones observed by the Sioux. During the birth, the mother must shut her mouth. Father and mother eat neither deer meat nor salmon until the child's navel is healed. Disregard of this taboo, so the Yurok believed, is the cause of convulsions in the child.

The newborn is not breast-fed for ten days, but is given a nut soup from a tiny shell. The breast feeding begins with Indian generosity and frequency. However, unlike the Sioux, the Yurok have a definite weaning time around the sixth month—that is, around the teething period: a minimal breast-feeding period for American Indians. Weaning is called "forgetting the mother" and, if necessary, is enforced toward the end of the first year by the mother's going away for a few days. The first solid food is salmon or deer meat well salted with seaweed. Salty foods are the Yurok's "sweets." The attempt at accelerating autonomy by early weaning seems to be part of a general tendency to encourage the baby to leave the mother and her support as soon as this is possible and bearable. It begins in utero. The pregnant woman eats little, carries much wood, and preferably does work which forces her to bend over forward, so that the fetus "will not rest against her spine"—i.e., relax and recline. She rubs her abdomen often, especially when daylight is waning, in order to keep the fetus awake, and to forestall an early tendency to regress to the state of prehistory which, as we saw, is the origin of all neuroses. Later, not only does early weaning further require him to release his mother; the baby's legs are left uncovered in the Yurok version of the cradleboard, and from the twentieth day on they are massaged by the grandmother to encourage early creeping. The parents' co-operation in this matter is assured by the rule that they may resume intercourse when the baby makes vigorous strides in creeping. The baby is kept from sleeping in the late afternoon and early evening, lest dusk close his eyes forever. The first postnatal crisis, therefore, has a different quality for the Yurok child from the one experienced by the little Sioux. It is characterized by the close proximity in time of teething, enforced weaning, encouraged creeping, and the mother's early return to old sex ways and new childbirths.

We have referred to the affinity between the Sioux baby's oral train-

ing and the desirable traits of a hunter of the plains; and we would expect the Yurok newborn to find a systematically different reception. And,
indeed, the Yurok child is exposed to early and, if necessary, abrupt weaning before or right after the development of the biting stage, and this after
being discouraged by a number of devices from feeling too comfortable
in, with, and around his mother. He is to be trained to be a fisherman:
one who has his nets ready for a prey which (if he only behaves nicely
and says "please" appropriately) will come to him. The Yurok attitude toward supernatural providers is a lifelong fervent "please" which seems to
be reinforced by a residue of infantile nostalgia for the mother from
whom he has been disengaged so forcefully. The good Yurok is characterized by an ability to cry while he prays in order to gain influence over
the food-sending powers beyond the visible world. Tearful words, such
as "I see a salmon," said with the conviction of self-induced hallucination,
will, so he believes, draw a salmon toward him. But he must pretend that
he is not too eager, lest the supply elude him, and he must convince himself that he means no real harm. According to the Yurok, the salmon says:
"I shall travel as far as the river extends. I shall leave my scales on nets and
they will turn into salmon, but I, myself, shall go by and not be killed."

This concentration on the sources of food is not accomplished without a second phase of oral training at the age when the child "has
sense"—i.e., when he can repeat what he has been told. It is claimed that
once upon a time, a Yurok meal was a veritable ceremony of self-restraint.
The child was admonished never to grab food in haste, never to take it
without asking for it, always to eat slowly, and never to ask for a second
helping—an oral puritanism hardly equaled among other primitives.
During meals, a strict order of placement was maintained and the child
was taught to eat in prescribed ways; for example, to put only a little food
on the spoon, to take the spoon up to his mouth slowly, to put the spoon
down while chewing the food—and above all, to think of becoming
rich during the whole process. There was supposed to be silence during
meals so that everybody could keep his thoughts concentrated on money
and salmon. This ceremonial behavior may well have served to lift to the
level of a kind of hallucination that nostalgic need for intake which may
have been evoked by the early weaning from the breast and from contact with the mother, at the stage of strong biting wishes. All "wishful
thinking" was put in the service of economic pursuits. A Yurok could
make himself see money hanging from trees and salmon swimming in the

river during the off season, and he believed that this self-induced hallu-cinatory thought would bring action from the Providers. Later, the en-ergy of genital daydreams is also harnessed to the same economic endeavor. In the "sweat house" the older boy will learn the dual feat of thinking of money and *not* thinking of women.

The fables told to children underline in an interesting way the ugli-ness of lack of restraint. They isolate one outstanding item in the phys-iognomy of animals and use it as an argument for "clean behavior":

The buzzard's baldness is the result of his having impatiently put his whole head into a dish of hot soup.

The greedy eel gambled his bones away.

The hood of the ever-scolding blue jay is her clitoris, which she tore off and put on her head once when she was enviously angry with her husband.

The bear was always hungry. He was married to the blue jay. One day they made a fire and the bear sent the blue jay to get some food. She brought back only one acorn. "Is that all?" the bear said. The blue jay got angry and threw the acorn in the fire. It popped all over the place, and there was acorn all over the ground. The bear swallowed it all down and got awfully sick. Some birds tried to sing for him, but it did not help. Nothing helped. Finally the hummingbird said, "Lie down and open your mouth," and then the hummingbird zipped right through him. This re-lieved him. That's why the bear has such a big anus and can't hold his feces.

This, then, leads us to the anal phase. In Yurok childhood, there seems to be no specific emphasis on feces or on the anal zone, but there is a gen-eral avoidance of all contaminations caused by the contact of antagonis-tic fluids and contents. The infant learns early that he may not urinate into the river or into any subsidiary brook because the salmon that swims in the river would not like to float in the body's fluids. The idea, then, is not so much that urine is "dirty," but that fluids of different tube systems are antagonistic and mutually destructive. Such lifelong and systematic avoidance calls for special safeguards built into personality and identity; and, indeed, the official behavior of the Yurok shows all the traits which psychoanalysis, following Freud and Abraham, has found to be of typi-cal significance in patients with "anal fixations": compulsive ritualization; pedantic bickering; suspicious miserliness; retentive hoarding, etc. Com-pulsiveness in our society is often the expression of just such a general avoidance of contaminations, focused by phobic mothers on the anal zone; but in our culture it is reinforced by excessive demands for a punctuality and orderliness which are absent from Yurok life.

The groundwork for the Yurok's genital attitudes is laid in the child's earlier conditioning, which teaches him to subordinate all instinctual drives to economic considerations. The girl knows that virtue, or shall we say an unblemished name, will gain her a husband who can pay well, and that her subsequent status, and consequently her children's and her children's children's status, will depend on the amount her husband will offer to her father when asking for her. The boy, on the other hand, wishes to accumulate enough wealth to buy a worthwhile wife and to pay in full. If he were to make a worthy girl prematurely pregnant—i.e., before he could pay her price in full—he would have to go into debt. And among the Yurok, all deviant behavior and character disorders in adults are explained as a result of the delinquent's mother or grandmother or great-grandmother not having been "paid for in full." This, it seems, means that the man in question was so eager to marry that he borrowed his wife on a down payment without being able to pay the installments. He thus proved that in our terms his ego was too weak to integrate sexual needs and economic virtues. Where sex does not interfere with wealth, however, it is viewed with leniency and humor. The fact that sex contact necessitates purification seems to be considered a duty or a nuisance, but does not reflect on sex as such or on individual women. There is no shame concerning the surface of the human body. If the young girl between menarche and marriage avoids bathing in the nude before others, it is to avoid offending by giving evidence of menstruation. Otherwise, everybody is free to bathe as he pleases in whatever company.

As we have seen, Sioux children learned to associate the locomotor and genital modes with hunting. The Sioux, in his official sexuality, was more phallic-sadistic in that he pursued whatever roamed: game, enemy, woman. The Yurok in all of this is more phobic and suspicious. He avoids being snared. For it even happened to God: the creator of the Yurok world was an extraordinarily lusty fellow who roamed around and endangered the world with his lawless behavior. His sons prevailed upon him to leave this world. He promised to be a good god, but as he ventured down the coast farther than any sensible and well-bred person would do, he found the skate woman lying on the beach, invitingly spreading her legs. (The skatefish, the Yurok say, look like "a woman's inside.") He could not resist her. But as soon as he had entered her, she held on to him with her vagina, wrapped her legs around him, and abducted him. This story serves to demonstrate where centrifugal, wandering, and lawless lust will lead. In the lawfully restricted Yurok world which was established by the delinquent creator's overconscientious sons, a sensible man avoids being "snared" by the wrong woman or at the wrong time or place—"wrong" meaning any circumstances that would compromise his assets as an economic being. To learn to avoid this means to become a "clean" individual, an individual with "sense."

4. COMPARATIVE SUMMARY

The worlds of the Sioux and the Yurok are primitive worlds according to the criteria employed earlier. They are highly ethnocentric, only concerned with tribal self-regulation in relation to a specific segment of nature, and with the development of sufficient tools and appropriate magic. We have found the Yurok world to be oriented along cautiously centripetal lines, whereas we found the Sioux to be vigorously centrifugal.

As a society the Yurok had almost no hierarchic organization. All emphasis was on mutual vigilance in the daily observance of minute differences of value. There was little "national" feeling, and, as I have neglected to point out, no taste for war whatsoever. Just as the Yurok could believe that seeing salmon meant making salmon come, he obviously also took it for granted that he could keep war away by simply not seeing potential enemies. Upriver Yurok are known to have ignored hostile tribes who traversed their territory in order to fight downriver Yurok. War was a matter of those concerned directly, not one of national or tribal loyalty.

Thus they felt secure in a system of avoidances: avoidance of being drawn into a fight, into a contamination, into a bad business deal. Their individual lives began with an early banishment from the mother's breast, and with subsequent instruction (for boys) to avoid her, to keep out of her living quarters, and to beware of snaring women in general. Their mythology banishes the creator from this world by having him snared and abducted by a woman. While the fear of being caught thus dominated their avoidances, they lived every moment for the purpose of snatching an advantage from another human being.

In the Yurok world, the Klamath River may be likened to a nutritional canal, and its estuary to a mouth and throat forever opened toward the horizon whence the salmon come; their world-image thus starkly suggests the oral mode of incorporation. All through the year the prayers of the Yurok world go out in that direction, protesting humility and denying the wish to hurt. Once a year, however, the Yurok tearfully lure their god back into this world just long enough to assure his good will—and to snare his salmon. As the Sioux world finds its highest expression in the performances surrounding the Sun Dance, the Yurok world dramatizes all it stands for during those exalted days when, with utmost communal effort and organization, it builds the fish dam: gradually closing, as if they were gigantic jaws, the two parts extended from the opposite shores of the river. The jaws close and the prey is trapped. The creator once more rejuvenates the world by grudgingly bequeathing it parts of himself, only to be banished for another year. Again, as in the case of the Sioux, this ceremonial climax follows a cycle of rituals which deals with the dependence of the people on supernatural providers. At the same time, the ceremonial represents a grandiose collective play with the themes of earliest danger in the individual life cycle: the ontogenic loss of the mother's breast at the biting stage corresponds to the phylogenetic danger of possible loss of the salmon supply from across the ocean. Here the conclusion is inevitable that the great themes of fertility and fecundity find their symbolic expression in an equation of the sacred salmon with the paternal phallus and the maternal nipple: the organ which generates life and that which nurtures it.

During the rejuvenation festivals—that is when their prayer was reinforced by technological teeth—the Yurok were not permitted to cry, for anyone who cried would not be alive in a year. Instead, "the end of the dam building is a period of freedom. Jokes, ridicule, and abuse run riot; sentiment forbids offense; and as night comes, lovers' passions are inflamed" (Kroeber). This one time, then, the Yurok behaved as licentiously as his phallic creator, proud that by an ingenious mixture of engineering and atonement he had again accomplished the feat of his world: to catch his salmon—and have it next year, too.

To be properly avoidant and yet properly avid, the individual Yurok must be *clean*; i.e., he must pray with humility, cry with faith, and hallucinate with conviction, as far as the Supernatural Providers are concerned; he must learn to make good nets, to locate them well, and to collaborate in the fish dam, as his technology requires; he must trade and haggle with stamina and persistence when engaged in business with his fellow men; and he must learn to master his body's entrances, exits, and interior tubeways in such a manner that nature's fluid-ways and supply routes (which are not accessible to scientific understanding and technical influence) will find themselves magically coerced. In the Yurok world, then, homogeneity rests on an integration of economic ethics and magic morality with geographic and physiological configurations. We have outlined in what way this integration is prepared in the training of the young organism.[3]

In trying to gain access to the meaning, or even the mere configurations, of Yurok behavior we have not been able to avoid analogies with what is considered deviant or extreme behavior in our culture. Within his everyday behavior the Yurok cries to his gods "like a baby"; he hallucinates in his meditation "like a psychotic"; he acts "like a phobic" when confronted with contamination; and he tries to act avoidant, suspicious, and stingy "like a compulsive neurotic." Am I trying to say that the Yurok *is* all of this or that he behaves *"as if"*?

The anthropologist who has lived long enough among a people can tell us what his informants care to enlarge upon, and whether what the people are said to be doing actually corresponds to what can be observed in daily and yearly life. Observations which would indicate whether or not traditional traits, such as nostalgia or avarice or retentiveness, are also dominant personal traits in typical individuals, are still rare. Take the Yurok's ability to pantomime a crying helpless being or a deeply grieved mourner. True, in characterizing the Yurok's institutionalized claiming of recompense, Kroeber, during a few minutes of one seminar evening, used the expressions "whining around," "fussing," "bickering," "crying out," "self-pity," "excuses a child might give," "claimants who make nuisances of themselves," etc. Does this mean that the Yurok anywhere within his technology is more helpless, more paralyzed by sadness, than are members of a tribe which does not develop these "traits"? Certainly not; his institutionalized helplessness *eo ipso* is neither a trait nor a neurotic symptom. It does not interfere with the individual's efficiency in meeting technological demands which were adequate for the segment of nature within which the Yurok lives. His crying is based on the learned and conditioned ability to dramatize an infantile attitude which the culture chooses to preserve and to put at the disposal of the individual, to be used by him and his fellow men within the limited area of magic. Such an institutionalized attitude neither spreads beyond its defined area nor makes impossible the development to full potency of its opposite. It is probable that the really successful Yurok was the one who could cry most heartbreakingly or haggle most effectively in some situations and be full of fortitude in others—that is, the Yurok whose ego was strong enough to synthesize orality and "sense." In comparison, oral and anal "types" whom we may be able to observe today in our culture are bewildered people who find themselves victims of overdeveloped organ modes without the corresponding homogeneous cultural reality.

The configuration of Yurok retentiveness seems to be as alimentary as it is anal: it includes the demanding mouth and the storing stomach as well as the stingy sphincters. It thus is prototypal also for the anal tendency to accumulate creatively for the sake of making the most of the collected values which belong to the whole social system, where they in turn give communal pleasure, prestige, and permanence.

Where the anal character in our culture approaches the neurotic, it often appears to be a result of the impact on a retentive child of a certain type of maternal behavior in Western civilization, namely, a narcissistic and phobic overconcern with matters of elimination. This attitude helps to overdevelop retentive and eliminative potentialities and to fixate them in the anal zone. It creates strong social ambivalence in the child, and it remains an isolating factor in his social and sexual development.

The Yurok's "pleasure of final evacuation and exhibition of stored-up material" is most conspicuous at dances, when, toward morning, the Yurok with a glowing face produces his fabulous treasures of obsidian or of headwear ornamented with woodpecker scalps. Here, the institutionalized obstinacy which made it possible for him to accumulate these treasures seems counteracted by the highly social experience of seeing his treasures enhance the prestige of the whole tribe. What I am arguing here is that neurosis is an individual state in which irrational trends are irreconcilably split off from a relatively advanced rationality; while primitivity is a state of human organization in which pre-rational thinking is integrated with whatever rationality is made possible by the technology.

Because both irrational and pre-rational "logic" makes use of magical images and impulses, Freud could shed light on the second as he deciphered the first; but the study of the ego—and that is, to me, the study of the interdependence of inner and social organization—must as yet determine the function of magic thinking in different human states.

Furthermore, if we know the official behavior required for successful participation in the traditional spectacle of a certain culture, we stand only at the beginning of the inquiry into the "character" of individuals: for to know how generous or how thrifty a people or an individual "is," we must know not only what the verbalized and the implied values of his culture are, but also what provisions are made for an individual's "getting away" with transgressions. Each system, in its own way, tends to make similar people out of all its members, but each in a specific way also permits exemptions and deductions from the demands with which it thus taxes the individuality of the individual ego. It stands to reason that these exemptions are less logical and much less obvious, even to the people themselves, than are the official rules.

Let it be stated, then, that in describing conceptual and behavioral configurations in the Yurok and in the Sioux world, we have not attempted to establish their respective "basic character structures." Rather, we have concentrated on the configurations with which these two tribes try to synthesize their concepts and their ideals in a coherent design for living. This design inculcates efficiency in their primitive ways of technology and magic and protects them from individual anxiety which might lead to panic: the anxiety among the Plains hunters over emasculation and immobilization, among the Pacific fishermen over being left without provisions. To accomplish this a primitive culture seems to use childhood in a number of ways: it gives specific meanings to early bodily and interpersonal experience in order to create the right combination of organ modes and the proper emphasis on social modalities; it carefully and systematically channelizes throughout the intricate pattern of its daily life the energies thus provoked and deflected; and it gives consistent supernatural meaning to the infantile anxieties which it has exploited by such provocation.

In doing all this, a society cannot afford to be arbitrary and anarchic. Even "primitive" societies must avoid doing just what our analogistic thinking would have them do. They cannot afford to create a community of wild eccentrics, of infantile characters, or of neurotics. In order to create people who will function effectively as the bulk of the people, as energetic leaders, or as useful deviants, even the most "savage" culture must strive for what we vaguely call a "strong ego" in its majority or at least in its dominant minority—i.e., an individual core firm and flexi-

ble enough to reconcile the necessary contradictions in any human organization, to integrate individual differences, and above all to emerge
from a long and unavoidably fearful infancy with a sense of identity and
an idea of integrity. Undoubtedly each culture also creates character
types marked by its own mixture of defect and excess; and each culture
develops rigidities and illusions which protect it against the insight that
no ideal, safe, permanent state can emerge from the blueprint it has
gropingly evolved. Nevertheless, we may do well to try to understand
the nature of these "instinctive" blueprints, as mankind works toward a
different kind of adaptation, at once more rational, more conscious, and
more universal.

A NEUROLOGICAL CRISIS
IN A SMALL BOY: SAM

from *Childhood and Society*

E arly one morning, in a town in northern California, the mother of a small boy of three was awakened by strange noises emanating from his room. She hurried to his bed and saw him in a terrifying attack of some kind. To her it looked just like the heart attack from which his grandmother had died five days earlier. She called a doctor, who said that Sam's attack was epileptic. He administered sedatives and had the boy taken to a hospital in a near-by metropolis. The hospital staff were not willing to commit themselves to a diagnosis because of the patient's youth and the drugged state in which he had been brought in. Discharged after a few days, the boy seemed perfectly well; his neurological reflexes were all in order.

One month later, however, little Sam found a dead mole in the back yard and became morbidly agitated over it. His mother tried to answer his very shrewd questions as to what death was all about. He reluctantly went to sleep after having declared that his mother apparently did not know either. In the night he cried out, vomited, and began to twitch around the eyes and the mouth. This time the doctor arrived early enough to observe the symptoms which culminated in a severe convulsion over the whole right side of his body. The hospital concurred in diagnosing the affliction as epilepsy, possibly due to a brain lesion in the left hemisphere.

When, two months later, a third attack occurred after the boy had accidentally crushed a butterfly in his hand, the hospital added an amendment to its diagnosis: "precipitating factor: psychic stimulus." In other words, because of some cerebral pathology this boy probably had a lower threshold for convulsive explosion; but it was a psychic stimulus, the idea of death, which precipitated him over his threshold. Otherwise neither his birth history, nor the course of his infancy, nor his neurological condition between attacks showed specific pathology. His general health was excellent. He was well nourished, and his brain waves at the time only indicated that epilepsy "could not be excluded."

What was the "psychic stimulus"? Obviously it had to do with death: dead mole, dead butterfly—and then we remember his mother's remark that in his first attack he had looked just like his dying grandmother.

Here are the facts surrounding the grandmother's death:

Some months before, the father's mother had arrived for her first visit to the family's new home in X. There was an undercurrent of excitement which disturbed the mother more deeply than she then knew. The visit had the connotation of an examination to her: had she done well by her husband and by her child? Also there was anxiety over the grandmother's health. The little boy, who at that time enjoyed teasing people, was warned that the grandmother's heart was not too strong. He promised to spare her, and at first everything went well. Nevertheless, the mother seldom left the two alone together, especially since the enforced restraint seemed to be hard on the vigorous little boy. He looked, the mother thought, increasingly pale and tense. When the mother slipped away for a while one day, leaving the child in her mother-in-law's care, she returned to find the old woman on the floor in a heart attack. As the grandmother later reported, the child had climbed on a chair and had fallen. There was every reason to suspect that he had teased her and had deliberately done something which she had warned him against. The grandmother was ill for months, failed to recover, and finally died a few days before the child's first attack.

The conclusion was obvious that what the doctors had called the "psychic stimulus" in this case had to do with his grandmother's death. In fact, the mother now remembered what at the time had seemed irrelevant to her—namely, that Sam, on going to bed the night before the attack, had piled up his pillows the way his grandmother had done to avoid congestion and that he had gone to sleep in an almost sitting position—as had the grandmother.

Strangely enough, the mother insisted that the boy did not know of his grandmother's death. On the morning after it occurred she had told him that the grandmother had gone on a long trip north to Seattle. He had cried and said, "Why didn't she say good-by to me?" He was told that there had not been time. Then, when a mysterious, large box had been carried out of the house, the mother had told him that his grandmother's books were in it. But Sam had not seen the grandmother either bring or use such a lot of books, and he could not quite see the reason for all the tears shed over a box of books by the hastily congregated relatives. I doubted, of course, that the boy had really believed the story; and indeed, the mother had puzzled over a number of remarks made by the little teaser. Once when she had wanted him to find something which he did not want to look for, he had said mockingly, "It has gone on a lo-ong trip, all the way to See-attle." In the play group which he later joined as part of the treatment plan, the otherwise vigorous boy would, in dreamy concentration, build innumerable variations of oblong boxes, the openings of which he would carefully barricade. His questions at the time justified the suspicion that he was experimenting with the idea of how it was to be locked up in an oblong box. But he refused to listen to his mother's belated explanation, now offered almost pleadingly, that the grandmother had, in fact, died. "You're lying," he said. "She's in Seattle. I'm going to see her again."

From the little that has been said about the boy so far, it must be clear that he was a rather self-willed, vigorous, and precociously intelligent little fellow, not easily fooled. His ambitious parents had big plans for their only son: with his brains he might go east to college and medical school, or maybe to law school. They fostered in him a vigorous expression of his intellectual precocity and curiosity. He had always been willful and from his first days unable to accept a "no" or a "maybe" for an answer. As soon as he could reach, he hit—a tendency which was not considered unsound in the neighborhood in which he had been born and raised: a neighborhood mixed in population, a neighborhood in which he must have received at an early age the impression that it was good to learn to hit first, just in case. But now they lived, the only Jewish family, in a small but prosperous town. They had to tell their little boy not to hit the children, not to ask the ladies too many questions, and—for heaven's sake and also for the sake of business—to treat the Gentiles gently. In his earlier milieu, the ideal image held out for a little boy had been that of a tough guy (on the street) and a smart boy (at home). The problem now was to become quickly what the Gentiles of the middle class would call "a nice little boy, in spite of his being Jewish." Sam had done a remarkably intelligent job in adjusting his aggressiveness and becoming a witty little teaser.

Here the "psychic stimulus" gains in dimensions. In the first place, this had always been an irritable and an aggressive child. Attempts on the part of others to restrain him made him angry; his own attempts at restraining himself resulted in unbearable tension. We might call this his *constitutional intolerance,* "constitutional" meaning merely that we cannot trace it to anything earlier; he just always had been that way. I must add, however, that his anger never lasted long and that he was not only a very affectionate, but also an outstandingly expressive and exuberant child, traits which helped him adopt the role of one who commits good-natured mischief. About the time of his grandmother's arrival, however, something, it now appeared, had robbed him of his humor. He had hit a child, hard. A little blood had trickled, ostracism had threatened. He, the vigorous extrovert, had been forced to stay at home with his grandmother, whom he was not allowed to tease.

Was his aggressiveness part of an epileptic constitution? I do not know. There was nothing feverish or hectic about his vigor. It is true that his first three major attacks were all connected with ideas of death and two later ones with the departures of his first and second therapists, respectively. It is also true that his much more frequent minor attacks—which consisted of staring, gagging, and swooning from which he would recover with the worried words, "What happened?"—often occurred immediately after sudden aggressive acts or words on his part. He might throw a stone at a stranger, or he might say, "God is a skunk," or, "The whole world is full of skunks," or (to his mother), "You are a stepmother." Were these outbursts of primitive aggression for which he was then forced to atone in an attack? Or were they desperate attempts at discharging with violent action a foreboding of an impending attack?

These were the impressions I had gathered from the doctor's case history and the mother's reports when I took over the boy's treatment about two years after the onset of his illness. And soon I was to witness one of his minor spells. We had played dominoes, and in order to test his threshold I had made him lose consistently, which was by no means easy. He grew very pale and all his sparkle dimmed out. Suddenly he stood up, took a rubber doll, and hit me in the face, hard. Then his glance turned into an aimless stare, he gagged as if about to vomit, and swooned slightly. Coming to, he said in a hoarse and urgent voice, "Let's go on," and gathered together his dominoes, which had tumbled over. Children are apt to express in spatial configurations what they cannot or dare not say. As he rearranged them hurriedly, he built an oblong, rectangular configuration: a miniature edition of the big boxes he had liked to build previously in the nursery school. The dominoes all faced inward. Now fully conscious, he noticed what he had done and smiled very faintly.

I felt that he was ready to be told what I thought I understood. I said, "If you wanted to see the dots on your blocks, you would have to be inside that little box, like a dead person in a coffin."

"Yes," he whispered.

"This must mean that you are afraid you may have to die because you hit me."

Breathlessly, "Must I?"

"Of course not. But when they carried your grandmother away in the coffin you probably thought that you made her die and therefore had to die yourself. That's why you built those big boxes in your school, just as you built this little one today. In fact, you must have thought you were going to die every time you had one of those attacks."

"Yes," he said, somewhat sheepishly, because he had actually never admitted to me that he had seen his grandmother's coffin, and that he knew she was dead.

Here one might think we have the story. In the meantime, however, I had worked with the mother also and had learned of her part in it—an essential portion of the whole account. For we may be sure that whatever deep "psychic stimulus" may be present in the life of a young child, it is identical with his mother's most neurotic conflict. Indeed, the mother now succeeded in remembering, only against severe emotional resistance, an incident when, in the middle of her busiest preparations for the mother-in-law's arrival, Sam had thrown a doll into her face. Whether he had done this "deliberately" or not, he had aimed only too well; he had loosened one of her front teeth. A front tooth is a precious possession in many ways. His mother had hit him right back, harder and with more anger than she had ever done before. She had not exacted a tooth for a tooth, but she had shown a rage which neither she nor he had known was in her.

Or had he known it before she did? This is a crucial point. For I believe that this boy's low tolerance for aggression was further lowered by the over-all connotation of violence in his family. Above and beyond individual conflict, the whole milieu of these children of erstwhile fugitives from ghettos and pogroms is pervaded by the problem of the Jew's special fate in the face of anger and violence. It had all started so significantly with a God who was mighty, wrathful, and vindictive, but also sadly agitated, attitudes which he had bequeathed to the successive patriarchs all the way from Moses down to this boy's grandparents. And it all had ended with the chosen but dispersed Jewish people's unarmed helplessness against the surrounding world of always potentially violent Gentiles. This family had dared the Jewish fate, by isolating itself in a Gentile town; but they were carrying their fate with them as an inner reality, in the midst of these Gentiles who did not actively deny them their new, if somewhat shaky, security.

Here it is important to add that our patient had been caught in this, his parents' conflict with their ancestors and with their neighbors, at the worst possible time for him. For he was going through a maturational stage characterized by a developmental intolerance of restraint. I refer to the rapid increase in locomotor vigor, in mental curiosity, and in a sadistic kind of infantile maleness which usually appears at the age of three or four, manifesting itself according to differences in custom and individual temperament. There is no doubt that our patient had been precocious in this as in other respects. At that stage any child is apt to show increased intolerance of being restrained from moving willfully and from asking persistently. A vigorous increase in initiative both in deed and in fantasy makes the growing child of this stage especially vulnerable to the talion principle—and he had come uncomfortably close to the tooth-for-a-tooth penalty. At this stage a little boy likes to pretend that he is a giant because he is afraid of giants, for he knows all too well that his feet are much too small for the boots he wears in his fantasies. In addition, precocity always implies relative isolation and disquieting imbalance. His tolerance, then, for his parents' anxieties was specifically low at the time when the grandmother's arrival added latent ancestral conflicts to the social and economic problems of the day.

This, then, is our first "specimen" of a human crisis. But before further dissecting the specimen, let me say a word about the therapeutic procedure. An attempt was made to synchronize the pediatric with the psychoanalytic work. Dosages of sedatives were gradually decreased as psychoanalytic observation began to discern, and insight to steady, the weak spots in the child's emotional threshold. The stimuli specific for these weak areas were discussed not only with the child but also with his father and mother so that they too, could review their roles in the disturbance and could gain some insight before their precocious child could overtake them in his understanding of himself and of them.

One afternoon soon after the episode in which I was struck in the face, our little patient came upon his mother, who lay resting on a couch. He put his hand on her chest and said, "Only a very bad boy would like to jump on his mommy and step on her; only a very bad boy would want to do that. Isn't that so, Mommy?" The mother laughed and said, "I bet you would like to do it now. I think quite a good little boy might think that he wanted to do such a thing, but he would know that he did not really want to do it"—or something like that: such things are hard to say, and wording is not too important. What counts is their spirit, and the implication that there are two different ways of wanting a thing, which can be separated by self-observation and communicated to others. "Yes," he said, "but I won't do it." Then he added, "Mr. E. always asks me why I throw things. He spoils everything." He added quickly, "There won't be any scene tonight, Mommy."

Thus the boy learned to share his self-observation with the very mother against whom his rages were apt to be directed, and to make her an ally of his insight. To establish this was of utmost importance, for it made it possible for the boy to warn his mother and himself whenever he felt the approach of that peculiar cosmic wrath or when he perceived the (often very slight) somatic indications of an attack. She would immediately get in touch with the pediatrician, who was fully informed and most co-operative. He would then prescribe some preventive measure. In this way minor seizures were reduced to rare and fleeting occurrences which the boy gradually learned to handle with a minimum of commotion. Major attacks did not recur.

The reader, at this point, may rightfully protest that such attacks in a small child might have stopped anyway, without any such complicated procedures. This is possible. No claim is advanced here of a cure of epilepsy by psychoanalysis. We claim less—and, in a way, aspire to more.

We have investigated the "psychic stimulus" which at a particular period in the patient's life cycle helped to make manifest a latent potentiality for epileptic attacks. Our form of investigation gains in knowledge as it gives insight to the patient, and it corrects him as it becomes a part of his life. Whatever his age, we apply ourselves to his capacity to examine himself, to understand, and to plan. In doing so, we may effect a cure or accelerate a spontaneous cure—no mean contribution when one considers the damage done by the mere habitualness and repetitiveness of such severe neurological storms. But in claiming less than the cure of the epilepsy, we would in principle like to believe that with therapeutic investigations into a segment of one child's history we help a whole family to accept a crisis in their midst as a crisis in the family history. For a psychosomatic crisis is an emotional crisis to the extent to which the sick individual is responding specifically to the latent crises in the significant people around him.

This, to be sure, has nothing to do with giving or accepting *blame* for the disturbance. In fact, the mother's very self-blame, that she may have caused damage to the child's brain with that one hard slap, constituted much of the "psychic stimulus" we were looking for: for it increased and reinforced that general fear of violence which characterized the family's history. Most of all, the mother's fear that she may have harmed him was a counterpart and thus an emotional reinforcement of what we finally concluded was the really dominant pathogenic "psychic stimulus" which Sam's doctors wanted us to find—namely, the boy's fear *that his mother too, might die* because of his attack on her tooth and because of his more general sadistic deeds and wishes.

No, blame does not help. As long as there is a sense of blame, there are also irrational attempts at restitution for the damage done—and such guilty restitution often results only in more damage. What we would hope that the patient and his family might derive from our study of their history is deeper humility before the processes which govern us, and the ability to live through them with greater simplicity and honesty. What are they?

The nature of our case suggests that we begin with the processes *inherent in the organism*. We shall in these pages refer to the organism as a process rather than as a thing, for we are concerned with the homeostatic quality of the living organism rather than with pathological items which might be demonstrable by section or dissection. Our patient suffered a somatic disturbance of a kind and an intensity which suggest the possibility of a somatic brain irritation of anatomic, toxic, or other origin. Such damage was not demonstrated, but we must ask what burden its presence would place on the life of this child. Even if the damage were demonstrable, it would, of course, constitute only a potential, albeit necessary, condition to convulsion. It could not be considered the cause of the convulsion, for we must assume that quite a number of individuals live with similar cerebral pathology without ever having a convulsion. The brain damage, then, would merely facilitate the discharge of tension, from whatever source, in convulsive storms. At the same time, it would be an ever present reminder of an inner danger point, of a low tolerance for tension. Such an inner danger can be said to decrease the child's threshold for outer dangers, especially as perceived in the irritabilities and anxieties of his parents, whose protection is needed so sorely, precisely because of the inner danger. Whether the brain lesion thus would cause the boy's temperament to be more impatient and more irritable, or whether his irritability (which he shared with other relatives and to which he was exposed in other relatives) would make his brain lesion more significant than it would in a boy of a different kind among different people—this is one of the many good questions for which there is no answer.

All we can say, then, is that at the time of the crisis Sam's "constitution" as well as his temperament and his stage of development had specific trends in common; they all converged on the intolerance of restrictions in locomotor freedom and aggressive expression.

But then, Sam's needs for muscular and mental activity were not solely of a physiological nature. They constituted an important part of his personality development and thus belonged to his defensive equipment. In dangerous situations Sam used what we call the "counterphobic" defense mechanism: when he was scared, he attacked, and when faced with knowledge which others might choose to avoid as upsetting, he asked questions with anxious persistence. These defenses, in turn, were well suited to the sanctions of his early milieu, which thought him cutest when he was toughest and smartest. With a shift in focus, then, many of the items originally listed as parts of his physiological and mental make-up prove to belong to a second process of organization, which we shall call *the organization of experience in the individual ego.* As will be discussed in detail, this central process guards the coherence and the individuality of experience by gearing the individual for shocks threatening from sudden discontinuities in the organism as well as in the milieu; by enabling it to anticipate inner as well as outer dangers; and by integrating endowment and social opportunities. It thus assures to the individual a sense of coherent individuation and identity: of being one's self, of being all right, and of being on the way to becoming what other people, at their kindest, take one to be. It is clear that our little boy tried to become an intelligent teaser and questioner, a role which he had first found to be successful in the face of danger and which he now found provoked it. We have described how this role (which prepared him well for the adult role of a Jewish intellectual) became temporarily devaluated by developments in neighborhood and home. Such devaluation puts the defensive system out of commission: where the "counterphobic" cannot attack, he feels open to attack and expects and even provokes it. In Sam's case, the "attack" came from a somatic source.

"Roles," however, grow out of the third principle of organization, the *social.* The human being, at all times, from the first kick *in utero* to the last breath, is organized into groupings of geographic and historical coherence: family, class, community, nation. A human being, thus, is at all times an organism, an ego, and a member of a society and is involved in all three processes of organization. His body is exposed to pain and tension; his ego, to anxiety; and as a member of a society, he is susceptible to the panic emanating from his group.

Here we come to our first clinical postulates. That there is no anxiety without somatic tension seems immediately obvious; but we must also learn that there is no individual anxiety which does not reflect a latent concern common to the immediate and extended group. An individual feels isolated and barred from the sources of collective strength when he (even though only secretly) takes on a role considered especially evil, be it that of a drunkard or a killer, a sissy or a sucker, or whatever colloquial designation of inferiority may be used in his group. In Sam's case, the grandmother's death had only confirmed what the Gentile children (or rather, their parents) had indicated, namely that he was an overwhelmingly bad boy. Behind all of this, of course, there was the fact that he was different, that he was a Jew, a matter by no means solely or even primarily brought to his attention by the neighbors: for his own parents had persistently indicated that a little Jew had to be especially good in order not to be especially bad. Here our investigation, in order to do justice to all the relevant facts, would have to lead back into history at large; it could do nothing less than trace the fate of this family back from Main Street to a ghetto in a far eastern province of Russia and to all the brutal events of the great Diaspora.

We are speaking of three processes, the somatic process, the ego process, and the societal process. In the history of science these three processes have belonged to three different scientific disciplines—biology, psychology, and the social sciences—each of which studied what it could isolate, count, and dissect: single organisms, individual minds, and social aggregates. The knowledge thus derived is knowledge of facts and figures, of location and causation; and it has resulted in argument over an item's allocation to one process or another. Our thinking is dominated by this trichotomy because only through the inventive methodologies of these disciplines do we have knowledge at all. Unfortunately, however, this knowledge is tied to the conditions under which it was secured: the organism undergoing dissection or examination; the mind surrendered to experiment or interrogation; social aggregates spread out on statistical tables. In all of these cases, then, a scientific discipline prejudiced the matter under observation by actively dissolving its total living situation in order to be able to make an isolated section of it amenable to a set of instruments or concepts.

Our clinical problem, and our bias, are different. We study individual human crises by becoming therapeutically involved in them. In doing so, we find that the three processes mentioned are three aspects of one process—i.e., human life, both words being equally emphasized. Somatic tension, individual anxiety, and group panic, then, are only different ways in which human anxiety presents itself to different methods of investigation. Clinical training should include all three methods, an ideal to which the studies in this book are gropingly dedicated. As we review each relevant item in a given case, we cannot escape the conviction that the meaning of an item which may be "located" in one of the three processes is co-determined by its meaning in the other two. An item in one process gains relevance by giving significance to and receiving significance from items in the others. Gradually, I hope, we may find better words for such *relativity in human existence.*

Of the catastrophe described in our first specimen, then, we know no "cause." Instead we find a convergence in all three processes of specific intolerances which make the catastrophe retrospectively intelligible, retrospectively probable. The plausibility thus gained does not permit us to go back and undo causes. It only permits us to understand a continuum, on which the catastrophe marked a decisive event, an event which now throws its shadow back over the very items which seem to have caused it. The catastrophe has occurred, and we must now introduce ourselves as a curing agent, into the post-catastrophic situation. We will never know what this life was like before it was disrupted, and in fact we will never know what this life was like before we became involved in it. These are the conditions under which we do therapeutic research.

TOYS AND REASONS

from *Childhood and Society*

[Paraphrasing Freud, we have called play the royal road to the understanding of the infantile ego's efforts at synthesis. We have observed an example of a failure of such synthesis. We shall now turn to childhood situations which illustrate the capacity of the ego to find recreation and self-cure in the activity of play; and to therapeutic situations in which we were fortunate enough to be able to help a child's ego to help itself.]

1. PLAY, WORK, AND GROWTH

Let us take as our text for the beginning of this more reassuring chapter a play episode described by a rather well-known psychologist. The occasion, while not pathological, is nevertheless a tragic one: a boy named Tom Sawyer, by verdict of his aunt, must whitewash a fence on an otherwise faultless spring morning. His predicament is intensified by the appearance of an age mate named Ben Rogers, who indulges in a game.

It is Ben, the man of leisure, whom we want to observe with the eyes of Tom, the working man.

> He took up his brush and went tranquilly to work. Ben Rogers hove in sight presently—the very boy, of all boys, whose ridicule he had been dreading. Ben's gait was the hop-skip-and-jump—proof enough that his heart was light and his anticipations high. He was eating an apple, and giving a long, melodious whoop, at intervals, followed by a deep-toned ding-dong-dong, ding-dong-dong, for he was personating a steamboat. As he drew near, he slackened speed, took the middle of the street, leaned far over to starboard and rounded to ponderously and with laborious pomp and circumstance—for he was personating the *Big Missouri,* and considered himself to be drawing nine feet of water. He was boat and captain and engine-bells combined, so he had to imagine himself standing on his own hurricane-deck giving the orders and executing them:
>   . . . "Stop the stabboard! Ting-a-ling-ling! Stop the labboard! Come ahead on the stabboard! Stop her! Let your outside turn over slow! Ting-a-ling-ling! Chow-ow-ow! Get out that head-line! *Lively* now! Come—out with your spring-line—what're you about there! Take a turn round that stump with the bight of it! Stand by that stage, now— let her go! Done with the engines, sir! Ting-a-ling-ling! *Sh't! sh't! sh't!"* (trying the gauge-cocks).
>   Tom went on whitewashing—paid no attention to the steamboat. Ben stared a moment, and then said:
>   "Hi-*yi! You're* up a stump, ain't you! . . . You got to work, hey?"

My clinical impression of Ben Rogers is a most favorable one, and this on all three counts: organism, ego, and society. For he takes care of the body by munching an apple; he simultaneously enjoys imaginary control over a number of highly conflicting items (being a steamboat and parts thereof, as well as being the captain of said steamboat, and the crew obeying said captain); while he loses not a moment in sizing up social reality when, on navigating a corner, he sees Tom at work. By no means reacting as a steamboat would, he knows immediately how to pretend sympathy though he undoubtedly finds his own freedom enhanced by Tom's predicament.

Flexible lad, we would say. However, Tom proves to be the better psychologist: he is going to put Ben to work. Which shows that psychology is at least the second-best thing to, and under some adverse circumstances may even prove superior to ordinary adjustment.

In view of Ben's final fate it seems almost rude to add interpretation to defeat, and to ask what Ben's play may mean. I presented this question to a class of psychiatric social-work students. Most of the answers were, of course, of the traumatic variety, for in what other way could Ben become accessible to "case work"? Ben must have been a frustrated boy, the majority agreed, to take the trouble to play so strenuously. The possible frustrations ranged from oppression by a tyrannical father from whom he escapes in fantasy by becoming a bossy captain, to a bedwetting or toilet trauma of some kind which now made him want to be a boat drawing nine feet of water. Some answers concerned the more obvious circumstance that he wanted to be big, and this in the form of a captain, the idol of his day.

My contribution to the discussion consisted of the consideration that Ben is a growing boy. To grow means to be divided into different parts which move at different rates. A growing boy has trouble in mastering his gangling body as well as his divided mind. He wants to be good, if only out of expediency, and always finds he has been bad. He wants to rebel, and finds that almost against his will he has given in. As his time perspective permits a glimpse of approaching adulthood he finds himself acting like a child. One "meaning" of Ben's play could be that it affords his ego a temporary victory over his gangling body and self by making a well-functioning whole out of brain (captain), the nerves and muscles of will (signal system and engine), and the whole bulk of the body (boat). It permits him to be an entity within which he is his own boss, because he obeys himself. At the same time, he chooses his metaphors from the tool world of the young machine age, and anticipates the identity of the machine god of his day: the captain of the *Big Missouri*.

Play, then, is a function of the ego, an attempt to synchronize the bodily and the social processes with the self. Ben's fantasy could well contain a phallic and locomotor element: a powerful boat in a mighty stream makes a good symbol. A captain certainly is a fitting father image, and, beyond that, an image of well-delineated patriarchal power. Yet the emphasis, I think, should be on the ego's need to master the various areas of life, and especially those in which the individual finds his self, his body, and his social role wanting and trailing. To hallucinate ego mastery and yet also to practice it in an intermediate reality between phantasy and actuality is the purpose of play—but play, as we shall see presently, is the undisputed master of only a slim margin of existence. What is play—and what is it not? Let us consult language, and then return to children.

The sunlight playing on the waves qualifies for the attribute "playful" because it faithfully remains within the rules of the game. It does not really interfere with the chemical world of the waves. It insists only on an intermingling of appearances. These patterns change with effortless rapidity and with a repetitiveness which promises pleasing phenomena within a predictable range without ever creating the same configuration twice.

When man plays he must intermingle with things and people in a similarly uninvolved and light fashion. He must do something which he has chosen to do without being compelled by urgent interests or impelled by strong passion; he must feel entertained and free of any fear or hope of serious consequences. He is on vacation from social and economic reality—or, as is most commonly emphasized: he *does not work.* It is this opposition to work which gives play a number of connotations. One of these is "mere fun"—whether it is hard to do or not. As Mark Twain commented, "constructing artificial flowers . . . is work, while climbing the Mont Blanc is only amusement." In Puritan times and places, however, mere fun always connoted sin; the Quakers warned that you must "gather the flowers of pleasure in the fields of duty." Men of equally Puritan mind could permit play only because they believed that to find "relief from moral activity is in itself a moral necessity." Poets, however, place the emphasis elsewhere: "Man is perfectly human only when he plays," said Schiller. Thus play is a borderline phenomenon to a number of human activities and, in its own playful way, it tries to elude definition.

It is true that even the most strenuous and dangerous play is by definition not work; it does not produce commodities. Where it does, it "goes professional." But this fact, from the start, makes the comparison of adult and child's play somewhat senseless; for the adult is a commodity-producing and commodity-exchanging being, whereas the child is only preparing to become one. To the working adult, play is re-creation. It permits a periodical stepping out from those forms of defined limitation which are his social reality.

Take *gravity:* to juggle, to jump, or to climb adds unused dimensions to the awareness of our body. Play here gives a sense of divine leeway, of excess space.

Take *time*: in trifling, in dallying, we lazily thumb our noses at this, our slave-driver. Where every minute counts, playfulness vanishes. This puts competitive sports on the borderline of play: they seem to make concessions to the pressure of space and time, only to defeat this very pressure by a fraction of a yard or of a second.

Take *fate* and *causality*, which have determined who and what we are, and where. In games of chance we re-establish equality before fate, and secure a virgin chance to every player willing to observe a few rules which, if compared with the rules of reality, seem arbitrary and senseless. Yet they are magically convincing, like the reality of a dream, and they demand absolute compliance. Let a player forget that such play must remain his free choice, let him become possessed by the demon of gambling, and playfulness vanishes again. He is a gambler, not a player.

Take *social reality*, and our defined cubicles in it. In play-acting we can be what in life we could not or would not be. But as the play-actor begins to believe in his impersonation he comes closer to a state of hysteria, if not worse; while if he tries, for purposes of gain, to make others believe in his "role" he becomes an impostor.

Take our *bodily drives*. The bulk of the nation's advertising effort exploits our wish to play with necessity, to make us believe, for example, that to inhale and to eat are not pleasurable necessities, but a fanciful game with ever new and sensuous nuances. Where the need for these nuances becomes compulsive, it creates a general state of mild addiction and gluttony, which ceases to transmit a sense of abundance and, in fact, produces an undercurrent of discontent.

Last but not least, in *love life* we describe as sex play the random activities preceding the final act, which permit the partners to choose body part, intensity, and tempo ("what, and with which, and to whom," as the limerick has it). Sex play ends when the final act begins, narrowing choice, dictating tempo, and giving rein to "nature." Where one of the preparatory random acts becomes compelling enough to completely replace the final act, playfulness vanishes and perversion begins.

This list of playful situations in a variety of human endeavors indicates the narrow area within which our ego can feel superior to the confinement of space and time and to the definitiveness of social reality—free from the compulsions of conscience and from impulsions of irrationality. Only within these limitations, then, can man feel at one with his ego; no wonder he feels "only human when he plays." But this presupposes one more most decisive condition: he must play rarely and work most of the time. He must have a defined role in society. Playboys and gamblers are both envied and resented by the working man. We like to see them exposed or ridiculed, or we put them to worse than work by forcing them to live in luxurious cages.

The playing child, then, poses a problem: whoever does not work shall not play. Therefore, to be tolerant of the child's play the adult must invent theories which show either that childhood play is really work—or that it does not count. The most popular theory and the easiest on the observer is that the child is *nobody yet,* and that the nonsense of his play reflects it. Scientists have tried to find other explanation for the freaks of childish play by considering them representative of the fact that childhood is neither here nor there. According to Spencer, play uses up *surplus energy* in the young of a number of mammalians who do not need to feed or protect themselves because their parents do it for them. However, Spencer noticed that wherever circumstances permit play, tendencies are "simulated" which are "unusually ready to act, unusually ready to have their correlative feelings aroused." Early psychoanalysis added to this the "cathartic" theory, according to which play has a definite function in the growing being in that it permits him to work off pent up emotions and to find imaginary relief for past frustrations.

In order to evaluate these theories, let us turn to the game of another boy, Tom's junior. He lived near another mighty river, the Danube, and his play was recorded by another great psychologist, Sigmund Freud, who wrote:[1]

Without the intention of making a comprehensive study of these phenomena, I availed myself of an opportunity which offered of elucidating the first game invented by himself of a boy eighteen months old. It was more than a casual observation, for I lived for some weeks under the same roof as the child and his parents, and it was a considerable time before the meaning of his puzzling and continually repeated performance became clear to me.

The child was in no respect forward in his intellectual development; . . . but he made himself understood by his parents and the maidservant, and had a good reputation for behaving "properly." He did not disturb his parents at night; he scrupulously obeyed orders about not touching various objects and not going into certain rooms; and above all he never cried when his mother went out and left him for hours together, although the tie to his mother was a very close one: she had not only nourished him herself, but had cared for him and brought him up without any outside help. Occasionally, however, this well-behaved child evinced the troublesome habit of flinging into the corner of the room or under the bed all the little things he could lay his hands on, so that to gather up his toys was often no light task. He accompanied this by an expression of interest and gratification, emitting a loud, long-drawn-out "O-o-o-oh" which in the judgment of the mother (one that coincided with my own) was not an interjection but meant "go away" [*fort*]. I saw at last that this was a game, and that the child used all his toys only to play "being gone" [*fort sein*] with them. One day I made an observation that confirmed my view. The child had a wooden reel with a piece of string wound round it. It never occurred to him, for example, to drag this after him on the floor and so play horse and cart with it, but he kept throwing it with considerable skill, held by the string, over the side of his little draped cot, so that the reel disappeared into it, then said his significant "O-o-o-oh" and drew the reel by the string out of the cot again, greeting its reappearance with a joyful *"Da"* [there]. This was therefore the complete game, disappearance and return, the first act being the only one generally observed by the onlookers, and the one untiringly repeated by the child as a game for its own sake, although the greater pleasure unquestionably attached to the second act. . . . This interpretation was fully established by a further observation. One day when the mother had been out for some hours she was greeted on her return by the information "Baby o-o-o-oh" which at first remained unintelligible. It soon proved that during his long lonely hours he had found a method of bringing about his own disappearance. He had discovered his reflection in the long mirror which nearly reached to the ground and had then crouched down in front of it, so that the reflection was "fort."

To understand what Freud saw in this game we must note that at the time he was interested in (and, in fact, writing about) the strange phenomenon of the "repetition compulsion"—i.e., the need to re-enact painful experiences in words or acts. We have all experienced the occasional need of talking incessantly about a painful event (an insult, a quarrel, or an operation) which one might be expected to want to forget. We know of traumatized individuals who, instead of finding recovery in sleep, are repeatedly awakened by dreams in which they re-experience the original trauma. We also suspect that it is not so innocently accidental that some people make the same mistakes over and over again; that they "co-incidentally" and in utter blindness marry the same kind of impossible partner from whom they have just been divorced; or that a series of analogous accidents and mishaps always must happen just to *them*. In all of these cases, so Freud concluded, the individual unconsciously arranges for variations of an original theme which he has not learned either to overcome or to live with: he tries to master a situation which in its original form had been too much for him by meeting it repeatedly and of his own accord.

As Freud was writing about this, he became aware of the solitary play described and of the fact that the frequency of the main theme (something or somebody disappears and comes back) corresponded to the intensity of the life experience reflected—namely, the mother's leaving in the morning and her return at night.

This dramatization takes place in the play sphere. Utilizing his mastery over objects, the child can arrange them in such a way that they permit him to imagine that he is master of his life predicament as well. For when the mother had left him, she had removed herself from the sphere of his cries and demands; and she had come back only when it happened to suit her. In his game, however, the little boy has the mother by a string. He makes her go away, even throws her away, and then makes her come back at his pleasure. He has, as Freud put it, *turned passivity into activity*; he plays at doing something that was in reality done to him.

Freud mentions three items which may guide us in a further social evaluation of this game. First, the child threw the object away. Freud sees in this a possible expression of revenge—"If you don't want to stay with me, I don't want you"—and thus an additional gain in active mastery by an apparent growth of emotional autonomy. In his second play act, however, the child goes further. He abandons the object altogether and, with the use of a full-length mirror, plays "going away" from himself and returning to himself. He is now both the person who is being left and the person who leaves. He has become master by incorporating not only the person who, in life, is beyond his control, but the whole situation, with *both* its partners.

This is as far as Freud goes with his interpretation. But we may make a point of the fact that the child greets the returning mother with the information that he has learned to "go away" from himself. The game alone, as reported by Freud, could have become the beginning of an increasing tendency on the child's part to take life experiences into a solitary corner and to rectify them in fantasy, and only in fantasy. Let us assume that at the mother's return the child were to show complete indifference, extending his revenge to the life situation and indicating that he, indeed, can now take care of himself, that he does not need her. This often happens after the mother's first excursions: she rushes back, eager to embrace her child, only to be met by a bland face. She may then feel rejected and turn against or away from the unloving child, who is thus easily made to feel that the vengeance in the game of throwing away and his subsequent boast has hit its mark too well, that he has indeed made the mother go away for good, whereas he has only tried to recover from being abandoned by her. Thus the basic problem of being left and leaving would not be improved by its solution in solitary play. Our little boy, however, told his mother of his play, and we may assume that she, far from being offended, demonstrated interest and maybe even pride in his ingenuity. He was then better off all around. He had adjusted to a difficult situation, he had learned to manipulate new objects, and he had received loving recognition for his method. All this is in "child's play."

But does the child's play—so a frequent question goes—always "mean" something personal and sinister? What if ten children, in horse-and-buggy days, begin to play with reels on strings, pulling them behind themselves and playing horsie? Must it mean anything to one of them over and beyond what it seems to mean to all?

As we have said already, children, if traumatized, choose for their dramatizations play material which is available in their culture and manageable at their age. What is available depends on the cultural circumstances and is therefore common to all children who share these circumstances. Bens today do not play steamboat but use bicycles as more tangible objects of co-ordination—which does not prevent them from imagining, on the way to school or the grocery, that they are flying through the air and machine-gunning the enemy; or that they are the Lone Ranger himself on a glorious Silver. What is manageable, however, depends on the child's power of co-ordination, and therefore is shared only by those who have reached a certain level of maturation. What has a *common meaning* to all the children in a community (i.e., the idea of having a reel and string represent a living thing on a leash) may have a *special meaning* to some (i.e., all those who have just learned to manipulate reel and string and may thus be ready to enter a new sphere of participation and communal symbolization). Yet all of this may have, in addition, a *unique meaning* to individual children who have lost a person or an animal and therefore endow the game with a particular significance. What these children "have by the string" is not just any animal—it is the personification of a particular, a significant, and a lost animal—or person. To evaluate play the observer must, of course, have an idea of what all the children of a given age in a given community are apt to play. Only thus can he decide whether or not the unique meaning transcends the common meaning. To understand the unique meaning itself requires careful observation, not only of the play's content and form, but also of accompanying words and visible affects, especially those which lead to what we shall describe . . . as "play disruption."

In order to approach the problem of anxiety in play, let us consider the activity of building and destroying a tower. Many a mother thinks that her little son is in a "destructive stage" or even has a "destructive personality" because, after building a big, big tower, the boy cannot follow her advice to leave the tower for Daddy to see, but instead *must* kick it and make it collapse. The almost manic pleasure with which children watch the collapse in a second of the product of long play labor has puzzled many, especially since the child does not appreciate it at all if his tower falls by accident or by a helpful uncle's hand. He, the builder, must destroy it himself. This game, I should think, arises from the not so distant experience of sudden falls at the very time when standing upright on wobbly legs afforded a new and fascinating perspective on existence. The child who consequently learns to *make* a tower "stand up" enjoys causing the same tower to waver and collapse: in addition to the active mastery over a previously passive event, it makes one feel stronger to know that there is somebody weaker—and towers, unlike little sisters, can't cry and call Mummy. But since it is the child's still precarious mastery over space which is thus to be demonstrated, it is understandable that watching somebody else kick one's tower may make the child see himself in the tower rather than in the kicker: all fun evaporates. Circus clowns later take over when they obligingly fall all over the place from mere ineptness, and yet continue to challenge gravity and causality with ever renewed innocence: there are, then, even big people who are funnier, dumber, and wobblier. Some children, however, who find themselves too much identified with the clown cannot stand his downfalls: to them they are "not funny." This example throws light on the beginning of many an anxiety in childhood, where anxiety around the child's attempt at ego mastery finds unwelcome "support" from adults who treat him roughly or amuse him with exercises which he likes only if and when he himself has initiated them.

The child's play begins with and centers on his own body. This we shall call *autocosmic play*. It begins before we notice it as play, and consists at first in the exploration by repetition of sensual perceptions, of kinesthetic sensations, of vocalizations, etc. Next, the child plays with available persons and things. He may playfully cry to see what wave length would serve best to make the mother reappear, or he may indulge in experimental excursions on her body and on the protrusions and orifices of her face. This is the child's first geography, and the basic maps acquired in such interplay with the mother no doubt remain guides for the ego's first orientation in the "world." Here we call as a witness Santayana:[2]

> ... Far, far in a dim past, as if it had been in another world or in a prenatal condition, Oliver remembered the long-denied privilege of sitting in his mother's lap. It had been such a refuge of safety, of softness, of vantage: You were carried and you were enveloped in an amplitude of sure protection, like a king on his throne, with his faithful bodyguard many ranks deep about him; and the landscape beyond, with its messengers and its motley episodes, became the most entertaining of spectacles, where everything was unexpected and exciting, yet where nothing could go wrong; as if your mother herself had been telling you a story, and these pictures were only the illustrations to it which painted themselves in your listening mind.

The *microsphere*—i.e., the small world of manageable toys—is a harbor which the child establishes, to return to when he needs to overhaul his ego. But the thing-world has its own laws: it may resist reconstruction, or it may simply break to pieces; it may prove to belong to somebody else and be subject to confiscation by superiors. Often the microsphere seduces the child into an unguarded expression of dangerous themes and attitudes which arouse anxiety and lead to sudden play disruption. This

is the counterpart in waking life of the anxiety dream; it can keep children from trying to play just as the fear of night terror can keep them
from going to sleep. If thus frightened or disappointed in the microsphere, the child may regress into the autosphere, daydreaming, thumb-
sucking, masturbating. On the other hand, if the first use of the
thing-world is successful and is guided properly, the pleasure of mastering toy things becomes associated with the mastery of the traumata
which were projected on them, and with the prestige gained through
such mastery.

Finally, at nursery-school age playfulness reaches into the *macrosphere,*
the world shared with others. First these others are treated as things, are
inspected, run into, or forced to "be horsie." Learning is necessary in
order to discover what potential play content can be admitted only to
fantasy or only to autocosmic play; what content can be successfully represented only in the microcosmic world of toys and things; and what
content can be shared with others and forced upon them.

As this is learned, each sphere is endowed with its own sense of reality
and mastery. For quite a while, then, solitary play remains an indispensable
harbor for the overhauling of shattered emotions after periods of rough
going in the social seas. This, and the fact that a child can be counted upon
to bring into the solitary play arranged for him whatever aspect of his ego
has been ruffled most, form the fundamental condition for our diagnostic reliance on "play therapy," which will be discussed next.

What is infantile play, then? We saw that it is not the equivalent of
adult play, that it is not recreation. The playing adult steps sideward into
another reality; the playing child advances forward to new stages of mastery. I propose the theory that the child's play is the infantile form of the
human ability to deal with experience by creating model situations and
to master reality by experiment and planning. It is in certain phases of
his work that the adult projects past experience into dimensions which
seem manageable. In the laboratory, on the stage, and on the drawing
board, he relives the past and thus relieves leftover effects; in reconstructing the model situation, he redeems his failures and strengthens his
hopes. He anticipates the future from the point of view of a corrected
and shared past.

No thinker can do more and no playing child less. As William Blake
puts it: "The child's toys and the old man's reasons are the fruits of the
two seasons."

2. PLAY AND CURE

Modern play therapy is based on the observation that a child made insecure by a secret hate against or fear of the natural protectors of his play in family and neighborhood seems able to use the protective sanction of an understanding adult to regain some play peace. Grandmothers and favorite aunts may have played that role in the past; its professional elaboration of today is the play therapist. The most obvious condition is that the child has the toys and the adult for himself, and that sibling rivalry, parental nagging, or any kind of sudden interruption does not disturb the unfolding of his play intentions, whatever they may be. For to "play it out" is the most natural self-healing measure childhood affords.

Let us remember here the simple, if often embarrassing, fact that adults, when traumatized, tend to solve their tension by "talking it out." They are compelled, repeatedly, to describe the painful event: it seems to make them "feel better." Systems designed to cure the soul or the mind make ritual use of this tendency by providing, at regular intervals, an ordained or otherwise sanctioned listener who gives his undivided attention, is sworn not to censure arbitrarily or to betray, and bestows absolution by explaining how the individual's problem makes sense in some larger context, be it sin, conflict, or disease. The method finds its limitations where this "clinical" situation loses the detachment in which life can be reflected, and itself becomes a passionate conflict of dependence and hostility. In psychoanalytic terms, the limitation is set by the tendency (especially strong in neurotics) to transfer basic conflicts from their original infantile setting into every new situation, including the therapeutic one. This is what Freud meant when he said that the treatment itself, at first, becomes a "transference neurosis." The patient who thus transfers his conflict in all its desperate immediacy becomes at the same time resistive to all attempts at making him see the situation in a detached way, at formulating its meaning. He is *in resistance*; in a war to end all wars, he becomes more deeply embroiled than ever. At this point, non-psychoanalytic therapeutic efforts often end; the patient, it is said, cannot or does not want to get well or is too inferior to comprehend his obligations in treatment. Therapeutic psychoanalysis, however, begins at this point. It makes systematic use of the knowledge that no neurotic is undivided in his wish to get well and of necessity transfers his dependences and hostilities to the treatment and the person of the therapist. Psycho-analysis acknowledges and learns from such "resistances."

This phenomenon of *transference* in the playing child, as well as in the verbalizing adult, marks the point where simple measures fail—namely, when an emotion becomes so intense that it defeats playfulness, forcing an immediate discharge into the play and into the relationship with the play observer. The failure is characterized by what is to be described here as *play disruption*—i.e., the sudden and complete or diffused and slowly spreading inability to play. We saw such play disruption occur, on my provocation, in Ann's case, when she had to leave me and my tempt-ing toys in order to rejoin her mother. [See *Childhood and Society,* Chap-ter 2.] Similarly, we saw Sam trapped by his overpowering emotions in the middle of a game. In both cases we used play observation as an inci-dental diagnostic tool. I shall now introduce a little girl who, although she came for diagnostic purposes only, led me through a full cycle of play dis-ruption and play triumph, and thus offered a good example of the way in which the ego, flooded by fear, can regain its synthesizing power through playful involvement and disengagement.

Our patient is Mary. She is three years old. She is a somewhat pale brunette, but looks (and is) intelligent, pretty, and quite feminine. When disturbed, however, she is said to be stubborn, babyish, and shut-in. Re-cently she has enriched her inventory of expression by nightmares and by violent anxiety attacks in the play group which she has recently joined. All that the play group teachers can say is that Mary has a queer way of lifting things and has a rigid posture: and that her tension seems to in-crease in connection with the routines of resting and going to the toilet. With this information at hand we invite Mary to our office.

Maybe a word should be said here about the thoroughly difficult sit-uation which ensues when a mother brings a child for observation. The child has not chosen to come. He often does not feel sick at all in the sense that he has a symptom which he wishes to get rid of. On the con-trary, all he knows is that certain things and, most of all, certain people make him feel uncomfortable and he wishes that we would do something about these things and people—not about him. Often he feels that some-thing is wrong with his parents, and mostly he is right. But he has no words for this and, even if he did have, he has no reason to trust us with such weighty information. On the other hand, he does not know what the parents have told us about him—while God only knows what they have told the child about us. For the parents, helpful as they may wish to be and necessary as they are as initial informants, cannot be trusted in these matters: the initial history given is often distorted by the wish to justify (or secretly punish) themselves or to punish (and unconsciously justify) somebody else, perhaps the grandparents who "told you so."

In this case, my office was in a hospital. Mary had been told that she was coming to discuss her nightmares with me—a man whom she had never seen before. Her mother had consulted a pediatrician regarding these nightmares and Mary had heard the mother and the doctor argue over the possible indication for a tonsillectomy. I had hoped, therefore, that she would notice that the appointments of my office indicated a strictly non-medical affair and that she would give me a chance in simple and straightforward terms to acknowledge the purpose of her visit, to tell her that I was not a doctor and then to make clear that we were going to play together in order to get acquainted. Such explanations do not quite settle a child's doubts, but they may permit him to turn to the toys and do something. And as soon as he does *something* we can observe what he selects and repudiates in our standard inventory of toys. Our next step, then, will be guided by the meaning thus revealed.

Mary holds on to her mother as she enters my office. When she offers me her hand it is both rigid and cold. She gives me a brief smile, then turns to her mother, puts her arms around her, and holds her close to the still open door. She buries her head in her mother's skirt as if she wanted to hide in it, and responds to my advances only by turning her head to me—now with tightly closed eyes. Yet she *had* for a split moment looked at me with a smile that seemed to convey an interest—as if she wanted to see whether or not the new adult was going to understand fun. This makes her flight to her mother seem somewhat dramatic. The mother tries to encourage her to look at the toys, but Mary again hides her face in her mother's skirt and repeats in an exaggeratedly babyish voice, "Mommy, mommy, mommy!" A dramatic young lady: I am not even quite sure that she is not hiding a smile. I decide to wait.

Mary does make a decision. Still holding on to her mother, she points to a (girl) doll and says several times quickly and babyishly, "What that, what that?" After the mother has patiently explained that it is a dolly, Mary repeats "Dolly, dolly, dolly," and suggests in words not understandable to me that the mother take off the dolly's shoes. The mother tries to make her perform this act herself, but Mary simply repeats her demand. Her voice becomes quite anxious, and it seems that we may have tears in a moment.

Now the mother asks if it is not time for her to leave the room and wait outside as she has told Mary she would. I ask Mary whether we can let her mother go now and she, unexpectedly, makes no objection, not even when she suddenly finds herself without anybody to lean on. I try to start a conversation about the name of the doll, which the mother has left in Mary's hand. Mary grasps it firmly around the legs and suddenly, smiling mischievously, she begins to touch various things in the room with the doll's head. When a toy falls from the shelf, she looks at me to see whether she has gone too far; when she sees me smile permissively she laughs and begins to push smaller toys, always with the doll's head, in such a way that they fall too. Her excitement increases. With special glee she stabs with the doll's head at a toy train which is on the floor in the middle of the room. She overturns all the cars with growing evidence of a somehow too exciting kind of fun. As the engine overturns she suddenly stops and becomes pale. She leans with her back against the sofa, holds the doll vertically over her lower abdominal region, and lets it drop on the floor. She picks it up again, holds it over the same region, and drops it again. While repeating this several times, she begins first to whine and then to yell, "Mommy, mommy, mommy."

The mother re-enters, sure that communication has failed, and asks Mary whether she wants to go. I tell Mary that she may go if she wishes but that I hope she will be back in a few days. Quickly calmed, she leaves with her mother, saying good-by to the secretary outside as if she had had a pleasant visit.

Strangely enough, I too felt that the child had made a successful if interrupted communication. With small children, words are not always necessary at the beginning. I had felt that the play was leading up to a conversation; and at any rate the child had conveyed to me by counterphobic activity what her danger was. The fact of the mother's anxious interruption was, of course, as significant as the child's play disruption. Together, they probably explain the child's babyish anxiety. But what had she communicated with this emotional somersault, this sudden hilarity and flushed aggressiveness, and this equally sudden inhibition and pale anxiety?

The discernible mode content had been *pushing* things, not with her hand but with the doll as an extension of her hand; and then *dropping* the same doll from the genital region.

The doll as an extension of the hand was, as it were, a pushing tool. This suggests that she may not dare to touch or push things with her bare hand and reminds me of her teachers' observation that she seemed to touch or lift things in her own special way. This, together with the general rigidity in her extremities, suggests that Mary may be worried about her hands, maybe as aggressive tools.

The transfer of the doll to the lower abdominal region followed by her strangely obsessive and repetitive dropping leads to the further suggestion that she was dramatizing the loss from that region of an aggressive tool, a pushing instrument. The attacklike state which overcame her at this point reminds me of something which I learned long ago: severe hysterical attacks in adult women have been interpreted as dramatizations representing both partners in an imagined scene. Thus, one hand in tearing off the patient's dress may dramatize an aggressor's approach, while the other, in clutching it, may represent the victim's attempt to protect herself. Mary's attack impressed me as being of such a nature: by dropping the doll several times, panicky and yet as if obsessed, she seemed to be inexorably driven to dramatize both the robbed and the robber.

But what was to be stolen from her? Here we would have to know which meaning is more relevant, the doll's use as an aggressive tool—or the doll as a baby. In this play hour the dropped doll had first been the prolongation of an extremity and a tool of (pushing) aggression, and then something lost in the lower abdominal region under circumstances of extreme anxiety. Does Mary consider a penis such an aggressive weapon, and does she dramatize the fact that she does not have one? From the mother's account it is entirely probable that on entering the nursery school Mary was given her first opportunity to go to the toilet in the presence of boys and visits to the toilet were said to be occasions for anxiety.

I am thinking of the mother when she raps on the door. She has left the child, now quite composed, outside to come back and add something to Mary's biography. Mary was born with a sixth finger which was removed when she was approximately six months old; there is a scar on her left hand. Just prior to the outbreak of her anxiety attacks, Mary had repeatedly and urgently asked about this scar ("What that, what that?") and had received the routine answer that it was "just a mosquito bite." The mother agreed that the child when somewhat younger could easily have been present when her congenital anomaly was mentioned. Mary, the mother adds, has recently been equally insistent in her sexual curiosity.

We can now understand better the fact that Mary feels uneasy about the aggressive use of her hand, which has been robbed of a finger, and that she may equate the scar on her hand and her genital "scar," the lost finger and the absent penis. Such an association would also bring into juxtaposition the observation of sex differences in the play school and the immediate question of a threatening operation.

Before Mary's second visit, her mother offered this further information: Mary's sexual curiosity had recently received a specific blow when her father, irritable because of a regional increase in unemployment which threatened his means of livelihood, had shown impatience with her during her usual morning visit to him in the bathroom. In fact, he had shoved her out of the room. As he told me later, he had angrily repeated the words, "You stay out of here!" She had liked to watch the shaving process and had also on recent occasions (to his slight annoyance) asked about his genitals. A strict adherence to a routine in which she could do, say, and ask the same thing over and over again had always been a necessary condition for Mary's inner security. She was "heartbroken" over the consequent exclusion from the father's toilet.

We also discussed the fact (which I have already mentioned) that Mary's disturbed sleep and foul breath had been attributed by a pediatrician to a bad condition of the tonsils, and that the mother and the physician had engaged in a discussion in front of Mary as to whether she needed an immediate operation or not. *Operation,* then, and *separation* are seen to be the common denominators: the actual operation on the finger, the anticipated operation of the tonsils, and the mythical operation by which boys become girls; the separation from her mother during play-school hours, and the estrangement from her father. At the end of the first hour of play observation, then, this was the closest we could come to meanings on which all of the play elements and biographic data seemed to converge.

The antithesis of play disruption is play satiation, play from which a child emerges refreshed as a sleeper from dreams which "worked." Disruption and satiation are very marked and very clear only in rare cases. More often they are diffused and must be ascertained by detailed study. But not so in Mary's case. During her second appointment she obliged me with a specimen of play satiation as dramatic as that of her play disruption.

At first Mary again smiles bashfully at me. Again she turns her head away, holding on to her mother's hand and insisting that the mother come with her into the room. Once in the room, however, she lets her mother's hand go and, forgetting about the mother's and my presence, she begins to play animatedly and with obvious determination and goal-mindedness. I quickly close the door and motion the mother to sit down, because I do not want to disturb the play.

Mary goes to the corner where the blocks are on the floor. She selects two blocks and arranges them in such a way that she can stand on them each time she comes to the corner to pick up more blocks. Thus, play begins again with an extension of extremities, this time her feet. She now collects a pile of blocks in the middle of the room, moving to the corner and back without hesitation. Then she kneels on the floor and builds a small house for a toy cow. For about a quarter of an hour she is completely absorbed in the task of arranging the house so that it is strictly rectangular and at the same time fits tightly about a toy cow. She then adds five blocks to one long side of the house and experiments with a sixth block until its position satisfies her (see Figure 10).

This time, then, the dominant emotional note is peaceful play concentration with a certain maternal quality of care and order. There is no climax of excitement, and the play ends on a note of satiation; she has built something, she likes it, now the play is over. She gets up with a radiant smile—which suddenly gives place to a mischievous twinkle. I do not realize the danger I am about to fall victim to, because I am too fascinated by the fact that the close-fitting stable looks like a hand—with a sixth finger. At the same time it expresses the "inclusive" mode, a female-protective configuration, corresponding to the baskets and boxes and cradles arranged by little and big girls to give comfort to small things. Thus we see, so I muse, two restorations in one: The configuration puts

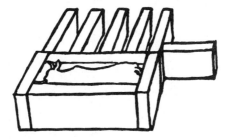

Figure 10

the finger back on the hand and the happily feminine pattern belies the "loss from the genital region" previously dramatized. The second hour's play thus accomplishes an expression of restoration and safety—and this concerning the same body parts (hand, genital region) which in the play disruption of the first hour had appeared as endangered.

But, as I said, Mary has begun to look teasingly at me. She now laughs, takes her mother's hand, and pulls her out of the room, saying with determination, "Mommy, come out." I wait for a while, then look out into the waiting room. A loud and triumphant, "Thtay in there!" greets me. I strategically withdraw, whereupon Mary closes the door with a bang. Two further attempts on my part to leave my room are greeted in the same way. She has me cornered.

There is nothing to do but to enter into the spirit of the game. I open the door slightly, quickly push the toy cow through the opening, make it squeak, and withdraw it. Mary is beside herself with pleasure and insists that the game be repeated a few times. She gets her wish, then it is time for her to go home. When she leaves she looks triumphantly and yet affectionately at me and promises to come back. I am left with the task of figuring out what has happened.

From anxiety in the autosphere in the first hour, Mary had now graduated to satiation in the microsphere—and to triumph in the macrosphere. She had taken the mother out of my space and locked me into it. This game had as content: a man is teasingly locked into his room. It was only in connection with this playful superiority that Mary had decided to talk to me, and this in no uncertain terms. "Thtay in there!" were the first words she had ever addressed to me! They were said clearly and in a loud voice, as if something in her had waited for the moment when she would be free enough to say them. What does that mean?

I think we have here the consummation of a play episode by way of a "father transference." It will be remembered that from the moment Mary came into my room at the beginning of the first contact she showed a somewhat coquettish and bashful curiosity about me, which she immediately denied by closing her eyes tightly. Since it can be expected that she would transfer to me (the man with toys) a conflict which disturbed her usually playful relationship with her father, it seems more than probable that in this game she was repeating with active mastery ("Thtay in there") and with some reversal of vectors (out-in) the situation of exclusion of which she had been a passive victim at home ("Stay out of here").

To some this may seem like a lot of complicated and devious reasoning for such a little girl. But here it is well to realize that these matters are difficult for rational thinking only. It would indeed be difficult to think up such a series of play tricks. It is even difficult to recognize and analyze it. But it happens, of course, unconsciously and automatically: here, never underestimate the power of the ego—even of such a little girl.

This episode is presented to illustrate the self-curative trend in spontaneous play; for play therapy and play diagnosis must make systematic use of such self-curative processes. They may help the child to help himself—and they may help us to advise the parents. Where this fails, more complicated methods of treatment (child psychoanalysis)[3] must be initiated—methods which have not been discussed in this chapter. With advancing age, prolonged conversation would take the place of play. Here, however, it was my purpose to demonstrate that a few play hours can serve to inform us of matters which the child could never verbalize. Trained observers, in the possession of numerous data, can see from a few play contacts which of these data are acutely relevant to the child, and why. In Mary's case, her play disruption and her play satiation, if seen in the framework of all the known circumstances, strongly suggest that a variety of past and future, real and imagined events had been incorporated into a system of mutually aggravating dangers. In her second play hour, she disposed of them all: she restored her finger, reassured herself, reaffirmed her femininity—and told the big man off. Such play peace gained must, however, be sustained by new insight on the part of the parents.

Mary's parents accepted (and partly themselves suggested) the following recommendations. Mary's curiosity in regard to her scar, her genitals, and her operation required a truthful attitude. She needed to have other children, especially boys, visit her for play at her home. The matter of the tonsils called for the decision of a specialist, which could be candidly communicated to the child. It did not seem wise to awaken and to restrain her during her nightmares; perhaps she needed to fight her dreams out, and there would be opportunity to hold her lightly and to comfort her when she awoke spontaneously. The child needed much activity; playful instruction in rhythmic motion might relax some of the rigidity in her extremities, which, whatever the initial cause, may have been at least aggravated by fearful anticipation since hearing for the first time about the mysterious amputation of her finger.

When Mary, a few weeks later, paid me a short visit, she was entirely at home and asked me in a clear, loud voice about the color of the train I had taken on my vacation. It will be remembered that she overturned a toy engine on the occasion of her first visit: now she could talk about engines. A tonsillectomy had proved unnecessary; the nightmares had ceased; Mary was making free and extensive use of the new play companions provided in and near her home. There was a revived play relationship with her father. He had intuitively made the most of Mary's sudden enraptured admiration for shining locomotives. He took her for regular walks to the railroad yards where together they watched the mighty engines.

Here the symbolism which has pervaded this clinical episode gains a new dimension. In the despair of play disruption, the toy engine apparently had a destructive meaning in some context with phallic-locomotor anxiety: when Mary pushed it over, she apparently had that awesome "Adam, where art thou" experience which we first observed in Ann. [See *Childhood and Society*, Chapter 2.] At the time, Mary's play relationship to her father had been disrupted, and this (as she could not know or understand) because of his worries over a possible disruption of his work status. This she seems to have interpreted entirely in terms of her maturational state and of her changes in status: and yet her reaction was not unrelated to the unconscious meaning of the father's actions. For threatened loss of status, threatened marginality, often result in an unconscious attempt by more stringent self-control and by purified standards to regain the ground lost or at least to keep from slipping any further. This, I believe, made the father react in a less tolerant way to the little girl's exploration, thus offending and frightening her in the general area which was already disturbed. It was, then, this area which appeared in her play in a condensed form, while she attempted, from the frightfulness of isolation, to work her way back to playful mutuality. Thus do children reflect and, where play fails, carry over into their own lives, the historical and economic crises of their parents.

Neither Mary's play nor the insight it provided could change the father's economic worries. But the moment he recognized the impact of his anxieties on his daughter's development, he realized that from a long-range point of view her anxieties mattered much more than the threatened change of his work status. In fact, actual developments did not confirm his apprehensions.

The father's idea of taking walks to the engine yards was felicitous. For the real engines now became symbols of power shared by father and daughter alike and sustained by the whole imagery of the machine culture in which this child is destined to become a woman.

Thus at the end of any therapeutic encounter with a child the parent must sustain what the adult patient must gain for himself: a realignment with the images and the forces governing the cultural development of his day, and from it an increased promise of a sense of identity.

But here, at last, we must try to come to a better description and definition of what we mean by identity.

3. THE BEGINNINGS OF IDENTITY

A. Play and Milieu

The emerging identity bridges the stages of childhood when the bodily self and the parental images are given their cultural connotations; and it bridges the stage of young adulthood, when a variety of social roles become available and, in fact, increasingly coercive. We will try to make this process more tangible, by looking first at some infantile steps toward identity and then at some cultural impediments to its consolidation.

A child who has just found himself able to walk, more or less coaxed or ignored by those around him, seems driven to repeat the act for the pure delight of functioning, and out of the need to master and perfect a newly initiated function. But he also acts under the immediate awareness of the new status and stature of "one who can walk," with whatever connotation this happens to have in the co-ordinates of his culture's space-time—be it "one who will go far," "one who will be able to stand on his own feet," "one who will be upright," or "one who must be watched because he might go too far." The internalization of a particular version of "one who can walk" is one of the many steps in child development which (through the coincident experience of physical mastery and of cultural meaning, of functional pleasure and of social prestige) contribute on each step to a more realistic self-esteem. This self-esteem grows to be a conviction that one is learning effective steps toward a tangible future, and is developing into a defined self within a social reality. The growing child must, at every step, derive a vitalizing sense of actuality from the awareness that his individual way of mastering experience (his ego synthesis) is a successful variant of a group identity and is in accord with its space-time and life plan.

In this children cannot be fooled by empty praise and condescending encouragement. They may have to accept artificial bolstering of their self-esteem in lieu of something better, but their ego identity gains real strength only from wholehearted and consistent recognition of real accomplishment—i.e., of achievement that has meaning in the culture. We have tried to convey this when discussing problems of Indian education, but yield to a more lucid statement:[4]

Dr. Ruth Underhill tells me of sitting with a group of Papago elders in Arizona when the man of the house turned to his little three-year-old granddaughter and asked her to close the door. The door was heavy and hard to shut. The child tried, but it did not move. Several times the grandfather repeated: "Yes, close the door." No one jumped to the child's assistance. No one took the responsibility away from her. On the other hand there was no impatience, for after all the child was small. They sat gravely waiting until the child succeeded and her grandfather gravely thanked her. It was assumed that the task would not be asked of her unless she could perform it, and having been asked, the responsibility was hers alone just as if she were a grown woman.

The essential point of such child training is that the child is from infancy continuously conditioned to responsible social participation, while at the same time the tasks that are expected of it are adapted to its capacity. The contrast with our society is very great. A child does not make any contribution of labor to our industrial society except as it competes with an adult; its work is not measured against its own strength and skill but against high-geared industrial requirements. Even when we praise a child's achievements in the home, we are outraged if such praise is interpreted as being of the same order as praise of adults. The child is praised because the parent feels well disposed, regardless of whether the task is well done by adult standards or not and the child acquires no sensible standard by which to measure its achievement. The gravity of a Cheyenne Indian family ceremoniously making a feast out of a little boy's first snowbird is far removed from our behavior. At birth the little boy was presented with a toy bow and arrow, and from the time he could run about, serviceable bows and arrows suited to his stature were specially made for him by the man of the family. Animals and birds were brought to his awareness in a graded series beginning with those most easily taken, and as he brought in his first of each species his family duly made a feast of it, accepting his contribution as gravely as the buffalo his father brought. When he finally killed a buffalo, it was only the final step of his childhood conditioning, not a new adult role with which his childhood experience had been at variance.

It dawns on us, then, that the theories of play which are advanced in our culture and which take as their foundation the assumption that in children, too, play is defined by the fact that it is not work, are really only one of the many prejudices by which we exclude our children from an early source of a sense of identity.

But then, with primitives it is a different matter. Their cultures are exclusive. Their image of man begins and ends with their idea of a strong or clean Yurok or Sioux, in their defined segments of nature. In our civilization the image of man is expanding. As it becomes more individuated, it also tends to include untold millions in new regions, nations, continents, and classes. New syntheses of economic and emotional safety are sought in the formation of new national and social entities based on more inclusive identities.

Primitive tribes have a direct relationship with the sources and means of production. Their techniques are extensions of the human body; their magic is a projection of body concepts. Children in these groups participate in technical and magic pursuits. Body and environment, childhood and culture may be full of dangers, but they are all one world. This world may be small, but it is culturally coherent. The expansiveness of civilization, on the other hand, its stratification and specialization, make it impossible for children to include in their ego-synthesis more than segments of the society which is relevant to their existence. History itself has become a temporal environment to be adjusted to. Machines, far from remaining tools and extensions of man's physiological functions, destine whole organizations of people to be extensions of machinery. Childhood, in some classes, becomes a separate segment of life, with its own folklore, its own literature.

The study of contemporary neuroses, however, points to the significance of this lag between child training and social actuality. Neuroses

contain, so we find, unconscious and futile attempts to adjust to the het-
erogeneous present with the magic concepts of a more homogeneous
past, fragments of which are still transmitted through child training. But
mechanisms of adjustment which once made for evolutionary adaptation,
tribal integration, caste coherence, national uniformity, etc., are at loose
ends in an industrial civilization.

No wonder, then, that some of our troubled children constantly break
out of their play into some damaging activity in which they seem to us
to "interfere" with our world; while analysis reveals that they only wish
to demonstrate their right to find an identity in it. They refuse to become
a specialty called "child," who must play at being big because he is not
given an opportunity to be a small partner in a big world.

B. Son of a Bombardier

During the last war a neighbor of mine, a boy of five, underwent a change
of personality from a "mother's boy" to a violent, stubborn, and disobe-
dient child. The most disquieting symptom was an urge to set fires.

The boy's parents had separated just before the outbreak of war. The
mother and the boy had moved in with some women cousins, and when
war began the father had joined the air force. The women cousins frequently expressed their disrespect for the father, and cultivated babyish
traits in the boy. Thus, to be a mother's boy threatened to be a stronger
identity element than to be a father's son.

The father, however, did well in war; in fact, he became a hero. On the
occasion of his first furlough the little boy had the experience of seeing
the man he had been warned not to emulate become the much-admired
center of the neighborhood's attention. The mother announced that she
would drop her divorce plans. The father went back to war and was soon
lost over Germany.

After the father's departure and death the affectionate and dependent
boy developed more and more disquieting symptoms of destructiveness
and defiance, culminating in fire setting. He gave the key to the change
himself when, protesting against his mother's whipping, he pointed to a
pile of wood he had set afire and exclaimed (in more childish words), "If
this were a German city, you would have liked me for it." He thus indicated that in setting fires he fantasied being a bombardier like the father,
who had told of his exploits.

We can only guess at the nature of the boy's turmoil. But I believe that we see here the identification of a son with his father, resulting from a suddenly increased conflict at the very close of the oedipus age. The father, at first successfully replaced by the "good" little boy, suddenly becomes both a newly vitalized ideal and a concrete threat, a competitor for the mother's love. He thus devaluates radically the boy's feminine identifications. In order to save himself from both sexual and social disorientation, the boy must, in the shortest possible time, regroup his identifications; but then the great competitor is killed by the enemy—a fact which increases the guilt for the competitive feeling itself and compromises the boy's new masculine initiative which becomes maladaptive.

A child has quite a number of opportunities to identify himself, more or less experimentally, with habits, traits, occupations, and ideas of real or fictitious people of either sex. Certain crises force him to make radical selections. However, the historical era in which he lives offers only a limited number of socially meaningful models for workable combinations of identification fragments. Their usefulness depends on the way in which they simultaneously meet the requirements of the organism's maturational stage and the ego's habits of synthesis.

To my little neighbor the role of the bombardier may have suggested a possible synthesis of the various elements that comprise a budding identity: his temperament (vigorous); his maturational stage (phallic-urethral-locomotor); his social stage (oedipal) and his social situation; his capacities (muscular, mechanical); his father's temperament (a great soldier rather than a successful civilian); and a current historical prototype (aggressive hero). Where such synthesis succeeds, a most surprising coagulation of constitutional, temperamental, and learned reactions may produce exuberance of growth and unexpected accomplishment. Where it fails, it must lead to severe conflict, often expressed in unexpected naughtiness or delinquency. For should a child feel that the environment tries to deprive him too radically of all the forms of expression which permit him to develop and to integrate the next step in his identity, he will defend it with the astonishing strength encountered in animals who are suddenly forced to defend their lives. And indeed, in the social jungle of human existence, there is no feeling of being alive without a sense of ego identity. Deprivation of identity can lead to murder.

I would not have dared to speculate on the little bombardier's conflicts had I not seen evidence for a solution in line with our interpretation.

When the worst of this boy's dangerous initiative had subsided, he was observed swooping down a hill on a bicycle, endangering, scaring, and yet deftly avoiding other children. They shrieked, laughed, and in a way admired him for it. In watching him, and hearing the strange noises he made, I could not help thinking that he again imagined himself to be an airplane on a bombing mission. But at the same time he gained in playful mastery over his locomotion; he exercised circumspection in his attack, and he became an admired virtuoso on a bicycle.

One should learn from such an example that re-education must seize upon the forces mobilized for playful integration. On the other hand, the desperate intensity of many a symptom must be understood as the defense of a step in identity development which to the child promises integration of the rapid changes taking place in all areas of his life. What to the observer looks like an especially powerful manifestation of naked instinct is often only a desperate plea for the permission to synthesize and sublimate in the only way possible. We can therefore expect our young patients to respond only to therapeutic measures which will help them to acquire the prerequisites for the successful completion of their identity. Therapy and guidance may attempt to substitute more desirable for less desirable items, but the total configuration of the developing identity elements soon becomes unalterable. It follows that therapy and guidance by professionals are doomed to failure where the culture refuses to provide an early basis for an identity and where opportunities for appropriate later adjustments are missing.

Our little son of a bombardier illustrates a general point. Psychosocial identity develops out of a gradual integration of all identifications. But here, if anywhere, the whole has a different quality from the sum of its parts. Under favorable circumstances children have the nucleus of a separate identity early in life; often they must defend it even against the necessity of overidentifying with one or both of their parents. These processes are difficult to study in patients, because the neurotic self has, by definition, fallen prey to overidentifications which isolate the small individual both from his budding identity and from his milieu.

C. Black Identity

But what if the "milieu" is determined to let live only at the expense of a permanent loss of identity?

Consider, for example, the chances for a continuity of identity in the American Negro child. I know a colored boy who, like our boys, listens every night to Red Rider. Then he sits up in bed, imagining that he is Red Rider. But the moment comes when he sees himself galloping after some masked offenders and suddenly notices that in his fancy Red Rider is a colored man. He stops his fantasy. While a small child, this boy was extremely expressive, both in his pleasures and in his sorrows. Today he is calm and always smiles; his language is soft and blurred; nobody can hurry him or worry him—or please him. White people like him.

Negro babies often receive sensual satisfactions which provide them with enough oral and sensory surplus for a lifetime, as clearly betrayed in the way they move, laugh, talk, sing. Their forced symbiosis with the feudal South capitalized on this oral-sensory treasure and helped to build a slave's identity: mild, submissive, dependent, somewhat querulous, but always ready to serve, with occasional empathy and childlike wisdom. But underneath a dangerous split occurred. The Negro's unavoidable identification with the dominant race, and the need of the master race to protect its own identity against the very sensual and oral temptations emanating from the race held to be inferior (whence came their mammies), established in both groups an association: light—clean—clever—white, and dark—dirty—dumb—nigger. The result, especially in those Negroes who left the poor haven of their Southern homes, was often a violently sudden and cruel cleanliness training, as attested to in the autobiographies of Negro writers. It is as if by cleansing, a whiter identity could be achieved. The attending disillusionment transmits itself to the phallic-locomotor stage, when restrictions as to what shade of girl one may dream of interfere with the free transfer of the original narcissistic sensuality to the genital sphere. Three identities are formed: (1) mammy's oral-sensual "honey-child"—tender, expressive, rhythmical; (2) the evil identity of the dirty, anal-sadistic, phallic-rapist "nigger"; and (3) the clean, anal-compulsive, restrained, friendly, but always sad "white man's Negro."

So-called opportunities offered the migrating Negro often only turn out to be a more subtly restricted prison which endangers his only historically successful identity (that of the slave) and fails to provide a reintegration of the other identity fragments mentioned. These fragments, then, become dominant in the form of racial caricatures which are underscored and stereotyped by the entertainment industry. Tired of his own caricature, the colored individual often retires into hypochondriac invalidism as a condition which represents an analogy to the dependence and the relative safety of defined restriction in the South: a neurotic regression to the ego identity of the slave.

I have mentioned the fact that mixed-blood Indians in areas where they hardly ever see Negroes refer to their full-blood brothers as "niggers," thus indicating the power of the dominant national imagery which serves to counterpoint the ideal and the evil images in the inventory of available prototypes. No individual can escape this opposition of images, which is all-pervasive in the men and in the women, in the majorities and in the minorities, and in all the classes of a given national or cultural unit. Psychoanalysis shows that the unconscious evil identity (the composite of everything which arouses negative identification—i.e., the wish not to resemble it) consists of the images of the violated (castrated) body, the ethnic outgroup, and the exploited minority. Thus a pronounced he-man may, in his dreams and prejudices prove to be mortally afraid of ever displaying a woman's sentiments, a Negro's submissiveness, or a Jew's intellectuality. For the ego, in the course of its synthesizing efforts, attempts to subsume the most powerful evil and ideal prototypes (the final contestants, as it were) and with them the whole existing imagery of superior and inferior, good and bad, masculine and feminine, free and slave, potent and impotent, beautiful and ugly, fast and slow, tall and small, in a simple alternative, in order to make one battle and one strategy out of a bewildering number of skirmishes.

While children may feel that colored people have become dark by a dirtying process, colored people may consider whites a bleached form of colored man. In either case there is the idea of a washable layer.

All folks was born black, an' dem what's turnt white, dey jest had more sense. Angel of de Lord come down an' told de ontire bunch to meet on de fo'th Friday at de dark o' de moon an' wash deyselves in Jordan. He oxplained to 'em dat dey'd all turn white an' straighten de kinks outen deir hair. Angel kept preachin' an' preachin', but dem fool niggers didn't pay him no mind. Angel can't teach a nigger nothin'. When de fo'th Friday come a mighty little sprinklin' of 'em went down to de river an' commenced to scrub. Water was mighty low. 'Twarn't like Old Missip'—'scusin' de Lord's river,—'twarn't no more'n a creek. You jest oughter seed dat crowd o' niggers settin' on de fence snickerin' at dem what went in washin'. Snickerin' an' throwin' slams. More niggers dan you ever see in Vicksburg on circus day.

Dem what went in de river kept scrubbin' and washin', special deir hair to git de kinks out. Old Aunt Grinny Granny—great-grand-mammy of all dem niggers—she sot on a log all day long, eatin' cheese and crackers and lowratin' dem what was washin'. When fust dark come, she jumped up and clapped her hands: "Fore Gawd, dem nig-gers *is* gittin' white!" Grinny Granny jerked off her head handkercher an' went tumblin' down de bank to wash her hair, an' all dem fool nig-gers followed her. But de water was all used up, jest a tiny drap in de bottom, no more'n enough to moisten de palms o' deir hands and de soles o' deir feet. So dat's why a nigger is white in dem places.[5]

Folklore here makes use of a factor which racial prejudice (shared by black and white alike) has in common with sexual prejudice (also shared, deep down, by man and woman alike). The differentiating factor, whether it is the darker color of the skin or the non-male form of the genitals, is assumed to have *happened* to the less-endowed, in the form of some over-sight or punishment; and it is more or less outspokenly treated as a blem-ish.

The Negro, of course, is only the most flagrant case of an American minority which by the pressure of tradition and the limitation of op-portunity is forced to identify with its own evil identity fragments, thus jeopardizing whatever participation in an American identity it may have earned.

What may be called an individual's ego space-time thus preserves the social topology of his childhood surroundings as well as the image of his own body, with its social connotations. To study both it is essential to correlate a patient's childhood history with the history of his family's sedentary residence in prototypal areas (East), in "backward" areas (South), or in "forward" areas (western and northern frontier), as these areas were gradually incorporated into the American version of the Anglo-Saxon cultural identity; his family's migration from, through, and to areas which at various periods may have represented the extreme sedentary or the extreme migratory pole of the developing American character; the family's religious conversions or digressions, with their class implications; abortive attempts at becoming standardized on a class level and the loss or abandonment of that level. Most important is that segment of the family's history which provided the last strong sense of cultural identity.

All of this impresses us with the dangers awaiting the minority-group American who, having successfully graduated from a marked and well-guided stage of autonomy, enters the most decisive stage of American childhood: that of initiative and industry. As indicated, minority groups of a lesser degree of Americanization are often privileged in the enjoyment of a more sensual early childhood. Their crisis comes when their mothers, losing trust in themselves and using sudden correctives in order to approach the vague but pervasive Anglo-Saxon ideal, create violent discontinuities; or where, indeed, the children themselves learn to disavow their sensual and overprotective mothers as temptations and a hindrance to the formation of a more American personality.

On the whole, it can be said that American schools successfully meet the challenge of training children of play-school age and of the elementary grades in a spirit of self-reliance and enterprise. Children of these ages seem remarkably free of prejudice and apprehension, preoccupied as they still are with growing and learning and with the new pleasures of association outside their families. This, to forestall the sense of individual inferiority, must lead to a hope for "industrial association," for equality with all those who apply themselves wholeheartedly to the same skills and adventures in learning. Individual successes, on the other hand, only expose the now overly encouraged children of mixed backgrounds and of somewhat deviant endowments to the shock of American adolescence: the standardization of individuality and the intolerance of "differences."

A lasting ego identity, we have said, cannot begin to exist without the trust of the first oral stage; it cannot be completed without a promise of fulfillment which from the dominant image of adulthood reaches down into the baby's beginnings and which, by the tangible evidence of social health, creates at every step of childhood and adolescence an accruing sense of ego strength. Thus, before entering further into identity problems of our time we must now recognize the place of identity in the human life cycle.

II

ON PSYCHOANALYSIS AND HUMAN DEVELOPMENT

E ven as he explored America, and so doing, the various lives of children, Erikson kept returning to his chosen field of inquiry, to psychoanalysis as a way of responding to people, to their problems as they affect their manner of living at home and working on jobs. He makes quite clear, in *Childhood and Society,* his intellectual loyalty to the psychoanalytic ideas and the mode of human observation and engagement which he as a young man learned—if Anna Freud was his "training analyst," Sigmund Freud was her "supervisor," to summon words now used in psychoanalytic institutes. Once, asked about his contemporary (1970) relationship to his profession's tenets, its way of seeing and putting things, Erikson spoke forthrightly but guardedly: "Look, this [psychoanalysis] is my work, and I'm glad for that. But I have never felt that we honor Freud by refusing to give his theories the critical attention he, in fact, always gave them. He was a careful thinker and writer, both— I mean by that [the use of the word "careful"] his concern for what he'd thought and how he said what he thought, spoke it, wrote it. In my five years in Vienna I never felt the need to be indoctrinated, nor the desire of others to do that. We were all trying to find ourselves, of course, but we weren't inclined (not then, not there) to turn ourselves into a sect (to use a word!), a secular one or a religious one. Freud had faith, needless to say—but it was a faith in the individual's ability to use the intellect, and doing that, to understand what is driving him, what makes him shudder with fear or tremble with foreboding. When some of us, who are called his 'followers,' start hanging on his every word, then we are giving up (surrendering) our own obligation to use our minds (to give thought to what an important psychological explorer, I think of him, discovered). So, that is where I stand—loyal to a discipline that has meant so very much to me, and grateful for all it enables in any of us who choose to use it, for ideas in general, and for ideas about themselves!"

A profession of deeply and sincerely meant reflection, conviction, rather than reflexive adherence, not to mention submission, I remember thinking. In all his essays, in the books that include them, Erikson was ever the Freudian, literally, in that he kept a picture of Freud on the wall of his study in Widener Library, at Harvard University, and mentioned him often, and with a clear acknowledgment of what those years in Vienna continued throughout his life to mean to him. He had no interest in a dissent that would turn into a parting of intellectual company, a departure with increasingly hard misgivings, demurrers, refutations, and refusals that would escalate into denunciations, an ideological movement of sorts. "There the issue is the disagreeing theorist's intent as much as [that of] his followers," observed Erikson as he took on the "separations" (he called them) of Jung and Adler from Freud, and made quite evident his lack of interest in leading any such insurrection of ideas.

In his tribute to Freud as "the first psychoanalyst" (an attribution that itself conveys both a historical-minded originality and a poetic eloquence) Erikson makes clear his desire that we, his interested readers, come to know the person of ideas, and of leadership, who made such a difference in so many lives, and in our assumptions about what we think or desire or fear, and why we do so—in short, that we come to know the man whose work in W. H. Auden's words became "a whole climate of opinion." In a sense, we can thank Erikson for helping along that cultural outcome, so that now, sixty years after Freud's death and the occasion of Auden's moving tribute, many of us in America know that "first psychoanalyst," know how his concepts make sense in therapeutic work or in the way we regard growing up—hence the value of the writing included in this section on the "nature of clinical evidence," and on the "life cycle." Indeed, Erikson's great contribution to us who speak English is his determined insistence that we understand (in familiar or colloquial language) how things work in our minds when we go awry, or when our sons and daughters, step by step, come to terms with their changing bodies, their increasing capacity to comprehend what is possible for them to think and do. Not least, Erikson insisted that we experience connection deep down, muscularly, through the everyday formality of human affiliation.

As one reads Erikson on stages and phases of childhood and adolescence, on life and its spurts, gains, the back and forth movements, the slips or setbacks that give way to new demonstrations of capability, of confidence, one thinks of the American master psychologist and philosopher William James, who realized right away (on Freud's American visit) what psychoanalysis would come to mean in America. Indeed, were he here with us, James would applaud the one who carried complex concepts, stated in German, and indebted to a classical tradition of expression, right into the midst of the American heartland—making a distant terminology available to those of us eager to speak in an earthy, feisty way about our day-to-day activities of head, heart, spirit. A visitor to us turned into a translator, an interpreter for us—and the ever-traveling William James, whose letters to his brother, Henry, abounded in psychological observations of various nations and their citizens as he came upon them, would surely have appreciated (with a comrade's nod of recognition) Erikson's quiet yet forceful reconciliation of American vernacular with the wisdom others acquired across the Atlantic and across the years of Western civilization.

THE FIRST
PSYCHOANALYST

from *Insight and Responsibility*

The 100th birthday of Sigmund Freud presented an occasion to introduce a new generation of German students to an event in the history of European thought which had been all but obliterated by National Socialist teaching: the discovery of psychoanalysis. The following address was delivered at a ceremony held jointly by the universities of Frankfurt and Heidelberg, at the University of Frankfurt, on May 6, 1956.

I t is a solemn and yet always a deeply incongruous occasion when we select an anniversary to honor a man who in lonely years struggled through a unique experience and won a new kind of knowledge for mankind. To some of us, the field created by Sigmund Freud has become an absorbing profession, to some an inescapable intellectual challenge, to all the promise (or threat) of an altered image of man. But any sense of proprietary pride in the man to be honored this year should be sobered by the thought that we have no right to assume that we would have met his challenge with more courage than his contemporaries did in the days when his insights were new. It seems fitting to use his centenary to review some of the dimensions of lonely discovery.

It is not easy (unless it be all too easy) for a "Freudian" to speak of the man who *was* Freud, of a man who grew to be a myth before our eyes. I knew Freud when he was very old, and I was young. Employed as a tutor in a family friendly to him I had the opportunity of seeing him on quiet occasions, with children and with dogs, and at outings in the mountains. I do not know whether I would have noticed Freud in a crowd. His notable features were not spectacular: the finely domed forehead, the dark, unfathomable eyes, and certain small indomitable gestures—they all had become part of that inner containment which crowns the old age of good fighters.

I was an artist then, which can be a European euphemism for a young man with some talent, but nowhere to go. What probably impressed me most was the fact that this doctor of the mind, this expert of warped biography, had surrounded himself in his study with a small host of little statues: those distilled variations of the human form which were created by the anonymous artists of the archaic Mediterranean. Certainly, of Freud's field, of conflict and complaint and confession, there was no trace in their art. This respect for form, so surprising in a man who had unearthed mankind's daimonic inner world, was also obvious in his love for proud dogs and for gaily bright children. I vaguely felt that I had met a man of rare dimensions, rare contradictions.

When I became a psychoanalyst myself, this same old man—now remote from the scene of training and gathering—became for me what he is for the world: the writer of superb prose, the author of what seems like more than one lifetime's collected works: a master, so varied in his grandiose one-sidedness that the student can manage to understand only one period of his work at a time. Strangely enough, we students knew little of his beginnings, nothing of that mysterious self-analysis which he alluded to in his writings. We knew people whom Freud had introduced into psychoanalysis, but psychoanalysis itself had, to all appearances, sprung from his head like Athena from the head of Zeus.

The early Freud became better known to us only a very few years ago, through the accidental discovery of intimate letters written before the turn of the century. They permitted us to envisage Freud the beginner, the first, and for a decade, the only, psychoanalyst. To pay homage to him means, in the passage of time, to acknowledge a lasting bond and yet also to take leave of what is now history.

For orientation and comparison, let us consider the circumstances of another discovery of the nineteenth century, the discovery of a man who was also lonely and calumniated, and who was also eventually recognized as a changer of man's image: Charles Darwin. Darwin came upon his evolutionary laboratory, the Galapagos Islands, on a voyage which was not part of an intended professional design. In fact, he had failed in medicine, not for lack of talent, it would seem, but partially because of an intellectual selectivity which forbade him to learn passively—a self-protective selectivity of the kind for which old Bernard Shaw, in retrospect, patted himself on the back when he said, "My memory rejects and selects; and its selections are not academic. . . . I congratulate myself on this."

Once embarked on the *Beagle,* however, and on his way to his "laboratory," Darwin showed that dogged, that prejudiced persistence which is one condition for an original mind's becoming a creative one. He now fully developed his superior gift, namely, "noticing things which easily escape attention, and observing them carefully." His physical stamina was inexhaustible. His mind proved ready for the laboratory and the laboratory seemed to have waited for him. He could fully employ sweeping configurations of thought which had ripened in him: cutting across existing classifications which assumed a parallel, linear origin of all species from a common pool of creation, he saw everywhere transitions, transmutations, variations, signs of a dynamic struggle for adaptation. The law of natural selection began to "haunt him." And he perceived that man must come under the same law: "I see no possible means of drawing the line and saying, here you must stop."

Darwin, at the age of twenty-seven, went home with his facts and theory, and traveled no more. He gave the scientific world a few papers primarily on geological subjects; then he withdrew to the country, to work for twenty years on the *Origin of Species*: he *made* it a long and lonely discovery. He now became physically incapacitated by insomnia, nausea, and chills. His doctor-father could not diagnose his disease, but declared his son too delicate for a career out in the world. The son became a life-long invalid. If his hypersensitivity was a sign of hereditary degeneracy, as some doctors believe, then there never was a degenerate guided more wisely in the utilization of his degeneracy by an inner genius of economy. For, "I could . . . collect facts bearing on the origin of species . . . when I could do nothing else from illness." Not that Darwin did not realize what this restriction of his lifespace did to him: when, at the end, even Shakespeare seemed so "intolerably dull" as to nauseate him, he deplored the "curious and lamentable loss of the higher aesthetic tastes" and spoke of an "enfeeblement of the emotional part of our nature."

I do not wish to speculate here on the dynamics of a psychoneurosis in a man like Darwin. But I do know that a peculiar malaise can befall those who have seen too much, who, in ascertaining new facts in a spirit seemingly as innocent as that of a child building with blocks, begin to perceive the place of these facts in the moral climate of their day. "We physicists have known sin," Oppenheimer has said; but it does not take the use of scientific data for mankind's material destruction to make a scientist feel or behave as if he had sinned. It is enough to have persisted, with the naïveté of genius, in the dissolution of one of the prejudices on which the security and the familiarity of the contemporary image of man is built. But a creative man has no choice. He may come across his supreme task almost accidentally. But once the issue is joined, his task proves to be at the same time intimately related to his most personal conflicts, to his superior selective perception, and to the stubbornness of his one-way will: he must court sickness, failure, or insanity, in order to test the alternative whether the established world will crush him, or whether he will disestablish a sector of this world's outworn fundaments and make place for a new one.

Darwin only dealt with man's biological origins. His achievement, and his "sin," was a theory that made man part of evolved nature. In comparing Darwin's approach to nature with his approach to man, a recent biographer remarks half-jokingly, "In any case, no man afflicted with a weak stomach and insomnia has any business investigating his own kind."

As we now turn to Freud, the psychological explorer, I hope to make the reader wonder whether anybody *but* one at least temporarily afflicted with psychosomatic symptoms, one temporarily sick of his own kind, could or would investigate his own species—provided that he had the inclination, the courage, and the mental means of facing his own neurosis with creative persistence. A man, I will submit, could begin to study man's inner world only by appointing his own neurosis that angel with whom he must wrestle and whom he must not let go until his blessing, too, has been given.

What was Freud's Galapagos, what species fluttered what kinds of wings before his searching eyes? As has often been pointed out derisively, his creative laboratory was the neurologist's office, the dominant species hysterical ladies—"Fräulein Anna O.," "Frau Emmy v. N.," "Katarina" (not a Fräulein, because she was a peasant).

Freud was thirty when, in 1886, he became the private doctor of such patients. He had not expected to be a practitioner; he had, in fact, received his medical degree belatedly. His mind, too, had been "selective." At the age of seventeen he had chosen medicine, in preference to law and politics, when he heard Goethe's "Ode to Nature": the unveiling of nature's mysteries, not the healing of the sick, provided the first self-image of a doctor. Then came *his* professional moratorium. As in an ascetic reaction to romantic indulgence he committed himself to the physiological laboratory and to the monastic service of physicalistic physiology. What geology was to Darwin, physiology was to Freud: a schooling in method. The ideology of the physicalistic physiologic method of the time was formulated in an oath by two of its outstanding teachers, DuBois Reymond and Brücke: "to put in power this truth: No other forces than the common physical chemical ones are active within the organism. . . . One has either to find the specific way or form of their action by means of the physical mathematical method, or to assume new forces equal in dignity to the chemical physical forces inherent in matter."[1] *New forces equal in dignity*—we shall return to this phrase.

When Freud exchanged the academic monastery for the medical parsonage, he had fully developed a style of work which would have sufficed for an impressively productive lifetime. He had published many papers on physiological and neurological subjects, and had two major works in preparation. Thus, when he became a practicing neurologist, he left a future behind him. But he had married the girl who had waited for him, and he wanted a family, in fact, a large one; he had earned the right to have confidence in himself.

Yet, a future anticipated in a man's configurations of thought means more than time not yet spent. To give up the laboratory meant to relinquish a work-discipline and a work-ideology to which Freud had been deeply committed. The work of a specialist catering to the epidemiological market was lacking in what Freud nostalgically called an inner tyrant, i.e., a great principle. Luckily, he had met an older practitioner, Dr. Joseph Breuer, who had shown him that there was a laboratory hidden in the very practice of neurology.

Freud's new laboratory, then, were patients, mostly women, who brought him symptoms which only an overly-serious and searching observer could accept as constituting a field activated by dignified forces. These ladies suffered from neuralgic pains and anesthesias, from partial paralyses and contractions, from tics and convulsions, from nausea and finickiness, from the inability to see and from visual hallucinations, from the inability to remember and from painful floods of memory. Popular opinion judged the ladies to be spoiled, just putting on airs—"attention-getting" some of us would call it today. The dominant neuropathology of the day, however, assumed some of their disturbances to be a consequence of hereditary degenerative processes in the brain. Freud, too, had learned to treat these patients like partially decerebrated bundles, or like children without a will: he had learned to apply massage and electricity to the affected body part and to dominate the patient's will by hypnosis and suggestion. He might, for example, order the hypnotized patient to laugh out loud when encountering in the future a certain thought or a person or place, the sight of which had previously caused a fit or a paralysis. The awakened patient did laugh out loud, but more often than not, she would become afflicted again, and in connection with something else.

But Freud, like Darwin, could not believe in linear descent—in this instance, of isolated symptoms from defects of the brain. In an array of symptoms he, too, looked for a common principle, a struggle for equilibrium, a clash of forces. And he was convinced that challenging phenomena must have a hidden history. As Freud listened to his hypnotized patients, he realized that they were urgently, desperately offering him series of memories which, seemingly fragmentary, were like variations in search of a theme—a theme which was often found in a historical model event.

Here no detail could be too trivial for investigation. A patient suffers from a persistent illusion of smelling burned pancakes. All right, the smell of burned pancakes shall be the subject of exhaustive analysis. As this smell is traced to a certain scene and the scene vividly remembered, the sensation disappears, to be replaced by the smell of cigars. The smell of cigars is traced to other scenes, in which a man in an authoritative position was present, and in which disturbing subjects had been mentioned in a connection which demanded that the patient control her feelings.

It fits our image of those Victorian days—a time when children in all, and women in most circumstances were to be seen but not heard—that the majority of symptoms would prove to lead back to events when violently aroused affects (love, sex, rage, fear) had come into conflict with narrow standards of propriety and breeding. The symptoms, then, were delayed involuntary communications: using the whole body as spokesman, they were saying what common language permits common people to say directly: "He makes me sick," "She pierced me with her eyes," "I could not swallow that insult," or, as the song has it, "I'm gonna wash that man right out of my hair." Freud the neurologist now became "haunted" by the basic conviction that any neurotic symptom, traced along a path of associated experiences (not of neurological pathways), would lead to the revival in memory of earlier and earlier conflicts, and in doing so would yield a complete history of its origin.

As Freud proceeded with his reconstruction of the pasts of his patients, a dangerous insight dawned on him; such conflicts as his patients revealed were, in principle, shared by all men. It would be hard, indeed, "to draw the line and say here you must stop." He became aware of the fact that man, in principle, does not remember or understand much of what is most significant in his childhood, and more, that he does not want to. Here, a mysterious *individual prehistory* seemed to loom up, as important for psychology as Darwin's biological prehistory was for biology.

But Darwin had at his disposal the whole tradition of an ancient science. For Freud's psychologic findings, there were, at first, only physiologic methods, his own speculations, and the sayings of writers and philosophers, who, in their way, it seemed, had known it all. Yet, it appears to be part of a creative man's beginnings that he may change his field and yet maintain the manner of work which became part of his first identity as a worker. Freud had investigated the nature of brain lesions by slicing the brains of young animals and foeti. He now investigated memories as representative cross sections of a patient's emotional condition. In successive memories, he traced trends which led, like pathways, to the traumatic past; there experiences of a disruptive nature loomed like lesions interfering with growth. Thus, the search for traumatic events in the individual's forgotten prehistory, his early childhood, replaced the search for lesions in early development.

Psychology, of course, is the preferred field for a transfer of configurations of thought from other fields. The nature of things, or better, man's logical approach to things, is such that analogies—up to a point—reveal true correspondences. But the history of psychology also reveals how consistently neglectful and belated man is in applying to his own nature methods of observation which he has tried out on the rest of nature. That man, the observer, is in some essential way set off from the observed world, is clear. But this difference calls for a constant redefinition in the light of new modes of thought. Only thus can man keep wisely different rather than vainly so. Before Copernicus, vanity as well as knowledge insisted that the earth must be in the exact nodal center of God's universe. Well, we know now where we are. Before Darwin, man could claim a different origin from the rest of the animal world with whom he shares a slim margin of the earth's crust and atmosphere. Before Freud, man (that is, man of the male sex and of the better classes) was convinced that he was fully conscious of all there was to him, and sure of his divine values. Childhood was a mere training ground, in charge of that intermediary race, women.

In such a world female hysteria was implicitly acknowledged by men and men doctors as a symptom of the natural inferiority, the easy degeneracy, of women. When Freud presented to the Vienna Medical Society a case of *male* hysteria, the reaction of his colleagues convinced him that years of isolation lay ahead of him. He accepted it then and there: he never visited that society again. Yet, their reaction proved to be only one small aspect of a memorable crisis in which a new science was almost stillborn, by no means only because of professional isolation, but also because of disturbances in the instrument of observation, the observer's mind. Freud's early writings and letters permit us to see a threefold crisis: a crisis in therapeutic technique; a crisis in the conceptualization of clinical experience; and a personal crisis. I shall try to indicate in what way all three crises were, in essence, one, and that they were the necessary dimensions of discovery in psychology.

First, then, Freud's change in technique. The textbooks describe it as the replacement of the cathartic and the suggestive methods by the psychoanalytic one. In Freud's *Studies in Hysteria,*[2] however, a pervasive change in the doctor-patient relationship is clearly traced. Freud judged some of his patients to be outstanding in character and talents, rather than degenerate. He began to let himself be led by the sequence and the nature of their communications. With amused surprise he would admit that a hypnotized patient, in suggesting to him that he should stop interrupting her with his authoritative suggestions, had a point. She fortified her point by unearthing memories which he would not have suspected. He realized that in hypnosis the patients had at their disposal a depth of understanding and a freedom of affect which they did not marshal in normal life. This he had not imposed by suggestion: it was their judgment and their affect, and if they had it in hypnosis, it was part of them. Perhaps, if he treated them like whole people, they would learn to realize the

wholeness which was theirs. He now offered them a conscious and direct partnership: he made the patient's healthy, if submerged, part his
partner in understanding the unhealthy part. Thus was established one
basic principle of psychoanalysis, namely, that *one can study the human
mind only by engaging the fully motivated partnership of the observed individual,
and by entering into a sincere contract with him.*

But a contract has two partners, at least. The changed image of the patient changed the self-image of the doctor. He realized that habit and
convention had made him and his fellow physicians indulge in an autocratic pattern, with not much more circumspection or justification than
the very paternal authorities who he now felt had made the patients sick
in the first place. He began to divine the second principle of psychoanalysis, namely, that *you will not see in another what you have not learned to
recognize in yourself.* The mental healer must divide himself as well as the
patient into an observer and an observed.

The intellectual task faced here, namely psychoanalytic insight and
communication, was a massive one. Today, it is difficult to appreciate the
psychosocial task involved. Freud had to relinquish a most important ingredient of the doctor role of the times: the all-knowing father role,
which was safely anchored in the whole contemporary cult of the paternal male as the master of every human endeavor except the nursery
and the kitchen. This should not be misunderstood: Freud did not,
overnight, become a different man. Indeed, there are many who will see
nothing in the nature of renunciation of paternalism in him. But we are
not speaking here of opinions and roles in the modern sense, of personalities subject to change like the body styles of automobiles which retain
little logical relation to the inner motor of the thing, nor to the laws of
the road. True roles are a matter of a certain ideologic-esthetic unity, not
of opinions and appearances. True change is a matter of worthwhile
conflict, for it leads through the painful consciousness of one's position
to a new conscience in that position. As Justice Holmes once said, the first
step toward a truer faith is the recognition that *I,* at any rate, am *not* God.
Furthermore, roles anchored in work-techniques are prepared in the in-
tricacies of a man's life history. Whoever has suffered under and identified with a stern father must become a stern father himself, or else find
an entirely different quality of moral strength, an equal measure of
strength. Young Martin Luther's religious crisis is a transcendent example of the heights and the depths of this problem.

Freud, as we have seen, had sought a new inner tyrant in a work-ideology shared with esteemed minds. He had relinquished it. Now, he discarded the practicing neurologist's prevailing role of dominance and of license. This, then, is the first aspect of Freud's crisis: he had to create a new therapeutic role for which there was no ideological niche in the tradition of his profession. He had to create it—or fail.

The second problem which isolated Freud in those years was the course taken by his search for the "energy of equal dignity" which might be the quantity and the power in mental life; for the mental mechanisms which normally maintain such power in a state of constancy; and for those inner conditions which unleash its destructiveness. The power, as we saw, was first perceived as "affect," the disturbance in the machine, as a "damming up." A long treatise recently found with some of Freud's letters reveals the whole extent of Freud's conflict between the creative urge to say in psychological terms what only literature had known before him, and on the other hand, his desperate obedience to physiology. The treatise is called "A Psychology for Neurologists."[3] It was written in 1895, sent to his friend Fliess, and forgotten. Freud introduces it thus: "The intention of this project is to furnish us with a psychology which shall be a natural science: its aim, that is, is to represent psychical processes as quantitatively determined states of specifiable material particles and so to make them plain and void of contradictions." Freud proceeds to develop a model for the organization of these "particles," a sensitive machine for the management of qualities and quantities of excitation, such as are aroused by external and internal stimuli. Physical concepts are combined with histological concepts to create a kind of neuronic Golem, a robot, in which even consciousness and thought are mechanistically explainable on the basis of an over-all principle of inner constancy. Here Freud, at the very beginning of his career as a psychologist, tried to create a mind-robot, a thinking-machine, in many ways related to the mechanical and economic as well as the physiological configurations of his day. As Freud wrote triumphantly to his friend: "Everything fell into place, the cogs meshed, the thing really seemed to be a machine which in a moment would run of itself." But one month after Freud had sent this conception to his friend, he recanted it. "All I was trying to do," he writes, "was to explain defense (against affect), but I found myself explaining something from the very heart of nature. I found myself wrestling with the whole of psychology. Now I want to hear no more of it." He now calls the psychology a "kind of aberration." This manuscript, found only accidentally, documents in a dramatic way the pains to which a discoverer will go *not* to haphazardly ignore the paths of his tradition, but to follow them instead to their absurd limit, and to abandon them only when the crossroad of lone search is reached.

In the meantime, clinical work had brought Freud within sight of his crossroad. His patients, he had become convinced, were suffering primarily from the "damming up" of one irrepressible "affect," namely, sexual sensuality, the existence of which had been consistently denied by their overclothed parents, while engaged in only with furtive shame and degradation by many of their mothers. In the epidemiological fact of widespread female hysteria, Freud faced the specific symptoms of the Victorian age, the price paid, especially by women, for the hypocritical double standard of the sexes in the dominant classes, the masters of commerce and the would-be masters of industrial power. However, the most glaring epidemiological fact (compare poliomyelitis, or juvenile delinquency) does not receive clarification until a seasoned set of theoretical configurations happens to suggest a specific approach. In introducing the energy concept of a sexual libido, which from birth onward is the fuel in all desiring and loving, and which our mind-machine must learn to transform according to our goals and ideals—in this concept Freud found at once the most fitting answer to the questions posed by his patients' memories, and the theory most consistent with his search for a "dignified force." But alas, it was also the most irrationally repugnant solution thinkable in his prudish times, and a solution of emotional danger to the observer. For, indeed, where "to draw the line"?

Here Freud's genetic fervor led to a faulty reconstruction. Certain of being on the right track, and yet shaken by inner and outer resistances, he overshot the mark. In search for a pathogenic Ur-event, he was led to regard as historically real the patients' accounts of passive sexual experiences in the first years of childhood, and to consider the fathers of the patients the perpetrators in such events. He later confessed: "The analysis had led by the correct path to such infantile sexual traumas, and yet, these were not true. Thus, the basis of reality had been lost. At that time, I would gladly have dropped the whole thing." But finally, "I reflected that if hysterics trace back their symptoms to imaginary traumas, then this new fact signified that they create such scenes in fantasy, and hence psychic reality deserves to be given a place next to actual reality." Freud would soon be able to describe psychic reality systematically as the domain of fantasy, dream, and mythology, and as the imagery and language of a universal unconscious, thus transforming into a scientific dimension what had been age-old intuitive knowledge.

In the meantime, had his error detracted from the "dignity" of sexuality? It does not seem so. Knowing what we know today, it is obvious that somebody had to come sometime who would decide that it would be better for the sake of the study of human motivation to call too many rather than too few things sexual, and then to modify the hypothesis by careful inquiry. For it was only too easy to do what had become civilization's "second nature," that is, in the face of the man's sexual and aggressive drives forever to beat a hasty retreat into romanticism and religionism, into secrecy, ridicule, and lechery. The patients' fantasies were sexual, and something sexual must have existed in their early years. Freud later called that something *psychosexuality,* for it encompasses the fantasies as well as the impulses, the psychology as well as the biology in the earliest stages of human sexuality.

Today one can add that Freud's error was not even as great as it seemed. First of all, sexual (if not always genital) seductions of children do occur, and are dangerous to them. But more important, the general provocation and exploitation of the child's immature emotions by parent and grandparent for the sake of their own petty emotional relief, of suppressed vengefulness, of sensual self-indulgence, and of sly righteousness must be recognized not only as evident in case histories, but as a universal potentiality often practiced and hypocritically rationalized by very "moral" individuals, indeed. Samuel Butler's *The Way of All Flesh* is probably the most forceful statement on record. What today is decried as "momism" in the United States existed in analogous form in the father's role in the Victorian world: it is only necessary to think of Hitler's official account of his father-hate, and the appeal of this account for millions of young Germans, to know that this is a smoldering theme of general explosiveness. In finding access to the altogether fateful domain of man's prolonged childhood, Freud discovered that infantile man, in addition to and often under the guise of being trained, is being ruefully exploited, only to become in adulthood nature's most systematic and sadistic ex-

ploiter. Freud's search thus added another perspective of as yet unfore-
seeable importance to the image of man.

Yet, this discovery, too, had to pass through its lonely stage. Freud had
made a significant mistake, and he was not one to shirk the responsibility for it either publicly or privately. He made it part of his self-analysis.

We know about this first self-analysis in history from the letters, already
mentioned, which Freud wrote to Dr. Wilhelm Fliess of Berlin. The extent and the importance of Freud's friendship with Fliess was not even
suspected until the letters revealed it.

The two doctors met for what they called their "congresses," long
weekends in some mountainous city or town. Their common heritage of
education permitted them to roam in varied conversation, as they walked
vigorously through the countryside. Freud seems to have shared Nietzsche's impression that a thought not born in locomotion could not be
much good. But among the theories discussed by the two doctors, there
were many which never saw the light of publication. Thus, Fliess, for
many years, was the first and only one to share Freud's thinking.

Psychoanalysts do not seem to like this friendship much; Fliess, after all,
was not even a psychoanalyst. Some of us now read of Freud's affection
for this man wishing we could emulate that biographer of Goethe who,
in the face of Goethe's claim that at a certain time he had dearly loved a
certain lady, remarks in a footnote: "Here Goethe is mistaken." Freud, we
now say, must have overestimated this friendship in an irrational, almost
pathological way. But what, after all, do thinkers need friends for? So that
they can share speculations, each alternately playing benevolent authority to the other, each being the other's co-conspirator, each serving as ap-
plauding audience, and as cautioning chorus. Freud calls Fliess his *"Other
one,"* to whom he can entrust what is not ready for "the *others.*" Fliess, at
any rate, seems to have had the stature and the wide education which
permitted Freud to entrust him with "imaginings, transpositions, and
guesses." That Freud's imaginings turned out to be elements of a true vision and a blueprint for a science, while Fliess's ended in a kind of mathematical mysticism, provides no grounds to belittle the friendship. The
value of a friend may sometimes be measured by the magnitude of the
problem which we leave behind with him.

The friendship seems to have been unmarred by irrational disturbances, until, in 1894, Freud consulted Fliess in regard to his own symptoms and moods, which he condenses in the word *Herzelend*—something like "misery of the heart." Fliess had cauterized swellings in Freud's nose and had urged him to give up his beloved cigars. Suddenly, the intellectual communication appears jammed: "I have not looked at your excellent case histories," Freud writes, and indicates that his latest communication to Fliess "was abandoned in the middle of a sentence." He continues: "I am suspicious of you this time, because this heart business [*Herzangelegenheit*] of mine is the first occasion on which I have ever heard you contradict yourself." At this time, Freud speaks of his discoveries with the anguish of one who has seen a promised land which he must not set his foot on: "I have the distinct feeling," he writes, "that I have touched on one of the great secrets of nature." This tedium of thought seems to have joined the "heart misery" and was now joined by a mistrust of his friend. He wrote, "Something from the deepest depths of my own neurosis has ranged itself against my taking a further step in understanding of the neuroses, and you have somehow been involved."

Freud, at this point, had developed toward Fliess what later, when he understood it, he called a transference, i.e., that peculiar mixture of overestimation and mistrust, which man is so especially ready to bestow on people in significant positions—doctors and priests, leaders and kings, and other superiors, competitors, and adversaries. It is called transference, because, where it is neurotic, it is characterized by the blurring of an adult relationship through the transfer to it of infantile loves and hates, dependencies and impotent rages. Transference thus also implies a partial regression to childish attitudes. It was this very area which, at that time, Freud was trying to understand in his patients. Yet, in Freud, it was quite obviously related to the processes of creativity. We have seen how young Freud, in his student days, had subdued an almost incestuous eagerness to "unveil nature" by the compensatory concentration on laboratory work. He had thus postponed a conflict by realizing only one part of his identity. But when, in his words, he "touched on one of the secrets of nature," he was forced to realize that other, that more creative identity. For any refuge in the established disciplines of scientific inquiry was, as the project proved, forever closed. It is in those moments when our divided selves threaten to drag each other down, that a friend, as Nietzsche said, becomes the life-saver which keeps us afloat and together.

Freud thus discovered another principle in his new work, namely, that *psychological discovery is accompanied by some irrational involvement of the observer, and that it cannot be communicated to another without a certain irrational involvement of both.* Such is the stuff of psychology; here it is not enough to put on an armor of superiority or aloofness in the hope that, like the physicist's apron, it will protect vital organs against the radiation emanating from the observed. Here, only the observer's improved insight into himself can right the instrument, protect the observer, and permit the communication of the observed.

In his transference to Fliess, Freud recognized one of the most important transferences of all: the transfer of an early father-image on later individuals and events. And here we can recognize the pervasiveness in these crises of the great father theme. We saw this theme in Freud's determination not to play autocratic father to patients already crushed by autocracy; we recognized this theme as the core of his tendentious error in the genetic reconstruction of his patients' childhood; and we observe it in his filial reactions to Fliess. A dream, he now reported to Fliess, had clearly revealed to him the fact, and the explanation for the fact, that an irrational wish to blame all fathers for their children's neuroses had dominated him. Yet, one senses at the same time the need of the creative man to have his creativity sired, as it were, by an overvalued friend—a need which often leads, and in Freud's life periodically led, to almost tragicomic involvements.

Having established, then, both the actual and the fantastic aspects of a universal father-image, Freud now could break through to the first prehistoric *Other* of them all: the loving mother. He was free to discover the whole Oedipus complex, and to recognize it as a dominant theme in literature and in mythologies around the world. Only then could he understand the full extent to which he, when sick and bewildered, had made a parent-figure out of Fliess, so that that mystic *Other* might help him analyze himself "as if he were a stranger." He concluded that "self-analysis is really impossible, otherwise there would be no illness . . . I can only analyze myself with objectively acquired knowledge." This insight is the basis for what later became the training analysis, that is, the preventive and didactic psychoanalytic treatment of every prospective psychoanalyst.

The friendship, for other reasons too, had outlived itself. It ended when Freud, in a way, could least afford to lose it, namely, around the turn of the century, after the appearance of *The Interpretation of Dreams.*[4]

Freud then, as later, considered this book his most fundamental contribution; he then also believed it to be his last. And, as he wrote, "not a leaf has stirred." For months, for years, there were no book reviews, no sales to speak of. Where there was interest, it was mostly disbelief and calumniation. At this time, Freud seems temporarily to have despaired of his medical way of life. Fliess offered a meeting at Easter. But this time Freud refused. "It is more probable that I shall avoid you," he writes. "I have conquered my depression, and now . . . it is slowly healing. . . . In your company . . . your fine and positive biological discoveries would rouse my innermost (impersonal) envy. . . . I should unburden my woes to you and come back dissatisfied . . . no one can help me in what depresses me, it is my cross, which I must bear." A few letters later, he refers to his patients' tendency to prolong the treatment beyond the acquisition of the necessary insight: "Such prolongation is a compromise between illness and health which patients themselves desire, and . . . the physician must therefore not lend himself to it." It is clear that he has now recognized such "prolongation" and "compromise" in his friendship as well, and that he will refuse to permit himself a further indulgence in the dependence on Fliess. But he will sorely miss him—"my one audience," as he calls him.

In the course of this friendship a balance was righted: feminine intuition, childlike curiosity, and artistic freedom of style were recognized and restored as partners of the masculine "inner tyrant" in the process of psychological discovery. And Fliess? According to him the friendship was ship-wrecked on the age-old rock of disputed priorities: Freud, he said, envied him. And, indeed, Freud had expressed envy that Fliess worked "with light, not darkness, with the sun and not the unconscious." But it does not seem probable that Freud would have changed places with him.

These, then, were the dimensions of the crisis during which and through which psychoanalysis was born. During these years Freud at times expressed some despair and confessed to some neurotic symptoms which reveal phenomenological aspects of a creative crisis. He suffered from a "railroad phobia" and from acute fears of an early death—both symptoms of an over-concern with the all too rapid passage of time. "Railroad phobia" is an awkwardly clinical way of translating what in German is *Reisefieber*—a feverish combination of pleasant excitement and anxiety. But it all meant, it seems, on more than one level that he was "coming too late," that he was "missing the train," that he would perish before reaching some "promised land." He could not see how he could complete what he had visualized if every single step took so much "work, time and error." As is often the case, such preoccupation with time leads to apprehension centered in the heart, that metronome and measure of endurance.

In the letters the theme of time overlaps with a geographic restlessness. He thinks of emigrating, maybe to Berlin, to England, or to America. Most striking is a theme of European dimensions, namely, an intense, a "deeply neurotic" urge to see Rome. At first, he wants to arrange to meet his friend, his "one audience," there. But he writes, "We are not in Rome yet," or, "I am further away from Rome than at any time since we met, and the freshness of youth is notably declining." Only when his fundamental work, *The Interpretation of Dreams,* is published, does Freud decide to spend Easter in Rome: "Not that there is any justification for it, I have achieved nothing yet [*es is nichts erreicht*] and in any case, circumstances will probably make it impossible."

What did Rome mean to Freud? It was a highly "overdetermined" and thus a highly condensed theme. We recognize in it the fate of Hannibal, who had kindled the imagination of the Jewish boy: the Semitic warlord had never conquered Rome. Beyond this, the Eternal City is the goal of many roads, all of which are superbly condensed in the final wish which Freud sent to Fliess: "Next Easter in Rome." Here we recognize the educated German's eternal *Sehnsucht* for Italy *("dahin, dahin");* the Israelite's longing for the ancestral home as expressed in the prayer at Passover, "Next year in Jerusalem"; and within it all a remnant of that infantile wonder once experienced by the little Jewish boy on the holiday of resurrection, under the eager guidance of the Kinderfrau, his Catholic nanny. I know that this kind of "over-determination," embracing various periods of a man's life and, at the same time, reconciling ambivalent divisions in his affects and in his imagery, seems to lack the parsimony of other sciences: but such is the material of psychoanalysis.

Only in the very last of the letters to Fliess does Freud seem to have found his position in time and space: "I have readers . . . the time is not yet ripe for followers." The last letter, written in the last year of the 19th century, admits, "We are terribly far ahead of our time." Freud is now forty-four years of age.

But lest anyone form the faulty image of a lamentably torn and tormented man and physician, it must be reported that the Freud of those years was what to all appearances we would call a well-adjusted individual, and what then was a decent and able one: a man who took conscientious care of all the patients who found their way to his door, who with devotion and joy raised a family of six children, who was widely-read and well-groomed, traveled with curiosity, walked (or, as we would say, exercised) with abandon, loved good food and wine wisely, and his cigars unwisely. His "railroad phobia" did not keep him from traveling. And, when he wrote about his being *"arbeitsunfähig"* (unable to work), he meant that his writing was not keeping up with his aspirations. But he was not too "well-adjusted" to entertain the dreams, the passions, and the fears adhering to extraordinary vision; nor too "decent" to approach a few things in life with decisive, with ruthless integrity. All of which in a way he could ill afford, for the times were bad for a medical specialist; it was the time of one of the first economic depressions of the modern industrial era, it was a time of poverty in plenty. Nor did the self-analysis "reform" or chasten Freud. Some of the vital conflicts which pervaded the friendship with Fliess remained lifelong, as did some of the early methodological habits: in *Totem and Taboo,* Freud again reconstructed—this time on the stage of history—an "event" which, though an unlikely happening in past actuality, yet proved most significant as a timeless theme. But that early period of Freud's work gave to the new method of inquiry its unique direction, and with it gave its originator that peculiar unity of peculiarities which makes up a man's identity, thus forming the cornerstone of his kind of integrity, and posing his challenge to contemporaries and generations to come.

Freud's self-revelations in the *Interpretation of Dreams* as well as in his letters have provided ample leeway to both his friends and his adversaries for placing emphasis on one or the other of the inner contradictions which characterize genius. Any exclusive emphasis, however, on the infantile or the great, the neurotic or the creative, the emotional or the intellectual, the medical or the psychological aspects of a creative crisis sacrifices essential components. Here, I like to quote a sentence which

Professor Cornford puts into the mouth of Pythagoras: "What is your warrant for valuing one part of my experience and rejecting the rest? If I had done so, you would never have heard my name."

The unique direction given by Freud to the new method of inquiry consisted of the introduction into psychology of a system of co-ordinates which I can only summarize most briefly. His early energy concept provided the *dynamic-economic* co-ordinate, dealing with drives and forces and their transformations. A *topographic-structural* co-ordinate emerged from his study of the partitions within that early mind-robot; while the *genetic* co-ordinate takes account of the origin and the development in stages of both drive and structure.[5] Generations of psychoanalysts have endeavored to find proper places for each new observation and each new theory in these co-ordinates, which thus have provided a method of cross-checking not easily appreciated by the untrained. On the other hand, Freud's case-studies have given to the study of lives a daimonic depth to be found before him only in drama, in fiction, and in the confessions of men endowed with passionate introspection.

Since those early days of discovery, psychoanalysis has established deep and wide interrelationships with other methods of investigation, with methods of naturalist observation, of somatic examination, of psychological experiment, of anthropological field work, and of historical research. If, instead of enlarging on all these, I have focused on the early days, and on the uniqueness of the original Freudian experience, I have done so because I believe that an innovator's achievement can be seen most dramatically in that moment when he, alone against historical adversity and inner doubts, and armed only with the means of persuasion, gives a new direction to human awareness—new in its focus, new in its method, and new in its inescapable responsibility.

The dimensions of Freud's discovery are contained in a triad which, in a variety of ways, remains basic to the practice of psychoanalysis, but also to its application. It is the triad of a *therapeutic contract,* a *conceptual design,* and *systematic self-analysis.*

In psychoanalytic practice, this triad can never become routine. As new categories of suffering people prove amenable to psychoanalytic therapy, new techniques come to life, new aspects of the mind find clarification, and new therapeutic roles are created. Today, the student of psychoanalysis receives a training psychoanalysis which prepares him for the emotional hazards of his work. But he must live with the rest of mankind in this era of what we may call anxiety-in-plenty, and neither his personal life nor the very progress of his work will spare him renewed conflicts, be his profession ever so recognized, ever so organized. Wide recognition and vast organization, in fact, will not assure—they may even endanger—the basic triad, for which the psychoanalyst makes himself responsible, to wit: that as a clinician he accept his contract with the patient as the essence of his field of study and relinquish the security of seemingly more "objective" methods; that as a theorist he maintain a sense of obligation toward continuous conceptual redefinition and resist the lure of seemingly more profound or of more pleasing philosophic short cuts; and finally, that as a humanist he put self-observant vigilance above the satisfaction of seeming professional omnipotence. The responsibility is great. For, in a sense, the psychoanalytic method must remain forever a "controversial" tool, a tool for the detection of that aspect of the total image of man which in a given historical period is being neglected or exploited, repressed or suppressed by the prevailing technology and ideology—including hasty "psychoanalytic" ideologies.

Freud's triad remains equally relevant in the applications of psychoanalysis to the behavioral sciences, and to the humanities. An adult studying a child, an anthropologist studying a tribe, or a sociologist studying a riot sooner or later will be confronted with data of decisive importance for the welfare of those whom he is studying, while the strings of his own motivation will be touched, sometimes above and sometimes well below the threshold of awareness. He will not be able, for long, to escape the necessary conflict between his emotional participation in the observed events and the methodological rigor required to advance his field and human welfare. Thus, his studies will demand, in the long run, that he develop the ability to include in his observational field his human obligations, his methodological responsibilities, and his own motivations. In doing so, he will, in his own way, repeat that step in scientific conscience which Freud dared to make.

That shift in self-awareness, however, cannot remain confined to professional partnerships such as the observer's with the observed, or the doctor's with his patient. It implies a fundamentally new *ethical orientation of adult man's relationship to childhood*: to his own childhood, now behind and within him; to his own child before him; and to every man's children around him.

But the fields dealing with man's historical dimension are far apart in their appraisal of childhood. Academic minds, whose long-range perspectives can ignore the everyday urgencies of the curative and educative arts, blithely go on writing whole world histories without a trace of women and children, whole anthropological accounts without any reference to the varying styles of childhood. As they record what causal chain can be discerned in political and economic realities, they seem to shrug off as historical accidents due to "human nature" such fears and rages in leaders and masses as are clearly the residue of childish emotions. True, scholars may have been justly repelled by the first enthusiastic intrusion of doctors of the mind into their ancient disciplines. But their refusal to consider the historical relevance of human childhood can be due only to that deeper and more universal emotional aversion and repression which Freud himself foresaw. On the other hand, it must be admitted that in clinical literature (and in literature turned altogether clinical) aversion has given place to a faddish preoccupation with the more sordid aspects of childhood as though they were the final determinants of human destiny.

Neither of these trends can hinder the emergence of a new truth, namely that the collective life of mankind, in all its historical lawfulness, is fed by the energies and images of successive generations; and that each generation brings to human fate an inescapable conflict between its ethical and rational aims and its infantile fixations. This conflict helps drive man toward the astonishing things he does—and it can be his undoing. It is a condition of man's humanity—and the prime cause of his bottomless inhumanity. For whenever and wherever man abandons his ethical position, he does so only at the cost of massive regressions endangering the very safeguards of his nature.

Freud revealed this regressive trend by dissecting its pathological manifestations in individuals. But he also pointed to what is so largely and so regularly lost in the ambivalent gains of civilization: he spoke of "the child's radiant intelligence"—the naive zest, the natural courage, the unconditional faith of childhood which become submerged by excessive ambitions, by fearful teaching and by limited and limiting information.

Now and again, we are moved to say that a genius preserved in himself the clear eye of the child. But do we not all too easily justify man's mass regressions by pointing to the occasional appearance of leaders of genius? Yet, we know (and are morbidly eager to know) how tortured a genius can be by the very history of his ascendance, and how often a genius is driven to destroy with one hand as he creates with the other.

In Freud, a genius turned a new instrument of observation back on his childhood, back on all childhood. He invented a specific method for the detection of that which universally spoils the genius of the child in every human being. In teaching us to recognize the daimonic evil in children, he urged us not to smother the creatively good. Since then, the nature of growth in childhood has been studied by ingenious observers all over the world: never before has mankind known more about its own past— phylogenetic and ontogenetic. Thus, we may see Freud as a pioneer in a self-healing, balancing trend in human awareness. For now that technical invention readies itself to conquer the moon, generations to come may well be in need of being more enlightened in their drivenness, and more conscious of the laws of individuality; they may well need to appreciate and to preserve more genuine childlikeness in order to avoid utter cosmic childishness.

Freud, before he went into medicine, wanted to become a lawyer and politician, a lawmaker, a *Gesetzgeber*. When, in 1938, he was exiled from his country, he carried under his arm a manuscript on Moses, the supreme law-giver of the Jewish people whose unique fate and whose unique gifts Freud had accepted as his own. With grim pride he had chosen the role of one who opens perspectives on fertile fields to be cultivated by others. As we look back to the beginnings of his work, and forward to its implications, we may well venture to say: Freud the physician in finding a method of healing himself in the very practice of emotional cure has given a new, a psychological rationale for man's laws. He has made the decisive step toward a true interpretation of the psychological with the technological and the political in the human order.

If, in the meantime, others see in him primarily the destroyer of precious illusions, if not of essential values, I would remind you of an event that took place in this city, Frankfurt am Main. It was from here that, in 1930, the Secretary of the Goethe Prize Committee informed Freud of his award, which was later received for her ailing father by Anna Freud, in a ceremony in the old (and now rebuilt) *Roemer.* In his dedication the Secretary suggested that "the Mephistophelic bend toward ruthless dis-illusion was the inseparable counterpart of the Faustian veneration of man's creative potentials." In his letter of acceptance Freud affirmed that nobody had recognized more clearly his "innermost personal motives."

THE NATURE OF CLINICAL
EVIDENCE

from *Insight and Responsibility*

The first lecture focused on the origin (and the originator) of psychoanalysis at the turn of the century. The second is an exposition of the
meaning of clinical experience for a psychoanalyst half a century later.
This lecture was given as a contribution to an interdisciplinary symposium
on "Evidence and Inference" at the Massachusetts Institute of Technology,
in 1957.

The letter which invited me to this symposium puts into the center of my assignment the question, *"How does a . . . clinician really
work?"* It gives me generous latitude by inquiring about the psychotherapist's reliance on *intuition* ("or some other version of personal
judgment") or on *objectified tests* ("relatively uniform among clinicians of
different theoretical persuasions"). And it concludes: "To the extent that
intuition plays a role, in what way does the clinician seek to discipline its
operation: by his conceptual framework? by long personal experience?"
This emphasizes, within the inquiry of how a clinician works, the question of how he thinks.

Such an invitation is a hospitable one, encouraging the guest, as it
were, to come as he is. It spares the clinician whatever temptation he
might otherwise feel to claim inclusion in the social register of long established sciences by demonstrating that he, too, can behave the way they
do. He can state from the outset that all four: intuition and objective data,
conceptual framework and experience are acceptable as the corners of
the area to be staked out; but also, that in one lecture he can offer no
more than phenomenological groundwork of a markedly personal nature.

The invitation in my case is addressed to a psychotherapist of a particular "persuasion": my training is that of Freudian psychoanalyst, and I help in the training of others—in the vast majority physicians—in this method. I shall place vocation over persuasion and try to formulate how the nature of clinical evidence is determined by a clinician's daily task. If I, nevertheless, seem to feel beholden to Freud's conceptual system—that is, a system originated around the turn of this century by a physician schooled in physicalist physiology—the reason is not narrowly partisan: few will deny that from such transfer of physicalistic concepts to psychology new modes of clinical thinking have developed in our time.

"Clinical," of course, is an old word. It can refer to the priest's administrations at the deathbed as well as to medical ministrations to the sick. In our time and in the Western world, the scope of the clinical is expanding rapidly to include not only medical but also social considerations, not only physical well-being but also mental health, not only matters of cure but also of prevention, not only therapy but also research. This means that clinical work is now allied with many brands of evidence and overlaps with many methodologies. In the Far East, the word "clinical" is again assuming an entirely different historical connotation, insofar as it concerns mind at all: in Communist China the "thought analyst" faces individuals considered to be in need of reform. He encourages sincere confessions and self-analyses in order to realign thoughts with "the people's will." There is much, infinitely much to learn about the ideological implications of concepts of mental sickness, of social deviancy, and of psychological cure. Yet, I feel called upon to speak of the nature of evidence gathered in the psychotherapeutic encounter.

Let me briefly review the elements making up the clinical core of medical work as the encounter of two people, one in need of help, the other in the possession of professional methods. Their *contract* is a therapeutic one: in exchange for a fee, and for information revealed in confidence, the therapist promises to act for the benefit of the individual patient, within the ethos of the profession. There usually is a *complaint,* consisting of the description of more or less circumscribed pain or dysfunction, and there are *symptoms,* visible or otherwise localizable. There follows an attempt at an *anamnesis,* an etiological reconstruction of the disturbance, and an *examination,* carried out by means of the physician's naked senses or supported by instruments, which may include laboratory methods. In evaluating the evidence and in arriving at diagnostic and prognostic inferences (which are really the clinical form of a *prediction*), the physician *thinks clinically*—that is, he scans in his mind different *models* in which different modes of knowledge have found condensation: the *anatomical* structure of the body, the *physiological* functioning of body parts, or the *pathological* processes underlying classified disease entities. A clinical prediction takes its clues from the complaint, the symptoms, and the anamnesis, and makes inferences based on a rapid and mostly pre-conscious cross-checking against each other of anatomical, physiological, and pathological models. On this basis, a *preferred method of treatment* is selected. This is the simplest clinical encounter. In it the patient lends parts of himself to an examination and as far as he possibly can, ceases to be a person, i.e., a creature who is more than the sum of its organs.

Any good doctor knows, however, that the patient's complaint is more extensive than his symptoms, and the state of sickness more comprehensive than localized pain or dysfunction. As an old Jew put it (and old Jews have a way of speaking for the victims of all nations): "Doctor, my bowels are sluggish, my feet hurt, my heart jumps—and you know, Doctor, I myself don't feel so well either." The treatment is thus not limited to local adjustments; it must, and in the case of a "good" doctor automatically does, include a wider view of the complaint, and entail corresponding *interpretations* of the symptom to the patient, often making the "patient himself" an associate observer and assistant doctor. This is especially important, as subsequent appointments serve a *developing treatment-history*, which step by step verifies or contradicts whatever predictions had been made and put to test earlier.

This, then, for better or for worse, is the traditional core of the clinical encounter, whether it deals with physical or with mental complaints. But in the special case of the *psychotherapeutic encounter*, a specimen of which I intend to present and to analyze presently, three items crowd out all the others, namely, *complaint, anamnesis,* and *interpretation.* What goes on in the therapist's mind between the verbal complaint addressed to him and the verbal interpretation given in return—this, I take it, is the question to be examined here. But this means: in what way can the psychological clinician make his own perception and thought reliable in the face of the patient's purely verbal and social expression, and in the absence of nonverbal supportive instruments? At this point I am no longer quite so sure that the invitation to "tell us how a . . . clinician really works" was so entirely friendly, after all. For you must suspect that the psychotherapist, in many ways, uses the setting and the terminology of a medical and even a laboratory approach, claiming recourse to an anatomy, a physiology, and a pathology of the mind, without matching the traditional textbook clarity of medical science in any way. To put it briefly, the element of subjectivity, both in the patient's complaints and in the therapist's interpretations, may be vastly greater than in a strictly medical encounter, although this element is in principle not absent from any clinical approach.

Indeed, there is no choice but to put subjectivity in the center of an inquiry into evidence and inference in such clinical work as I am competent to discuss. The psychotherapist shares with any clinician the Hippocratic fact that hour by hour he must fulfill a *contract* with individuals who offer themselves to cure and study. They surrender much of their most personal inviolacy in the expectation that they will emerge from the encounter more whole and less fragmented than when they entered it. The psychotherapist shares with all clinicians the further requirement that even while facing most intimate and emotional matters, he must maintain intellectual inner contact with his conceptual models, however crude they may be. But more than any other clinician the psychotherapist must include in his field of observation a *specific self-awareness* in the very act of perceiving his patient's actions and reactions. I shall claim that there is a core of *disciplined subjectivity* in clinical work—and this both on the side of the therapist and of the patient—which it is neither desirable nor possible to replace altogether with seemingly more objective methods— methods which originate, as it were, in the machine-tooling of other kinds of work. How the two subjectivities join in the kind of disciplined understanding and shared insight which we think are operative in a cure—that is the question.

First, a word about "history taking," as the anamnesis is called today. In clinics, this is often done by "intake" workers, as if a patient, at the moment of entering treatment, could give an objective history of his sickness, and could reserve until later a certain fervent surrender to "the doctor." In the treatment proper, of course, much of this history will be reported again in significant moments. Whether or not the psychotherapist will then choose to dwell on the patient's past, however, he will enter his life history and join the grouping of individuals already significant in it. Therefore, without any wish to crowd him, I think I would feel methodologically closest to the historian in this symposium.

R. G. Collingwood defines as an historical process one "in which the past, so far as it is historically known, survives in the present." Thus being "itself a process of thought . . . it exists only in so far as the minds which are parts of it know themselves for parts of it." And again: "History is the life of mind itself which is not mind except so far as it *both lives in historical process and knows itself as so living.*"[1]

However, it is not my task to argue the philosophy of history. The analogy between the clinician and the historian as defined by Collingwood to me centers in the case-historian's function in the art of history-taking, of becoming part of a life history. Here the analogy breaks down; it could remain relevant only if the historian were also a kind of clinical statesman, correcting events as he records them, and recording changes as he directs them. Such a conscious clinician-historian-statesman may well emerge in the future.

Let me restate the psychotherapeutic encounter, then, as an historical one. A person has declared an emergency and has surrendered his self-regulation to a treatment procedure. Besides having become a subjective *patient,* he has accepted the role of a formal *client.* To some degree, he has had to interrupt his autonomous life-history as lived in the unselfconscious balances of his private and his public life in order, for a while, to "favor" a part-aspect of himself and to observe it with the diagnostic help of a curative method. "Under observation," he becomes self-observant. As a patient he is inclined, and as a client often encouraged, to historicize his own position by thinking back to the onset of the disturbance, and to ponder what world order (magic, scientific, ethical) was violated and must be restored before his self-regulation can be reassumed. He participates in becoming a *case,* a fact which he may live down socially, but which, nevertheless, may forever change his view of himself.

The clinician, in turn, appointed to judge the bit of interrupted life put before him, and to introduce himself and his method into it, finds himself part of another man's most intimate life history. Luckily he also remains the functionary of a healing profession with a systematic orientation, based on a coherent world image—be it the theory that a sick man is beset by evil spirits or under the temptation of the devil, the victim of chemical poisons or of faulty heritage, racked by inner conflicts, or blinded by a dangerous ideology. In inviting his client to look at himself with the help of professional theories and techniques, the clinician makes himself part of the client's life history, even as the client becomes a case in the history of healing.

In northern California I knew an old Shaman woman who laughed merrily at my conception of mental disease, and then sincerely—to the point of ceremonial tears—told me of her way of sucking the "pains" out of her patients. She was as convinced of her ability to cure and to understand as I was of mine. While occupying extreme opposites in the history of American psychiatry, we felt like colleagues. This feeling was based on some joint sense of the historical relativity of all psychotherapy: the relativity of the patient's outlook on his symptoms, of the role he assumes by dint of being a patient, of the kind of help which he seeks, and of the kinds of help which are eagerly offered or are available. The old Shaman woman and I disagreed about the locus of emotional sickness, what it "was," and what specific methods would cure it. Yet, when she related the origin of a child's illness to the familial tensions existing within her tribe, when she attributed the "pain" (which had got "under a child's skin") to his grandmother's sorcery (ambivalence), I knew she dealt with the same forces, and with the same kinds of conviction, as I did in my professional nook. This experience has been repeated in discussions with colleagues who, although not necessarily more "primitive," are oriented toward different psychiatric persuasions.

The disciplined psychotherapist of today finds himself heir to medical methods and concepts, although he may decide to counteract these with a determined turn to existential or social views concerning his person-to-person encounter in the therapeutic setting. At any rate, he recognizes his activities as a function of life-historical processes, and concludes that in his sphere one makes history as one records it.

It is in such apparent quicksand that we must follow the tracks of clinical evidence. No wonder that often the only clinical material which impresses some as being at all "scientific" is the more concrete evidence of the auxiliary methods of psychotherapy—neurological examination, chemical analysis, sociological study, psychological experiment, etc.—all of which, strictly speaking, put the patient into non-therapeutic conditions of observation. Each of these methods may "objectify" *some* matters immensely, provide inestimable supportive evidence for *some* theories, and lead to independent methods of cure in *some* classes of patients. But it is not of the nature of the evidence provided in the psychotherapeutic encounter itself.

To introduce such evidence, I need a specimen. This will consist of my reporting to you what a patient *said* to me, how he *behaved* in doing so and what I, in turn, *thought* and *did*—a highly suspect method. And, indeed, we may well stand at the beginning of a period when consultation rooms (already airier and lighter than Freud's) will have, as it were, many more doors open in the direction of an enlightened community's resources, even as they now have research windows in the form of one-way screens, cameras, and recording equipment. For the kind of evidence to be highlighted here, however, it is still essential that, for longer periods or for shorter ones, these doors be closed, soundproof, and impenetrable.

By emphasizing this I am not trying to ward off legitimate study of the setting from which our examples come. I know only too well that many of our interpretations seem to be of the variety of that given by one Jew to another in a Polish railroad station. "Where are you going?" asked the first. "To Minsk," said the other. "To Minsk!" exclaimed the first, "you say you go to Minsk so that I should believe you go to Pinsk! You are going to Minsk anyway—so why do you lie?" There is a widespread prejudice that the psychotherapist, point for point, uncovers what he claims the patient "really," and often unconsciously, had in mind, and that he has sufficient Pinsk-Minsk reversals in his technical arsenal to come out with the flat assertion that the evidence is on the side of his claim. It is for this very reason that I will try to demonstrate what method there may be in clinical judgment. I will select as my specimen the most subjective of all data, a dream-report.

A young man in his early twenties comes to his therapeutic hour about midway during his first year of treatment in a psychiatric hospital and reports that he has had the most disturbing dream of his life. The dream, he says, vividly recalls his state of panic at the time of the "mental breakdown" which had caused him to interrupt his studies for missionary work abroad and enter treatment. He cannot let go of the dream; it seemed painfully real on awakening; and even in the hour of reporting, the dream-state seems still vivid enough to threaten the patient's sense of reality. He is afraid that this is the end of his sanity.

THE DREAM: "There was a big face sitting in a buggy of the horse-and-buggy days. The face was completely empty, and there was horrible, slimy, snaky hair all around it. I am not sure it wasn't my mother." The dream report itself, given with wordy plaintiveness, is as usual followed by a variety of seemingly incidental reports of the events of the previous day which, however, eventually give way to a rather coherent account of the patient's relationship with his deceased grandfather, a country parson. In fact, he sees himself as a small boy with his grandfather crossing a bridge over a brook, his tiny hand in the old man's reassuring fist. Here the patient's mood changes to a deeply moved and moving admission of desperate nostalgia for the rural setting in which the values of his Nordic immigrant forebears were clear and strong.

How did the patient get from the dream to the grandfather? Here I should point out that we consider a patient's "associations" our best leads to the meaning of an as yet obscure item brought up in a clinical encounter, whether it is a strong affect, a stubborn memory, an intensive or recurring dream, or a transitory symptom. By associated evidence we mean everything which comes to the patient's mind during and after the report of that item. Except in cases of stark disorganization of thought, we can assume that what we call the synthesizing function of the ego will tend to associate what "belongs together," be the associated items ever so remote in history, separate in space, and contradictory in logical terms. Once the therapist has convinced himself of a certain combination in the patient of character, intelligence, and a wish to get well, he can rely on the patient's capacity to produce during a series of therapeutic encounters a sequence of themes, thoughts, and affects which seek their own concordance and provide their own cross-references. It is, of course, this basic synthesizing trend in clinical material itself which permits the clinician to observe with "free-floating attention," to refrain from undue interference, and to expect sooner or later a confluence of the patient's search for curative clarification and his own endeavor to recognize and to name what is most relevant, that is, to give an *interpretation*.

At the same time, everything said in an hour is linked with the material of previous appointments. It must be understood that whatever insight can result from one episode will owe its meaning to the fact that it clarifies previous questions and complements previous half-truths. Such *evidential continuity* can be only roughly sketched here; even to account for this one hour would take many hours. Let me only mention, then, the seemingly paradoxical fact that during his previous hour the patient had spoken of an increased well-being in his work and in his life, and had expressed trust in and even something akin to affection for me.

As to the rest of the hour of the dream-report I listened to the patient, who faced me in an easy chair, with only occasional interruptions for the clarification of facts or feelings. Only at the conclusion of the appointment did I give him a résumé of what sense his dream had made to me. It so happened that this interpretation proved convincing to us both and, in the long run, strategic for the whole treatment. (These are the hours we like to report.)

As I turn to the task of indicating what inferences helped me to formulate one of the most probable of the many possible meanings of this dream-report, I must ask you to join me in what Freud has called "free-floating attention," which—as I must now add—turns inward to the observer's ruminations even as it attends the patient's "free associations" and which, far from focusing on any one item too intentionally, rather waits to be impressed by recurring themes. These themes will, first faintly but ever more insistently, signal the nature of the patient's message and its meaning. It is, in fact, the gradual establishment of strategic intersections on a number of tangents that eventually makes it possible to locate in the observed phenomena that central core which comprises the "evidence."

I will now try to report what kinds of considerations will pass through a psychotherapist's mind, some fleetingly, others with persistent urgency, some hardly conscious in so many words, others nearly ready for verbalization and communication.

Our patient's behavior and report confront me with a therapeutic crisis, and it is my first task to perceive where the patient stands as a client, and what I must do next. What a clinician must do first and last depends, of course, on the setting of his work. Mine is an open residential institution, working with severe neuroses, some of the borderline of psychosis or psychopathy. In such a setting, the patients may display, in their most regressed moments, the milder forms of a disturbance in the sense of reality; in their daily behavior, they usually try to entertain, educate, and employ themselves in rational and useful ways; and in their best moments, they can be expected to be insightful and to do proficient and at times creative work. The hospital thus can be said to take a number of calculated risks, and to provide, on the other hand, special opportunities

for the patient's abilities to work, to be active, and to share in social responsibilities. That a patient will fit into this setting has been established
in advance during the "evaluation period." The patient's history has been
taken in psychiatric interviews with him and perhaps with members of
his family; he has been given a physical examination by a physician and
has been confronted with standardized tests by psychologists who perform their work "blindly," that is, without knowledge of the patient's history; and finally, the results have been presented to the whole staff at a
meeting, at the conclusion of which the patient himself was presented by
the medical director, questioned by him and by other staff members,
and assigned to "his therapist." Such preliminary screening has provided
the therapist with an over-all diagnosis which defines a certain range of
expectable mental states, indicating the patient's special danger points and
his special prospects for improvement. Needless to say, not even the best
preparation can quite predict what depths and heights may be reached
once the therapeutic process gets under way.

The original test report had put the liability of our patient's state into
these words: "The tests indicate border-line psychotic features in an inhibited, obsessive-compulsive character. However, the patient seems to be
able to take spontaneously adequate distance from these border-line tendencies. He seems, at present, to be struggling to strengthen a rather precarious control over aggressive impulses, and probably feels a good deal
of anxiety." The course of the treatment confirmed this and other test results. Thus, a dream-report of the kind just mentioned, in a setting of this
kind, will first of all impress the clinical observer as a diagnostic sign. This
is an "anxiety dream." Such a dream may happen to anybody, and a mild
perseverance of the dream state into the day is not pathological as such.
But this patient's dream appears to be only the visual center of a severe
affective disturbance: no doubt if such a state were to persist, it could pre-
cipitate him into a generalized panic such as brought him to our clinic
in the first place. The report of this horrible dream which intrudes itself
on the patient's waking life now takes its place beside the data of the tests
and the range and spectrum of the patient's moods and states as observed
in the treatment, and shows him on the lowest level attained since admission, i.e., relatively closest to an *inability* "to take adequate distance
from his borderline tendencies."

The first "prediction" to be made is whether this dream is the sign of
an impending collapse, or, on the contrary, a potentially beneficial clini-

cal crisis. The first would mean that the patient is slipping away from me and that I must think, as it were, of the emergency net; the second, that he is reaching out for me with an important message which I must try to understand and answer. I decided on the latter alternative. Although the patient acted as if he were close to a breakdown, I had the impression that, in fact, there was a challenge in all this, and a rather angry one. This impression was, to some extent, based on a comparison of the present hour and the previous one when the patient had seemed so markedly improved. Could it be that his unconscious had not been able to tolerate this very improvement? The paradox resolves itself if we consider that cure means the loss of the right to rely on therapy; for the cured patient, to speak with Saint Francis, would not so much seek to be loved as to love, and not so much to be consoled as to console, to the limit of his capacity. Does the dream-report communicate, protesting somewhat too loudly, that the patient is still sick? Is his dream sicker than the patient is? I can explain this tentative diagnostic conclusion only by presenting a number of inferences of a kind made very rapidly in a clinician's mind, and demonstrable only through an analysis of the patient's verbal and behavioral communications and of my own intellectual and affective reactions.

The experienced dream interpreter often finds himself "reading" a dream-report as a practitioner of medicine scans an X-ray. Especially in the cases of wordy or reticent patients or of lengthy case reports, a dream often lays bare the stark inner facts.

Let us first pay attention to the dream images. The main item is a large face without identifying features. There are no spoken words, and there is no motion. There are no people in the dream. Very apparent, then, are omissions. An experienced interpreter can state this on the basis of an implicit inventory of dream configurations against which he checks the individual dream production for present and absent dream configurations. This implicit inventory can be made explicit as I have myself tried to do in a publication reviewing Freud's classic first analysis of a "dream specimen."[2] The dream being discussed, then, is characterized by a significant omission of important items present in most dreams: motion, action, people, spoken words. All we have instead is a motionless image of a faceless face, which may or may not represent the patient's mother.

But in trying to understand what this image "stands for," the interpreter must abandon the classic scientific urge (leading to parsimonious explanation in some contexts but to "wild" interpretation in this one) to look for the one most plausible explanation. He must let his "free-floating" clinical attention and judgment lead him to all the *possible* faces which may be condensed in this one dream face and then decide what *probable meaning* may explain their combined presence. I will, then, proceed to relate the face in the dream to all the faces in my patient's hierarchy of significant persons, to my face as well as those of his mother and grandfather, to God's countenance as well as to the Medusa's grimace. Thus, the probable meaning of an empty and horrible face may gradually emerge.

First myself, then. The patient's facial and tonal expression reminded me of a series of critical moments during his treatment when he was obviously not quite sure that I was "all there" and apprehensive that I might disapprove of him and disappear in anger. This focused my attention on a question which the clinician must consider when faced with any of his patient's productions, namely, his own place in them.

While the psychotherapist should not force his way into the meanings of his patient's dream images, he does well to raise discreetly the masks of the various dream persons to see whether he can find his own face or person or role represented. Here the mask is an empty face, with plenty of horrible hair. My often unruly white hair surrounding a reddish face easily enters my patients' imaginative productions, either in the form of a benevolent Santa Claus or that of a threatening ogre. At that particular time, I had to consider another autobiographic item. In the third month of therapy, I had "abandoned" the patient to have an emergency operation which he, to use clinical shorthand, had ascribed to his evil eye. At the time of this dream-report I still was on occasion mildly uncomfortable—a matter which can never be hidden from such patients. A sensitive patient will, of course, be in conflict between his sympathy, which makes him want to take care of me, and his rightful claim that I should take care of him—for he feels that only the therapist's total presence can provide him with sufficient identity to weather his crises. I concluded that the empty face had something to do with a certain tenuousness in our relationship, and that one message of the dream might be something like this: "If I never know whether and when you think of yourself rather than attending to me, or when you will absent yourself, maybe die, *how can I have or gain what I need most—a coherent personality, an identity, a face?"*

Such an indirect message, however, even if understood as referring to the immediate present and to the therapeutic situation itself, always proves to be "overdetermined," that is, to consist of a *condensed code* transmitting a number of other messages, from other life situations, seemingly removed from the therapy. This we call *"transference."* Because the inference of a "mother transference" is by now an almost stereotyped requirement, and thus is apt to lead to faulty views concerning the relationship of past and present, I have postponed, but not discarded, a discussion of the connection between the patient's implied fear of "losing a face" with his remark that he was not sure the face was not his mother's. Instead, I put first his fear that he may yet lose himself by losing me too suddenly or too early.

Clinical work is always research in progress, and I would not be giving a full account of the clinician's pitfalls if I did not discuss in passing the fact that this patient's dream happened to fit especially well into my research at the time. This can be a mixed blessing for the therapeutic contract. A research-minded clinician—and one with literary ambitions, at that—must always take care lest his patients become footnotes to his favorite thesis or topic. I was studying in Pittsburgh and in Stockbridge the "identity crises" of a number of young people, college as well as seminary students, workmen and artists. My purpose was to delineate further a syndrome called *"identity-confusion,"* a term which describes the inability of young people in the late 'teens and early twenties to establish their station and vocation in life, and the tendency of some to develop apparently malignant symptoms and regressions.[3] Such research must re-open rather than close questions of finalistic diagnosis. Perhaps there are certain stages in the life cycle when even seemingly malignant disturbances are more profitably treated as *aggravated life crises* rather than as diseases subject to routine psychiatric diagnosis. Here the clinician must be guided by the proposition that if he can hope to save only a small subgroup, or, indeed, only one patient, he must disregard existing statistical verdicts. For one new case, understood in new ways, will soon prove to be "typical" for a whole class of patients.

But any new diagnostic impression immediately calls for epidemiological considerations. What we have described as a therapeutic need in one patient, namely, to gain identity by claiming the total presence of his therapist, is identical with *the need of young people anywhere* for ideological affirmation. This need is aggravated in certain critical periods of history, when young people may try to find various forms of "confirmation" in groups that range from idealistic youth movements to criminal gangs.[4]

The young man in question was one among a small group of our patients who came from theological seminaries. He had developed his symptoms when attending a Protestant seminary in the Middle West where he was training for missionary work in Asia. He had not found the expected transformation in prayer, a matter which both for reasons of honesty and of inner need, he had taken more seriously than many successful believers. To him the wish to gaze through the glass darkly and to come "face to face" was a desperate need not easily satisfied in some modern seminaries. I need not remind you of the many references in the Bible to God's "making his face to shine upon" man, or God's face being turned away or being distant. The therapeutic theme inferred from the patient's report of an anxiety dream in which a face was horribly unrecognizable thus also seemed to echo relevantly this patient's religious scruples at the time of the appearance of psychiatric symptoms—the common denominator being a *wish to break through to a provider of identity*.

This trend of thought, then, leads us from the immediate clinical situation (and a recognition of my face in the dream face) to the developmental crisis typical for the patient's age (and the possible meaning of facelessness as "identity-confusion"), to the vocational and spiritual crisis immediately preceding the patient's breakdown (and the need for a divine face, an existential recognition). The "buggy" in the dream will lead us a step further back into an earlier identity crisis—and yet another significant face.

The horse and buggy is, of course, an historical symbol of culture change. Depending on one's ideology, it is a derisive term connoting hopelessly old-fashioned ways, or it is a symbol of nostalgia for the good old days. Here we come to a trend in the family's history most decisive for the patient's identity crisis. The family came from Minnesota, where the mother's father had been a rural clergyman of character, strength, and communal esteem. Such grandfathers represent to many today a world of homogeneity in feudal values, "masterly and cruel with a good conscience, self-restrained and pious without loss of self-esteem." When the patient's parents had moved from the north country to then still smog-covered Pittsburgh, his mother especially had found it impossible to over-come an intense nostalgia for the rural ways of her youth. She had, in fact, imbued the boy with this nostalgia for a rural existence and had demon-strated marked disappointment when the patient, at the beginning of his identity crisis (maybe in order to cut through the family's cultural con-flict), had temporarily threatened to become somewhat delinquent. The horse and buggy obviously is in greatest ideological as well as techno-logical contrast to the modern means of locomotor acceleration, and, thus, all at once a symbol of changing times, of identity-confusion, and of cultural regression. Here the horrible motionlessness of the dream may reveal itself as an important configurational item, meaning some-thing like being stuck in the middle of a world of competitive change and motion. And even as I inferred in my thoughts that the face sitting in the buggy must *also* represent the deceased grandfather's, also framed by white hair, the patient spontaneously embarked (as reported above) on a series of memories concerning the past when his grandfather had taken him by the hand to acquaint him with the technology of an old farm in Minnesota. Here the patient's vocabulary had become poetic, his de-scription vivid, and he had seemed to be breaking through to a genuinely positive emotional experience. Yet as a reckless youngster he had defied this grandfather shortly before his death. Knowing this, I sympathized with his tearfulness which, nevertheless, remained strangely perverse, and sounded strangled by anger, as though he might be saying: "One must not promise a child such certainty, and then leave him."

Here it must be remembered that all "graduations" in human devel-opment mean the abandonment of a familiar position, and that all growth—that is, the kind of growth endangered in our patients—must come to terms with this fact.

We add to our previous inferences the assumption that the face in the dream (in a *condensation* typical for dream images) also "meant" the face of the grandfather who is now dead and whom as a rebellious youth the patient had defied. The immediate clinical situation, then, the history of the patient's breakdown and a certain period in his adolescence are all found to have a common denominator in the idea that the patient wishes to *base his future sanity on a countenance of wisdom and firm identity* while, in all instances, he seems to fear that his anger may have destroyed, or may yet destroy, such resources. The patient's desperate insistence on finding security in prayer and, in fact, in missionary work, and yet his failure to find peace in these endeavors belongs in this context.

It may be necessary to assure you at this point that it is the failure of religious endeavor, not religiosity or the need for reverence and service, which is thereby explained. In fact, there is every reason to assume that the development of a sense of fidelity and the capacity to give and to receive it in a significant setting is a condition for a young adult's health, and of a young patient's recovery.

The theme of the horse and buggy as a rural symbol served to establish a possible connection between the nostalgic mother and her dead father; and we now finally turn our attention to the fact that the patient, half-denying what he was half-suggesting, said, "I am not sure it wasn't my mother." Here the most repetitious complaint of the whole course of therapy must be reviewed. While the grandfather's had been, all in all, the most consistently reassuring countenance in the patient's life, the mother's pretty, soft, and loving face had since earliest childhood been marred in the patient's memory and imagination by moments when she seemed absorbed and distorted by strong and painful emotions. The tests, given before any history-taking, had picked out the following theme: "The mother-figure appears in the Thematic Apperception Tests as one who seeks to control her son by her protectiveness of him, and by 'self-pity' and demonstrations of her frailty at any aggressive act on his part. She is, in the stories, 'frightened' at any show of rebelliousness, and content only when the son is passive and compliant. There appears to be considerable aggression, probably partly conscious, toward this figure." And indeed, it was with anger as well as with horror that the patient would repeatedly describe the mother of his memory as utterly exasperated, and this at those times when he had been too rough, too careless, too stubborn, or too persistent.

We are not concerned here with accusing this actual mother of having behaved this way; we can only be sure that she appeared this way in certain retrospective moods of the patient. Such memories are typical for a certain class of patients, and the question whether this is so because they have in common a certain type of mother or share a typical reaction to their mothers, or both, occupies the thinking of clinicians. At any rate many of these patients are deeply, if often unconsciously, convinced that they have caused a basic disturbance in their mothers. Often, in our time, when corporal punishment and severe scolding have become less fashionable, parents resort to the seemingly less cruel means of presenting themselves as deeply hurt by the child's willfulness. The "violated" mother thus tends to appear more prominently in images of guilt. In some cases this becomes an obstacle in the resolution of adolescence—as if a fundamental and yet quite impossible restitution were a condition for adulthood. It is in keeping with this trend that the patients under discussion here, young people who in late adolescence face a breakdown on the borderline of psychosis, all prove to be partially regressed to the earliest task in life, namely, the acquisition of a sense of basic trust strong enough to balance that sense of basic mistrust to which newborn man (most dependent of all young animals and yet endowed with fewer inborn instinctive regulations) is subject in his infancy. We all relive earlier and earliest stages of our existence in dreams, in artistic experience, and in religious devotion, only to emerge refreshed and invigorated. These patients, however, experience such partial regression in a lonely, sudden, and intense fashion, and most of all with a sense of irreversible doom. This, too, is in this dream.

The mother's veiled presence in the dream points to a complete omission in all this material: there is no father either in the dream or in the associated themes. The patient's father images became dominant in a later period of the treatment and proved most important for the patient's eventual solution of his spiritual and vocational problems. From this we can dimly surmise that in the present hour the grandfather "stands for" the father.

On the other hand, the recognition of the mother's countenance in the empty dream face and its surrounding slimy hair suggests the discussion of a significant symbol. Did not Freud explain the Medusa, the angry face with snake-hair and an open mouth, as a *symbol of the feminine void,* and an expression of the masculine horror of femininity? It is true that some of the patient's memories and associations (reported in other sessions in connection with the mother's emotions) could be easily traced to infantile observations and ruminations concerning "female trouble," pregnancy, and post-partum upsets. Facelessness, in this sense, can also mean inner void, and (from a male point of view) "castration." Does it, then, or does it not contradict Freudian symbolism if I emphasize in this equally horrifying but entirely empty face a representation of facelessness,

of loss of face, of lack of identity? In the context of the "classical" interpretation, the dream image would be primarily symbolic of a sexual idea
which is to be warded off, in ours a representation of a danger to the continuous existence of individual identity. Theoretical considerations would
show that these interpretations do not exclude each other. In this case a
possible controversy is superseded by the clinical consideration that a
symbol to be interpreted must first be shown to be immediately relevant.
It would be futile to use sexual symbolism dogmatically when acute interpersonal needs can be discerned as dominant in strongly concordant
material. The sexual symbolism of this dream was taken up in due time,
when it reappeared in another context, namely that of manhood and sexuality, and revealed the bisexual confusion inherent in all identity conflict.

Tracing one main theme of the dream retrospectively, we have recognized it in four periods of the patient's life—all four premature graduations which left him with anger and fear over what he was to abandon
rather than with the anticipation of greater freedom and more genuine
identity: the present treatment—and the patient's fear that by some act of
horrible anger (on his part or on mine or both) he might lose me and
thus his chance to regain his identity through trust in me; his immediately preceding religious education—and his abortive attempt at finding
through prayer that "presence" which would cure his inner void; his earlier youth—and his hope to gain strength, peace, and identity by identifying himself with his grandfather; and, finally, early childhood—and his
desperate wish to keep alive in himself the charitable face of his mother
in order to overcome fear, guilt, and anger over her emotions. Such re-
dundancy points to a central theme which, once found, gives added
meaning to all the associated material. The theme is: "Whenever I begin
to have faith in somebody's strength and love, some angry and sickly
emotions pervade the relationship, and I end up mistrusting, empty, and
a victim of anger and despair."

You may be getting a bit tired of the clinician's habit of speaking for
the patient, of putting into his mouth inferences which, so it would
seem, he could get out of him for the asking. The clinician, however, has
no right to test his reconstructions until his trial formulations have combined into a comprehensive interpretation which feels right to him, and
which promises, when appropriately verbalized, to feel right to the pa-

tient. When this point is reached, the clinician usually finds himself compelled to speak, in order to help the patient in verbalizing his affects and images in a more communicative manner, and to communicate his own impressions.

If according to Freud a successful dream is an attempt at representing a wish as fulfilled, the attempted and miscarried fulfillment in this dream is that of finding a face with a lasting identity. If an anxiety dream startling the dreamer out of his sleep is a symptom of a derailed wish-fulfillment, the central theme just formulated indicates at least one inner disturbance which caused the miscarriage of basic trust in infancy.

It seemed important to me that my communication should include an explicit statement of my emotional response to the dream-report. Patients of the type of our young man, still smarting in his twenties under what he considered his mother's strange emotions in his infancy, can learn to delineate social reality and to tolerate emotional tension only if the therapist can juxtapose his own emotional reactions to the patient's emotions. Therefore, as I reviewed with the patient some of what I have put before you, I also told him without rancor, but not without some honest indignation, that my response to his account had included a feeling of being attacked. I explained that he had worried me, had made me feel pity, had touched me with his memories, and had challenged me to prove, all at once, the goodness of mothers, the immortality of grandfathers, my own perfection, and God's grace.

The words used in an interpretation, however, are hard to remember and when reproduced or recorded often sound as arbitrary as any private language developed by two people in the course of an intimate association. But whatever is said, a therapeutic interpretation, while brief and simple in form, should encompass a *unitary theme* such as I have put before you, a theme common at the same time to a dominant trend in the patient's relation to the therapist, to a significant portion of his symptomatology, to an important conflict of his childhood, and to corresponding facets of his work and love life. This sounds more complicated than it is. Often, a very short and casual remark proves to have encompassed all this; and the trends *are* (as I must repeat in conclusion) very closely related to each other in the patient's own struggling mind, for which the traumatic past is of course a present frontier, perceived as acute conflict. Such an interpretation, therefore, joins the patient's and the therapist's modes of problem-solving.

Therapists of different temperament and of various persuasions differ as to what constitutes an interpretation: an impersonal and authoritative explanation, a warm and parental suggestion, an expansive sermon, or a sparse encouragement to go on and see what comes up next. The intervention in this case, however, highlights one methodological point truly unique to clinical work, namely, the disposition of the clinician's "mixed" feelings, his emotions and opinions. The evidence is not "all in" if he does not succeed in using his own emotional responses during a clinical encounter as an evidential source and as a guide in intervention, instead of putting them aside with a spurious claim to unassailable objectivity. It is here that the prerequisite of the therapist's own psychoanalytic treatment as a didactic experience proves itself essential, for the personal equation in the observer's emotional response is as important in psychotherapy as that of the senses in the laboratory. Repressed emotions easily hide themselves in the therapist's most stubborn blind spots.

I do not wish to make too much of this, but I would suggest in passing that some of us have, to our detriment, embraced an objectivity which can only be maintained with self-deception. If "psychoanalyzed" man learns to recognize the fact that even his previously repudiated or denied impulses may be "right" in their refusal to be submerged without a trace (the traces being his symptoms), so he may also learn that his strongest ethical judgments are right in being persistent even if modern life may not consider it intelligent or advantageous to feel strongly about such matters. Any psychotherapist, then, who throws out his ethical sentiments with his irrational moral anger, deprives himself of a principal tool of his clinical perception. For even as our sensuality sharpens our awareness of the orders of nature, so our indignation, admitted and scrutinized for flaws of sulkiness and self-indulgence, is, in fact, an important tool both of therapy and of theory. It adds to the investigation of what, indeed, has happened to sick individuals and offers a suggestion of where to look for those epidemiological factors that should and need not happen to anybody. But this means that we somehow harbor a model of man which could serve as a scientific basis for the postulation of an ethical relation of the generations to each other; and that we are committed to this whether or not we abrogate our partisanship in particular systems of morality.

A certain combination of available emotion and responsive thought, then, marks a therapist's style and is expressed in minute variations of facial expression, posture, and tone of voice. The core of a therapeutic intervention at its most decisive thus defies any attempt at a definitive account. This difficulty is not overcome by the now widespread habit of advocating a "human," rather than a "technical" encounter. Even humanness can be a glib "posture," and the time may come when we need an injunction against the use in vain of this word "human," too.

What do we expect the patient to contribute to the closure of our evidence? What tells us that our interpretation was "right," and, therefore, proves the evidence to be as conclusive as it can be in our kind of work? The simplest answer is that this particular patient was amused, delighted, and encouraged when I told him of my thoughts and my feelings over his unnecessary attempts to burden me with a future which he could well learn to manage—a statement which was not meant to be a therapeutic "suggestion" or a clinical slap on the back, but was based on what I knew of his inner resources as well as of the use he made of the opportunities offered in our clinical community. The patient left the hour—to which he had come with a sense of dire disaster—with a broad smile and obvious encouragement. Otherwise, only the future would show whether the process of recovery had been advanced by this hour.

But then, one must grant that the dream experience itself was a step in the right direction. I would not want to leave you with the impression that I accused the patient of pretending illness, or that I belittled his dream as representing sham despair. On the contrary, I acknowledged that he had taken a real chance with himself and with me. Under my protection and the hospital's he had hit bottom by chancing a repetition of his original breakdown. He had gone to the very border of unreality and had gleaned from it a highly condensed and seemingly anarchic image. Yet that image, while experienced as a symptom, was in fact a kind of creation, or at any rate a condensed and highly meaningful communication and challenge, to which my particular clinical theory had made me receptive. A sense of mutuality and reality was thus restored, reinforced by the fact that while accepting his transferences as meaningful, I had refused to become drawn into them. I had played neither mother, grandfather, nor God (this is the hardest), but had offered him my help as defined by my professional status in attempting to understand what was behind his helplessness. By relating the fact that his underlying anger aroused mine, and that I could say so without endangering either myself or him, I could show him that in his dream he had also confronted anger in the image of a Medusa—a Gorgon which, neither of us being a hero, we could yet slay together.

The proof of the correctness of our inference does, of course, not always lie in the patient's immediate assent. I have, in fact, indicated how this very dream experience followed an hour in which the patient had assented too much. Rather, the proof lies in the way in which the communication between therapist and patient "keeps moving," leading to new and surprising insights and to the patient's greater assumption of responsibility for himself. In this he is helped, if hospitalized, by the social influences of the "therapeutic community," and by well-guided work activities—all of which would have to be taken into account, if I were concerned here with the nature of *the therapeutic process* rather than with that of clinical evidence. But it is important to remember that only in a favorable social setting, be it the private patient's private life or the hospitalized patient's planned community, can the two main therapeutic agents described here function fully: the insight gained into the pathogenic past, and the convincing presence of a therapeutic relationship which bridges past and future.

I may now confess that the initial invitation really requested me to tell you "how a *good* clinician works." I have replaced this embarrassing little word with dots until now when I can make it operational. It is a mark of the good clinician that much can go on in him without clogging his communication at the moment of therapeutic intervention, when only the central theme may come to his awareness. Since a clinician's identity as a worker is based (as is anybody else's) on decisive learning experiences during the formative years of his first acquaintance with the field of his choice, he cannot avoid carrying with him some traditional formulations which may range in their effect from ever helpful clarifications to burdening dogmatisms. In a good clinician, such formulations have become a matter of implicit insight and of a style of action. On the other hand, he must also be able to call his ruminations to explicit awareness when professional conferences permit their being spelled out—for how else could such thinking be disciplined, shared, and taught? Such sharing and teaching, in turn, if it is to transcend clinical impressionism, presupposes a communality of conceptual approaches. I cannot give you today more than a suggestion that there is a systematic relationship between clinical observation on the one hand and, on the other, such conceptual points of view as Freud has introduced into psychiatry: a *structural* point of view denoting a kind of anatomy of the mind, a *dynamic* point of view denoting a kind of physiology of mental forces, a *genetic* point of view reconstructing the growth of the mind and the stages marking its strengths and its dangers, and finally, an *adaptive* point of view.[5] But even as such propositions are tested on a wide front of inquiry (from the direct observation of children and perception experiments to "metapsychological" discussion), it stands to reason that clinical evidence is characterized by an immediacy which transcends formulations ultimately derived from mechanistic patterns of thought.

The "points of view" introduced into psychiatry and psychology by Freud are, at this time, subject to a strange fate. No doubt, they were the bridges by which generations of medical clinicians could apply their anatomical, physiological, and pathological modes of thinking to the workings of the mind. Probably also, the neurological basis of behavior was thus fruitfully related to other determinants; I myself cannot judge the fate of Freud's neurological assumptions as such. A transfer of concepts from one field to another has in other fields led to revolutionary clarifications and yet eventually also to a necessary transcendence of the borrowed concepts by newer and more adequate ones. In psychoanalysis, the fate of the "points of view" was pre-ordained: since on their medical home ground they were based on visible facts such as organs and functions, in the study of the mind they sooner or later served improper reifications, as though libido or the death-instinct or the ego really existed. Freud was sovereignly aware of this danger, but always willing to learn by giving a mode of thought free reign to see to what useful model it might lead. He also had the courage, the authority, and the inner consistency to reverse such a direction when it became useless or absurd. Generations of clinical practitioners cannot be expected to be equally detached or authoritative. Thus it cannot be denied that in much clinical literature the clinical evidence secured with the help of inferences based on Freud's theories has been increasingly used and slanted to verify the original theories. This, in turn, could only lead to a gradual estrangement between theory and clinical observation.

I should, therefore, say explicitly which of the traditional psychoana-

lytic concepts have remained intrinsic to my clinical way of thinking. I
would say that I have to assume that the patient is (to varying degrees)
unconscious of the meaning which I discern in his communications, and
that I am helping him by making fully conscious what may be totally repressed, barely conscious, or simply cut off from communication. By
doing so, however, I take for granted an effective wish on his part (with
my help) to see, feel, and speak more clearly. I would also assume a *regressive trend,* a going back to earlier failures in order to solve the past
along with the present. In doing so, however, I would not give the past
a kind of fatalistic dominance over the present: for the temporal rear can
be brought up only where the present finds consolidation. I would also
acknowledge the power of *transference,* i.e., the patient's transfer to me of
significant problems in his past dealings with the central people in his life;
but I would know that only by playing my role as a new person in his
present stage of life can I clarify the inappropriateness of his transferences
from the past. In this past, I would consider libidinal attachments and relationships of dependence and of abandonment of paramount importance: but I would assume, in line with everything that we have learned
about human development, that these relationships were not disturbed
only by a *libidinal disbalance.* Such disbalance, in fact, is part of a *missed mutuality* which kept the child from realizing his potential strength even as
the parent was hindered in living up to his potentialities by the very failure of mutuality in relation to this child. You will note, then, that in naming the rock-bottom concepts of repression and regression, transference
and libido, I have tried to keep each linked with the observation and experience of the clinical encounter as a new event in the patient's life history. You would find other clinical workers similarly groping for a
position which permits them to honor the therapeutic contract as they
use and advance the theory of the field. At the end, the therapist's chosen intervention and the patient's reactions to it are an integral part of the
evidence provided in the therapeutic encounter. It is from such experience that the psychotherapist goes back to his drawing board, back to his
models of the mind, to the blueprints of intervention, and to his plans for
the wider application of clinical insight.

I have given you an example which ends on a convincing note, leaving
both the patient and the practitioner with the feeling that they are a

pretty clever pair. If it were always required to clinch a piece of clinical evidence in this manner, we should have few convincing examples. To tell the truth, I think that we often learn more from our failures—if indeed we can manage to review them in the manner here indicated. But I hope to have demonstrated that there is enough method in our work to force favorite assumptions to become probable inferences by cross-checking the patient's diagnosis and what we know of his type of illness and state of physical health; his stage of development and what we know of the "normative" crisis of his age-group; the co-ordinates of his social position and what we know of the chances of a man of his type, intelligence, and education in the social actuality of our time. This may be hard to believe unless one has heard an account of a *series of such encounters* as I have outlined here, the series being characterized by a progressive or regressive shift in all the areas mentioned: such is the evidence used in our clinical conferences and seminars.

Much of clinical training, in fact, consists of the charting of such series. In each step, our auxiliary methods must help us work with reasonable precision and with the courage to revise our assumptions and our techniques systematically, if and when the clinical evidence should show that we overestimated or underestimated the patient or ourselves, the chances waiting for him in his environment, or the usefulness of our particular theory.

In order to counteract any subjectivity and selectivity, whole treatments are now being sound-filmed so that qualified secondary observers can follow the procedure and have certain items repeated many times over, sometimes in slow motion. This will be important in some lines of research, and advantageous in training. Yet, it confronts a second observer or a series of observers with the task of deciding on the basis of their reactions, whether or not they agree with the judgments of the original observer made on the basis of his unrecordable reactions. Nor does the nature of clinical evidence change in such new developments as group-psychotherapy, where a therapist faces a group of patients and they face one another as well, permitting a number of combinations and variations of the basic elements of a clinical encounter. Clinical evidence, finally, will be decisively clarified, but not changed in nature, by a sharpened awareness (such as now emanates from sociological studies) of the psychotherapist's as well as the patient's position in society and history.

The relativity implicit in clinical work may, to some, militate against its scientific value. Yet, I suspect, that this very relativity, truly acknowledged, will make the clinicians better companions of today's and tomorrow's scientists than did the attempts to reduce the study of the human mind to a science identical with traditional natural science. I, therefore, have restricted myself to giving an operational introduction to the clinician's basic view which asserts that scientists may learn about the nature of things by finding out what they can do *to* them, but that the clinician can learn of the true nature of man only in the attempt to do something *for* and *with* him. I have focused, therefore, on the way in which clinical evidence is grounded in the study of what is *unique* to the *individual* case—including the psychotherapist's involvement. Such uniqueness, however, would not stand out without the background of that other concern, which I have neglected here, namely the study of what is *common* to verifiable *classes* of cases.

HUMAN STRENGTH AND
THE CYCLE OF
GENERATIONS

from *Insight and Responsibility*

With this lecture the focus shifts from the inner and outer hazards of ego development to those basic human strengths which have evolved with man's prolonged childhood and with his institutions and traditions. This lecture is an expansion of an address given for the Psychoanalytic Institute and the Mt. Zion Medical Center in San Francisco, in 1960, in memory of Sophie Mirviss, M.D.

1. A SCHEDULE OF VIRTUES

The psychoanalyst has good reason to show restraint in speaking about human virtue. For in doing so lightly he could be suspected of ignoring the evidential burden of his daily observations which acquaints him with the "much furrowed ground from which our virtues proudly spring." And he may be accused of abandoning the direction of Freudian thought in which conscious values can find a responsible re-evaluation only when the appreciation of the unconscious and of the irrational forces in man is firmly established.

Yet the very development of psychoanalytic thought, and its present preoccupation with "ego strength," suggests that human strength be reconsidered, not in the sense of nobility and rectitude as cultivated by moralities, but in the sense of "inherent strength." For I believe that psychoanalysts, in listening to life-histories for more than half a century, have developed an "unofficial" image of the strengths inherent in the individual life cycle and in the sequence of generations. I think here of those most enjoyable occasions when we can agree that a patient has really improved—not, as the questionnaires try to make us say, markedly improved, or partially improved—but essentially so. Here, the loss of symptoms is mentioned only in passing, while the decisive criterion is an increase in the strength and staying power of the patient's concentration on pursuits which are somehow right, whether it is in love or in work, in home life, friendship, or citizenship. Yet, we truly shy away from any systematic discussion of human strength. We recognize, for example, an inner affinity between the earliest and deepest mental disturbances and a radical loss of a basic kind of hope; or between the relation of compulsive and impulsive symptoms and a basic weakness in will. Yet, we are not curious to know what the genetic or dynamic determinants of a state of hope or of a state of controlled will power really are. In fact, we do our tortured best to express what we value in terms of double negatives; a person whom we would declare reasonably well is relatively resistant to regression, or somewhat freer from repression, or less given to ambivalence than might be expected. And yet we know that in a state of health or of mental and affective clarity a process of order takes over which is not and cannot be subsumed under the most complete list of negatives. Some of this process we call "ego-synthesis," and we gradually accumulate new observations under this heading. But we know that this process too, in some men in some moments and on some occasions, is endowed with a total quality which we might term "animated" or "spirited." This I certainly will not try to classify. But I will submit that, without acknowledging its existence, we cannot maintain any true perspective regarding the best moments of man's balance—nor the deepest of his tragedy.

In what follows I intend to investigate, then, first the developmental roots and later the evolutionary rationale of certain basic human qualities which I will call virtues. I do so, partially because I find the plural "strengths" awkward, but most of all because the word virtue serves to make a point. In Latin virtue meant virility, which at least suggests the combination of *strength, restraint,* and *courage* to be conveyed here, although we would, of course, hesitate to consider manliness the official virtue of the universe, especially since it dawns on us that womanhood may be forced to bear the larger share in saving humanity from man's climactic and catastrophic aspirations. But old English gave a special meaning to the word "virtue" which does admirably. It meant *inherent strength* or *active quality,* and was used, for example, for the undiminished potency of well preserved medicines and liquors. Virtue and spirit once had interchangeable meanings—and not only in the virtue that endowed liquid spirits. Our question, then, is: what "virtue goes out" of a human being when he loses the strength we have in mind, and "by virtue of" what strength does man acquire that animated or spirited quality without which his moralities become mere moralism and his ethics feeble goodness?

I will call "virtue," then, certain human qualities of strength, and I will relate them to that process by which ego strength may be developed from stage to stage and imparted from generation to generation.

A seeming paradox of human life is man's collective power to create his own environment, although each individual is born with a naked vulnerability extending into a prolonged infantile dependence. The weakness of the newborn, however, is truly relative. While far removed from any measure of mastery over the physical world, newborn man is endowed with an appearance and with responses which appeal to the tending adults' tenderness and make them wish to attend to his needs; which arouse concern in those who are concerned with his well-being; and which, in making adults care, stimulate their active care-taking. I employ the repetition of the words tending, concern, and caring, not for poetic effect, but in order to underscore the fundamental fact that, in life in general and in human life in particular, the vulnerability of being newly born and the meekness of innocent needfulness have a power all their own. Defenseless as babies are, they have mothers at their command, families to protect the mothers, societies to support the structure of families, and traditions to give a cultural continuity to systems of tending and training. All of this, however, is necessary for the human infant to evolve humanly, for his environment must provide that outer wholeness and continuity which, like a second womb, permits the child to develop his separate capacities in distinct steps, and to unify them in a series of psychosocial crises.

In recent years, psychiatry has concerned itself with the mother-child relationship, and has at times burdened it with the whole responsibility for man's sanity and maturation. This concentration on earliest development seemed to find powerful support in the young science of ethology, which analyzes the innate mechanism by which mother animal and young animal release in each other the behavior necessary for the survival of the young—and thus the species. However, a true ethological comparison must juxtapose the first period in animal life (such as the nest-occupancy of certain birds) with man's whole pre-adult life, including adolescence. For man's psychosocial survival is safeguarded only by vital virtues which develop in the interplay of successive and overlapping generations, living together in organized settings. Here, living together means more than incidental proximity. It means that the individual's life-stages are "interliving," cogwheeling with the stages of others which move him along as he moves them. I have, therefore, in recent years, attempted to delineate the whole life-cycle as an integrated psychosocial phenomenon, instead of following what (in analogy to teleology) may be called the "originological" approach, that is, the attempt to derive the meaning of development primarily from a reconstruction of the infant's beginnings.

When it comes to naming the basic virtues, with which human beings steer themselves and others through life, one is at first tempted to make up new words out of Latin roots. Latin always suggests expertness and explicitness, while everyday words have countless connotations. To optimists they make virtues sound like gay and easy accomplishments, and to pessimists, like idealistic pretences. Yet when we approach phenomena closer to the ego, the everyday words of living languages, ripened in the usage of generations, will serve best as a basis of discourse.

I will, therefore, speak of *Hope, Will, Purpose,* and *Competence* as the rudiments of virtue developed in childhood; of *Fidelity* as the adolescent virtue; and of *Love, Care,* and *Wisdom* as the central virtues of adulthood. In all their seeming discontinuity, these qualities depend on each other. Will cannot be trained until hope is secure, nor can love become reciprocal until fidelity has proven reliable. Also, each virtue and its place in the schedule of all virtues is vitally interrelated to other segments of human development, such as the stages of psychosexuality which are so thoroughly explored in the whole of psychoanalytic literature,[1] the psychosocial crises,[2] and the steps of cognitive maturation.[3] These schedules I must take for granted, as I restrict myself to a parallel timetable of the evolving virtues.

If we ascribe to the healthy infant the rudiments of *Hope,* it would, indeed, be hard to specify the criteria for this state, and harder to measure it: yet he who has seen a hopeless child, knows what is *not* there. Hope is both the earliest and the most indispensable virtue inherent in the state of being alive. Others have called this deepest quality *confidence,* and I have referred to *trust* as the earliest positive psychosocial attitude, but if life is to be sustained hope must remain, even where confidence is wounded, trust impaired. Clinicians know that an adult who has lost all hope, regresses into as lifeless a state as a living organism can sustain. But there is something in the anatomy even of mature hope which suggests that it is the most childlike of all ego-qualities, and the most dependent for its verification on the charity of fate; thus religious sentiment induces adults to restore their hopefulness in periodic petitionary prayer, assuming a measure of childlikeness toward unseen, omnipotent powers.

Nothing in human life, however, is secured in its origin unless it is verified in the intimate meeting of partners in favorable social settings. The infant's smile inspires hope in the adult and, in making him smile, makes him wish to give hope; but this is, of course, only one physiognomic detail which indicates that the infant by his trustful search for experience and assurance, awakens in the giver a strength which he, in turn, is ready and needful to have awakened and to have consolidated by the experience of mutuality.

Hope relies for its beginnings on the new being's first encounter with *trustworthy maternal persons,* who respond to his need for *intake* and *contact* with warm and calming envelopment and provide food both pleasurable to ingest and easy to digest, and who prevent experience of the kind which may regularly bring too little too late. This is far from being a merely instinctive, or a merely instinctual matter. Biological motherhood needs at least three links with social experience: the mother's past experience of being mothered; a conception of motherhood shared with trustworthy contemporary surroundings; and an all-enveloping world-image tying past, present, and future into a convincing pattern of providence. Only thus can mothers provide.

Hope is verified by a combination of experiences in the individual's "prehistoric" era, the time before speech and verbal memory. Both psychoanalysis and genetic psychology consider central in that period of growth the secure apperception of an "object." The psychologists mean by this the ability to perceive the *enduring quality* of the *thing world* while psychoanalysts speak loosely of a first love-object, i.e., the experience of the care-taking person as a *coherent being,* who reciprocates one's physical and emotional needs in expectable ways and therefore deserves to be endowed with trust, and whose face is recognized as it recognizes. These two kinds of object are the first knowledge, the first verification, and thus the basis of hope.

Hope, once established as a basic quality of experience, remains independent of the verifiability of "hopes," for it is in the nature of man's maturation that concrete hopes will, at a time when a hoped-for event or state comes to pass, prove to have been quietly superseded by a more advanced set of hopes. The gradual widening of the infant's horizon of active experience provides, at each step, verifications so rewarding that they inspire new hopefulness. At the same time, the infant develops a greater capacity for renunciation, together with the ability to transfer disappointed hopes to better prospects; and he learns to dream what is imaginable and to train his expectations on what promises to prove possible. All in all, then, maturing hope not only maintains itself in the face of changed facts—it proves itself able to change facts, even as faith is said to move mountains. From an evolutionary point of view, it seems that hope must help man to approximate a measure of that rootedness possessed by the animal world, in which instinctive equipment and environment, beginning with the maternal response, verify each other, unless catastrophe overtakes the individual or the species. To the human infant, his mother *is* nature. She must *be* that original verification, which, later, will come from other and wider segments of reality. All the self-verifications, therefore, begin in that inner light of the mother-child-world, which Madonna images have conveyed as so exclusive and so secure: and, indeed, such light must continue to shine through the chaos of many crises, maturational and accidental.

To chance some first formulations: *Hope is the enduring belief in the attainability of fervent wishes, in spite of the dark urges and rages which mark the beginning of existence.* Hope is the ontogenetic basis of faith, and is nourished by the adult faith which pervades patterns of care.

An exclusive condition of hopefulness, translated into various imaginable worlds, would be a paradise in nature, a Utopia in social reality, and a heaven in the beyond. In the individual, here and now, it would mean a maladaptive optimism. For true hope leads inexorably into conflicts between the rapidly developing self-will and the will of others from which the rudiments of will must emerge. As the infant's senses and his muscles grasp at opportunities for more active experience, he faces the double demand for self-control and for the acceptance of control from others. *To will* does not mean to be willful, but rather to gain gradually the power of increased judgment and decision in the application of drive. Man must learn to will what can be, to renounce as not worth willing what cannot be, and to believe he willed what is inevitable.

Here, no doubt, is the genetic origin of the elusive question of Free Will, which man, ever again, attempts to master logically and theologically. The fact is that no person can live, no ego remain intact without hope and will. Even philosophical man who feels motivated to challenge the very ground he stands on, questioning both will and hope as illusory, feels more real for having willed such heroic enquiry; and where man chooses to surrender his sense of having willed the inevitable to gods and leaders, he fervently endows them with what he has renounced for himself.

The rudiments of will are acquired, in analogy to all basic qualities, as the ego unifies experiences on fronts seemingly remote from one another: awareness and attention, manipulation, verbalization, and locomotion. The training of the eliminative sphincters can become the center of the struggle over inner and outer control which resides in the whole muscle system and its double executive: individual co-ordination and social guidance. A sense of defeat (from too little or too much training) can lead to deep *shame* and a compulsive *doubt* whether one ever really willed what one did, or really did what one willed.

If will, however, is built securely into the early development of the ego it survives, as hope does, the evidences of its limited potency, for the maturing individual gradually incorporates a knowledge of what is expectable and what can be expected of him. Often defeated, he nevertheless learns to accept the existential paradox of making decisions which he knows "deep down" will be predetermined by events, because making decisions is part of the evaluative quality inherent in being alive. Ego strength depends, above all, on the sense of having done one's active part in the chain of the inevitable. And as it is with lesser hopes, so it is with small wills (if the word is permitted). They do not really seem worth despairing over when the moment of testing arrives, provided only that growth and development have enough leeway to present new issues, and that, all in all, expectable reality proves more satisfactory and more interesting than fantasy.

Will, therefore, is the unbroken determination to exercise free choice as well as self-restraint, in spite of the unavoidable experience of shame and doubt in infancy. Will is the basis for the acceptance of law and necessity, and it is rooted in the judiciousness of parents guided by the spirit of law.

The social problem of will is contained in the words "good will." The good will of others obviously depends on a mutual limitation of wills. It is during the second and third year that the child must yield to new-comers. It is now the task of judicious parenthood to honor the privileges of the strong and yet protect the rights of the weak. It will gradually grant a measure of self-control to the child who learns to control willfulness, to offer willingness, and to exchange good will. But in the end the self-image of the child will prove to have been split in the way in which man is apt to remain split for the rest of his life. For even as the ideal ("pre-ambivalent," as we say) image of the loving mother brought with it the child's self-image as reflecting that mother's true recognition of the child as hers and as good, so does the ambivalently loved image of the controlling parent correspond to an ambivalently loved self, or rather selves. From here on, the able and the impotent, the loving and the angry, the unified and the self-contradictory selves will be part of man's equipment: truly a psychic fall from grace. In view of this inner split, only judicious parenthood, feeling itself part of a reasonably just civic and world order, can convey a healing sense of justice.

We now come to the third vital virtue: *Purpose.* And taking the principles of presentation for granted, we can now be briefer.

It is inherent in infantile man's prolonged immaturity that he must train the rudiments of will in situations in which he does not quite know what he wants and why, which makes his willfulness at times rather desperate. By the same token he must develop in "mere" fantasy and play the rudiments of purpose: a temporal perspective giving direction and focus to concerted striving. Play is to the child what thinking, planning, and blueprinting are to the adult, a trial universe in which conditions are simplified and methods exploratory, so that past failures can be thought through, expectations tested. The rules of play cannot be altogether imposed by the will of adults: toys and playmates are the child's equals. In the toy world, the child "plays out" the past, often in disguised form, in the manner of dreams, and he begins to master the future by anticipating it in countless variations of repetitive themes. In taking the various role-images of his elders into his sphere of make-believe, he can find out how it feels to be like them before fate forces him to become, indeed, like some of them. But if it seems that he spends on his play a sincere purposefulness out of proportion to what he soon must learn, namely, what things are "really for," what their "real purpose" is, we underestimate the evolutionary necessity for representational play in an animal who must learn to bind together an inner and an outer world, a remembered past and an anticipated future, before he can learn to master the tools used in co-operation, the roles distributed in a community, and the purposes pursued in a given technology.

Thus infantile play (like mature man's inspired toys: dance, drama, ritual) affords an intermediate reality in which purposefulness can disengage itself from fixations on the past. It seems significant that play is most intense when the period of infantile sexuality comes to an end and when that great human barrier, the universal "incest-taboo," is met. Sexual drive and purposeful energy must now be diverted from the very parental persons who first awakened the child's tenderness, sensuality, and amorphous sexual fantasies; and it is diverted toward a future first of fantastic but then more and more of realizable goals.

Play, in young animals, too, is predicated upon parental protection from hunger and from danger. In man it is, furthermore, dependent on protection from unmanageable conflict. The play age relies on the existence of the *family in one of its exemplary forms,* which must gradually delineate where play ends and irreversible purpose begins, where fantasy is no longer permissible and to-be-learned reality all-demanding: only thus is conscience integrated. It is not always understood that one of the main rationales for marital and familial loyalty is the imperative need for inner unity in the child's conscience at the very time when he can and must envisage goals beyond the family. For the voices and images of those adults who are now internalized as an *inner voice* must not contradict each other too flagrantly. They contribute to the child's most intense conscience development—a development which separates, once and for all, play and fantasy from that future which is irreversible. Threats, punishments, and warnings all have in common the designation of certain acts (and by implication, thoughts) as having a social and, indeed, eternal reality which can never be undone. Conscience accepts such irreversibility as internal and private, and it is all the more important that it incorporate the ethical example of a family purposefully united in familial and economic pursuits. This alone gives the child the inner freedom to move on—to whatever school setting his culture has ready for him.

Purposefulness is now ready to attach itself gradually to a sense of reality which is defined by what *can be attained* and by what can be *shared in words*. Thus, conscience, the consistent inner voice which delineates permissible action and thought, finds a powerful ally in the structure of language which verifies a shared actuality.

Purpose, then, is the courage to envisage and pursue valued goals uninhibited by the defeat of infantile fantasies, by guilt, and by the foiling fear of punishment. It invests ideals of action and is derived from the example of the basic family. It is the strength of aim-direction fed by fantasy yet not fantastic, limited by guilt yet not inhibited, morally restrained yet ethically active. That man began as a playing child, however, leaves a residue of play-acting and role-playing even in what he considers his highest purposes. These he sees, as an adult, enacted in the tableaux of his past history; these he projects on a larger and more perfect future stage; and these he dramatizes in the ceremonial present with uniformed players in ritual arrangements.

W hat shall we call the next virtue? *Competence* comes closest to what I have in mind, although my friend, R. W. White, has reserved it for a principle active in all living.[4] Yet, it should not be too difficult to agree that a quality which endows all living should yet have its epigenetic crisis during one stage of the life cycle. A sense of competence, at any rate, characterizes what eventually becomes *workmanship*. Ever since his "expulsion from paradise," of course, man has been inclined to protest work as drudgery or as slavery, and to consider most fortunate those who seemingly can choose to work or not to work. The fact, however, is that man *must* learn to work, as soon as his intelligence and his capacities are ready to be "put to work," so that his ego's power may not atrophy.

Evolution has brought to pass that man, when he approaches the age of instruction in the basic elements of his culture's technology, is the most unspecialized of all animals. The rudiments of hope, will, and purpose anticipate a future of only dimly anticipated tasks. Now the child needs to be shown basic methods leading to the identity of a technical way of life. For (contrary to modern apostles of infantile Eros) infantile sexuality lacks any chance of competence, and if R. W. White would wish to oppose his theory of competence to the psychoanalytic theory of infantile sexuality, he could point out that in childhood the transitory investment of instinctual energy in erotic possibilities is intense, and often fateful, but that its dividends in satisfaction and completion are extremely limited. It makes sense, then, that a period of psychosexual latency should permit the human to develop the tool possibilities of body, mind, and thing-world and to postpone further progress along sexual and sensual lines until they become part of a larger area of social responsibility.

In school, what "works" in the fabric of one's thought and in the use of one's physical co-ordination can be found to "work" in materials and in co-operative encounters: a self-verification of lasting importance. All cultures, therefore, meet this stage with the offer of instruction in perfectible skills leading to practical uses and durable achievements. All cultures also have their logic and their "truths" which can be learned, by exercise, usage, and ritual. Where literacy is a common basis for future specialization, the rules of grammar and of algebra, of course, form a more abstract demonstration of the workings of reality. Thus the rudiments of competence and of reasonableness prepare in the child a future sense of workmanship without which there can be no "strong ego." Without it man feels inferior in his equipment, and in his ability to match an ever-increasing radius of manageable reality with his capacities.

The child at this stage, then, is ready for a variety of specializations and will learn most eagerly techniques in line with that *ethos of production* which has already entered his anticipations by way of ideal examples, real or mythical, and which now meets him in the persons of instructive adults and co-operative peers. It is thus that individual man develops at each stage a significant gain in human evolution by joining a larger section of his culture. In this case his developing capacities permit him to apprehend the basic materials of technology, and the elements of reasoning which make techniques teachable.

Competence, then, is the free exercise of dexterity and intelligence in the completion of tasks, unimpaired by infantile inferiority. It is the basis for co-operative participation in technologies and relies, in turn, on the logic of tools and skills.

When man's sexuality matures in puberty, he is not yet ready to be a mate or a parent. There is, in fact, a real question whether early freedom in the direct use of his sexuality would make man freer as a person and as a guarantor of the freedom of others. At any rate, a youth's ego-balance is decidedly endangered by the double uncertainty of a newly matured sexual machinery which must be kept in abeyance in some or all of its functions while he prepares for his own place in the adult order. His consequent impulsiveness alternating with compulsive restraint is well-known and well-described. In all of this, however, an "ideological" seeking after an inner coherence and a durable set of values can always be detected; and I would call the particular ego-quality which emerges, with and from adolescence, *Fidelity*.[5]

Fidelity is the ability to sustain loyalties freely pledged in spite of the inevitable contradictions of value systems. It is the cornerstone of identity and receives inspiration from confirming ideologies and affirming companions.

In youth, such truth verifies itself in a number of ways: a high sense of duty, accuracy, and veracity in the rendering of reality; the sentiment of truthfulness, as in sincerity and conviction; the quality of genuineness, as in authenticity; the trait of loyalty, of "being true"; fairness to the rules of the game; and finally all that is implied in devotion—a freely given but binding vow, with the fateful implication of a curse befalling traitors. When Hamlet, the emotional victim of his royal parents' faithlessness, poses the question, "To be or not to be," he demonstrates in word and deed that to him "to be" is contingent on being loyal (to the self, to love, to the crown) and that the rest is death. Cultures, societies, religions offer the adolescent the nourishment of some truth in rites and rituals of confirmation as a member of a totem, a clan, or a faith, a nation or a class, which henceforth is to be his super-family; in modern times we also find powerful ideologies which claim and receive the loyalty (and, if demanded, an early death) from youth. For youth needs, above all, confirming adults and affirming peers. Identity owes its evolutionary and historical significance to the fact that, so far, social groups of men, no longer constituting a species in nature and not yet the mankind of history, have needed to feel with vanity or conviction that they were of some *special* kind, which promised to each individual the participation in a select identity.

Tribal, national, and class identity, however, demand that man consider otherness inimical, and at least some men have overdefined others as enemies, treating them with an arbitrary ferocity absent from the animal world. At any rate, the need for superior status-identity combined with technological pride has made man exploit and annihilate other men with complete equanimity. Whatever level of technology man has reached he can regress to archaic pursuits with a vengeance: he can hunt down men of another race or nation or class; he can enslave them in masses; he can trade them out of property and liberty; he can butcher them in public "furors" or discreetly design their mass destruction. Perhaps even more astonishing, he can treat his own children as "others": as "soil" to be implanted with his values; as animals to be whipped and tamed; as property to be disposed of; and as cheap labor to be exploited. All this, at one time or another, has been a part of an ethos of a technology so self-righteous that even highminded men could not afford to act otherwise without seeming to be traitors to some superiority, or despoilers of some solidarity. In our era of limitless technological expansion, therefore, the question will be what man can afford and decide *not* to use, *not* to invent, and *not* to exploit—and yet save his identity.

But here we enter the domain of ethical values. Identity and fidelity are necessary for ethical strength, but they do not provide it in themselves. It is for adult man to provide content for the ready loyalty of youth, and worthy objects for its need to repudiate. As cultures, through graded training, enter into the fiber of young individuals, they also absorb into their lifeblood the rejuvenative power of youth. Adolescence is thus a vital regenerator in the process of social evolution; for youth selectively offers its loyalties and energies to the conservation of that which feels true to them and to the correction or destruction of that which has lost its regenerative significance.

Loyal and legal are kindred words. He who can be loyal can bind himself legally—or decide to remain deviant or become revolutionary in loyalty to an overdue rejuvenation. As the young adult selects those who in turn will select him—as members, friends, mates, and co-workers—he completes the foundation for the adult virtues. His identity and his style of fidelity define his place in what history has determined as his environment; but so does his society define itself by the way it absorbs (or fails to absorb) his powers of solidarity.

In our day, ideologies take over where religion leaves off, presenting themselves (in addition to other, more practical claims) as historical perspectives on which to fasten individual faith and collective confidence. As religions do, they counteract a threatening sense of alienation with positive ritual and affirmative dogma, and with a rigorous and cruel ban on alienisms in their own ranks or in foreign enemies. They do not hesitate to combine magic with technique by amplifying the sound of One Voice speaking out of the night, and by magnifying and multiplying One Face in the spotlights of mass gatherings. Most relevant in the present connection, however, is the way in which ideologies tie dogmas to new scientific and technological developments. For it must be obvious that science and technology in our day provide a most immediate form of verification by the material riches available to all who are willing and able to work, and, above all, to help to make things work.

That *Love* is the greatest of human virtues, and, in fact, the dominant virtue of the universe, is so commonly assumed that it will be well to consider once more its evolutionary rationale, and to state why love is here assigned to a particular stage and a particular crisis in the unfolding human life cycle. Does not love bind together every stage? There are, to be sure, many forms of love, from the infant's comfortable and anxious attachment to his mother to the adolescent's passionate and desperate infatuation; but love in the evolutionary and generational sense is, I believe, the transformation of the love received throughout the preadolescent stage of life into the care given to others during adult life.

It must be an important evolutionary fact that man, over and above sexuality, develops a selectivity of love: I think it is the *mutuality of mates and partners in a shared identity,* for the mutual verification through an experience of finding oneself, as one loses oneself, in another. For let me emphasize here that identity proves itself strongest where it can take chances with itself. For this reason, love in its truest sense presupposes both identity and fidelity. While many forms of love can be shown to be at work in the formation of the various virtues, it is important to realize that only graduation from adolescence permits the development of that intimacy, the selflessness of joined devotion, which anchors love in a mutual commitment. Intimate love thus is the guardian of that elusive and yet all-pervasive power in psycho-social evolution: the power of *cultural and personal style,* which gives and demands conviction in the shared patterns of living, guarantees individual identity in joint intimacy, and binds into a "way of life" the affiliations of procreation and of production.

The love of young adulthood is, above all, a *chosen,* an *active* love, no matter what the methods of matrimonial selection are which make such a choice a pre-condition for familiarity or lead to it by a process of gradual familiarization. In either case, the problem is one of transferring the experience of being cared for in a parental setting, in which one happened to grow up, to a new, an adult affiliation which is actively chosen and cultivated as a mutual concern.

The word "affiliation" literally means to adopt somebody as a son— and, indeed, in friendships and partnerships young adults become sons of each other, but sons by a free choice which verifies a long hope for kinship beyond (incestuous) blood-bonds. From here on, ego-strength depends on an affiliation with others who are equally ready and able to share in the task of caring for offspring, products, and ideas.

Adult sexuality is marked by genitality, by the capacity for a full and mutual consummation of the sexual act. An immense power of verification pervades this meeting of bodies and temperaments after a hazardously long childhood, which, as the study of neuroses has revealed in detail, can severely prejudice the capacity for psychosexual mutuality. Freud observed that mature genitality alone guarantees that combination (by no means easily acquired, nor easily maintained) of intellectual clarity, sexual mutuality, and considerate love, which anchors man in the actuality of his responsibilities.

We have, so far, said nothing about the differences between the sexes, and for once, this neglect has a justification. For it is only in young adulthood that the biological differences between the sexes—and I believe that they are decisive from the beginning—pass their psychosocial crisis and result in a polarization of the two sexes within a joint life-style. The previously established virtues are preparatory to such polarization and to such style, as are all the physical powers and cognitive capacities developing up to and through adolescence. Competence as such is an intersexual virtue, and so is fidelity. One could make a point for an evolutionary rationale which would explain why sexual differences should not fully divide the sexes until competence and fidelity permit their division to be one of polarization, that is, one of mutual enhancement of experience and of distribution of labor within a stylized pattern of love and care. Such a rationale of human development would also suggest that the sexes are less different in regard to the capacities and virtues which further communication and cooperation; while the differences are greatest where divergence is of the essence, that is, in the counterpoints of love life and the divided functions of procreation.[6] One could say, then, that the sexes are most similar in the workings of the ego, which—being closest to consciousness, language, and ethics—must serve both to integrate the fact of sexual mutuality and bipolarity.

Love, then, is mutuality of devotion forever subduing the antagonisms inherent in divided function. It pervades the intimacy of individuals and is thus the basis of ethical concern.

Yet, love can also be joint selfishness in the service of some territoriality, be it bed or home, village or country. That such "love," too, characterizes his affiliations and associations is at least one reason for man's clannish adherence to styles which he will defend "as if his life depended on them." His ego's coherence, his certainty of orientation, *do* depend on them; and it is for this reason that ego-panic can make man "go blind" with a rage which induces him, in the righteous defense of a shared identity, to sink to levels of sadism for which there seems to be no parallel in the animal world.

C*are* is a quality essential for psychosocial evolution, for we are the teaching species. Animals, too, instinctively encourage in their young what is ready for release, and, of course, some animals can be taught some tricks and services by man. Only man, however, can and must extend his solicitude over the long, parallel, and overlapping childhoods of numerous offspring united in households and communities. As he transmits the rudiments of hope, will, purpose, and competence, he imparts meaning to the child's bodily experiences, he conveys a logic much beyond the literal meaning of the words he teaches, and he gradually outlines a particular world image and style of fellowship. All of this is necessary to complete in man the analogy to the basic, ethological situation between parent animal and young animal. All this, and no less, makes us comparable to the ethologist's goose and gosling. Once we have grasped this interlocking of the human life stages, we understand that adult man is so constituted as to *need to be needed* lest he suffer the mental deformation of self-absorption, in which he becomes his own infant and pet. I have, therefore, postulated an instinctual and psychosocial stage of "generativity" beyond that of genitality. Parenthood is, for most, the first, and for many, the prime generative encounter[7] yet the perpetuation of mankind challenges the generative ingenuity of workers and thinkers of many kinds. And man *needs* to teach, not only for the sake of those who need to be taught, and not only for the fulfillment of his identity, but because facts are kept alive by being told, logic by being demonstrated, truth by being professed. Thus, the teaching passion is not restricted to the teaching profession. Every mature adult knows the satisfaction of explaining what is dear to him and of being understood by a groping mind.

Care is the widening concern for what has been generated by love, necessity, or accident; it overcomes the ambivalence adhering to irreversible obligation.

Generativity, as the instinctual power behind various forms of selfless "caring," potentially extends to whatever a man generates and leaves behind, creates and produces (or helps to produce). The ideological polarization of the Western world which has made Freud the century's theorist of sex, and Marx that of work, has, until quite recently, left a whole area of man's mind uncharted in psychoanalysis. I refer to man's *love for his works and ideas as well as for his children,* and the necessary self-verification which adult man's ego receives, and must receive, from his labor's challenge. As adult man needs to be needed, so—for the strength of his ego and for that of his community—he requires the challenge emanating from what he has generated and from what now must be "brought up," guarded, preserved—and eventually transcended.

Man's creation of all-caring gods is not only an expression of his persisting infantile need for being taken care of, but also a projection onto a super-human agency of an ego-ideal. This agency has to be strong enough to guide (or at least forgive) man's propensity for freely propagating offspring, causing events and creating conditions which, ever again, prove to be beyond him. It is obvious, however, that man must now learn to accept the responsibility which evolution and history have given him, and must learn to guide and planfully restrain his capacity for unlimited propagation, invention, and expansion. And here I emphatically include woman, when I speak of man. For woman's preparation for care is anchored more decisively in her body, which is, as it were, the morphological model of care, at once protective abode and fountain of food.

Modern man, forced to limit his fertility, is apt to consider the matter of procreative involvement resolved by the technical possibility of making a conscious choice in the matter of fertilization. For such choice, men must be readied. Yet an ever so "safe" love life, if accompanied by a mere avoidance of offspring and a denial of generativity, could be, in some, as severe a source of inner tension as the denial of sexuality itself has been. There could well arise the specific guilt of playing with the "fire of creation." It is essential, therefore, that the control of procreation be guided not only by an acknowledgment of man's psychosexual needs, but also by a universal sense of generative responsibility toward all human beings brought planfully into this world. This would include (beyond contraceptives and food packages) the joint guarantee to each child of a chance for such development as we are outlining here.

As we come to the last stage, we become aware of the fact that our civilization really does not harbor a concept of the whole of life, as do the civilizations of the East: "In office a Confucian, in retirement a Taoist." In fact, it is astonishing to behold, how (until quite recently and with a few notable exceptions) Western psychology has avoided looking at the range of the whole cycle.[8] As our world-image is a one-way street to never ending progress interrupted only by small and big catastrophes, our lives are to be one-way streets to success—and sudden oblivion. Yet, if we speak of a cycle of life we really mean two cycles in one: the cycle of one generation concluding itself in the next, and the cycle of individual life coming to a conclusion. If the cycle, in many ways, turns back on its own beginnings, so that the very old become again like children, the question is whether the return is to a childlikeness seasoned with wisdom—or to a finite childishness. This is not only important within the cycle of individual life, but also within that of generations, for it can only weaken the vital fiber of the younger generation if the evidence of daily living verifies man's prolonged last phase as a sanctioned period of childishness. Any span of the cycle lived without vigorous meaning, at the beginning, in the middle, or at the end, endangers the sense of life and the meaning of death in all whose life stages are intertwined.

Individuality here finds its ultimate test, namely, man's existence at the entrance to that valley which he must cross alone. I am not ready to discuss the psychology of "ultimate concern." But in concluding my outline,

I cannot help feeling that the order depicted suggests an existential com-plementarity of the great Nothingness and the actuality of the cycle of generations. For if there is any responsibility in the cycle of life it must be that one generation owes to the next that strength by which it can come to face ultimate concerns in its own way—unmarred by debilitating poverty or by the neurotic concerns caused by emotional exploitation.

For each generation must find the wisdom of the ages in the form of its own wisdom. Strength in the old, therefore, takes the form of wisdom in all of its connotations from ripened "wits" to accumulated knowledge and matured judgment. It is the essence of knowledge freed from tem-poral relativity.

Wisdom, then, is detached concern with life itself, in the face of death itself. It maintains and conveys the integrity of experience, in spite of the decline of bodily and mental functions. It responds to the need of the on-coming generation for an integrated heritage and yet remains aware of the rela-tivity of all knowledge.

Potency, performance, and adaptability decline; but if vigor of mind combines with the gift of responsible renunciation, some old people can envisage human problems in their entirety (which is what "integrity" means) and can represent to the coming generation a living example of the "closure" of a style of life. Only such integrity can balance the de-spair of the knowledge that a limited life is coming to a conscious con-clusion, only such wholeness can transcend the petty disgust of feeling finished and passed by, and the despair of facing the period of relative helplessness which marks the end as it marked the beginning.

There are the leaders, of course, and the thinkers, who round out long productive lives in positions in which wisdom is of the essence and is of service. There are those who feel verified in a numerous and vigorous progeny. But they, too, eventually join the over-aged who are reduced to a narrowing space-time, in which only a few things, in their self-contained form, offer a last but firm whisper of confirmation.

2. EVOLUTION AND EGO

As I reviewed with you an epigenetic schedule of emergent virtues, you were, no doubt, as concerned as I am over the probability that this ascending list will be eagerly accepted by some as a potential inventory for tests of adjustment, or as a new production schedule in the manufacture of desirable children, citizens, and workers. But all such attempts will be shortlived, because they will not work, not even on paper. Others may foresee the use of the schedule as a new set of ideals, to be held up with moral fervor: this by their very nature *these* virtues cannot be. But perhaps we should be more concerned about the list itself, as it stands, for my selection of virtues and their distribution throughout the cycle of life may well appear rather arbitrary. I remember here, with some discomfort, one of my favorite Viennese stories. An Austrian Emperor was asked to pass judgment on the model of a baroque statue which was to adorn one of Vienna's squares. He studied it for a while with the concentration expected of a patron of the arts and then decreed with authority: "It needs some more faith-hope-and-charity down there on the left." Have I viewed the whole of life the way the Emperor judged the statue?

I hope to have indicated that these emergent virtues are not external ornaments easily added or omitted according to the fancies of esthetic or moral style. This whole "body" of virtues is, in fact, anchored in three different systems which I would like to remark on in some detail. They are: *epigenesis* in individual development; the *sequence of generations*; and the *growth of the ego.* Let me first approach epigenesis.

At a meeting in 1955, a number of workers in child development discussed the question of whether there were discernible "general stages" in childhood—stages clearly encompassing *(englobe)* the different functions of body and mind—which develop at the same time and yet seem to maintain such remarkable autonomy from each other.[9] Jean Piaget was one of the discussants and was, as usual, both sharply rigorous in the pursuit of known method, and amusing in his asides. He doubted the existence of such unified stages on physiological grounds, reiterating that, for example, the dental, skeletal, cerebral, and endocrine systems grow and develop at their own rates. He took for granted that, in the healthy child, there is, at any given time, a high degree of *functional unity,* that is, an ability to reconcile and co-ordinate the growth patterns of all the physiological as well as the mental and emotional functions. This he called the *unity of personality.* But he discarded, as unproven, any claim of having found the principles governing this functional unity at a given stage in such a way that a *structural unity* for that particular stage could be demonstrated. Offering himself as an example of a personality *"multiple, divisée et contradictoire,"* he granted that on professional occasions he could force himself to be quite serious, while on other (unspecified) occasions, he had to consider himself rather childish or was apt to behave like an adolescent. In other words, there are conflicts:

> "Je ne réalise pas l'unité structurale. La seule unité structurale que je me connais est l'unité du personnage social que je répresente, mais qui ne recouvre pas tout. Comment voulez-vous donc qu'il y ait une unité structurale chez l'enfant si elle n'existe pas chez l'adult?"

I would like, however, to approach the question of structural unity on the basis of clinical, developmental, and evolutionary speculation. Not that I could even begin to suggest methods of inquiry approaching the rigor demanded by Piaget, and exemplified in his synthesis of the experimental and the clinical. Most of us have our roots in one or the other, in the experimental or the clinical methods; that is, we know man either when he is well enough to lend parts of himself for study in suitable settings, or sick enough to fall apart into discernible fragments of behavior. The workers who turn to the first, the experimental method, are on the whole cautious in making any promises regarding their ability to reveal man's nature. But it is clear that their methodological modesty disguises the expectation that all their reliable data added together will eventually be equal to the total functioning of man—if, indeed, man could only be prevailed upon to realize that life would be much more manageable if he would consent to be the sum of his reliably investigated parts. I belong to another breed, the clinicians, who are modest and vain in different ways. Much less cautious, we speak with relative ease of the core of man's personality and of stages in its development. But then, our subjects want to become whole; and the clinician must have some theories and methods which offer the patient a whole world to be whole in. Mistaking our patients' gratitude for verification, we are sometimes sure that we could explain or even guide mankind if it would only consent to be our collective patient.

Piaget has been singularly successful in avoiding either of these illusions. The remark quoted was, of course, meant to pretend naïveté; and if I am not mistaken, he usually allows for such weakness in a discussion just before he turns politely but deftly on the clinicians present. At any rate, in his remark about his own behavior the terms "childlike" and "adolescent" should be in quotation marks. For Piaget would claim both too much and too little if he were to insist that what he refers to as a remnant of childishness is truly childlike, or his allegedly adolescent streak truly youthful. When "childlike," an adult may be surprisingly, or charmingly, or ridiculously childlike—for an adult; and when "adolescent," goodnaturedly or exuberantly or shockingly adolescent. But he is structurally an adult because his adulthood determines the nature and the use he makes of what is left of his earlier selves and what is presaged of his future ones, including his ability to remark on them in a sovereign and strategic manner.

Piaget's remark will serve, however, as an *illustration of a principle* which I wish to employ in charting the strengths of the ego at different stages of life—which are, of course, the structural basis of man's functional unity at such stages. I have used this principle of epigenesis in a number of other publications, in the form of a chart such as this:

STAGE C	"childlike" adult	"adolescent" adult	adult adult
STAGE B	"childlike" adolescent	adolescent adolescent	"adult" adolescent
STAGE A	childlike child	"adolescent" child	"adult" child

Figure 1

The child is childlike in Stage A, the adolescent adolescent in Stage B, and the adult adult in Stage C—in *this sequence,* for each stage represents a certain *period* during which (healthy) body and mind provide the *potentials* and the (true) community the corresponding *opportunities* for the accomplishment of such unity. Where processes of disease or disintegration upset this order, the childish or "childlike" adult would still be structurally different from a playing child; the precocious or "adult" adolescent different from an adult philosopher; and the unchildlike or "adolescent" child from an exuberant or brooding adolescent. However, we clinicians must admit that we understand crises typical for certain stages better than the stages themselves, and know the cubicles with the quotation marks better than those without. In psychoanalysis the stages of childhood were first identified with their typical inner crises, and their crises with the (mostly unconscious) instinctual wishes which gave them their urgency and provided their core-conflict. What man, at a given stage, had wanted unconsciously became that stage, and the sum of such stages, man; and even in Piaget's remark, reflecting somewhat of a caricature of clinical thinking, there is the suggestion that an adult who must admit that he harbors adolescent and infantile trends forfeits to that extent the claim of an adult structural unity.

It must be granted here that one is not an adult adult (nor was a childlike child, nor became an adolescent adolescent) without what Piaget calls conflict—a matter to which I would give a more normative and developmental status by calling it crisis. In fact, to each such unity corresponds a major crisis; and whenever, for whatever reason, a later crisis is severe, earlier crises are revived.

In presenting my schedule of emerging virtues, I have also implied, but not spelled out, the existence of developmental crises. I must briefly define this ancient little word. In clinical work (as in economics and politics) crisis has increasingly taken on half of its meaning, the catastrophic half, while in medicine a crisis once meant a turning point for better or for worse, a crucial period in which a decisive turn *one way or another* is unavoidable. Such crises occur in man's total development sometimes more noisily, as it were, when new instinctual needs meet abrupt prohibitions, sometimes more quietly when new capacities yearn to match new opportunities, and when new aspirations make it more obvious how limited one (as yet) is. We would have to talk of all these and more if we wanted to gain an impression of the difficult function—of functional unity. I have tried to take into account the double aspect of such crises by assigning double terms to the psychosocial stages which I have previously postulated.[10] Thus—to mention only three—infancy would culminate in a crisis in which basic trust must outweigh basic mistrust, adolescence in a crisis in which identity must prove stronger than role confusion, while in old age only integrity can balance despair. However, I will not deal in detail here with the psychosocial basis of those unifying strengths which I have called basic virtues.

It is not easy to admit, while speaking with some conviction of an evolving ground plan, that one does not yet know how to observe or to formulate its components. In this first attempt to name basic properties of the "strong" person (matters so far left to moralists and theologians), I have given these properties their everyday names: this is what they look like when observed in others; this is what they feel like when possessed; and this, above all, seems absent when "virtue goes out" of a person. Now, the negative of this kind of virtue cannot be vice; rather, it is a weakness, and its symptoms are disorder, dysfunction, disintegration, anomie. But "weakness" fails to convey the complexity of disturbance and to account for the particular rage which accumulates whenever man is hindered in the activation and perfection of the virtues outlined here. Only when active tension is restored, do things fall into place, strongly and simply. I, for one, remember with pleasure the exclamation of a patient: "You sure know how to de-complicate things!" Such flattery, however, is only as good as the surprise behind it: one cannot pre-decomplicate things. In this sense, the list of virtues only points to an order which, I believe, will be found to be violated in every new form of perplexing disorder and restored in its (always surprising) resolution. To consider such order, then, is a matter of long range study and contemplation: for the virtues seem to me to point to principles of cohesion as well as to defects in the "fiber" of generations and institutions.

To call hope in this context a vital virtue means only to name that basic minimum without which the most highly valued and espoused hopes become irrelevant; it means to mark the limits of the socio-genetic efficacy of all values. For values which do not secure the re-emergence of the order of these vital strengths (whatever their genetic disposition and their individual nature) in each generation, are apt to lose—well, their virtue.

In an epigenetic development of the kind here envisaged, each item has its time of ascendance and crisis, yet each persists throughout life. Hope is the first and most basic and yet it is also the most lasting; it is the most stable and yet acquires new qualities, depending on the general stage reached. Thus, in adulthood, hope may have become invested in a formulated faith or endow an implicit one. Similarly, the rudiments of will become part of an adult's determination, both in the sense of his capacity to exert strong will over others and in his necessary self-control.

I would not be ready by any means to complete this list. The point to be made is merely that what thus grows in steps is part of an ensemble in which no part must have missed its original crisis, its further meta-morphoses, and its re-integration into each later stage. Thus, hope in in-fancy already has an element of willfulness which, however, cannot be challenged as yet in the way it must be when the crisis of will arrives in the play age. That a baby already has some tiny developmental Anlage which will grow to become wisdom after a long life—that will be harder to defend against all but the most fanatic devotees of infancy. (On the other hand, Lao-tse, so I am told, does mean "old child . . .")

But it is true that the over-all stages of development in the human being cannot be grasped before what Piaget calls the "functional unity of the personality" is better understood. As human strengths, the virtues listed here are obviously superordinated to the psychosexual and psy-chosocial schedules, in the sense that they are an expression of their in-tegration, even though the specific time within a stage, when such unity is reached, and the mechanisms by which it comes about are not yet known. What Freud calls oral libido obviously endows the experiences from which hope emerges. Both can only arise, and must arise, in in-fancy. On the other hand, oral libido would not find its place in the unity of the personality (and that means, as we have seen, in the unity of the generational process) without a strong and pervading hopefulness. This over-all state, however, depends on much more than a successful orality, even if there were such a thing as a successful libido on its own. It depends on the verifications, in social reality, of all the maturing part-functions of organism and mind. There is really no use, then, in asking what comes first: the ensemble arises with its parts and the parts with the ensemble; even though each part when first revealed by a new method may impress its finder as being the cause and the beginning of all other parts. Freud saw this when he called his instinct theory his "mythology." Myths do not lie, but they find new forms closer to ob-servation.

Whatever is built into human development also has an evolutionary ra-tionale. I have implied that I consider this to be true for the basic virtues. But the use of the word virtue in proximity to the term evolution im-mediately suggests one of the dreaded "naturalist fallacies." I use the word virtue in this context, however, not in order to read moral intentions into evolution, but in order to discern adaptive strengths which have emerged from it. Now it is obvious that man, who according to Waddington[11] "goes in for ethicizing," has built on the vital virtues moral and religious superstructures which impress us not only with their occasional capacity to lift man up but also to cause his frequent total downfall. For this very reason, however, we must recognize in human development that substructure and rockbottom of vital strengths which assure human adaptation from generation to generation. Geneticists hesitate to specify genetically transmitted "dispositions" by which man is born ready to negotiate with a social environment, not only for his full physiological stature and cognitive expanse, but also for a set of vital strengths which will make him the effective bearer of offspring, producer of tools, and carrier of tradition. Yet, Waddington recognizes not only that man "goes in for ethicizing," but that he is, by nature, an "authority acceptor." This, I think, will do as the minimum genetic acknowledgment necessary to assume inborn dispositions ensuring and negotiating sequences of generations living in organized societies. Within these processes, then, the vital virtues enumerated and tentatively named here are not lofty ideals (this they become, in fact, in their hour of relative weakness) but essential qualities arising from the convergence, in each life and in each generation, of unfolding capacities with existing institutions. If motherhood inspires hope, if ideological institutions provide grounds for fidelity, and if patterns of co-operation foster love, then each depends on the sequence of all, and all on some original total disposition emerging in that total cultural milieu, of which human motherhood is a part. The disposition, to be sure, is for Hope, not for a particular variety of prescribed hopes; it is for Fidelity and not for particular loyalties and devotions which, in fact, may sharply contrast with each other from ideology to ideology; it is for Love, and not for a particular cultural combination of love with sexual and social mores.

To complete my discourse in which the word evolutionary has appeared so regularly, I should admit that the thoughts which I am advancing here were partially provoked by a request from Sir Julian Huxley to contribute to a volume called, "The Humanist Frame."[12] For this he encouraged me to "write what you have long wanted to say," and what emerged is the scheme which I have presented here. To discuss further the dialectics of evolution and ego, I must reach back to the world-view, or better the world mood, which has emerged from both Darwin's and Freud's investigations, and which is to blame, I think, for our hesitation in studying human strength.

Darwinism and Freudian psychoanalysis have successively focused on what is popularly considered man's "lower nature": the descent and evolution of the genus man from a pre-human state of animality; the emergence of civilized man from degrees of savagery and barbarism; and the evolution of individual man from the stages of infantility. They have shown the relation of rational man's everyday irrationalities to insanity, and revealed political man's propensity for mob anarchy. Each of these insights at first met with derision and disbelief, but soon assumed the form of modern myths. Popular thought (and that includes specialists in non-biological fields) has generalized Darwin's theory as a "tooth-and-claw" struggle for survival, in which the crown of creation would go to what T. H. Huxley called the "gladiatorial" type of man. Similarly, popular thought (and that includes scientists not familiar with the advancements of psychoanalysis) has crudely over-simplified Freud's theory of inner conflict. It clings to the earliest formulation of this conflict and conceives of it as an inner tooth-and-claw struggle between ravenous instincts (the impersonal "Id") and cruel conscience (the moralistic "Super-Ego"). Thus the moral alternatives seemingly implicit in Darwin's and Freud's discoveries have been over-dramatized—as if mankind were taking revenge on these fearless men by forcing them into the role of tragic high priests in the cult of "facing man's lower nature," a nature which could now be faced with moralistic derision, or with an acceptance which soon excused everything. That double myth of an inner and outer struggle to the death has made it difficult for both biology and psychoanalysis to come to grips with the question of man's strength. Yet if man's future were dependent on his unbridled "instincts" or his overweening conscience alone, it could predictably end in species-wide suicide—in the name of the highest principles.

But the problem is not all one of popularization. The scientific (and ethical) necessity to view man's repudiated origins and his "lower nature" with an unflinching eye has led the scientific observer himself into an untenable dualism. G. G. Simpson, in the very conclusion of the book *Behavior and Evolution,* edited by him, makes reference to the essay on the evolution of human behavior by Roe and Freedman:

With all this behind us, and with us, we are—who can doubt it?—sexual, aggressive, and acquisitive; in closing, my only regret is that Freedman and Roe intentionally omitted from this list the characteristic best exemplified in and by this book—exploratory curiosity.[13]

And indeed, the two authors of that essay, while lining up with admirable clarity all the data suggested by clinical observation, tend to attach to these data interpretations derived from psychiatric work, and describe man, as it were, with his "inside out," a nearly helpless victim of repression, conflict, and ambivalence. This endows the primates with an image of the infant reconstructed from clinical experience. Thus (as Simpson suggests), they seem to have forgotten themselves and excluded from evolution what they are doing when they write about evolution. Here, they have followed a tradition which characterizes psychoanalysis, as well. Freud's model of man consists primarily of the processes which he observed when, with such primeval courage, he looked into himself as he looked into his patients; but the model had no place for the judicious observer, the curious man. Science, morality, and himself Freud "took for granted."

Yet, both Darwin and Freud have given us the means to re-evaluate conscience itself, which was seen by Darwin as "by far the most important . . . of all the differences between man and the lower animals" yet solely devoted to "the welfare of the tribe—not that of the species, nor that of an individual member of the tribe." And it was Freud who revealed the instinctual crudeness and tribal cruelty in much of man's morality. History since Freud and Darwin has amply illustrated the limitations and dangers of a tribal conscience, especially when it is in the possession of modern technology.

Julian Huxley, at his best, summed the matter up at the end of his Romanes Lecture:

The peculiar difficulties which surround our individual moral adjustment are seen to be largely due to our evolutionary history. Like our prolonged helplessness in infancy, our tendency to hernia and sinusitis, our troubles in learning to walk upright, they are a consequence of our having developed from a simian ancestry. Once we realize that the primitive super-ego is merely a makeshift developmental mechanism, no more intended to be the permanent central support of our morality than is our embryonic motochord intended to be the permanent central support of our bodily frame, we shall not take its dictates so seriously (have they not often been interpreted as the authentic Voice of God?), and shall regard its supersession by some more rational and less cruel mechanism as the central ethical problem confronting every human individual.[14]

This passage expresses a view to which, in fact, psychoanalysis is dedicated both as a clinical technique and a system of thought. Every step in treatment and every act of clarification is directed toward the "supersession by some more rational and less cruel mechanism." This view is also well prepared for by an aspect of Freud's thought which has not provoked the imagination of other scientists as has his instinct theory: I refer to his ego-psychology.

Freud's concept of the ego is as old as psychoanalysis itself, and was, in fact, brought along from Freud's physiologic days. Freud first,[15] then Anna Freud,[16] and finally Heinz Hartmann[17] have worked consistently on the refinement of the concept. Yet, this "structural" part of Freud's work seems to have less appeal. Psychologists have continued to refer to the field of psychoanalysis as primarily concerned with the "affective," and biologists prefer to think of psychoanalysis as covering the sexual or, at best, the "emotional" only. It is obvious, I think, that the shock caused by Freud's earlier systemizations of the dichotomy of instinct and super-ego has been absorbed so slowly, and with so much emotional ambivalence, that Freud's later thoughts have simply not reached the attention of the majority of scientific workers. And even where the psychoanalytic concept of the ego has permeated, it has been immediately drawn into the imagery of man's "lower nature," and into the popular meaning of ego, namely, an inflated self. Thus a church-historian, in one of the best of our academic journals, could suggest that a psychoanalytic study of Luther's identity crisis was meant to show that Luther started the Reformation merely "for the satisfaction of his ego." To that extent has the popular "ego" as a designation of modern man's vain sense of a self-made Self (a precarious sense, subject to sudden deflation by the pricks of fate—and of gossip) penetrated the vocabulary even of the learned. But it happens to designate the opposite of the psychoanalytic meaning; therefore in all but the most specialized circles, it is still necessary to say what the ego is not.

The psychoanalytic meaning of ego designates it as an inner–psychic regulator which organizes experience and guards such organization *both* against the untimely impact of *drives* and the undue pressure of an over-weening *conscience*. Actually, ego is an age-old term which in scholastics stood for the *unity* of body and soul, and in philosophy in general of the *permanency* of conscious experience. Psychoanalysis, of course, has not concerned itself with matters of soul and has assigned to consciousness a limited role in mental life by demonstrating that man's thoughts and acts are co-determined by unconscious motives which, upon analysis, prove him to be both worse and better than he thinks he is. But this also means that his motives as well as his feelings, thoughts, and acts, often "hang to-gether" much better than he could (or should) be conscious of. The ego in psychoanalysis, then, is analogous to what it was in philosophy in ear-lier usage: a selective, integrating, coherent, and persistent agency central to personality formation. William James still used the term in this sense: in his letters, he speaks not only of "the ego's active tension," but also of the "enveloping ego to make continuous the times and spaces not nec-essarily coincident of the partial egos."[18] But then, his self-observation had brought him close to the study of impaired states in which the ego was first revealed in its weakness, and then recognized as a control regu-lator of remarkable endurance and power.

Psychoanalysis, then, while first concentrating on the vicissitudes of in-stinctual forces in man (as recognizable in clinical symptoms and univer-sal symbolisms, in dreams and in myths, in the stages of ontogeny and the evolution of the species), never ceased its work in the second area of in-quiry, namely, on that "coherent organization of mental processes" which, in this caldron of forces and drives, assures a measure of individuality, in-telligence, and integrity. Only the measure of the measure varied. The original awe of the inner conflicts which motivate man made his ego seem to be a pathetic compromiser between the Id, which had a mo-nopoly on all instinctual fuel of man's "animal-nature" and the Super-Ego, which could claim the support of all-knowing priests, all-powerful parents, and all-embracing institutions. No wonder that, at the time, the ego seemed to Freud like a rider who is "obliged to guide (his horse) where it wants to go." Gradually, however, the study of the human ego, the guardian of individuality, revealed it to be the inner "organ" which makes it possible for man to bind together the two great evolutionary de-velopments, his *inner life* and his *social planning*.

The ego was gradually seen to be an organ of active mastery, not only in defending the inviolacy of the person against excessive stimulation from within the organism or from the environment, but also in integrating the individual's adaptive powers with the expanding opportunities of the "expectable" environment. The ego thus is the guardian of *meaningful experience,* that is, of experience individual enough to guard the unity of the person; and it is adaptable enough to master a significant portion of reality with a sense, in this world of blind and unpredictable forces, of being in an *active state.* This means that a "strong ego" is the psychological precondition for that freedom which has alternately been specified as the effort through which the inevitable comes to pass—or the will to choose what is necessary.

But I must say in passing that over the years I have become less intolerant of the popular misunderstanding of the term "ego," for it covers, as folklore often does, a deeper truth. Up to a point, the ego can be understood as a guardian of man's individuality, that is, his indivisibility. But in the midst of other individualities, equally indivisible, the ego must guard and does guard certain prerogatives which man cannot afford to be without and which he therefore will maintain both with secret delusions (such as are revealed in his dreams and daydreams) and in those collective illusions which often guide his history. Some of these prerogatives are a sense of *wholeness,* a sense of *centrality* in time and space, and a sense of *freedom of choice.* Man cannot tolerate to have these questioned beyond a certain point, either as an individual among his fellow men, or as a member of a group among other groups. It is for this reason that in individual memories and in collective history man rearranges experience in order to restore himself as the cognitive center and the source of events. He has crowned all-powerful kings and created all-knowing gods, endowing them with all the ego-ism the individual cannot do without: a central position in violent events; a sense of having willed and created fate itself; a certainty of being eternal and immortal; a conviction of being able to know the secret of life; the ability of being totally aware of goings-on everywhere and of influencing whatever one wishes to change. To restore this necessity of ego-ism in his own little self, man has also found means (inspirational, artistic, toxic) to be "beside himself" in order to feel himself to be more than himself. With all due respect, I see the latest version of this inexorable inner need in those post-Darwinists who insist that man, now that he recognizes himself as a part of evolution, and may learn to steer some of it by dint of this recognition, becomes the crown and the goal of it instead of a creature who does well if he manages to restore or undo what he has upset and wrought in the tiny and dark corner that he, at best, can know. When faced with one of the customary apotheoses of man by an otherwise strict scientist, I am apt to remember the remark of a co-ed who expressed the depth of our darkness in the direct way reserved to women. Her escort had just mused aloud that life was a strange thing, indeed. There was a silence which he took for inspired consent. But she asked quietly: ". . . as compared with what?"

If the super-ego, then, has guarded man's morality but also has made him its slave, the ego, more adaptively, permits him a measure of human balance, yet not without dangerous illusions—dangerous, I should add, because of the destructive rage which accompanies their failure. In this sense, the basic virtues enumerated here have their illusory side which can develop into grand delusions of vain virtuousness, and lead to specific rages of disillusionment. Yet each is indispensable, and each is necessary for that ensemble which is man at his most balanced; while all in moments of humor and wisdom, in prayer, meditation, and self-analysis, can be charitably transcended.

But where, in animal nature, is the precursor of human ego? Man has always tended to project what he calls his own "animal nature"—that is, his id-superego split—on animals, comparing, for example, his ravenousness with the eating style of dogs, or his rage with that of provoked tigers. Whole "bestiaries" attribute to animals the lowest vices as well as the conflicts of man. A recent calendar relates a medieval view according to which a lion never overeats, adding, "and when he feels he might overeat, he puts his paw in his mouth to prevent himself." So here, too, man ascribes to the lion an inner life by which he becomes aware of an illicit wish and actively prevents himself from "giving in," even as our conscience struggles with our desires. On the other hand, our abysmal ambivalence leads us to see also our most exalted virtues in the image of animals: we are as courageous as lions, as meek as lambs, or we see in the quiet glance of a dark-eyed beauty the mysterious eyes of a doe. What we do not ascribe to animals, and are usually surprised to find in reports and in moving pictures made in their natural habitat, is a certain built-in balance, a restraint and discipline within their ecological niche of survival and activity. For an analogy to what we call ego, we may have to contemplate a certain chaste restraint and selective discipline in the life of even the "wildest" animals: a built-in regulator which prevents (or "inhibits") carnivorous excess, inappropriate sexuality, useless rage, and damaging panic, and which permits rest and play along with the readiness to attack when hungry or intruded upon. Similarly, different species of animals share environments with a minimum of mutual interference or distraction, each minding its own section of the environment unless, and until, vital interests prove to intersect. Thus, the state of the adapted animal is defined by what we might call *ecological integrity*; a combination of mutual regulation and reciprocal avoidance which safeguards adaptation within the characteristic environment and with other species sharing it. Man, who has evolved into a creature who is always in the process of readjusting to historical change in his man-made world, obviously overreacts (in suffering, for example, from affect-incontinence as Konrad Lorenz has said): for him to live up, on his level, to the animal's adaptive integrity would call for a mutual regulation of inner motivation and technical-social invention which he seems to approach only during certain glorious but unpredictable periods. But whether for new glory or mere survival, he must now take his place more consciously in the succession of generations within his psychosocial universe.

We cannot overlook for a moment that so far in his history man has realized the blueprint of his potentialities only in fragments. There are many reasons for this. History records the triumphs of perfectibility attained in certain eras and areas, and presents us with examples of human perfectibility, transient and yet preserved in forms and words speaking to us with the utter presence which Rilke, in his *Duino Elegies,* ascribes to lovers: *"So weit sind's wir"*—"that much is truly ours." Thus we recognize the perfection of harmonious growth in the Greek realization of an excellent body and an excellent mind—a harmony counterpointed by the tragedies, and the death of Socrates. We recognize the perfection of charity in the words of Christ and St. Francis, against the background of the last Passion. And we see the emergence of technological and organizational perfection in our time, reaching to the stars and preparing the stage for species-wide tragedy. But history has, on the whole and until recently, lacked both the method and the intent to demonstrate the dynamic relation between these triumphs and the inner distortions and social sacrifices imposed alike on elites and masses. With the possible advent of world democracy and with the necessity that every child born be a child chosen to be born and guaranteed by a world community an equal degree of opportunity, the function and the consciousness of history will change radically.

The cogwheeling stages of childhood and adulthood are, as we can see in conclusion, truly a system of *generation* and *regeneration*—for into this system flow, and from this system emerge, those social attitudes to which the institutions and traditions of society attempt to give unity and permanence.

This, then, is the most immediate connection between the *basic virtues* and the *essentials of an organized human community:* adults are organized (among other reasons) for the purpose of deriving from the collectivity and from its tradition a fund of reassurance and a set of methods which enable them to meet the needs of the next generation in relative independence of the vicissitudes of individual fate. Trustworthy motherliness, thus, needs a trustworthy "universe," and the religion of women can be observed to have a different quality from that of men. The womanly verification of faith lies less in a logic which permits action without guilt than in what the woman can do with faith itself, namely, give hope and establish trust in new humans.

Human strength, then, depends on a total process which regulates at the same time the *sequence of generations* and the *structure of society.* The ego is the regulator of this process in the individual.

To use, once more, hope as an example: the emergence of this vital quality can be seen as defined by three co-ordinates: the relation of the mother's motherhood to her own past childhood; the mother-child relation itself; and the relation of both to institutions providing faith in procreation. All three are set to augment hope: the mother's own past has left her with the wish and the necessity to pass on that hope which emanated from her mother(s) and from her culture. Her infant's hope, once awakened, maintained, and developed has the power to augment hope in all around him. At the same time, however, the adults entrusted with the maintenance of an infant's hope need some societal confirmation and restoration of hope, whether it is offered by religious ritual or inspired and informed advice, or both. Once given, this reassurance is reflected in the gradual transformation of the small individual's generalized hopefulness into a faith related to the predominant assumptions concerning the order of the universe. And as he grows up, he will not only become ready to transmit such faith (in the form of hope) to his progeny, but he will also contribute to the preservation or change of those institutions which preserve a tradition of faith.

What begins as hope in the individual infant is in its mature form faith, a sense of superior certainty not essentially dependent on evidence or reason, except where these forms of self-verification become part of a way of life binding technology, science, and new sources of identity into a coherent world-image. It is obvious that for the longest period of known history religion has monopolized the traditional formulation and the ritual restoration of faith. It has shrewdly played into man's most child-like needs, not only by offering eternal guarantees for an omniscient power's benevolence (if properly appeased) but also by magic words and significant gestures, soothing sounds and soporific smells—an infant's world. This has led to the interpretation that religion exploits, for the sake of its own political establishment, the most infantile strivings in man. This it undoubtedly does. Yet at the height of its historical function it has played another, corresponding role, namely that of giving concerted expression to adult man's need to provide the young and the weak with a world-image sustaining hope. Here it must not be forgotten that religious world-images have at least contained some recognition (and this is more than radical rationalism could claim until the advent of psychoanalysis) of the abysmal alienations—from the self and from others—which are the human lot. For along with a fund of hope, an inescapable alienation is also bequeathed to life by the first stage, namely, a sense of a threatening separation from the matrix, a possible loss of hope, and the uncertainty whether the "face darkly" will brighten again with recognition and charity.

Will, in turn, matures to be the ego's disposition over the strength of controlled drive. Such will-power, however, must join the will of others in such a way that drive remains powerful and resourceful in all, even as it is restrained by voluntary self-abnegation and ready obedience. The institution which gives "eternal" form to such judiciousness is the law. The judiciousness which governs the training of the small individual's willfulness in its infantile beginnings is thus carried on by the individual and, as a social demand, carried into institutions which guard the traditional and support a balance of leadership and followership, of privilege and obligation, of voluntary action and coercion. To its majesty organized man surrenders the disposition over the leftovers of willfulness in himself and in others, half hoping and half fearing that he himself may get away with small transgressions once in a while, even while watching his neighbors with coercive righteousness. The law's majesty, on the other hand, relies on interpretation, and ambiguous decision as well as ambivalent obedience remain its daily diminutions. Thus institutions, too, suffer from the past: from the phylogenetic past which, at a critical time, attempted to take an "eternal" principle out of the flux of time, and to transform it into a set of laws so formulated as to anticipate all future contingencies; and the ontogenetic past common to all citizens, namely, their "law training" in childhood and all its inconsistencies. Whether, as children, they learned to believe in justice because they had learned to admire judiciousness and to love righteousness, or to hate the willfulness of others, the law is now a requirement for ego-strength. Emotions as well as social logic will participate in the maintenance of a balance of privileges, obligations, and prohibitions.

The dependence of any institution on rejuvenation by the emotional investment of generations brings with it a persistent double danger. Even as the individual, in frantic search of his earliest hope-giving relationship, may end up lost in delusions and addictions, so are religions, when they lose their bonds with living ethics, apt to regress to the fostering of illusory and addictive promises or empty fantasy. And even as the individual, under the impact of his infantile training in domestic law and order, can become "compulsive," i.e., excessively controlled by and concerned with the mechanisms of inner control, so organized law can become machinery using the letter to subdue the spirit which was to be safeguarded. One can speak, then, of "sick" institutions, but only as long as one specifies the adaptive mechanisms which have bogged down in mere repetitiveness; and as long as one does not indulge in the assumption that psychiatric enlightenment as such will heal society.

It seems probable, then, that what we have called basic virtues emerging from the dealings of generations with each other have their counterparts in the spirit of those human institutions which attempt to formalize and to safeguard such dealings. Without seeking a simple correspondence within any one virtue and any institution, I would posit a mutual activation and replenishment between the virtues emerging in each individual life cycle and the strengths of human institutions. In whatever way we may learn to demonstrate this, virtue in the individual and the spirit of institutions have evolved together, are one and the same strength. From the stages and virtues such individual dispositions as faith, judiciousness, moral purpose, technical efficiency, ideological devotion, ethical responsibility, and detached sagacity flow into the life of institutions. Without them, institutions wilt; but without the spirit of institutions pervading the patterns of care, love, instruction, and training, no virtue could emerge from the sequence of generations. However there is no one-to-one connection between single virtues and single institutions, such as churches, law courts, or economic establishments.

A survey may suggest premature conclusions concerning a large area, details of which remain as yet inaccessible to more systematic approaches. But a "long view" may at least clarify where, in general, one is going. It seems beyond question to me that a theory which is "to glean from psychopathology contributions to normal psychology," must complement observations of childhood with a view of adulthood, supplement a theory of the libido with a conception of other sources of energy, and fortify a concept of the ego with insights into the nature of social institutions.

An attempt to construct a ground plan of human strength, however, could be accused of neglecting diversities, of contributing to the fetish of deadly norms, and thus to the undermining of the individual as a hero or a rebel, an ascetic or a mere person of singularity. Yet, the life processes will always lead to more diversity than we can comfortably manage with our insights, our cures, and our aspirations. And so will man's reaction to the diversity of conditions. In the processes of socio-genetic change we can ascribe a long-range meaning to the idiosyncratic individualist and to the deviant as well as to the obedient conformist. True *adaptation,* in fact, is maintained with the help of loyal rebels who refuse to adjust to "conditions" and cultivate an indignation in the service of a *to-be-restored wholeness* without which psychosocial evolution and all of its institutions would be doomed. When Camus says that faith is sin, he says it in a form and in a context which forcefully suggests that he "cares" to relive and to restate faith beyond any compromise which, as a child, he was forced to accept.

Where do we stand?

In our time, for the first time, one human species can be envisaged, with one common technology on one globe and some surrounding "outer space." The nature of history is about to change. It cannot continue to be the record of high accomplishments in dominant civilizations, and of their disappearance and replacement. Joint survival demands that man visualize new ethical alternatives fit for newly developing as well as over-developed systems and identities. A more universal standard of perfection will mediate more realistically between man's inner and outer worlds than did the compromises resulting from the reign of moral absolutes; it will acknowledge the responsibility of each individual for the potentialities of all generations and of all generations for each individual, and this in a more informed manner than has been possible in past systems of ethics.

As we have seen, the individual ego can be strong only through a mutual guarantee of strength given to and received by all whose life-cycles intertwine. Whatever chance man may have to transcend the limitations of his ego seems to depend on his prior ability, in his one and only life cycle, to be fully engaged in the sequence of generations. Thus, the study of those miracles of everyday life which we have attempted to describe as the emergence of basic virtues seems indispensable to an appraisal of the process man partakes in, of the stuff he must work with, and of the strength he can count on, as he attempts to give a more unified direction to his future course.

III

ON LEADERS

Throughout his own pioneering life as a theorist, teacher, writer, to the point that he became a leading man of ideas, lectured at a leading university, wrote for leading journals, attracted a substantial cohort of eager students, young colleagues (as members of his seminars, section men or women in his courses), Erik Erikson wanted to know what makes for leadership—who becomes what kind of commanding figure for whom. As the pages ahead indicate, even when Erikson was examining psychoanalysis as a practitioner and theoretician, and as a literary and social essayist, he chose to do so as a biographer, an admiring one determined to emphasize chronology. Freud's breakthrough, we are asked to realize, eventuated in the assumption of an occupational position or role, in an intellectual achievement, and, in Erikson's views, a historical triumph: Freud was "the first" in what would be a long line of successors, including Erikson himself, whose essay "The First Psychoanalyst" accomplished with verve a narrative or expository feat all its own.

This biographical side of Erikson's interests and writing would become an important aspect of his reflective life—arguably, the ultimate mainstay of his reputation as a leader himself (intellectual, psychoanalytic), and one who took the measure of other leaders: Sigmund Freud, whom he knew firsthand in Austria, and others available to him through their words, deeds. The range of studies that addressed those various individuals is impressive to consider. Gorky came first—a Russian storyteller who became quite something else, Erikson (the astute storyteller) reminds us, a legend for a Russia that went through great tumult but needed desperately to secure its past. Luther was next, the one who challenged a religion's authority, that of the Catholic Church and its popes, only to become the founder of another religion, the ultimate authority in whose name that religion pursued its practices and evangelized its doctrines over the generations—the Lutheranism young Erikson surely knew of, during his life in Germany, even as he would know, during his middle years, what had happened to the Lutheran Church (its members all over Hitler's Third Reich in consort with the Nazis, some ministers even proudly, rather than ashamedly, wearing swastikas into and out of their church services). It was no easy task for the author of *Young Man Luther* to try to do justice to a minister's, a theologian's, historical and ideological achievements, even as in this century his surviving church has had to come to terms with what some in it let happen to themselves, or let happen to others hatefully ignored or condemned. In his book on Luther, Erikson really found his way as a thoroughgoing biographer, and consequently, his prose shines throughout, his ideas, too, with their subtlety, their compelling interest, the psychological and religious narrative they tell.

Years after the book on Luther, we all met, through Erikson, our wide-ranging president Thomas Jefferson. In the Jefferson lectures a German-born psychoanalyst spoke of our third president, his astonishing capacity to leap over constraints and barriers that have curbed others like him, powerful or talented. In a sense the telling of Jefferson's nature brought Erikson as close to America's heart and soul as he could possibly get: a foreign-born observer become, as an elder, the chosen recipient of a nation's intellectual honor. Not least, Erikson would give us *Gandhi's Truth,* perhaps his most praised book, the one accorded the highest awards he'd receive. India's Mahatma receives close scrutiny, indeed; his ethical efforts, positions, accomplishments, are resolutely told, but as well, some of his less appealing sides are confronted by a biographer who wanted to do justice to a political philosophy of nonviolence, while also mentioning those small errors of omission, of commission, to which even our saintly, if not at times holy, men and women occasionally fall heir. When Erikson dares confront that kind of moral ambiguity, however, he is at pains to be compassionate, tactful, and broadly understanding of a great moral and political leader's complex, unnerving life: such lives are often lived under exceptionally demanding, taxing circumstances, with grave threats around many corners, as Gandhi well knew, even as he tried to keep his (nonviolent) composure, hold fast and true to his political creed, his spiritual values.

Some of us who knew Erikson were quite aware that Gandhi might well be the last person whose life he'd try to understand, evoke, portray, given his advancing age upon completion of that effort—though we also knew how interested he was not only in Christianity, but in *its* leader. Even as the essay on Freud might have been placed in this section, linked to these biographical studies, which were the pride and joy of Erikson's writerly and analytic life, his last essay, which appears some pages down the line, because of its content and focus, was a hint, perhaps it can be said, of what an Erikson who lived to, say, one hundred, clearheaded and energetic, might have given us, but alas, could not—a portrait of the Jesus who walked the land of ancient Palestine, trying so very hard to touch and heal, to persuade and suggest and convince and console and inspire. For very sure, we can assume, as with all his biographical approaches to leaders, that a book on Jesus by him would have been carefully appreciative. For Erikson a leader of ethical or aesthetic reputation, distinction, deserves respectful interest and a writer's full, empathic responsiveness—a contrast, indeed, with the pitiably reductionist, jargon-filled biographic accounts certain psychoanalytically disposed writers have seen fit to impose on us, *their* motives as worth knowing as the ones they so relentlessly and ungenerously attribute to their "subjects."

THE LEGEND OF MAXIM
GORKY'S YOUTH¹

from *Childhood and Society*

I t is difficult today to learn much about Russia that is certain, relevant, and articulate at the same time. What little I know has recently been crystallized around the imagery of an old and yet vital Russian moving picture, and especially around the countenance of a boy who is its hero.

The moving picture tells the Bolshevik legend of Maxim Gorky's childhood. As before with the National Socialist version of Hitler's childhood, I shall analyze the imagery in relation to the geographic locus and the historical moment of its origin.² In some significant respects the two legends are not dissimilar. They both show a growing, self-willed youngster in bitter fight with a father who is a merciless tyrant yet himself a senile failure. Both Hitler and Gorky in adolescence fell mentally ill with the senselessness of existence and the futility of rebellion. They became intellectual proletarians, close to utter despair. It is an ironic coincidence that both were known on the police books of their respective countries as "paperhangers." But here the analogy ends.

Gorky became a writer, not a politician. True, after the Russian rev-

olution he continued to remain an idol of the Soviet state. He returned
to Russia, and he died there. Whether his death was mysterious or merely
mystified for political reasons we do not know. At his bier Molotov compared his loss to that of Lenin himself. But the reason for this national
stature certainly does not lie in doctrinaire fanaticism or in political as-
tuteness on the part of Gorky. For he, the friend of Lenin, said: "Differences of outlook ought not to affect sympathies; I never gave theories and
opinions a prominent place in my relation to people." In fact, one gath-
ers that both Lenin and Stalin were exceptionally lenient with Gorky in
ignoring certain acquaintances of his who were of questionable orthodoxy. The answer lies in the fact that Gorky, consciously and stubbornly,
was a writer of and for the people. He, the "vagrant" and the "provincial," lived in a double exile, one from the Tsarist police and the other
from the intellectual circles of his time. His *Reminiscences* show how
calmly and deliberately he delineated himself even in the presence of
such overpowering idols as Tolstoy.

Like Tolstoy, Gorky belongs to that epoch of Russian realism which
made literate Russia so cruelly self-observant and so miserably self-
conscious. But his writing did not surrender to the self-intoxication of
misery which pervades that of his greater contemporaries. He did not
end up in a fatal deadlock of good and evil, a final surrender to the
demons of the past, as did Tolstoy and Dostoevsky. Gorky learned to observe and to write simply, because he saw "the necessity of representing
exactly certain—most rare and positive—phenomena of actuality." The
moving picture portrays the growth of this frame of mind. Beyond that,
it illustrates a Russian dilemma, a Bolshevik dilemma, and, as I shall try
to show, the dilemma of a "protestant" frame of mind belatedly emerging in the countries of the East.

The film is an old one. At first it makes impossible demands on American eyes and ears. But in content, it seems easy as a fairy tale. It flows
along as a loose and sentimental narrative apparently designed to bring
the hero, little Alyosha, close to the heart of audiences who recognize
in it all their native Russia and their childhood, and who at the same
time know that this Alyosha will some day be the great Gorky. In the
Russians who saw the picture with me it left only nostalgic pensiveness,
and no aftertaste of political controversy. The legend is its own propaganda.

1. THE LAND AND THE MIR

At the beginning there is the Russian trinity: empty plains, Volga, balalaika. The vast horizons of central Russia reveal their dark emptiness; and immediately balalaika tunes rise to compassionate crescendos, as if they were saying, "You are not alone, we are all here." Somewhere along the Volga broad river boats deliver bundled-up people into isolated villages and crowded towns.

The vastness of the land and the refuge of the small, gay community thus are the initial theme. One is reminded of the fact that "mir," the word for village, also means world, and of the saying, "Even death is good if you are in the mir." A thousand years ago the Vikings called the Russians "the people of the stockades" because they had found them huddling together in their compact towns, thus surviving winters, beasts, and invaders—and enjoying themselves in their own rough ways.

A bulky boat docks by a pier, which is crowded with festive friends. Among them, a group of relatives close in on two arrivals: Varvara, the widowed mother, and her boy, Alyosha. His handsome little face first appears, wide-eyed and open-mouthed, as he emerges from behind his mother's long full skirts, eyeing with awe the noisy relatives who embrace and engulf them. And indeed, as he dares to show more of his face, practical jokers test the stamina of his curiosity. A mischievous little cousin puts out his tongue and hoots at him; an uncle grasps his nose and gently presses it in synchronization with the ship's whistle. A handsome young man laughs loudly when he sees him, good-naturedly so, but one cannot be sure. Finally, the boy is clouted on the head and pushed into a small boat.

The family is then seen marching up the center of the street tramping heavily in compact closeness, like a procession of pilgrims, or maybe a band of prisoners—or both. Undercurrents of hostile gossip become louder. Somebody whispers, "They are still fighting over their shares of the old man's property." Somebody suggests that Alyosha's widowed mother has come home to exact another dowry from her father. The grandmother, whose large frame leads the procession, whisperingly wails, "Children, children," as if the measure of progeny were overflowing.

Now we see this large family at home, crowded into a small room and immersed in a sequence of strange moods. A balalaika suggests tentative tunes of misery and nostalgia. As if in lieu of a prayer before the meal which is laid out before them, these people indulge in musical self-commiseration, together and yet each in his own preoccupied way. Old Gregory expresses the theme most strikingly: in rhythm with the song he beats his own head. It is not clear which he is enjoying more, the rhythm or the beating.

But as if enough were enough, Uncle Yakov's expression suddenly changes. He takes a sip (of vodka?), he smells a whiff (of an onion?) and plays a gay and rhythmic tune, singing some nonsense of crickets and roaches. There is an immediate and electrifying crescendo, too fast for a Western mind to comprehend. Then we see Gypsy dance the squatting dance.

Gypsy is young and handsome; and as he loosens his sleeves, pulls his shirttails out, and generally "unties" himself, he gives the most relaxedly vigorous performance of the whole picture. He leaps in the air, slaps his heels, and kicks his legs out from under him. The whole crowded room responds, as if in a gay earthquake. The furniture rocks, dishes jiggle, even the water in the decanter sways.

This most manly performance somehow is then replaced with a scene of generous femininity. The grandmother herself is prevailed upon to dance. Grandmother is really an enormous old woman, heavily wrapped in clothing, with a square head and broad face, and with a smile like the dawn. This heavy creature manages to be first childishly shy, then girlishly pleased, and then to move her strong frame in a sincerely serene fashion suggesting utter charm and lightness. She does not move her feet much, her body remains straight and regal; but as she slowly turns, she extends first one, then both of her arms, lifting her heavy shawl, as if baring to everybody her broad breasts.

At this moment she suddenly stops, pales, and draws her shawl around her shoulders. The music stops, motion freezes. All eyes stare at the door; grandfather has entered. To be sure: we had not even missed him. Yet nothing could be stronger than the implication that it was only in his absence that grandmother could bare her heart and her body to her children.

These vigorous scenes mark a happy beginning, or rather the reference to a happy past. As Westerners we had better prepare ourselves for the fact that there is no happy ending in this movie: no love story, no success story. What we see at the beginning is the remembrance of things past; at the end there will be a future of which only one thing is certain: it will be bitter. "Gorky" means "bitter."

For the grandfather has entered, and with him miserliness and the hate of men. His face is tense, his motions jerky; he is all secretive excitement. It seems that instead of joining them he left to buy a tablecloth, a white tablecloth. As he childishly shows it around, it becomes plain that to him the white tablecloth is a symbol of his status: He is trying to use the reception for an egotistic display of the fact that he is now rich enough to be able to afford a white tablecloth. He is the owner of a small dyeing establishment, yet exposed to proletarization.

Immediately whispers and shouts take up the question of his property. When is he going to retire, to distribute his wealth to his already nearly middle-aged sons?

As angry whispers increase, the grandfather shouts in a shrill, senile way: "Silence! I give to no one!" His voice betrays the despair but also the last strength of a cornered animal. The grandfather's shouting is like a signal for murderous glances between his sons. Soon the sons roll on the floor fighting one another in drunken rage. The grandfather's coat gets entangled and his sleeve is torn. He (quite surprisingly) turns against his wife. "Witch!" he whines. "You gave birth to wild animals!"—a theme to be remembered.

As the guests disperse in panic, as the festive table becomes a ruin, poor little Alyosha flees to the top of the stove, the refuge of babies. He has seen enough for his first day. So far he has not said a word. What it all meant and what it will mean to him in the end can be seen only in the way he acts or indeed refrains from participating, as his position is elaborated in a sequence of encounters.

So that we may concentrate on the nature of these encounters, I shall briefly outline the whole story.

Alyosha's father, Maxim Pyeshkov, had left the house of his in-laws, the Kashirins, years ago. He has died in a faraway region. Varvara, his wife, and Alyosha are forced to return to her family. The Kashirins are a greedy lot. The uncles (Vanya and Yakov) want the senile grandfather to turn his dye factory over to them. He refuses. At first they get even with him in "practical jokes." He revenges himself by flogging his small grandsons. One of the uncles sets fire to the establishment, and the disintegration of the family begins. Alyosha's mother eventually finds refuge in a marriage to a petty official and moves to the city. Alyosha is left with his grandparents and must witness the grandfather's economic and mental decline. He finds friends outside of the family first among the servants, then among the children of the town. At home, there are old Gregory, the foreman who during the fire loses his eyesight, and Ivan ("Gypsy"), the apprentice, who later dies. In the streets Alyosha befriends a gang of homeless boys and a crippled youngster, Lyenka. Most decisive, however, is his encounter with a mysterious boarder, who is later arrested by the police as an "anarchist." At the end we see Alyosha, now perhaps twelve or fourteen, set a resolute face toward the horizon. He leaves decay behind. Little is said of what lies ahead.

Throughout these scenes Alyosha does not say or do much. He participates rarely, but he observes eagerly, and mostly he reacts by refraining from participation. Such dramatization by non-action is hardly a feature of what we Westerners consider a story.

By studying the omissions as much as the commissions, I gradually became convinced that the very meaning of these scenes is that of way stations in the boy's resistance to temptation: temptations of a kind completely strange to us.

To translate it into terms of our radio announcements: will Alyosha submit to his grandmother's primitive fatalism? Will his mother's betrayal make him a pessimist? Will his grandfather's sadism provoke him into patricidal rage—and futile remorse? Will the fratricidal uncles induce him to share their crimes—and their drunken soul-baring? Will the blind and the crippled arouse paralyzing pity and cheap charity in him? Will it all deflect him from becoming a new Russian—from becoming Gorky?

Each scene and each significant person thus represents a temptation to regress to the traditional morality and to the ancient folkways of his people, to remain bound by the traditional superego within and by serfdom without. On the positive side, Alyosha is seen to become sure of himself, as if he had taken a secret vow; and he seems to devote himself with deepening fidelity to an unformulated goal.

Westerners, of course, have learned to identify what we here call temptations with the quaintness of the Russian soul—and with its brand of Christianity. And we get angry if people do not stick to the brand of soul which they have advertised and which has become their easy label. But we must try to understand: Alyosha, by virtue of his fate as a displaced Pyeshkov among the Kashirins, demonstrates the way stations of an emergent new Russian frame of mind, a Russian individualism. No

Luther, no Calvin has shown him new recesses of the mind; and no founding fathers and pioneers have opened up uncharted continents where he might overcome his inner and his outer serfdom. By himself, and in secret agreement with kindred minds, he must learn to protest, and to develop—in the very widest sense—a "protestant" morality.

2. THE MOTHERS

We have met with a display of grandmother's strength, charm, and generosity in the reception scene. By far the greatest temptation, and the one which accompanies Alyosha to the very end, is that of finding refuge in his grandmother's peace of mind (as—at the very beginning of the picture—he hid in his mother's full skirts) and becoming part of her calm conscience. This old woman seems to represent the matter-of-factness of the earth, the self-evident strength of the flesh, and the native stoutness of the heart. Her maternal generosity is boundless. Not only did she bear and nurse the Kashirin breed, whom she has learned to endure; she also found and fondled Gypsy, making the homeless boy free and gay.

It becomes increasingly clear to Alyosha that the grandmother is even nursing the wailing grandfather along. In the fatal matter of property distribution, her principles are simple if "unprincipled": "Give it away," she says; "you will feel better." And in the face of the old man's horror she says, "I'll go begging for you." At the same time she lets the senile man beat her, simply going down on her knees as if he had actually been strong enough to push her down. Alyosha is bewildered. "You are stronger than he!" he cries. "Yes," she acknowledges, "but he is my husband." Soon she becomes Alyosha's mother as well. For as Varvara leaves the grandmother says simply: "I will be his grandmother *and* his mother."

This woman seems to know no law but that of giving; no principles except the complete trust in her own inner endurance: in this she obviously symbolizes the primitive trust of the people, their ability to survive and to persist, and yet also their weakness in enduring what will ultimately enslave them.

Alyosha comes to accept the grandmother's grandiose endurance as something from another world. This world, it seems, is the oldest Russia and the deepest stratum of her—and his—identity. It is the primitive

Russia which persisted through the early Christian era, when wooden images survived forced baptisms and naïve Christianizations. It is the peace of mind of the original stockade, the primitive mir which had found some organization close to the earth and some faith in animistic dealings with the wild forces in nature. Grandmother still uses animistic practices in secret. She remembers the old ballads and can say them simply and forcefully. She is not afraid of God or of the elements. She proves to be on quite good terms with fire, which throughout the picture symbolizes destructive passion.

During the great fire grandmother enters the burning house to remove a bottle of vitriol; and she easily calms the horse which is rearing and plunging. "Did you really think I would let you burn in there?" she says, and the horse seems to be reassured. She accepts the passions of men as she accepts the fire: both are external if unavoidable evils. It is as if she had lived long before passions had made men ambitious, greedy, and, in turn, childishly repentant; and as if she expected to outlast it all.

Her passion, then is compassion. Even when she prays to God, she is most intimate with Him, as if He really resided in the icon right in front of her. Her approach is that of equality, or even that of a mother asking something of a child of hers who had happened to become God. She does not need to be destructive in her passion, because her conscience is without cruelty. Thus she is a primitive Madonna, a mother of God and man, and of spirits, too.

The grandmother thus assumes that place in the boy's life which women in Russia play traditionally for "anybody's" children: the role of the babushka, and that of the nyanya: women who are at home in this world because (and often only as long as) they make it a home for others. Like the big stove in the center of the house, they can be relied upon eternally—a reliance of the kind which makes a people endure and permits it to wait, to wait so long that reliance becomes apathy and stamina becomes serfdom.

Alyosha must not only learn to leave his mothers, but more, to leave without a residue of sinfulness which makes a straying soul penitently hold on to mother symbols: as if, in tearing himself away, he had destroyed his mother. For much of the morbid and unrestrained surrender of the soul had its source in the necessity of overcoming an overwhelming sense of having ravished and abandoned the maternal origin and of restoring by soul-fusion the earliest sense of home, of paradise.

That home, it seems, is not of necessity the real mother. There are series and degrees of motherhood in peasant Russia which prevent an exclusive mother-fixation and give the child a rich inventory of giving and frustrating mother-images. The babushka is and remains the representative of the mother-image of infancy, unmarred by the growing boy's oedipal jealousies.

In our picture Alyosha's "real" mother becomes vague and almost without a will of her own; she gradually recedes, first as a source of strength and then as an object of affection. There is a moment at the beginning when this mother, to protect her child, proudly sails into one of the unkind uncles, kicking him over like a piece of furniture. At this point Alyosha gives in to temptation and says loudly, "My mother is strong." The poor boy has to eat these words later, when he is flogged by his grandfather, while his awe-stricken mother can only whimper, "Don't do it, papasha." "*Now* is your mother strong?" echoes the mean little cousin. The weakness of women is not physical. It is that they "give in."

While the grandmother is a law unto herself and is unprincipled only because she antedates the principles of formulated morality, the mother chooses the hypocritical safety of petty officialdom. She sells herself in marriage to a uniformed lackey of a man, and explains to the boy that thus will she be able to buy freedom for him. This once, this single once, he acts violently, passionately. He insults the mother's suitor, throws himself on his bed, and cries as a child cries. As she leaves she immerses him once more in her physical presence, by enfolding him in her shawl. But there is no suggestion that he intends to follow her, to take advantage of her personal and social betrayal. "It seems to be your fate to stay with me," says old Kashirin. The boy is silent and grim.

One wonders: The traditional division and diffusion of motherhood in peasant Russia probably made the world a more reliable home, since mothering was not dependent on one frail relationship but was a matter of homogeneous atmosphere. And yet a bitter nostalgia was plainly related to the mother's turning to "another man," or the mother's permitting herself otherwise to be degraded and destroyed—or so it sometimes seems in the literature. As to Alyosha's new father, remember that Hitler's father, too, was an official, a member of the servile and yet officious "middling" class.

The Alyosha of the moving picture determinedly swallows his nostalgia. What such "swallowed nostalgia" did to the real Gorky we shall see

later when discussing his fits of anger and contempt and his strange attempt at suicide in young manhood. His writing long suffered from nostalgia. Chekhov wrote to him: "[Your] lack of restraint is felt especially
in the description of nature . . . in your description of women . . . and in
your love scenes. You speak a great deal about waves . . ."[3] Gorky worked
hard to overcome this weakness.

3. SENILE DESPOT AND CURSED BREED

The grandfather is a little man with "reddish beard, green eyes, and hands
that seemed to be smeared with blood, the dye had so eaten into the skin.
His abuse and prayers, his jests and moralizing, all merged in some strange
way into a rasping, caustic whine that ate like rust into one's heart."[4] The
movie reflects this description faithfully. The grandfather is depicted as
the destroyer of all boyish gaiety. He is a man dependent to the point of
childishness on his money and on his wife's strength. A sadistic-retentive
miser, he gradually regresses to the dependence of a beggar.

The variables of his character become most apparent in the flogging
scene. The anger of the man, which flared up at the violent end of the
reception scene, smoulders on. We become acquainted with the dye establishment where the uncles, hunched over their sewing, furtively think
of mean revenge. Practical jokes again precede more direct destruction.
The uncles make Sasha heat grandfather's thimble over a flame and put
it back in place. As he puts his outstretched finger into it, he "nearly goes
through the ceiling" with pain. But the grandfather's very core is invaded
when Alyosha, in his only boyish prank, is led by the other boys to dye
the new tablecloth, to destroy its whiteness. The grandfather decides to
flog the boys—on the Sabbath, after church.

The flogging is shown in slow detail: the grandfather's cold preparations; the women's dramatic but impotent intervention; the whining of
the whip and the writhing of the small bodies. Gypsy must hold them
down on the bench of torture.

After the flogging Alyosha lies in bed—on his face, for his back is
marked with long, thin welts. Suddenly the grandfather enters. The boy
views him first suspiciously, then angrily. But the grandfather dangles
nicely shaped cookies before his eyes. The boy kicks him, the old man ig-

nores it. Kneeling down by the boy's bed, he pleads with him: "You are not suffering for nothing, it will all add up." The sadist thus introduces the masochistic theme that suffering is good for salvation, that as we suffer we stack up credit for ourselves on a heavenly board of accounting. But he goes further. He speaks of his own sufferings as a Volga boatman, in his youth. When you draw barges in bare feet along river beaches with sharp stones, "your eyes fill, your soul weeps, your tears drop," he says with deep emotion. Again, the implication is that a man's suffering explains and excuses his imparting further suffering on those weaker than himself, a Russian form of saying, "What was good enough for me is good enough for you." The boy does not seem moved. He makes no gesture of peace; nor does he repay the outpouring of the grandfather's soul with an exchange of commiseration. The grandfather is called away.

Another temptation has passed: that of acquiring in a moment of torment an identification with the tormentor and with his sado-masochistic reasoning. If the boy had permitted his anger at this moment to turn into pity, if he had let his soul pour out to the tormentor who was opening his own soul to him, he would have acquired that pattern of masochistic identification with authority which apparently has been a strong collective force in the history of Russia. The Tsar, as the little white father, was just such a symbol of pitied autocracy. Even the man whom history called Ivan the Terrible was to his people only Ivan the Severe, for he claimed that as a child he had suffered under the cruelty of the court oligarchy.

The grandfather's sado-masochistic mood-swings are illustrated in other scenes. As his property slips away from him he wails before the icon, "Am I a worse sinner than the others?" The icon does not answer. But the grandmother takes him into her arms, almost on her lap. She calms him and promises to go begging for him. He collapses on her in foolish fondness, only to rally suddenly and to knock her down in a rage of jealousy, for he claims she loves the cursed breed more than she loves him. The implication is obvious that his wife is his property and his property is a kind of substitute mother without whom he cannot live. The "privileged owner's" utter defeat in the oedipal game is, of course, one of the implicit propagandistic notes of the picture—just as the defeat of Hitler's father was a necessary note in his imagery. The grandfather becomes more and more senile, and becomes useless as a provider.

In one of the final scenes Alyosha brings his fight with his grandfather to victorious conclusion. He has just given grandmother a coin which he has earned; she looks tenderly at him. At this point Alyosha becomes aware of his grandfather's eyes, which are narrowed down with hate. Alyosha takes on the challenge and a duel of the eyes ensues. The boy's eyes become thin as razor blades and it is as if the two wanted to pierce and cut one another with their glances. They both know that this is the end, and that the boy must leave. But he leaves undefeated.

This cutting of eye by eye is an impressive encounter. Yet there is something Russian about this particular use of the eye as an aggressive and defensive weapon. In Russian literature there is endless variation in the use of the eye as a soulful receptor, as an avid grasper, and as the very organ for mutual soulful surrender. In regard to the great models of political and literary life, however, the emphasis is on the eye as an incorruptible instrument for the manipulation of the future. Gorky's description of Tolstoy is typical: "With sharp eyes, from which neither a single pebble nor a single thought could hide itself, he looked, measured, tested, compared." Or again, his eyes are "screwed up as though straining to look into the future."

Equally typical is Trotsky's description of Lenin: "When Lenin, his left eye narrowed, receives a wireless containing a speech he resembles a devilishly clever peasant who does not let himself be confused by any words, or deluded by any phrases. That is highly intensified peasant shrewdness, lifted to the point of inspiration."[5]

The scene of the grandfather sitting by the bedside of his bruised grandson, in that shabby hut, begging his forgiveness, somehow reminded me of a famous Russian painting showing a similar scene in a palace: Ivan the Terrible sits by the corpse of his oldest son, whom he has murdered. Paternal violence à la Kashirin characterizes Russia's leading families from the beginning of history, and it permeates the literature of the prerevolutionary epoch. In both it developed to heights of crude violence unknown in comparable regions and periods of history. The coincidence of these two scenes invites a digression into history.

The original Slavs were peaceful and prolific peasants, hunters, and stockade dwellers. About a thousand years ago they asked Rurik, a Viking, to undertake their protection against nomadic invaders from the south. They apparently thought to buy, against reasonable concessions, peace and the permission to maintain the status quo of hunting with primitive weapons, of cultivating the soil with their crude wooden tools, and of worshiping their wooden idols and nature gods. Whatever forced them to surrender their autonomy to those shiningly armored, light-skinned warriors of the north, they received more protection than they had bargained for. The protectors begot sons who wanted to be in on the protection business. "Foreigners" muscled in. Soon, protecting the people against other protectors became an established occupation. The first prince initiated the grand-prince system, a kind of rank-order of residences for his sons which led to endless feuds over the cities which first emerged: Kiev and Novgorod. Such feuds were repeated over and over in smaller and larger segments of the land, making the people at last wish and pray for the one "strong father," the central authority who would unite the various sons even if he had to murder them all. Thus in early Russian history the stage was set for the interplay of the people who needed guidance and protection against enemies; the oligarchic protectors who became petty tyrants; and the central super-tyrant who was a captive of the oligarchy and a secret redeemer.

The protectors forcibly introduced Christianity (of the Byzantine variety) and with it another hierarchy which forever remained locked in conflict with itself and with the worldly princes. While both the princes and the priests had their cultural and often their ethnic origins in a variety of other lands, they gradually began to perform the spectacle which the books call Russian history: a sequence of dynastic struggles which not only survived the terrible Tartar invasion but gained in violent momentum and national scope. By way of counterpoint, these led to the establishment of a nation, of a Russian Christianity, and of a Russian tsardom: in the fifteenth century Moscow became "the third Rome" and Ivan III the first ruler of all the Russians and the Protector of the True Faith. He made ancient Russia into a national state; his son expanded this Russian state over its numerous and varied neighbors.

With Ivan the Terrible the tradition, existing since the tenth century, of "quarrelsome and murderous sons" reached its climax. Parricide had abounded in high circles for centuries. But Ivan, whom history calls "the Terrible," slew his oldest, his favorite, son with his own hands. He (like old Kashirin at bruised Alyosha's bedside) blamed his sufferings as a boy for the cruel madness of his manhood. The people agreed. As I have pointed out, they did not call him the Terrible, as did history; they called

him the Severe. For had he not been the victim of the oligarchic aristocracy—his enemies, and the people's—who had made his boyhood
miserable? And indeed this first Tsar had turned in his saner moments to
the people, had permitted them to petition him, had initiated judiciary
reforms and introduced printing. In his insaner states he continued to
gloat over lists of murdered aristocrats, only to indulge, in turn, in the
most abject remorse. The people idolized and gladly strengthened the authority of this Tsar in order to keep the princes, aristocrats, and middle
classes in check.

As centralization progressed and national organization developed, the
paradoxes of Russian history became self-perpetuating. For one: with
every step toward organized and centralized statehood in this immense
land, the number of middlemen increased. They governed and policed
"for the Tsar," they taught school and collected taxes, and they extorted
and corrupted. It is an old theme in Russia that every progress on a national scale is paid for with new power to a bureaucracy—which explains
an "inborn" hostile indifference of the people both to progress in general and to the contemporary oligarchy in particular.

Secondly, every step toward Westernization and enlightenment led to
increased serfdom. Ivan, in pursuit of his holy "severity," robbed the peasants of their right to change masters on St. George's day. Catherine,
friend and enlightened correspondent of Voltaire, gave away 800,000
crown slaves to be tortured and sold at will by individual aristocratic
owners. And when much later Alexander II liberated twenty million
slaves, because he feared that they might liberate themselves, he only exposed them to landlessness, proletarization, and at best the necessity of
tilling with antiquated tools small portions of land to be paid for in installments.

But what interests us here is the third paradox: the people's tacit permission for these tsars to behave in a grandiosely irrational way. Peter the
Great, a precocious boy and impetuous like Ivan, was Russia's first emperor and the greatest of Russia's monarchic reformers. He, too, murdered his oldest son, although with progressing civilization he used his
secret police, not a club in his own hands. In addition to such outright
family murders, there were in Russian history all kinds of strange regency
arrangements. There were mysterious and immensely popular pretenders,
alleged sons of murdered tsars, who, like Alyosha, came back to challenge
the evildoers; and who were almost holy by mere virtue of not belong-

ing to the dominant "cursed breed." Maybe the height of oedipal atrocity was reached when near-demented Tsar Paul (the people called him the Poor), at the death of his mother Catherine, had his father (whom she had murdered) exhumed and put beside her. He forced her numerous lovers to stand splendid military guard over the decomposition of the imperial corpses.

Historians take it for granted that such is "history." But how explain not only a people's passive consent to but passionate altruistic identification with such imperial tragedies and comedies? Why should a sturdy and prolific people have bowed to foreign protectors? Why did it admit their system into its national life, involving its very life style ever deeper in a relationship of mutual possessedness? Is the explanation to be sought first in the superiority of murderous nomads and wild beasts, and then in the impotence of this immense population against the armed oligarchy?

The answer is probably that forms of leadership are defined not only by the historical dangers to be warded off by the work of organization; they must also serve the public display of popular phantasies and anticipations. Monarchs, even if foreign (and often, because they are foreign) become visible safeguard of a people's weak inner moral forces; aristocratic elites, personifications of dimly perceived new ideals. It is for this purpose that monarchs and aristocrats may and must play out on the stage of history the full cycle of irrational conflict: they must sin more defiantly and atone more deeply, and finally emerge with increased personal and public stature. While they try to accomplish this cycle, the people will gladly serve as their whispering chorus and their sacrificial animals. For the grandiose sin of a few promises total salvation to all.

This, then, is more than a "projection" either of inner badness (the id) or of inexorable conscience. I think it has also a collective ego function; it serves the development of a better-defined national and moral identity. Ivan and Peter are great, not in spite of the tragic passions which seemingly marred their stature as leaders, but because they could display on a gigantic scale the tragedy of early patriarchal organization and its inner counterpart, the superego; and because in doing so, they advanced national consciousness and national conscience, each by a decisive step. Maybe our concept of history must be expanded to include an analysis of the dynamic demands made by the governed masses on their most "self-willed" masters who thus are forced to act out the conflicts of human evolution on the macrocosmic stage of history: in this sense, perhaps, kings are the toys of the people. In later stages of civilization their tragedies and comedies are transferred to a fictitious macrocosm, the stage, and finally, to the microcosm of fiction.

We can now see the historical mission of Russian realistic literature: it put the tragedy of patricide and fratricide back into the ordinary Russian himself—to be read by the literate.[6] Such literary pronouncement of individual responsibility parallels the growth of political responsibility. Russian literature and Russian history were late and explosive in reaching—in one terrifyingly condensed century—the preliminary stages of an effective literary consciousness and of a political conscience, while the backwardness of the vast peasant masses continued to reflect a primitive historical level which the West had left behind in Hellenic days.

Let us pause here also to remember that at the time of the Russian revolution four-fifths of the Russian population were peasants. The gigantic task of the outer transformation and inner conversion of these masses of peasants can hardly be overestimated, not because they wanted another form of government, but because they had never thought of an organized interlocking of their daily lives with any form of government.

The moving picture's characterization of the moody "breed" points to at least one collective complex of a singularly archaic character which has kept the peasant masses of Russia (and, in fact, of much of the Eurasian continent) in inner serfdom as their outer serfdom was assured by princes and priests. I refer to the psychological consequences of an ancient technological upheaval: the agricultural revolution. Here the mysteries of prehistory are as deep as those of early childhood. They both force us to mythologize in order to gain the beginning of an understanding.

In connection with the hunters and fishermen of prehistoric North America we employed one key which opened certain primitive rituals to interpretation. We pointed out that pre-literate human beings try to understand and to master the great Unknown in its expansion in space and time by projecting the attributes of human structure and growth on it: thus geographic environment is personified, and historical past is endowed with the imagery of human childhood. In this sense, then, the earth becomes a mother who, once upon a time, gave of her own free will. The transition from nomadic to agricultural life implied the usurpation of segments of land, and their partition; the violation of the soil with coercive tools; the subjugation of the earth as an enforced provider. Whatever inner evolution accompanied this technological step, it was (as myths and rituals attest) associated with that primal sin which, in individual life, consists of the first awareness of the violent wish to control the mother with the maturing organs of bite and grasp.

The "cursed breed" then represents the children who in their rapacity would jealously usurp and destroy the mother; and the men, whom the task of collectively tilling the soil made ambitious, jealous, and exploitive. Thus the sense of a primal guilt, which we discussed earlier, chains the peasant to the cycle of sorrowful atonement and manic feasting as it makes him dependent on the productive year. Christianity, of course, took hold of this self-perpetuating cycle and superimposed on it its own yearly calendar of sin and expiation, of death and redemption.

I can conclude this dark subject only by referring to a memoir of Gorky's which betrays the identification of cultivated earth and conquered woman and the manic challenge of her master.[7]

He [Chekhov] used to say:

"If every man did all he could on the piece of earth belonging to him, how beautiful would this world be!"

I had started to write a play called Vasska Busslaev and one day I read to him Vasska's boastful monologue:

> "Ha, were I only endowed with more strength and power
> I'd breathe a hot breath—and make the snows melt!
> I'd go round the earth and plough it through and through!
> I'd walk for years and years and build town after town,
> Put up churches without number, and grow gardens without end;
> I'd adorn the earth—as though it were a maiden fair;
> Clasp it in my arms—as though it were my bride;
> Lift it to my heart, and carry it to God: . . . .
>
> "I'd have given it to you, Lord, as a fine gift—
> Only—no—it would not do—I am too fond of it myself!"

Chekhov liked this monologue very much, and coughing excitedly said:

"That's very fine indeed! Very true, and very human! In this lies

the essence of all philosophy. Man has made the earth habitable—
therefore he must also make it comfortable for himself."

He shook his head in obstinate affirmation and repeated:

"He will!"

He asked me to read Vasska's boastful speech over again. I did so and
he listened attentively to the end, then he remarked:

"The last two lines are unnecessary—they are impertinent. There is
no necessity for that. . . ."

4. THE EXPLOITED

A. Saint and Beggar

Gypsy, the foundling, was not born in sin like the rest of the breed, the
uncles, the "wild animals." Not having been born in sin, he has, as the
grandmother puts it, a "simple soul." He has a graceful body, as he well
demonstrated in his squatting dance, while the other men seem wooden
and unfree in their motions and when drunk or enraged are like trucks
without brakes. Not being anybody's son, Gypsy expects no property and
envies none. It is as if his orphanhood suggested immaculate conception.
And, indeed, in a subtle way, Gypsy is pictured as a primal Christian, charitable and always in hope.

Gypsy speaks to Alyosha of his dead father. He was different: *he understood.* For this reason he was hated by the Kashirins. Here a theme is
introduced which is later taken up at the appearance of the anarchist, the
representative of those who understand and accept homelessness. They
are hated by the fathers and their rapacious sons as bearers of an entirely
new principle which cannot be fought with old weapons: they read,
think, plan. Thus it is Gypsy who provides Alyosha's eager soul with the
imagery of his future identity.

Gypsy recognizes those who understand but he himself does not "understand." He has another fault and is dangerously different in another
way: he is *"good."* After the flogging his arm shows bloody welts, and he
confesses cheerfully that in holding the boy down on the bench he had
let his arms absorb the heaviest blows. "I took the blows for love," he tells
the spellbound boy, whose heart goes out to him. But then Gypsy ex-
pounds on methods of how to take blows. Don't shrink back, he tells

him, but try to relax. And shout as much as you wish. He confesses that he has taken so many blows that his hide would make good book covers.

Again, the implication of this scene is not formulated. But it seems to concern the temptation of naïve non-violence, of Christian goodness, and of learning to endure the pains of the world by adjusting to its beatings. Alyosha is touched and fascinated, but remains reserved. And indeed, soon after, Gypsy dies in a picturesque and symbolic way and he must bear the loss.

One of the uncles wants to erect a huge cross for his dead wife (whom, as Gypsy knows, he has murdered). He asks Gypsy to help him carry it up the designated hill. As everybody can see, the enormous cross is too heavy for one man. But Gypsy in childlike pride boasts that he can carry it on his back—all alone. Alyosha for a moment feels an urge to help him; the audience trembles with fear that the little boy may try to help support that big cross, but then—as at several highly critical moments—Alyosha simply lets himself be deflected, and leaves his friend to his fate.

In a scene obviously intended to suggest Calvary, Gypsy is seen in silhouette stumbling up a faraway hill with the huge cross on his bent back. It apparently crushes him, for soon he is carried back to the house, where he dies on the floor. A little white mouse, with which he has endlessly entertained himself and the children, escapes from his clothing and runs over to Alyosha, who catches it. It is as if Gypsy's "white soul" had found a new home, in Alyosha.

If the grandmother represents the primitive folkways, and the grandfather and the uncles the greedy era of the ownership of lands and goods and wives and titles, then Gypsy is the simple saint of a primitive Christian era. He is cheerfully good, and charitable to the end.

This boy Alyosha, then, watches the pre-ordained destruction around him and yet maintains a sleepwalker's surefootedness in the avoidance of fatal involvements and of traditional pitfalls. Does Alyosha have no sympathy, no morality?

Take his encounter with old Gregory, the very individual who drags him away as Gypsy's Calvary approaches (for Gregory, nearly blind, can see what lies ahead). He is an impressive, a prophetic figure. But he has worked in the grandfather's dye factory for nearly four decades, and faces unemployment when his waning eyesight is gone. Because the grandfather refuses to take care of him, Gregory will have to go begging. Alyosha is horrified. "I will go with you," he cries compassionately. "I will lead you by the hand!"

But after the fire, as blinded Gregory stumbles around with out-stretched arms, miserably calling Alyosha, the boy hides from him and lets him stumble on alone in his eternal night. Two or three times he is later shown following Gregory, then a beggar on the street and on the fair-ground. In fact, Alyosha stalks Gregory as if fascinated by the sight.

The Western movie-goer cannot help thinking what a touching picture they would make together, the tall blinded patriarchal figure and the boy who leads him by the hand. He envisages an ending where the tormented grandfather reforms and sends out a statewide alarm for the two, when it may be almost too late. The sheriff's posse or the state motorcycle patrol reaches the old man and the small boy just as they are about to reach a bridge weakened by a flooded river. . . .

But it is clear that what we are watching in this picture is the emergence of a new frame of mind, which to us is primarily characterized by its omissions. What is omitted, again and again, is action based on a sense of guilt. Thus neither remorse nor reform seem to count in this new frame of mind. What counts is critical caution, incorruptible patience, absolute avoidance of wrong action, the ripening of clear inner direction, and then—action.[8]

The Western observer at this point decides that the picture has less than a moral, that it is amoral. It may be, however, that the picture merely poses moral alternatives quite different from those to which our Judaeo-Christian world is committed. When Alyosha avoids being drawn into the temptation of sacrificing his young life to the blind old man he breaks, it is true, a promise to an individual—a promise possibly made on the basis of a sense of shared guilt, a sense that he should make up for his grandfather's economic sins. Opposed to this "temptation" however, there is an inner vow, a vow to follow a direction, an as yet indistinct plan which, instead of the self-perpetuation of inner guilt, will lead to co-operative action beyond good and evil. Such a vow is personified by another member of the cast: the anarchist.

But a final scene should be noted which in its crude imagery shows the utter contempt of the new generation for the moral collapse of the old. As the by now thoroughly senile grandfather begs his way through the crowd at the fair, old Gregory, his erst-while foreman, responds to his wail and hands him a piece of bread. The grandfather, now recognizing the blind man, throws the bread away, crying: "You have eaten me out of my house!" It is a cruel scene, from our point of view; but little Alyosha turns away from it, not even with visible disgust. To leave the ruins of men and systems behind seems to be a job which does not call for any expenditure of emotion.

B. The Stranger

All this time there is a man in the village, in fact in a room of grandfather's house, who belongs nowhere and speaks with no one. He is not a serf, and yet he owns nothing; he has nothing to sell, and yet he seems to eat. He calls himself a chemist, yet he does not seem to hold a job. With his black hair, his high forehead, and his sharp, bespectacled eyes, he looks like a youngish, somewhat starved Trotsky.

As Alyosha one day trustingly slides through this man's window into his underground room, the man quickly hides a book. Then he calmly gases the boy out of his room by opening a bottle with some malodorous vapors. The boy is offended, but even more fascinated.

He sees the man again at a meeting at which the grandmother sings ancient legends and ballads. In simple and strong words we hear her recite a long legend which contains the sentence: *"Behind the conscience of others he did not hide."* At this the man gets strangely excited as if hearing an oracle. He mumbles something concerning "the people, our people" (which apparently refers to the quality of old folk wisdom) and leaves the room hurriedly. It may be symbolical that, thus swayed with emotions, he leaves his glasses behind. At any rate, Alyosha picks them up.

In the next scene Alyosha sees the strange man lying in the grass on top of the cliff overlooking the river. The man hardly thanks him for the glasses. In fact, he somewhat rudely indicates that the boy may sit beside him if he can manage to be quiet and to join his contemplative mood. Thus this man, the river, the vast horizon, and a new frame of mind become and remain associated. The man's commanding presence seems to proclaim that you must be able to be silent; you must be able to meditate; you must be willing to envisage the distant horizon. Explicitly he says: "You must remember all the legends the grandmother knows. You must learn to read and to write." Alyosha is astonished, but apparently takes a deep liking to the man's fervor and sincerity.

Their friendship does not last long; or rather, their friendship must outlast a very short acquaintance, for the greedy grandfather forces the stranger to vacate his room and the man decides to leave town.

A gang of homeless boys accompany him to the river. But he puts his arm on Alyosha's shoulder. According to the English caption, he passionately tells the boy: "One must learn how to take life." He says this with such missionary fervor that one senses a significance in it which surpasses the words used. Here we must turn linguist.

The man's gestures indicate that he means "take" in the sense of grasping or holding on, and not in the sense of enduring or holding out. Yet when I saw the picture the first time, my Russian interpreter insisted that the man had said *"brat' "*—take = endure. For reasons to be discussed presently, this difference seemed so basic that I persisted in inquiring into the origin of the discrepancy between the word and the gesture. And indeed, in the book on which this movie is based, the revolutionary says: "One must know how to take (Russian *wzyat'*) each single thing. Do you understand? It is very difficult to learn how to take *(wzyat')." Wzyat'* means "to take" in the sense of "grasp." It is apparent, then, that the word but not the meaning was lost somewhere between the book and the picture.

The meaning is: One must learn not to wait until one is given, one must grasp what one wants and hold on to it. We have discussed this alternative in connection with the social modalities of the oral stages. Obviously this man does not only mean to say that one must grasp, but also that one must do so with a good conscience, with a new conscience; that one must grasp and not regress from sheer sense of sin over having grasped.

As we shall see, this determined "grasping," paired with a resistance against sinking back into dependence, is of outstanding importance in the Bolshevik psychology. We have already reported on Alyosha's piercing, cutting way of reacting to the grandfather's hateful glance; we have pointed to the importance of focusing, comprehending, grasping in vision and foresight; and we have shown his incorruptibility of purpose, irrespective of personal feelings.

It later becomes apparent that the stranger was a revolutionary. The police were looking for him. They caught up with him somewhere beyond the horizon; for one day when a miserable group of shabby, shackled prisoners pass through Alyosha's street on their way to the boat and to Siberia, the stranger is among them, pale and ghostlike but almost gay.

The caption says, "Thus ended my friendship with the first of a series of strangers in their own country—the best people."

Alyosha, then, has come face to face with a member of the underground of professional revolutionaries, called for a time intelligentsia because of their religious belief in the necessity not only of reading and writing but also of mental discipline as the salvation from apathy, lethargy, and serfdom.

C. Fatherless Gang and Legless Child

As the anarchist disappears, Alyosha seems to grow in stature. He now has a goal, a fellowship. We must remember that his father, too, "understood"—and disappeared. Yet we are horrified to watch this mere boy identify with the martyred ghost of a man whose ethos was contained in a few obscure remarks. Alyosha is a mere child; where is his childhood, who are his age mates? Does he ever play?[9]

We saw the abortive participation in the practical jokes of his cousins and their malicious and devious ways of getting even with the old man. The flogging scene—or, shall we say, the greater maturity following the grandfather's moral defeat after the flogging scene—put an end to that. In a later scene, as Alyosha looks around the neighborhood, he comes across a group of well-fed children who with stones and yells have fallen upon an idiot boy. Alyosha immediately stands up for the idiot, whereupon they turn on him by calling him a "Kashirin." He protests, "I am a Pyeshkov." Like boys all the world over, they end up by throwing words at one another: Kashirin! Pyeshkov! Kashirin! Pyeshkov! But as the boys begin to beat and kick him, a gang of starved and ragged young creatures appears suddenly, frees him, and immediately befriends him.

This gang consists of homeless boys—"proletarians" in the original sense. Alyosha becomes one of them, economically, in that he joins their occupation of searching garbage pits for items that can be sold to junk dealers; spiritually, in that he shares their feeling that they cannot rely on their parents—if, indeed, they have any. Thus in a few scenes Alyosha's proletarization is dramatically demonstrated. He, a fatherless Pyeshkov, takes the side of the idiot boy who is born with inferior endowment; he associates with those who have sunk below all caste and class. In one impressive scene he stumbles upon the fact that one of the gang, a boy with Asiatic features, does not even know where he came from. Alyosha

laughs; it is the last display of thoughtless gaiety. Seeing the Asiatic's despair and rage, he becomes immune to one more temptation: to be proud
of the name Pyeshkov. (As we know, he later chose his father's first name,
Maxim, and the last name Gorky, which means bitter.)

Now he is a proletarian too. After "work" he and his gang lie up on
the cliff—that mild elevation from which the dispossessed look toward
the horizon and the future. There they dream—of what? Of keeping pigeons so that they can set them free: "I love to see pigeons circling in the
bright summer sky."

This suggestion of freedom is counterpointed by one more encounter.
One day Alyosha hears a gay young voice from a cellar window. He follows the voice and finds Lyenka, a crippled boy, in bed. His legs are paralyzed, they "don't live, they are just there," as he explains. He is thus
imprisoned in his cellar. But he proves to be living in a world of his own,
a world of play and daydreams. He keeps little animals in boxes and
cages. They must share his captivity. But he lives for the day when he will
see the meadows and the prairie, and then he will open all the little
boxes and set the animals free. In the meantime they are his microcosm:
they reflect the world outside. One little roach is "the landlord," another
the "official's wife." The very oppressors of the real world are the captives
of his play world. It is as if his crippled state permitted him to be the only
child with a playful mind in the picture. His laugh is the gayest and freest;
his eyes are full of a delighted sparkle. His sense of power seems to know
no bounds; he is sure, he tells Alyosha excitedly, that "a mouse could grow
to be a horse."

Seeing the boy's love for the animal companions of his imprisonment
and his necessity and ability to invest a small thing like a mouse with
mythical possibilities, Alyosha after a faint trace of hesitation gives him
Gypsy's white mouse. This little mouse, we remember, had been Gypsy's
dying gift to him. It was his last link to gaiety; it was his last toy. Why does
he give it away? Is it pity, charity? Again Alyosha seems to grow in moral
stature by sacrificing a comfort, and by resisting a temptation: the temptation to play, to dream, to hang on to fetishistic substitutes which make
prisons more bearable, and thus add to their shackles. He knows that he
will have to go without a toy. Thus, each of Alyosha's acts (or refusals to
act) is like a vow. One after another, the bridges of regression are cut and
the infantile comforts of the soul forever denied.

Lyenka, however, can get free only if somebody will make him free, will give him legs. And this is what Alyosha puts the "gang" to work on. From among the treasures which they salvage from the garbage heaps, they save items of machinery out of which they build him a carriage, a mechanical prosthesis of locomotor freedom.

D. The Swaddled Baby

The figure of Lyenka does not seem to be taken from Gorky's book. I do not know who invented it. But it seems significant that this most emotive and gay of all the children is, as it were, the least motional. His delight reaches to the horizons, but his legs are tied, "are not alive, just there." This suggests a discussion of an outstanding Russian problem of child training which has assumed an almost ludicrous prominence in recent discussions of the Russian character: swaddling.

Is the Russian soul a swaddled soul? Some of the leading students of Russian character, to which I owe my first acquaintance with this moving picture, definitely think so.[10]

In the great Russian peasant population, and to a varying degree in all the regions and classes which shared and continue to share the common cultural heritage of the great central plains of Russia, the item of child care called swaddling was developed to an extreme. While the custom of bandaging newborn infants is widespread, the ancient Russian extreme insists that the baby be swaddled up to the neck, tightly enough to make a handy "log of wood" out of the whole bundle, and that swaddling be continued for nine months, for the greater part of the day and throughout the night. Such procedure does not result in any lasting locomotor deficiency, although the unswaddled infant apparently has to be taught to crawl.

When asked why babies must be swaddled, simple Russians have answered with astonishment: What other way was there to carry a baby and to keep him warm through a Russian winter? And besides, how could one otherwise keep him from scratching and harming himself, and of scaring himself with the sight of his own hands? Now it is probably true that a swaddled baby, especially when just unswaddled, has not sufficient mastery over his own movements to keep from scratching and hitting himself. The further assumption that *therefore* he has to be swaddled again is a favorite trick of cultural rationalization. It makes a particular pattern of infant-restraint culturally self-supporting. You must swaddle the infant to protect him against himself; this causes violent vasomotor needs in him; he must remain emotionally swaddled in order not to fall victim to wild emotion. This, in turn, helps to establish a basic, a preverbal, indoctrination, according to which people, for their own good, must be rigidly restrained, while being offered, now and then, ways of discharging compressed emotion. Thus, swaddling falls under the heading of those items of child training which must have a significant relation to the world image of the whole culture.

And indeed, there is no literature which, like the Russian, abounds in vasomotor excess. People in Russian fiction seem both isolated and effusive. It is as if each individual were strangely imprisoned in himself as in a restraining box of strangled emotions. Yet he is forever seeking other souls by sighing, paling, and blushing, by weeping and fainting. Many of the characters populating this literature seem to live for the moment when some intoxication—glandular, alcoholic, or spiritual—will permit a temporary fusion of emotion, often only an illusory mutuality which must end in exhaustion. But we need not look beyond the motion picture under discussion: if daily Russian reality of young Gorky's time manifested a fraction of the loudness, intensity, and variety of emotional expression which we see in this picture, the small child's awareness of emotion must be vivid and kaleidoscopic.

It is interesting to reflect, then, that the swaddled baby, when he becomes aware of such emotionality, is himself hindered from responding to it in a "motional" way, such as kicking with arms and legs or moving his fingers. He is hindered from lifting his head, from grasping support, and from extending his visual field over the auditory sources of the perceived commotion. Such an arrangement can, indeed, be thought of as burdening the vasomotor system with the task of buffeting and balancing all these vivid impressions. Only during the periodical experience of being unswaddled would the baby partake of his elders' effusiveness.

However, in order to evaluate the significance of an item of child training such as swaddling in the totality of a culture's configuration, it would be necessary to assume not a single one-way chain of causality in the sense that Russians are the way they are—or like to appear or to picture themselves—because they have been swaddled. As in our discussion of other cultures we must rather assume a reciprocal amplification of a number of themes. Thus the almost universal—and incidentally, quite practical—custom of swaddling would have received amplification as a result of that synthesizing trend which put geography, history, and human childhood over a few common denominators. We observe a configurational affinity between these facts of Russian tradition.

1. The compact social life in a lonely stockade isolated in the rigors of the central plains and its periodic liberation after the spring thaws;
2. The long periods of tight swaddling alternating with moments of rich interchange of joyous affection at the time of unswaddling; and
3. The sanctioned behavior of wooden endurance and apathetic serfdom on the one hand, and on the other, periodic emotional catharsis achieved by effusive soul-baring.

Historically and politically seen, swaddling, then, would appear to be part of a system of stubborn institutions which have helped to support and prolong the Russian combination of serfdom and "soul." And, indeed, Gorky said in his play *Philistines*: "When a man is tired of lying on one side, he turns over on the other, but when he is tired of the conditions in which he lives he only grumbles. Then make an effort—and *turn over!*" A man, properly motivated, can make an effort to turn over or indeed, as we would say, to get up; but in the face of the adversity of being chained to certain conditions his mind may act according to its earliest experience of being tied down. And what the swaddled baby can do least of all is turn over. He can only sink back, give in, be patient, and hallucinate, dwelling on his vasomotor sensations and on the adventures of his bowels, till the moment of locomotor liberation comes again upon him.

Something of this kind may well be symbolized by Lyenka, the child with the greatest emotion and with the most impaired motion; the child with the most vivid imagination and the greatest dependence on others. When Alyosha gives him the little white mouse it is as if he were growing beyond the necessity of holding on to a play fetish and to dreams of omnipotence such as swaddled and imprisoned souls may be in need of. He does not pity Lyenka. Rather, he recognizes his state, compares it with his own, and acts accordingly. He sees to it that Lyenka gets mechanized legs—but he does not identify with him.

While the motion picture does not show Alyosha and his gang at play, Gorky's *Reminiscences* gives an account of a fantastic game indulged in by these young "outlaws." As we shall see, Gorky's interpretation of this game is entirely in tune with the theories advanced in our chapter on play.

> As a lad of about ten I used to *lie down under a ballast train,* competing in audacity with my chums, one of whom, the postman's son, played the game with particular cool-headedness. It is an almost safe amusement, provided the furnace of the locomotive is raised high enough and the train is moving up-hill, not down-hill—for then the brake-chains of the cars are tightly stretched, and can't strike you or, having caught you, fling you on to the sleepers. For a few seconds you experience an eerie sensation, you *try to press as flat and close to the ground* as possible, and with the exertion of your whole will to *overcome the passionate desire to stir, to raise your head.* You feel that the stream of iron and timber, rushing over you, tears you off the ground and *wants to drag you off* somewhere, and the rumble and grinding of the iron rings as it were in your bones. Then, when the train has passed, you lie motionless for a minute or more, *powerless to rise,* seeming to swim along after the train; and it is as if your body stretches out endlessly, grows, *becomes light, melts into air,* and—the next moment you will be flying above the earth. It is very pleasant to feel all this.
>
> "What fascinated you in such an absurd game?" asked Andreyev.
>
> I said that perhaps we were testing the power of our wills, by opposing to the mechanical motion of huge masses the conscious immobility of our puny little bodies.
>
> "No," he replied, "that is too good; no child could think of that."
>
> Reminding him of how children love to "tread the cradle"—to swing on the supple ice of a new frozen pond or of a shallow river-bank, I said that they generally liked dangerous games.[11]

I have italicized those passages which suggest (in accordance with our theories of trauma and play) a further meaning in this game. An audacious gang could be said here to challenge a ballast train to provide them with an experience in which the essential elements of a childhood trauma common to all are eerily repeated: immobility and violent motion, utter powerlessness and the lightest of emotion.

Whatever the "swaddling hypothesis" proves or fails to prove in regard to the transformation of infantile experience into juvenile and adult patterns, it does seem to point to configurations of experience singularly alive in Russian behavior and imagination.

In the moving picture, Alyosha does not participate in any games. He keeps his eyes open, if often narrow with inquisitiveness: he "lifts his head," focuses his vision, tries to apprehend and to perceive with clarity and to concentrate with discipline—all of this in order eventually to grasp life. The picture says more about the things he frees himself *from,* than about the things he wants to be free *for.*

5. THE PROTESTANT

Alyosha is leaving. The gang accompanies him to the fields. On the little wagon, now completed, they take Lyenka along. Lyenka is beside himself with joy and anticipation: he is in motion and he is going to set his animals free. In a scene which would well have marked the happy ending of the movie in any other culture, Lyenka throws his precious birds up in the air and lets them take to their wings and to the endless spaces. But as the gang waves and shouts good-by, Alyosha simply and un-emotionally sets his face toward the horizon.

Where is he going, the youth with steel in his eyes? The picture does not say. Obviously he is leaving to become Gorky, and beyond that, to become a new kind of Russian. What became of young Gorky, and what marked the new Russian?

Gorky went to study in the University of Kazan. "If anybody had proposed to me 'Go and study, but on condition that you'll be publicly birched every Sunday on Nikolayewsky Square' I most likely would have agreed."[12] But he soon felt the discrimination against him as a penniless peasant. He therefore became a student in what he called the "free" university of the revolutionary youth.

But Gorky had always been sensitive and impressionable, and his basic, sentimental sadness was counteracted only by his determination to "grasp" life, almost to force it to respond to his faith. His discipline as a writer consisted of a struggle to say the essential by using fewer words. Against a deeply nostalgic trend young Gorky determined to develop a heart that could grasp, yet love, a soul with teeth in it. As with so many of his like-minded contemporaries, the struggle nearly killed him.

At the age of twenty he attempted suicide by shooting himself in the side. "I lay the blame of my death," he wrote in a remarkable suicide note, "on the German poet Heine who invented a *toothache of the heart*. . . . It will be seen from my passport that I am A. Pyeshkov, but from this note, I hope, nothing will be seen."[13] He will now forgive us if we do see a meaningful relationship between this toothache of the heart and his, and his nation's struggle to overcome regressive nostalgia and "to learn to grasp life." The term used had, indeed, been invented by the bitterly (or may we say bitingly) nostalgic Heine, who recommended as a remedy for the heart's toothaches a certain tooth-powder invented by Bertold Schwarz—the inventor of gunpowder. Gorky later formulated to Chekhov his depressive period as a time of "stony darkness," of *"immobility forever poised."* Having broken the deadlock by risking self-destruction, he recovered and set out to wander and to work.

"I have come into the world not to compromise," he said in his first epic poem. Alyosha had followed Gregory and all the others, watching in order to find out where he should and should not be involved in living the life of the people; Gorky literally stalked people and situations to see where he could wrest from life, as a homeless wanderer, those "rare and positive" phenomena which would keep his faith alive.

His analytic incorruptibility "lifted to the point of inspiration" is never more epically expressed than in the famous letter which he wrote upon the receipt of the gripping news that old Tolstoy had wandered off from home, wife, and estate.[14]

> . . . There is a dog howling in my soul and I have a foreboding of some misfortune. Yes, newspapers have just arrived and it is already clear: you at home are beginning to "create a legend"; idlers and good-for-nothings have gone on living and have now produced a saint. Only think how pernicious it is for the country just at this moment, when the heads of disillusioned men are bowed down, the souls of the majority empty, and the souls of the best full of sorrow. Lacerated and starving they long for a legend. They long so much for alleviation of pain, for the soothing of torment. And they will create just what he desires, but what is not wanted—the life of a holy man and saint.
>
> . . . Well, now he is probably making his last assault in order to give his ideas the highest possible significance, so that he might assert his ho-

liness and obtain a halo. That is dictatorial, although his teaching is justified by the ancient history of Russia and by his own sufferings of genius. Holiness is attained by flirting with sin, by subduing the will to live. People do desire to live, but he tries to persuade them: "That's all nonsense, our earthly life." It is very easy to persuade a Russian of this: he is a lazy creature who loves beyond anything else to find an excuse for his own inactivity.

. . . A strange impression used to be produced by his words: "I am happy, I am very happy, I am too happy." And then immediately afterwards: "To suffer." To suffer—that too was true in him. I don't doubt it for a second, that he, only half convalescent, would have been really glad to be put into prison, to be banished, in a word to embrace a martyr's crown.

In the last analysis, he saw in Tolstoy's conversion the ancient curse of Russia:[15]

. . . He always greatly exalted immortality on the other side of this life, but he preferred it on this side. A writer, national in the truest and most complete sense, he embodied in his great soul all the defects of his nation, all the mutilations we have suffered by the ordeals of our history; his misty preaching of "non-activity," of "non-resistance to evil," the doctrine of passivism, all this is the unhealthy ferment of the old Russian blood, envenomed by Mongolian fatalism and almost chemically hostile to the West with its untiring creative labor, with its active and indomitable resistance to the evils of life. What is called Tolstoy's "anarchism" essentially and fundamentally expresses our Slav anti-Statism, which, again, is really a national characteristic, ingrained in our flesh from old times, our desire to scatter nomadically. Up to now we have indulged that desire passionately, as you and everyone else know. We Russians know it too, but we always break away along the lines of least resistance; we see that this is pernicious, but still we crawl further and further away from one another; and these mournful cockroach journeyings are called "the history of Russia," the history of a State which has been established almost incidentally, mechanically—to the surprise of the majority of its honest-minded citizens—by the forces of the Variags, Tartars, Baltic Germans, and petty officials. . . .

In viewing this motion picture and in trying to determine what Alyosha became free *for,* it is hard to avoid two pitfalls, a biographical and a historical one. It seems clear that Alyosha, as the collective myth of the film, has great affinity to Gorky's image of himself, to his ideals, and to the legend which he, as any great writer, worked so hard to become. Yet the real Gorky's ways of solving, by creativity and by neurosis, the problem which he shouldered as a youth, is tangential to our discussion.

The historical pitfall would lie in a hostile comparison of this picture's simple humanity and earthiness, its implicit revolutionary spirit, with the stilted and stagnant revolutionary "line" which we have become used to in what reaches us now of Soviet writings and movies. Beyond the cruel abuse of revolutions by the super-managers whom they bring to power, we must look for the root of revolution in the needs of the led—and the misled.

The importance of the picture for this book lies in its simple relevance for a few psychological trends which are basic to revolutions in general; and specifically to those in areas which face industrialization while still immersed in the imagery of an ancient agricultural revolution. True, our motion picture offers for discussion only some of the imagery of one of these areas: the great Russian plains. While other ethnic areas would call for the consideration of different or related imageries, yet Russia has so far been as decisive and pervading an influence in the Communist revolution as, say, the Anglo-Saxons were in the history of America.

To summarize: In the imagery suggested by this movie, the grandmother has a dominant place. She seems to represent the people in their mystical unity with flesh and earth: good in itself but cursed by the greediness of the "breed": Paradise lost. To become or remain a party to the grandmother's strength would mean surrender to timelessness, and eternal bondage to the faith of primitive economy. It is that faith which makes the primitive hang on to the methods of ancient tools and of magical influence over the forces of nature; it is that faith which, in turn, provides him with a simple remedy for any sense of sin: projection. Badness all lies in evil forces, in spirits, in curses: you must regulate them with magic—or be possessed by them. To the Bolshevik revolutionary the grandmother's goodness reaches back into times before good and evil entered the world; and, one assumes, it reaches into the far future when classless society will overcome the morality of greed and exploitation. In the meantime grandmother is a danger. She is the political apathy of the

Russian's very timelessness and childish trust. Maybe she is the virtue, as it has been put recently, which permits the Kremlin to wait, and the Russian people to wait longer.

A second set of images seems to concern the wood-fire dichotomy. The uncles, and the other men, are stout, square, heavy, awkward, and dull, like logs of wood; but they are highly combustible. They are wood— and they are fire. The swaddled "log of wood" with its smoldering vaso-motor madness, the wooden Russian people with their explosive souls: are such images leftovers of a very recent or, in Russia, even contempo-rary *wooden age*? Wood provided the material for the stockades as well as for the overheated ovens through the long winters. It was the basic ma-terial for tools. But it also incorporated the danger of being consumed by its own combustibility. Houses and villages and wood supplies burned beyond recovery—a fatal tendency in view of the fact that the forests themselves perished in fires and receded from prairies and marshes. What magic means were invoked to save them?

A third set of images centers in *iron* and *steel*. In the picture it is pre-sent only in the appearance of the little wheel for Lyenka's cart. The scav-enger boys find it, but instead of turning it into money they use it to complete the prosthesis for Lyenka's locomotor liberation. But then, the wheel takes a special place among the basic human inventions. It goes be-yond the tools which represent mere extensions of and prostheses for the limbs; moving within itself, it is basic for the idea of the machine, which, man-made and man-driven, yet develops a certain autonomy as a me-chanical organism.

Beyond this, however, steel is, in many ways, suggested as a symbol of the new frame of mind. While the wood and fire imagery suggests a cyclic personality structure characterized by apathetic drudgery, childlike trust, sudden outbreaks of consuming passion, and a sense of depressing doom, the imagery of steel suggests incorruptible realism and enduring, disciplined struggle. For steel is forged in fire, but it is not combustible or subject to destruction by fire. To master it means to triumph over the weakness of the flesh-soul and the deadness and combustibility of the wood-mind. As it is forged, steel forges a new generation and a new elite. Such, at least, must be the connotation of names like Stalin (steel) and Molotov (hammer), and of official behavior which underscores with-out cessation the incorruptibility of Bolshevik perception, the long range of its vision, its steel-like clarity of decision, and the machine-like firm-

ness of action. On the defensive, such composure again becomes wood-
enness—or combustible oratory.

We see now where Gorky meant to stand and where this motion picture of the early days of the Russian revolution puts him: into that van-
guard of revolutionaries called the "intelligentsia," which—with all its
morbid ruminations—prepared the new morality by learning to grasp
and hold, first facts and ideas, and then political and military control itself. It is hard for us to realize what superhuman inspiration seemed involved at the time in Lenin's decision to ask the workers and peasants on
the collapsing fronts to hold on to their guns; and what a miracle it must
have seemed that the worn-out masses complied. It was Gorky who
called writers "the engineers of society," and, in turn, spoke of an inventor as "a poet in the domain of scientific technique, who arouses that sensible energy which creates goodness and beauty." As the revolution
established itself, the highly educated and in many ways Westernized intellectual elite gave place to a planned, meticulously trained elite of political, industrial, and military engineers who believed themselves to be
the aristocracy of the historical process itself. They are our cold, our
dangerous adversaries today.

But there was a time when the intelligentsia wanted passionately to be
of the people and for the people; and, no doubt, they once amplified and
were amplified by a dark and illiterate tendency in the Russian masses (or,
at any rate, in a decisive segment of these masses) to find its national identity in a mystical international cause. In Alyosha we see the son of a mystic and earthy past as well as a potential founding father of an industrial
world future.

The American farmer's boy is the descendant of Founding Fathers who
themselves were rebel sons. They had refused to hide behind any crown
or cross. They were heirs of a reformation, a renaissance, the emergence
of nationalism and of revolutionary individualism. They had before them
a new continent which had not been their motherland and which had
never been governed by crowned or ordained fathers. This fact permitted an exploitation of the continent which was crudely masculine, rudely
exuberant, and, but for its women, anarchic. The Americans have, if any
people has, fulfilled Chekhov's dream. They have made conquered earth
comfortable and machinery almost pleasant, to the ambivalent envy of

the rest of the world. Protestantism, individualism, and the frontier to-gether created an identity of individual initiative which in industrializa-tion found its natural medium. In an earlier chapter [in *Childhood and Society*] we pointed to the problems which this identity faced as the con-tinent was gradually exploited in its width and depth, and as voracious initiative began to eat into the human resources of the nation; and we have pointed to some of the derivatives of the protestant revolution.

I shall now try to make more explicit what I meant earlier when re-ferring to Alyosha's new frame of mind as a form of delayed Eastern protestantism.

The temptations Alyosha turns away from—and a protestant turns away from and against—are not dissimilar to those which the early Protestants felt emanated from Rome: the enchantment of God as a spirit that enters through the senses as the light of the stained windows, the fume of the incense, and the lullaby of the chant; the mystic immer-sion in the mass; the "clinical" view of life as a childhood disease of the soul; and most of all, the permission "to hide behind another's con-science."

If we turn to the community of men which Alyosha seems to be turning toward, the parallelism with protestant patterns becomes even clearer. For from a centralized organization for mediated salvation (and thus the exploitation of infantile and primitive fears) Alyosha and his comrades turn to the establishment of a responsible elite. Their means of selection is not faith in the Invisible, but conduct within a community which examines, selects, and judges. Their conscience is not based on the paroxysms of the sin-and-expiation cycle, but on a discipline of mind. This discipline determines their form of sacrifice, which is the emphasis on a systematic discipline of the senses rather than on spectacular atone-ment. Their state of salvation is not determined by the inner glow of faith and of love for the believers, but in disciplined success in this world, in a determined alignment with contemporary economic and technical forces. Their damnation and their death is not the consciousness of sin and the certainty of hell, but the exclusion from the revolutionary com-munity, and even the self-exclusion from the historical process, a moral annihilation compared with which death from whatever hand is a mere biological trifle.

The framework of this Eastern protestant reorientation is of course radically different from the Western one; it is proletarian and industrial, and it is Russian and Orthodox. The latter two elements have determined the pitfalls of this orientation and the enormity of its tragedy.

We can continue and conclude our analogy here. The Communist Party, in absorbing an emerging protestantism, could not tolerate an important protestant ingredient: *sectarianism*. To maintain absolute power it felt the need for absolute unity. The party's desperate and finally cruel attempts at warding off sectarian splits are well documented in the minutes of its early conventions, which were characterized by a hair-splitting most reminiscent of ecclesiastic history: the issues were the *truth* of dialectic history, the *infallibility* of the Politburo, and the mystic *wisdom* of the masses. We know how this hair-splitting ended.

Max Weber's prediction that an attempt at dictatorship for the proletariat could only lead to a dictatorship of the middleman, of bureaucracy, now proves to have been prophetic. Again, the Russian people believe in one man in the Kremlin, whom they do not blame for the cruelties of his middlemen and whom they believe to be their defender against usurpers and exploiters, foreign and domestic.

As of today, they believe this honestly, because their is nothing else that they could believe on the basis of what they know. Therefore, their best is invested in this belief. Our devoted studies should concern the fact that the original emergence of a revolutionary frame of mind in Russia and Asia, volcanic as it was, may have been an attempt, and in view of the historical process an unavoidable one, to approach the stage of human conscience which characterized our protestant revolution. Whether or not a few men on the Eurasian continent or some nervous council of ministers will plunge us into war—we do not know. But it may well be that the future—with or without war—will belong to those who will harness the psychological energies freed from the wasteful superstitions of ancient agricultural moralities on the European, Asiatic, and African continents. Physics, in learning to split the atom, has released new energy, for peace and for war. With the help of psychoanalysis we can study another kind of energy which is released when the most archaic part of our conscience is "split." As civilization enters into an industrialized era, such a split is inevitable. The enormous energy thus released can be benevolent, and it can be malevolent. In the end, it may be more decisive than material weapons.

As we Americans, with the friendly coerciveness of a Paul Bunyan (the Russians would say, a Vassily Buslaiev), throw gadgets and robots into the world market, we must learn to understand that we help to create revolutionized economic conditions. We must be able to demonstrate to grim Alyoshas everywhere that our new and shiny goods (so enticingly wrapped in promises of freedom) do not come to them as so many more sedatives to make them subservient to their worn-out upper classes, as so many more opiates to lull them into the new serfdom of hypnotized consumership. They do not want to be granted freedom; what they want is to be given the opportunity to grasp it, as equals. They do not want progress where it undermines their sense of initiative. They demand autonomy, together with unity; and identity together with the fruits of industry. We must succeed in convincing the Alyoshas that—from a very long-range point of view—their protestantism is ours and ours, theirs.

THE FIT IN THE CHOIR

from *Young Man Luther*

1

Three of young Luther's contemporaries (none of them a later follower of his) report that sometime during his early or middle twenties, he suddenly fell to the ground in the choir of the monastery at Erfurt, "raved" like one possessed, and roared with the voice of a bull: *"Ich bin's nit! Ich bin's nit!"*[1] or *"Non sum! Non sum!"*[2] The German version is best translated with "It isn't me!" the Latin one with "I am *not!*"

It would be interesting to know whether at this moment Martin roared in Latin or in German; but the reporters agree only on the occasion which upset him so deeply: the reading of Christ's *ejecto a surdo et muto daemonio*—Christ's cure of a man possessed by a *dumb spirit.*[3] This can only refer to Mark 9:17: "And one of the multitude answered and said, Master, I have brought unto thee my son, which hath a dumb spirit." The chroniclers considered that young Luther was possessed by demons—the religious and psychiatric borderline case of the middle ages—and that he showed himself possessed even as he tried most loudly to deny it. "I am *not,*" would then be the childlike protestation of somebody who has been called a name or has been characterized with loathsome adjectives: here, dumb, mute, possessed.

We will discuss this alleged event first as to its place in Luther's life history, and then, as to its status in Luther's biography.

The monk Martinus entered the Black Monastery of the Augustinians in Erfurt when he was twenty-one years old. Following a vow made in an attack of acute panic during a severe thunderstorm, he had abruptly and without his father's permission left the University of Erfurt, where he had just received with high honors the degree of a master of arts. Behind the monk lay years of strict schooling supported only with great sacrifice by his ambitious father, who wanted him to study the law, a profession which at that time was becoming the springboard into administration and politics. Before him lay long years of the most intense inner conflicts and frequently morbid religious scruples; these eventually led to his abandonment of monasticism and to his assumption of spiritual leadership in a widespread revolt against the medieval papacy. The fit in the choir, then, belongs to a period when his career, as planned by his father, was dead; when his monastic condition, after a "godly" beginning, had become problematic to him; and when his future was as yet in an embryonic darkness. This future could have been divined by him only in the strictest (and vaguest) term of the word, namely, as a sense of a spiritual mission of some kind.

It is difficult to visualize this young man, later to become so great and triumphant, in the years when he took that chance on perdition which was the very test and condition of his later greatness. Therefore, I shall list a few dates, which may be of help to the reader.

EVENTS OF MARTIN'S YOUTH

Born in 1483, Martin Luther	1483
entered the University of Erfurt at seventeen;	1501
received his master's degree at twenty-one, and	1505
entered the monastery, having vowed to do so	
during a thunderstorm.	
Became a priest and celebrated his first Mass at the	1507+
age of twenty-three; then fell into severe doubts and	
scruples which may have caused the "fit in the choir."	

Became a doctor of theology at the age of   1512+
    twenty-eight; gave his first lectures on the
    Psalms at the University of Wittenberg, where
    he experienced the "revelation in the tower."

At thirty-two, almost a decade after the episode in the   1517
    choir, he nailed his ninety-five theses on the church
    door in Wittenberg.

The story of the fit in the choir has been denied as often as it has been repeated; but its fascination even for those who would do away with it seems to be great. A German professor of theology, Otto Scheel, one of the most thorough editors of the early sources on Luther's life, flatly disavows the story, tracing it to that early hateful biography of Luther written by Johannes Cochläus in 1549.[4] And yet, Scheel does not seem to be able to let go of the story. Even to him there is enough to it so that in the very act of belittling it he grants it a measure of religious grandeur: "Nicolaus Tolentinus, too," he writes "when he knelt at the altar and prayed, was set upon by the Prince of Darkness. But precisely in this visibly meaningful (sinnfaellig) struggle with the devil did Nicolaus prove himself as the chosen armour of the Lord. . . . Are we to count it to Luther's damnation if he, too, had to battle with the devil in a similarly meaningful way?"[5] He appeals to Catholic detractors: "Why not measure with the same yardstick?" And in a footnote he asks the age-old question: "Or was Paul's miraculous conversion also pathological?" Scheel, incidentally, in his famous collection of documents on Luther's development, where he dutifully reprints Cochläus' version, makes one of his very rare mistakes by suggesting that the biblical story in question is Mark 1:23, where a "man with an unclean spirit . . . *cried out*" and was *silenced* by Christ.[6] However, the *surdus* and *mutus daemonius* can hardly refer to this earlier passage in Mark.

Scheel is a Protestant professor of theology. For him the principal task is explaining as genuinely inspired by a divine agency those attacks of unconsciousness and fits of overwhelming anxiety, those delusional moments, and those states of brooding despair which occasionally beset young Luther and increasingly beset the aging man. To Scheel they are all *geistlich,* not *geistig*—spiritual, not mental. It is often troublesome to try to find one's way through the German literature on Luther, which refers to various mental states as *"Seelenleiden"* (suffering of the soul) and *"Geis-teskrankheit,"* (sickness of the spirit)—terms which always leave it open whether soul or psyche, spirit or mind, is afflicted. It is especially troublesome when medical men claim that the reformer's "suffering of the soul" was mainly *biologically* determined. But the *professor*—as we will call Scheel when we mean to quote him as the representative of a particular academic-theological school of Luther biography—the professor insists, and in a most soberly circumstantial biography, that all of Luther's strange upsets came to him straight down from heaven: *Katastrophen von Gottes Gnaden.*

The most famous, and in many ways rightly infamous, detractor of Luther's character, the Dominican Heinrich Denifle, Sub-Archivar of the Holy See, saw it differently. For him such events as the fit in the choir have only an inner cause, which in no way means a decent conflict or even an honest affliction, but solely an abysmal depravity of character. To him, Luther is too much of a psychopath to be credited with honest mental or spiritual suffering. It is only the Bad One who speaks through Luther. It is, it must be, Denifle's primary ideological premise, that nothing, neither mere pathological fits, nor the later revelations which set Luther on the path to reformation, had anything whatsoever to do with divine interference. "Who," Denifle asks, in referring to the thunderstorm, "can prove, for himself, not to speak of others, that the alleged inspiration through the Holy Ghost really came from above . . . and that it was not the play of conscious or unconscious self-delusion?"[7] Lutheranism, he fears (and hopes to demonstrate) has tried to lift to the height of dogma the phantasies of a most fallible mind.

With his suspicion that Luther's whole career may have been inspired by the devil, Denifle puts his finger on the sorest spot in Luther's whole spiritual and psychological make-up. His days in the monastery were darkened by a suspicion, which Martin's father expressed loudly on the occasion of the young priest's first Mass, that the thunderstorm had really been the voice of a *Gespenst,* a ghost; thus Luther's vow was on the borderline of both pathology and demonology. Luther remained sensitive to this paternal suspicion, and continued to argue with himself and with his father long after his father had no other choice than to acknowledge his son as a spiritual leader and Europe's religious strong man. But in his twenties Martin was still a sorely troubled young man, not at all able to express either what inspired or what bothered him; his great-

est worldly burden was certainly the fact that his father had only most reluctantly, and after much cursing, given his consent (which was legally
dispensable, anyway) to the son's religious career.

With this in mind, let us return to Mark 9:17–24. It was a father who
addressed Christ: "Master I have brought unto Thee my son, which hath
a dumb spirit. . . . and he asked his father, how long is it ago since this
came unto him? And he said, Of a child. . . . Jesus said unto him, If thou
canst believe, all things are possible to him that believeth. . . . And straightway the father of the child cried out, and said with tears, Lord, I believe;
help thou mine unbelief." Two cures, then, are suggested in the Bible passage: the cure of a son with a dumb spirit, after a father has been cured
of a weak faith. The possibility of an "inner-psychological" kernel in
Martin's reaction to this passage will thus deserve to be weighed carefully,
although with scales other than those used by Father Denifle—to whom
we will refer as the *priest,* whenever we quote him as a representative of
a clerical-scholastic school in Luther biography.

But now to another school of experts. An extremely diligent student
of Luther, the Danish psychiatrist, Dr. Paul J. Reiter, decides unequivo-
cally that the fit in the choir is a matter of severest psychopathology. At
most, he is willing to consider the event as a relatively benign hysterical
episode; even so, he evaluates it as a symptom of a steady, pitiless, "endogenous" process which, in Luther's middle forties, was climaxed by a
frank psychosis. *Endogenous* really means biological; Reiter feels that
Luther's attacks cannot "with the best of will" be conceived of as links
"in the chain of meaningful psychological development."[8] It would be
futile, then, to try to find any "message," either from a divine or an inner
source, in Luther's abnormalities other than indications of erratic upsets
in his nervous system. Reiter considers the years in which we are most
interested—when Luther was twenty-two to thirty—as part of one long
Krankheitsphase, one drawn-out state of nervous disease, which extended
to the thirty-sixth year; these years were followed by a period of "manic"
productivity, and then by a severe breakdown in the forties. In fact, he
feels that only a pitifully small number of Luther's years were really characterized by the reformer's famous "robust habitual state"—which means
that Luther was like himself only very rarely, and most briefly. Reiter considers at least Luther's twenties as a period of neurotic, rather than of psychotic, tension, and he acknowledges the crisis of this one period as the
only time in Luther's life when his ideological search remained mean-

ingfully related to his psychological conflicts; when his creativity kept pace with his inner destructive processes; and when a certain "limited intellectual balance" was reached.

We will make the most of the license thus affirmed by the *psychiatrist,* as we shall call Reiter when we quote him as the representative of a medical-biological school in Luther-biography. This class of biographers ascribes Luther's personal and theological excesses to a sickness which, whether "seated" in brain, nervous system, or kidneys, marks Luther as a biologically inferior or diseased man. As to the event in the choir, Reiter makes a strange mistake. Luther, he says, could not have been conscious, for he called out with "utmost intentionally . . . 'That's me!' " *(Ich bin's)*[9]—meaning, the possessed one of the evangelium. Such a positive exclamation would do away with a good part of the meaning which we will ascribe to the event in the choir; however, three hundred pages earlier in the same book, Reiter, too, tells the story in the traditional way, making Martin call out: "That's *not* me."[10]

And how about a psychoanalyst? The professor and the psychiatrist frequently and most haughtily refer to a representative of the "modern Freudian school"—Professor Preserved Smith, then of Amherst College, who, beside writing a biography of Luther,[11] and editing his letters,[12] wrote, in 1915, a remarkable paper: "Luther's Early Development in The Light of Psychoanalysis."[13] I use the word "beside" deliberately, for this paper impresses one as being a foreign body in Smith's work on Luther; it is done, so to speak, with the left hand, while the right and official hand is unaware. "Luther," Smith claims, "is a thoroughly typical example of the neurotic quasi-hysterical sequence of an infantile sex-complex; so much so, indeed, that Sigismund [sic] Freud and his school could hardly have found a better example to illustrate the sounder part of their theory than him."[14] Smith musters the appropriate data to show (what I, too, will demonstrate in detail) that Luther's childhood was unhappy because of his father's excessive harshness, and that he was obsessively preoccupied with God as an avenger, with the Devil as a visible demon, and with obscene images and sayings. Smith unhesitatingly characterizes "the foundation-stones of early Protestantism . . . as an interpretation of Luther's own subjective life." Outstanding in Luther's morbid subjectivity is his preoccupation with "concupiscence" which Smith, contrary to all evidence, treats as if to Luther it had been a mere matter of sexual "lust." Smith in fact (while conceding that "it is to his great credit that there is good reason to believe he never sinned with women") attributes Luther's great preoccupation with concupiscence to his losing battle with masturbation.

It is instructive to see what an initial fascination and temporary indoctrination with "Freudian" notions can do to a scholar, in particular perhaps to one with a Puritan background: the notions remain in his thinking like a foreign body. In order to make the masturbation hypothesis plausible, Smith, obviously a thorough student of the German sources, flagrantly misinterprets a famous statement of Luther's. Luther reported repeatedly that at the height of his monastic scruples he had confessed to a trusted superior, "not about women, but about *die rechten Knotten.*"[15] This phrase means "the real knots"; in the language of the peasant, it means the knotty part of the tree, the hardest to cut. This reference to real hindrances Smith suspects is a hint at masturbation, although the sound of the words does not suggest anything of the kind, and although at least on one occasion Luther specifies the knots as transgressions against *die erste Taffel*[16] that is, the first commandment concerning the love of God the Father. This would point to Luther's increasing and obsessive-blasphemous ambivalence toward God, partially a consequence (and here Smith is, of course, correct and is seconded by the psychiatrist) of a most pathological relationship to his father; which, in turn provides the proper context for Luther's sexual scruples. Professor Smith, incidentally, translates the reported outcry in the choir as "It is not I!"— words which I doubt even a New Englander would utter in a convulsive attack.

Although the professor, the priest, and the psychiatrist refer to Smith as "the psychoanalyst," I myself cannot characterize him in this way, since his brilliant but dated contribution appears to be an isolated exercise of a man who, to my knowledge, never systematically pursued psychoanalysis either in practice or in theory.

2

Why did I introduce my discussion of Luther with this particular event in the choir, whose interpretation is subject to so many large and small discrepancies?

As I tried to orient myself in regard to Luther's identity crisis by studying those works which promised to render the greatest number of facts and references for independent study, I heard him, ever again, roar in rage, and yet also in laughter: *Ich bin's nit!* For with the same facts (here and there altered, as I have indicated, in details precisely relevant to psychological interpretation), the professor, the priest, the psychiatrist, and others as yet to be quoted each concocts his own Luther; this may well be the reason why they all agree on one point, namely, that dynamic psychology must be kept away from the data of Luther's life. Is it possible that they all agree so that each may take total and unashamed possession of him, of the great man's charisma?

Take the professor. As he sifts the sources minutely and masterfully establishes his own versions, a strange belligerence (to judge from Freud's experience not atypical of the German scientific scene of the early part of this century) leads him to challenge other experts as if to a duel. He constantly imputes to them not only the ignorance of high school boys, but also the motives of juveniles. This need not bother us; such duels spill only ink and swell only footnotes. But the emerging image of Luther, erected and defended in this manner, assumes, at decisive moments, some of the military qualities of the method; while otherwise it remains completely devoid of any psychological consistency. At the conclusion of the professor's first volume, only a soldierly image suffices to express his hopes for sad young Martin behind whom the gates of the monastery have just closed: "Out of the novice Luther," he writes, "the warrior shall be created, whom the enemy can touch neither with force nor with cunning, and whose soul, after completion of its war service, will be led to the throne of the judge by archangel Michael."[17] *Kriegsdienst* is the metallic German word for war service, and the professor makes the most of the biblical reference to God as El Zebaoth, the master of the armies of angels; he even makes God share the Kaiser's title *Kriegsherr.* Everything extraordinary, then, that happens to Luther is *befohlen,* ordered from above, without advance notice or explanation and completely without intention or motivation on Luther's part; consequently, all psychological speculation regarding motivation is strictly *verboten.* No wonder that Luther's "personality" seems to be put together from scraps of conventional images which do not add up to a workable human being. Luther's parents and Luther himself are pasted together; their ingredients are the characteristics of the ordinary small-town German: simple, hardworking,

earnest, straightforward, dutiful folk *(bieder, tuechtig, gehorsam,* and *wacker).*
The myth to be created, of course, is that God selects just such folk to
descend on in a sudden "catastrophic" decision.

Boehmer,[18] whom I would place in the same school, although equally
well-informed, is milder and more insightful. Yet for him, too, Luther's father is a harsh, but entirely well-meaning, sturdy, and healthy type, until
suddenly, without any warning whatsoever, he behaves "like a madman"
when his son enters the monastery. Boehmer acts as if such a childish explosion were a German father's prerogative and above any psychologizing.

Scheel's book is a post–World War I heir of two trends in the Lutheran
writing of history, initiated by two men and never surpassed by others:
the universalistic-historical trend of the great von Ranke,[19] the "priestly
historian," whose job it was to find in the conflicting forces of history
"the holy hieroglyph of God"; the other, a theological-philosophical
trend (sometimes fusing, sometimes sharply separating philosophy and religion) begun by the elder Harnack.[20] We will return to this last point of
view when we come to the emergence of Luther's theology.

Denifle the Dominican priest, also an acknowledged scholar and authority on late medieval institutions of learning (he died a few days before he was to receive an honorary degree from the University of
Cambridge), as well as most powerful detective of Luther's often rather
free quotations from and reinterpretations of theological doctrine, feels
obliged to create a different image of Luther. To him he is an *Umsturz-
mensch,* the kind of man who wants to turn the world upside down
without a plan of his own. To Denifle, Luther's protestant attitude introduced into history a dangerous kind of revolutionary spirit. Luther's special gifts, which the priest does not deny, are those of the demagogue and
the false prophet—falseness not only as a matter of bad theology, but as
a conscious falsification from base motives. All of this follows from the
priest's quite natural thesis that war orders from above, such as the professor assumes to have been issued to Luther, could only be genuine if
they showed the seal and the signature of divinity, namely, signs and miracles. When Luther prayed to God not to send his miracles, so that he
would not become proud and be deflected from the Word by Satan's
delusions, he only discarded grapes which were hanging as high as heaven
itself: for the faintest possibility of any man outside the Church receiving such signs had been excluded for all eternity by the verification of
Jesus as God's sole messenger on earth.

Denifle is only the most extreme representative of a Catholic school of Luther biography, whose representatives try hard to divorce themselves from his method while sharing his basic assumption of a gigantic moral flaw in Luther's personality. The Jesuit Grisar[21] is cooler and more dissecting in his approach. Yet he too ascribes to Luther a tendency for "egomanic self-delusion," and suggests a connection between his self-centeredness and his medical history; thus Grisar puts himself midway between the approaches of the priest and of the psychiatrist.

Among all of Luther's biographers, inimical or friendly, Denifle seems to me to resemble Luther most, at least in his salt-and-pepper honesty, and his one-sided anger. "Tyrolean candor," a French biographer ascribes to him.[22] The Jesuit is most admirable in his scholarly criticism of Luther's theology; most lovable in his outraged response to Luther's vulgarity. Denifle does not think that a true man of God would ever say "I gorge myself *(fresse)* like a Bohemian and I get drunk *(sauff)* like a German. God be praised. Amen,"[23] although he neglects the fact that Luther wrote this in one of his humorous letters to his wife at a time when she was worried about his lack of appetite. And he seriously suggests that the sow was Luther's model of salvation. I cannot refrain from translating here the quotation on which Denifle bases this opinion, which offers a contrast to Scheel's martial image and, as such, is an example of a radically different and yet equally scholarly suggestion for the real core of Luther's personality.

In an otherwise hateful pamphlet written in his middle forties, Luther relaxes into that folksy manner which he occasionally also used in his sermons. What he wants to make clear is that there is a prereligious state of mind. "For a sow," he writes, "lies in the gutter or on the manure as if on the finest feather bed. She rests safely, snores tenderly, and sleeps sweetly, does not fear king nor master, death nor hell, devil or God's wrath, lives without worry, and does not even think where the clover *(Kleien)* may be. And if the Turkish Caesar arrived in all his might and anger, the sow would be much too proud to move a single whisker in his honor. . . . And if at last the butcher comes upon her, she thinks maybe a piece of wood is pinching her, or a stone. . . . The sow has not eaten from the apple, which in paradise has taught us wretched humans the difference between good and bad."[24] No translation can do justice to the gentle persuasiveness of these lines. The priest, however, omits the argument in which they appear: Luther is trying to persuade his readers that the as yet expected Messiah of the Jews could not make a man's life a tenth as good as that of a sow, while the coming of Christ has done more, has put the whole matter of living on a higher plane. And yet one cannot escape the fact that in Luther's rich personality there was a soft spot for the sow so large that Denifle correctly considers it what I will call one of Luther's identity elements. Oftentimes when this element became dominant, Luther could be so vulgar that he became easy game for the priest and the psychiatrist, both of whom quote with relish: "Thou shalt not write a book unless you have listened to the fart of an old sow, to which you should open your mouth wide and say 'Thanks to you, pretty nightingale; do I hear a text which is for me?' "[25] But what writer, disgusted with himself, has not shared these sentiments—without finding the right wrong words?

The Danish psychiatrist, in turn, offers in his two impressive volumes as complete an account of Luther's "environment, character, and psychosis" as I have come across. His study ranges from the macrocosm of Luther's times to the microcosm of his home and home town, and includes a thorough discussion of his biological make-up and of his lifelong physical and emotional symptoms. But the psychiatrist lacks a theory comprehensive enough for his chosen range. Psychoanalysis he rejects as too dogmatic, borrowing from Preserved Smith what fragments he can use without committing himself to the theory implied. He states his approach candidly: it is that of a psychiatrist who has been consulted on a severe case of manifest psychosis (diagnosis: manic-depressive, à la Kraepelin) and who proceeds to record the presenting condition (Luther's acute psychosis in his forties) and to reconstruct the past history, including the twenties. He shows much insight in his asides; but in his role of bedside psychiatrist, he grimly sticks to his central view by asserting that a certain trait or act of Luther's is "absolutely typical for a state of severe melancholia" and "is to be found in every psychiatric textbook." The older Luther undoubtedly approached textbook states, although I doubt very much that his personal meetings with the devil were ever true hallucinations, or that his dramatic revelations concerning his mental suffering can be treated on the same level as communications from a patient.

Furthermore, when it comes to the younger Luther and the psychiatrist's assertion that his *tentationes tristitiae*—that sadness which is a traditional temptation of the *homo religiosus*—is among the "classical traits in the picture of most states of depression, especially the endogenous ones,"[26] we must be decidedly more doubtful. For throughout, this psychiatric textbook version of Luther does not compare him with other examples of sincere religious preoccupation and corresponding genuine giftedness, but with some norm of *Ausgeglichenheit*—an inner balance, a simple enjoyment of life, and an ordinary decency and decided direction of effort such as normal people are said to display. Though the psychiatrist makes repeated allowances for Luther's genius, he nevertheless demands of him a state of inner repose which, as far as I know, men of creative intensity and of an increasing historical commitment cannot be expected to be able to maintain. At any rate, he points out that even in his last years Luther's "psychic balance was not complete," his inner state only "relatively harmonious." Using this yardstick of normality, the psychiatrist considers it strange that Luther could not accept his father's reasonable plans and go ahead and enjoy the study of law; that he could not be relaxed during his ordination as other young priests are; that he could not feel at home in as sensible and dignified a regime as that of an Augustinian monastery; and that he was not able, much later, to sit back and savor with equanimity the fruits of his rebellion. The professor, too, finds most of this surprising; but he assumes that God, for some divine reason, needled Luther out of such natural and sensible attitudes; the psychiatrist is sure that the needling was done from within, by endogenous mental disease.

I do not know about the kind of balance of mind, body, and soul that these men assume is normal; but if it does exist, I would expect it least of all in such a sensitive, passionate, and ambitious individual as young Luther. He, as many lesser ones like him, may have had good inner reasons to escape premature commitments. Some young people suffer under successes which, to them, are subjectively false, and they may even shy away as long as they possibly can from what later turns out to be their true role. The professor's and the psychiatrist's image of normality seems an utterly incongruous measure to use on a future professional reformer. But then the psychiatrist (with the priest) not only disavows God's hand in the matter, he also disregards, in his long list of character types and somatotypes, the existence of a *homo religiosus* circumscribed and proved not necessarily by signs and miracles, but by the inner logic of his way of life, by the logic of his working gifts, and by the logic of his effect on society. To study and formulate this logic seems to me to constitute the task at hand, if one wishes to consider the total existence of a man like Luther.

I will conclude this review of a few of the most striking and best-informed attempts at presenting prejudiced versions of Luther's case with one more quotation and one more suggested Luther image. This image comes from sociology, a field certainly essential to any assessment of the kind to which our authors aspire. I could not, and would not, do without *The Social Basis of the German Reformation* although its author, R. Pascal, a social scientist and historical materialist, announces with the same flatness which we have encountered in the other biographers how well he could manage without me and my field. "The principle underlying [Luther's contradictions]," he states, "is not logical, it is not psychological. The consistency amid all these contradictions is the consistency of class-interest."[27]

This statement is, perhaps, the most Marxist formulation in the economic-political literature of Luther's personality and his influence on the subsequent codevelopment of protestantism and capitalism. (The most encompassing book with this economic-political point of view is by Ernst Troeltsch[28]; the most famous, at least in this country, those of Weber[29] and of Tawney.[30]) I am not smiling at it in superiority, any more than I am smiling at the statements of the dogmatic professor of theology, the Dominican scholar, or the "constitutional" psychiatrist. For each cites valid data, all of which, as we shall see, complement each other. It is necessary, however, to contemplate (if only as a warning to ourselves) the degree to which in the biography of a great man "objective study" and "historical accuracy" can be used to support almost any total image necessitated by the biographer's personality and professed calling; and to point out that biographers categorically opposed to systematic psychological interpretation permit themselves the most extensive psychologizing—which they can afford to believe is common sense only because they disclaim a defined psychological viewpoint. Yet there is always an implicit psychology behind the explicit antipsychology.

One of the great detractors of Luther, Jacob Burckhardt, who taught Nietzsche to see in Luther a noisy German peasant who at the end waylaid the march of Renaissance man, noted: "Who are we, anyway, that we can ask of Luther . . . that [he] should have fulfilled *our* programs? . . . This concrete Luther, and no other, existed; he should be taken for what he was" *(Man nehme ihn wie er gewesen ist)*.[31]

But how does one take a *great* man "for what he was"? The very adjective seems to imply that something about him is too big, too awe-ful, too shiny, to be encompassed. Those who nonetheless set out to describe the whole man seem to have only three choices. They can step so far back that the great man's contours appear complete, but hazy; or they can step closer and closer, gradually concentrating on a few aspects of the great man's life, seeing one part of it as big as the whole, or the whole as small as one part. If neither of these works, there is always polemics; one takes the great man in the sense of appropriating him and of excluding others who might dare to do the same. Thus a man's historical image often depends on which legend temporarily overcomes all others; however, all these ways of viewing a great man's life may be needed to capture the mood of the historical event.

3

The limitations of my knowledge and of the space at my disposal for this inquiry preclude any attempt to present a new Luther or to remodel an old one. I can only bring some newer psychological considerations to bear on the existing material pertaining to one period of Luther's life. As I indicated in Chapter I, the young monk interests me particularly as a young man in the process of becoming a great one.

It must have occurred to the reader that the story of the fit in the choir attracted me originally because I suspected that the words "I am *not!*" revealed the fit to be part of a most severe identity crisis—a crisis in which the young monk felt obliged to protest what he was *not* (possessed, sick, sinful) perhaps in order to break through to what he was or was to be. I will now state what remains of my suspicion, and what I intend to make of it.

Judging from an undisputed series of extreme mental states which attacked Luther throughout his life, leading to weeping, sweating, and fainting, the fit in the choir could well have happened; and it could have happened in the specific form reported, under the specific conditions of Martin's monastery years. If some of it is legend, so be it; the making of legend is as much part of the scholarly rewriting of history as it is part of the original facts used in the work of scholars. We are thus obliged to accept half-legend as half-history, provided only that a reported episode does not contradict other well-established facts; persists in having a ring of truth; and yields a meaning consistent with psychological theory.

Luther himself never mentioned this episode, although in his voluble later years he was extraordinarily free with references to physical and mental suffering. It seems that he always remembered most vividly those states in which he struggled through to an insight, but not those in which he was knocked out. Thus, in his old age, he remembers well having been seized at the age of thirty-five by terror, sweat, and the fear of fainting when he marched in the Corpus Christi procession behind his superior, Dr. Staupitz, who carried the holy of holies. (This Dr. Staupitz, as we will see, was the best father figure Luther ever encountered and acknowledged; he was a man who recognized a true *homo religiosus* in his subaltern and treated him with therapeutic wisdom.) But Staupitz did not let Luther get away with his assertion that it was Christ who had frightened him. He said, *"Non est Christus, quia Christus non terret, sed consolatur."* (It couldn't have been Christ who terrified you, for Christ consoles.)[32] This was a therapeutic as well as a theological revelation to Luther, and he remembered it. However, for the fit in the choir, he may well have had an amnesia.

Assuming then that something like this episode happened, it could be considered as one of a series of seemingly senseless pathological explosions; as a meaningful symptom in a psychiatric case-history; or as one of a series of religiously relevant experiences. It certainly has, as even Scheel suggests, *some* marks of a "religious attack," such as St. Paul, St. Augustine, and many lesser aspirants to saintliness have had. However, the inventory of a total revelation always includes an overwhelming illumination and a sudden insight. The fit in the choir presents only the symptomatic, the more pathological and defensive, aspects of a total revelation: partial loss of consciousness, loss of motor coordination, and automatic exclamations which the afflicted does not know he utters.

In a truly religious experience such automatic exclamations would sound as if they were dictated by divine inspiration; they would be positively illuminating and luminous, and be intensely remembered. In Luther's fit, his words obviously expressed an overwhelming inner need to deny an accusation. In a full religious attack the positive conscience of faith would reign and determine the words uttered; here negation and rebellion reign: "I am *not* what my father said I was and what my conscience, in bad moments, tends to confirm I am." The raving and roaring suggest a strong element of otherwise suppressed rage. And, indeed, this young man, who later became a voice heard around the world, lived under monastic conditions of silence and meditation; at this time he was submissively subdued, painfully sad, and compulsively self-inspective—too much so even for his stern superiors' religious taste. All in all, however, the paroxysm occurred in a holy spot and was suggested by a biblical story, which places the whole matter at least on the borderline between psychiatry and religion.

If we approach the episode from the psychiatric viewpoint, we can recognize in the described attack (and also in a variety of symptomatic scruples and anxieties to which Martin was subject at the time) an intrinsic ambivalence, an inner two-facedness, such as we find in all neurotic symptoms. The attack could be said to deny in its verbal part ("I am not") what Martin's father had said, namely, that his son was perhaps possessed rather than holy; but it also proves the father's point by its very occurrence in front of the same congregation who had previously heard the father express his anger and apprehension. The fit, then, is both unconscious obedience to the father and implied rebellion against the monastery; the words uttered both deny the father's assertion, and confirm the vow which Martin had made in that first known anxiety attack during a thunderstorm at the age of twenty-one, when he had exclaimed, "I want to be a monk."[33] We find the young monk, then, at the crossroads of obedience to his father—an obedience of extraordinary tenacity and deviousness—and to the monastic vows which at the time he was straining to obey almost to the point of absurdity.

We may also view his position as being at the crossroads of mental disease and religious creativity and we could speculate that perhaps Luther received in three (or more) distinct and fragmentary experiences those elements of a total revelation which other men are said to have acquired in one explosive event. Let me list the elements again: physical paroxysm; a degree of unconsciousness; an automatic verbal utterance; a command to change the over-all direction of effort and aspiration; and a spiritual revelation, a flash of enlightenment, decisive and pervasive as a rebirth. The thunderstorm had provided him with a change in the over-all direction of his life, a change toward the anonymous, the silent, and the obedient. In fits such as the one in the choir, he experienced the epileptoid paroxysm of ego-loss, the rage of denial of the identity which was to be discarded. And later in the experience in the tower, he perceived the light of a new spiritual formula.

The fact that Luther experienced these clearly separate stages of religious revelation might make it possible to establish a psychological rationale for the conversion of other outstanding religionists, where
tradition has come to insist on the transmission of a total event appealing to popular faith. Nothing, to my mind, makes Luther more a man of
the future—the future which is our psychological present—than his utter
integrity in reporting the steps which marked the emergence of his identity as a genuine *homo religiosus.* I emphasize this by no means only because it makes him a better case (although I admit it helps), but because
it makes his total experience a historical event far beyond its immediate
sectarian significance, namely, a decisive step in human awareness and responsibility. To indicate this step in its psychological coordinates is the
burden of this book.

Martin's general mood just before he became a monk, a mood into
which he was again sliding at the time of the fit in the choir, has been
characterized by him and others as a state of *tristitia,* of excessive sadness.
Before the thunderstorm, he had rapidly been freezing into a melancholy
paralysis which made it impossible for him to continue his studies and to
contemplate marriage as his father urged him to do. In the thunderstorm, he had felt immense anxiety. Anxiety comes from *angustus,* meaning to feel hemmed in and choked up; Martin's use of *circumvallatus*—all
walled in—to describe his experience in the thunderstorm indicates he
felt a sudden constriction of his whole life space, and could see only one
way out: the abandonment of all of his previous life and the earthly future it implied for the sake of total dedication to a new life. This new life,
however, was one which made an institution out of the very configuration of being walled in. Architecturally, ceremonially, and in its total
world-mood, it symbolized life on this earth as a self-imposed and self-
conscious prison with only one exit, and that one, to eternity. The acceptance of this new frame of life had made him, for a while, peaceful
and "godly"; at the time of his fit, however, his sadness was deepening
again.

As to this general veil of sadness which covered the conflicts revealed
so explosively in the choir, one could say (and the psychiatrist has said it)
that Martin was sad because he was a melancholic; and there is no doubt
that in his depressed moods he displayed at times what we would call the
clinical picture of a melancholia. But Luther was a man who tried to distinguish very clearly between what came from God as the crowning of

a worthwhile conflict, and what came from defeat; the fact that he called defeat the devil only meant he was applying a diagnostic label which was handy. He once wrote to Melanchthon that he considered him the weaker one in public controversy, and himself the weaker in private struggles—"if I may thus call what goes on between me and Satan."[34] One could also say (and the professor has said it) that Martin's sadness was the traditional *tristitia,* the melancholy world mood of the *homo religiosus;* from this point of view, it is a "natural" mood, and could even be called the truest adaptation to the human condition. This view, too, we must accept to a point—the point where it becomes clear that Martin was not able in the long run to embrace the monastic life so natural to the traditional *tristitia;* that he mistrusted his sadness himself; and that he later abandoned this melancholic mood altogether for occasional violent mood swings between depression and elation, between self-accusation and the abuse of others. Sadness, then, was primarily the over-all symptom of his youth, and was a symptom couched in a traditional attitude provided by his time.

4

Youth can be the most exuberant, the most careless, the most self-sure, and the most unselfconsciously productive stage of life, or so it seems if we look primarily at the "once-born." This is a term which William James adopted from Cardinal Newman; he uses it to describe all those who rather painlessly fit themselves and are fitted into the ideology of their age, finding no discrepancy between its formulation of past and future and the daily tasks set by the dominant technology.

James[35] differentiates the once-born from those "sick souls" and "divided selves" who search for a second birth, a "growth-crisis" that will "convert" them in their "habitual center of . . . personal energy." He approvingly quotes Starbuck to the effect that "conversion is in its essence a normal adolescent phenomenon" and that "theology . . . brings those means to bear which will intensify the normal tendencies" and yet also shorten "the period by bringing the person to a definite crisis." James (himself apparently the victim in his youth of a severe psychiatric crisis) does not make a systematic point of the fact that in his chapters on the

Sick Soul, the Divided Self, and Conversion, his illustrations of spontaneous changes in the "habitual center of personal energy" are almost exclusively people in their late teens and early twenties—an age which can be most painfully aware of the need for decisions, most driven to choose new devotions and to discard old ones, and most susceptible to the propaganda of ideological systems which promise a new world-perspective at the price of total and cruel repudiation of an old one.

We will call what young people in their teens and early twenties look for in religion and in other dogmatic systems an *ideology*. At the most it is a militant system with uniformed members and uniform goals; at the least it is a "way of life," or what the Germans call a *Weltanschauung*, a world-view which is consonant with existing theory, available knowledge, and common sense, and yet is significantly more: an utopian outlook, a cosmic mood, or a doctrinal logic, all shared as self-evident beyond any need for demonstration. What is to be relinquished as "old" may be the individual's previous life; this usually means the perspectives intrinsic to the life-style of the parents, who are thus discarded contrary to all traditional safeguards of filial devotion. The "old" may be a part of himself, which must henceforth be subdued by some rigorous self-denial in a private life-style or through membership in a militant or military organization; or, it may be the world-view of other castes and classes, races and peoples: in this case, these people become not only expendable, but the appointed victims of the most righteous annihilation.

The need for devotion, then, is one aspect of the identity crisis which we, as psychologists, make responsible for all these tendencies and susceptibilities. The need for repudiation is another aspect. In their late teens and early twenties, even when there is no explicit ideological commitment or even interest, young people offer devotion to individual leaders and to teams, to strenuous activities, and to difficult techniques; at the same time they show a sharp and intolerant readiness to discard and disavow people (including, at times, themselves). This repudiation is often snobbish, fitful, perverted, or simply thoughtless.

These constructive and destructive aspects of youthful energy have been and are employed in making and remaking tradition in many diverse areas. Youth stands between the past and the future, both in individual life and in society; it also stands between alternate ways of life. As I pointed out in "The Problem of Ego-Identity,"[36] ideologies offer to the members of this age-group overly simplified and yet determined answers to exactly those vague inner states and those urgent questions which arise in consequence of identity conflict. Ideologies serve to channel youth's forceful earnestness and sincere asceticism, as well as its search for excitement and its eager indignation, toward that social frontier where the struggle between conservatism and radicalism is most alive. On that frontier, fanatic ideologists do their busy work and psychopathic leaders their dirty work; but there, also, true leaders create significant solidarities.

In its search for that combination of freedom and discipline, of adventure and tradition, which suits its state, youth may exploit (and be exploited by) the most varied devotions. Subjecting itself to hardship and discipline, it may seek sanctioned opportunities for spatial dispersion, follow wandering apprenticeships, heed the call of frontiers, man the outposts of new nations, fight (almost anybody's) holy wars, or test the limits of locomotive machine-power. By the same token it is ready to provide the physical power and the vociferous noise of rebellions, riots, and lynchings, often knowing little and caring less for the real issues involved. On the other hand, it is most eager to adopt rules of physical restriction and of utter intellectual concentration, be it in the study of ancient books, the contemplation of monkhood, or the striving for the new—for example, in the collective "sincerity" of modern thought reform. Even when it is led to destroy and to repudiate without any apparent cause, as in delinquent gangs, in colonies of perverts and addicts, or in the circles of petty snobs, it rarely does so without some obedience, some solidarity, some hanging on to elusive values.

Societies, knowing that young people can change rapidly even in their most intense devotions, are apt to give them a *moratorium,* a span of time after they have ceased being children, but before their deeds and works count toward a future identity. In Luther's time the monastery was, at least for some, one possible psychosocial moratorium, one possible way of postponing the decision as to what one is and is going to be. It may seem strange that as definite and, in fact, as eternal, a commitment as is expressed in the monastic vow could be considered a moratorium, a means of marking time. Yet in Luther's era, to be an ex-monk was not impossible; nor was there necessarily a stigma attached to leaving a monastic order, provided only that one left in a quiet and prescribed way—as for example, Erasmus did, who was nevertheless offered a cardinalate in his old age; or that one could make cardinals laugh about themselves, as the runaway monk Rabelais was able to do. I do not mean to suggest that those who chose the monastery, any more than those who choose other forms of moratoria in different historical coordinates (as Freud did, in committing himself to laboratory physiology, or St. Augustine to Manichaeism) *know* that they are marking time before they come to their crossroad, which they often do in the late twenties, belated just because they gave their all to the temporary subject of devotion. The crisis in such a young man's life may be reached exactly when he half-realizes that he is fatally overcommitted to what he is not.

As a witness to the predicament of over-commitment let me quote an old man who, looking back on his own youth, had to admit that no catastrophe or failure stopped him in his tracks, but rather the feeling that things were going meaninglessly well. Somehow events in his life were coming to a head, but he felt that he was being lived by them, rather than living them. A man in this predicament is apt to choose the kind of lonely and stubborn moratorium which all but smothers its own creative potential. George Bernard Shaw describes his crisis clearly and unsparingly.[37]

"I made good in spite of myself, and found, to my dismay, that Business, instead of expelling me as the worthless imposter I was, was fastening upon me with no intention of letting me go. Behold me, therefore, in my twentieth year, with a business training, in an occupation which I detested as cordially as any sane person lets himself detest anything he cannot escape from. In March, 1876 I broke loose."

Breaking loose meant to leave family and friends, business and Ireland, and to avoid the danger of success without identity, of a success unequal to "the enormity of my unconscious ambition." He thus granted himself a prolongation of the interval between youth and adulthood. He writes: ". . . when I left my native city I left this phase behind me, and associated no more with men of my age until, after about eight years of solitude in this respect, I was drawn into the Socialist revival of the early eighties, among Englishmen *intensely serious* and *burning with indignation* at *very real* and *very fundamental evils* that affected *all the world.*" (The words I have italicized in this statement are almost a list of the issues which dominate Martin's history.) In the meantime, Shaw apparently avoided opportunities, sensing that "Behind the conviction that they could lead to nothing that I wanted, lay the unspoken fear that they might lead to something I did not want." We have to grant some young people, then, the paradoxical fear of a negative success, a success which would commit them in a direction where, they feel, they will not "grow together."

Potentially creative men like Shaw build the personal fundament of their work during a self-decreed moratorium, during which they often starve themselves, socially, erotically, and, last but not least, nutritionally, in order to let the grosser weeds die out, and make way for the growth of their inner garden. Often, when the weeds are dead, so is the garden. At the decisive moment, however, some make contact with a nutriment specific for their gifts. For Shaw, of course, this gift was literature. As he dreamt of a number of professional choices, "of literature I had no dreams at all, any more than a duck has of swimming."

He did not dream of it, but he did it, and with a degree of ritualization close to what clinicians call an "obsessive compensation." This often balances a temporary lack of inner direction with an almost fanatic concentration on activities which maintain whatever work habits the individual may have preserved. "I bought supplies of white paper, demy size, by sixpence-worths at a time; folded it in quarto; and condemned myself to fill five pages of it a day, rain or shine, dull or inspired. I had so much of the schoolboy and the clerk still in me that if my five pages ended in the middle of a sentence I did not finish it until the next day. On the other hand, if I missed a day, I made up for it by doing a double task on the morrow. On this plan I produced five novels in five years. It was my professional apprenticeship. . . ." We may add that these five novels were not published for over fifty years, at which time Shaw, in a special introduction, tried to dissuade the potential buyer from reading them, while recommending to his attention their biographical importance. To such an extent was Shaw aware of their true function and meaning; although his early work habits were almost pathological in their compulsive addictiveness, they were auto-therapeutic in their perseverance: "I have risen by sheer gravitation, too industrious by acquired habit to stop working (I work as my father drank)." There is a world of anguish, conflict, and victory in this small parenthesis; for to succeed, Shaw had to inwardly defeat an already outwardly defeated father some of whose peculiarities (for example, a strange sense of humor) contributed to the son's unique greatness, and yet also to that specific failure that is in each greatness. Shaw's autobiographical remarks do not leave any doubt about the true abyss which he, one of the shyest of religious men, faced in his youth before he had learned to cover his sensitivities by appearing on the stage of history as the great cynic ("in this I succeeded only too well"), while using the theatre to speak out of the mouth of the Maid of Orleans.

As was indicated in the preface, Freud and Darwin are among the great men who came upon their most decisive contribution only after a change of direction and not without neurotic involvement at the time of the breakthrough to their specific creativity. Darwin failed in medicine, and had, as if accidentally, embarked on a trip which, in fact, he almost missed because of what seem to have been psychosomatic symptoms. Once aboard the *Beagle,* however, he found not only boundless physical vigor, but also a keen eye for unexplored details in nature, and a creative discernment leading straight to revolutionary insights: the law of natural selection began to haunt him. He was twenty-seven years old when he came home; he soon became an undiagnosed and lifelong invalid, able only after years of concentrated study to organize his data into a pattern which convincingly supported his ideas. Freud, too, was already thirty when, as if driven to do so by mere circumstance, he became a practicing neurologist and made psychiatry his laboratory. He had received his medical degree belatedly, having decided to become a medical scientist rather than a doctor at the age of seventeen. His moratorium, which gave him a basic schooling in method while it delayed the development of his specific gift and his revolutionary creativity, was spent in (then physicalistic) physiology. And when he at last did embark on his stupendous lifework, he was almost delayed further by neurotic suffering. However, a creative man has no choice. He may come across his supreme task almost accidentally. But once the issue is joined, his task proves to be at the same time intimately related to his most personal conflicts, to his superior selective perception, and to the stubbornness of his one-way will: he must court sickness, failure, or insanity, in order to test the alternative whether the established world will crush him, or whether he will disestablish a sector of this world's outworn fundaments and make a place for a new one.[38]

Darwin dealt with man's biological origins. His achievement, and his sin, was a theory that made man part of nature. To accomplish this, and only for this, he was able to put his neurosis aside. Freud, however, had to "appoint his own neurosis that angel who was to be wrestled with and not to be let go, until he would bless the observer." Freud's wrestling with the angel was his working through of his own father complex which at first had led him astray in his search for the origins of the neuroses in childhood. Once he understood his own relationship to his father, he could establish the existence of the universal father image in man, break through to the mother image as well, and finally arrive at the Oedipus complex, the formulation of which made him one of the most controversial figures in the history of ideas. In *The Interpretation of Dreams*,[39] Freud gave psychoanalysis its orientation as the study of unconscious motivation in the normal as well as the pathological, in society as well as the individual. At the same time he freed his own creativity by self-analysis and was able to combine strict observation with disciplined intuition and literary craftsmanship.

This general discussion of the qualities of that critical area between neurosis and creativity will introduce the state of mind which engulfed Martin at the time of the fit in the choir. Even the possibly legendary aspects of this fit reflect an unconscious understanding on the part of the legend-makers, here Martin's monastic brothers, as to what was going on inside him. In the next chapter [in *Young Man Luther*] we will analyze what little is known of Martin's childhood. Then we will trace the subsequent personality change which made it possible for the young man who in the choir was literally felled by the power of the need to negate to stand before his emperor and before the Pope's emissary at the Diet of Worms twelve years later and affirm human integrity in new terms: "My conscience is bound by God's words. Retract anything whatsoever I neither can nor will. For to act against one's conscience is neither safe nor honorable."[40]

God's words: he had, by then, become God's "spokesman," preacher, teacher, orator, and pamphleteer. This had become the working part of his identity. The eventual liberation of Luther's voice made him creative. The one matter on which professor and priest, psychiatrist and sociologist, agree is Luther's immense gift for language: his receptivity for the written word; his memory for the significant phrase; and his range of verbal expression (lyrical, biblical, satirical, and vulgar) which in English is paralleled only by Shakespeare.

The development of this gift is implicit in the dramatic outcry in the choir of Erfurt: for was it not a "dumb" spirit which beset the patient before Jesus? And was it not muteness, also, which the monk had to deny by thus roaring "like an ox"? The theme of the Voice and of the Word, then, is intertwined with the theme of Luther's identity and with his influence on the ideology of his time.

We will therefore concentrate on this process: how young Martin, at the end of a somber and harsh childhood, was precipitated into a severe identity crisis for which he sought delay and cure in the silence of the monastery; how being silent, he became "possessed"; how being possessed, he gradually learned to speak a new language, *his* language; how being able to speak, he not only talked himself out of the monastery, and much of his country out of the Roman Church, but also formulated for himself and for all of mankind a new kind of ethical and psychological awareness: and how, at the end, this awareness, too, was marred by a return of the demons, whoever they may have been.

THE MEANING OF
"MEANING IT"

from *Young Man Luther*

1

In Goethe's day it became fashionable for German and Nordic men of the arts and sciences to divide their lives into the periods "before" and "after" their first trip to Italy—as if a thinking and feeling man's humanist awareness was fully ripe only after Nordic discipline and thought had been combined with the style and sensuality of the Mediterranean.

Luther, too, went to Rome. What we know of this visit and of his reactions, however, indicates not only a monastic self-restriction, but also a decidedly provincial unawareness of the nature and the culture of the South, and a strange anonymity, considering the fact that ten years later he became the Pope's effective antagonist. In the autumn of 1510 he set out for Rome on foot, one of two monks who were to present in the Vicar General's office in Rome an urgent appeal from a number of Augustinian monasteries of the Saxon congregation. These monasteries were opposed to plans already decreed by a papal bull, on recommendation of the General of the Order, Mariano de Genazzano, to give Staupitz, just appointed provincial general of all of Saxony, sweeping power to reorganize the twenty-nine monasteries of his congregation. Twenty-two of the monasteries had approved the plans; but seven ob-

jected, among them Nuremberg and Erfurt, the two largest and most influential. Over Staupitz's head they decided to send two representatives
to Rome. The official spokesman was probably an older monk from
Nuremberg; his mandatory *socius itinerarius* (for an Augustinian never
traveled alone) was Father Luther from Erfurt. Exactly what mixture of
political principle, inescapable obedience, local loyalty, or personal ambivalence was responsible for Martin's selection for this errand is impossible to know.

By its very absence of any overt sensation, Martin's journey was an
event strange to behold. The future reformer, acting as chaperon to an
older monk on a regional routine errand to the capital, crosses Southern
Germany and Northern Italy, climbs over the Alps and the Apennines, all
on foot, and mostly in abominable weather, finally "comes upon the Italian Renaissance," and notices nothing; just as nobody notices anything
unusual about him.

He passed through Florence, where, as yet a public novelty of a few
years, Michelangelo's gigantic David stood on the porch of the Signoria,
a sculptured declaration of the emancipation of youth from dark giants.
Little more than a decade before, Savonarola had been burned in Florence: a man of fiery sincerity; a man who, like Martin, had tried academic life, and had found it ideologically wanting; who also had left home
to become a monk, and, at the age of twenty-nine, after a long latency
as an orator, had burst out preaching against the papal Antichrist. He also
became the leader not only of a local political movement, but of an international movement of rebellious northerners. Luther later called him
a saint; but there is every reason to believe that at the time of this journey both the visual splendor and the passionate heroism of the Renaissance were to him primarily Italian, and foreign; the social leadership of
Savonarola, with its Christian utopianism, must have seemed far removed
from whatever Protestant yearning Martin may have felt. What he did
notice in Florence was the devoted and quiet *Riformazione* which went
along with the noisy and resplendent *Risorgimento*: he admired the personal service rendered to the poor by anonymous aristocrats; he noted the
hygienic and democratic administration of hospitals and orphanages.

He and his companion completed their extramural duties in as short
a time as possible (as monks should) and took advantage of their trip (as
was then routine) to make a general confession at the very center of
Christendom. He first beheld The City, as many travelers and pilgrims

before and after him, from a certain spot on the ancient Via Cassia; he reached his order's host monastery immediately after having entered through the Porta del Popolo. Once established, Martin seems to have gone about his errand like a representative of some firm or union who accompanies an official to the federal capital to see the secretary of a department about an issue already decided against them. He spent much time commuting from his hotel to the department, and more time there in waiting rooms; never saw the secretary himself, and left without knowing the disposition of their appeal. In the meantime, he saw the sights which one must see and attempted to be properly impressed; also he heard a lot of gossip which, when he returned home, he undoubtedly distributed as inside information. All in all, however, the inner workings of the capital have remained mysterious to him.

In one respect, however, Martin differed from most travelers. Although he accepted most of the trip with sober thought, he approached certain of the routine sights with the fervor of a most desperate pilgrim. His attempt to devote himself, in his spare time, to some highly promoted observances in Rome seems to indicate a last endeavor on his part to settle his inner unrest with ceremonial fervor, by the accomplishment of works.

Those who visualize the beggar-monk awed by the splendor of ancient Rome and seething with vociferous indignation about papal luxury will be disappointed to hear first of all that the city of Rome, at that time, was primarily a wasteland of rubble which Martin had to cross on his daily walks from the Augustinian monastery near the Chiesa Santa Maria del Popolo to the center of town. The ancient city had not been restored since the Normans had burned it in 1084. The only architectural signs of life were monasteries, hunting lodges, and the summer houses of the aristocracy; and the only human signs of life were hordes of brigands. A medieval city, with only twice as many people as Erfurt, and with very little of Erfurt's sedate merchant spirit functioned in the flatlands of the Tiber. Papal Rome itself had the character of an administrative capital with ministries, legations, financial houses, hotels, and inns; it was, at the time, deserted by all important functionaries, who had followed the Pope to a warfront. Every monastic order had a central office in Rome, as well as a mother monastery; but a monk on business would not get any closer to the Vatican than the office of his order's procurator. Martin was able to meet only some bureaucrats, lobbyists, the shyster lawyers, and the political agents attached to the various office-holders; and the prostitutes of both sexes who beset them all.

As for Renaissance splendor, the city architecture did not reflect much of it as yet. Imposing avenues had been planned and partially laid out; and a few grandiose palaces, with rather stern and simple exteriors, had been erected to house the Renaissance which was on the move to Rome. But whatever existed of uniform styles of life and of art was confined mostly to the exclusive interiors of these palaces; the streets were still medieval in character. Michelangelo was at work on the ceilings of the Sistine Chapel, and Raphael was adorning the walls of the Pope's chambers; but these projects were private, and excluded, if not the *popolo* of aristocrats, certainly the populace at large, and all undistinguished foreigners. St. Peter's was in the process of being rebuilt, many of the old buildings having been torn down to make space for that imperial edifice which would not be completed for another century. What in style was a renaissance of Caesarian antiquity, no doubt seemed primarily Italian to the busy German monk; he was interested in works of art only for the sake of some curious historical circumstance, or gigantic proportions, or some surprising realism of technique which always impresses those who have not specifically learned to enthuse about a new style.

In his provincial eagerness to absorb the spiritual possibilities of Rome, Martin visited the seven churches, fasting all the way, in order to be ready for communion in St. Peter's, the last and most important. He had no thought of disengaging himself from the flourishing relic business, and he went eagerly to see the arms of his beloved St. Anne, which were displayed in a church separately from the rest of her bones. He saw with awe the halves of the bodies of St. Peter and of St. Paul, which had been weighed to prevent injustice to the church harboring the other halves. The churches were proud of these saintly slices: some later saints, immediately after their souls' departures, had been carefully boiled to prepare their bones for immediate shipment to worthy bidders. With these and other relics, the various churches maintained a kind of permanent fair where one could see, for a fee, Jesus's footprint in a piece of marble, or one of Judas's silver coins. One sight of this coin could save the viewer fourteen hundred years in purgatory; the wanderer along the holy road from the Lateran Church to St. Peter's had done his afterlife as much good as by a pilgrimage to the holy sepulchre in Jerusalem. And so much cheaper.

It is easy to say that the relics were just for the people and that the

Church's intellectuals worked hard to reconcile faith and reason. Luther was, and always remained, one of the people; and like highly intelligent men of any age who do not challenge the propaganda of their government or the advertisements of the dominant economic system, Martin had become accustomed to the worst kind of commercialism. Back in Wittenberg Fredric was displaying such relics as a branch of the Burning Bush of Moses, thorns from the Crown of Thorns, and some of the straw of the Manger. The display even included a hair and a drop of milk from the Virgin herself. Later, of course, Luther raged against both the commercialism and the inanity of such "stinking" practices; in Rome, he still so much wanted to be of the people that he did not really rouse from his medieval twilight world. Only his obsessional symptoms stirred. He ran like a "mad saint" through all the churches in vain, finally advancing up the twenty-eight steps of the Lateran Church on his knees, saying a paternoster on each step in the conviction that each paternoster would free a soul from purgatory (without that soul being consulted, as he dared to comment only years later). Arriving on the top, all he could think was: "Who knows whether it is true?" But then, on the way up he had entertained the classical obsessional thought that he "almost" wished his parents dead so that he could use this golden opportunity to save them more surely.

Also typically, he was bothered most by affronts against the very observance which caused the greatest scruples in himself, namely, the Mass. He was horrorstricken when he heard German courtesans laugh and say that the Roman priests, under their breath, were murmuring *"Panis es, panis manebis, vinum es, vinum manebis"*—Bread and wine thou art, and shall always be. And, indeed, the priests' driving hurry was more than obvious to him, the slow pious German, who had come determined to celebrate the Mass faultlessly at the traditional altars, and get the most value out of the occasion. He did not like to be told, *"Passa, passa*—Hurry up, get on." In Sebastian's Basilica, he saw seven priests celebrate Mass at one altar in just one hour. Worst of all, they did not know Latin, and their careless, furtive, undisciplined gestures seemed a mockery. He had desired above all to say Mass on a Saturday in front of the entrance to the chapel *Sancta Sanctorum*; for this act would contribute materially to his mother's salvation. But alas, the rush was too great; some mothers, Martin's included, never had a chance. So he went and ate a salted herring. All these hindrances and nuisances, however, were to Martin at the time expres-

sions of the Italian national character, not of the Church's decline. He felt
at home in only one church in Rome: Santa Maria dell' Anima, the German church, whose sacristan he remembered long and well.

Luther later mentioned (as far as the records show) only a few impressions of the seventy days of traveling, and they are all utilitarian. He
admired the grandiose aqueducts in Rome, and he gave the Florentine
aristocrats high praise for their well-run orphanages and hospitals, ignoring whatever other merits they may have prided themselves on. He
judged the old St. Peter's acoustics to be as bad as those of the dome in
Cologne and the cathedral in Ulm. He liked the fertile valley of the Po;
but Switzerland was a "country full of sterile mountains."

Luther ignored the Renaissance and never referred to the esthetic
quality of a single one of its statues or pictures, painters, or writers;
this is a historical as well as a personal footnote. It takes time, especially
for deeply preoccupied people, to comprehend the unity of the beginnings of an era which later will be so neatly classified in history books.
Even today, when history has reached the height of journalistic self-
consciousness, important trends and events can remain invisible before
our eyes. If Luther did not notice the Renaissance, that does not in itself
mean that he was not a man of the Renaissance. Erasmus, who had been
in Rome a year earlier, and had had access to the papal chambers, never
mentioned Michelangelo or Raphael. And Martin was, most of all, a religious egotist who had not learned to speak to either man or God, nor
to speak glamorously and in a revitalized vernacular as the Renaissance
demanded. He was a provincial Saxon who had studied Latin, Greek, and
Hebrew, and who had still to create, out of his own explosive needs, the
German language with which to speak to his own people.

The traveler of today, however, will find in the Uffizi in Florence,
among the grandiose works of Renaissance painting, Cranach's small, exquisite, and sober portrait of Martin Luther.

2

At this point one could easily fall into the mistake of St. Thomas' colleagues, and be too impressed with what the dumb (and in this case, even
German) ox did *not* say. Some have wondered how, in the space of a few

years, such a man could grow into a great reformer. Others have suspected that as he was retracing his steps over the wintry Alps, he was
seething with well-formulated indignation. Above all, however, his behavior on this trip, and his later utterances concerning it, have been used
to bolster the image of Luther as a medieval man, utterly untouched by
the Renaissance, to which he seemed blind.

Visually unreceptive he was, to an extraordinary degree. I propose this
consideration, however: Luther simply had not reached the end of his
creative latency. An original thinker often waits a long time not only for
impressions, but also for his own reactions. (Freud was unreceptive to
"musical noise," Darwin nauseated by higher literature. Freud did not become a psychoanalyst, nor Darwin an evolutionist, until they had reached
the end of their twenties.) In the meantime he lives, as it were, in his pre-
conscious, storing up in other than verbal images what impressions he receives, and keeping his affects from premature conclusions. One could say
that Luther was compulsively retentive, or even that he was mentally and
spiritually "constipated"—as he was apt to be physically all his life. But
this retentive tendency (soon to alternate with an explosive one) was
part of his equipment; and just as we assume that psychosexual energies
can be sublimated, we must grant that a man can (and must) learn to derive out of the modes of his psychobiological and psychosexual make-
up the prime modality of his creative adaptation. The image of Martin
inhibited and reined in by a tight retentiveness must be supplemented by
one which shows him taming his affects and restraining his speech until
he would be able to say in one and the same explosive breath what he
had come to really *mean,* what he really had thought through. In order
to know himself what he thinks, such a "total" man is dependent on his
need to combine intellectual meaning with an inner sense of meaning it.
My main proposition is that, after he had come thus to *mean* it, Luther's
message (in the first form of his early lectures) did contain a genuine Renaissance attitude. But since a renaissance emerges *against* something, it
is necessary to discuss briefly those elements of the dogma which to
Luther and his contemporaries were ideological alternatives, and which
he restated, rejuvenated, or repudiated in his early lectures.

Our problem centers around the contribution of religious dogma and
practice to the sense of identity of an age. All religions assume that a
Higher Identity inhabits the great unknown; men of different eras and
areas give this Identity a particular appearance or configuration from

which they borrow that part of their identity which we may call *existential,* since it is defined by the relation of each soul to its mere existence. (In this context we should not be sidetracked by such monastic-ascetic techniques as those that systematically diminish man's sense of an individual identity; for they may be rather a supreme test of having a pretty firm one.) The particular Christian combination of a Higher Identity in the form of a Personal Maker of an absolutist moral bent, and a father figure who became more human in heaven as he became more totalitarian on earth was, we suggest, gradually robbing medieval man of just that existential identity which religion owed him.

As was pointed out in the Prologue [of *Young Man Luther*], the matter is never strictly a religious one, even though the medieval Church could claim a monopoly on official ideologies. The question always involves those events, institutions, and individuals which actually influence the world-image at a given time in such a way that the identity needs of individuals are vitally affected, whether such influence is or is not quite conscious, generally intended, officially sanctioned, or specifically enforced. The problem is a psychohistorical one, and I can do no more than suggest it. There are two sides to it: what makes an ideology *really* effective at a given historical moment? and what is the nature of its effects on the individuals involved?

Consider for a brief moment certain great names of our time, which prides itself on a dominant identity enhanced by scientific truth. Darwin, Einstein, and Freud—omitting Marx, who was a conscious and deliberate ideological craftsman—would certainly deny that they had any intention of influencing, say, the editorials, or the vocabulary, or the scrupulosity of our time in the ways in which they undoubtedly did and do. They could, in fact, refute the bulk of the concepts popularly ascribed to them, or vaguely and anonymously derived from them, as utterly foreign to their original ideas, their methodology, and their personal philosophy and conduct. Darwin did not intend to debase man to an animal; Einstein did not preach relativism; Freud was neither a philosophical pansexualist nor a moral egotist. Freud pointed squarely to the psychohistorical problem involved when he said that the world apparently could not forgive him for having revised the image of man by demonstrating the dependence of man's will on unconscious motivation, just as Darwin had not been forgiven for demonstrating man's relationship to the animal world, or Copernicus for showing that our earth is off-center.

Freud did not foresee a worse fate, namely that the world can absorb such a major shock by splintering it into minor half-truths, irrelevant exaggerations, and brilliant distortions, mere caricatures of the intended design. Yet somehow the shock affects the intimate inner balance of many, if not all, contemporary individuals, obviously not because great men are understood and believed, but because they are felt to represent vast shifts in man's image of the universe and of his place in it—shifts which are determined concomitantly by political and economic developments. The tragedy of great men is that they are the leaders and yet the victims of ideological processes.

From time to time, a great institution tries to monopolize, to stabilize, and to master the ideological process. The Church was such an institution. I shall try to reformulate from this point of view some of the main ideological influences which affected Luther's observances and studies.

Christianity, like all great movements, had its heroic era, repeatedly appealed to as a mythical justification, but rarely recaptured in earnest.

What is known of the early Christians of the Paulinian era creates the impression that they lived in the kind of clean and clear atmosphere which exists only after a catastrophic storm. This storm, of course, was Christ's passion. He had died for all men. To his followers, for a while, the merry-go-round of destruction and restoration which characterizes man's cycle of war and peace, festivals and carnivals, intoxication and remorse, had come to rest. The legend of Christ conveyed that total presence and absolute transcendence which is the rarest and the most powerful force among men. A few simple words had once more penetrated the disguises and pretenses of this world, words which at one and the same time were part of the language of the child, the language of the unconscious, and the language of the uncorrupted core of all spiritual tradition. Once again the mortal vulnerability of the individual soul had become the very backbone of its spiritual strength; the very fragility of a new beginning promised to move mountains. Death, fully accepted, became the highest identity on earth, superseding the need for smaller identities, and assuring at least one unquestionable equality for poor and rich, sick and healthy, ignorant and erudite. The disinherited (disinherited in earthly goods, and in social identity) above all desired to hear and rehear those words which made their inner world, long stagnant and dead, reverberate with forgotten echoes; this desire made them believe that God, from somewhere in the outer spaces, spoke through a chosen man on a definable historical occasion. Because the savior used the biological parable of a sonship of God, they believed in a traceable divine descendance of the son. But alas, having hardly made a God out of the son, they brought the Father down to a level where He seems much too human—for such a son.

The early Christians could be brothers and sisters, eating together without murderous envy, and together partaking of Him Who had commanded them to do so. They were able to ignore obsessive laws of observance, and improvise ritual and conduct as faith seemed to suggest—for had not the Son's uncorrupted self-sacrifice been accepted as valid by the Father of all fathers? History was dead. They could ignore the horizontal of worldly organization, that exchange of bewildering different currencies, all dirty from too much handling, and forever mutually contradictory in exchange value, forever cheating somebody, and most often everybody; they could concentrate on the vertical which connects each man's soul with the higher Identity in heaven, bringing down the currency of charity, and taking faith back up to Him. Occasionally in world history, communities like the early Christians have existed, and do exist, like a field of flowers, even though no one would mistake the single member for a lily, as St. Paul did not. What gave them, as a community, a glow greater than the sum of their individual selves was the identity of knowing transcendence: "We know, therefore we are—in eternity." St. Paul said to them, as if he were speaking to a garden of children: "You may all prophesy one by one, that all may learn, and all may be comforted."[1] Such identity, vulnerable as it seems, is indestructible in its immediate conviction, which carries within it a sense of reality common to good proselytizers and good martyrs.

I saw a small and transient example of the gaiety of *Agape* only two decades ago, in a small pueblo in our Southwest. Though excommunicated by the Roman Church for an act of collective disobedience, the pueblo was preparing for a religious holiday, I think Easter. The men were mending the adobe walls of the church, the young people formed a chain to hand buckets of water from the brook, and the women, dressed in gay colors, were scrubbing and washing the church. Where the altar had been, an elder sat, wrinkled, shrewd, and dignified; he was the oldest and the newest priest, and was supervising the construction of a madonna, an enormous ball of colorful cloth topped by a tiny crowned head. Somewhere on her global bosom there lay a tiny pink baby doll. Instead of candles this goddess was surrounded by magnificent cornstalks. One could not help feeling that the concordant gaiety which bound these people together in the improvisation of a religion, combining the best of the old and the new, was a response to having been freed from the supervision of the law. In ignoring the excommunication they gained a gay energy from the historical vacuum. Some, of course, sulked and worried in their houses; and in the background was the absent priest, who was being sacrificially murdered by the proceedings.

Those early Christians did play havoc with the organized world, the horizontal relation of things and events in space and time. Unhistorically, unhierarchically, and unconditionally, they treated as of no substance or avail the Jewish identity of patriarchal law, the Roman identity of world-citizenship, and the Greek identity of body-mind harmony. All human order was only of this world, which was coming to a foreseeable end.

Christianity also had its early organizational era. It had started as a spiritual revolution with the idea of freeing an earthly proletariat for victory in another world after the impending withering of this one. But as always, the withering comes to be postponed; and in the meantime, bureaucracies must keep the world in a state of preparedness. This demands the administrative planning and the theoretical definition of a double citizenship: one vertical, to take effect *when*; and one horizontal, always in effect *now*. The man who first conceived of and busily built the intersection of the horizontal and the vertical was St. Paul, a man converted out of a much too metropolitan identity conflict between Jewish rabbi, Roman citizen, and Greek philosopher not to become an empire-builder and doctrine-former. His much-traveled body reached Rome only to be beheaded; but his organizational testament merged with that of Christ's chosen successor, the sturdy Peter, to eventually establish in the capital of the horizontal empire of Rome a permanent anchorage and earthly terminal for all of man's verticals. (Luther, in his first theological restatements, was identifying with Paul's evangelical identity: he did not know, until it was to be foisted on him, how much he was preparing to identify with Paul's managerial fervor, his ecclesiastic identity, as well.)

The sacrifice, in whose blood the early gnostic identity had flourished, was gradually sacrificed to dogma; and thus that rare sublimation, that holiday of transcendence, which alone had been able to dissolve the forces of the horizontal, was forfeited. Philosophically and doctrinally, the main problem became the redefinition of the sacrifice so that its magic would continue to bind together, in a widening orbit, not only the faith of the weak and the simple, but also the will of the strong, the initiative of the ambitious, and the reason of the thinking. In each of these groups, also, the double citizenship meant a split identity: an eternal, always impending, one, and one within a stereotyped hierarchy of earthly estates. For all of these groups an encompassing theology had to be formulated and periodically reformulated.

The philosophers thus had their task set out for them: the theoretical anchoring of the vertical in the horizontal in such a way that the identities of the horizontal would remain chained to each other in a hierarchical order which would continue to receive its values and its style from the Church. To maintain itself, an ideological monopoly must assure all the stereotyped roles it creates, from the bureaucratic and ceremonial center to the militant and defensive outposts on the periphery, a sense of invigorating independence, without weakening their common bond to the centralized source of a common Super-Identity. The Roman Church, more than any other church or political organization, succeeded in making an ideological dogma—formulated, defended, and imposed by a central governing body—the exclusive condition for *any* identity on earth. It made this total claim totalitarian by using terror. In this case (as in others) the terror was not always directly applied to quivering bodies; it was predicted for a future world, typically in such a way that nobody could quite know whom it would hit, or when. That a man has or may have done something mortally bad, something which may or may not ruin his eternal after-condition, makes his status and inner state totally dependent on the monopolists of salvation, and leaves him only the identity of a potential sinner. As in the case of all terror, the central agency can always claim not to be responsible for the excessive fervor of its operatives; in fact, it may claim it has dissuaded its terrorists by making periodic energetic pronouncements. These, however, never reach the lowly places where life in the raw drives people into being each others' persecutors, beginning with the indoctrination of children.

One philosophical problem, then, involved the definition of the vertical's earthly anchorage in the Church, its unseen destination in heaven, and the kind of traffic it would bear back and forth. This is the question of man's identity in the hidden face of God, and of God's in the revealed face of man; it includes the possibility of ever receiving an inkling of mutual recognition as through a glass darkly, or the shadow of a smile. The philosophers did not shirk concreteness and substantiality; and all the concepts we will mention must be understood to be as thing-like as we can conceive them to be: who is man in this world of things? what equipment does he have to approach God in the hope of making contact, to be heard and perhaps to be given a message? Who is God? and where, and what equipment does He use to partake in life on earth, for the sake of whatever investment He may have in it? The idea that Christ had been divinity become mortal and had returned to be next to and in God again became dogma only centuries after his death, at which time the question became involved in the nascent scientific curiosity (then guided entirely by philosophy) which called for answers combining gnostic immediacy with philosophic speculation, and with naturalist observation; all within a framework of obedience to the Church's dogma.

Plato's Absolute Good, the world of pure ideas, was for thinking people the strongest contender to the idea of a personal god; its pole was the Absolute Bad, the world of special appearances and worldly involvements. Christianity defended itself, as it absorbed them, against Platonism and Aristotelianism; thus, questions of the relatively greater identity and of the differential initiative of the two worlds became paramount. Does he who learns to recognize the more real also become more real—and more virtuous into the bargain? And who has the initiative in the matter? Is God waiting for our moves, or is He moving us? Do we have the leeway of some initiative? if so, how do we know of it and learn to use it—and when do we forfeit it?

It has been said that Descartes's "I think, therefore I am" marked the end of medieval philosophy, which began with St. Augustine, who saw in man's ability to think the proof not only of God's existence, but also of God's grace. Augustine thought that man's "inner light" is the realization of the *infusio caritatis,* so that we may speak of a *caritative* or *infused iden-*

tity. It is precisely because Augustine centered all his theology in faith that Luther called him the greatest theologian since the apostles and before Luther. Augustine (as Luther, later) made no concession about the completeness of *perditio,* man's total lostness, nor is he less relentlessly convinced that only God has Being by Himself. "Things," he says, "are and are not; they are because from God they derive existence; they are not because they only *have* being, they *are* not being. . . . they exist not all at once, but by passing away and succeeding, they together complete the universe, whereof they are a portion."[2] Man, without grace, would obviously be no different: he, too, passes away. Without grace, the identity of man is also one of the mere succession of men. But God gave him a mind and a memory, and thus the rudiment of an identity.

> These things do I within, in that vast court of my memory. For there are present within me, heaven, earth, sea, and whatever I could think on therein, besides what I have forgotten. There also meet I with myself, and recall myself, and when, where, and what I have done, and under what feelings. There be all which I remember, either on my own experience or other's credit. Out of the same store do I myself with the past continually combine fresh and fresh likenesses of things which I have experienced, or, from what I have experienced, have believed: and thence again infer future actions, events and hopes, and all these again I reflect on, as present. . . . Sure I am that in it Thou dwellest, since I have remembered Thee ever since I learnt Thee, and there I find Thee, when I call Thee to remembrance.[3]

In spite of Augustine's pessimistic statements about man's total perdition, then, he does seem to be rather glad to meet himself face to face in his own memory. Nonetheless, it is a gift of God's *caritas* that he *can* thus meet himself, for, as Paul said: "Who maketh thee to differ from another? and what hast thou that thou didst not receive?"[4] To look at himself in his own memory without being grateful to God would be narcissism—what Augustine calls *praesumptio* which, together with *superbia,* constitutes man's greatest sin: egomania. For man forfeited all free will when he was born human, and thus sick in origin *(morbus originis)*. Because of Christ's sacrifice, he is able to receive through baptism redemption from the sins of previous generations; but he is still burdened with *concupiscentia,* with the "touchwood, the tinder, of sin" *(fomes peccati)*. He is only a *homo naturalis,* but does have the chance that his mind might be recreated by the infusion of God's grace, and that he might become a *homo spiritualis.*

To Augustine, *concupiscentia* was covetousness, and thus *libido,* which is not sin, but only the stuff sin is made of; it becomes sin through man's *consensus.* By a free act of love, God can give man the ability *not* to identify with his own drives. But should man sin, there is still God's *misericordia indebita,* his pity, which is available even to the undeserving. Thus, whatever we are and become, what we can do and will do, is all a gift from God: *Ex Deo nobis est, non ex nobis.* But for all his renunciation of free will, Augustine shows a pathway up the vertical whose waysigns are *fruitio* and *perfectio.* His theology, compared with those that followed, is a maternal one; in it the wretched human being is forever reassured that, because of Christ's sacrifice, he is born with a chance in life; growth, and fruition, and possible perfection are open to him; and he may always expect his share, and more, of the milk of grace.

St. Augustine saved the Church from Platonism by embracing and converting it; St. Thomas did the same with the Aristotelianism which reemerged in the middle ages, intellectually ornamented by the medical and mystical Arabs and Jews. Platonism, the orientation toward the Idea, was, through St. Thomas' work, augmented by a new orientation toward the facts and forces of Nature. God, the *prima veritas* and the primary good, was shown to reveal Himself in His creation as the prime Planner and Builder. He was the *causa causans*; although man was only a *causa secunda,* he could feel necessary both as a planned part of this created world, and as its contemplator and theorist.

Aristotle had left Plato intact, but complemented him: God was the *sola gratia,* and it remained of prime importance to distinguish between *quod est ex gratia* and *quod est ex libero arbitrio*—that which originates in God's love, and that which man can accomplish with his God–given reason and free will. God was the only Being which, "being to all beings the cause of their being," was His own necessity. But it is clear that Aristotle permitted reason and will a greater leeway; they were active participants in the "creativity of creatures," which gave man's identity an independent method of self-verification. In theological terms, this process was one of reading God's goodness from the *ordo* which he had manifested in the world. Man could practise his power of observation by contemplating forms and similarities, images and ideas; he could establish causalities and eventually translate them into experiments, and thus become God's assistant planner and mover. In St. Augustine the currency which passed along the vertical between the two worlds was faith and love. St. Thomas added the currency of perceived form and order. God's message was perceivable in the *ordo divina*; man's equipment included the ability to perceive order; and there was prescribed order in the inner formability of man. So that he can negotiate among all these orders, man is given a number of organs: intuitive vision; perception on the basis of faith; and recognition *per rationem rationalem*. Man's reason, in turn, is given a high enough place in the order of things so that even matters of good and bad can, and in fact, must, be reasoned out. This may lead to no more than a *certitudo conjecturae*; but at any rate, St. Thomas reserves a place for active and reasonable conjecture where before there was room for only faith and hope. In this philosophy man as a contemplator acquires a new identity, that of a "theorist." We may, therefore, speak of Thomism as centering in a *rational identity*: the identity verified by a divine order perceived by reason.

It is clear that through Thomism theology acquired as its own those Aristotelian strivings for observation and speculation which became dominant in the Renaissance. But man's equipment for observation and reason still needed divine encouragement to give it the *perseverantia* to utilize the *cooperatio* between the two worlds. A greater synthesis between Antiquity and Christianity, Reason and Faith, could not be conceived; its immediate results were a dignified piety, immaculate thought, and an integrated cosmology well-suited to the hierarchic and ceremonial style of the whole era. Luther's question, however, was whether, in this synthesis, problems of conscience are not drawn into the sphere of reason, rather than reason being incorporated into faith.

St. Thomas, an architectural thinker and himself an expression of the *ordo* in which he recognized God's message, was also representative of the highest expression of the medieval identity: the grandiose as well as minute *stylization* which characterized the cathedrals, built for eternity, and the ceremonies, which allegorized God's order in the microcosm of special occasions. Ceremonialism permits a group to behave in a symbolically ornamental way so that it seems to represent an ordered universe; each particle achieves an identity by its mere interdependency with all the others. In ceremonial stylization, the vertical and the horizontal met; the Church's genius for hierarchic formulization spread from the Eucharist to the courts, the market places, and the universities, giving the identity of medieval man an anchor of colors, shapes, and sounds. The medieval ceremonialist also tried to place man in a symbolic and allegoric order, and in the static eternity of estates and castes, by drawing up minute and detailed laws of conduct: thus man partook of a gigantic as well as a minute order by giving himself ceremonial identities set apart by extravagantly differentiated roles and costumes.

It must be added, however, that active self-perpetuation and self-verification in the ceremonial microcosms were restricted to small groups of ecclesiastic and secular aristocracies. The masses could participate only as onlookers, as the recipients of a reflection of a reflection. This parasitic ceremonial identity lost much of its psychological power when the excessive stylization of the ruling classes proved to be a brittle defense against the era's increasing dangers; the plague and syphilis, the Turks, and the discord of popes and princes. At the same time, the established order of material and psychological warfare (always so reassuring a factor in man's sense of borrowed godliness) was radically overthrown by the invention of gunpowder and of the printing press.

The daily intellectual and religious life to which Luther was exposed in college and monastery was stimulated by three isms: the great philosophical antithesis of realism and nominalism; and religious mysticism.

Realism was the assumption of a true substantive existence of the world of ideas. Its quite unphilosophical alliance with the fetichistic adoration of relics (messengers from the other world, like fragments of meteors from the skies) could not be illustrated better than by the fact that St. Thomas, immediately after his death, was boiled by his confreres so that they could sever, by one industrial act, the perishable flesh from the pile of negotiable bones. Realistic thought had little influence on Luther, the dogmatist; but it dominated the *Zeitgeist* which often emerged in Luther's more informal utterances, especially in its alliance with demonism. We know Luther to have been a lifelong addict of demonic thought, which he managed to keep quite separate from his theological thought and his scientific judgment. The devil's behind maintained a reality for him which—because his intellect and his religious intuition

seemed to function on different planes—could be said to verge on the
paranoid were it not at the same time representative of a pervading medieval tendency. As Huizinga puts it:

> Now, it is in the domain of faith that realism obtains, and here it is to
> be considered rather as the mental attitude of a whole age than as a
> philosophic opinion. In this larger sense it may be considered inher-
> ent in the civilization of the Middle Ages and as dominating all ex-
> pressions of thought and of the imagination. . . .[5]

All realism, in the medieval sense, leads to anthropomorphism. Having attributed a real existence to an idea, the mind wants to see this idea
alive, and can only effect this by personifying it. In this way allegory is
born. It is not the same thing as symbolism. Symbolism expresses a
mysterious connection between two ideas, allegory gives a visible form
to the conception of such a connection. Symbolism is a very profound function of the mind, allegory is a superficial one. It aids symbolic thought to express itself, but endangers it at the same time by
substituting a figure for a living idea. The force of the symbol is easily
lost in the allegory. . . .[6]

The Church, it is true, has always explicitly taught that sin is not a
thing or an entity. But how could it have prevented the error, when
everything concurred to insinuate it into men's minds? The primitive
instinct which sees sin as stuff which soils or corrupts, which one
should, therefore, wash away, or destroy, was strengthened by the extreme systematizing of sins, by their figurative representation, and even
by the penitentiary technique of the Church itself. In vain did Denis
the Carthusian remind the people that it was but for the sake of comparison that he calls sin a fever, a cold and corrupted humour—popular thought undoubtedly lost sight of the restrictions of dogmatists.[7]

The following passage gives us the medieval background for some of
Luther's occasional preoccupation with bodily zones and modes:

> The infusion of divine grace is described under the image of the ab-
> sorption of food, and also of being bathed. A nun feels quite deluged
> in the blood of Christ and faints. All the red and warm blood of the
> five wounds flowed through the mouth of Saint Henry Suso into his
> heart. Catherine of Sienna drank from the wound in His side. Others

drank of the Virgin's milk, like Saint Bernard, Henry Suso, Alain de la Roche.

Now, whereas the celestial symbolism of Alain de la Roche seems artificial, his infernal visions are characterized by a hideous actuality. He sees the animals which represent the various sins equipped with horrible genitals, and emitting torrents of fire which obscure the earth with their smoke. He sees the prostitute of apostasy giving birth to apostates, now devouring them and vomiting them forth, now kissing them and petting them like a mother.[8]

Huizinga's analysis prepares us for the issue of indulgences. Realism, just as it served to give supernatural reality to the "dirt" on earth, also gave monetary substance to grace itself, establishing the vertical as a canal system for that mysterious substance of supreme ambivalence which both the unconscious and mysticism alternately designate as gold and as dirt. The idea of a heavenly treasure of the works of supererogation was an ancient one; but the capitalist interpretation of a reserve which the Church can dispose of by retail was officially formulated only in 1343 by Clement VI, who established the dogma that the wide distribution of the treasure would lead to an increase in merit—and thus to continued accumulation of the treasure. In this dogma realism took a form which Luther eventually fought in his opposition to the cash-and-carry indulgences which were supposed to instantly affect the condition of a soul in purgatory— the way a coin can immediately be heard as it drops into the collector's box.

The dangers to man's identity posed by a confused realism allied with a popular demonology are obvious. The influences from the other world are brought down to us as negotiable matter; man is able to learn to master them by magical thinking and action. But momentary victories of magic over an oppressive superreality do not, in the long run, either develop man's moral sense or fortify a sense of the reality of his identity on this globe.

The systematic philosophical content of German mysticism is small, indeed, and Luther did not read Tauler, the most systematic mystic, until after he had established the basic tenets of his own theology. Tauler was the exponent of an ism which is one of the constant, if extreme, poles of spiritual possibilities. For Tauler, God begins where all categories and differentiations end *(on allen underscheit);* he is the Unborn Light *(ein ungeschaffen Licht).* To reach him, one must be able to develop the *raptus,* the rapt state of complete passivity in which man loses his name, his attributes, and his will. He must achieve something for which only the German language has a proper word—*Gelassenheit,* meaning a total state of *letting* things be, letting them come and go. This includes also the all-Christian condition of accepting total guiltiness, but without excessive remorse or melancholy. Thus, returning to one's inner darkness and nebulousness *(nebulas et tenebras)* one becomes ready for the *Einkehr,* the homecoming to the *Seelengrund,* the ground and womb of spiritual creation. Here is the meeting-ground for the wedding *(das Hochgezeit),* and God becomes, for an instant, mightily active; his coming is as quick as a glance *(in einem snellen Blicke)* which cuts through all the ways of the world *(ueber alle die Wise und die Wese in einem Blicke).* But mind you, this ray of light from God's eye does not penetrate to him who attempts to look at God; it comes only to one who is in a state of total receptivity, free of all striving.[9]

We are here confronted with a system which retreats far behind the gnostic position, and far below the trust position of infancy. It is the return to a state of symbiosis with the matrix, a state of floating unity fed by a spiritual navel cord. We may call it the *passive identity.* Its clear parallel with, and its differentiation as German mysticism from, other Western or Eastern systems must not occupy us here. Luther adored it from afar (he wrote a preface to Tauler's works); but he was intellectually and temperamentally unfit for it, and somehow afraid of it.

The great common sense identity based on the view that things are things, and ideas, ideas, was mainly established by Occam; his influence helped to change the meaning of the term *realism* into "things as they are." Occamism was eagerly ideologized at a time when the empire of faith was threatening to fall apart into all-too-concrete, all-too-human entities: a God with the mind of a usurer, a lawyer, and a police chief; a family of saints, like holy aunts and uncles, with whom people made deals, instead of approaching the distant Father; a Church that had become a state, and a Pope who was a warring prince; priests who had lost their own awe and failed to inspire it in other people, and thus became more contemptible as they became only too understandable; observances which at the earthly end of the vertical were measured in hard cash, and at the other, in aeons of purgatory.

Occam, or at any rate Occamism, severed the vertical from the horizontal. One might almost say it made parallels out of them. Such entities as God, soul, or spirit were not considered to be matters accessible to the mind down here. God has no ascertainable attributes and does not underlie any generalities which we can "think." We cannot know His intentions or His obligations: his *potentia is absoluta*. He has *infinita latitudo*, and there is no way of obliging or coercing Him by developing the right disposition, be it ever so saintly. All we can hope is that when the judgment comes we will prove acceptable to Him, and that He will grant us an *extenuatio legis*. All we can do is to obey the Church (which Occam disobeyed) and be reasonable *(ratio recta spes)*, for we can assume that even God's laws are subject to logic. Gerson, the famous French Occamist, who was one of Luther's favorite authors and whose pastoral writings were obligatory reading for all student priests, even suggested that one could expect God not to be too unreasonable in His decisions on judgment day.

As to this world, single things do have a concrete and immediate reality, as man's intuitive knowledge clearly perceives. But a symbol of a thing is nothing but *flatus vocis*, a burst of verbal air. Ideas, or universals, do not exist, except in *significando*, in the mental operations by which we give them meaning. We have no right to attribute to them the quality of thingness, and then to proceed to increase their quantity as our fancy might lead us to do: *Non est ponenda pluralitas sine necessitate* is the famous sentence which establishes the law of parsimony, a law which sharpened the search of the natural sciences, and now hounds psychology with its demand to reduce man, too, to a model of a minimal number of forces and mechanisms.

All in all, then, Occam's nominalism is a medieval form of skepticism and empiricism which antedates the philosophy of enlightenment. Some historians attribute to Occam operations of thought mature enough to antedate the mathematics of Descartes. But one can well see why, to some Catholic thinkers, Occamist became an adjective worse than Pelagian. And, in many ways, Occam was an abortive Luther. He, too, called the Pope an Antichrist; he, too, supported the princes' supremacy over the Curia; he, too, was attracted by the absolutism of an earlier form of

Christianity, which was forever embarrassing to the Church: Franciscan communism. But Occam was at heart a pragmatic philosopher; and although Luther's own shrewdness appreciated Occam's practical scepticism, it was Occam's demonstration that the vertical could not be approached at all by way of the horizontal which impressed Martin. Occam showed that faith as an individual experience had been lost in all the cathedral building and hierarchy arranging, in all the ceremonializing of life and formalizing of thought. The dream of a predictable vertical anchored in an orderly horizontal was failing the most faithful, and leaving the faithless to the overwhelming dangers of the day.

In contrast to these medieval trends of thought, what did the Renaissance man think of his relative reality on this planet?

First of all, he recovered man's identity from its captivity in the eleventh heaven. He refused to exist on the periphery of the world theater, a borrowed substance subject to God's whims. He was anthropocentric, and existed out of his own substance—created, as he somewhat mechanically adds, by God. This substance was his executive center. His geographic center, because of his own efforts, turned out to be peripheral to the solar system: but what did lack of cosmic symmetry matter, when man had regained a sense of his own center? Ficino, one of the prime movers of the Platonic Academy of Lorenzo the Magnificent's Florence, made this clear. The soul of man, he says, "carries in itself all the reasons and models of the lower things that it recreates as it were of its own. It is the center of all and possesses the forces of all. It can turn to and penetrate this without leaving that, for it is the true connection of things. Thus, it can rightly be called the center of nature."[10] And Pico della Mirandola, the author of *On the Dignity of Man* (1494) celebrated the "highest and most marvelous felicity of man! . . . To him it is granted to have whatever he chooses, to be whatever he wills. On man when he came to life, the Father conferred the seeds of all kinds and the germs of every way of life. . . . Who would not admire this chameleon?"[11]

The human theater of life, according to this humanist school, is circumscribed for each by the power of that specific endowment which in him happens to be blessed with the gift of workmanship, be he painter or sculptor, astronomer, physician, or statesman. For Leonardo, it was the trained, intent eye, the "knowing how to see," which was "the natural point," in which "the images of our hemisphere enter and pass together with those of all the heavenly bodies. . . . in which they merge and become united by mutually penetrating and intersecting each other." "These are the miracles . . . forms already lost, mingled together in so small a space, it can recreate and reconstitute."[12] Michelangelo found this center in the hand which, guided by intellect, can free the conception "circumscribed in the marble's excess."[13]

This view again anchors the human identity in the hierarchy of organs and functions of the human body, especially insofar as the body serves (or is) the mind. Renaissance sensuality (in contrast to the medieval alternation of asceticism and excess) tried to make the body an intuitive and disciplined tool of reality; it did not permit the body to be sickened with sinfulness, nor the mind to be chained to a dogma; it insisted on a full interplay between man's senses and intuitions and the world of appearances, facts, and laws. As Leonardo put it: "Mental things which have not gone through the senses are vain and bring forth no truth except detrimental."[14] But this implies disciplined sensuality, *"exact fantasy,"* and makes the verification of our functioning essence dependent on the meeting between our God-given mental machinery and the world into which God has put us. We need no proof of His identity nor of ours as long as, at any given time, an essential part of our equipment and a segment of His world continue to confirm each other. This is the law of operating inside nature.

Ficino strained this point of view to its ideological limit; his statement in many ways has remained the ideological test and limit of our own world image: "Who could deny," he says, "that man possesses as it were almost the same genius as the Author of the heavens? And who could deny that man could somehow also make the heavens, could he only obtain the instruments and the heavenly material?"[15]

It cannot escape those familiar with psychoanalytic theory that the Renaissance is the ego revolution *par excellence.* It was a large-scale restoration of the ego's executive functions, particularly insofar as the enjoyment of the senses, the exercise of power, and the cultivation of a good conscience to the point of anthropocentric vanity were concerned, all of which was regained from the Church's systematic and terroristic exploitation of man's proclivity for a negative conscience. Latin Christianity in Martin's time tended to promise freedom from the body at the price of the absolute power of a negative external conscience: negative

in that it was based on a sense of sin, and external in that it was defined
and redefined by a punitive agency which alone was aware of the rationale of morality and the consequences of disobedience. The Renaissance gave man a vacation from his negative conscience, thus freeing the
ego to gather strength for manifold activity. The restoration of ego vanity to a position over superego righteousness, also established an ideological Utopia which found expression in Ficino's statement. Renaissance
man was free to become what Freud called a god of protheses, and the
question of how to dispose of this god's bad conscience came to occupy
not only theology, but also psychiatry.

Nietzsche, Luther's fellow-Saxon, prided himself on being the belated
German spokesman of the Renaissance and Europe's gay moralist.
Wrongly informed about Luther's trip to Rome and believing his ninety-
five theses to have been a German peasant's revolt against the Renaissance, Nietzsche blamed on Luther's untimely interference the failure of
the Medici to imbue the papacy with a Renaissance spirit mature enough
to completely absorb medieval spirituality. Nietzsche felt that Luther had
forced the Church into the defensive instead, and had made it develop
and reinforce a reformed dogma, a mediocrity with survival value. Erasmus, also, four hundred and fifty years before Nietzsche, had blamed
Luther for ruining the dreams of Humanism. It is true that Luther *was*
completely blind to the visual splendor and the sensual exquisiteness of
the Renaissance, just as he was furiously suspicious of Erasmus' intellectuality: *"Du bist nicht fromm,"* he wrote to him. "You do not know what
true piety is."[16] And although for a few years Luther occupied the stage
of history with some of the exhibitionistic grandeur of a Renaissance
man, there is no doubt that he concluded his life in an obese provincial-
ity.

Yet one could make a case that Martin, even as he hiked back to Erfurt, was preparing himself to do the dirty work of the Renaissance, by
applying some of the individualistic principles immanent in the Renaissance to the Church's still highly fortified homeground—the conscience
of ordinary man. The Renaissance created ample leeway for those in art
and science who had their work confirmed by its fruits, that is, by aesthetic, logical, and mathematical verification. It freed the visualizer and
the talker, the scholar and the builder—without, however, establishing either a truly new and sturdy style of life, or a new and workable morality. The great progress in pictorialization, verbalization, and material

construction left, for most of the people, something undone on an inner frontier. We should not forget that on his deathbed Lorenzo the Magnificent, who died so young and so pitifully soon after he had withdrawn to the country to devote the rest of his life to the "enjoyment of leisure with dignity," sent for Savonarola. Only the most strongly principled among Lorenzo's spiritual critics would do as his last confessor. Ficino, who in his youth addressed his students as "beloved in Plato," became a monk in his forties; Pico, who wrote *On the Dignity of Man* when he was a mere youth, died in his early thirties a devout follower of Savonarola, and considering a monastic life. These were all men who somehow had loved women, or at any rate their own maleness, too much; altogether womanless men, like Leonardo and Michelangelo, found and recognized the defeat of the male self in grandiose ways. Surely existential despair has never been represented more starkly than in the Sistine man facing eternal damnation, nor essential human tragedy with more dignity than in Michelangelo's Pieta. One must review the other Madonnas of the Renaissance (della Robbia's, del Sarto's, Raphael's) who are shown with the boy Jesus making a gay and determined effort to stand on his own feet and to reach out for the world, to appreciate Michelangelo's unrealistic and unhistorical sculpture—an eternally young mother holding on her lap the sacrificial corpse of her grown and aged son. A man's total answer to eternity lies not in what he says at any one period of his life, but in the balance of all his pronouncements at all periods. Psychologically speaking, Renaissance man contained within himself the same contradictions which are the burden of all mortals. History ties together whatever new ideological formulations most fitly correspond to new conquests over matter, and lets the men drop by the wayside.

Luther accepted for his life work the unconquered frontier of tragic conscience, defined as it was by his personal needs and his superlative gifts: *"Locus noster,"* he said in the lectures on the Psalms, *"in quo nos cum Deo, sponsas cum sponsa, habitare debet . . . est conscientia."*[17] Conscience is that inner ground where we and God have to learn to live with each other as man and wife. Psychologically speaking, it is where the ego meets the superego; that is, where our self can either live in wedded harmony with a positive conscience or is estranged from a negative one. Luther comes nowhere closer to formulating the auditory threat, the voice of wrath, which is internalized in a negative conscience than when he speaks of the "false Christ" as one whom we hear expostulate *"Hoc non fecisti,*"[18] "Again, you have not done what I told you"—a statement of the kind which identifies negatively, and burns itself into the soul as a black and hopeless mark: *conscientia cauterisata.*

Hans' son was made for a job on this frontier. But he did not create the job; it originated in the hypertrophy of the negative conscience inherent in our whole Judaeo-Christian heritage in which, as Luther put it: "Christ becomes more formidable a tyrant and a judge than was Moses."[19] But the negative conscience can become hypertrophied only when man hungers for his identity.

We must accept this universal, if weird, frontier of the negative conscience as the circumscribed *locus* of Luther's work. If we do, we will be able to see that the tools he used were those of the Renaissance: fervent return to the original texts; determined anthropocentricism (if in Christocentric form); and the affirmation of his own organ of genius and of craftsmanship, namely, the voice of the vernacular.

3

After his return from Rome, Martin was permanently transferred to the Wittenberg monastery. Some say that he was pushed out by the Erfurt Augustinians, some, that he was pulled to Wittenberg by Staupitz's influence. The fact is that his friend John Lang had to go, too; a few years later, Luther's influence over the whole province was so great that he was able to appoint Lang prior back at Erfurt.

Martin's preaching and teaching career started in earnest in Wittenberg, never to be interrupted until his death. He first preached to his fellow-monks (an elective job), and to townspeople who audited his intramural sermons. He became pastor of St. Mary's. As a professor, he lectured both to monks enrolled in advanced courses, and to the students in the university. Forced to speak his mind in public, he realized the rich spectrum of his verbal expression, and gained the courage of his conflicted personality. He learned to preach to the heart and to lecture to the mind in two distinct styles. His sermons were for the uplift of the moment; in his lectures, he gradually and systematically developed as a thinker.

Luther the preacher was a different man from Martin the monk. His posture was manly and erect, his speech slow and distinct. This early Luther was by no means the typical pyknic, obese and round-faced, that he became in his later years. He was bony, with furrows in his cheeks, and a stubborn, protruding chin. His eyes were brown and small, and must have been utterly fascinating, judging by the variety of impressions they left on others. They could appear large and prominent or small and hidden; deep and unfathomable at one time, twinkling like stars at another, sharp as a hawk's, terrible as lightning, or possessed as though he were insane. There was an intensity of conflict about his face, which might well impress a clinician as revealing the obsessive character of a very gifted, cunning, and harsh man who possibly might be subject to states of uncontrolled fear or rage. Just because of this conflicted countenance, Luther's warmth, wit, and childlike candor must have been utterly disarming; and there was a total discipline about his personality which broke down only on rare occasions. It was said about Luther that he did not like to be looked in the eye, because he was aware of the revealing play of his expression while he was trying to think. (The same thing was said of Freud; and he admitted that his arrangement for the psychoanalytic session was partially due to his reluctance "to be stared at.")

Martin's bearing gradually came to contradict the meekness demanded of a monk; in fact, his body seemed to be leaning backward so that his broad forehead was imperiously lifted toward the sky; his head sat on a short neck, between broad shoulders and over a powerful chest. Some, like Spalatin, the elector's chaplain and advisor, admired him unconditionally; others, like the elector himself, Frederic the Wise, felt uncomfortable in his presence. It is said that Luther and the elector, who at times must have lived only a short distance from him and to whose cunning diplomacy and militant protection he would later owe his survival, "personally never met" to converse, even though the elector often heard him preach—and on some occasions, preach against him and the other princes.

As a preacher and lecturer, Luther combined a command of quotations from world literature with a pervading theological sincerity. His own style developed slowly out of the humanistic preoccupation with sources, the scholastic love of definitions, and the medieval legacy of (to us, atrocious) allegory. He almost never became fanciful. In fact, he was soon known for a brusqueness and a folksy directness which was too much for some of his humanist friends, who liked to shock others in more so-

phisticated ways: but Luther, horrors! was one who "meant it." It could
not have endeared him to Erasmus that of all the animals which serve
preachers for allegories and parables, Luther came to prefer the sow; and
there is no doubt but that in later years his colorful earthiness sometimes
turned into plain porcography. Nervous symptoms harassed his preaching; before, during, or after sermons he was on occasion attacked by
dizziness. The popular German term of dizziness is *Schwindel,* a word
which has a significant double meaning, for it is also used for the fraud-
ulent acts of an impostor. And one of his typical nightmares was that he
was facing a congregation, and God would not send him a *Konzept.*

But I think the psychiatrist misjudges his man when he thinks that endogenous sickness alone could have kept Luther from becoming a well-
balanced *(ausgeglichen)* creature when his preaching brought him success.
After all, he was not a Lutheran; or, as he said himself, he was a mighty
bad one. On the frontier of conscience, the dirty work never stops, the
lying old words are never done with, and the new purities remain forever dimmed. Once Luther had started to come into his own as a
preacher, he preached lustily, and at times compulsively, every few days;
when traveling, he preached in hospitable churches and in the market-
place. In later years when he was unable to leave his house because of
sickness or anxiety, he would gather wife, children, and house guests
about him and preach to them.

To Luther, the inspired voice, the voice that means it, the voice that
really communicates in person, became a new kind of sacrament, the
partner and even the rival of the mystical presence of the Eucharist. He
obviously felt himself to be the evangelical giver of a substance which
years of suffering had made his to give; an all-embracing verbal generosity developed in him, so that he did not wish to compete with professional talkers, but to speak to the people so that the least could understand
him: "You must preach," he said, "as a mother suckles her child." No other
attitude could, at the time, have appealed more to members of all
classes—except Luther's preaching against taxation without representation which, in 1517, made him a national figure. By then, he had at his
command the newly created machinery of communication. Within ten
years thirty printers in twelve cities published his sermons as fast as he or
the devoted journalists around him could get manuscripts and transcripts
to them. He became a popular preacher, especially for students; and a gala
preacher for the princes and nobles.

Luther the lecturer was a different man from either preacher or monk. His special field was Biblical exegesis. He most carefully studied the classical textbooks *(Glossa, Ordinaria, and Lyra),* and his important predecessors among the Augustinians; he also kept abreast of the humanist scholars of his time and of the correctives provided by Erasmus's study of the Greek texts and Reuchlin's study of the Hebrew texts. He could be as quibbling a linguist as any scholasticist and as fanciful as any humanist. In his first course of lectures he tries the wings of his own thoughts; sometimes he bewilders himself, and sometimes he looks about for companions, but finally he soars his own lonesome way. His fascinated listeners did not really know what was happening until they had a national scandal on their hands, and by that time Luther's role had become so political and ideological that his early lectures were forgotten and were recovered only in the late nineteenth and early twentieth centuries. Because of Luther's habit of telescoping all of his theological prehistory into the events of 1517, when he became a celebrity, it has only been recognized in this century that his theology was already completed in outline when he burst into history. Then it became politics and propaganda; it became Luther as most of us know him.

But we are interested here in the beginnings, in the emergence of Martin's thoughts about the "matrix of the Scriptures." Biblical exegesis in his day meant the demonstration—scholarly, tortured, and fanciful—of the traditional assumption that the Old Testament was a prophecy of Christ's life and death. The history of the world was contained in the Word: the book of Genesis was not just an account of creation, it was also a hidden, an allegorical, index of the whole Bible up to the crowning event of Christ's passion. Exegesis was an ideological game which permitted the Church to reinterpret Biblical predictions of its own history according to a new theological line; it was a high form of intellectual and linguistic exercise; and it provided an opportunity for the display of scholastic virtuosity. There were rules, however; some education and some resourcefulness were required to make things come out right.

The medieval world had four ways of interpreting Biblical material: literally *(literaliter),* which put stress on the real historical meaning of the text; allegorically *(allegorice),* which viewed Biblical events as symbolic of Christian history, the Church's creation, and dogma; morally *(tropologice),* which took the material as figurative expression of proper behavior for a man of faith; and anagogically *(anagogice),* which treated the material as an expression of the life hereafter. Luther used these techniques for his own purposes, although he always tried to be sincere and consistent; for example, he felt that the demand for circumcision in the Old Testament foretold his new insight that outer works do not count; but this interpretation also expresses the idea that the covenant of circumcision stressed humility by its attack on the executive organ of male vainglory. Luther's ethical search gradually made him discard the other categories of exegesis and concentrate on the moral one: *tropologicem esse primarium sensum scripturae*.[20] The scriptures to him became God's advice to the faithful in the here and now.

The Book of Psalms was the subject of the first series of lectures given by the new *lector bibliae* in the academic year 1513–14. Tradition suggested that King David the Psalmist ought to be interpreted as an unconscious prophet whose songs prefigured what Christ would say to God or to the Church, or what others would say to or about Christ. Our point here is to establish the emergence of Lutherisms from the overripe mixture of neoplatonic, sacramental, mystical, and scholastic interpretations; but we must remember that the personal conflict and the theological heresy on which we will focus were firmly based in what was then scholarly craftsmanship and responsible teaching. Nothing could make this more clear than the fact that no eyebrows were raised at what Martin said: and that as far as he was concerned, what he said was good theology and dedicated to the service of his new function within the Church. Furthermore, despite the impression early Lutherisms give, Luther maintained in his sermons and in his lectures a disciplined dedication to his metier, and allowed his personality expression only in matters of divine conviction. When he discussed a certain depth of contrition in his lectures, he could confess simply, "I am very far from having reached this myself";[21] but on the day he was to leave for Worms to face the Emperor, he preached in the morning without mentioning his imminent departure for that historical meeting.

His series of lectures, at the rate of one lecture a week, extended over a two-year course. Luther took the job of being a professor rather unprofessionally hard. He meticulously recorded his changes of mind, and accounted for insights for which he found the right words only as he went along with editorial honesty. "I do not yet fully understand this,"[22] he would tell his listeners. "I did not say that as well the last time as I did today." *Fateamur nos proficere scribendo et legendo,*[23] he pleaded: We must learn to become more proficient as we write and read. He does not try to hide his arbitrariness ("I simply rhymed the abstract and the concrete together"),[24] or an occasional tour de force: "All you can do with a text that proves to have a hard shell is to bang it at a rock and it will reveal the softest kernel *(nucleum suavissimum)."*[25] For these words he congratulated himself by marks on the margins. It is obvious that his honesty is a far cry from the elegant arbitrariness of the scholastic divines, and their stylized methods of rationalizing gaps between faith and reason. Luther's arbitrariness is part of a working lecture in which both rough spots and polish are made apparent. The first lectures on the Psalms impress one as being a half-finished piece of work; and Luther's formulations fully matured only in the lectures on Paul's Epistles to the Romans (1515–16). But concerned as we are here with the solution of an extended identity crisis rather than with a completed theology, we will restrict ourselves to the first emergence of genuine Lutherisms in the lectures on the Psalms.

4

Rather dramatic evidence exists in Luther's notes on these lectures for the fact that while he was working on the Psalms Luther came to formulate those insights later ascribed to his revelation in the tower, the date of which scholars have tried in vain to establish with certainty. As Luther was reviewing in his mind Romans 1:17, the last sentence suddenly assumed a clarity which pervaded his whole being and "opened the door of paradise" to him: "For therein is the righteousness of God revealed from faith to faith: as it is written, *The just shall live by faith."* The power of these words lay in a new perception of the space-time of life and eternity. Luther saw that God's justice is not consigned to a future day of judgment based on our record on earth when He will have the "last word." Instead, this justice is in us, in the here and now; for, if we will only perceive it, God has given us faith to live by, and we can perceive it by understanding the Word which is Christ. We will discuss later the circumstances leading to this perception; what interests us first of all is its relation to the lectures on the Psalms.

In a remarkable study published in 1929, Erich Vogelsang demonstrated that the insights previously attributed exclusively to Luther's rev-

elation in the tower, and often ascribed to a much later time, appear fully
and dramatically early in these lectures. Whether this means, as Vogelsang
claims, that the revelation really "took place" while Luther was occupied
with the lectures, that is, late in the year 1513, is a theological controversy
in which I will not become involved. My main interest is in the fact that
at about the age of thirty—an important age for gifted people with a delayed identity crisis—the wholeness of Luther's theology first emerges
from the fragments of his totalistic reevaluations.

Vogelsang's study is remarkable because he weeds out of Luther's text
statements which are, in fact, literal quotations from older scholars; Vogelsang thus uncovers the real course and crescendo of Luther's original
remarks. Moreover, he studies usually neglected dimensions of the original text, dimensions which are not visible in the monumental Weimar
Edition. For instance, there is the "archeological" dimension—the layers
of thought to be seen in the preparatory notes for the lectures, in the
transcripts of the lectures, and in later additions written or pasted into the
text. Vogelsang studied the kinds of paper and ink used, noted variations
in handwriting, and analyzed the fluctuating personal importance attached by Luther himself to various parts of his notes, indicated by underscorings and by marginal marks of self-applause. Vogelsang discovered
the path of a spiritual cyclone which cut right through the texts of the
lectures on the Psalms: "When Luther, in the *Psalmenkolleg* faces the task
of offering his listeners an *ex professo* interpretation of the passage, *in
justitia tua libera me* [and deliver me in thy righteousness], this task confronts him with a quite personal decision, affects him like a clap of thunder, and awakes in him one of the severest temptations, to which he later
could think back only with trembling for the duration of his life."[26]

This much was acknowledged by old Luther: "When I first read and
sang in the Psalms," he said, *"in justitia tua libera me,* I was horror-stricken
and felt deep hostility toward these words, God's righteousness, God's
judgment, God's work. For I knew only that *justitia dei* meant a harsh
judgment. Well, was he supposed to save me by judging me harshly? If
so, I was lost forever. But *gottlob,* when I then understood the matter and
knew that *justitia dei* meant the righteousness by which He justifies us
through the free gift of Christ's justice, then I understood the *grammat-
ica,* and I truly tasted the Psalms."[27]

Vogelsang finds interesting bibliographical and graphological evidence
of Luther's struggle. "In the whole *Dresdener Psalter,*" he writes, "there is

no page which bears such direct witness to personal despair as does the *Scholie* to Psalm 30:1 [Psalm 31 in the King James' version]. He who has trained his ear in steady dealings with these lectures here perceives a violence and passion of language scarcely found anywhere else. The decisive words, *in justitia tua libera me,* Luther jumps over in terror and anxiety, which closes his ear to the singularly reassuring passage, 'Into thine hand, I commit my spirit' [Psalm 31:5, King James version]."[28] Remember what Scheel said about Martin's *tentatio* during his first Mass: that he seemed blind to the reassuring passage which referred to Christ as the mediator, and preferred to test the rock bottom of his despair, "because there was no real faith." Vogelsang continues: "He immediately proceeds with 'Have mercy upon me, O Lord,' (the handwriting here is extremely excited and confused; he adds a great number of underscorings) and prays with trembling conscience in the words of the sixth Psalm [Psalm 7, King James version]—*'Ex intuitu irae dei.'* And even as the text of the 31st Psalm is about to call him out of his temptation with the words *'in te speravi Domine,'* ['But I trusted in Thee, O Lord'] he deflects the discussion only more violently back to the words of the sixth Psalm."[29]

Although Vogelsang does not make a point of it, it cannot escape us that these psalms are expressions of David's accusations against his and (so he likes to conclude) the Lord's enemies; in them David vacillates between wishing the wrath of God and the mercy of God upon the heads of his enemies. There are other passages in Psalm 31 which Luther ignores, besides those which Vogelsang mentioned: "Pull me out of the net that they had laid privily for me: for thou art my strength";[30] and "I have hated them that regard lying vanities: but I trust in the Lord."[31] Luther probably had enemies at the time in Erfurt. But there was another enemy who, "regarding lying vanities," had "privily laid a net" for Martin; had not his father, thwarted in his vain plans for his son, put a curse on his son's spiritual life, predicted his temptations, predicted, in fact, his coming rebellion? In Martin's struggle for justification, involving the emancipation of his obsessive conscience from his jealous father and the liberation of his thought from medieval theology, this new insight into God's pervading justice could not, psychologically speaking, be experienced as a true revelatory solution without some disposition of his smouldering hate. We will come back to this point when we discuss Luther's identification with Christ; for the Psalmist's complaint about his enemies reminds us of the social setting of Christ's passion. He, too, was mockingly challenged to prove his sonhood of God: "He trusted in God; let him deliver him now, if he will have him: for he said, I am the Son of God."[32]

When the lectures on the Psalms reached Psalm 71:2, Luther again faced the phrase, "Deliver me in thy righteousness," again preceded (Psalm 70) by "Let them be turned back for a reward of their shame that say, Aha, aha." But now his mood, his outlook, and his vocabulary had undergone a radical change.[33] He twice quotes Romans 1:17 (the text of his revelation in the tower) and concludes *"Justitia dei . . . est fides Christi"*: Christ's faith is God's righteousness. This is followed by what Vogelsang calls a dithyrambic sequence of new and basically "Protestant" formulations, a selection of which we will review presently. These formulations center in Luther's final acceptance of Christ's mediatorship, and a new concept of man's sonhood of God.

This was the breakthrough. In these lectures, and only in these, Luther quotes St. Augustine's account of his own awakening four times: in the very first lecture; in connection with the dramatic disruption caused by Psalm 31; and twice in connection with Psalm 71.

It seems entirely probable, then, that the revelation in the tower occurred sometime during Luther's work on these lectures. Alternatively, instead of one revelation, there may have been a series of crises, the first perhaps traceable in this manuscript on the Psalms, the last fixed in Luther's memory at that finite event which scholars have found so difficult to locate in time.

The finite event seems to be associated in Luther's mind with a preceding period of deep depression, during which he again foresaw an early death. The reported episode has been viewed with prejudice because of its *place* of occurrence. Luther refers to a *Secretus locus monachorum, hypocaustum,* or *cloaca*; that is, the monks' secret place, the sweat chamber, or the toilet. According to Scheel, this list originates from one transcript of a table-talk of 1532, when Luther is reported to have said *"Dise Kunst hatt mir der Spiritus Sanctus auff diss Cl. eingeben"*: the holy spirit endowed me with this art on the Cl.[34] Rorer, whom the very critical Scheel considers the most reliable of the original reporters, transcribes Cl. as cloaca. Nevertheless, Scheel dismisses this interpretation; and indeed, no other reported statement of Luther's has made mature men squirm more uncomfortably, or made serious scholars turn their noses higher in contemptuous disbelief. The psychiatrist concedes that Cl. does refer to the toilet; but, of all people, he haughtily concludes that after all, it is not relevant *where* important things happen.

This whole geographic issue, however, deserves special mention exactly because it *does* point up certain psychiatric relevances. First of all, the locality mentioned serves a particular physical need which hides its emotional relevance only as long as it happens to function smoothly. Yet, as the psychiatrist himself points out, Luther suffered from lifelong constipation and urine retention. Leaving the possible physical causes or consequences of this tendency aside, the functions themselves are related to the organ modes of retention and elimination—in defiant children most obviously, and in adults through all manner of ambivalent behavior. There can be little doubt that at this particular time, when Martin's power of speech was freed from its infantile and juvenile captivity, he changed from a highly restrained and retentive individual into an explosive person; he had found an unexpected release of self-expression, and with it, of the many-sided power of his personality.

Those who object to these possibly impure circumstances of Martin's spiritual revelation forget St. Paul's epileptic attack, a physical paroxysm often accompanied by a loss of sphincter control, and deny the total involvement of body and soul which makes an emotional and spiritual experience genuine. Scholars would prefer to have it happen as they achieve their own reflected revelations—sitting at a desk. Luther's statement that he was, in fact, sitting somewhere else, implies that in this creative moment the tension of nights and days of meditation found release throughout his being—and nobody who has read Luther's private remarks can doubt that his total being always included his bowels. Furthermore, people in those days expressed much more openly and conceptualized more concretely than we do the emotional implications (and the implication in our emotions) of the primary bodily functions. We permit ourselves to understand them in a burlesque show, or in circumstances where we can laugh off our discomfort; but we are embarrassed when we are asked to acknowledge them in earnest. Then we prefer to speak of them haughtily, as though they were something we have long left behind. But here the suppressed meaning betrays itself in the irrational defensiveness; for what we leave behind, with emotional repudiation, is at least unconsciously associated with dirt and feces. St. Paul openly counted all the glittering things which he had abandoned for Christ "but dung."

A revelation, that is, a sudden inner flooding with light, is always as-sociated with a repudiation, a cleansing, a kicking away; and it would be entirely in accord with Luther's great freedom in such matters if he were to experience and to report this repudiation in frankly physical terms. The cloaca, at the "other end" of the bodily self, remained for him some-times wittily, sometimes painfully, and sometimes delusionally alive, as if it were a "dirt ground" where one meets with the devil, just as one meets with God in the *Seelengrund,* where pure being is created.

The psychiatric relevance of all this is heightened by the fact that in later years, when Luther's freedom of speech occasionally deteriorated into vulgar license, he went far beyond the customary gay crudity of his early days. In melancholy moods, he expressed his depressive self-repudiation also in anal terms: "I am like ripe shit," he said once at the dinner table during a fit of depression (and the boys eagerly wrote it down), "and the world is a gigantic ass-hole. We probably will let go of each other soon."[35] We have no right to overlook a fact which Luther was far from denying: that when he, who had once chosen silence in order to restrain his rebellious and destructive nature, finally learned to let him-self go, he freed not only the greatest oratory of his time, but also the most towering temper and the greatest capacity for dirt-slinging wrath.

The problem is not how extraordinary or how pathological all this is, but whether or not we can have one Luther without the other. We will return to this question in conclusion. In the meantime, what we know of Martin's autocratic conscience, and what we begin to know of his tempestuous temperament, will stand us in good stead as we see the lec-turer find his balance and his identity in the act of lecturing, and with them, some new formulations of man's relation to God and to himself.

In what follows, themes from Luther's first lectures are discussed side by side with psychoanalytic insights. Theological readers will wonder whether Luther saved theology from philosophy only to have it exploited by psychology; while psychoanalysts may suspect me of trying to make space for a Lutheran God in the structure of the psyche. My purposes, however, are more modest: I intend to demonstrate that Luther's redefi-nition of man's condition—while part and parcel of his theology—has striking configurational parallels with inner dynamic shifts like those which clinicians recognize in the recovery of individuals from psychic

distress. In brief, I will try to indicate that Luther, in laying the foundation for a "religiosity for the adult man," displayed the attributes of his
own hard-won adulthood; his renaissance of faith portrays a vigorous recovery of his own ego-initiative. To indicate this I will focus on three
ideas: the affirmation of voice and word as the instruments of faith; the
new recognition of God's "face" in the passion of Christ; and the redefinition of a just life.

After 1505 Luther had made no bones about the pernicious influence
which "rancid Aristotelianism" had had on theology. Scholasticism had
made him lose faith, he said; through St. Paul he had recovered it. He put
the problem in terms of organ modes, by describing scholastic disputa-
tions as *dentes* and *linguae*: the teeth are hard and sinister, and form words
in anger and fury; the tongue is soft and suavely persuasive. Using these
modes, the devil can evoke purely intellectual mirages *(mira potest suggere
in intellectu).*[36] But the organ through which the word enters to replen-
ish the heart is the ear *(natura enim verbi est audiri),*[37] for it is in the nature
of the word that it should be heard. On the other hand, faith comes from
listening, not from looking *(quia est auditu fides, non ex visu).*[38] Therefore,
the greatest thing one can say about Christ, and about all Christians, is
that they have *aures perfectas et perfossas:*[39] good and open ears. But only
what is perceived at the same time as a matter *affectionalis* and *moralis* as
well as intellectual can be a matter sacred and divine: one must, therefore,
hear before one sees, believe before one understands, be captivated before one captures. *Fides est "locus" animae:*[40] faith is the seat, the organ of
the soul. This had certainly been said before; but Luther's emphasis is not
on Augustinian "infusion," or on a nominalist "obedience," but, in a truly
Renaissance approach, on a self-verification through a God-given inner
"apparatus." This *locus,* this apparatus, has its own way of seeking and
searching—and it succeeds insofar as it develops its own *passivity.*

Paradoxically, many a young man (and son of a stubborn one) becomes
a great man in his own sphere only by learning that deep passivity which
permits him to let the data of his competency speak to him. As Freud said
in a letter to Fliess, "I must wait until it moves in me so that I can perceive it: *bis es sich in mir ruehrt und ich davon erfahre."*[41] This may sound
feminine, and, indeed, Luther bluntly spoke of an attitude of womanly
conception—*sicut mulier in conceptu.*[42] Yet it is clear that men call such attitudes and modes feminine only because the strain of paternalism has
alienated us from them; for these modes are any organism's birthright, and

all our partial as well as our total functioning is based on a metabolism of passivity and activity. Mannish man always wants to pretend that he made himself, or at any rate, that no simple woman bore him, and many puberty rites (consider the rebirth from a kiva in the American Southwest) dramatize a new birth from a spiritual mother of a kind that only men understand.

The theology as well as the psychology of Luther's passivity is that of man in the *state of prayer,* a state in which he fully means what he can say only to God: *Tibi soli peccavi,* I have sinned, not in relation to any person or institution, but in relation only to God, to *my* God.

In two ways, then, rebirth by prayer is passive: it means surrender to God the Father; but it also means to be reborn *ex matrice scripturae nati,*[43] out of the matrix of the scriptures. "Matrix" is as close as such a man's man will come to saying "mater." But he cannot remember and will not acknowledge that long before he had developed those wilful modes which were specifically suppressed and paradoxically aggravated by a challenging father, a mother had taught him to touch the world with his searching mouth and his probing senses. What to a man's man, in the course of his development, seems like a passivity hard to acquire, is only a regained ability to be active with his oldest and most neglected modes. Is it coincidence that Luther, now that he was explicitly teaching passivity, should come to the conclusion that a lecturer should feed his audience as a mother suckles her child? Intrinsic to the kind of passivity we speak of is not only the memory of having been given, but also the identification with the maternal giver: "the glory of a good thing is that it flows out to others."[44] I think that in the Bible Luther at last found a mother whom he could acknowledge: he could attribute to the Bible a generosity to which he could open himself, and which he could pass on to others, at last a mother's son.

Luther did use the words *passiva* and *passivus* when he spoke Latin, and the translation *passive* must be accepted as correct. But in German he often used the word *passivisch,* which is more actively passive, as passific would be. I think that the difference between the old modalities of *passive* and *active* is really that between *erleben* and *handeln,* of being in the state of *experiencing* or of *acting.* Meaningful implications are lost in the flat word *passivity*—among them the total attitude of living receptively and through the senses, of willingly "suffering" the voice of one's intuition and of living a *Passion*: that total passivity in which man regains, through considered self-sacrifice and self-transcendence, his active position in the face of nothingness, and thus is saved. Could this be one of the psychological riddles in the wisdom of the "foolishness of the cross?"

To Luther, the preaching and the praying man, the measure in depth of the perceived presence of the Word was the reaction with a total affect which leaves no doubt that one "means it." It may seem paradoxical to speak of an affect that one could not thus mean; yet it is obvious that rituals, observances, and performances do evoke transitory affects which can be put on for the occasion and afterward hung in the closet with one's Sunday clothes. Man is able to ceremonialize, as he can "automatize" psychologically, the signs and behaviors that are born of the deepest reverence or despair. However, for an affect to have a deep and lasting effect, or, as Luther would say, be *affectionalis* and *moralis,* it must not only be experienced as nearly overwhelming, but it must also in some way be affirmed by the ego as valid, almost as chosen: one means the affect, it signifies something meaningful, it is significant. Such is the relative nature of our ego and of our conscience that when the ego regains its composure after the auditory condemnation of the absolutist voice of conscience we mean what we have learned to believe, and our affects become those of positive conscience: faith, conviction, authority, indignation—all subjective states which are attributes of a strong sense of identity and, incidentally, are indispensable tools for strengthening identity in others. Luther speaks of matters of faith as experiences from which one will profit to the degree to which they were intensive and expressive *(quanto expressius et intensius).* If they are more *frigidus,* however, they are not merely a profit missed, they are a terrible deficit confirmed: for man without intense convictions is a robot with destructive techniques.

It is easy to see that these formulations, once revolutionary, are the commonplaces of today's pulpits. They are the bases of that most inflated of all oratorical currency, credal protestation in church and lecture hall, in political propaganda and in oral advertisement: the protestation, made to order for the occasion, that truth is only that which one means with one's whole being, and lives every moment. We, the heirs of Protestantism, have made convention and pretense out of the very sound of meaning it. What started with the German *Brustton der Ueberzeugung,* the manly chestiness of conviction, took many forms of authoritative appeal, the most recent one being the cute sincerity of our TV announcers. All this only indicates that Luther was a pioneer on one of our eternal inner frontiers, and that his struggle must continue (as any great man's must) exactly at that point where his word is perverted in his own name.

Psychotherapists, professional listeners and talkers in the sphere of affectivity and morality know only too well that man seldom really knows what he really means; he as often lies by telling the truth as he reveals the truth when he tries to lie. This is a psychological statement; and the psychoanalytic method, when it does not pretend to deliver complete honesty, over a period of time reveals approximately what somebody really means. But the center of the problem is simply this: in truly significant matters people, and especially children, have a devastatingly clear if mostly unconscious perception of what other people really mean, and sooner or later royally reward real love or take well-aimed revenge for implicit hate. Families in which each member is separated from the others by asbestos walls of verbal propriety, overt sweetness, cheap frankness, and rectitude tell one another off and talk back to each other with minute and unconscious displays of affect—not to mention physical complaints and bodily ailments—with which they worry, accuse, undermine, and murder one another.

Meaning it, then, is not a matter of credal protestation; verbal explicitness is not a sign of faith. Meaning it, means to be at one with an ideology in the process of rejuvenation; it implies a successful sublimation of one's libidinal strivings; and it manifests itself in a liberated craftsmanship.

When Luther listened to the scriptures he did not do so with an unprejudiced ear. His method of making an unprejudiced approach consisted of listening both ways—to the Word coming from the book and to the echo in himself. "Whatever is in your disposition," he said, "that the word of God will be unto you."[45] Disposition here means the inner configuration of your most meant meanings. He knew that he meant it when he could say it: the spoken Word was the activity appropriate for his kind of passivity. Here "faith and word become one, an invincible whole." "*Der Glawb und das Worth wirth gantz ein Ding und ein unuberwintlich ding.*"[46]

Twenty-five times in the Lectures on the Psalms, against once in the Lectures on the Romans, Luther quotes two corresponding passages from Paul's first Epistle to the Corinthians. The first passage:

22. For the Jews require a sign, and the Greeks seek after wisdom;
23. But we preach Christ crucified, unto the Jews a stumblingblock, and unto the Greeks foolishness;
25. Because the foolishness of God is wiser than men; and the weak ness of God is stronger than men.[47]

This paradoxical foolishness and weakness of God became a theological absolute for Luther: there is not a word in the Bible, he exclaimed, which is *extra crucem,* which can be understood without reference to the cross; and this is all that shall and can be understood, as Paul had said in the other passage:

1. And I, brethren, when I came to you, came not with excellency of speech or of wisdom, declaring unto you the testimony of God.
2. For I determined not to know any thing among you, save Jesus Christ, and him crucified.
3. And I was with you in weakness, and in fear, and in much trembling.[48]

Thus Luther abandoned any theological quibbling about the cross. He did not share St. Augustine's opinion that when Christ on the cross exclaimed *Deus meus, quare me derelequisti,* He had not been really abandoned, for as God's son and as God's word, He *was* God. Luther could not help feeling that St. Paul came closer to the truth when he assumed an existential paradox rather than a platonic fusion of essences; he insists on Christ's complete sense of abandonment and on his sincere and active premeditation in visiting hell. Luther spoke here in passionate terms very different from those of medieval adoration. He spoke of a man who was unique in all creation, yet lives in each man; and who is dying *in* everyone even as he died *for* everyone. It is clear that Luther rejected all arrangements by which an assortment of saints made it unnecessary for man to embrace the maximum of his own existential suffering. What he had tried, so desperately and for so long, to counteract and overcome he now accepted as his divine gift—the sense of utter abandonment, *sicut jam damnatus,*[49] as if already in hell. The worst temptation, he now says, is not to have any; one can be sure that God is most angry when He does not seem angry at all. Luther warns of all those well-meaning *(bone intentionarii)* religionists who encourage man "to do what he can": to forestall sinning by clever planning; to seek redemption by observing all occasions for rituals, not forgetting to bring cash along to the limit of their means; and to be secure in the feeling that they are as humble and as peaceful as "it is in them to be." Luther, instead, made a virtue out of what his superiors had considered a vice in him (and we, a symptom), namely, the determined search for the rock bottom of his sinfulness: only thus, he says, can man judge himself as God would: *conformis deo est et verax et justus.*[50] One could consider such conformity utter passivity in the face of God's judgment; but note that it really is an active self-observation, which scans the frontier of conscience for the genuine sense of guilt. Instead of accepting some impersonal and mechanical absolution, it insists on dealing with sincere guilt, perceiving as "God's judgment" what in fact is the individual's own truly meant self-judgment.

Is all this an aspect of personal adjustment to be interpreted as a set of unconscious tricks? Martin the son, who on a personal level had suffered deeply because he could not coerce his father into approving his religiosity as genuine, and who had borne with him the words of this father with an unduly prolonged filial obedience, assumes now on a religious level a volitional role toward filial suffering, perhaps making out of his protracted sonhood the victory of his Christlikeness. In his first Mass, facing the altar—the Father in heaven—and at the same time waiting to face his angry earthly father, Martin had "overlooked" a passage concerning Christ's mediatorship. Yet now, in finding Christ in himself, he establishes an inner position which goes beyond that of a neurotic compromise identification. He finds the core of a praying man's identity, and advances Christian ideology by an important step. It is clear that Luther abandoned the appreciation of Christ as a substitute who has died "for"—in the sense of "instead of"—us; he also abandoned the concept of Christ as an ideal figure to be imitated, or abjectly venerated, or ceremonially remembered as an event in the past. Christ now becomes the core of the Christian's identity: *quotidianus Christi adventus,*[51] Christ is today here, in me. The affirmed passivity of suffering becomes the daily Passion and the Passion is the substitution of the primitive sacrifice of others with a most active, most masterly, affirmation of man's nothingness—which, by his own masterly choice, becomes his existential identity.

The men revered by mankind as saviors face and describe in lasting words insights which the ordinary man must avoid with all possible self-deception and exploitation of others. These men prove their point by the magic of their voices which radiate to the farthest corner of their world and out into the millennia. Their passion contains elements of choice, mastery, and victory, and sooner or later earns them the name of King of Kings; their crown of thorns later becomes their successor's tiara. For a little while Luther, this first revolutionary individualist, saved the Saviour from the tiaras and the ceremonies, the hierarchies and the thought-police, and put him back where he arose: in each man's soul.

Is this not the counterpart, on the level of conscience, to Renaissance anthropocentrism? Luther left the heavens to science and restricted himself to what he could know of his own suffering and faith, that is, to what he could mean. He who had sought to dispel the angry cloud that darkened the face of the fathers and of The Father now said that Christ's life *is* God's face: *qui est facies patris.*[52] The Passion is all that man can know of God: his conflicts, duly faced, are all that he can know of himself. The last judgment is the always present self-judgment. Christ did not live and die in order to make man poorer in the fear of his future judgment, but in order to make him abundant today: *nam judicia sunt ipsae passiones Christi quae in nobis abundant.*[53] Look, Luther said at one point in these lectures (IV, 87), how everywhere painters depict Christ's passion as if they agreed with St. Paul that we know nothing but Christ crucified.[54] The artist closest to Luther in spirit was Dürer, who etched his own face into Christ's countenance.

The characteristics of Luther's theological advance can be compared to certain steps in psychological maturation which every man must take: the internalization of the father-son relationship; the concomitant crystallization of conscience; the safe establishment of an identity as a worker and a man; and the concomitant reaffirmation of basic trust.

God, instead of lurking on the periphery of space and time, became for Luther "what works in us." The way *to* Him is not the effortful striving toward a goal by "doing what you can"; rather, His way is what moves from inside: *via dei est, qua nos ambulare facit.*[55] God, now less of a person, becomes more personal for the individual; and instead of constituting a threat to be faced at the end of all things, He becomes that which always begins—in us. His son is therefore always reborn: *"ita et nos semper oportet nasci, novari, generari"*: It therefore behooves us to be reborn, renovated, regenerated.[56] To "do enough" means always to begin: *"Proficere est nihil aliud nisi semper incipere."*[57] The intersection of all the paradoxes of the vertical and the horizontal is thus to be found in man's own divided nature. The two *regna,* the realist sphere of divine grace and the naturalist sphere of animality, exist in man's inner conflicts and in his existential paradoxes: *"Die zwo Personen oder zweierlei ampt,"*[58] the two personalities and the two callings which a Christian must maintain at the same time on this earth.

It does not matter what these two personalities "are." Theologians, philosophers, and psychologists slice man in different ways, and there is no use trying to make the sections coincide. The main point to be made here is Luther's new emphasis on man in *inner* conflict and his salvation through introspective perfection. Luther's formulation of a God known to individual man only through the symbolism of the Son's Passion redefined the individual's existence in a direction later pursued in both Kierkegaard's existentialism and Freud's psychoanalysis—methods which lead the individual systematically to his own borders, including the border of his religious ecstasies.

Let us rephrase somewhat more psychologically what we have just put in theological terms. What we have referred to as the negative conscience corresponds in many ways to Freud's conceptualization of the pressure put by the superego on the ego. If this pressure is dominant in an individual or in a group, the whole quality of experience is overshadowed by a particular sense of existence, an intensification of certain aspects of subjective space and time. Any fleeting moment of really bad conscience can teach us this, as can also, and more impressively, a spell of melancholy. We are then strangely constricted and paralyzed, victims of an inner voice whispering sharply that we are far from that perfection which alone will do when the closely impending, but vague and unpredictable, doom arrives; in spite of that immediacy, we are as yet sinners, not quite good enough, and probably too far gone. Any temporary relief from this melancholy state (into which Luther, at the height of his worldly success, sank more deeply than ever before) is only to be had at the price of making a painful deal with the voice, a deal which offers the hope that maybe soon we will find the platform for a new start; or maybe at the hour of trial we will find that according to some unknown scale we will prove barely but sufficiently acceptable, and so may pass—pass into heaven, as some proud minds have asked, by just *getting by?* In the meantime, our obsessive scrupulosity will chew its teeth out and exercise its guts on the maybe-soons, the already-almosts, the just-a-bit-mores, the not-yet-quites, the probably-next-times. Not all minds, of course, naturally exercise themselves in this way; but everybody does it to some degree, and almost anybody can be prevailed upon to participate by an ideological system which blocks all exits except one, that one adorned with exactly matching symbols of hope and despair, and guarded by the system's showmen, craftsmen, and torturers.

To some individuals, however, such a state becomes, for personal reasons, habitual: from these people the religionists in any field are recruited. Whole peoples may elaborate this potential state into a world image. William James remarked that the Latin races seem to be able more easily to split up the pressure of evil into "ills and sins in the plural, removable in detail," while the Germanic races tend to erect one "Sin in the singular, and with a capital S . . . ineradicably ingrained in our natural subjectivity, and never to be removed by any piecemeal operation."[59] If this is true, climate may have much to do with it: the more decided retreat of the sun to the danger point of disappearance in the Nordic winter, the protracted darkness and the fatal cold which last over periods long enough to convey a sense of irretrievability or at any rate to enforce a totalistic adjustment to such a possibility. Just because Luther's periodic states of melancholy repeatedly forced him to accept despair and disease as final, and death as imminent, he may have expressed in his pessimistic and philosophically most untenable concepts (such as the total predestination of individual fate, independent of personal effort) exactly that cold rock bottom of mood, that utter background of blackness, which to Northern people is the condition of spring:

> *Der Sommer ist hart fuer der Tuer*
> *Der Winter ist vergangen*
> *Die zarten Blumen gehn herfuer;*
> *Der das hat angefangen*
> *Der wird es auch vollenden.*

This only says that winter is gone and summer is at the door, and that the flowers are coming up; and that Whoever has begun such a process will surely complete it.

A predominant state of mind in which the ego keeps the superego in victorious check can reconcile certain opposites which the negative conscience rigidly keeps separate; ego-dominance tends to be holistic, to blend opposites without blunting them. In his state of personal recovery, Luther (like any individual recovering from an oppressive mental state) had recourse to massive totalisms from which he derived the foundation stones for a new wholeness. The whole person includes certain total states in his balances: we are, Luther proclaimed, totally sinners *(totus homo peccator)* and totally just *(totus homo justus),* always both damned and blessed, both alive and dead. We thus cannot strive, by hook or by crook, to get from one absolute stage into another; we can only use our God-given organs of awareness in the here and now to encompass the paradoxes of the human condition. Psychologically speaking, this means that at any given moment, and in any given act or thought, we are codetermined to a degree which can never become quite conscious by our drives *and* by our conscience. Our ego is most powerful when it is not burdened with an excessive denial of our drives, but lets us enjoy what we can, refute what we must, and sublimate according to our creativity—always making due allowance for the absolutism of our conscience, which can never be appeased by small sacrifices and atonements, but must always remain part of the whole performance. Luther thus said in his terms what Freud formulated psychologically, namely, that only on the surface are we ever entirely driven *or* completely just; in our depths we are vain when we are most just, and bad conscience can always be shown to be at work exactly when we are most driven by lust or avarice. But this same inner psychological condition saves God (theologically speaking) from that impossible characteristic for which Martin had not been able to forgive him, namely, that of being The Father only in certain especially meritorious moments, rather than for all eternity, as he should be. To the ego, eternity is always now.

Luther's strong emphasis on the here and now of the spiritual advent, and on the necessity of always standing at the beginning, *(semper incipere)* is not only a platform of faith, it is akin to a time-space quality dominating the inner state which psychoanalysts call "ego-strength." To the ego the past is not an inexorable process, experienced only as preparation for an impending doom; rather, the past is part of a present mastery which employs a convenient mixture of forgetting, falsifying, and idealizing to fit the past to the present, but usually to an extent which is neither unknowingly delusional nor knowingly dishonest. The ego can resign itself to past losses and forfeitings and learn not to demand the impossible of the future. It enjoys the illusion of a present, and defends this most precarious of all assumptions against doubts and apprehensions by remembering most easily chains of experiences which were alike in their unblemished presentness. To the healthy ego, the flux of time sponsors the process of identity. It thus is not afraid of death (as Freud has pointed out vigorously); it has no concept of death. But it *is* afraid of losing mastery over the negative conscience, over the drives, and over reality. To lose any of these battles is, for the ego, living death; to win them again and again means to the ego something akin to an assumption that it is causing its own life. In theological terms, *creaturae procedunt ex deo libere et voluntarie et non naturaliter:*[60] what lives, proceeds from God freely and voluntarily, not naturally, that is, not by way of what can be explained biologically.

Luther's restatements about the total sinfulness and the total salvation which are in man at any given time, can easily be shown to be alogical. With sufficient ill will they can be construed as contrived to save Martin's particular skin, which held together upswings of spiritual elations and cursing gloominess, not to speak of lusts for power and revenge, women, food, and beer. But the coexistence of all these contradictions has its psychologic—as has also the fury of their incompatibility. Martin's theological reformulations imply a psychological fact, namely, that the ego gains strength *in practice,* and *in affectu* to the degree to which it can accept at the same time the total power of the drives and the total power of conscience—*provided* that it can nourish what Luther called *opera manum dei,*[61] that particular combination of work and love which alone verifies our identity and confirms it. Under these conditions, apparent submission becomes mastery, apparent passivity the release of new energy for active pursuits. We can make negative conscience work for the aims of the ego only by facing it without evasion; and we are able to manage and creatively utilize our drives only to the extent to which we can acknowledge their power by enjoyment, by awareness, and through the activity of work.

If the ego is not able to accomplish these reconciliations, we may fall prey to that third inner space-time characterized by the dominance of what Freud called the *id.* The danger of this state comes from what Freud considered biological instincts which the ego experiences as beneath and outside itself while at the same time it is intoxicated by them. Dominance by the id means that time and space are arranged in one way—toward wish fulfillment. We know only that our tension rises when time and circumstances delay release and satisfaction, and that our dri-venness is accelerated when opportunities arise. The self-propelled will tends to ignore all that has been learned in the past and is perceived in the present, except to the extent to which past and present add fuel to the goal-directedness of the wish. This id-intoxication, as Luther for-mulated so knowingly, can become total poisoning especially when it is haughtily denied.

Some monastic methods systematically descend to the frontiers where all ego dangers must be faced in the raw—where an overweening con-science is appeased through prayer, drives tamed by asceticism, and the pressure of reality is itself defeated by the self's systematic abandonment of its identity. But true monasticism is a late development and is possible only to a mature ego. Luther knew why he later said that nobody under thirty years of age should definitely commit himself to it.

Luther's redefinitions of work have probably been more misunderstood than any other of his formulations, except, naturally, those pertaining to sex. In both these sensitive areas, theory and practice have become com-pletely separated. In trying to decide what a great man meant by his original formulations, it is always good to find out what he was talking *against* at the time, or what previous overstatement he was trying to cor-rect, for greatness is based on an excessive restatement of some previous overstatement, usually made by others, often by the master himself. To the extent that the restatement momentarily sharpens our perception of our own frontiers, it will live, even though the concepts themselves become the focus of the next period's overstatement. When Luther spoke about works and work, he was speaking against a climate of opinion which, in matters of religion, asked a man how much he had done of what there was in him (or in his pocketbook) to do. When Luther spoke against works, he spoke against holy busywork which has nothing whatsoever to do with the nature or the quality of devoted craftsmanship.

Luther felt that the Christianity of his time had forgotten St. Paul's and Christ's Christianity and had reverted to "Jewish, Turkish, and Pelagian" notions, particularly in putting so much emphasis on the fulfillment of prescribed rituals. We need only remember his own obsession in Rome with the collection of free and not so free coupons to heaven to know what he meant. He later caricatured this attitude: "He runs to St. James,

Rome, Jerusalem, here, there; prays to St. Brigit, this, that; fasts today, to-morrow; confesses here, there; asks this one, that one—and yet does not find peace."[62] He considered this a regression to "the law" in Judaism, in which he felt there was an excess of righteousness expressed in meticu-lous observances. In the obsessive fulfillment of detailed rituals, as he knew only too well, the negative conscience takes over, dividing every minute of the day into a miniature last judgment. The small self-salvations thus gained come to count as virtue—a virtue which has no time for faith and leaves not a moment's peace to others, if it can help it. Much is in the language here, in English as well as German: those who *do* what is right *(richtig)* think that they *are* right *(recht)* and claim that they *have* the right to lord it over others *(rechthaben)*.

Against this inner psychic sequence Luther, in accord with his whole new space-time configuration, re-emphasized the spirit in which a thing is done from the start for its own sake. Nobody is just, he said, because he does just works; the works are just *if* the man is just: *quia justus, opera justa*. As he says in one of his teutonic restatements of a biblical saying: "What would it avail you, if you did do miracles, and strangled all the Turks *(alle Turcken erwurgkist)* and yet would sin against love?"[63]

In matters of sex and work misquotation is easy. Even Nietzsche mis-understood Luther in the matter of work, claiming that exercise and practice are every bit as necessary for good work as is faith, and often are the forerunners of faith. Nietzsche was writing against Schopenhauer's as-ceticism and pessimism at the time, and was intent on reinstating will and action as prime virtues. He ignored the fact that Luther was against works, but very much for work; and that he sanctified even such activi-ties as piling up manure, washing babies, and cleaning up the house, if they were done with faith.

As far as Luther's attitude toward his own work is concerned, only when he was able to make speaking his main occupation could he learn to know his thoughts and to trust them—and also trust God. He took on the lectures, not with pious eagerness, but with a sense of tragic conflict; but as he prepared and delivered them, he became affectively and intel-lectually alive. This is not works; it is work, in the best sense. In fact, Luther made the verbal work of his whole profession more genuine in the face of a tradition of scholastic virtuosity. His style indicates his con-viction that a thing said less elegantly and meant more truly is better work, and better craftsmanship in communication.

There is a psychological truth implicit in Luther's restatement. People with "well-functioning egos" do good work if they can manage to "mean" the work (for whatever reason or for whoever's sake) which they must do. This is not always easily arranged, by any means, and we should not be too glib with the term "strong ego." Many individuals should not do the work which they are doing, if they are doing it well at too great inner expense. Good work it may be in terms of efficiency; but it is also bad works. The point is, not how efficiently the work is done, but how good it is for the worker in terms of his lifetime within his ideological world. The work's individual goodness will be reflected in some technical goodness which is more than the sum of mastered procedures. In his insistence on the importance of the spirit of work Luther antedated Marx; but, of course, neither politically nor economically did he foresee progress as a new dimension of ideology, although he helped to make man free for it. His was a craftsman's point of view; and he considered one craft as good a way to personal perfection as another; but also as bad a potential lifelong prison as another.

We live always in all three space-times; certain alternations of emphases differentiate us from one another. We are all alternately driven and conscience-stricken some of the time; but usually we manage to live in a dominant ego space-time, despite the world-image which totalitarian powers of spirit, sword, or dollar may continuously try to impose on us. Each historical period has its lacunae of identity and of style; each best of all possible worlds has its tensions and crazes which attest to its peculiar excesses of drivenness and constriction. Man never lives entirely in his time, even though he can never live outside it; sometimes his identity gets along with his time's ideology, and sometimes it has to fight for its life. But it is only when an overwhelming negative conscience like Martin's is linked with the sensitivity and the power-drive of a Luther that a new positive conscience arises to sow ideological seeds into fresh furrows of historical change. And perhaps all such fresh starts have in common the ego qualities which I have tried to circumscribe in this discussion.

Luther's theology contains an unsolved personal problem which is more accessible to psychoanalysis than is the theology itself. This unsolved personal problem becomes obvious later, when the suddenly changed course of his life endangers the identity which he had won as a lecturer and preacher; and even more obvious when the crisis of middle age brings to the fore again that inner store of self-hate, and that murderous intolerance of disobedience which in the lectures on the Psalms had been relatively balanced—within Luther's identity as a lecturer.

God himself thus joins the benevolent paternal images. Luther interprets Psalm 102:13, "Thou shalt arise, and have mercy upon Zion," in these words: "This arising, this standing up, means the sweetest and most gracious becoming human on the part of God, for here He has come to us so that He may lift us up to Himself."[64]

The study of Luther's earliest lectures shows that in his self-cure from deep obsessive struggles he came, almost innocently, to express principles basic to the mastery of existence by religious and introspective means. As he stated in his notes for the lectures on Romans, in which he came much closer to perfection as a professor and to clarity as a dogmatist: "Perfect self-insight is perfect humility; perfect humility is perfect knowledge; perfect knowledge is perfect spirituality."[65] At the same time Luther crowns his attempt to cure the wounds of this wrath by changing God's attributes: instead of being like an earthly father whose mood-swings are incomprehensible to his small son, God is given the attribute of *ira misericordiae*—a wrath which is really compassion. With this concept, Luther was at last able to forgive God for being a Father, and grant Him justification.

Only a very independent mind could thus restate the principles of pre-Roman Christianity; and only a righteously simple man could delude himself into believing that if he let the Roman Church live, she would let him preach. This self-deception had not ended when Luther nailed the ninety-five theses on the church door in Wittenberg—not a defiant gesture in itself, but rather scholastic routine. But circumstances, to be recounted in the concluding chapter, used his theory of the spiritual negligibility of works as the backbone of an economic revolt. All of Northern Germany jumped at the opportunity to limit Roman taxation on what seemed like sound theological grounds, in the argument, the Germans began to hear the voice that argued, and it sounded like the kind of voice they had long been waiting for.

Luther grew elatedly into his role of reformer. How he thus changed identities—he who had denied his father's wish that he should become a secular leader by choosing monastic silence instead—we can only sketch. It is clear, however, that the negative conscience which had been aggravated so grievously by Martin's paternalistic upbringing had only waited (as such consciences always do) for an opportunity to do to others in some measure what had been done to him.

EPILOGUE

from *Young Man Luther*

1

To relegate Luther to a shadowy greatness at the turbulent conclusion of the Age of Faith does not help us see what his life really stands for. To put it in his own words:

"I did not learn my theology all at once, but I had to search deeper for it, where my temptations took me."[1] *"Vivendo, immo moriendo et damnando fit theologus, non intelligendo, legendo, aut speculando"*:[2] A theologian is born by living, nay dying and being damned, not by thinking, reading, or speculating.

Not to understand this message under the pretense of not wanting to make the great man too human—although he represented himself as human with relish and gusto—only means to protect ourselves from taking our chances with the *tentationes* of our day, as he did with his. Historical analysis should help us to study further our own immediate tasks, instead of hiding them in a leader's greatness.

I will not conclude with a long list of what we must do. In too many books the word "must" increases in frequency in inverse relation to the number of pages left to point out how what must be done might be done. I will try, instead, to restate a few assumptions of this book in order to make them more amenable to joint study.

When Luther challenged the rock bottom of his own prayer, he could not know that he would find the fundament for a new theology. Nor did Freud know that he would find the principles of a new psychology when he took radical chances with himself in a new kind of introspective analysis. I have applied to Luther, the first Protestant at the end of the age of absolute faith, insights developed by Freud, the first psychoanalyst at the end of the era of absolute reason; and I have mentioned seemingly incidental parallels between the two men. A few weightier connections must be stated in conclusion.

Both men endeavored to increase the margin of man's inner freedom by introspective means applied to the very center of his conflicts; and this to the end of increased individuality, sanity, and service to men. Luther, at the beginning of ruthless mercantilism in Church and commerce, counterpoised praying man to the philosophy and practice of meritorious works. Subsequently, his justification by faith was absorbed into the patterns of mercantilism, and eventually turned into a justification of commercialism by faith. Freud, at the beginning of unrestricted industrialization, offered another method of introspection, psychoanalysis. With it, he obviously warned against the mechanical socialization of men into effective but neurotic robots. It is equally obvious that his work is about to be used in furtherance of that which he warned against: the glorification of "adjustment." Thus both Doctor Luther and Doctor Freud, called great by their respective ages, have been and are apt to be resisted not only by their enemies, but also by friends who subscribe to their ideas but lack what Kierkegaard called a certain strenuousness of mental and moral effort.

Luther, as we saw, instituted a technique of prayer which eminently served to clarify the delineation of what we, to the best of our knowledge, really mean. Freud added a technique (totally inapplicable to people who do not really mean anything at all) which can make us understand what it means when we insist we mean what we, according to our dreams and symptoms, cannot mean deep down. As to prayer, Luther advocated an appeal to God that He grant you, even as you pray, the good intention with which you started the prayer: *ut etiam intentionem quam presumpsisti ipse tibi dat*. Centuries later Freud postulated an analogous rigor for genuine introspection, namely, the demand that one take an especially honest look at one's honesty.

Luther tried to free individual conscience from totalitarian dogma; he meant to give man credal wholeness, and, alas, inadvertently helped to increase and to refine authoritarianism. Freud tried to free the individual's insight from authoritarian conscience; his wholeness is that of the individual ego, but the question is whether collective man will create a world worth being whole for.

Luther accepted man's distance from God as existential and absolute, and refused any traffic with the profanity of a God of deals; Freud suggests that we steadfastly study our unconscious deals with morality and reality before we haughtily claim free will, or righteously good intentions in dealings with our fellowmen.

Luther limited our knowledge of God to our individual experience of temptation and our identification in prayer with the passion of God's son. In this, all men are free and equal. Freud made it clear that the structure of inner *Konflict,* made conscious by psychoanalysis and recognized as universal for any and all, is all we can know of ourselves—yet it is a knowledge inescapable and indispensable. The devoutly sceptical Freud proclaimed that man's uppermost duty (no matter what his introspective reason would make him see, or his fate suffer) was *das Leben auszuhalten*: to stand life, to hold out.

In this book I have described how Luther, once a sorely frightened child, recovered through the study of Christ's Passion the central meaning of the Nativity; and I have indicated in what way Freud's method of introspection brought human conflict under a potentially more secure control by revealing the boundness of man in the loves and rages of his childhood. Thus both Luther and Freud came to acknowledge that "the child is in the midst." Both men perfected introspective techniques permitting isolated man to recognize his individual patienthood. They also reasserted the other pole of existence, man's involvement in generations: for only in facing the helplessness and the hope newly born in every child does mature man (and this *does* include woman) recognize the irrevocable responsibility of being alive and about.

2

Let us consider, then, what we may call the metabolism of generations.

Each human life begins at a given evolutionary stage and level of tradition, bringing to its environment a capital of patterns and energies; these are used to grow on, and to grow into the social process with, and also as contributions to this process. Each new being is received into a style of life prepared by tradition and held together by tradition, and at the same time disintegrating because of the very nature of tradition. We say that tradition "molds" the individual, "channels" his drives. But the social process does not mold a new being merely to housebreak him; it molds generations in order to be remolded, to be reinvigorated, by them. Therefore, society can never afford merely to suppress drives or to guide their sublimation. It must also support the primary function of every individual ego, which is to transform instinctual energy into patterns of action, into character, into style—in short, into an identity with a core of integrity which is to be derived from and also contributed to the tradition. There is an optimum ego synthesis to which the individual aspires; and there is an optimum societal metabolism for which societies and cultures strive. In describing the interdependence of individual aspiration and of societal striving, we describe something indispensable to human life.

In an earlier book, I indicated a program of studies which might account for the dovetailing of the stages of individual life and of basic human institutions. The present book circumscribes for only one of these stages—the identity crisis—its intrinsic relation to the process of ideological rejuvenation in a period of history when organized religion dominated ideologies.

In discussing the identity crisis, we have, at least implicitly, presented some of the attributes of any psychosocial crisis. At a given age, a human being, by dint of his physical, intellectual, and emotional growth, becomes ready and eager to face a new life task, that is, a set of choices and tests which are in some traditional way prescribed and prepared for him by his society's structure. A new life task presents a *crisis* whose outcome can be a successful graduation, or alternatively, an impairment of the life cycle which will aggravate future crises. Each crisis prepares the next, as one step leads to another; and each crisis also lays one more cornerstone for the adult personality. I will enumerate all these crises (more thoroughly treated elsewhere) to remind us, in summary, of certain issues in Luther's life; and also to suggest a developmental root for the basic human values of faith, will, conscience, and reason—all necessary in rudimentary form for the identity which crowns childhood.

The first crisis is the one of early infancy. How this crisis is met decides whether a man's innermost mood will be determined more by basic trust or by basic mistrust. The outcome of this crisis—apart from accidents of heredity, gestation, and birth—depends largely on the quality of maternal care, that is, on the consistency and mutuality which guide the mother's ministrations and give a certain predictability and hopefulness to the baby's original cosmos of urgent and bewildering body feelings. The ratio and relation of basic trust to basic mistrust established during early infancy determines much of the individual's capacity for simple faith, and consequently also determines his future contribution to his society's store of faith—which, in turn, will feed into a future mother's ability to trust the world in which she teaches trust to newcomers. In this first stage we can assume that a historical process is already at work; history writing should therefore chart the influence of historical events on growing generations to be able to judge the quality of their future contribution to history. As for little Martin, I have drawn conclusions about that earliest time when his mother could still claim the baby, and when he was still all hers, inferring that she must have provided him with a font of basic trust on which he was able to draw in his fight for a primary faith present before all will, conscience, and reason, a faith which is "the soul's virginity."

The first crisis corresponds roughly to what Freud has described as orality; the second corresponds to anality. An awareness of these correspondences is essential for a true understanding of the dynamics involved.

The second crisis, that of infancy, develops the infantile sources of what later becomes a human being's will, in its variations of willpower and wilfulness. The resolution of this crisis will determine whether an individual is apt to be dominated by a sense of autonomy, or by a sense of shame and doubt. The social limitations imposed on intensified wilfulness inevitably create doubt about the justice governing the relations of grown and growing people. The way this doubt is met by the grown-ups determines much of a man's future ability to combine an unimpaired will with ready self-discipline, rebellion with responsibility.

The interpretation is plausible that Martin was driven early out of the trust stage, out from "under his mother's skirts," by a jealously ambitious father who tried to make him precociously independent from women, and sober and reliable in his work. Hans succeeded, but not without storing in the boy violent doubts of the father's justification and sincerity; a lifelong shame over the persisting gap between his own precocious conscience and his actual inner state; and a deep nostalgia for a situation of infantile trust. His theological solution—spiritual return to a faith which is there before all doubt, combined with a political submission to those who by necessity must wield the sword of secular law—seems to fit perfectly his personal need for compromise. While this analysis does not explain either the ideological power or the theological consistency of his solution, it does illustrate that ontogenetic experience is an indispensable link and transformer between one stage of history and the next. This link is a psychological one, and the energy transformed and the process of transformation are both charted by the psychoanalytic method.

Freud formulated these matters in dynamic terms. Few men before him gave more genuine expression to those experiences which are on the borderline between the psychological and the theological than Luther, who gleaned from these experiences a religious gain formulated in theological terms. Luther described states of badness which in many forms pervade human existence from childhood. For instance, his description of shame, an emotion first experienced when the infant stands naked in space and feels belittled: "He is put to sin and shame before God . . . this shame is now a thousand times greater, that a man must blush in the presence of God. For this means that there is no corner or hole in the whole of creation into which a man might creep, not even in hell, but he must let himself be exposed to the gaze of the whole creation, and stand in the open with all his shame, as a bad conscience feels when it is really struck. . . ."[3] Or his description of doubt, an emotion first experienced when the child feels singled out by demands whose rationale he does not comprehend: "When he is tormented in *Anfechtung* it seems to him that he is alone: God is angry only with him, and irreconcilably angry against him: then he alone is a sinner and all the others are in the right, and they work against him at God's orders. There is nothing left for him but this unspeakable sighing through which, without knowing it, he is supported by the Spirit and cries 'Why does God pick on me alone?' "[4]

Luther was a man who would not settle for an easy appeasement of these feelings on any level, from childhood through youth to his manhood, or in any segment of life. His often impulsive and intuitive formulations transparently display the infantile struggle at the bottom of the lifelong emotional issue.

His basic contribution was a living reformulation of faith. This marks him as a theologian of the first order; it also indicates his struggle with the ontogenetically earliest and most basic problems of life. He saw as his life's work a new delineation of faith and will, of religion and the law: for it is clear that organized religiosity, in circumstances where faith in a world order is monopolized by religion, is the institution which tries to give dogmatic permanence to a reaffirmation of that basic trust—and a renewed victory over that basic mistrust—with which each human being emerges from early infancy. In this way organized religion cements the faith which will support future generations. Established law tries to formulate obligations and privileges, restraints and freedoms, in such a way that man can submit to law and order with a minimum of doubt and with little loss of face, and as an autonomous agent of order can teach the rudiments of discipline to his young. The relation of faith and law, of course, is an eternal human problem, whether it appears in questions of church and state, mysticism and daily morality, or existential aloneness and political commitment.

The third crisis, that of initiative versus guilt, is part of what Freud described as the central complex of the family, namely, the Oedipus complex. It involves a lasting unconscious association of sensual freedom with the body of the mother and the administrations received from her hand; a lasting association of cruel prohibition with the interference of the dangerous father; and the consequences of these associations for love and hate in reality and in phantasy. (I will not discuss here the cultural relativity of Freud's observations nor the dated origin of his term; but I assume that those who do wish to quibble about all this will feel the obligation to advance systematic propositions about family, childhood, and society which come closer to the core, rather than go back to the periphery, of the riddle which Freud was the first to penetrate.) We have reviewed the strong indications of an especially heavy interference by Hans Luder with Martin's attachment to his mother, who, it is suggested, secretly provided for him what Goethe openly acknowledged as his mother's gift— *"Die Frohnatur, die Lust zu fabulieren"*: gaiety and the pleasure of confabulation. We have indicated how this gift, which later emerged in Luther's poetry, became guilt-laden and was broken to harness by an education designed to make a precocious student of the boy. We have also traced its relationship to Luther's lifelong burden of excessive guilt. Here is one of Luther's descriptions of that guilt: "And this is the worst of all these ills, that the conscience cannot run away from it-self, but it is always present to itself and knows all the terrors of the crea-ture which such things bring even in this present life, because the ungodly man is like a raging sea. The third and greatest of all these horrors and the worst of all ills is to have a judge."[5] He also said, "For this is the na-ture of a guilty conscience, to fly and to be terrified, even when all is safe and prosperous, to convert all into peril and death."[6]

The stage of initiative, associated with Freud's phallic stage of psycho-sexuality, ties man's budding will to phantasy, play, games, and early work, and thus to the mutual delineation of unlimited imagination and aspira-tion and limiting, threatening conscience. As far as society is concerned, this is vitally related to the occupational and technological ideals per-ceived by the child; for the child can manage the fact that there is no re-turn to the mother as a mother and no competition with the father as a father only to the degree to which a future career outside of the narrower family can at least be envisaged in ideal future occupations: these he learns to imitate in play, and to anticipate in school. We can surmise that for little Martin the father's own occupation was early precluded from an-ticipatory phantasy, and that a life of scholarly duty was obediently and sadly envisaged instead. This precocious severity of obedience later made it impossible for young Martin to anticipate any career but that of un-limited study for its own sake, as we have seen in following his path of obedience—in disobedience.

In the fourth stage, the child becomes able and eager to learn system-atically, and to collaborate with others. The resolution of this stage de-cides much of the ratio between a sense of industry or work completion, and a sense of tool-inferiority, and prepares a man for the essential in-gredients of the ethos as well as the rationale of his technology. He wants to know the *reason* for things, and is provided, at least, with rationaliza-tions. He learns to use whatever simplest techniques and tools will pre-pare him most generally for the tasks of his culture. In Martin's case, the tool was literacy, Latin literacy, and we saw how he was molded by it—and how later he remolded, with the help of printing, his nation's liter-ary habits. With a vengeance he could claim to have taught German even to his enemies.

But he achieved this only after a protracted identity crisis which is the main subject of this book. Whoever is hard put to feel identical with one set of people and ideas must that much more violently repudiate another set; and whenever an identity, once established, meets further crises, the danger of irrational repudiation of otherness and temporarily even of one's own identity increases.

I have already briefly mentioned the three crises which follow the crisis of identity; they concern problems of intimacy, generativity, and integrity. The crisis of intimacy in a monk is naturally distorted in its heterosexual core. What identity diffusion is to identity—its alternative and danger—isolation is to intimacy. In a monk this too is subject to particular rules, since a monk seeks intentional and organized isolation, and submits all intimacy to prayer and confession.

Luther's intimacy crisis seems to have been fully experienced and resolved only on the Wartburg; that is, after his lectures had established him as a lecturer, and his speech at Worms as an orator of universal stamp. On the Wartburg he wrote *De Votis Monasticis,* obviously determined to take care of his sexual needs as soon as a dignified solution could be found. But the intimacy crisis is by no means only a sexual, or for that matter, a heterosexual, one: Luther, once free, wrote to men friends about his emotional life, including his sexuality, with a frankness clearly denoting a need to share intimacies with them. The most famous example, perhaps, is a letter written at a time when the tragicomedy of these priests' belated marriages to runaway nuns was in full swing. Luther had made a match between Spalatin and an ex-nun, a relative of Staupitz. In the letter, he wished Spalatin luck for the wedding night, and promised to think of him during a parallel performance to be arranged in his own marital bed.[7]

Also on the Wartburg, Luther developed, with his translation of the Bible, a supreme ability to reach into the homes of his nation; as a preacher and a table talker he demonstrated his ability and his need to be intimate for the rest of his life. One could write a book about Luther on this theme alone; and perhaps in such a book all but the most wrathful utterances would be found to be communications exquisitely tuned to the recipient.

Owing to his prolonged identity crisis, and also to delayed sexual intimacy, intimacy and generativity were fused in Luther's life. We have given an account of the time when his generativity reached its crisis, namely, when within a short period he became both a father, and a leader of a wide following which began to disperse his teachings in any number of avaricious, rebellious, and mystical directions. Luther then tasted fully the danger of this stage, which paradoxically is felt by creative people more deeply than by others, namely, a sense of *stagnation,* experienced by him in manic-depressive form. As he recovered, he proceeded with the building of the edifice of his theology; yet he responded to the needs of his parishioners and students, including his princes, to the very end. Only his occasional outbursts expressed that fury of repudiation which was mental hygiene to him, but which set a lasting bad example to his people.

3

We now come to the last, the integrity crisis which again leads man to the portals of nothingness, or at any rate to the station of *having been.* I have described it thus:

> Only he who in some way has taken care of things and people and has adapted himself to the triumphs and disappointments adherent to being, by necessity, the originator of others and the generator of things and ideas—only he may gradually grow the fruit of these seven stages. I know no better word for it than ego integrity. Lacking a clear definition, I shall point to a few constituents of this state of mind. It is the ego's accrued assurance of its proclivity for order and meaning. It is a post-narcissistic love of the human ego—not of the self—as an experience which conveys some world order and some spiritual sense, no matter how dearly paid for. It is the acceptance of one's one and only life cycle as something that had to be and that, by necessity, permitted of no substitutions: it thus means a new, a different, love of one's parents. It is a comradeship with the ordering ways of distant times and different pursuits, as expressed in the simple products and sayings of such times and pursuits. Although aware of the relativity of all the various life styles which have given meaning to human striving, the possessor of integrity is ready to defend the dignity of his own life style against all physical and economic threats. For he knows that an individual life is the accidental coincidence of but one life cycle with but one segment of history; and that for him all human integrity stands or falls with the one style of integrity of which he partakes. The style of integrity developed by his culture or civilization thus becomes the

"patrimony of his soul," the seal of his moral paternity of himself (*". . . pero el honor/Es patrimonio del alma"*: Calderon). Before this final solution, death loses its sting.[8]

This integrity crisis, last in the lives of ordinary men, is a lifelong and chronic crisis in a *homo religiosus.* He is always older, or in early years suddenly becomes older, than his playmates or even his parents and teachers, and focuses in a precocious way on what it takes others a lifetime to gain a mere inkling of: the questions of how to escape corruption in living and how in death to give meaning to life. Because he experiences a breakthrough to the last problems so early in his life maybe such a man had better become a martyr and seal his message with an early death; or else become a hermit in a solitude which anticipates the Beyond. We know little of Jesus of Nazareth as a young man, but we certainly cannot even begin to imagine him as middle-aged.

This short cut between the youthful crisis of identity and the mature one of integrity makes the religionist's problem of individual identity the same as the problem of existential identity. To some extent this problem is only an exaggeration of an abortive trait not uncommon in late adolescence. One may say that the religious leader becomes a professional in dealing with the kind of scruples which prove transitory in many all-too-serious postadolescents who later grow out of it, go to pieces over it, or find an intellectual or artistic medium which can stand between them and nothingness.

The late adolescent crisis, in addition to anticipating the more mature crises, can at the same time hark back to the very earliest crisis of life— trust or mistrust toward existence as such. This concentration in the cataclysm of the adolescent identity crisis of both first and last crises in the human life may well explain why religiously and artistically creative men often seem to be suffering from a barely compensated psychosis, and yet later prove superhumanly gifted in conveying a total meaning for man's life; while malignant disturbances in late adolescence often display precocious wisdom and usurped integrity. The chosen young man extends the problem of his identity to the borders of existence in the known universe; other human beings bend all their efforts to adopt and fulfill the departmentalized identities which they find prepared in their communities. He can permit himself to face as permanent the trust problem which drives others in whom it remains or becomes dominant into denial, despair, and psychosis. He acts as if mankind were starting all over with his own beginning as an individual, conscious of his singularity as well as his humanity; others hide in the folds of whatever tradition they are part of because of membership, occupation, or special interests. To him, history ends as well as starts with him; others must look to their memories, to legends, or to books to find models for the present and the future in what their predecessors have said and done. No wonder that he is something of an old man (a *philosophus,* and a sad one) when his age-mates are young, or that he remains something of a child when they age with finality. The name Lao-tse, I understand, means just that.

The danger of a reformer of the first order, however, lies in the nature of his influence on the masses. In our own day we have seen this in the life and influence of Gandhi. He, too, believed in the power of prayer; when he fasted and prayed, the masses and even the English held their breath. Because prayer gave them the power to say what would be heard by the lowliest and the highest, both Gandhi and Luther believed that they could count on the restraining as well as the arousing power of the Word. In such hope great religionists are supported—one could say they are seduced—by the fact that all people, because of their common undercurrent of existential anxiety, at cyclic intervals and during crises feel an intense need for a rejuvenation of trust which will give new meaning to their limited and perverted exercise of will, conscience, reason, and identity. But the best of them will fall asleep at Gethsemane; and the worst will accept the new faith only as a sanction for anarchic destructiveness or political guile. If faith can move mountains, let it move obstacles out of *their* way. But maybe the masses also sense that he who aspires to spiritual power, even though he speaks of renunciation, has an account to settle with an inner authority. He may disavow their rebellion, but he is a rebel. He may say in the deepest humility, as Luther said, that "his mouth is Christ's mouth"; his nerve is still the nerve of a usurper. So for a while the world may be worse for having had a vision of being better. From the oldest Zen poem to the most recent psychological formulation, it is clear that "the conflict between right and wrong is the sickness of the mind."[9]

The great human question is to what extent early child training must or must not exploit man's early helplessness and moral sensitivity to the degree that a deep sense of evil and of guilt become unavoidable; for such a sense in the end can only result in clandestine commitment to evil in the name of higher values. Religionists, of course, assume that because a sense of evil dominated them even as they combated it, it belongs not only to man's "nature," but is God's plan, even God's gift to him. The answer to this assumption is that not only do child training systems differ in their exploitation of basic mistrust, shame, doubt, and guilt—so do religions. The trouble comes, first, from the mortal fear that instinctual forces would run wild if they were not dominated by a negative conscience; and second, from trying to formulate man's optimum as negative morality, to be reinforced by rigid institutions. In this formulation all man's erstwhile fears of the forces and demons of nature are reprojected onto his inner forces, and onto the child, whose dormant energies are alternatively vilified as potentially criminal, or romanticized as altogether angelic. Because man needs a disciplined conscience, he thinks he must have a bad one; and he assumes that he has a good conscience when, at times, he has an easy one. The answer to all this does not lie in attempts to avoid or to deny one or the other sense of badness in children altogether; the denial of the unavoidable can only deepen a sense of secret, unmanageable evil. The answer lies in man's capacity to create order which will give his children a disciplined as well as a tolerant conscience, and a world within which to act affirmatively.

4

In this book we are dealing with a Western religious movement which grew out of and subsequently perpetuated an extreme emphasis on the interplay of initiative and guilt, and an exclusive emphasis on the divine Father-Son. Even in this scheme, the mother remains a counterplayer however shadowy. Father religions have mother churches.

One may say that man, when looking through a glass darkly, finds himself in an inner cosmos in which the outlines of three objects awaken dim nostalgias. One of these is the simple and fervent wish for a hallucinatory sense of unity with a maternal matrix, and a supply of benevolently powerful substances; it is symbolized by the affirmative face of charity, graciously inclined, reassuring the faithful of the unconditional acceptance of those who will return to the bosom. In this symbol the split of autonomy is forever repaired: shame is healed by unconditional approval, doubt by the eternal presence of generous provision.

In the center of the second nostalgia is the paternal voice of guiding conscience, which puts an end to the simple paradise of childhood and provides a sanction for energetic action. It also warns of the inevitability of guilty entanglement, and threatens with the lightning of wrath. To change the threatening sound of this voice, if need be by means of partial surrender and manifold self-castration, is the second imperative demand which enters religious endeavor. At all cost, the Godhead must be forced to indicate that He Himself mercifully planned crime and punishment in order to assure salvation.

Finally, the glass shows the pure self itself, the unborn core of creation, the—as it were, preparental—center where God is pure nothing: *ein lauter Nichts,* in the words of Angelus Silesius. God is so designated in many ways in Eastern mysticism. This pure self is the self no longer sick with a conflict between right and wrong, not dependent on providers, and not dependent on guides to reason and reality.

These three images are the main religious objects. Naturally, they often fuse in a variety of ways and are joined by hosts of secondary deities. But must we call it regression if man thus seeks again the earliest encounters of his trustful past in his efforts to reach a hoped-for and eternal future? Or do religions partake of man's ability, even as he regresses, to recover creatively? At their creative best, religions retrace our earliest inner experiences, giving tangible form to vague evils, and reaching back to the earliest individual sources of trust; at the same time, they keep alive the common symbols of integrity distilled by the generations. If this is partial regression, it is a regression which, in retracing firmly established pathways, returns to the present amplified and clarified.[10] Here, of course, much depends on whether or not the son of a given era approaches the glass in good faith: whether he seeks to find again on a higher level a treasure of basic trust safely possessed from the beginning, or tries to find a birthright denied him in the first place, in his childhood. It is clear that each generation (whatever its ideological heaven) owes to the next a safe treasure of basic trust; Luther was psychologically and ideologically right when he said in theological terms that the infant *has* faith if his community *means* his baptism. Creative moments, however, and creative periods are rare. The process here described may remain abortive or outlive itself in stagnant institutions—in which case it can and must be associated with neurosis and psychosis, with self-restriction and self-delusion, with hypocrisy and stupid moralism.

Freud has convincingly demonstrated the affinity of some religious ways of thought with those of neurosis.[11] But we regress in our dreams, too, and the inner structures of many dreams correspond to neurotic symptoms. Yet dreaming itself is a healthy activity, and a necessary one. And here too, the success of a dream depends on the faith one has, not on that which one seeks: a good conscience provides that proverbially good sleep which knits up the raveled sleeve of care. All the things that made man feel guilty, ashamed, doubtful, and mistrustful during the daytime are woven into a mysterious yet meaningful set of dream images, so arranged as to direct the recuperative powers of sleep toward a constructive waking state. The dreamwork fails and the dream turns into a nightmare when there is an intrusion of a sense of foreign reality into the dreamer's make-believe, and a subsequent disturbance in returning from that superimposed sense of reality into real reality.

Religions try to use mechanisms analogous to dreamlife, reinforced at times by a collective genius of poetry and artistry, to offer ceremonial dreams of great recuperative value. It is possible, however, that the medieval Church, the past master of ceremonial hallucination, by promoting the reality of hell too efficiently, and by tampering too successfully with man's sense of reality in this world, eventually created, instead of a belief in the greater reality of a more desirable world, only a sense of nightmare in this one.

I have implied that the original faith which Luther tried to restore goes back to the basic trust of early infancy. In doing so I have not, I believe, diminished the wonder of what Luther calls God's disguise. If I assume that it is the smiling face and the guiding voice of infantile parent images which religion projects onto the benevolent sky, I have no apologies to render to an age which thinks of painting the moon red. Peace comes from the inner space.

5

The Reformation is continuing in many lands, in the form of manifold revolutions, and in the personalities of protestants of varied vocations.

I wrote this book in Mexico, on a mirador overlooking a fishing village on Lake Chapala. What remains of this village's primeval inner order goes back to pre-Christian times. But at odd times, urgent church bells call the populace to remembrance. The church is now secular property, only lent to the Cura; and the priest's garb is legally now a uniform to be worn only in church or when engaged in such business as bringing the host to the dying. Yet, at night, with defensive affront, the cross on the church tower is the only neon light in town. The vast majority of the priest's customers are women, indulging themselves fervently in the veneration of the diminutive local madonna statue, which, like those in other communities, is a small idol representing little-girlishness and pure motherhood, rather than the tragic parent of the Savior, who, in fact, is little seen. The men for the most part look on, willing to let the women have their religion as part of women's world, but themselves bound on secular activity. The young ones tend toward the not too distant city of Guadalajara, where the churches and cathedrals are increasingly matched in height and quiet splendor by apartment houses and business buildings.

Guadalajara is rapidly turning into a modern city, the industrial life of which is dominated by the products and techniques of the industrial empire in the North; yet, the emphasis is on Mexican names, Mexican management. A postrevolutionary type of businessman is much in evidence: in his appearance and bearing he protests Mexican maleness and managerial initiative. His modern home can only be called puritan; frills and comforts are avoided, the lines are clean and severe, the rooms light and barren.

The repudiation of the old is most violently expressed in some of the paintings of the revolution. In Orozco's house in Guadalajara one can see beside lithographs depicting civil war scenes with a stark simplicity, sketches of vituperative defamation of the class he obviously sprang from: his sketches swear and blaspheme as loudly as any of the worst pamphlets of Martin Luther. In fact, some of the most treasured murals of the revolution vie with Cranach's woodcuts in their pamphleteering aimed at an as yet illiterate populace. But will revolutions against exploiters settle the issue of exploitation, or must man also learn to raise truly less exploitable men—men who are first of all masters of the human life cycle and of the cycle of generations in man's own lifespace?

On an occasional trip to the capital, I visit ancient Guanajuato where the university, a formidable fortress, has been topped by fantastic ornamental erections in order to overtower the adjoining cathedral which once dominated education. The cathedral wall bears this announcement about death, judgment, inferno, and eternal glory:

> *La Muerta que es puerta de la Eternidad*
> *El Judicio que decidera la Eternidad*
> *El Infierno que es la habitacion de la desgraciada Eternidad*
> *La Gloria que es la masion de la feliz Eternidad*

The area of nearby Lake Patzcuaro is dominated by an enormous statue erected on a fisherman's island. The statue depicts the revolutionary hero Morelos, an erstwhile monk, his right arm raised in a gesture much like Luther's when he spoke at Worms. In its clean linear stockiness and stubborn puritanism the statue could be somewhere in a Nordic land; and if, in its other hand, it held a mighty book instead of the handle of a stony sword, it could, for all the world, be Luther.

THE PERSPECTIVE OF THE
MOUNT

from *Dimensions of a New Identity*

The view from Monticello, as contained in the *Notes on the State of Virginia,* was written, we said, at the lowest moment of Jefferson's career when the political survival of the continent, of Virginia, and of the author himself was at stake. I pointed to a few of the writer's identity elements visible in that work; we will summarize those in conclusion. But now to the review of the actions and sayings of Jesus—a review of a very different kind, which Jefferson undertook during the second half of his life, and, in fact, at the height of his career as a statesman. Because of the central prominence in it of the Sermon on the Mount, I will characterize this outlook as the Perspective of the Mount.

In 1801, Jefferson had become president with an overwhelming mandate from the people, though not without being exposed to such slanderous reportage as was to become typical for American campaigns but which could only deeply offend a man who, on the one hand, was so jealous of his public image, and yet so ready to disavow ambition and to withdraw to Monticello. Furthermore, the attacks on him concerned those most sensitive and central aspects of a man's life which Jefferson never aired in public: his personality, his (very) private life, and his religion. As he once put it, "I not only write nothing on religion, but rarely permit myself to speak of it, and never but in reasonable society." And so, during his first presidential campaign, he had to tolerate with silence the most sinister insinuations concerning the devastating consequences for the whole country of an atheist administration. And, indeed, all his life Jefferson avoided public Christian display and loud sectarian controversies and shunned any contrivance with clerical power struggles: "To the corruptions of Christianity I am, indeed, opposed; but not to the genuine precepts of Jesus himself. I am a Christian in the only sense in which he wished anyone to be; sincerely attached to his doctrines in preference to all others; ascribing to himself every *human* excellence; and believing that he never claimed any other."

Such a well-defined position, however, he could assume only on the basis of having surveyed the Scriptures with great care, if (again) a care which was guided by that pervasive sense of privileged selectivity which characterized his struggle for human integrity within his historical reality. And so, we must visualize an American president in the beginning of the nineteenth century spending evenings going over the New Testament, comparing its versions in Latin and Greek, French and English, and asking himself line for line whether or not it spoke to him as the voice of Jesus. These "authentic" parts he cut out and pasted together in a booklet which he called, "THE PHILOSOPHY OF JESUS OF NAZARETH extracted from the account of his life and teachings as given by Matthew, Mark, Luke and John. Being an abridgement of the New Testament for the use of the Indians, unembarrassed with matters of fact or faith beyond their comprehension." Whatever the fate of his subtitle, it does seem to suggest the writer's intent to present something of a native, an American Gospel.

This, the historians tell us, refers to the compilation which was completed in the years 1804–05, was shown only to very few intimates, and then disappeared. It has been reconstructed only recently and is said to be more personal and more revealing than another compilation, completed in the 1820s which, in turn, was called the *Life and Morals of Jesus of Nazareth,* and came to public attention when it reached the National Museum in 1895. For our purposes and for this lecture, this second compendium will and must do.

We owe ourselves a review of this effort, for it bespeaks some awareness, on the part of an American president, of the fact that one pole of any identity, in any historical period, relates man to what is forever contemporary, namely, eternity. And it permits us to sketch, if only in broad strokes, this pole of identity, as it deals with the awareness of death. We all dimly feel that our transient historical identity is the only chance in all eternity to be alive as somebody in a here and a now. We, therefore, dread the possibility, of which we are most aware when deeply young or very old, that at the end we may find that we have lived the wrong life or not really lived at all. This dread seems incomparably greater than that of death itself, after a fulfilled life—awful as the sudden cessation of life always is. Therefore, human communities, whether they consist of a tribe set in a segment of nature, or of a national empire spanning the territory and the loyalties of a variety of peoples, must attempt to reinforce that sense of identity which promises a meaning for the cycle of life within a world view more real than the certainty of death. Paradoxically speaking, however, to share such a transient sense of being indestructible, all participants must accept a ritual code of mortality and immortality which (whether it promises a rebirth on earth or in heaven) includes the privilege and the duty, if need be, to die a heroic, or at any rate a shared death, while also being willing and eager to kill or help kill those on "the other side" who share (and live and kill and die for) another world view. The motto of this immortality, whether in combat or competition, can be said to be "kill and survive."

The men who inspire and accomplish such a world view we call great and we bestow a form of immortality on them: While they must die, as we must, their image, cast in metal, seems to survive indestructibly in the monuments of our town squares or in the very rock of Mount Rushmore.

But there is the other, the transcendent, effort at insuring salvation through a conscious acceptance of finiteness. It emphasizes nothingness instead of an insistence on somebodyness. It is "not of this world," and instead of a competition for the world's goods (including those securing the earthly identity) it seeks human brotherhood in self-denial. It courts death or, at any rate, self-denial as a step toward a more real and everlasting life. It prefers self-sacrifice to killing. And it visualizes the men and women who can make this aspect of existence convincing, not as great and immortal, but as saintly and as partaking of an eternal life. This way of identity is personified by the great religious leaders who in their own words represent the naked grandeur of the I that transcends all earthly identity in the name of Him who *is* I Am. The motto of this world view could be said to be "die and become."

History shows how these two forms of an immortal identity find their most elaborate communal expressions in empires and religions, which may remain infinitely antagonistic to each other or attempt reconciliation and collusion when priestly empires make political deals with the worldly ones. They may attempt to hasten with holy wars the salvation of the right-minded and the damnation of the rest. Reformations and revolutions upset such collaborations (until they form their own) and demand ideological commitment to one truth or the other. The main point of reviewing such grand schemes in such limited space is the suggestion that the readiness for both extremes, that is, for a defined identity in space and time and a transcendent one is given in all human beings. The biblical division of human duties allocated to Caesar and God makes the basic point that without a physical existence in an earthly regime there can be no defined self as a seat for an I in search of transcendence and no social order to support or to complement a religious domain. And it appears to have been the interplay between empires and world religions which in past history has worked toward a unified identity on earth.

Where the state succeeds in making the motto "kill and survive" so imperative that the voice of "die and become" is being silenced, religious men must oppose the state and, as some of our friends have done, put their bodies on the line. I have attempted to demonstrate with the means at my disposal Mahatma Gandhi's application of a nonviolent method to both national and spiritual liberation as the most systematic attempt in our times, significantly born on the other side of the globe, to a unification of action and faith in a self-aware, all-human identity. "God," he said, "appears to you only in action." Jefferson could have said that. And if Gandhi meant nonviolent action, I think one can find a strong temperamental trend—"peace is my passion"—toward solutions without violence in Jefferson's policies. In the meantime, it bespeaks Jefferson's, the nation builder's, classical sense of balance that he attempted to accommodate the postrevolutionary and the dominant religious identity to each other—for the sake of a new actuality with infinite possibilities.

It is this widest context—at the time underscored, no doubt, by a deep conflict between political triumph and the need for privacy—which gives significance to Jefferson's secret scholarly effort, even though radical religionists will characterize it more as pragmatic compromise with an economic ideal than as an existential commitment. As a friend of mine, great minister and activist, exclaimed when he found me studying

this matter, "Oh, for that Jeffersonian faith: Christianity without sin!" A
political cynic, in turn, may well suspect that Jefferson, when he undertook this work in the midst of violent political controversies, may have
identified with Jesus as the one who drove the Hamiltonians out of the
temple treasury. But let us see.

"I have," so Jefferson wrote in two letters, "made a wee little book
which I call the Philosophy of Jesus; it is a paradigm of his doctrines,
made by cutting the texts out of the [New Testament] and arranging
them on the pages of a blank book in a certain order of time or subject."
And, "The result is an octavo of forty-six pages of pure and unsophisti-
cated doctrines such as were professed and acted on by the *unlettered*
Apostles, the Apostolic Fathers, and the Christians of the first century.
The matter which is evidently his . . . is as easily distinguishable as dia-
monds in a dunghill."

Whatever latent motives, political or personal, will be found in the reconstructed early version, its base line, as it were, is the image which Jefferson had of the person of Jesus—an image of a very special son of the
countryside: "His parentage was obscure, his condition poor; his education null; his natural endowments great; his life correct and innocent; he
was meek, benevolent, patient, firm, disinterested, and of the sublimest
eloquence."

My theological friends tell me that the selections of the later compendium in four languages stand up well under modern Bible research,
which, in its own way, has entered the psychohistorical arena by asking
what each particular Gospel writer, at what particular place and in what
particular time, wrote for what audience, and what we may reconstruct
of the writer's life history and personality before we undertake to see
through all the haze of his self-expression and propagandistic effort who
the man Jesus may have been and what he really said. Jefferson, we will
not be surprised to hear, selected fully half of Matthew—the Gospel
writer whom the scholars judge to be most "lucid, calm, tidy, and judicious." There are lesser portions of the others. The longest coherent section and the centerpiece of it all is the Sermon on the Mount, which sets
the tone for the rest. The whole is above all a narrative, recording Jesus'
travels and relating mainly facts—and not a single miracle! But it does report the parables which make the kingdom so agriculturally concrete.
The kingdom of heaven is like "there was a landowner who planted a
vineyard," or "like a mustard seed," or like "a treasure lying buried in the

field." All this, it is clear, can be made to fit the agricultural destiny of the new world, where transcendence must emerge above all, from work, and where, therefore, actuality is faith, and faith, actuality.

If I, in my turn, may be permitted to be selective in my emphases, there is always the story which I would relate here even if Jefferson had not included it in his Gospel—as he luckily did: "And he came to Capernaum: and being in the house he asked them, 'What was it that ye disputed among yourselves by the way?'

"But they held their peace: for by the way they had disputed among themselves, who should be the greatest.

"And he sat down, and called the twelve, and saith unto them, 'If any man desire to be first, the same shall be last of all, and servant of all.'

"And he took a child, and set him in the midst of them: and when he had taken him in his arms, he said unto them,

" 'Whosoever shall receive one of such children in my name, receiveth me; and whosoever shall receive me, receiveth not me, but him that sent me.' " (Mark 9: 33–38)

A child, not a boy or a girl; a child in its sensory, sensual, and cognitive wholeness, not yet defined in sexual roles and not yet overdefined by economic ones. Such a one has that childlikeness, which to regain in the complexities of adult life, is the beginning of the kingdom. All else is history.

Jefferson's selection is, of course, as interesting in its omissions as it is in its commitments. The context of today's lecture permits me to point out, that what Jefferson discards as a "dunghill" is, in fact, the Gospel writers' pamphletistic attempt to convince their readers that Jesus is the product and the prophet of the coherent world vision prophesied by the books, and that he only confirmed, even as he renewed and restated, the Judaic world with its dooms and promises and, above all, its ethnic utopia. Jefferson obviously felt that this falsified rather than verified Jesus' most pervasive and most rebellious presence as well as the nature of the salvation he envisaged. And, indeed, it can be seen in many Gospel passages that Jesus was most diffident about the traditional, ceremonial, and professional roles which his followers wanted to foist on him, even as he was, in fact, diffident whenever the crowd wanted to define him in terms of his personal identity, his familial or geographic origin. At the end, so it seems he felt, only the final agony of the crucifixion could verify his transcendent identity. Jefferson excludes the story of the resurrection, but it is clear that he believed in the singular presence of Jesus among men.

If some critics miss all references to contrition in Jefferson's Gospel, it is true that the founding fathers did not go for what Thomas Paine called "theological inventions" which seduce man "to contemplate himself an outcast, at an immense distance from his Creator, so that he lost his sense for true religion." Faith in action demanded, as we saw, an intrinsic unity of divine and historical design.

But let me tell you what I find missing in Jefferson's selections. I miss, and I think not only out of professional pique, all references to Jesus' healing mission. Jesus' own diffidence in regard to his very success in the traditional healer's role explains well why Jefferson would want to omit all such references as an undue attempt to prove the legitimacy of Jesus by emphasizing his competence as a miracle doctor. And, we may add, Jefferson believed in the preventive powers of an active life more than he did in the healing arts, including the radical practices of his friend Dr. Rush. (Jefferson was once heard to say that when he saw two doctors in conversation, he scanned the sky for an approaching buzzard.) But I cannot forgive him for omitting the story which we need dearly so as to remain oriented in the history of healing concepts which, as I must show, change with any new identity. To me, the decisive therapeutic event in the Gospels appears in Luke 8: 48, and Mark 5: 25–35. It is the story of a woman who had lost not only blood for twelve years, but also all her money on physicians who had not helped her at all.

"When she had heard of Jesus, [the woman] came in the press behind, and touched his garment.

"For she said, 'If I may touch but his clothes, I shall be whole.'

"And straightway the fountain of her blood was dried up; and she felt in her body that she was healed of that plague.

"And Jesus, immediately knowing in himself that virtue had gone out of him, turned him about in the press, and said, 'Who touched my clothes?'

"And his disciples said unto him, 'Thou seest the multitude thronging thee, and sayest thou, Who touched me?'

"And he looked round about to see her that had done this thing.

"But the woman fearing and trembling, knowing what was done in her, came and fell down before him, and told him all the truth.

"And he said unto her, 'Daughter, thy faith hath made thee whole; go in peace, and be whole of thy plague.' "

This story conveys themes which renew their urging presence in each age: There is the assumption of certain quantities lost and regained and with them a quality of wholeness. Jesus, too, notices that a quantity of virtue has passed from him to her—and this as she touched him, and not (according to the age-old technique) as his hand touched her. He felt her touch even in the general press that surrounded him, and this solely because her faith thus magnetically attracted some of his strength before he quite knew it. There could be no doubt, then, that it was her faith in his mission that had made her whole. This story is an exalted illustration of that dynamic element, that electric force which has always fascinated the healing professions, not the least in Jefferson's times when Rush as well as Franklin became acquainted with Mesmer's attempts to physicalize this quantity and its transfer, and again in our time when Freud assumed the misplacement of quantities of love and hate to be intrinsic to emotional disturbance, and transference essential for their cure.

Transformations in the over-all sense of identity (and it is obvious that the polarization of the Greco-Roman Empire and the Christian kingdom was such a transformation which eventually also influenced the new identity made in America) bring with them new approaches to sickness and madness. These are characterized by a greater internalization of the cause as well as the cure of the sickness ("your faith will make you whole") and thus by a greater ethical awareness on the parts of both healer and to-be-healed. How, in our time, insight thus joined faith as the therapeutic agent of wholeness, even as the theorizing about mysterious quantities continued—that, too, we will return to in the second lecture.

PROTEAN PRESIDENT

from *Dimensions of a New Identity*

L et me, in conclusion, attempt to connect a few of the psychohistorical themes which have emerged in this lecture with the point
of view I would represent before that imaginary academy con-
voked to integrate the data of Jefferson's life and personality.

Sooner or later, of course, Jefferson was to be called a *Protean* man. But
this word is as elusive as the mythical figure whose name it bears, for as
it means a man of many appearances, this meaning itself is hard to take
hold of. It can and does denote a many-sided man of universal stature; a
man of many gifts, competent in each; a man of many appearances, yet
centered in a true identity. But it can also mean a man of many disguises;
a man of chameleonlike adaptation to passing scenes; a man of essential
elusiveness. According to our historical formula, however, any of these
designations in a man of such stature, would have to be seen in relation
to the new identity emerging in his time. As part of a self-made man a
Protean personality would convey the ability to make many things of
oneself, and this in a semideliberate and rebellious fashion. And, indeed,
Jefferson, who always seems to anticipate with some lucky phrase whatever interpretation one comes to attach to him, once spoke of his early
resolution "not to wear any other character than that of a farmer," which

implies that he had a choice and chose an over-all appearance related to a specific work role. Such a role Jefferson could carry through with a special flair and not without coming into some poignant conflict with other roles. When, in the White House, he greeted the first British ambassador and his lady in worn-out slippers, he knew well what he meant to dramatize, considering his cold and formal reception, years before, at the Royal Court. The White House was the national homestead of free farmers.

Among the themes contributing to Jefferson's individual identity, in addition to natural aristocrat, I had occasion to mention several elements of intellectual and esthetic style: The amateur and the surveyor, the educator and the ideologue. Each of these elements could have been specialized in an occupational identity. Instead, they all pervaded a rich alternation of occupational roles: farmer and architect, statesman and scholar. But they were all guided by passionate choices of commitment (and here identity comes of age) to causes that needed to be taken care of competently. These, in turn, permitted Jefferson to combine contradictory modes of action—such as his grandiose expansionism as a statesman, who doubled the territory of the United States (and had it duly surveyed) during his administration, and the capacity and sometimes desperate need for seclusion in his private domain.

Even though Jefferson attests to no kinship with Goethe (whose language was one of the few truly foreign to him), my European education often makes me think of this man who was Jefferson's contemporary. He, too, integrated his many-sidedness in a carefully cultivated façade. Jefferson the amateur could, in fact, fall in love with façades such as the Roman temple in Nîmes ("No Madam . . . to fall in love . . . with a house . . . is not without precedent in my history"). Maybe one must have been brought up in classical humanism to know that to say somebody loved façades, including his own, is no slur. This classical façade, no doubt, had much to do with the Greco-Roman stance cultivated by that other new, that Renaissance identity, which did so much to balance the Judaeo-Christian heritage of contrition. I would go further and say that Jefferson's tremendous correspondence, of which he himself kept such careful duplicates, constituted careful, craftsmanlike work on the desired historical appearance, even though he claimed to be fond of letter writing just because it so genuinely preserved "the warmth and presence of fact and feeling," and, in the life of some, "the only full and genuine journal of life." Jefferson's personality comes through exactly where he can combine, with supreme artistry, both façade and feeling, and ever again surprise others with a convincing informality well suited to his physical appearance of natural roughness and, yet, genuinely elegant stature. Where fact and feeling could not be surely fitted into the frame which he wished to immortalize, he destroyed even his correspondence, as he did that with his mother and his wife.

Such alternation of effusiveness and reserve makes, of course, any approach to a man's private personality hazardous. But we have no right to accuse him of the deliberate sabotage of our efforts which belong to such a different period. Yet, we remain curious as to what was behind the façade, and we want to know what such a façade cost a man in pained concerns about loss of face, in some deviousness of self-defense under attack, and in loneliness. He always held his head high, but, so it seems, only at the price of that occasional headache such as the one that befell him high up on the Natural Bridge. His outstanding symptom was incapacitating migraine, for weeks at a time. And he could fall to the ground and lie there as if lifeless in desperate mourning.

A façade exists to be seen, and in ascribing to an individual the intention or the need to maintain one, we must also ask who are his needy and obliging onlookers. And here, we may remember the history of monuments, not to speak of portraiture which, in Jefferson's time, combined a certain warmth of expression with a stance of reserve, uprightness, and farsightedness to which Jefferson's (and Washington's) body height and profiles lent themselves perfectly. Such façades arouse admiration to the point of canonization, for the exalted image of the human stature permits us to participate in the glorified uprightness which we, the vertical species on earth, need in order to hold our own heads high. But a façade also provides disbelief and suspicion, ranging all the way from the mild assertion that in some ways the hero seems to be human (meaning like us) to the pleasure of finding cracks in the great façade. All this can be transcended in some systematic fashion, only in the attempt to detect in the façade a truth which includes us, the beholders.

The analysis of how a person comes to choose such a public image, even though he himself may at times react diffidently to it, may begin with the call emanating from the historical situation. Jefferson's times demanded some self-aggrandizement in the service of the new, almost instant ancestral past which American history had to create. Besides the obligation to make his special gifts serve the new regime, and this with some grandeur (refreshingly counteracted in Franklin's humor), there must also be a special capacity to put such gifts to work.

In his study of Leonardo, Freud conceded that artistic gift as such escapes analysis. But so does any giftedness: For a gift there can be no itemized bill. The whole ecology of greatness, therefore, transcends many of the assumptions which clinical work has suggested regarding the inner economy of a person. They remain applicable, of course, to any leader's symptomatic behavior, which means either that he himself suffers from attacks beyond his control and comprehension, or, indeed, that he is judged by his intimates not to be quite himself. Where this leads to impulsive criminal acts transgressing what is expectable or tolerable in the ordinary collusions of any system of power, clinical considerations will, of course, help clarify events. Otherwise, the facile or biased use of psychiatric terms can only blind the observer to the historical issues at stake.

For example, it must be said that such a love of façade could not exist without a strong degree of that love of one's own image which we, technically, call narcissism. It was Narcissus who so fell in love with his own likeness as mirrored in a spring—a likeness reminding him of his dead twin sister—that he was unable to abandon it and perished by the side of the stream. The true—and potentially malignant—danger of narcissism, then, is a tendency in adolescence and beyond, to remain totally (and bisexually) absorbed in oneself instead of losing oneself in engagements with others. But it is obvious that a leader like Jefferson, whatever dangers of narcissism he may have harbored, as he sees himself mirrored in the imagery of a present and vital people, answers their call for leadership artfully and competently. And he was no show off: Not even in the defense of his eloquent authorship of the Declaration of Independence was he able to engage in oratory; while in his presidency, from the day of his inauguration he toned down public ceremony and private protocol, and this quite in contrast to the regal ceremonialism introduced by Washington.

A word about the child in the man. When I read to you some of Jefferson's descriptions of nature (and we have now added his love of beautiful buildings), you no doubt sensed in him a deep nostalgia which seems to have been lifelong—was it for that mysterious mother about whom, partially because he kept her from us, we as yet know so little? But how can one begin to analyze such a trend as unconscious in a man who

could say of himself, when he finally retired to Monticello, "I fold myself into the arms of retirement"?

In rebuilding Monticello beyond all need (and he confessed to any true
designer's delight in "putting up, and pulling down") he crowned the
building with an octagonal dome, thus adding an equally dominant maternal element to the strong façade. He had once been "violently smit-
ten" when beholding what is now the Palais de la Légion d'Honneur in
Paris. But the Monticello dome is said to have been inspired by that of
the Hall aux Bleds where he had first met a lady whom we will introduce presently. All one can say of this whole trend of nostalgia, then, is
that while it endangered his composure at times, his ethos of self-made
masculinity permitted and enabled him to plan his own maternal shrine,
and to "fold himself into its arms." Retired, he spent his last years de-
signing, founding, and caring for the University of Virginia, providing for
future generations a cupola symbolizing an Alma Mater, and embracing
"the human mind in this hemisphere." Let us not forget, then, to add *designer* to the essential elements of his identity.

All this was many years after Jefferson's married life had come to an
abrupt end. Shortly after he had written the *Notes on the State of Virginia,*
and before he turned forty, his wife died. He later said, "My history . . .
would have been as happy a one as I could have asked could the objects
of my affection have been immortal. But all the favors of fortune have
been embittered by domestic losses. Of six children I have lost four, and
finally their mother." In fact, only Martha, the oldest, survived him, being,
while she was young, mothered by him as much as fathered, and later a
maternal companion to him as much as a daughter.

The question of this widower's love life has haunted biographic imagination. It moves into the center of interpretation in our time when a
man's sexuality has been recognized (from Nietzsche on) as prototypical
for his personal style, not to speak of Freudian "libidinal economy" or
Kinseyan "outlets." We do not easily give it credence, as Freud himself
did, that special powers of sublimation may be assumed to exist in persons of such passionate devotion and minute service to public causes. At
any rate, over the years, only two women have been mentioned as possible companions. One is Maria Cosway, an Englishwoman whom he
loved and lost while in Paris. His love for her is freely proclaimed in some
now famous letters. When these were published as late as 1945, the reviewer in the *New York Times* remarked with a biographer's jealousy that

they were "worthy of a better subject." But that graceful and vivacious, if undoubtedly somewhat flighty, woman (she, too, an Anglo-Saxon at home in Mediterranean culture), may have represented for him, as Carl Binger suggests, a Jungian "Anima" that is something of a female counterpart—a twin, indeed—whose presence evoked both a sense of wholeness and a rare quality of interplay. I will come back to the tragicomic end of this affair in the second lecture.

And, then, there is Jefferson's alleged liaison in later years, back on the plantation, with a much younger mulatto woman who is said to have borne him several children. The available data oscillate between conveying something that seems possible to something even probable. But here, too, an essential matter to be settled first is the attitude of the biographers. The term *African Venus* has attached itself to this woman, although she was only one-quarter black, and, in fact, the half-sister (sharing the same father) of Jefferson's much bemourned wife. Jefferson's possible fathering of her children is refuted as an act of unthinkable miscegenation, although these children would have been only one-eighth black and were, as we know from Jefferson's own *Farm Book,* permitted to disappear when they reached maturity, in order to pass into the general population. Here there arise questions of value, tact, and tolerance which (in my imaginary academy) only a consortium of women and men could approach psychohistorically. For what, one must ask at last, would these Southern ladies, and domestic slaves have known and felt about their being relatives? And what would it have meant for Jefferson whose only son died unnamed, at the age of three weeks, to send into safe oblivion a mulatto son who, in fact, is said to have looked very much like him? These and many more questions will have to be accommodated before this liaison, if factual, also can become real—for us. Whatever biographers will conclude in regard to such intimate matters, and, no doubt, many incidences and utterances will be shown to be indicative of regressive trends, Jefferson was a man of rare adult stature, caring intensely and competent to take care of what he undertook—publicly and privately. If he deserves the name founding father, he certainly deserved that of father. His lapses and defeats, too, must be seen in this larger context of a mature consummation of the cycle of life.

As for the pervasive Protean quality—does this not make him intensely American and both prototypical and unique among the leaders of his time? It is hard to believe today—for we believe we started it in our time—how conscious these early Americans were of the job of developing an American character out of the regional and generational polarities and contradictions of a nation of immigrants and migrants. And *character* here, again, meant many things: the clear differentiation of a new identity transcending and yet aware of its links to those left behind in the mother countries; a new typology embodying a cast of clearly drawn, and often overdrawn, characters depicted in highly self-conscious formative novels; and the moral strength demanded of self-made men, not to become the forever adjustable puppets of new conditions and improvised mores. For the overwhelming quantitative changes (there were ten million Americans by the time of Jefferson's death) soon began to defy the founders' design. Just because of this once-in-history chance for self-made newness, this country has experienced greater expansiveness and yet also deeper anguish than have other countries; and few nations have seen their ideals and their youth divided, as has this country in the recurring divisions of a national identity. Was the happiness guaranteed in the Declaration that of wealth and of technological power or that of an all-human identity such as resides primarily in the free person? Is there any other country which continues to ask itself not only "What will we produce and sell next?" but everagain "Who are we anyway?" which may well explain this country's hospitality to such concepts as the identity crisis which, for better or for worse, now seem almost native to it.

The monumental achievement of Jeffersonian biography, then, as it stands and as it is still developing, can find some complement in psychohistorical approaches. The emotional hazards of doing biographical and historical work have become conscious to every Jefferson scholar. Jefferson's image does not settle for less. If such work awakens new aspirations in history writing, it also suggests a certain resignation concerning that definitive biography or history that is forever about to be written. Maybe all that can be hoped for is a conscious and disciplined assessment of the true relativity of the best of historical data, and of our own lives as observers.

Let me present a few excerpts from Jefferson's correspondence with his daughter, and remind you of one more period in his life, a veritable crisis of the middle years, midway between his Virginia governorship and his presidency. You may remember that the low point of his political career (when he wrote the *Notes on the State of Virginia*) was followed by the deepest personal sorrow, the death of his wife. Having undergone an extraordinary period of mourning, he had ceased to resist the call of national office, especially since it revived an old dream—to live in Paris. There (now in his mid-forties and minister to France), he had fallen in love with a younger Englishwoman—married, as were all his women friends. She was an artist who seems to have freed in him much of his lighter side, as he was to attest somewhat mournfully in "The Head and the Heart," that most famous love letter known to have been written by a future president of the United States—so far. I promised to report to you the end of this affair. On one of his last walks with the lady in a Paris park, Jefferson must, as we would say in basic American, have jumped the traces, for he fell and broke his right wrist, one of those joints the strategic function of which is fully realized only when it is put out of commission; and for Jefferson it was the wrist that moved the bow of his beloved violin, and that guided the pen with which he wrote his letters. He himself, as usual, not only felt the deeper meaning in this event but could express it in one or two sentences: "How the right hand became disabled would be a long story for the left to tell. It was by one of those follies from which good cannot come, but ill may," he wrote to a young friend at the time.

One could, and others rightfully will, make much of this event and this confession. At any rate, a few weeks of unparalleled emotional freedom had ended in a fall and a permanent injury.

Jefferson went to take the cure in Southern France where he received a letter from his daughter, Martha, now in her middle teens, who had joined him in France to go to school near Paris. She wrote, "Titus Livius puts me out of my wits. I cannot read a word by myself, and I read of it very seldom with my master; however, I hope I shall soon be able to take it up again."

Anyone who knows the stern and schoolmasterly tone of some of Jefferson's letters to his young daughters realizes that this passage was prime provocation. And it worked. He answered, "I do not like your saying that you are unable to read the ancient print of your Livy, but with the aid of your master. We are always equal to what we undertake with resolution." And he warns her, "If at any moment, my dear, you catch yourself in idleness, start from it as you would from the precipice of a gulph" for "idleness begets ennui, ennui the hypochondria, and that a diseased body." This, I must admit, is a formula for health which my training has denied me. (And yet it seems to be alive, for the other day a New York taxi driver, zigzagging down Fifth Avenue at the rush hour, warned me, "Don't let it worry you. It would make you sick.") Jefferson reinforces his clinical threats with patriotic admonition: "It is part of the American character to consider nothing as desperate; to surmount every difficulty by resolution and contrivance. Remote from all other aid, we are obliged to invent and to execute; to find means within ourselves and not to lean on others." And he concludes, "No laborious person was yet hysterical." This veritable syndrome of threats—idleness and ennui, hypochondria and disease, unAmericanism and hysteria—permits me to remind you of the negative identity, that necessary counterpart of any positive one. It is really as if (as Kai Erikson suggests in his book, *Wayward Puritans*) any new identity harbored a line-up of deviancies which define the boundaries (here marked by a "precipice" and a "gulph") of the officially sanctioned character.

Equally memorable is the adolescent (and very American) daughter's undaunted and pointed answer, which exposes the father's moralistic stance: "I hope your wrist is better and I am inclined to think that your voyage is rather for your pleasure than for your health. I hope, however, it will answer both purposes. . . . I shall take up my Livy, as you desire it. I shall begin it again, as I have lost the thread of the history. As for the hysterics, you may be quiet on that head, as I am not lazy enough to fear them." That his daughter could thus talk back to him, and teasingly so, bespeaks Jefferson's own personal balance between a strong morality and a rebellious spirit—a combination probably fostered in him by *his* father. This daughter, Martha, as we recounted, was to be the only one of his children to survive him and maintain throughout his later life a fascinating role as womanly companion, even while she was bearing thirteen children to her husband.

If Thomas Jefferson here sounds somewhat punitive toward a daughter who seems to be well able to take it, we cannot even begin to recount how slowly in his time cruel treatment of children became transformed into mere "psychological warfare." Normal man, so proud and yet so vulnerable in his resolution and contrivance seems to feel righteously justified in teaching a lesson to those who are helpless, because they are dependent, or those who he feels could help it, but are too weak in character.

Physical binding, flogging, and cold water treatments only gradually gave way to moral instruction. And as to the other deviants included in the negative identity, for example, people gone mad, they were chained and kept in dark and narrow places, their scalps were shaved and blistered, their bodies bled and purged. Patrick Henry, the great orator, when at home, had to feed his raving wife who was chained in the cellar. Rush (whose son, himself a doctor, became criminally and hopelessly insane) was one of the first to recognize the emotional origins of some sickness and of most madness, and to advocate occupational therapy as well as hygiene and kindness, even for psychotics. Yet, while madness could be caused by moral factors, the result remained physical, and Dr. Rush was a fanatic bloodletter. As for criminals, Jefferson himself, as a young lawyer and lawgiver, compiled a list of amputatory punishments of the most concrete eye-for-an-eye logic. This list, too, is contained, albeit inconspicuously, in the *Notes on the State of Virginia*. He was appalled about this later; and it must be said that when he had undertaken this assignment for a legislative committee he had attempted to limit the application of capital punishment by making circumscribed mutilation seem logical and just.

The point to be made here, is that the treatment of those who deviate from the path of adult normality, is somehow related to the way each individual treats threatening deviations in himself: It is as if the configurations of outer suppression are related to those of inner repression. Thus, if we make children stand in a corner or stay in some enclosure, if we incarcerate (even suspected) delinquents in narrow or overcrowded cells, or, as it were excarcerate dissenters beyond our borders and excommunicate and ban nonbelievers, the logic, not to speak of the benefit of such arrangement is certainly doubtful—but not so our satisfaction in having done to the transgressors what they had coming to them. There were, no doubt, practical reasons for confining orphans as well as psychotics, syphilitics, and destitutes in one jail-like building as was still done in Jefferson's time. But one may get an inkling from his letter how the positive identity must ever fortify itself by drawing the line against undesirables, even as it must mark itself off against those negative potentials which each man must confine and repress, deny and expel, brand and torture, within himself.

Yet Jefferson, the educator, was aware of the fact (and this way ahead of his time and especially of his own social setting) that cruelly punitive and vindictive behavior on the part of adults was dangerous for children not only when vented against them but also when done to others and witnessed by them. Here, I will end my introductory quotations by repeating once more a memorable passage which we must have before us in this lecture, too: "If a parent could find no motive either in his philanthropy or his self-love, for restraining the intemperance of passion towards his slave, it should always be a sufficient one that his child is present. . . . The parent storms, the child looks on, catches the lineaments of wrath, puts on the same airs in the circle of smaller slaves, gives a loose to his worst of passions, and thus nursed, educated, and daily exercised in tyranny, cannot but be stamped by it with odious peculiarities. The man must be a prodigy who can retain his manners and morals undepraved by such circumstances."

Philanthropy here means more than doing good, self-love more than pride, the children's presence more than an embarrassing circumstance. Together, they represent the informed love of humanity—in others, in himself, and in his children—which alone can help man to overcome his worst passion: The punitiveness by which he destroys not only those whom he beats into submission, but also takes risks with his own chance of truly respecting himself. Today, such passion is well disguised (so some adults think) when expressed in mechanized punitiveness on a large and more impersonal scale in far away countries against those not of our kind. Yet, it is literally brought home to our children by the media, and one wonders whether it does not threaten a whole generation with what Jefferson had in mind when he used the words "odious peculiarities."

All of this brings us to Jefferson's most famous saying which is, in fact, quoted on the invitation to these lectures: "The earth belongs always to the living." This he underscored by adding: "The dead have neither powers nor rights over it." Jefferson originally meant by this the legal mortgaging of the next generation by the attachment of the father's debts on the real estate inherited by the son. He himself had suffered under such a loaded inheritance from his father-in-law. But soon, and, of course, quite in the spirit of the revolution, this saying was applied to the whole problem of laws which force future generations to abide by a legal logic not affirmed by their own experience, and thus by the "sovereignty of the living generation." Merrill Peterson has called this "at once the most original and the most radical of Jefferson's political ideas." And, indeed, Jefferson as a lawgiver was forever preoccupied with matters of the generations, with the right to education and with freedom of (informed) conscience. And it was, indeed, Jefferson who once said (and some of the younger ones among you have asked me to confirm that he said it), "God forbid that we should ever be twenty years without . . . a rebellion." Why twenty years? Did he, maybe, refer not only to history but also to the life cycle: God forbid anybody should be twenty years old without having rebelled? At any rate, twenty years is about the span of human development needed for the individual to acquire a sense of identity firm and informed enough to act: which requires enough experience to acknowledge the power of facts and the facts of power; enough practical idealism to attach infantile ideals to live persons and issues; and enough rebellious commitment to the future to leave behind some of the internalized debt of infantile guilt.

Jefferson's saying, like all great sayings, remains alive as man's experience expands. Where his "earth" meant at first the earth under our feet, bounded by property lines in a new land still defining its over-all boundaries, it has come to mean to us the globe inhabited by one mankind, if not a spaceship in the perspective of outer space. If inheritance meant material enrichment or indebtedness transferred to the inheritors from those who wanted to leave something behind to perpetuate their name, today we are aware of the way in which older generations mortgage the inner ground of living. We know that each new generation carries within it a conscience weighted down with debts of guilt as well as of compliance implanted in the helplessness of childhood. But we also know that the resulting cruelty of man to man and of man to himself is grounded in the course of evolution and the history of civilization. To chart the tragic closeness of the best and the worst in man today also means to relate the fatal affinity of humanity's triumphs to its inhuman self-negation. But instead of preaching the loftier aspects conveyed by our string of quotations, let me attempt to bring out their import for human development. For, to summarize this introduction, the basic declaration that all men are created equal can mean to us only that all individuals are born with some capacity to develop and that each child born has a right to expect a chance to develop such potential. And to be born, mind you, from here on, means to be either chosen to be born or, alas, to have been born by default. In either case, it must mean the right to live in a community which chooses to guarantee, because it knows it lives by, the fullest development of each of its members.

Since our insight into problems of identity, like so many other fundamental insights, has originated in clinical thought, let me say here a word
about Freud. We have learned to take it for granted that a neuropsychia-
trist has become one of the great enlightening influences in the Western
world. Each age, of course, has its own idea of what liberates inner man,
and I have, in these lectures, pointed to an over-all trend in the conceptualization of inner unfreedom. I quoted in detail a Gospel passage emphasizing the sufferer's faith as the decisive factor in her cure. Turning to
Jefferson's time, I reported how Rush, trained in Europe, gained remarkable insights into mental dynamics. He anticipated Freud when, for example, he claimed that depression "may be induced by causes that are
forgotten; or by the presence of objects which revive the sensation of
distress with which at one time it was associated, but without reviving the
cause of it in the memory." These brief illustrations, so distant from each
other in time and context, may yet indicate a trend which more and more
places the cause of mental disturbance in the victim's inner life and its cure
in an inner resolve—according to Rush's advice, to keep clean and busy.
Freud's moral as well as clinical sense made him, too, discard the laying on
of hands which was still done in hypnosis, and remove himself from any
other role of authority except the voice that encourages insight into the
cause of the distress and helps such insight along by interpretation. But the
idea of a disturbing quantity remained: Some evil substance which in
the Gospels was driven into swine, in Rush's time was still let out with bad
blood and today is shocked out electrically. In Freud's time, too, there was
the idea of a cathartic experience, the abreaction of imprisoned emotion.
But here it was to serve the facilitation of insight, that is the utilization of
the patient's own ego strength for his own transformation. Thus, in helping another set of outcasts (the hysterics that Jefferson had held up warn-
ingly to his daughter) to respect themselves and to understand their own
history, he created methods and concepts applicable not only to all kinds
of deviants, but to the history of so-called normal man himself. By this
means he extended man's responsibility for his own unconscious and especially for the development of his children by lifting the repression that
had beclouded and falsified early development. And so he made possible
a certain foresight in regard to the generational processes in which Jefferson was so passionately interested. He did so by replacing some previously
erratic hindsight with systematic insight.

But Freud was also the first thinker to predict that such new findings as his could by the very nature of things never be accepted without an inner resistance which, in fact, he considered part of the normal workings of the mind. So we are, or we should be, prepared for the fact that such resistances join other defensive reactions against insights which seem to rob us of our self-made certainty. Freud, in this respect, compared his own ideas with those of Copernicus and Darwin as "disturbers of mankind's sleep"; I think that we must add to this illustrious list Marx, and Freud's contemporary, Einstein.

In fact, I would nominate the idea of relativity in the physical world and the concept of the unconscious in man's inner world (and I include in this Marx's discovery of a class unconscious) as two such disturbing extensions of human consciousness in our time. And I would postulate that any new identity must develop the *courage of its relativities* and the *freedom of its unconscious resources*; which includes facing the anxiety aroused by both. Man always reprojects on himself what he has managed to conceptualize in the universe; history teaches what theories of the universe come to mean to everyday man. And relativity has come to suggest relativism—an idea, of course, foreign to Einstein. But then, you may remember, or I do, that even outstanding German scientists in Einstein's time considered his work *abscheulich*—repugnant. It gave them a moral shudder. Gerald Holton rightly corrects them and us: "Relativity Theory," he says, "of course, does not find that truth depends on the point of view of the observer but, on the contrary, reformulated the laws of physics so that they hold good for every observer, no matter *how he moves or where he stands.* Its central meaning is that the most valued truths in science are wholly independent of the point of view." I have italicized the words which should remind us of the psychological importance of a *standpoint* in order to clarify the paradoxical relationship between major scientific upheavals and the human ego's aforementioned criteria: centrality, originality, choice, initiative—and identity. Centrality seems endangered if the earth is not in the center of the universe; originality, if we are descended from a lower species; choice and initiative, if what we think we are doing is decisively influenced by unconscious motivation. Thus new facts, demonstrated by men who can play with facts with utmost sincerity, and who, in their competence and certainty have the courage to stand alone and can thus risk both sanity and acceptance, often seem to shatter what we continue to think must be real. The paradox is that these facts and theories increase human power over nature (and human nature) enormously, but create a lag between what we know and what we can "realize"—a dangerous situation, indeed.

In response to this new consciousness, there are many reactions. Some are joyful and resourceful, creating a new leeway in inventiveness and thoughtfulness; but I think it is my task to point, rather, to the age-old extremes of too narrow and too wide identities. There is, then, the attempt to preserve the old new identity that contends all the more grimly that one can and must be consciously self-made, fabricated, a do-it-yourself personality in the American tradition, a tradition which perpetuates a kind of old-fashioned stance now relying on the reactionary possession of privileged interests and organized powers. This old new identity is marked by a disdainful punitiveness toward those who, instead, experiment with different identities, and this at their own pace.

Among the young—or now not so young anymore—there are those who mistrust the whole identity concept as another trick of the older generation, designed to impose traditional restraints on what one might become if one refused to make anything of oneself and merely continued to improvise, to drift. These young people seem to be permissive toward themselves and disdainful primarily toward those who believe so strenuously that they know who they are. But this does not mean that they are not seeking what they are denying. For even where new forms of consciousness and new social patterns arise in bewildering alternation, the fundamental need for a familiar identity, as we saw, changes ever so slowly. And so, the search for a revolutionary identity often leads to stances belonging to other eras and bygone proletariats.

Identity is safest, of course, where it is grounded in activities. When we meet a new person, we usually want to know what he does, and then, how he does what he does. For a need for competence, too, is well anchored in development, and most importantly, the stage of identity grows out of the school age, that is, the stage when work competence and gamesmanship emerge out of the matured ability to play meaningfully, and, in play and work, to entertain ideal images of initiative. But such ideals of future competence always remain beset with some infantile guilt over the usurpation of roles previously occupied by parental figures; and the question is always whether such a subjective usurpation will find sanction in a competence of performance verified by the objective nature of things. For this reason, a new identity will be very much attached to an intimate mastery of a set of skills dictated by the state of science and technology as well as the arts, and no attempt to "humanize" life should belittle or bedevil this mastery itself. Competence without conviction, to be sure, is not more than a form of fact-slavery; but conviction without competence is less than liberation.

HOMO RELIGIOSUS

from *Gandhi's Truth*

A t the time of the Ahmedabad strike, Gandhi was forty-eight years
old: middle-aged Mahatma, indeed. That the very next year he
emerged as the father of his country only lends greater importance to the fact that the middle span of life is under the dominance of
the universal human need and strength which I have come to subsume
under the term *generativity*. I have said that in this stage a man and a
woman must have defined for themselves what and whom they have
come to care for, what they care to do well, and how they plan to take
care of what they have started and created. But it is clear that the great
leader creates for himself and for many others new choices and new
cares. These he derives from a mighty drivenness, an intense and yet flexible energy, a shocking originality, and a capacity to impose on his time
what most concerns him—which he does so convincingly that his time
believes this concern to have emanated "naturally" from ripe necessities.
And historians must agree, for they are able only to study the confluences
in what has come to pass and to be recorded—unless, of course, they
come to the conclusion (and not a few have done so) that India, if not
much better, would certainly not be much worse off if the man had
never lived. And, indeed, compared with the charismatic men of his

time, Gandhi and his "inner voice" may seem more moodily personal, more mystically religious, and more formless in ideology than any of them. There is nothing more consistent in the views of Gandhi's critics than the accusation of inconsistency: at one time he is accused of sounding like a socialist, and at another a dreamy conservative; or, again, a pacifist and a frantic militarist; a nationalist, and a "communalist"; an anarchist and a devotee of tradition; a Western activist, and an Eastern mysticist; a total religionist and yet so liberal that he could say he saw God even in the atheist's atheism. Did this polymorphous man have a firm center?

If, for the sake of the game, I should give his unique presence a name that would suit my views, I would call him a *religious actualist*. In my clinical ruminations I have found it necessary to split what we mean by "real" into that which can be known because it is demonstrably correct (factual reality) and that which feels effectively true in action (actuality).[1] Gandhi absorbed from Indian culture a conception of truth *(sat)* which he attempted to make actual in all compartments of human life and along all the stages which make up its course. I will in the next section make the most of the claim that the Mahatma (in spite of his enmity toward all erotism) was a mighty good bodily specimen—as is attested in motion pictures which show him to be so much more agile and of one piece than most men seem to be.

At the same time, he was as actual an Indian as can be imagined, aware that the great majority of his country's massive population was held together only by an ancient culture which, even if disintegrating, was all there was for India to rely on in the face of irreversible modernization. As an Indian, he had been born a Bania, and it was as a Bania and a Gujarati that he entered on the fateful path toward an all-Indian Mahatmaship. But while he learned to utilize craftily what was his first professional identity, namely, that of a barrister English style, and while he then became a powerful politician Indian style, he also strove to grasp the "business" of religious men, namely, to keep his eyes trained upon the all-embracing circumstance that each of us exists with a unique consciousness and a responsibility of his own which makes him at the same time zero and everything, a center of absolute silence, and the vortex of apocalpytic participation. A man who looks through the historical parade of cultures and civilizations, styles, and isms which provide most of us with a glorious and yet miserably fragile sense of immortal identity, defined status, and collective grandeur faces the central truth of our nothingness—and, *mirabile dictu,* gains power from it.

Gandhi's actualism, then, first of all consisted in his knowledge of, and his ability to gain strength from, the fact that nothing is more powerful in the world than conscious nothingness if it is paired with the gift of giving and accepting actuality. It is not for me to say what this power *is*; yet obviously it demands the keenest of minds and a most experienced heart, for otherwise it would be crushed between megalomania and self-destruction. As for the rest of mankind, I have an inkling that our response to such a man rests on the need of all men to find a few who plausibly take upon themselves—and seem to give meaning to—what others must deny at all times but cannot really forget for a moment. Freud, in one of his "economic" moods, might well have said that, psychologically speaking, such men save others not so much from their sins (this Freud would not have claimed to know), but from the fantastic effort *not* to see the most obvious of all facts: that life is bounded by not-life.[2]

Indian culture has (as have all others) made out of this special mission of saintly men a universal and often utterly corrupt institution, and Gandhi was well aware of the fact that the Mahatmaship could type him to the point of in-actuality. He considered it all the more incumbent upon himself to make his spiritual power work in political realities—for which he brought along both a specific giftedness and favorable identifications. I think the man was right who said that Gandhi, when he listened to his inner voice, heard the clamor of the people. It may be just this alliance of inner voice and voice of mankind which must make such a man at times insensitive to those closest to him by familial bond.

Swaraj in the sense of home-rule *and* self-rule was Gandhi's "way": if the power of actuality—as we now may add—is the mutual maximization of greater and higher unity among men, then each must begin to become actual by combining what is given in his individual development and in his historical time. Gandhi, I think, would make his own those pronouncements of Luther which I once singled out as the essence of religious actualism: *Quotidianus Christi adventus*—Christ comes today; *via dei est qua nos ambulare facit*—God's way is what makes us move; *semper oportit nasci, novari, generari*—we must always be reborn, renewed, regenerated; *proficere est nihil aliud nisi semper incipere*—to do enough means nothing else than always to begin again. Thus, out of the acceptance of nothingness emerges what can be the most central and inclusive, timeless and actual, conscious and active position in the human universe. We have seen that Gandhi was never too proud to find universal meaning in petty circumstances, for he knew that one must build on the values of one's childhood as long as they are revalidated by experience, until one perceives a wider truth which may make them relative or obsolete. Thus Gandhi could be and remain a Jain—a religion which, of course, provides ritual choices in a multiplicity of images and values—and yet could also absorb some of the essence of other, all other, religions. By the same token, he could live in symbiosis with the technology of his time and yet comprehend and exploit the fact that some such symbolic and pragmatic item as the spinning wheel could dramatically activate in hundreds of thousands of localities what was at the time not at all ready for industrialization.

Here, as in many other aspects of his life, the appearance of inconsistency is only a function of the critics' confusion in regard to elusive ends and self-fulfilling means. For it is in the daily means that *dharma,* practicality, and ethics coincide, wherefore the devotee of the hum of the charkha is not necessarily further removed from actuality than is he who feels vitalized by the clang of industrial activity. If each worker continues with full attention to the mood and the style of his activity, and as long as this activity lifts him above otherwise fallow or regressive potentials, he adheres to the Gandhian dictum that means are "ends-in-the-making" or "ends in process."[3] A "true" man, then, will not remain fixated on either means or ends for their own sake. He will not permit himself or others to use foul means with the illusory justification that their continuance "for a little while longer" will end in a utopian future when the truth will at last become the universal means—whereupon the world will forever after be free for democracy, or free for communism, or free for the stateless society, or whatever. What is true now will, if not attended to, never be true again; and what is untrue now will never, by any trick, become true later. Therefore I would interpret, and interpret with humility, the truth-force of the religious actualist thus: to be ready to die for what is true now means to grasp the only chance to have lived fully.

The religious actualist, however, inevitably becomes a religious innovator, for his very passion and power will make him want to make actual for others what actualizes him. This means to create or recreate institutions, and it can mean the attempt to institutionalize nothingness. The Hindu concept of the life cycle, as we saw, allots a time for the learning of eternal concerns in youth, and for the experience of near-nothingness

at the end of life, while it reserves for the middle of life a time dedicated
to the "maintenance of the world," that is, a time for the most intense actualization of erotic, procreative, and communal bonds: in this period of
life, adult man *must* forget death for the sake of the newborn individual
and the coming generations. But the middle-aged do need all the more
the occasional man who can afford to remember, and they will travel regularly and far to partake of his elusive power. We have seen how deeply
Gandhi at times minded having to become a householder, for without his
becoming committed to a normal course of life by child marriage, he
might well have been a monastic saint instead of what he became: politician and reformer with an honorary sainthood. For the true saints are
those who transfer the state of householdership to the house of God, becoming father and mother, brother and sister, son and daughter, to all creation, rather than to their own issue. But they do this in established
"orders," and they create or partake in rituals which will envelop and give
peace to those who must live in transitory reality.

Actuality, however, is by no means a mere denial of nothingness. As I
indicated when discussing the Hindu life cycle, actuality is complementary to nothingness and, therefore, deeply and unavoidably endowed with
the instinctual energy and the elemental concern of generativity. Thus,
men and women in middle age are "assigned" by instinct and custom a
time to forget death so that they may maintain the life of their own kind.
Here is the origin of one kind of "greatness," the greatness of founding
fathers who stake out a territory and sanction its conquest; the greatness
of leaders who sanction the killing of those led by other kinds of leaders; and the greatness of young heroes who get killed in so killing. Here
also is the origin of all those mutual differentiations into dogmas and isms
which combine larger and larger human communities in power spheres
providing more inclusive identities. But alas, each such consolidation lives
off its exclusiveness and becomes a new example of a *pseudo species.*

Religious presence, however (while often allied with temporal power),
has an affinity to the experience of women, who in their hereness and
practical religiosity weave together in the chores of daily life what really
"maintains the world," and who—while heroes court death—can experience death as an intrinsic part of a boundless and boundlessly recreative
life.

Inept as all such talk is, it may at least suggest a fair approach to what
is most problematic in Gandhi. To be ascetic in the sense of Hindu *Brah-*

macharya is not just a matter of not being active sexually or of cutting off one's masculinity; it is a matter of stepping outside of the daily consolidation and maintenance of what the two sexes create and take care of together, united in an illusion made inescapably and brilliantly real by each child.

But the middle-aged leader is also burdened and burdens others with cares more profound and more tragic than is the usual lot. His idiosyncratic choices may come to create concerns greater than he and his followers can really promise to take care of in their lifetimes. For he must sanction the initiative of a committed following and an irreversibly united multitude: but who will sanction him, the sanctioner, and all that he has generated, originated, promised, at a time of life already more than half lived and yet already totally committed? Thus men like St. Augustine, Gandhi, and Freud write their great introspective works—*The Confessions, My Experiments with Truth, The Interpretation of Dreams*—in middle age and at the threshold of lonely greatness.

We have traced in Gandhi's life the father-son theme—which these men and others like them pursue with almost monotonous guiltiness in their diaries, autobiographies, and self-analyses. We saw this theme erupt like a play within a play in the letter in which the middle-aged Gandhi tells his son of a dream in which the son had done to him what he once had done to *his* ailing father. And we saw it again in the middle-aged man's filial surrender to the "pale" Viceroy. No doubt, both in relation to his sons and to the few men who *could* represent a father to him in his mature years, the Mahatma was highly ambivalent. But such ambivalence is not merely an expression of a sense of guilt telling grown-up Oedipus "I told you so"; in the case of a charismatic leader (as, indeed, in that of King Oedipus) it belongs intrinsically to the ceremonial role held by him who is forced by fate to usurp a position imposed on him, more or less against his will, by the charisma-hungry masses. Here it will not do to treat the data as if they had emerged from the treatment history of a patient significantly inhibited in his perception of the real and in his participation in the actual. We must see what is symptomatic of a "great" man's conflicts in the context of their actuality in the historical period which chooses to crown and to crucify him. And with all his mood-swings and confessions, Mahatma Gandhi could, for a moment in history, make his inner voice consonant with the trend of human history and—we shall come to that—evolution.

Who could deny then that Gandhi was "a man"? However, he was an Indian man engaged in politics but aspiring to saintliness. We were able to follow the infantile and juvenile antecedents of a deep conflict between phallicism and saintliness, and between paternal power and maternal care. But just because Gandhi was so free in providing us with conflictful memories as well as with confessions of "unmanly" aspirations, we must be sparing with our interpretations; for in his revealed life the abnormal and the supernormal vie with such disarming frankness that whatever we could diagnose as his neurosis simply becomes part of his personal *swaraj*, the home ground of his being—and a man must build on that.

I would add that in such a man, and especially in an innovator, much phallic maleness seems to be absorbed in the decisive wielding of influence—and in a certain locomotor drivenness. He must always be on the move, and he must be moving others along, an often excessive need which is only counterpointed, but never diminished, by a corresponding need to be moved by a higher inspiration—*qua mulier in conceptu* (like a woman in the act of conception), as Luther said unhesitatingly. To conceive, obviously, is the all-inclusive word for such moods and periods.

But I wonder whether there has ever been another political leader who almost prided himself on being half man and half woman, and who so blatantly aspired to be more motherly than women born to the job, as Gandhi did. This, too, resulted from a confluence of a deeply personal need and a national trend, for a primitive mother religion is probably the deepest, the most pervasive, and the most unifying stratum of Indian religiosity. Gandhi was able, in deep sorrow, to have engraved on a stone dedicated to the memory of Maganlal that the latter's death had "widowed" him; and Shankerlal did not mind telling Gandhi, who in jail had made him pray at dawn and spin for hours in the daytime: "The worst mother-in-law could not be as tough with her daughter-in-law as you are with me." Gandhi would answer (proving Shankerlal's point): "You will appreciate it later." But the feminine imagery seems to have come naturally. There has been much talk, of course, of Gandhi's love of home spinning, which—no matter what it had been in days past and was to be in the days of national khadi—was traditionally women's work. All such talk, however, would be countered by Gandhi with the simple admission that yes, he aspired to be half a woman, even as he had countered Churchill's slurring remark about the naked fakir with the assertion that yes, he wanted to be as naked as possible. He undoubtedly saw a kind of sublimated maternalism as part of the positive identity of a whole man, and certainly of a *homo religiosus*. But by then all overt phallicism had become an expendable, if not a detestable matter to him. Most men, of course, consider it not only unnecessary, but in a way, indecent, and even irreverent, to disavow a god-given organ of such singular potentials; and they remain deeply suspicious of a sick element in such sexual self-disarmament. And needless to say, the suspicion of psychological self-castration becomes easily linked with the age-old male propensity for considering the renunciation of armament an abandonment of malehood. Here, too, Gandhi may have been prophetic; for in a mechanized future the relative devaluation of the martial model of masculinity may well lead to a freer mutual identification of the two sexes.

This is a clinician's book, and for the sake of speculating on the eventual fate of Gandhi's maternalism and, indeed, bisexuality, I must now briefly mention that item from his very last years which is often and eagerly referred to in conversational gossip, East or West, and usually with a slur such as "You know, of course, that Gandhi had naked girls sleep with him when he was an old man."[4] The most authoritative account of the events leading to this story is given in Nirmal Bose's *My Days with Gandhi,*[5] and I have had an opportunity to discuss the matter with him. Considering the personages involved, however, I doubt that the story will ever be fully told.

As far as I can make out, two circumstances are condensed in the story. For one, on her deathbed, Kasturba had asked her husband to take her place as a mother to an orphaned young relative named Manu; and he had taken this role rather seriously, being concerned, for example, with the girl's physical development, and having her sleep on a mat at the foot-end of his own mat and later, on occasion, "in his bed"—whatever that designation may mean in sleeping arrangements which include neither bedsteads nor doors. The marked maternalism governing this relationship was later acknowledged in the very title of the young woman's memoir: *Bapu, My Mother.*[6]

This young girl, however, does not seem to have been the central figure in the major crisis which caused such unrest among Gandhi's friends. This occurred in the very last phase of Gandhi's life when the Mahatma was 77 and 78 years old, and when in Lear-like desperation he wandered among the storms and ruins of communal riots which seemed to mark an end of any hope of a unified India. At night he at times suffered from severe attacks of shivering; and he would ask some of his middle-aged women helpers to "cradle" him between them for bodily warmth. This some suspicious companions thought to go beyond fatherly or motherly innocence; and, in fact, some of his best friends parted ways with him when Gandhi made things immeasurably worse by claiming publicly that by having (sometimes naked) women near him at night he was test-ing his ability *not* to become aroused. This implied, of course, proving to himself by implication that he *could* be. This explanation is based on a deeply Indian preconception concerning seminal continence and men-tal potency. And, indeed, "If I can master this," the Mahatma is said to have remarked, "I can still beat Jinnah"—that is, prevent the partition of India. All this confounded the question as to whether the whole arrange-ment expressed a senile and eccentric self-testing, a belated need for younger women, or, indeed, a regression to an infantile need for moth-erly warmth. It could well have been all of these.

My comparison with Lear indicates how I, for one, would study such a story: as one of old age despair, characterized, of course, by the conflicts life had not settled. Lear, a widower, also wanted to be reassured (and re-assured excessively, as his youngest child told him) that his daughters loved and honored him: thus did the king try to secure his immortality as a father and a king. As for an old man's need for warmth, one may think of another king who "was old and stricken in years" and who, al-though covered at night with many clothes, "gat no heat."

> So they sought for a fair damsel throughout all the coasts of Israel, and found Ab-i-shag a Shu-nam-mite, and brought her to the king.
>   And the damsel was very fair, and cherished the king, and ministered to him: but the king knew her not. [I Kings I:3,4]

The method employed here even has a name: shunamitism; and it is said to have been also cultivated, long before King David, by the kings of northern India.[7] Gandhi, however, was not a king; and it was not enough for him to say that he knew these women not. His denial was not enough for him, because he apparently had to prove, to the last, that he was mas-ter of all his impulse life, and it was not enough for others who insisted to the bitter end that he prove, or forfeit, what *they* called sainthood.

The whole episode, as Bose brilliantly recognized at the time, points to a persistent importance in Gandhi's life of the theme of motherhood, both in the sense of a need to be a perfect and pure mother, and in the sense of a much less acknowledged need to be held and reassured, especially at the time of his finite loneliness. In this last crisis the Mahatma appears to have been almost anxiously eager to know what those who had studied the "philosophy" of that doctor in Vienna might say about him,[8] although he probably could do little with the interpretation offered by one of his friends, namely that his shivering was an orgasm-equivalent. Bose's main objection to the whole episode was well-taken: the women had too little choice either in being involved or in having their actions publicized, and the general tension was setting them against one another.

As to the Mahatma's public private life, all we can say is that here was a man who both lived and wondered aloud, and with equal intensity and depth, about a multiformity of inclinations which other men hide and bury in strenuous consistency. At the end, great confusion can be a mark of greatness, too, especially if it results from the inescapable conflicts of existence. Gandhi, one may conclude from all the parental themes we have recounted, had wanted to purify his relationship to his father by nursing and mothering him; and he had wanted to be an immaculate mother. But when, at the end, he was defeated in his aspiration to be the founding father of a united India, he may well have needed maternal solace himself.

But how about the Mahatma's followers? As I have indicated, he skillfully selected them for particular kinds of functions, often diagnosing with psychological acuity the identity conflicts of our witnesses, who met him in the rebellious days of their twenties and were attracted to him to the point that their lives fused, in variable degree, with his. The degree, I would judge, often depended on their willingness to sacrifice sexual and social freedom to the communal rules of the ashram. Those who escaped such commitment can now discuss the Mahatma more freely than those who did not, but they often do so in order to rationalize their escape; the real "inmates" almost never express ambivalence, although Gandhi himself was wont to recognize it teasingly. But surely, the reader will surmise, they must have told me, directly or indirectly, about the

emotional and irrational concomitants of such discipleship. And it is true
that the psychoanalyst in me was not so subdued by the amateur historian that I was without curiosity about the motivational patterns these
men and women may have shared. But here the question arises whether
one has a right, methodologically and ethically, to lay bare data pointing
to the unconscious motivations of trusting informants who have tried to
be of help in the reconstruction of an historical event. A number of informants shared with my witnesses a certain propensity to tell me of
memories, dreams, and daydreams that haunted them. Such data would
be offered during a drive through such traffic as nearly incapacitated my
"third ear," or during meals when I could and would not reach for writing paper, and sometimes as confidences offered, in my presence, to my
wife. Whether on my part a certain professional propensity for attracting
confidences was involved here, I could not know; but I am reasonably
sure that such data emerged in a mood of re-evoking the Mahatma's
image, which, in turn, awakened memories of more complex emotional
involvements. Varied as these moments were, it soon became clear that
they fell into two groups of themes. The first was *a deep hurt* which the
informant had inflicted on one of his parents or some guardian (uncle or
aunt) in such a way that the memory had become a kind of curse; and
we have seen how determinedly Gandhi helped some of his early followers to sever already frayed bonds. The second category is an obsessively intense wish *to take care* of abandoned people or animals, paired
with a strong sense of identification with all fatherless and motherless
creatures who have strayed too far from home.

All this "accidental" material combined with other data available to me
in creating a certain conviction that all these informants harbor a sense
(maybe unconscious, maybe un-verbalized) of having vastly outdistanced
their childhood loyalties, and with these, their personal *dharma,* by serving a man who had the power to impose his *dharma* on his contemporaries—a very special kind of guru who would make radical and total use
of an age-old emotional (and once well institutionalized) necessity for
finding a second, spiritual father. And I would think that the inner conflicts which lead a young person to such an unconventional leader, and
to acceptance of him, come to include a deep ambivalence toward that
leader. As we saw, Gandhi sought out his followers with a determination
tempered only with diplomatic reserve, and he did not hesitate, as it
were, to take over the spiritual parentage of these young people. Gandhi,

of course, always wanted to be sure that an applicant could be expected to do some essential thing really well, but he also demanded a potential of total devotion in his future followers. From a man with high academic qualifications, for example, he demanded to know only whether he would be willing "to become a scavenger." Scavenging included what in America we subsume under the word "dirty work," but it also literally meant cleaning latrines. In the name of truth and in the service of India, however, they had to accept what was his own family's plight, namely, that he belonged to all—and to none.

These young people, then, highly gifted in a variety of ways, seem to have been united in one personality "trait," namely, an early and anxious concern for the abandoned and persecuted, at first within their families, and later in a widening circle of intensified concern. At the same time, they were loyal rebels: loyal in their sorrow, determined in their rebellion. All this they offered Gandhi, displaying a wish to serve, which was determined as much by personality as by tradition. Gandhi's capacity both to arouse and to squelch ambivalence must have been formidable; but he put these men and women to work, giving direction to their capacity to care, and multiplying miraculously both their practical gifts and their sense of participation.

Followers, too, deserve a formula for the recorder or reviewer of history or life history. Whatever motivation or conflict followers may have in common as they join a leader[9] and are joined together by him has to be studied in all the complementarity of

1. their personal lives, that is
   a. the moment when they met the leader, their state of mind, and their stage of life;
   b. the place of that moment in their life history, especially in lifelong themes transferred to the leader;
2. their communities, insofar as these are relevant to their search for an identity by participation, that is
   a. their generation's search for leadership
   b. traditional and evolving patterns of followership.

As to the last point, Gandhi, as we saw, was a master not only in the selection and acquisition of co-workers, but also in assigning them to or using them in all manner of different tasks and ways of life—from the position of elected sons and daughters in his ascetic settlement to that of revolutionary organizers all over India and of aspirants for highest political power, including the prime ministership, for which he "needed a boy from Harrow."

But any explanation, psychoanalytic or other, of how followers became singly what they proved to be together, is relative to—well, to the historical moment. The first Satyagrahi was, of course, unique in the manner of his ascendance and comparable only with equally unique individuals. His followers, however, were characterized primarily by the fact of having found this particular unique man among their contemporaries at a crucial moment in their own lives as well as in history—and of having been selected by him. My data (unless the data should prove to be "typically Indian") may offer a fleeting glance into the mutual assimilation of motives which might take place in a self-chosen group making history together.

THE INSTRUMENT

from *Gandhi's Truth*

1. TACTICS

We have reported Gandhi's saying that God appears to you not in person but in action. But this also means that the full measure of a man—and that includes his unconscious motivation—can never be comprehended in isolation from his most creative action. What, then, is the essence of the social tools which Gandhi created?

Here I will roughly follow Joan Bondurant's indispensable treatment in her *Conquest of Violence,* which analyzes six Satyagraha campaigns in a fashion both scholarly and compassionate. If I do not fully accept either her discourse or her conclusions, it is, I believe, because she writes as a political scientist, whereas I must come to some psychological conclusions. Neither of us (she would agree) can hope to do more than approximate the meaning which Satyagraha had for its originator, his first followers, and the Indian masses. And both of us must restate these meanings in the terms of our disciplines and our days in the West: the truth (Gandhi would tell either of us) can only be revealed in the kind of appraisal which is *our* action. Satyagraha purports to be a strategy which depends, every minute, on the unmistakable experience of something as evasive as "the truth." I have tried to trace what truth had come to mean to Gandhi, throughout his development, in order to fathom what it may have meant to him in a given action; and even then the interpretation of his meaning was bound by our own imagery and terminology. If this seems too elusive even to attempt to formulate, I will ask the reader in how many connotations he has used the term "reality" throughout his life, or "virtue," or "health," not to speak of "identity"—all terms which serve to characterize the essence of a man's being and action.

Sat, we are told, means "it is." We can come closer to "what 'is' " only by asking further: in comparison with what, where, and when? In comparison with what might have been or what should be, or with what only seems to be or is only felt to be? Thus "what is" is obviously relative to any era's world-image, and to the methodologies which determine what questions are considered important and are asked relevantly. Yet, for each individual, "what is" will also depend on his personal way of facing being in all its relativity—relative to an absolute Being who alone is truth, or relative to non-being, or relative to becoming. Gandhi commits himself only to "the relative truth as I have conceived it," but he also clings firmly to the dictum that only insofar as we can commit ourselves on selected occasions "to the death" to the test of such truth in action—only to that extent can we be true to ourselves and to others, that is, to a joint humanity. This seems to call for an altogether rare mixture of detachment and commitment, and for an almost mystical conflux of inner voice and historical actuality. And in spite of the fact that it opens up wide every opportunity for self-deceit and the misuse of others, Gandhi, "in all modesty," considered it his mission to lead his contemporaries into "experimental" action. As he wrote to C. F. Andrews:

> I have taken up things as they have come to me and always in trembling and fear. I did not work out the possibilities in Champaran, Kheda or Ahmedabad nor yet when I made an unconditional offer of service in 1914. I fancy that I followed His will and no other and He will lead me "amid the encircling gloom."[1]

Yet there is no reason to question the fact that the sudden conviction that the moment of truth *had* arrived always came upon him as if from a voice which had spoken before he had quite listened. Gandhi often spoke of his inner voice, which would speak unexpectedly in the preparedness of silence—but then with irreversible firmness and an irresistible demand for commitment. And, indeed, even Nietzsche, certainly the Mahatma's philosophical opposite, claimed that truth always approached "on the feet of doves." That is, the moment of truth is suddenly there—unannounced and pervasive in its stillness. But it comes only to him who has lived with facts and figures in such a way that he is always ready for a sudden synthesis and will not, from sheer surprise and fear, startle truth away. But acting upon the inner voice means to involve others on the assumption that they, too, are ready—and when Gandhi listened to his inner voice, he often thought he heard what the masses were ready to listen to. That, of course, is the secret of all charismatic leadership, but how could he know it was "the truth"? Gandhi's answer would be: Only the readiness to suffer would tell.

Truthful action, for Gandhi, was governed by the readiness to get hurt and yet not to hurt—action governed by the principle of *ahimsa*. According to Bondurant "the only dogma in the Gandhian philosophy centers here: that the only test of truth is action based on the refusal to do harm."[2] With all respect for the traditional translation of *ahimsa,* I think Gandhi implied in it, besides a refusal not to do physical harm, a determination not to violate another person's essence. For even where one may not be able to avoid harming or hurting, forcing or demeaning another whenever one must coerce him, one should try even in doing so, not to violate his essence, for such violence can only evoke counter-violence, which may end in a kind of truce, but not in truth. For *ahimsa* as acted upon by Gandhi not only means not to hurt another, it means to respect the truth in him. Gandhi reminds us that, since we can not possibly know the absolute truth, we are "therefore not competent to punish"—a most essential reminder, since man when tempted to violence always parades as another's policeman, convincing himself that whatever he is doing to another, that other "has it coming to him." Whoever acts on such righteousness, however, implicates himself in a mixture of pride and guilt which undermines his position psychologically and ethically. Against this typical cycle, Gandhi claimed that only the voluntary acceptance of self-suffering can reveal the truth latent in a conflict—and in the opponent.

A few years ago I had occasion to talk on medical ethics to a graduating class of young doctors and found myself trying to reinterpret the Golden Rule in the light of what we have learned in clinical work, that is, in the encounter of two individuals as "unequal" as a therapist and a patient.[3]

I suggested that (ethically speaking) a man should act in such a way that he actualizes both in himself and in the other such forces as are ready for a heightened mutuality. Nothing I have read or heard since has dissuaded me from the conviction that one may interpret Gandhi's truth in these terms. In fact, Gandhi made a similar assumption when he viewed Satyagraha as a bridge between the ethics of family life and that of communities and nations.

Bondurant concludes that the "effect" of Gandhi's formulation was "to transform the absolute truth of the philosophical *Sat* to the relative truth of ethic principle capable of being tested by a means combining non-violent action with self-suffering."[4] The truth in any given encounter is linked with the developmental stage of the individual and the historical situation of his group: together, they help to determine the *actuality,* i.e., the potential for unifying action at a given moment. What Bondurant calls "veracity," then, must have actuality as well as reality in it, that is, it depends on acting passionately as well as on thinking straight; and acting passionately would include acting upon and being guided by what is most genuine in the other. Truth in Gandhi's sense points to the next step in man's realization of man as one all-human species, and thus to our only chance to transcend what we are.

I have attempted to sketch the whole configuration of actualities which led to Gandhi's choice of Ahmedabad as the setting for the Event: the compulsion coming from the Mahatma's individual past and from his cultural tradition as well as from the situational attraction as presented by Ambalal and Anasuya. Gandhi later had reason to repudiate this beginning, but not because any other place on earth would have been more suitable; for origins are inescapable. As to the reality of the situation, Gandhi always made his inner voice "hold its breath" for a while in order to give him time to study the facts; but the sum of the facts consisted not only of the statistics which proved the textile workers right, it also included the over-all political and economic situation which governs public opinion. The goal, in Ahmedabad, was 35 per cent—an increase considerable enough to be of help to the workers, moderate enough to be borne by the industry and to be tolerated by the public, and enough of a compromise to be symbolic. The objective was eventually reached. But it probably could have been reached with less spectacular means, sealed with no more than an announcement on the factory's bulletin board, and a notice in the local press. But the wider objective was that of establishing a method which would prove applicable to other social and national settings, even as in the local milieu it was to improve permanently the relation of each participant to himself (honor), to all others (cooperation), and to a common God (truth). All this, then, depended on stringent conditions which Bondurant summarizes under *rules, a code of conduct,* and certain orderly *steps.* Here I must select a few combinations.

As we saw, the essential preliminary steps in any of Gandhi's campaigns were an objective investigation of facts, followed by a sincere attempt at *arbitration.* Satyagraha must appear to be a last resort in an unbearable situation which allows for no other solution and is representative enough to merit a commitment of unlimited self-suffering. It, therefore, calls for a thorough *preparation* of all would-be participants, so that they may know the grievances as factually true and join in the conclusion that the agreed-upon goal is both just and attainable. But they must also be sure of being on the side of a truth which transcends all facts and is the true rationale for Satyagraha. Gandhi's helpers had to be convinced of all the basic propositions, and sufficiently so that they could promise to abide by the nonviolent code. In Ahmedabad, Gandhi was sure that not only the local mill workers, but workers anywhere in the world should refuse to accept conditions such as were then acute, even as he was sure that a man in Ambalal's position should not be permitted (because he should not permit himself) to insist on the defeat of the workers. But he also "picked" Ambalal because, in all his intransigence, Ambalal knew that Gandhi was right, and he respected his sister for standing up for reform—against him, her brother.

But to continue in a more general vein: in any campaign the widest *publicity* or (if one wishes) agitation was necessary in order to induce the public either to intervene in advance, or to provide public pressure in support of the action to be taken. That action, in fact, had to be *announced* in all detail in advance, with a clear *ultimatum* binding to all, and yet permitting the resumption of arbitration at any stage of the enfolding action—an arbitration, that is, conducive to face-saving all around. Therefore, an *action committee* created for this purpose would select such *forms of non-cooperation*—strike, boycott, civil disobedience—as would seem fitting as the *minimum force necessary to reach a defined goal*: no quick triumph would be permitted to spread the issue beyond this goal, nor any defeat to narrow it. The quality of such fitness, however, would vastly transcend the question of mere feasibility: for it would encompass *issues* which were at the same time central to the *practical* life of the community and *symbolic* for its future—as was for example, the land around a peasant's homestead in Champaran, or the right of Untouchables in a given locality to pass over a temple road on the way to work, or the right of all Indians to take from their sea, without paying taxes to a colonial government, the salt necessary to make their food palatable and their bodies resistant in the heat of their subcontinent.

We can see from this once-revolutionary list how the choice of issues in Gandhi's India has changed the legal conscience of mankind in regard to grievances and rights now taken for granted in many parts of the world. As to the rules for the resisters, they must *rely on themselves,* for both their suffering and their triumph must be their own; for this reason Gandhiji forbade his striking workers to accept outside support. The movement must *keep the initiative,* which includes the willingness to atone for miscalculations as well as the readiness to adapt to changes in the opponent, and to readjust both the strategy and (as far as they were negotiable) the goals of the campaign. And in all of this, the resister must be consistently *willing to persuade* and to enlighten, even as he remains ready *to be persuaded* and enlightened. He will, then, not insist on obsolete precedent or rigid principle, but will be guided by what under changing conditions will continue or come to feel true to him and his comrades, that is, will become *truer through action.*

Such truth, however, could not depend on individual impressions and decisions. It could reveal itself only as long as the resisters' actions remained co-ordinated and were guided by a code which was as firm as it was flexible enough to perceive changes—and to obey changing commands. The leader would have to be able to count on a discipline based on the Satyagrahi's commitment to suffer the opponent's anger without getting angry and yet also without ever submitting to any violent coercion by anyone; to remain so attuned to the opponent's position that he would be ready, on the leader's command, even to come to the opponent's help in any unforeseen situation which might rob him of his freedom to remain a counterplayer on the terms agreed upon; and to remain, in principle, so law-abiding that he would refuse co-operation with the law or law-enforcing agencies *only* in the chosen and defined issues. Within these limits, he would accept and even demand those penalties which by his chosen action he had willingly invoked against himself.

And then, there is the leader's self-chosen suffering, which is strictly "his business," as Gandhi would say with his mild-mannered rudeness. For there must be a leader, and, in fact, a predetermined succession of leaders, so that the leader himself can be free to invite on himself any suffering, including death, rather than hide behind the pretext that he was not expendable. As we saw, in the first national Satyagraha, Gandhi's arrest turned out to be *the* critical factor, even as the Ahmedabad Satyagraha floundered over the critical issue of Gandhi's decision to fast. For once the leader decides on a "true" course, he must have the freedom to restrain as well as to command, to withdraw as well as to lead and, if this freedom should be denied him by his followers, to declare a Satyagraha against them. If such singular power produces a shudder in the reader of today—indoctrinated as he is against "dictators"—it must not be forgotten that we are now speaking of the post–First World War years when a new kind of charismatic leadership would emerge, in nation after nation, filling the void left by collapsing monarchies, feudalisms, and patriarchies, with the mystic unity of the Leader and the Masses. And such was the interplay of the private and the public, the neurotic and the charismatic, during the period when these sons of the people assumed such a mystic authority, that we must recognize even that most personal of Gandhi's decisions, namely, his *fast,* as part of an "Indian leadership Indian style."

Fasting, we may consider in passing, is an age-old ritual act which can serve so many motivations and exigencies that it can be as corrupt as it can be sublime. As recently as January 1967, Pyarelal found it necessary to reassert in the Indian press the rules Gandhi had laid down for public fasting in a public issue. And Pyarelal concludes that fasting

> cannot be resorted to against those who regard us as their enemy, or on whose love we have not established a claim by dint of selfless service; it cannot be resorted to by a person who has not identified himself with, or worked for the cause he is fasting for; it cannot be used for gaining a material selfish end, or to change the honestly held opinion of another or in support of an issue that is not clear, feasible and demonstrably just. . . . To be legitimate, a fast should be capable of response.[5]

Gandhi, at one time, urged any individual or authority that was "fasted against" and which considered the fast to be blackmail "to refuse to yield to it, even though the refusal may result in the death of the fasting person." Obviously, only such an attitude would do honor to him who thus offers his own life. On the other hand, Gandhi insisted that the fasting person must be prepared to the end to discover or to be convinced of a flaw in his position. The Indian writer Raja Rao told me on a walk how a friend of his had written to Gandhi that he was going to fast in order to underline certain demands. Gandhi wrote back suggesting that the friend write down ten demands worthy of a fast and Gandhi would initial the list without reading it. The friend pondered the matter and thought of other ways to protest!

Everything that has been said here, however, should make us very cautious in referring to the outcome of a sincere fast or to any part of a genuine Satyagraha campaign as a "failure." For as we saw in the national *hartal* of 1919, the choice of withdrawal or suspension may be the only way in which the leader can keep the spiritual initiative and thus save the instrument—dented but not broken—for another day. In this sense, the Ahmedabad mill owners' yielding was not a "capitulation"; for in an ideal Satyagraha campaign both sides will have had a chance to make the outcome a mutually beneficial one—as was the case even with the Bania deal in Ahmedabad. And, of course, new principles far beyond any circumscribed "success" or "failure" are being forced on the imagination of a wider audience in any Satyagraha worthy of the name. At any rate, even today, the surviving mill owners are far from registering a sense of having given in. *"We* forced him to fast," one said; and another: "We were ready to grant that much, anyway"; while all agree that the Event radically changed labor relations in Ahmedabad and in India.

This brings us to a final item in the inventory of Satyagraha which, at least locally, is most far-reaching: it is what in Gandhian terminology is called the "constructive program." In Champaran, the failure most keenly felt by Gandhi (and this, I believe, *was* a failure in the sense of a lack of essential completion) was the absence of any lasting impact on the everyday lives of the people of Bihar. In Ahmedabad, as we saw, Gandhi insisted, in the very days of the strike, on consolidating the gains of labor initiated by Anasuya and subsequently sustained in many significant ways by Ambalal and the other mill owners—gains in the general concept of work as a dignifying activity in itself; in the solidarity of all the laborers, in factory conditions, and in the welfare of the worker population.

In conclusion, I shall describe the practical consequences of the strike in Ahmedabad. The gains were institutionalized in an industry-wide

Board of Arbitrators—the first members being Mangaldas Girardhas (then president of the Association, who had never wavered in his willingness to continue the plague bonus) and Gandhiji. Also, the Ahmedabad Textile Labor Association was founded—an organization given first rank in most nonpolitical treatises dealing with the Labor Movement in India. At the time of my first visit to Ahmedabad, the bustling activity of the T.L.A. provided by far the most vivid and most sustained "echo" of Gandhi's presence. The specific gains of labor relations, of course, seem barely to rise above the very minimum of what the post-industrial West would consider decent working and living conditions; and, indeed, some of the items brought up for arbitration in the years after the strike would hardly seem worthy of the attention of such powerful men—in any country, that is, other than India. But the critical point is that a great mill owner and a mahatma *would* discuss, say, toilet facilities, and follow up on it; that they *had* the joint authority to force the mill owners to make ever-so-grudging concessions; and that they *could* induce the mill workers to maintain discipline and to be restrained in their demands; while, in cases of insoluble discord, they *were* in a position to call on the best minds of the country to arbitrate. At any rate, it would be impossible to overrate the changes the post-strike days brought in regard to the concepts of work and collaboration. On one occasion, Anasuya told us, the Muslim workers stayed away from work on five consecutive days so that they could go to the station and greet a Muslim delegation which kept postponing arrival from day to day. Gandhi insisted that these workers work two extra days a month in order to make up for the sixty hours lost. They did. Anasuya went on to say that the workers would not have such discipline today, with Gandhiji gone. But when I asked whether they would even think of going to the station for five consecutive days today, she agreed that they (and the Association) had learned to respect their jobs too much for that.

In 1925 the membership of the T.L.A. had risen to 14,000; in 1959 it was 100,000, and as late as February 1967 the Indian newspaper *The Statesman* reported on the Ahmedabad Association as follows:

A Textile worker in Ahmedabad today is the highest paid among his colleagues elsewhere in the country. He was getting about 20% less wages than that prevailing in Bombay in 1920 when the Textile Labour Association came into being. But today his is 10% more.

This, the TLA leaders claim, is entirely attributable to the long spell of industrial peace in Ahmedabad, which, in its turn is the result of its general adherence to the principle of arbitration in settling labour disputes. In this respect, the TLA can certainly claim to be the pace-setter.

With its Rs 12-lakh [1,200,000 rupees] annual budget; a highly efficient secretariat to assist workers in their day-to-day grievances about service conditions; a bank the working capital of which rose to over Rs 5.3 crores [53,000,000 rupees] in 1963 from a mere Rs 31 lakhs [3,100,000 rupees] 15 years ago; a 200-strong paid cadre mainly to be among the workers in the mills and to act as liaison between them and the employer; and with over 100 cooperative societies run under its aegis, the Association has today an outfit easily comparable to the very best evolved by a trade union in a Western country.[6]

But the Association also became a school for national leaders, as we saw in the case of Shankerlal Banker (later the national chief of the khadi movement, in Gulzarilal Nanda (later Home Minister and acting Prime Minister), and even in the old firebrand Indulal Yagnik, who became the most vociferous opponent of the remnants of "feudalism" which he and many others claim still dominates Ahmedabad's labor peace. Others could be named; but we are concerned here only with one period and one Event, and with the instrument then tried and perfected.

This may be the place to come back to the question of why the Mahatma reported the strike the way he did in his Autobiography; and, more particularly, why he interrupted his report of the strike with an account of the snakes which infested the ashram grounds and yet refrained from harming anybody when treated with respectful *ahimsa*. If one cared to be a "busybody" of the psychoanalytic kind, one could make the most of the thematic sequence of these chapters. In the first of the three installments, Gandhi and his followers are shown to be up against recalcitrant mill owners; in the second, against poisonous snakes; and in the third, against mill owners again. Do snakes, then, "stand for" mill owners? This could suggest to a clinician a breakthrough of Gandhi's anger against the mill owners—an anger which he had expressly forbidden to himself as well as to the striking and starving workmen. If one can win over poisonous snakes by love and nonviolence, the hidden thought might be, one can reach the hearts of industrialists too. Or the suggestion might be that it would be more profitable to be kind to poisonous snakes than to industrialists—and here we remember that another Man of Peace, also using an analogy from the bestiary, once mused that big lazy camels might squeeze through where a rich man could not or would not.

If so, the interruption would only underscore the most obvious explanation for the Mahatma's treatment of the Ahmedabad incident, namely, mixed and conflicting feelings toward the mill owners and particularly toward Ambalal. Unnecessary to say, Indian Labour, insofar as it later followed (or talked) the line of Lenin, has considered Gandhi's relation to the mill owners utterly suspect and has never ceased to consider the Ahmedabad brand of labor peace "feudal" and "reactionary." In this they have had the quiet support of those mill owners who believe and admit that they, in fact, used Gandhi for their own purposes at the time and have used his memory ever since. For the Mahatma, however, this was not a matter of ideological propaganda or, indeed, economic interest. For if Satyagraha had in it the stuff to rival Lenin's liberation of labor, then the sole criterion for its success or failure was its inner purity. And this to the Mahatma always centered in the immediate situation and in his relation to concretely present men. Ambalal had supported Gandhi during the most critical period of the young ashram's existence. On this score alone Gandhi's wavering in his fast could be seen as unworthy of the leading Satyagrahi, and unworthy of the goal of *Moksha*.

The Autobiography, however, by its very division of chapters, betrays a conflict on another score. By the time Gandhi came to write the "columns" relating to the strike (rather late, in the 146th installment of a total of 167), he had taken Ambalal's side in an issue reaching into the depth and width of the historical necessity of anchoring Satyagraha in the *ahimsa* of Hinduism. In 1926 Ambalal, as he described it to me, had noticed from the window of his office in one of his mills that the workmen and their wives did not dare to sit by a well which had been a favorite luncheon spot and that the women would approach the well only armed with sticks. On inquiry he learned that an increasing number of ferocious-looking dogs were loose in the area around the mill, some looking clearly rabid. The municipality of Ahmedabad had apparently decided to dispose of its canine problems without breaking the injunction against the killing of animals by catching all stray dogs and letting them loose outside the city limits. Some workers—as is the wont of people who do not have enough to eat themselves—threw food to the emaciated animals, a sign for dozens of the creatures to converge on the well. Ambalal gave the municipality a week to round up the dogs and then requested the police to kill them. Considering arsenic cruel, they shot them. The cadavers were then loaded on carts which (for whatever reason) were pulled right through the old town—and this on a holiday. The Hindu populace was stunned, and many stores immediately closed in protest according to the ancient pattern of *hartal*—a storekeepers' strike. Ambalal's life was in danger.

Gandhi, however, immediately spoke up for him in *Young India*, a fact which aroused such a flood of correspondence that he had to defend himself in five successive issues. As always his defense was both practical and spiritual. In one Ahmedabad hospital more than a thousand cases of hydrophobia had been treated in the year 1925 and almost a thousand thus far in 1926. "In our ignorance," he wrote, "we must kill rabid dogs even as we might have to kill a man found in the act of killing people." As often, he seemed to contradict contradictions by adding new ones, but he concluded prophetically:

> They had attributed to me nonviolence as they understand it. Now they find me acting in a contrary manner and are angry with me. . . . I appreciate the motive behind it. I must try to reason with them patiently . . . it is a sin to feed stray dogs. It is a false sense of compassion. It is an insult to a starving dog to throw a crumb at him. Roving dogs do not indicate the civilization or compassion of the society; they betray on the contrary the ignorance and lethargy of its members. The lower animals are our brethren. I include among them the lion and the tiger. We do not know how to live with these carnivorous beasts and poisonous reptiles because of our ignorance. When man learns better, he will learn to befriend even these. Today he does not even know how to befriend a man of a different religion or from a different country.[7]

This new and highly controversial linkage of Gandhi's and Ambalal's names, then, complicated an issue calling for autobiographic clarification as one of his "experiments with truth," which appears to be the reason for the remarkable fact that Gandhi separates the introduction of the strike and the story of its conclusion with the installment on the ashram.

This installment does have a moral—Gandhi's lengthy protestation that in his ashrams there had never been any "loss of life occasioned by snake bite." This fact has since been confirmed by both residents and visitors. An old member of the ashram showed me the spot where, he said, Vinoba Bhave once sat when a big poisonous snake crawled under his clothes. He neither moved nor called out but patiently waited for a helper, who calmly folded up Vinoba's clothes and carried the whole bundle to the river. Now the difference between dogs insane with rabies and reptiles essentially minding their own business is not to be minimized; this, too, will be a subject indispensable to our more general conclusions. Here we are interested only in the fact that Gandhi, while telling the story of the strike, found it necessary to reiterate that his basic position on the killing of animals had remained intact.

2. RITUAL

I have now attempted to summarize some spiritual properties and some practical steps essential to the leverage of Satyagraha. There remain two fundamental doubts nagging not only incurable cynics but also many sympathizers, East and West: if the psychic energy needed for such an instrument is dependent on *Brahmacharya*—and Gandhi seemed to insist at least for himself and his immediate followers that it was—how manageable is this truth in the instinctual life of more ordinary men, and how alien to ordinary man's "instinctive" aggressiveness? In one word: how *natural* is it?

In line with his religious heritage, Gandhi could not tolerate any deliberate harm to animals. Intellectually, however, he was a popular kind of Darwinian, with all the ambivalence contained in the very terminology which makes man a "descendant" from creatures whom he considers far beneath him in instinctual restraint. When on the occasion of his visit to London he was asked to say a word to the American people, Gandhi said in a radio address: "Hitherto, nations have fought in the manner of the brute." This manner he specified as "wreaking vengeance," and he pronounced it "the law that governs brute creation . . . inconsistent with human dignity."[8] Now, in view of what we have learned about animals or men since then, we can not continue to assert that man without self-control is "no better than a brute," unless the implication is that—measured by the code of organisms—he is much, much worse. Yet, it must be remembered that only in the post-Darwinian period has mankind even begun to confront the shocking intelligence that he may be merely some special kind of mammal.

To absorb that shock has been the task of the century after Darwin; and so it comes about that Gandhi's contemporary, Freud, who loved proud dogs for their honesty in love and hate, and who advocated an insightful acceptance of sexuality, would say in turn: "Conflicts of interest between man and man are resolved, in principle, by the recourse to violence. It is the same in the animal kingdom, from which man cannot claim exclusion."[9] Freud thus comes to the grim conclusion that in man "the slaughter of a foe gratifies an instinctive craving." But when he assents to the old dictum that *homo* is *hominis lupus,* one may at least wonder whether he means that man is to man what wolf is to man or what wolf is to wolf.

At any rate, it can not be denied that such post-Darwinism represents the lowest common denominator in the thinking of the two men who invented two corresponding methods of dealing with our instinctuality in a nonviolent manner. It is a striking example of the boundness of even the greatest men in the imagery of their time.

Konrad Lorenz's book *On Aggression*[10] is probably the best known summary of intraspecies aggression in some of the higher animals. There is, of course, an endless display of skillful violence on the part of animals who go hunting, who set out to settle territorial competition, or who feel cornered by a superior enemy. Obviously, to aggress in the sense of *ad-gredere* and to defend in that of *de-fence* must be instinctive in any creature that occupies or moves in space in unison with his own kind and in both symbiotic and antagonistic relation to other kinds.

The question is: when and where does "natural" aggression become raving violence, and the instinctive technique of killing become senseless murder? The inhabitants of an Indian jungle live face to face with "beasts" in their domain; but even they consider an occasional "killer" among tigers something of an outlaw or a deviant, a creature whom one cannot come to terms with, and who, therefore, must be singled out and hunted down. A normal lion, however, when ready for the kill (and he kills only when hungry) shows no signs of anger or rage: he is "doing his job"—or so he appears to be when his physiognomy can be studied in the wilds through long-range lenses. Nor is there any pervasive tendency for mass annihilation in nature's book—except, apparently, in rodents such as rats, under particular conditions. Wolves on the chase (Dante's *bestia senza pace*) do not decimate healthy herds but pick out the stragglers who fall behind. Among themselves, they are capable of devoted friendship; and it is reported that when two wolves happen to get into a fight, there comes a moment when the one that begins to weaken bares his unprotected neck to his opponent, who, in turn, is instinctively inhibited from taking advantage of this now "nonviolent" situation.

A more ritual elaboration of such *instinctive pacific behavior* appears in the antler tournament among the Damstags. The tournament begins with a parade *à deux*: the stags trot alongside one another, whipping their antlers up and down. Then, suddenly, they stop in their tracks as if on command, swerve toward each other at a right angle, lower their heads until the antlers almost reach the ground, and crack them against each other. If it should happen that one of the combatants swerves earlier than the other, thus endangering the completely unprotected flank of his rival with the powerful swing of his sharp and heavy equipment, he instantly puts a brake on his premature turn, accelerates his trot, and continues the parallel parade. When both are ready, however, there ensues a full mutual confrontation and a powerful but harmless wrestling. The victor is the one who can hold out the longest, while the loser concedes the tournament by a ritualized disengagement which normally stops the attack of the victor. Lorenz suggests that there are untold numbers of analogous rituals of pacification among the higher animals; but he also points out (most importantly for us) that de-ritualization at any point results in violence to the death. Skeletons of stags whose antlers are entwined in death have been found; but they are victims of an instinctive ritual that failed.

We owe such observations not only to new techniques of extending our photographic vision into animal territory, but also to a new willingness on the part of observers to let some animals dwell in their own living space[11] or to enter into the animal's domain with not more than reasonable safeguards—reasonable in the sense that the animal under observation could not mistake such presence for anything but a nonviolent approach. An ethologist of this kind, however, has given up more than just excessive fear. He has accepted a measure of joint universe with the animal beyond all question of man's descent or ascent—not to speak of human condescension—and thus has let it become clear that some of the aggressive or fearful behavior ascribed to animals is a response to man's prejudices, projections, and apprehensions. We learn from such observation that "aggressive" behavior is elicited and stopped, displaced, or replaced under given *conditions*. For, as Lorenz says so characteristically, *"Jawohl, ein Trieb kann angetrieben werden"*: "Yes, indeed, a drive can be driven, an instinct instigated"—that is, by compelling circumstances. And by the same token, a drive can also remain latent and yet at a moment's provocation impel competent action. This, one would think, should make it unnecessary to apply to animal aggression (as I fear, Lorenz has done) the model of a Freudian instinct, which is essentially derived from sexuality—itself in man a much more ubiquitous, pervasive, and spontaneous drive than in animals.

"Instinct" has become an embarrassing term. Biologists are about to discard it and yet in psychoanalysis it is not expendable. When one uses it with too much of a biological connotation one is apt to imply what one did not mean to say. There is something instinctive and something instinctual about aggression, but one would hesitate to call aggression an "instinct." If one abandons the term altogether, however, one neglects the energetic and the driven aspect of man's behavior. Here is the crux of the matter: Freud's *Trieb* is something between the English "drive" and "instinct." In comparing the statements of animal psychologists with those of psychoanalysts, it is always useful to ask whether "instinct" is meant to convey something *instinctive* (an inborn pattern of adaptive competence), or something *instinctual* (a quantity of drive or drivenness, whether adaptive or not).[12]

If for comparative purposes we retain the term "instinct," it becomes clear that the aggressive acts as well as the pacific maneuvers of animals are *instinctive*—that is, pre-formed action patterns which under certain conditions can call on some ready drive energy for instantaneous, vigorous, and skillful release. This makes it quite unnecessary for the animal either to be unduly aroused or to inhibit himself in any individual or "moral" fashion. For the ritualization assures a pre-selection of opponents of nearly equal strength. Such opponents will be equally endowed with the capacity for the clocklike display of a whole set of scheduled and reciprocal reactions, and they will be equally ready for the assumption of either of the terminal roles (what *we* would call victor or vanquished) convincingly and effectively. Much of animal aggression is already thus "ritualized," as Julian Huxley was the first to put it. I have never been able to watch the angry-sounding seagulls, for example, without thinking that they would long since have burned up from emotion were not their behavior an instinctive "convention," invested with relatively small doses of the available drive and emotion—unless an "accident" happens. One can well see in such ritualization, as Konrad Lorenz does, an evolutionary antecedent of man's inborn propensity for a moral inhibition that prevents undue violence; and one could well (and I will) go further and see in Gandhi's Satyagraha the suggestion of a pacific confrontation that may be grounded not only in man's religiosity but also in instinctive patterns already common among some "brutes."

Yet, from everything we have said, it must be clear that for man this is by no means a simple return to nature. Rather it is an instance of man's capacity to let inspiration, insight, and conviction "cure" his instinctual complexity and to reinstate on a human level what in the animal is so innocently and yet so fatefully given. This is why Freud could say that the animal perishes when his environment changes too fast and too radically for his instinctive adaptation, while man, the great creator of his own environment, *"geht an seinen Trieben zugrunde"*—perishes from senseless instinctual needs. Thus man can eat, drink, and smoke, work and "love," curse, moralize, and sacrifice himself to death. For man's instinctual forces are never completely bound in adaptive or reasonable patterns; some are repressed, displaced, perverted, and often return from repression to arouse strictly human kinds of anxiety and rage. Here it must be conceded that even Gandhi's fanatic attempts to simplify his tastes, however moralistic in their scrupulosity, do contain a truth which was, at the same time, made accessible to insight by Freud. If the nutritional instinct, for example, guides the animal in finding and devouring an adequate amount of the right kind of food, this is very different from the oral-incorporative instinctuality which may make man spend a greater portion of his resources on alcohol and soda pop, on tobacco and coffee, than on the schooling of his children.

Thus, Gandhi's awareness of unfunctional drives in man and the necessity somehow to free himself from them—this awareness is essential to man's future. The question is what we will do with this awareness: reassert old moralisms, which, as Gandhi demonstrated in his own life, have a tendency to become as excessive as the drives they are meant to hold in check; or strive for a new ethics, based on new insights? At any rate, Freud could have meant to blame only an *"instinctual"* craving (even if he is translated as having blamed an "instinctive" one) for man's pleasure in torturing and killing an enemy. On the way, however, we must face once more how far civilized man may have sunk in some respects below the animal and probably also below his early human ancestors: for it is civilized man, morality and all, who is, or has become, in Loren Eiseley's terrible phrase, the lethal element in the universe. The question, then, is whether violence of the total kind, that is, characterized by irrational rage, wild riot, or systematic extermination, can be traced to our animal nature at all—or, for that matter, to our primitive forebears.

The motion picture *Dead Birds* shows with great esthetic skill how two tribes discovered only in this century in the New Guinea highlands indulge in regular, ritualized, and dramatized warfare, facing each other across an appointed battlefield in impressive warriors' plumage, advancing boisterously and retreating loudly in alternation. These tribes have many sinister rituals; their blatantly phallic bragging and their mutilation of female fingers can arouse nausea as well as awe. But with all such martial obsession, there is no attempt at annihilation, suppression, or enslavement; and while shouted contempt is part of the bragging display, these tribes must have maintained, for decades or centuries, a *convention of warfare,* in which the enemy can be trusted to abide by a certain ritualization which sacrifices to the martial ethos only a minimum number of individuals on either side. Here the existence of a cultural arrangement somewhere between the instinctual and the instinctive and somewhere also between tribal self-insistence and an intertribal league may well be assumed. Such warfare seems to typify a human potential; and if it can be said that "ritualization" in animals helps the participants to clarify *situational ambiguities* and to restore instinctive trust, the burden of human ritualization may well be the restoration of peace by the periodical settlement of *ambivalences* arising from man's division into pseudo-species.

Although Gandhi may indeed have sensed something of the ritual potential of *traditional warfare* when he perceived the necessity to transfer some of the discipline of soldierdom to militant nonviolence, it must be granted that it made little sense to send tens of thousands of Indians into the mechanized slaughter of the First World War, and to expect them there, of all places, to learn the bravery and chivalry necessary for Satyagraha.

For this we have learned since and are now fighting out with one another and within ourselves: even if human warfare has always included an element of uniformed ritual by which heroes were sacrificed to the survival and the immortality of idealized communal bodies, man's technological evolution has vastly outdistanced what adaptive value wars may once have had. Today we know that all this has evolved together and must be studied together: social identity and the hatred of "otherness," morality and righteous violence, inventiveness and mass murder. From the arrow released by hand to the warhead sent by intercontinental missile, man, the skillful and righteous attacker, has been transformed into a technician who can view his opponent as a mere target in a gunsight or on a map, or a statistic in a genocidal death sentence.

In 1954, Pyarelal related in *The Statesman* how a few hours before the end Gandhi was asked by a foreign journalist, "How would you meet the atom bomb . . . with nonviolence?" He answered, "I will not go underground, I will not go into shelter. I will come out in the open and let the pilot see I have not a trace of evil against him. The pilot will not see our faces from his great height, I know. But that longing in our hearts—that he will not come to harm—would reach up to him and his eyes would be opened." Utter foolishness? Maybe; and yet, perhaps, true for its very absurdity. For Gandhi's answer only dramatizes a basic nonviolent attitude which, while it must admittedly find new methods in an electronic and nuclear age, nevertheless remains a human alternative, enacted and demonstrated by the Mahatma as feasible in *his* times and circumstances. And as for the times ahead, has not the same technology which has given to man the means to incinerate himself also provided him with the techniques of facing his own kind over unlimited distances? And has he not, at the same time, also gained new introspective means to face himself and thus all others in himself, and himself in others?

If we add that man must learn to face himself as he faces all others, we imply that so far in history he has made every effort *not* to see that mankind is one species. If in this connection I have spoken of man's "pseudo-species" mentality, this concept intrigued Konrad Lorenz sufficiently to ascribe to me the term "pseudo-speciation," which I gladly appropriate. But what, stated once more, does it mean?

The term denotes the fact that while man is obviously one species, he appears and continues on the scene split up into groups (from tribes to nations, from castes to classes, from religions to ideologies) which provide their members with a firm sense of distinct and superior identity—and immortality. This demands, however, that each group must invent for itself a place and a moment in the very centre of the universe where and when an especially provident deity caused it to be created superior to all others, the mere mortals.[13]

One could go far back into prehistory and envisage man, the most naked and least identifiable animal by natural markings, and lacking, for all his self-consciousness, the identity of a species. He could adorn himself flamboyantly with feathers, pelts, and paints, and elevate his own kind into a mythological species, called by whatever word he had for *"the people."* At its friendliest, "pseudo" means only that something is made to appear to be what it is not; and, indeed, in the name of his pseudo-species man could endow himself and his universe with tools and weapons, roles and rules, with legends, myths, and rituals, which would bind his group together and give to its existence such super-individual significance as inspires loyalty, heroism, and poetry. One may assume that some tribes and cultures have for long periods peacefully cultivated just such an existence. What renders this "natural" process a potential malignancy of universal dimensions, however, is the fact that in times of threatening change and sudden upheaval the idea of being the foremost species must be reinforced by a fanatic fear and hate of other pseudo-species. That these others, therefore, must be annihilated or kept "in their places" by periodical warfare or conquest, by stringent legislation or local custom—that becomes a periodical and often reciprocal obsession of man.

At its unfriendliest, then, "pseudo" means that somebody is trying with all the semi-sincerity of propaganda to put something over on himself as well as on others: and I am afraid that I mean to convey just that. This "pseudo" aspect of man's collective identities can become dominant under the impact of historical and economic displacements, which make a group's self-idealization both more defensive and more exclusive. This process is so fundamental to man that, as modern history shows, the pseudo-species mentality refuses to yield even to gains in knowledge and experience acquired through progress. Even most "advanced" nations can harbor, and, in fact, make fanatically explicit, a mystical adherence to the mentality of the pseudo-species. The total victory of this mentality in an enlightened modern nation was exemplified in Hitler's Germany.

The most frightening aspect of pseudo-speciation, however, is the fact that a "species" which has come under the dominance of another is apt to incorporate the derisive opinion of the dominant "species" into its own self-estimation, that is, it permits itself to become infantilized, storing up within and against itself a rage which it dare not vent against the oppressor and, indeed, often dares not feel. This can become a curse from generation to generation, leading at first to occasional violence among the oppressed themselves until, at last, all the latent rage can rush into riotous manifestation at a moment when historical circumstances seem to invite and to sanction an explosion. It should not surprise us that such riotousness can be childishly gay even as it is carelessly destructive: for the oppressed have stood their oppression only by cultivating a defensive childlikeness and childishness in their individual lives and a fragmented primitivity in their cultural heritage. It stands to reason, then, that where an emphasis on the pseudo-species prevails—as in much of colonial history—the development of every participant individual is endangered by various combinations of guilt and rage which prevent true development, even where knowledge and expertise abound.

History provides, however, a way by which the pseudo-species mentality of warring groups can become disarmed, as it were, within a *wider identity.* This can come about by territorial unification: the *Pax Romana* embraced races, nations, and classes. Technological advances in universal "traffic," too, unite: seafaring, mechanized locomotion, and wireless communication each has helped to spread changes eventually contained in a sense of widening identity which helps to overcome economic fear, the anxiety of culture change, and the dread of a spiritual vacuum.[14]

We have seen in Gandhi's development the strong attraction of one of those more inclusive identities: that of an enlightened citizen of the British Empire. In proving himself willing neither to abandon vital ties to his native tradition nor to sacrifice lightly a Western education which eventually contributed to his ability to help defeat British hegemony—in all of these seeming contradictions Gandhi showed himself on intimate terms with the actualities of his era. For in all parts of the world, the struggle now is for the *anticipatory development of more inclusive identities.*

I submit, then, that Gandhi, in his immense intuition for historical actuality and his capacity to assume leadership in "truth in action," may have created a ritualization through which men, equipped with both realism and spiritual strength, can face each other with a mutual confidence analogous to the instinctive safety built into the animals' pacific rituals.

Instead of indulging in further speculation, however, let me come back to the concrete Event studied and sketch certain convergences of the Event and the patterns of pacific ritualization just described. In Ahmedabad, as on other occasions, Gandhi, far from waiting to be attacked so he could "resist passively" moved right in on his opponent by announcing what the grievance was and what action he intended to take: *engagement at close range* is of the essence in his approach. Thus, he gave his opponent the maximum opportunity for an informed response, even as he had based his demands on a thorough investigation of the facts. He told the workers not to demand more than what was fair and right but also to be prepared to *die* rather than demand less. He also saw to it that the issue was joined as one *among equals.* He explained that the mill owners' assets (money and equipment) and the workers' assets (capacity to work) depended on each other, and, therefore, were *equivalent* in economic power and dignity. In other words, they shared an inclusive identity, they were—so to say—of one species.

In this sense, he would not permit either side to undermine the other; even as the mill owners became virulent and threatening he forbade his workers to use counter-threats. He exacted from these starving people a pledge that they would abstain from any destruction, even of the opponent's good name. He thus not only avoided physical harm to machines or men (remember that the police appeared unarmed from the third day of the strike on) but also refused to let moralistic condemnation arouse anger in the opponent—and guilt feelings in the accuser.

He refused, then, to permit that cumulative aggravation of *bad conscience, negative identity,* and *hypocritical moralism* which characterizes the division of men into pseudo-species. In fact, he conceded to the mill owners that their errors were based only on a misunderstanding of their and their workers' obligations and functions, and he appealed to their "better selves." In thus demonstrating perfect trust in them, he was willing to proceed with daily improvisations leading to an interplay in which clues from the opponent determined the next step, although he was never willing to exploit any sudden appearance of weakness on the part of his opponent. The *acceptance of suffering,* and, in fact, of death, which is so basic to his "truth force," constitutes an *active choice without submis-*

sion to anyone: it includes the acceptance of punishment which one knew one courted. All of this is at once a declaration of non-intent to harm others, and (here the parallel to Konrad Lorenz's stags is most striking) an expression of a faith in the opponent's inability to persist in harming others beyond a certain point, provided, of course, that the opponent is convinced that he is not only not in mortal danger of losing either identity or rightful power, but may, in fact, acquire a more inclusive identity and a more permanent share of power.

Such faith, if disappointed, could cause the loss of everything—power, face, life—but the Satyagrahi would, in principle, choose death rather than a continuation of that chain of negotiated compromises which always eventually turn out to be the cause of future strife and murder. All this was imbedded in a style of presence and of attention. The mood of the Event was, above all, pervaded by a spirit of *giving the opponent the courage to change* even as the challenger remained ready to change with the events. At such periods of his life Gandhi possessed a Franciscan gaiety and a capacity to reduce situations to their bare essentials, thus helping others both to discard costly defenses and denials and to realize hidden potentials of good will and energetic deed.

This, I submit, actualizes something in man which for all its many abortive applications has nevertheless provided the spiritual and tactical rationale for a *revolutionary* kind of human ritualization which, in fact, may derive some of its obvious strength from an *evolutionary* potential, namely, the one so dramatically illustrated by the pacific rituals of animals. Here I am claiming something hopelessly complex and yet as simple as all the best things in life: for, indeed, only faith gives back to man the dignity of nature.

Gandhi's instrument itself, once innovated by one of the rarest of men under specific cultural and historical conditions, now exists in the images, impulses, and ritualizations of many who have become aware of it by what we may call "ritual-diffusion." It now calls for leaders who will re-innovate it elsewhere, sharing, no doubt, some of the personal or historical motivation of the first leader, the first followers, and those first led, but recombining this motivation with totally new elements. For if the instrument once was "the truth," it can and must become actual in entirely different settings, in which the necessary toolmaking may be based on a different and yet analogous tradition, and where the toolmakers come from different vocations and yet share converging goals. If truth is actuality, it can never consist of the mere repetition of ritualized acts or stances. It calls for reconstitution by a new combination of universal verities and social disciplines.[15]

3. INSIGHT

In returning once more to the correspondences between the method of Satyagraha and that of psychoanalytic insight, it is interesting to note that after World War I the Mahatma could be very sure that he was offering a political alternative to what he felt was Wilson's hypocritical peace moves in Versailles, while Freud (as we now know from his introduction to a book on Wilson allegedly co-authored by him and William C. Bullitt[16]) was equally aroused and equally certain that his method of psychological analysis was needed to show up a man like Wilson as a moralist of a deeply neurotic bent. Together, then, these men saw in Wilson, who for a brief moment in history had become the embodiment of lasting peace, the symbol instead of man's deep hypocrisy as expressed in that combination of contradictory attitudes which we must concede has proven to be the greatest danger to peace: the ceaseless perfection of armament paired with that righteous and fanatic kind of moralism which ever again can pivot from peace to war.

As Gandhi wrote to C. F. Andrews in 1919:

> The message of the West . . . is succinctly put by President Wilson in his speech delivered to the Peace Conference at the time of introducing the League of Nations Covenant: "Armed force is in the background in this programme, but it is in the background, and if the moral force of the world will not suffice, physical force of the world shall."[17]

But the Freudian movement was not alone in emphasizing therapeutic persuasion as a cure of man's aberrations. The period here under consideration saw the development of a systematic concern with "the minds of men" as strategic for both peace and war, adaptation and revolution. Thought-therapy as a means of curing the minds of men from political fixations and regressions has become familiar in Chinese thought reform. But it came as something of a shock when Khrushchev ascribed to another one of Gandhi's contemporaries these words:

> As a special duty of the Control Commission there is recommended a deep, individualized relationship with, and sometimes even a type of therapy for, the representatives of the so-called opposition—those who have experienced a psychological crisis because of failure in their Soviet or party career. An effort should be made to quiet them, to explain the matter to them in a way used among comrades, to find for them (avoiding the method of issuing orders) a task for which they are psychologically fitted.[18]

This, so Khrushchev claimed, was said by Lenin in 1920. Wherever it comes from, it is a remarkable formulation of therapeutic persuasion as a counterpoint to political terror. Among more recent revolutionaries, at least in Dr. Guevara's life, there seems to have been some intrinsic conflict between the passion to cure and the conviction that one must kill. That killing, in fact, may be a necessary self-cure for colonialized people was Dr. Frantz Fanon's conviction and message, which he carefully documented with psychiatric histories of torturers as well as with those of tortured men. An implicit therapeutic intent, then, seems to be a common denominator in theories and ideologies of action which, on the level of deeds, seem to exclude each other totally. What they nevertheless have in common is the intuition that violence against the adversary and violence against the self are inseparable; what divides them is the program of dealing with either.

Gandhi's way, as we have seen, is that of a double conversion: the hateful person, by containing his egotistic hate and by learning to love the opponent as human, will confront the opponent with an enveloping technique that will force, or rather permit, him to regain his latent capacity to trust and to love. In all these and other varieties of confrontation, the emphasis is not so much (or not entirely) on the power to be gained as on the cure of an unbearable inner condition. Some of the revolutionaries of today share with Gandhi the readiness to suffer and to die in the pursuit of their conviction that there are ills in the human condition which an insightful person must not tolerate. Gandhi could sympathize with proud and violent youth; but he believed that violence breeds violence from generation to generation and that only the combined insight and discipline of Satyagraha can really disarm man, or rather, give him a power stronger than all arms.

Important new insights often arise when men and women of imagination accept responsibility for a class of men previously bracketed, judged, and diagnosed as doomed to inferiority: the history of psychiatry and its influence on civilization also began with the insight gained by thoughtful practitioners that certain classes of mental patients were unjustly treated by others, including doctors, as though they were possessed by evil or doomed genetically—were a separate species, as it were. Clinical confrontation, too, revealed how the untruthfulness inherent in man's propensity for pseudo-speciation does violence to man.

I therefore will come back to the fact which provided one rationale for this book, namely, that Freud, when he listened to the "free associations" of his confused and yet intelligent and searching patients, heard *himself* and heard *man* in and through their revelations. In noticing the similarity of their imaginative productions to his own dreams, and of both to themes of mythology and literature, he really was "tapping" for clinical purposes a need to verbalize and to confess certain wishes and imaginings which are, in principle, universal themes but come to awareness and verbalization only under a variety of special conditions: from the dreams of the sleep state to daydreams and the content of creative production; from the ravings of insanity to artificially induced "consciousness expansion," and from impulsive confessions to systematic self-revelation in autobiographies. Both religion and politics have made rituals out of man's basic need to confess the past in order to purge it, while psychoanalysis has clarified the way in which many kinds of imaginative productions are also confessions. But psychoanalysis has done more than lay bare such productions; it has created a controlled situation for studying their emergence.

At the end of this discussion it should not come as a shocking conclusion that historicizing *as such* appears to be a process by which man recapitulates the past in order to render—or even surrender—it to the judgment of the future: an adaptive process. Psychoanalysis, then, may well become operative in curing the historical process of some of its built-in impediments and in providing the conscious insights which are unconsciously sought in all manner of indirect self-revelations. I mean to say here that man by understanding the way he historicizes may yet overcome certain stereotyped ways in which history repeats itself—ways which man can no longer afford.

Gandhi's and Freud's methods converge more clearly if I repeat: in both encounters only the militant probing of a vital issue by a nonviolent confrontation can bring to light what insight is ready on both sides. Such probing must be decided on only after careful study, but then the developing encounter must be permitted to show, step by step, what the power of truth may reveal and enact. At the end only a development which transforms both partners in such an encounter is truth in action; and such transformation is possible only where man learns to be nonviolent toward himself as well as toward others. Finally, the truth of Satyagraha and the "reality" of psychoanalysis come somewhat nearer to each other if it is assumed that man's "reality testing" includes an attempt not only to think clearly but also to enter into an optimum of mutual activation with others. But this calls for a combination of clear insight into our central motivations and pervasive faith in the brotherhood of man.

Seen from this vantage point, psychoanalysis offers a method of intervening nonviolently between our overbearing conscience and our raging affects, thus forcing our moral and our "animal" natures to enter into respectful reconciliation.

When I began this book, I did not expect to rediscover psychoanalysis in terms of truth, self-suffering, and nonviolence. But now that I have done so, I see better what I hope the reader has come to see with me, namely, that I felt attracted to the Ahmedabad Event not only because I had learned to know the scene and not only because it was time for me to write about the responsibilities of middle age, but also because I sensed an affinity between Gandhi's truth and the insights of modern psychology. That truth, and these insights, are the legacy of the first part of this century to its remainder. A concrete event has served to illustrate their origins in all the complexity of historical actuality. I did not undertake to do and could not do more than that. But as we historicize more consciously, we also assume some of the burden of tradition. Even one past event, seen in the light of a new awareness, must make it apparent that man denies and abandons the visions and the disciplines he has already acquired only at the risk of historical and personal regression.

MARCH TO THE SEA

from *Gandhi's Truth*

I n 1930, again in the fateful month of March, the Mahatma started a new campaign. He was now leaving Ahmedabad for good, vowing not to return before India had become fully independent. The departure was one of the most dramatic and inspired in history, and a brief account of it is a fitting conclusion to this book—for almost all the men and women, and some of the (then) children who became my friends in Ahmedabad were there the night of March 11. It was the night before the great trek, 200 miles down to the Arabian Sea, where the Mahatma would collect some grains of salt from India's ocean.

The 1920s had provided Gandhi with time for different seasons: a year of undisputed leadership of Congress and the nation, and two years in jail; the "silent year" and the years of autobiographic introspection; another year of despair and illness, and years of inner rebuilding and ambulatory reforming, from village to village.

Now the Mahatma felt ready to stake everything once more on a national Satyagraha—the Salt Satyagraha. For the Salt Act was to be the eminently practical and highly symbolic focus of this campaign of civil disobedience. It netted the English only £25 million out of the eight hundred million pounds yearly collected from India. But these revenues were drawn, literally, from the sweat of the poorest and from a commodity lavishly available to all along the thousands of miles of Indian seashore. One little town, Dandi, near Jalalpur on the entrance to the Gulf of Cambay, would be the scene for the gesture of freedom—and the bloodiest reprisals.

Again, a letter had been sent to the Viceroy: "Dear Friend. . . ." But this time there had been no equivocation: "I hold the British rule to be a curse." Yet: "I do not intend harm to a single Englishman or to any legitimate interest he may have in India." He had pleaded with the Viceroy "on bended knee" to work for the repeal of the Salt Act, reminding the Emperor's representative with his usual militancy *ad hominem* that his salary was five thousand times that of India's average income. He had concluded:

My ambition is no less than to convert the British people through non-violence, and thus make them see the wrong they have done to India. I do not seek to harm your people. I want to serve them even as I want to serve my own. . . .[1]

But His Excellency had only let him know through his secretary that he "regretted to learn," etc.

The evening of March 11, Gandhiji had held his last prayer meeting. To thousands he had announced:

In all probability this will be my last speech to you. Even if the Government allows me to march tomorrow morning, this will be my last speech on the sacred banks of the Sabarmati. Possibly these may be the last words of my life here.

I have already told you yesterday what I had to say. Today I shall confine myself to what you should do after my companions and I are arrested. The programme of the march to Jalalpur must be fulfilled as originally settled. The enlistment of volunteers for this purpose should be confined to Gujarat. From what I have seen and heard during the last fortnight, I am inclined to believe that the stream of civil resisters will flow unbroken.

But let there be not a semblance of breach of peace even after all of us have been arrested. We have resolved to utilize all our resources in the pursuit of an exclusively non-violent struggle. Let no one commit

a wrong in anger. This is my hope and prayer. I wish these words of
mine reached every nook and corner of the land.[2]

This time he could speak with more realistic assurance and less vain-
glorious hope. For this time there was an army at his command. This
army even had a uniform, if one denoting poverty and humility: it was
made of khadi, showed no rank, and was topped by the Gandhi cap, a fac-
simile of the jail prisoners' headgear. Gandhi was the leader; but other
commanders were posted all over the land: Vallabhbhai Patel would stay
in Ahmedabad, Rajagopolachari in Madras, Sen Gupta in Calcutta—and
Nehru in Allahabad: "Let nobody assume that after I am arrested there
will be no one left to guide you. It is not I, but Pandit Jawaharlal who is
your guide. He has the capacity to lead."

Whatever other measures of civil disobedience were indicated in various regions would be decided by responsible subleaders. Gandhi concentrated on the main issue:

> Wherever possible, civil disobedience of Salt laws should be started.
> These laws can be violated in three ways. It is an offence to manufac-
> ture salt wherever there are facilities for doing so. The possession and
> sale of contraband salt (which includes natural salt or salt earth) is also
> an offence. The purchasers of such salt will be equally guilty. To carry
> away the natural salt deposits on the sea-shore is likewise a violation of
> law. So is the hawking of such salt. In short, you may choose any one
> or all of these devices to break the salt monopoly.[3]

This time, a vast group of well-trained Satyagrahis were available, well
trained in controlling as well as in propagandizing large crowds. They all
were held together not only by a joint pledge but also (at least in Gandhi's
vicinity) by the rules of the ashram-in-motion which included the "three
essentials": prayer, spinning, and writing a diary.[4]

And such discipline was to be sorely needed; for this time, the tangible opponent was to be the army as well as the police—mostly Indians
in uniform, then, who were both goaded on by their contemptuous of-
ficers and themselves irritated to the extreme by the seemingly mocking
challenge of wave after wave of unarmed and yet militant civilians.

Among the many well-wishers stretched out on the grounds during
the night (for the month of March can be pleasant in Western India, not

yet too dry and not yet drenched by the monsoon) was the mill owner's wife Saraladevi ("my blood-sister") and her oldest children, daughter Mridula, then 17, who was to become one of Gandhi's dearest if always totally straightforward followers; Gautam, then only 12, who was to become Ambalal's successor; and Vikram, now in charge of India's nuclear development.

But alas, this time there was also the press, from all over India and from "the world." And then, not having been arrested as had been expected ("the government is puzzled and perplexed") Gandhi, in the morning, led his seventy-eight men and women out the gate of the ashram and down the road to Dandi. Among them were Anasuya, and Pyarelal, then a long-time secretary. Shankerlal, the organizer, had been sent ahead to select and prepare the places where the marchers would stop to eat and spin, pray and sleep. The Mahatma was then over sixty, but twelve miles a day for twenty-four days was "child's play." And, indeed, as the documentary films of the day attest, there was a certain gaiety about this pilgrimage through the festooned villages and along roads which the peasants had sprinkled against dust and bedecked with leaves against stones. And at the end, the Mahatma picked up some salt (which, in true Bania fashion, later was sold to the highest bidder nearby and netted 1,600 rupees)—a signal to do likewise for thousands all over the subcontinent who happened to be near the ocean. The raw material was brought inland to be prepared in pans on rooftops and then to be peddled—mostly "pretty awful stuff," as Nehru hardly had time to observe before he was arrested, one of the first of more than fifty thousand to be jailed. But except for some disturbances in Bengal, there was no violence to speak of in any part of India.

The very absence of violence, however, again aroused the police to pointed viciousness. The report of a British journalist, Webb Miller, has become the classical account of Satyagraha on the front line. Under the leadership of Sarojini Naidu and Manilal Gandhi (Devadas and Ramdas had already been arrested), 2,500 volunteers "attacked" the Dharasana Salt Works not far from Dandi.

> In complete silence the Gandhi men drew up and halted a hundred yards from the stockade. A picked column advanced from the crowd, waded the ditches, and approached the barbed-wire stockade. . . . Suddenly at a word of command, scores of native policemen rushed upon

the advancing marchers and rained blows on their heads with their steel-shod lathis. Not one of the marchers even raised an arm to fend off the blows. They went down like ten-pins. From where I stood I heard the sickening whack of the clubs on unprotected skulls. The waiting crowd of marchers groaned and sucked in their breath in sympathetic pain at every blow. Those struck down fell sprawling, unconscious or writhing with fractured skulls or broken shoulders. . . . The survivors, without breaking ranks, silently and doggedly marched on until struck down.

They marched steadily, with heads up, without the encouragement of music or cheering or any possibility that they might escape serious injury or death. The police rushed out and methodically and mechanically beat down the second column. There was no fight, no struggle; the marchers simply walked forward till struck down. . . .[5]

After that, the men in uniform, feeling defenseless in all their superior equipment, could think of doing only what seems to "come naturally" to uniformed men in similar situations: if they did not succeed in bashing in the volunteers' skulls, they kicked and stabbed them in the testicles. "Hour after hour stretcher-bearers carried back a stream of inert, bleeding bodies."[6]

What had the Satyagrahis accomplished? They did not take the Works; nor was the Salt Act formally abolished in its entirety. But this, the world began to realize, was not the point. The Salt Satyagraha had demonstrated to the world the nearly flawless use of a new instrument of peaceful militancy. May it only be added that after another stay in jail, Gandhi met the Viceroy for the famous Tea Party. After some compromises all around, Gandhi was invited to talks with the Viceroy. Churchill scoffed at the "seditious fakir, striding half-naked up the steps of the Viceroy's palace, to negotiate with the representative of the King-Emperor." But the Viceroy, Lord Irwin, has described the meeting as "the most dramatic personal encounter between a Viceroy and an Indian leader." When Gandhi was handed a cup of tea, he poured a bit of salt (tax-free) into it out of a small paper bag hidden in his shawl and remarked smilingly, "to remind us of the famous Boston Tea Party." Moniya and the Empire! The following year he would go to England for a Round Table Conference, the sole representative of Congress and a world leader now immensely popular even with the English masses. What followed in the Mahatma's and in India's life is well documented.[7]

In May 1930 Tagore wrote triumphantly to the *Manchester Guardian* that Europe had now lost her moral prestige in Asia. Weak Asia, he said, praising the Mahatma, "could now afford to look down on Europe where before she looked up." Gandhi, as I read him, might have said it differently: Asia could now look Europe in the eye—not more, not less, not up to, not down on. Where man can and will do that, there, sooner or later, will be mutual recognition.

IV

ON MORAL
MATTERS

F rom the last paragraphs of *Childhood and Society,* his still prominently important first book, to one of his last books, *Insight and Responsibility,* and his last published essay on "The Galilean Sayings," Erik Erikson was constantly giving much thought to ethics (and social ethics), to the rights and wrongs of this life as we come to know and experience them. He started doing so as he tried to understand a large nation, not without its own severe injustice. When he came to America, segregation was very much legally enforced in parts of the country, and African-Americans, by the millions, were voteless and often desperately impoverished. It is noteworthy that *Childhood and Society* has a section on "black identity" and, too, makes mention of "an interracial seminar." Not every psychoanalyst in the United States at the time of the book's publication (1950) was interested in such a grievous problem—indeed the biography by Sara Lawrence Lightfoot of her mother (*Balm in Gilead*), who was a "first psychoanalyst" of a different sort than Freud, the first black person to become one, is sadly and instructively full of stories that, in their sum, tell of an intelligent, forthright, honorable black woman's repeated dismissal at the hands of the whites who, of course, were her only psychoanalytic teachers, future colleagues, during her extended training. The book tells, alas, of an indifference and callousness, even of racism, that existed not only in relatively obscure Mississippi or Alabama sheriff's offices, but in the midst of the haute bourgeoisie of Manhattan, San Francisco, and elsewhere—the narrowness, self-importance, parochialism, and even meanness that can persist, no matter the "enlightenment" that psychoanalysis and higher education might claim or promise.

For Erikson, however, it seemed necessary and only proper that a study of struggling, incapacitated patients, or of "society" as it existed for the well-to-do, or for the poor and distantly removed (Native Americans on reservations, for example) be carried on closer at hand—at the psychoanalytic institutes and training centers, which he felt it fair and reasonable to include in his journey of sorts across our American social terrain. Had not Freud emphasized just such a necessity—that those of us who try to understand others ought to take a good and continuing look inward, at ourselves, the memories, even troubles, we bring to those clinical offices, but also the blind spots? Such a look, for Erikson, meant noticing the smug and even confining or narrowing points of view that all too often can get fitted into a host of self-serving rationalizations, excuses, justifications. Ever loyal to Freud in ways some psychoanalysts had no interest in being, Erikson wrote his concluding message of his first book with a powerfully candid acknowledgment of what was there, he knew, for the seeing and hearing—how success in a profession had brought its own hazards, its moral downside that one could readily recognize. As a consequence of his willingness to take the measure of his own professional kind, he dared hold little back, and the result was an arousing and morally energetic statement that many who admire him still consider one of his finest, most trenchant writing moments—even as his own analyst, Anna Freud, would take up the same line, less directly but no less evidently, in a speech she gave titled "Difficulties in the Path of Psychoanalysis" (1968). Both she and Erikson had seen a once boldly independent and ethically awake psychoanalysis become all too complacently satisfied with its accommodation to social "reality" (and power). At the time each of them spoke out (in the 1950s and 1960s), many of their friends and associates were talking and writing of a "value-free" psychoanalysis, and in a sense arguing that "science" ought (and can) aim to distance itself from a variety of attitudes, injustices, in the name of "objectivity," and to deliberately hold at bay a consideration of what ought be done in the name of certain virtues, causes.

The result was a kind of moral neutrality and an apathy, a coolness of manner and an excessive self-involvement that, alas, abstained from self-criticism, itself a moral act, as in the confessional tradition that St. Augustine knew well, but also as with secularists such as Rousseau and Tolstoy, not to mention Freud himself, his daughter, and their onetime student and analysand, Erik Erikson. Erikson's concluding remarks in *Childhood and Society* have no doubt served as a reminder to many that moral indignation can indeed wane, and alas, be excused in the name of a psychoanalytic experience used as a reason for self-absorption, hence a disregard of others in all their vulnerability. Such a development became "a straw in the wind of a changeable history," Erikson pointedly remarks in a stirring, worried exhortation that is a moral call to arms, lest, in the pursuit of psychological interpretation, that kind of inwardness, all moral and spiritual introspection, be set aside, even abandoned, lost.

Such an incisive and trenchantly explicit statement (an analysis, really, of "analysis" become socially, culturally, all too humanly, a kind of morally "unreflecting egoism," to draw on a phrase of George Eliot's in *Middlemarch*) would not be Erikson's last attempt to warn himself, his fellow psychoanalysts, and his readers of what can go wrong in the name of a tenacious indifference to moral action that is justified in the name of "reality" or "normality." The very title of one of Erikson's later books tells a long story, then: "insight and responsibility" linked and put on a book's jacket as a caveat, lest the former be perused with no concomitant felt requirement to find moral purpose and direction as a consequence of whatever self-awareness is obtained. Indeed, as if he wants to let that phrase become a book's proclamation, Erikson becomes wonderfully, expansively concerned with moral questions, invokes the Golden Rule, even addresses the Sermon on the Mount. Thereby he muses about contemporary psychoanalytic self-examination as some of us experience it—a lack of felt ethical "responsibility" that lives all too comfortably with "insight" achieved. He is worried not only for religious reasons but lest our lives fail to be morally affirmed through our daily existence. He held fast, in contrast, to the hope that our various "insights" be enacted, turned into the daily stuff of values, ideas, thoughtfully and insistently affirmed.

In the early 1970s, as a matter of fact, at a meeting attended by a host of psychiatrists and psychoanalysts, Erikson (then at work on Gandhi's life and on political activity as it is engaged, sometimes, with minds, even souls) spoke to us, eagerly assembled, about his intellectual struggle to make sense of a great leader (published eventually as *Gandhi's Truth*), but also about his "troubles" with a particular individual so much admired throughout the world. "When I learned about Gandhi," Erikson told us, "I kept wondering about his wife and children—and I have to admit, I worried about them." I was listening with a tape recorder, and with others there noted that he was especially candid and poignant as he shared his concerns, provoked by a writing project. "I had to have something out with him [Gandhi]," he told us, and then, this: "I sat there in a daze, unable to put on paper what was crossing my mind—until I felt the need, the desire, to write this man [Gandhi] a letter. He was dead, but he was certainly alive in my mind, and finally, there I was writing a letter to him—I told him (to be brief) that I wished he'd been as understanding and kindly at home with his family as he was in the world with all his associates and followers, and yes, with his enemies, the ones he was confronting and opposing. I guess I was trying to reconcile his brilliant capacity for political 'insight' with his family or everyday 'responsibilities'!"

I can still see, with those words spoken, Erikson's head lowered, even a momentary shake of the head—irony and ambiguity as almost heart-stopping in their capacity to give us much reflective pause. Erikson did, however, proceed; he spoke of Gandhi's spiritual and political triumphs, no matter his not altogether happy personal life as a family man, and of course, many of us in that room weren't totally surprised, because we'd seen such a disparity in many of our apparently successful young or older patients, but also in people like us, in ourselves upon occasion: achievement in school or college or in the worlds of law, business, medicine—yet, all the while, a failure to measure up humanly and therefore morally to the accomplishments being accumulated in classes or workplaces. Some years later, the novelist Walker Percy would summarize what we were discussing at that meeting when he described a character of his in *The Second Coming* as (to paraphrase) "one of those people who get all A's and flunk ordinary living"; and I recall well Erik Erikson, in his study, trying to say as much—though not as pointedly, and not with such a catching punch—when he mused: "It can happen that the qualities that make for good in one part of someone's life don't necessarily have the same effect on that person's 'other life,' you can call it." He became suggestive then—made mention of the "secret side of many brilliant people," or the "cost" of such accomplishments to others, those forsaken or ignored, even insulted or injured—a melancholy matter for all of us to ponder.

Still, our lecturer wanted to move us that day in another direction, stir us as he'd been stirred while he got to "know," as it were, Gandhi, through reading of him, taking in his letters and essays, his remembered remarks; and so we heard for a half hour or more about "grace," its workings and expression in a life as it connected to other lives—a remarkable spell descended on us, I recall feeling, as that presentation took place, and after it, our responsive discussion. Unfortunately, however, the word "grace," as Erikson eagerly and relaxedly used it, caused evident perplexity (even discomfort) in certain of his listeners, who began to move in their chairs, even whisper to one another. Finally, when the talk was over and we were all given the chance to raise our hands, address the speaker with questions or comments, a prominent psychoanalyst asked "what grace means," and then others, following the lead, posed further questions—wanted to know the "source" of grace, its "origins in child development," no less. I could see Erikson flushing, moving his right hand through his ample white hair, telltale signs, in him, of agitation, irritation, if not annoyance. At last, he indicated that he was ready to reply, to have his say—but he remained silent while he noted more hands, took more questions, listened to off-the-cuff remarks, each of them aimed at explaining grace, through resort to psychoanalytic conceptualization. Upon a last inquiring insistence ("How would you define grace?"), Erikson, sitting in a chair on a slightly raised platform in a hospital conference room, looked out a window toward the sky—and then, these words: "Look, if you have to ask, I'm afraid you'll never know." There we all were, and there our meeting ended—a hurried rush for the door, and surely, inevitably, later, the ticlike buzz of psychological reductionism (what *is* his problem that caused his evident anger?). But on his way home from the lecture, Erikson was glad for that moment: "You have to feel sorry for people who won't let anything or anyone *be*, who have to explain, explain, explain—but that's life, I'm afraid, for many of us who have stumbled into this profession of ours, and maybe I should have been more resigned (or amused!) back there, though there are times, maybe, when enough is enough!"

FROM "BEYOND ANXIETY"

from *Childhood and Society*

I would consider *tolerance-indignation* a dimension of the psychotherapist's work. Much has been said and is being said about the therapist's
moral detachment from the multitude of patients who bring to him
varieties of conflicts and solutions: naturally, he must let them find their
own style of integrity. But the analyst has gone further. In analogy to a
certain bird, he has tried to pretend that his values remained hidden because his classical position at the head of the "analytic couch" removed
him from the patient's visual field. We know today that communication
is by no means primarily a verbal matter: words are only the tools of
meanings. In a more enlightened world and under much more complicated historical conditions the analyst must face once more the whole
problem of judicious partnership which expresses the spirit of analytic
work more creatively than does apathetic tolerance or autocratic guidance. The various identities which at first lent themselves to a fusion
with the new identity of the analyst—identities based on talmudic argument, on messianic zeal, on punitive orthodoxy, on faddist sensationalism,
on professional and social ambition—all these identities and their cultural
origins must now become part of the analyst's analysis, so that he may be
able to discard archaic rituals of control and learn to identify with the

lasting value of his job of enlightenment. Only thus can he set free in himself and in his patient that remnant of judicious indignation without which a cure is but a straw in the changeable wind of history.

The "psychoanalytic situation" is a Western and modern contribution to man's age-old attempts at systematic introspection. It began as a psychotherapeutic method and has led to an encompassing psychological theory. I have emphasized in conclusion the possible implications of both theory and practice for a more judicious orientation in the unlimited prospects and dangers of our technological future.

THE GOLDEN RULE IN THE
LIGHT OF NEW INSIGHT

from *Insight and Responsibility*

One cannot long consider the responsibilities suggested by new insight without intruding on the domain of ethics. I was first encouraged to do so when asked to give the George W. Gay Lecture on Medical Ethics in the Harvard Medical School. The themes then presented are repeated and elaborated in the following and final address which was given for the University of Delhi and the India International Centre in New Delhi in January 1963.

W hen a lecture is announced one does not usually expect the title to foretell very much about the content. But it must be rare, indeed, that a title is as opaque as the one on your invitation to this lecture: for it does not specify the field from which new insight is to come and throw new light on the old principle of the Golden Rule. You took a chance, then, in coming, and now that I have been introduced as a psychoanalyst, you must feel that you have taken a double chance.

Let me tell you, therefore, how I came upon our subject. In Harvard College, I teach a course, "The Human Life Cycle." There (since I am by experience primarily a clinician) we begin by considering those aggravated *crises* which mark each stage of life and are known to psychiatry as potentially pathogenic. But we proceed to discuss the potential *strengths* which each stage contributes to human maturity. In either case, so psychiatric experience and the observation of healthy children tell us, much depends on the interplay of generations in which human strength can be revitalized or human weakness perseverated "into the second and third generation." But this leads us to the role of the individual in the sequence of generations, and thus to that evolved order which your scriptures call *Lokasangraha*—the "maintenance of the world" (in Professor Radhakrishnan's translation). Through the study of case-histories and of life-histories we psychoanalysts have begun to discern certain fateful and certain fruitful patterns of interaction in those most concrete categories (parent and child, man and woman, teacher and pupil) which carry the burden of maintenance from generation to generation. The implication of our insights for ethics had preoccupied me before I came here; and, as you will well understand, a few months of animated discussion in India have by no means disabused me from such concerns. I have, therefore, chosen to tell you where I stand in my teaching, in the hope of learning more from you in further discussion.

My base line is the Golden Rule, which advocates that one should do (or not do) to another what one wishes to be (or not to be) done by. Systematic students of ethics often indicate a certain disdain for this all-too-primitive ancestor of more logical principles; and Bernard Shaw found the rule an easy target: don't do to another what you would like to be done by, he warned, because his tastes may differ from yours. Yet this rule has marked a mysterious meeting ground between ancient peoples separated by oceans and eras, and has provided a hidden theme in the most memorable sayings of many thinkers.

The Golden Rule obviously concerns itself with one of the very basic paradoxes of human existence. Each man calls his own a separate body, a self-conscious individuality, a personal awareness of the cosmos, and a certain death; and yet he shares this world as a *reality* also perceived and judged by others and as an *actuality* within which he must commit himself to ceaseless interaction. This is acknowledged in your scriptures as the principle of Karma.

To identify self-interest and the interest of other selves, the Rule alternately employs the method of warning, "Do *not* as you would *not* be done by," and of exhortation, "Do, as you *would* be done by." For psychological appeal, some versions rely on a minimum of *egotistic prudence*, while others demand a maximum of *altruistic sympathy*. It must be admitted that the formula, "Do not to others what if done to you would cause you pain," does not presuppose much more than the mental level of the small child who desists from pinching when it gets pinched in return. More mature insight is assumed in the saying, "No one is a believer until he loves for his brother what he loves for himself." Of all the versions, however, none commit us as unconditionally as the Upanishad's, "he who sees all beings in his own self and his own self in all beings," and the Christian injunction, "love thy neighbor as thyself." They even suggest a true love and a true knowledge of ourselves. Freud, of course, took this Christian maxim deftly apart as altogether illusory, thus denying with the irony of the enlightenment what a maxim really is—and what (as I hope to show) his method may really stand for.

I will not (I could not) trace the versions of the Rule to various world religions. No doubt in English translation all of them have become somewhat assimilated to Biblical versions. Yet the basic formula seems to be universal, and it re-appears in an astonishing number of the most revered sayings of our civilization, from St. Francis' prayer to Kant's moral imperative and Lincoln's simple political creed: "As I would not be slave, I would not be master."

The variations of the Rule have, of course, provided material for many a discussion of ethics weighing the soundness of the logic implied and measuring the degree of ethical nobility reached in each. My field of inquiry, the clinical study of the human life cycle, suggests that I desist from arguing logical merit or spiritual worth and instead distinguish *variations in moral and ethical sensitivity* in accordance with stages in the development of human conscience.

The dictionary, our first refuge from ambiguity, in this case only confounds it: morals and ethics are defined as synonyms *and* antonyms of each other. In other words, they are the same, with a difference—a difference which I intend to emphasize. For it is clear that he who knows what is legal or illegal and what is moral or immoral has not necessarily learned thereby what is ethical. Highly moralistic people can do unethical things, while an ethical man's involvement in immoral doings becomes by inner necessity an occasion for tragedy.

I would propose that we consider *moral rules* of conduct to be based on a fear of *threats* to be forestalled. These may be outer threats of abandonment, punishment, and public exposure, or a threatening inner sense of guilt, of shame, or of isolation. In either case, the rationale for obeying a rule may not be too clear; it is the threat that counts. In contrast, I would consider *ethical rules* to be based on *ideals* to be striven for with a high degree of rational assent and with a ready consent to a formulated good, a definition of perfection, and some promise of self-realization. This differentiation may not agree with all existing definitions, but it is substantiated by the observation of human development. Here, then, is my first proposition: the moral and the ethical sense are different in their psychological dynamics, because the moral sense develops on an earlier, more immature level. This does not mean that the moral sense could be skipped, as it were. On the contrary, all that exists layer upon layer in an adult's mind has developed step by step in the growing child's, and all the major steps in the comprehension of what is considered good behavior in one's cultural universe are—for better and for worse—related to different stages in individual maturation. But they are all necessary to one another.

The response to a moral tone of voice develops early, and many an adult is startled when inadvertently he makes an infant cry, because his voice has conveyed more disapproval than he intended to. Yet, the small child, so limited to the intensity of the moment, somehow must learn the boundaries marked by "don'ts." Here, cultures have a certain leeway in underscoring the goodness of one who does not transgress or the evilness of one who does. But the conclusion is unavoidable that children can be made to feel evil, and that adults continue to project evil on one another and on their children far beyond the verdict of rational judgment. Mark Twain once characterized man as "the animal that blushes."

Psychoanalytic observation first established the psychological basis of a fact which Eastern thinkers have always known, namely, that the radical division into good and bad can be *the* sickness of the mind. It has traced the moral scruples and excesses of the adult to the childhood stages in which guilt and shame are ready to be aroused and are easily exploited. It has named and studied the "super-ego" which hovers over the ego as the inner perpetuation of the child's subordination to the restraining will of his elders. The voice of the super-ego is not always cruel and derisive, but it is ever ready to become so whenever the precarious balance which we call a good conscience is upset, at which times the secret weapons of this inner governor are revealed: the brand of shame and the bite of conscience. We who deal with the consequences in individual neuroses and in collective irrationality must ask ourselves whether excessive guilt and excessive shame are "caused" or merely accentuated by the pressure of parental and communal methods, by the threat of loss of affection, of corporal punishment, of public shaming. Or are they by now a proclivity for self-alienation which has become a part—and, to some extent, a necessary part—of man's evolutionary heritage?

All we know for certain is that the moral proclivity in man does not develop without the establishment of some chronic self-doubt and some truly terrible—even if largely submerged—rage against anybody and anything that reinforces such doubt. The "lowest" in man is thus apt to reappear in the guise of the "highest." Irrational and pre-rational combinations of goodness, doubt, and rage can re-emerge in the adult in those malignant forms of righteousness and prejudice which we may call *moralism*. In the name of high moral principles all the vindictiveness of derision, of torture, and of mass extinction can be employed. One surely must come to the conclusion that the Golden Rule was meant to protect man not only against his enemy's open attacks, but also against his friend's righteousness.

L est this view, in spite of the evidence of history, seem too "clinical," we turn to the writings of the evolutionists who in the last few decades have joined psychoanalysis in recognizing the super-ego as an evolutionary fact—and danger. The *developmental* principle is thus joined by an *evolutionary* one. Waddington[1] even goes so far as to say that super-ego rigidity may be an overspecialization in the human race, like the excessive body armor of the late dinosaurs. In a less grandiose comparison he likens the super-ego to "the finicky adaptation of certain parasites which fits them to live only on one host animal." In recommending his book, *The Ethical Animal,* I must admit that his terminology contradicts mine. He calls the awakening of morality in childhood a proclivity for "ethicizing," whereas I would prefer to call it moralizing. As do many animal psychologists, he dwells on analogies between the very young child and the young animal instead of comparing, as I think we must, the young animal with the pre-adult human, including the adolescent.

In fact, I must introduce here an amendment to my first, my "developmental" proposition, for between the development in childhood of man's *moral* proclivity and that of his *ethical* powers in adulthood, adolescence intervenes when he perceives the universal good in *ideological* terms. The imagery of steps in development, of course, is useful only where it is to be suggested that one item precedes another in such a way that the earlier one is necessary to the later ones and that each later one is of a higher order.

This "epigenetic" principle, according to which the constituent parts of a ground plan develop during successive stages, will be immediately familiar to you. For in the traditional Hindu concept of the life cycle the four intrinsic goals of life (Dharma, the orders that define virtue; Artha, the powers of the actual; Kama, the joys of libidinal abandon; and Moksha, the peace of deliverance) come to their successive and mutual perfection during the four stages, the ashramas of the apprentice, the householder, the hermit, and the ascetic. These stages are divided from each other by sharp turns of direction; yet, each depends on the previous one, and whatever perfection is possible depends on them all.

I would not be able to discuss the relation of these two foursomes to each other, nor ready to compare this ideal conception to our epigenetic views of the life cycle. But the affinities of the two conceptions are apparent, and at least the ideological indoctrination of the apprentice, the Brahmacharya, and the ethical one of the Grihasta, the householder, correspond to the developmental categories suggested here.

No wonder; for it is the joint development of cognitive and emotional powers paired with appropriate social learning which enables the individual to realize the potentialities of a stage. Thus youth becomes ready— if often only after a severe bout with moralistic regression—to envisage the more universal principles of a highest human good. The adolescent learns to grasp the flux of time, to anticipate the future in a coherent way, to perceive ideas and to assent to ideals, to take—in short—an *ideological* position for which the younger child is cognitively not prepared. In adolescence, then, an ethical view is approximated, but it remains susceptible to an alternation of impulsive judgment and odd rationalization. It is, then, as true for adolescence as it is for childhood that man's way stations to maturity can become fixed, can become premature end stations, or stations for future regression.

The moral sense, in its perfections and its perversions, has been an intrinsic part of man's *evolution,* while the sense of ideological rejuvenation has pervaded his *revolutions,* both with prophetic idealism and with destructive fanaticism. Adolescent man, in all his sensitivity to the ideal, is easily exploited by promises of counterfeit millennia, easily taken in by the promise of a new and arrogantly exclusive identity.

The *true* ethical sense of the young adult, finally, encompasses and goes beyond moral restraint and ideal vision, while insisting on concrete commitments to those intimate relationships and work associations by which man can hope to share a lifetime of productivity and competence. But young adulthood engenders its own dangers. It adds to the moralist's righteousness, and to the ideologist's fanatic repudiation of all otherness, the *territorial defensiveness* of one who has appropriated and staked out his earthly claim and who seeks eternal security in the super-identity of organizations. Thus, what the Golden Rule at its highest has attempted to make all-inclusive, tribes and nations, castes and classes, moralities and ideologies have consistently made exclusive again—proudly, superstitiously, and viciously denying the status of reciprocal ethics to those "outside."

If I have so far underscored the malignant potentials of man's slow maturation, I have done so not in order to dwell on a kind of dogmatic pessimism which can emerge all too easily from clinical preoccupation and often leads only to anxious avoidances. I know that man's moral, ideological, and ethical propensities can find, and have found on occasion, a sublime integration, in individuals and in groups who were both tolerant and firm, both flexible and strong, both wise and obedient. Above all, men have always shown a dim knowledge of their better potentialities by paying homage to those purest leaders who taught the simplest and most inclusive rules for an undivided mankind. I will have a word to say later about Gandhi's continued "presence" in India. But men have also persistently betrayed them, on what passed for moral or ideological grounds, even as they are now preparing a potential betrayal of the human heritage on scientific and technological grounds in the name of that which is considered good merely because it can be made to work—no matter where it leads. No longer do we have license to emphasize either the "positive" or the "negative" in man. Step for step, they go together: moralism with moral obedience, fanaticism with ideological devotion, and rigid conservatism with adult ethics.

Man's socio-genetic evolution is about to reach a crisis in the full sense of the word, a crossroads offering one path to fatality, and one to recovery and further growth. Artful perverter of joy and keen exploiter of strength, man is the animal that has learned to survive "in a fashion," to multiply without food for the multitudes, to grow up healthily without reaching personal maturity, to live well but without purpose, to invent ingeniously without aim, and to kill grandiosely without need. But the processes of socio-genetic evolution also seem to promise a new humanism, the acceptance by man—as an evolved product as well as a producer, and a self-conscious tool of further evolution—of the obligation to be guided in his planned actions and his chosen self-restraints by his knowledge and his insights. In this endeavor, then, it may be of a certain importance to learn to understand and to master the differences between infantile morality, adolescent ideology, and adult ethics. Each is necessary to the next, but each is effective only if they eventually combine in that wisdom which, as Waddington puts it, "fulfills sufficiently the function of mediating evolutionary advance."

At the point, however, when one is about to end an argument with a global injunction of what we *must* do, it is well to remember Blake's admonition that the common good readily becomes the topic of "the scoundrel, the hypocrite, and the flatterer"; and that he who would do some good must do so in "minute particulars." And indeed, I have so far spoken only of the developmental and the evolutionary principle, according to which the propensity for ethics grows in the individual as part of an adaptation roughly laid down by evolution. Yet, to grow in the individual, ethics must be generated and regenerated in and by the sequence of generations—again, a matter fully grasped and systematized, some will say stereotyped, in the Hindu tradition. I must now make more explicit what our insights tell us about this process.

Let me make an altogether new start here. Let us look at scientific man in his dealings with animals and let us assume (this is not a strange assumption in India) that animals, too, may have a place close to the "other" included in the Rule. The psychologists among you know Professor Harry Harlow's studies on the development of what he calls affection in monkeys.[2] He did some exquisite experimental and photographic work attempting, in the life of laboratory monkeys, to "control the mother variable." He took monkeys from their mothers within a few hours after birth, isolated them, and left them with "mothers" made out of wire, metal, wood, and terry cloth. A rubber nipple somewhere in their middles emitted piped-in milk, and the whole contraption was wired for body warmth. All the "variables" of this mother situation were controlled: the amount of rocking, the temperature of the "skin," and the exact incline of the maternal body necessary to make a scared monkey feel safe and comfortable. Years ago, when this method was presented as a study of the development of affection in monkeys, the clinician could not help wondering whether the small animals' obvious attachment to this contraption was really *monkey* affection or a fetishist addiction to inanimate objects. And, indeed, while these laboratory reared monkeys became healthier and healthier, and much more easily trained in technical know-how than the inferior animals brought up by mere monkey mothers, they became at the end what Harlow calls "psychotics." They sit passively, they stare vacantly, and some do a terrifying thing: when poked they bite themselves and tear at their own flesh until the blood flows. They have not learned to experience "the other," whether as mother, mate, child—or enemy. Only a tiny minority of the females produced offspring, and only one of them made an attempt to nurse hers. But science remains a wonderful thing. Now that we have succeeded in producing "psychotic" monkeys experimentally, we can convince ourselves that we have at last given scientific support to the theory that severely disturbed mother-child relationships "cause" human psychosis.

This is a long story; but it speaks for Professor Harlow's methods that what they demonstrate is unforgettable. At the same time, they lead us to that borderline where we recognize that the scientific approach toward living beings must be with concepts and methods adequate to the study of ongoing life, not of selective extinction. I have put it this way: one can study the nature of things by doing something *to* them, but one can really learn something about the essential nature of living beings only by doing something *with* them or *for* them. This, of course, is the principle of clinical science. It does not deny that one can learn by dissecting the dead, or that animal or man can be motivated to lend circumscribed parts of themselves to an experimental procedure. But for the study of those central transactions which are the carriers of socio-genetic evolution, and for which we must take responsibility in the future, the chosen unit of observation must be the generation, not the individual. Whether an individual animal or human being has partaken of the stuff of life can only be tested by the kind of observation which includes his ability to transmit life—in some essential form—to the next generation.

One remembers here the work of Konrad Lorenz, and the kind of "inter-living" research which he and others have developed, making—in principle—the life cycle of certain selected animals part of the same environment in which the observer lives his own life cycle, studying his own role as well as theirs and taking his chances with what his ingenuity can discern in a setting of sophisticated naturalist inquiry. One remembers also Elsa the Lioness, a foundling who was brought up in the Adamson household in Kenya. There the mother variable was not controlled, it was in control. Mrs. Adamson and her husband even felt responsible for putting grown-up Elsa back among the lions and succeeded in sending her back to the bush, where she mated and had cubs, and yet came back from time to time (accompanied by her cubs) to visit her human foster parents. In our context, we cannot fail to wonder about the built-in "moral" sense that made Elsa respond—and respond in very critical situations, indeed—to the words, "No, Elsa, no," *if* the words came from human beings she trusted. Yet, even with this built-in "moral" response, and with a lasting trust in her foster parents (which she transmitted to her wild cubs) she was able to live as a wild lion. Her mate, however, never appeared; he apparently was not too curious about her folks.

The point of this and similar stories is that our habitual relationship to what we call beasts in nature and "instinctive" or "instinctual" beastliness in ourselves may be highly distorted by thousands of years of superstition, and that there may be resources for peace even in our "animal nature" if we will only learn to nurture nature, as well as to master it. Today, we can teach a monkey, in the very words of the Bible, to "eat the flesh of his own arm," even as we can permit "erring leaders" to make of all mankind the "fuel of the fire." Yet, it seems equally plausible that we can also let our children grow up to lead "the calf and the young lion and the fatling together"—in nature and in their own nature.

To recognize one of man's prime resources, however, we must trace back his individual development to his *pre-moral* days, his infancy. His earliest social experimentation at that time leads to a certain ratio of basic trust and basic mistrust—a ratio which, if favorable, establishes the fundamental human strength: hope. This over-all attitude emerges as the newborn organism reaches out to its caretakers and as they bring to it what we will now discuss as *mutuality*. The failure of basic trust and of mutuality has been recognized in psychiatry as the most far-reaching failure, undercutting all development. We know how tragic and deeply pathogenic its absence can be in children and parents who cannot arouse and cannot respond. It is my further proposition, then, that all moral, ideological, and ethical propensities depend on this early experience of mutuality.

I would call mutuality a relationship in which partners depend on each other for the development of their respective strengths. A baby's first responses can be seen as part of an actuality consisting of many details of mutual arousal and response. While the baby initially smiles at a mere configuration resembling the human face, the adult cannot help smiling back, filled with expectations of a "recognition" which he needs to secure from the new being as surely as it needs him. The fact is that the mutuality of adult and baby is the original source of hope, the basic ingredient of all effective as well as ethical human action. As far back as 1895, Freud, in his first outline of a "Psychology for Neurologists," confronts the "helpless" newborn infant with a "help-rich" *("hilfreich")* adult, and postulates that their mutual understanding is "the primal source of all moral motives."[3] Should we, then, endow the Golden Rule with a principle of mutuality, replacing the reciprocity of both prudence and sympathy?

Here we must add the observation that a parent dealing with a child will be strengthened in *his* vitality, in *his* sense of identity, and in *his* readiness for ethical action by the very ministrations by means of which he secures to the child vitality, future identity, and eventual readiness for ethical action.

But we should avoid making a new Utopia out of the "mother-child relationship." The paradise of early childhood must be abandoned—a fact which man has as yet not learned to accept. The earliest mutuality is only a beginning and leads to more complicated encounters, as both the child and his interaction with a widening circle of persons grow more complicated. I need only point out that the second basic set of vital strengths in childhood (following trust and hope) is autonomy and will, and it must be clear that a situation in which the child's willfulness faces the adult's will is a different proposition from that of the mutuality of instilling hope. Yet, any adult who has managed to train a child's will must admit—for better or for worse—that he has learned much about himself and about will that he never knew before, something which cannot be learned in any other way. Thus each growing individual's developing strength "dovetails" with the strengths of an increasing number of persons arranged about him in the formalized orders of family, school, community, and society. But orders and rules are kept alive only by those "virtues" of which Shakespeare says (in what appears to me to be *his* passionate version of the Rule) that they, "shining upon others heat them and they retort that heat again to the first giver."

One more proposition must be added to the developmental and to the generational one, and to that of mutuality. It is implied in the term "activate," and I would call it the principle of *active choice*. It is, I think, most venerably expressed in St. Francis's prayer: "Grant that I may not so much seek to be consoled as to console; to be understood, as to understand; to be loved as to love; for it is in giving that we receive." Such commitment to an initiative in love is, of course, contained in the admonition to "love thy neighbor." I think that we can recognize in these words a psychological verity, namely, that only he who approaches an encounter in a (consciously and unconsciously) active and giving attitude, rather than in a demanding and dependent one, will be able to make of that encounter what it can become.

With these considerations in mind, then, I will try to formulate my understanding of the Golden Rule. I have been reluctant to come to this point; it has taken thousands of years and many linguistic acrobatics to translate this Rule from one era to another and from one language into another, and at best one can only confound it again, in a somewhat different way.

I would advocate a general orientation which has its center in whatever activity or activities gives man the feeling, as William James put it, of being "most deeply and intensely active and alive." In this, so James promises, each one will find his "real me"; but, I would now add, he will also acquire the experience that *truly worthwhile acts enhance a mutuality between the doer and the other—a mutuality which strengthens the doer even as it strengthens the other.* Thus, the "doer" and "the other" are partners in one deed. Seen in the light of human development, this means that the doer is activated in whatever strength is *appropriate to his age, stage, and condition,* even as he activates in the other the strength appropriate to *his* age, stage, and condition. Understood this way, the Rule would say that it is best to do to another what will strengthen you even as it will strengthen him— that is, what will develop his best potentials even as it develops your own.

This variation of the Rule is obvious enough when applied to the relation of parent and child. But does the uniqueness of their respective positions, which has served as our model so far, have any significant analogies in other situations in which uniqueness depends on a divided function?

To return to particulars, I will attempt to apply my amendment to the diversity of function in the two sexes. I have not dwelled so far on this most usual subject of a psychoanalytic discourse, sexuality. So much of this otherwise absorbing aspect of life has, in recent years, become stereotyped in theoretical discussion. Among the terminological culprits to be blamed for this sorry fact is the psychoanalytic term "love object." For this word "object" in Freud's theory has been taken too literally by many of his friends and by most of his enemies—and moralistic critics do delight in misrepresenting a man's transitory formulations as his ultimate "values." The fact is that Freud, on purely conceptual grounds, and on the basis of the scientific language of his laboratory days, pointed out that drive energies have "objects." But he certainly never advocated that men or women should treat one another as objects on which to live out their sexual idiosyncrasies.

Instead, his central theory of genitality which combines strivings of sexuality and of love points to one of those basic mutualities in which *a partner's potency and potentialities are activated even as he activates the other's potency and potentialities.* Freud's theory implies that a man will be more a man to the extent to which he makes a woman more a woman—and vice versa—because only two uniquely different beings can enhance their respective uniqueness for one another. A "genital" person in Freud's sense is thus more apt to act in accordance with Kant's version of the Golden Rule, in that he would so act as to treat humanity "whether in his person or in another, always as an end, and never as only a means." What Freud added to the ethical principle, however, is a methodology which opens to our inquiry and to our influence the powerhouse of inner forces. For they provide the shining heat for our strengths—and the smoldering smoke of our weaknesses.

I cannot leave the subject of the two sexes without a word on the uniqueness of women. One may well question whether or not the Rule in its oldest form tacitly meant to include women as partners in the golden deal. Today's study of lives still leaves quite obscure the place of women in what is most relevant in the male image of man. True, women are being granted *equality* of political rights, and the recognition of a certain *sameness* in mental and moral equipment. But what they have not begun to earn, partially because they have not cared to ask for it, is the *equal right to be effectively unique,* and to use hard-won rights in the service of what they uniquely represent in human evolution. The West has much

to learn, for example, from the unimpaired womanliness of India's modern women. But there is today a universal sense of the emergence of a
new feminism as part of a more inclusive humanism. This coincides with
a growing conviction—highly ambivalent, to be sure—that the future of
mankind cannot depend on men alone and may well depend on the fate
of a "mother variable" uncontrolled by technological man. The resistance
to such a consideration always comes from men and women who are
mortally afraid that by emphasizing what is unique one may tend to re-
emphasize what is unequal. And, indeed, the study of life histories confirms a far-reaching sameness in men and women insofar as they express
the mathematical architecture of the universe, the organization of logical thought, and the structure of language. But such a study also suggests
that while boys and girls can think and act and talk alike, they naturally
do not experience their bodies (and thus the world) alike. I have attempted to demonstrate this by pointing to sex differences in the struc-
turalization of space in the play of children.[4] But I assume that a
uniqueness of either sex will be granted without proof, and that the
"difference" acclaimed by the much-quoted Frenchman is not considered
only a matter of anatomical appointments for mutual sexual enjoyment,
but a psychobiological difference central to two great modes of life, the
paternal and the *maternal* modes. The amended Golden Rule suggests
that one sex enhances the uniqueness of the other; it also implies that
each, to be really unique, depends on a mutuality with an equally unique
partner.

From the most intimate human encounters we now turn to a professional, and yet relatively intimate, one: that between healer and patient.
There is a very real and specific inequality in the relationship of doctor
and patient in their roles of knower and known, helper and sufferer,
practitioner of life and victim of disease and death. For this reason medical people have their own and unique professional oath and strive to live
up to a universal ideal of "the doctor." Yet the practice of the healing arts
permits extreme types of practitioners, from the absolute authoritarian
over homes and clinics to the harassed servant of demanding mankind,
from the sadist of mere proficiency, to the effusive lover of all (well, almost all) of his patients. Here, too, Freud has thrown intimate and orig-

inal light on the workings of a unique relationship. His letters to his friend and mentor Fliess illustrate the singular experience which made him recognize in his patients what he called "transference"—that is, the patient's wish to exploit sickness and treatment for infantile and regressive ends. But more, Freud, recognized a "countertransference" in the healer's motivation to exploit the patient's transference and to dominate or serve, possess or love him to the disadvantage of his true function. He made systematic insight into transference *and* countertransference part of the training of the psychoanalytic practitioner.

I would think that all of the motivations necessarily entering so vast and so intricate a field could be reconciled in a Golden Rule amended to include a mutuality of divided function. Each specialty and each technique in its own way permits the medical man to *develop as a practitioner, and as a person, even as the patient is cured as a patient, and as a person.* For a real cure transcends the transitory state of patienthood. It is an experience which enables the cured patient to develop and to transmit to home and neighborhood an attitude toward health which is one of the most essential ingredients of an ethical outlook.

Beyond this, can the healing arts and sciences contribute to a new ethical outlook? This question always recurs in psychoanalysis and is usually disposed of with Freud's original answer that the psychoanalyst represents the ethics of scientific truth only and is committed to studying ethics (or morality) in a scientific way. Beyond this, he leaves *Weltanschauungen* (ethical world views) to others.

It seems to me, however, that the clinical arts and sciences, while employing the scientific method, are not defined by it or limited by it. The healer is committed to a highest good, the preservation of life and the furtherance of well-being—the "maintenance of life." He need not prove scientifically that these are, in fact, the highest good; rather, he is precommitted to this basic proposition while investigating what can be verified by scientific means. This, I think, is the meaning of the Hippocratic oath, which subordinates all medical method to a humanist ethic. True, a man can separate his personal, his professional, and his scientific ethics, seeking fulfillment of idiosyncratic needs in personal life, the welfare of others in his profession, and truths independent of personal preference or service in his research. However, there are psychological limits to the multiplicity of values a man can live by, and, in the end, not only the prac-

titioner, but also his patient and his research, depend on a certain unification in him of temperament, intellect, and ethics. This unification
clearly characterizes great doctors.

While it is true, then, that as scientists we must study ethics objectively,
we are, as professional individuals, committed to a unification of personality, training, and conviction which alone will help us to do our work
adequately. At the same time, as transient members of the human race, we
must record the truest meaning of which the fallible methods of our era
and the accidental circumstances of our existence have made us aware. In
this sense, there is (and always has been) not only an ethics governing
clinical work, and a clinical approach to the study of ethics, but also a
contribution to ethics of the healing orientation. The healer, furthermore, has now committed himself to prevention on a large scale, and he
cannot evade the problem of assuring ethical vitality to all lives saved from
undernourishment, morbidity, and early mortality. Man's technical ability and social resolve to prevent accidental conception makes every child
conceived a subject of universal responsibility.

As I approach my conclusion, let me again change my focus and devote
a few minutes to a matter political and economic as well as ethical:
Gandhi's "Rule."

In Ahmedabad I had occasion to visit Gandhi's ashram across the
Sabarmati River; and it was not long before I realized that in Ahmedabad
a hallowed and yet eminently concrete event had occurred which perfectly exemplifies everything I am trying to say. I refer, of course, to
Gandhi's leadership in the lock-out and strike of the mill-workers in
1918, and his first fast in a public cause. This event is well known in the
history of industrial relations the world over, and vaguely known to all
educated Indians. Yet, I believe that only in Ahmedabad, among surviving witnesses and living institutions, can one fathom the "presence" of
that event as a lastingly successful "experiment" in local industrial relations, influential in Indian politics, and, above all, representing a new
type of encounter in divided human functions. The details of the strike
and of the settlement need not concern us here. As usual, it began as a
matter of wages. Nor can I take time to indicate the limited political and
economic applicability of the Ahmedabad experiment to other industrial
areas in and beyond India. What interests us here, is the fact that Gandhi,

from the moment of his entry into the struggle, considered it an occasion not for maximum reciprocal coercion resulting in the usual compromise, but as an opportunity for all—the workers, the owners, and himself—"to rise from the present conditions."[5]

The utopian quality of the principles on which he determined to focus can only be grasped by one who can visualize the squalor of the workmen's living conditions, the latent panic in the ranks of the paternalistic millowners (beset by worries of British competition), and Gandhi's then as yet relative experience in handling the masses of India. The shadows of defeat, violence, and corruption hovered over every one of the "lofty" words which I am about to quote. But to Gandhi, any worthwhile struggle must "transform the inner life of the people." Gandhi spoke to the workers daily under the famous Babul Tree outside the medieval Shahpur Gate. He had studied their desperate condition, yet he urged them to ignore the threats and the promises of the millowners who in the obstinate fashion of all "haves" feared the anarchic insolence and violence of the "have nots." He knew that they feared him, too, for they had indicated that they might even accept his terms if only he would promise to leave and to stay away forever. But he settled down to prove that a just man could "secure the good of the workers while safeguarding the good of the employers"—the two opposing sides being represented by a sister and a brother, Anasuyabehn and Ambalal Sarabhai. Under the Babul Tree Gandhi announced the principle which somehow corresponds to our amended Rule: *"That line of action is alone justice which does not harm either party to a dispute."* By harm he meant—and his daily announcements leave no doubt of this—an inseparable combination of economic disadvantage, social indignity, loss of self-esteem, and latent vengeance.

Neither side found it easy to grasp this principle. When the workers began to weaken, Gandhi suddenly declared a fast. Some of his friends, he admitted, considered this "foolish, unmanly, or worse"; and some were deeply distressed. But, "I wanted to show you," he said to the workers, "that I was not playing with you." He was, as we would say, in dead earnest, and this fact, then as later, immediately raised an issue of local conscience to national significance. In daily appeals, Gandhi stressed variously those basic inner strengths without which no issue has "virtue," namely, will with justice, purpose with discipline, respect for work of any kind, and truthfulness. But he knew, and he said so, that these masses of

illiterate men and women, newly arrived from the villages and already exposed to proletarization, did not have the moral strength or the social solidarity to adhere to principle without strong leadership. "You have yet to
learn how and when to take an oath," he told them. The oath, the dead
earnestness, then, was as yet the leader's privilege and commitment. In the
end the matter was settled, not without a few Gandhian compromises to
save face all around, but with a true acceptance of the settlement originally proposed by Gandhi.

I do not claim to understand the complex motivations and curious
turns of Gandhi's mind—some contradicting Western rigidity in matters
of principle, and some, I assume, strange to Indian observers, as well. I can
also see in Gandhi's actions a paternalism which may now be "dated." But
his monumental simplicity and total involvement in the "experiment"
made both workers and owners revere him. And he himself said with
humorous awe, "I have never come across such a fight." For, indeed both
sides had matured in a way that lifted labor relations in Ahmedabad to a
new and lasting level. Let me quote only the fact that, in 1950, the
Ahmedabad Textile Labor Organization accounted for only a twentieth
of India's union membership, but for eighty per cent of its welfare ex-
penditures.

Such a singular historical event, then, reveals something essential in
human strength, in traditional Indian strength and in the power of
Gandhi's own personal transformation at the time. To me, the miracle of
the Ahmedabad experiment has been not only its lasting success and its
tenacity during those days of anarchic violence which after the great
partition broke down so many dams of solidarity, but above all, the spirit
which points beyond the event.

And now a final word on what is, and will be for a long time to come,
the sinister horizon of the world in which we all study and work: the international situation. Here, too, we cannot afford to live for long with a
division of personal, professional, and political ethics—a division endangering the very life which our professions have vowed to keep intact, and
thus cutting through the very fiber of our personal existence. Only in our
time, and in our very generation, have we come, with traumatic suddenness, to be conscious of what was self-evident all along, namely, that
in all of previous history the Rule, in whatever form, has comfortably co-

existed with warfare. A warrior, all armored and spiked and set to do to another what he fully expected the other to be ready to do to him, saw no ethical contradiction between the Rule and his military ideology. He could, in fact, grant to his adversary a respect which he hoped to earn in return. This tenuous coexistence of ethics and warfare may outlive itself in our time. Even the military mind may well come to fear for its historical identity, as boundless slaughter replaces tactical warfare. What is there, even for a "fighting man" in the Golden Rule of the Nuclear Age, which seems to say, "Do not unto others—unless you are sure you can do them in as totally as they can do you in"?

One wonders, however, whether this deadlock in international morals can be broken by the most courageous protest, the most incisive interpretation, or the most prophetic warning—a warning of catastrophe so all-consuming that most men must ignore it, as they ignore their own death and have learned to ignore the monotonous prediction of hell. It seems, instead, that only an ethical orientation, a direction for vigorous cooperation, can free today's energies from their bondage in armed defensiveness. We live at a time in which—with all the species-wide destruction possible—we can think for the first time of a species-wide identity, of a truly universal ethics, such as has been prepared in the world religions, in humanism, and by some philosophers. Ethics, however, cannot be fabricated. They can only emerge from an informed and inspired search for a more inclusive human identity, which a new technology and a new world image make possible as well as mandatory. But again, all I can offer you here is another variation of the theme. What has been said about the relationships of parent and child, of man and woman, and of doctor and patient, may have some application to the relationship of nations to each other. Nations today are by definition units at different stages of political, technological, and economic transformation. Under these conditions, it is all too easy for over-developed nations to believe that nations, too, should treat one another with a superior educative or clinical attitude. The point of what I have to say, however, is not underscored inequality, but respected uniqueness within historical differences. Insofar as a nation thinks of itself as a collective individual, then, it may well learn to visualize its task as that of maintaining mutuality in international relations. For the only alternative to armed competition seems to be the effort to *activate in the historical partner what will strengthen him in his historical development even as it strengthens the actor in his own develop-*

ment—toward a common future identity. Only thus can we find a common denominator in the rapid change of technology and history and transcend the dangerous imagery of victory and defeat, of subjugation and exploitation which is the heritage of a fragmented past.

Does this sound utopian? I think, on the contrary, that all of what I have said is already known in many ways, is being expressed in many languages, and practiced on many levels. At our historical moment it becomes clear in a most practical way that the doer of the Golden Rule, and he who is done by, is the same man, *is* man.

Men of clinical background, however, must not lose sight of a dimension which I have taken for granted here. While the Golden Rule in its classical versions prods man to strive *consciously* for a highest good and to avoid mutual harm with a sharpened awareness, our insights assume an *unconscious* substratum of ethical strength and, at the same time, unconscious arsenals of destructive rage. The last century has traumatically expanded man's awareness of unconscious motivations stemming from his animal ancestry, from his economic history, and from his inner estrangements. It has also created (in all these respects) methods of productive self-analysis. These I consider the pragmatic Western version of that universal trend toward self-scrutiny which once reached such heights in Asian tradition. It will be the task of the next generation everywhere to begin to integrate new and old methods of self-awareness with the minute particulars of universal technical proficiency.

It does not seem easy to speak of ethical subjects without indulging in some moralizing. As an antidote I will conclude with the Talmudic version of the Rule. Rabbi Hillel once was asked by an unbeliever to tell the whole of the Torah while he stood on one foot. I do not know whether he meant to answer the request or to remark on its condition when he said: "What is hateful to yourself, do not to your fellow man. That is the whole of the Torah and the rest is but commentary." At any rate, he did not add: "Act accordingly." He said: "Go, and learn it."

THE GALILEAN SAYINGS
AND THE SENSE OF *"I"*

from *The Yale Review*

1

Thomas Jefferson, newly inaugurated as president, spent many solitary evenings in the White House studying the gospels in various languages. He marked each passage "line for line," wondering whether or not it spoke to him with the true voice of Jesus, for he was interested only in "the genuine precepts of Jesus himself." "I am a Christian," he asserted, "in the only sense in which he wished anyone to be: sincerely attached to his doctrines in preference to all others; ascribing to himself every *human* excellence; and believing that he never claimed any other." Finally he cut the passages apart and pasted together those which passed his judgment, collecting them under the title of "The Philosophy of Jesus of Nazareth," with a subtitle dedicating this work to the American Indians. I do not intend to pursue here Jefferson's principles of selection: to mention only two omissions, there was no resurrection and there were no miracles, healing or otherwise. But there was, indeed, the Sermon on the Mount.

When I discussed this very private preoccupation of an American president in my 1973 Jefferson Lectures and described his search as one seeking the "authentic," I was not aware of (or not aware of the implications of) the fact that there had emerged in more recent times a whole

school of theologians who had developed a method called "form criticism" in order to discern with a certain methodological rigor which of
the early sayings of Jesus could reasonably be considered "authentic."
This work originated in Germany in the writings of Martin Dibelius
(1919), Rudolf Bultmann (1921), and, later, Joachim Jeremias (1947). In
this country, however, it has been most vividly reported by Norman Perrin of Chicago, who studied with Jeremias in Germany. His book *Redis-
covering the Teaching of Jesus* (1967) persuaded me to review some of Jesus'
sayings in the first, the Galilean, part of his ministry, when this unknown
rabbi addressed the strangely "mixed" populace of his native region.
Would the fact of their authenticity throw some additional light on the
singular and ever so far-reaching power of those words—words that had
been passed on by word of mouth before they were collected in written
accounts, and then (if in a later form) had become some of the most consistently remembered in history?

To begin, however, I must take a certain exception to the term "authentic," if, indeed, it is meant to convey more than the probable his-
toricity of some words, because it might seem to suggest that the gospel
writers' variations of these sayings are somehow "inauthentic." Now the
gospels themselves are a creative art form, characterized by a certain freedom of improvisation in reporting a sequence of lively and colorful
episodes, each describing within a native setting the encounters of Jesus
and the Galilean populace. But all this paperwork (as it were) was done
during the latter part of the first century, decades after Jesus' death, and,
in fact, it reviews his reported words in the light of his death and resurrection, which are reported as having taken place in the second part of
his ministry—that is, in Judaea, in Jerusalem. By then, the purpose of the
gospels obviously was to provide a testamental backbone for growing
Christian communities in and way beyond Palestine—communities such
as Jesus himself had never witnessed. All of this development had an authenticity of its own, in the form of a new tradition of ritualizations and
of worship suited to the individual writers' revelatory idiosyncrasies, to
the social trends of the day, and to the receptivity and concerns of readers at that historical moment. That all such traditional ritualization sooner
or later is apt to lead to some dead ritualisms is a subject to which we will
return repeatedly. But in its beginnings it all has its own historical "authenticity."

Maybe I emphasize all this because I must in my own small way make use of some psychoanalytical license in reflecting on a few of Jesus' sayings and in pointing to an inner logic which to me, as a modern person and a psychoanalyst in the Judaeo-Christian orbit, makes their authentication, well, authentic. To do so, however, I will first have to locate Jesus and the Galilee of his time in the geography and history of Judaism, and I will then have to coordinate that historical pursuit with a more contemporary search—one concerning a vital phenomenon that lies on the borderline of psychology and of theology. I am referring to the sense of *"I"* which is that most obvious and most elusive endowment of creatures with consciousness—and language. This phenomenon has been treated by some psychologists, and I will at a proper time refer to some early remarks made by Freud. William James (in his *Principles of Psychology*) approached the problem from a privileged point of view, namely, that of the professional thinker:

> Whatever I may be thinking of, I am always at the same time more or less aware of *myself*, of my *personal existence*. At the same time it is I who am aware; so that the total self of me, being as it were duplex, partly known and partly knower, partly object and partly subject, must have two aspects discriminated in it, of which for shortness we may call one the *Me* and the other the *I*.

> The I, or "pure ego," is a very much more difficult subject of inquiry than the Me. It is that which at any moment *is* conscious, whereas the Me is only one of the things which it is conscious *of*. In other words, it is the *Thinker;* and the question immediately comes up *what* is the thinker?

In reading this I hear somebody murmur, "I think, therefore I am (I think)." But what we are concerned with in these pages is the sense of *I* of all human beings (including the thinkers) who can join others in a sense of the *We* only by dint of a shared language which, in turn, must fit the way in which the prevailing world view influences not only the general outlook of all individuals in a given region but especially their readiness for a new revelatory voice. The *I*, after all, is the ground for the simple verbal assurance that each person is a center of awareness in a universe of communicable experience, a center so numinous that it amounts to a sense of being alive, and more, of being the vital condition of exis-

tence. At the same time, only two or more persons sharing a corresponding world image as well as language can, for moments, merge their
*I*s into a *We*. I will, then, report later what I have been able to discern of
the particular temporal and spatial dimensions on which depend the relative clarity of the sense of *I,* or, indeed, the peculiar dread which can im-
pair it.

To return now to biblical times, let me merely suggest here two questions. What may be the relation of all this to Moses' report that when he
asked God for his name he received the answer: *"I am that I am"?* And
what may be the relation of all this to the fact that Jesus, the messenger,
is (authentically) reported to have introduced rather than ended a number of his sayings with "Amen, but I say unto you"?

In the gospels, the ministry of Jesus begins as a provincial Galilean
event. How he is reported to have spoken, and to whom and in what
places, all suggest the Galilean landscape. The parables, in fact—generally
considered to be his most authentic art form—clearly reflect the fertile
agricultural countryside and the thriving fishing industry on Galilee's
sea. It is from those shores that Jesus recruited his first disciples—men
who, we thus learn, by no means joined him because they were hungry
or wayward, but who, when recruited imperiously on the edge of the sea,
at once followed his itinerary "all through Galilee." That his sayings traveled far, and quickly so, is made more probable by the fact that Galilee is
a province in Palestine's north. It is crossed by well-traveled highways that
in Jesus' day carried caravans of traders as well as streams of pilgrims
south—either along the Mediterranean shore or down the traversable
strip of land along the Jordan river to Jerusalem—and brought back trade
on the way north and northeast in the direction of Damascus. Accordingly (and according to Matthew) all of Jesus' healing and teaching is pictured as being done as he walked along ways and byways, stopping only
for an occasional wish to be alone with himself or with his disciples.

The beautiful and fertile countryside, transversed by interregional
roads, is only the geographic basis for a region of extremes, each of which
can be praised or blamed for the fact that Galilee first listened to Jesus. Extreme conditions could prevail everywhere in Palestine when (anybody's)
rioting armies were let loose. And yet there were peaceful, sedentary
populations in Greek cities, for example, or in the countryside populated
by Jewish landowners: a few were wealthy, but most were "smallholders,"
some of whom were busy with family handicrafts such as carpentry or

pottery, and some of whom employed hirelings or owned slaves. Among all these there was a population frequenting the synagogues, praying and learning the word. And then there was a haplessly migratory mass, often looking for work, such as unemployed hands and laborers—and younger sons. But Galilee, just because it was removed from the centers of Roman power, was also the "cradle" of Zealotism—movements of pious terrorists, waiting for their time, which always ended with a mass sacrifice of young lives. And then, again, there were those who felt defeated in all national (and that meant, of course, religious and national) matters who leaned toward all kinds of messianic movements and, naturally, were at first and long thereafter considered by some to be "unlettered rabble"— a natural audience for Jesus' preaching. The gospels retrospectively give their own descriptions of the social atmosphere of the ministry. They may describe Jesus and his disciples ambling through the fields on the sabbath or up the hills and down the valleys on a "workday," into clusters of villages and out again to neighboring countrysides, finding the level of faith too low for his ministry only near Nazareth, where Jesus "came from." And there was always the Sea of Galilee, either on calm days when he sat on a boat so as better to address the crowd ashore or miraculously to feed all those who had followed him, or, on occasions of severe storms, when it invited other miracles. Thus, curing and teaching, he was forever followed by a large crowd, including such figures as tax collectors and prostitutes who might not have felt welcome elsewhere. And from these crowds emerged, ever again, an individual help-seeker (a leper, a blind man, a man "possessed") or a seeker for help for relatives at home (a centurion, a president of a synagogue, a Canaanite woman). And, indeed, Jesus went into their houses to assist the sick (Peter's mother-in-law, say, who had a fever). But even when he was in a house, it was soon crowded—so much so that in one, some friends lowered a paralyzed man, tied to a bed, into Jesus' presence through a hole in the roof. (We will discuss later what Jesus said.) But on occasion he demanded the right to go up into the hills to pray by himself, or, indeed, to go up a hill and "take his seat" in order to speak to those who began to hear what he was saying; and it was on such an occasion that he delivered the Sermon on the Mount, followed by the Lord's Prayer, that incomparable variation of the Jewish Kaddish. To the crowds, however, he spoke in parables: was it (as the controversy goes) in order to hide the deeper truth from them or, rather, to teach it to them in an art form they would understand?

Here I must—as I will now and then—take recourse to the old Luther Bible which so often, in his German, seems to solve poetically what cannot so easily be decided intellectually. The gospel writers are unsure (perhaps because they want so badly to belong to those who understood the full meaning of Jesus' words) whether or not Jesus means to ascribe to the crowds some ability to sense the meaning of what he is saying by way of the parables. Matthew has Jesus say (to the disciples, to be sure): "This is why I speak to them in parables, because seeing they do not see, and hearing they do not hear, nor do they understand. With them indeed is fulfilled the prophecy of Isaiah which says: 'You shall indeed hear but never understand, and you shall indeed see but never perceive. For this people's heart has grown dull, and their ears are heavy of hearing, and their eyes they have closed, lest they should perceive with their eyes, and hear with their ears, and understand with their heart, and turn for me to heal them.' But blessed are your eyes, for they see, and your ears, for they hear. Truly, I say to you, many prophets and righteous men longed to see what you see, and did not see it, and to hear what you hear, and did not hear it" (Matthew 13:13–17).

I will not go here into the various translations of Jesus' words. Luther—who in creating the first German Bible rejuvenated the image of Jesus as he renewed the German language—resolves it all by suggesting that the parables, even if they do not make crowds "understand," can make them "hear with hearing ears" and "see with seeing eyes" *("mit hoerenden Ohren und sehenden Augen")*. Indeed, what else could be the purpose of such a special form of narration, if not that it can make you sense—its sense?

According to Matthew, however, the sayings were of less interest to the crowds than were the cures and the miracles, while Jesus seemed to feel driven by his compassion to cure as many as possible even where he also seemed to indicate that he regretted the excessive demand on his time for dramatic "signs" of the Kingdom's arrival. Furthermore, when we hear, as we will, some of the (authenticated!) words which accompanied his cures, it becomes clear that his declaration of being a shepherd of lost sheep expressed the intention to heal his contemporaries way beyond the mere undoing of the diseases or the misfortunes of some. And, indeed, his sayings, some of which at the time must have had a poetic form (maybe, in their native Aramaic, even some rhyming), were addressed to the malaise of faith which was then a national symptom reflecting the political (and in Judaism this was almost identical with the religious) conditions of that time.

The episodic art form of gospels such as St. Matthew's, then, one-sided as each may be, conveys the combination in Jesus' ministry of an extensive capacity to address the wide variety of groups found in Galilee, and yet to be, potentially, in contact with each individual encountered. In this connection, a scene stands out which I, as a psychoanalyst, felt I had good reason to quote in my Jefferson lectures, and this especially because Jefferson had omitted it from *his* authentic data. It is the story of a woman who had lost not only her blood for twelve years but also all her money on physicians, none of whom had helped her at all. Finding herself in a big crowd surrounding Jesus, she did not dare to, or could not, approach him directly, but she pressed in behind him and touched his garment.

> And straightway the fountain of her blood was dried up; and she felt in her body that she was healed of that plague. And Jesus, immediately knowing in himself that virtue had gone out of him, turned him about in the press, and said, "Who touched my clothes?" And his disciples said unto him, "Thou seest the multitude thronging thee, and sayest thou, 'Who touched me?' " And he looked round about to see her that had done this thing. But the woman fearing and trembling, knowing what was done in her, came and fell down before him, and told him all the truth. [Mark 5:29–34]

This illustrates Jesus' selective responsiveness to one person reaching out for him in a big crowd. What he then said to her—that will open up a whole new subject to us.

But now we have to leave Galilee. For at a certain point in Jesus' ministry there comes, in all three synoptic gospels, a decisive announcement according to which Jesus, "on leaving these parts, . . . came into the region of Judaea and the Transjordan" (Mark 10:1); or having "finished this discourse," he "left Galilee" (Matthew 19:1); or more goal-specifically: "As the time approached when he was to be taken up to heaven, he set his face resolutely toward Jerusalem" (Luke 9:51). His sacrifice of the Galilean style of ministry, then (Jesus is now thirty-three years old), is based on a clear-cut decision that he had to challenge—yes, nonviolently—the "powers that be" in Jerusalem. What followed was the Passion that eventually led to his being called Christ and made the Cross the

acclaimed symbol of the church to come. With this part of the story, vari-
ably elaborated as it is in the gospels, we will not deal in these pages. Yet,
we point to an additional justification for our concentration on the
Galilean part of the ministry in one of the very last words of the Passion
story. Mark (14:28) reports that Jesus and the disciples, right after the last
supper, went out to the Mount of Olives, where he added to all his sad
predictions of the disciples' impending betrayal a most touchingly intimate remark: "But after I am raised up I will go before you into Galilee."
His reported reference to the resurrection may not be authentic; but this
statement suggests on his part or on that of the witnesses what may well
have been a feeling shared with them by the earthly Jesus, namely, that
Galilee was home.

2

I have now circumscribed my overall theme: it is the relationship of Jesus'
Galilean sayings to what we call the human sense of *I,* in general; and
more specifically, what aspects of these sayings may have promised a pervasive healing quality for the historical and religious malaise of Jesus' time.
I will admit that beside and beyond this Galilean moment in human
evolution I wonder whether such reflections may throw some light on
other great sayings in that millennium, such as those attributed to Lao
Tse, and their role in Taoist religion. For, incidentally, the Reign or even
the Way seems to be a more persuasive designation for what in English
is called the Kingdom; and, indeed, the first Christians did refer to their
vision as the New Way.

    In order to be able to approach the Galilean sayings in their historical
setting, however, we must go beyond their Galilean time and place. We
have noted that Galilee in all the insularity of its countryside and its
seashore nonetheless served as a highway to Jerusalem and beyond to the
Hellenistic world and Rome. We must now follow this highway into
metropolitan Judaea and review some of the history which gave it its
place in the wider world. And on the way we must here and there approach the problem of the human *I* in its relation to the dimensions of
the world image suggested by past history and by contemporary historical change.

    I have suggested that the sense of *I* is one of the most obvious facts of existence—indeed, maybe *the* most obvious—and that it is, at the same time, one of the most elusive; wherefore psychologists are apt to consider it a philosophical rather than a psychological concern. I will discuss later how my teacher, Sigmund Freud, managed (almost) to ignore it. But it is true, of course, that this subjective sense dwells on the very border of our conscious existence, though no doubt its health is dependent on such qualities of our psychosocial life as our sense of identity. In the Bible, the most direct reference to the human *I* is in the form of an inner light, that is, of a luminosity of awareness. The original Galilean saying is reported in Matthew's account: "Nor do men light a lamp and put it under a bushel, but on a stand, and it gives light to all in the house" (5:15). "The eye is the lamp of the body. So, if your eye is sound, your whole body will be full of light, but if your eye is not sound, your whole body will be full of darkness. If, then, the light in you is darkness, how great is the darkness!" (6:22). And, indeed, our sense of *I* gives to our sensory awareness a numinous center. It is no wonder, then, that our most eloquent recent witness for the inner light is a blind man, Jacques Lusseyran, who lost his eyesight through an accident at the age of seven and a half. He later wrote (in "The Blind in Society"):

Barely ten days after the accident that blinded me, I made the basic discovery . . . I could not see the light of the world any more. Yet the light was still there. . . . I found it *in myself* and what a miracle!—it was intact. This "in myself," however, where was that? In my head, in my heart, in my imagination? . . . I felt how it wanted to spread out over the world. . . . The source of light is not in the outer world. We believe that it is only because of a common delusion. The light dwells where life also dwells: within ourselves. . . . The second great discovery came almost immediately afterwards. There was only one way to see the inner light, and that was to love.

This numinosity, however, seems lost when it is too eagerly concentrated on for its own sake, as if one light were asked to illuminate another. No wonder that dictionaries avoid the matter! I have before me a psychological dictionary which does not even mention *I*. My thesaurus, in turn, refers first to a "self-designating pronoun" and then to "the spiritual personality"—and nothing in between.

Actually, writers who take the sense of *I* seriously will first of all ask what is the *I*'s counterplayer. They may indeed begin with the second pronoun, *you*, and end with the soul's sense of a divine *Thou*. To my developmental orientation the most telling "map" depicting the development of the sense of *I* would be the whole list of personal pronouns, from *I* to *They*, as each one first gets to be pronounced and understood correctly in childhood, and then as it is meaningfully experienced and reexperienced throughout life. The beginnings of the sense of *I* itself, one should think, can only emerge in a newborn out of the counterplay with a sensed *You* in the maternal caretaker—whom we shall call the Primal Other; and it seems of vital importance that this Other, and, indeed, related Others, in turn experience the new being as a *presence* that heightens *their* sense of *I*. It is this interplay, I think, that helps the original sense of *I* gradually face another fundamental counterplayer, namely, *my Self*— almost an Inner Other. But the original interplay of *You* and *I* remains the model for a mutual recognition throughout life, up to a finite expectation to which St. Paul gave the explicitly religious form of an ultimate meeting now only vaguely sensed beyond "a glass, darkly" (the Ultimate Other, then).

Now, one glance at the list of all personal pronouns reveals a whole developmental program in their sequence: for while *I* and *you* form the original dyad, this dyad soon turns into a number of triads as a series of *he*'s or *she*'s (and, indeed, a world of *it*'s) become additional counterplayers within varied connotations: paternal, fraternal, sororal, and so on. And as this happens, the plural concepts *we, you*, and *they* become both verbal necessities and the bearers of important emotional involvements. Thus, the system of pronouns, beginning with *I* and *you*, is built into a ground plan ready to unfold in stages; and one can well see how each of them, once learned, serves a widening experience as it includes, on every stage, new counterplayers. Take, for example, the necessity—especially in any patriarchal and monotheistic system—to transfer some of the earliest forms of a sense of *I* from their maternal origin to strongly paternal and eventually theistic relationships. Or consider the crisis of adolescence as a transfer of the identity elements formed in childhood and youth to the productive milieu in which one expects to find one's psychosocial identity. Or, again, how the sense of *we* acquired in one's family of origin ("my kind") must be extended to the family and the community one marries into—and, indeed, to one's own new family in which one must help to generate new beings with their own sense of *I*.

Throughout this establishment of new boundaries of *We, Ourselves,* dictated as it is by the realities and the ideology of work and production, there also emerges a gradual demarcation of the decisive borderlines beyond which live those definitely other Others—those *they's* and *them's* whom one has learned to repudiate or to exclude as foreign, if not nonhuman altogether. These habitual rejections, in turn, have helped to give a clearer outline to one's own "true Self" or to those variant "selves" which are either proudly or fatalistically accepted as a self-description within the contemporary world of roles. And yet, throughout all these critical stages with all their involvements, there remains for the *I* a certain existential solitariness which, in these pages, we depict as seeking love, liberation, salvation. So we now return to such geographic and historical conditions as provide in any given period the basis for an ideological orientation in the widest sense of a Way of Life—the essential bridge between all *I*'s and their *We*'s.

When Jesus and his disciples crossed into Judaea, they abruptly entered a country in a most vulnerable condition. True, it was ready to view them as (possibly dangerous) outsiders, for Galilee's name in the exclusively Jewish population of Judaea was, in fact, "Galilee of the Gentiles," whose "north country" Aramaic was made fun of and whose strong admixture of militant zealots was feared by Romans and Jews alike. One of the predominant facts in Judaea was a precarious deal between the representatives of Rome, the occupying power, and the temple's Jewish aristocracy—a deal to keep Jerusalem safe enough to be forever hostess of the temple, the religious empire's sacred center and the central geographic reference of a people, the larger part of which was already living in the enclaves of a widespread Diaspora reaching to Rome, to Alexandria, and to Mesopotamia.

As we now approach such unique space-time configurations as *Diaspora*—configurations which can have quite ambiguous connotations for a nation's sense of existence—we might briefly reconsider the spatial sense established by the all-important fact in American history of a *frontier.* As an overall gestalt, the frontier gradually moved westward and northward until it joined the Pacific Ocean, and yet it still figures in many life plans and ventures, as well as, of course, memories—not to speak of habitual media themes. Let us not overlook, in passing, the configuration of im-migration which for so long—as it does in Israel today— expressed the eagerness of the new homecomers to have "made it," no matter what may have made them leave where they came from. "Frontier" has obviously played a significant role in the implicit images of "new deals" as well as the explicit slogan of a "new frontier." The same is true (or, significantly, *has* been true) for the American imagery of war, which always assumed that armies are *ex*-peditionary forces expected to fight on *foreign* fronts and not meant to wait for a potential enemy ever to *in*-vade. The personal sense of fate which depends on such shared space-time configurations can consist of the simplest of all defensive attitudes, such as who can do what to me—and what can I do to them if they do it. Radical changes in such habitual expectability and the totally new threat of total nuclear vulnerability are absorbed only very, very slowly into either the individual sense of existence or, indeed, the psychosocial and national identity. They demand and are in fact waiting for nothing less than a kind of revelatory reorientation of the whole world image as based on the acceptance of the undeniable facts of developing technology and on the capacity for new modes of ethical adaptation.

We come to the conclusion, then, that whatever a people's geographic and historical setting, its majority (or its leading aristocracy) must be assured of the reliability of a number of dominant space-time qualities which, in fact, correspond to the requirements of a sense of *I,* even as they cohere in a collective *We.* Among these we have mentioned a sense of *numinosity;* we now add a choice of *action,* of a *central position,* as well as a guarantee of *continuity* in time, and all marked by strong *boundaries*— a concept which will prove indispensable to a comparison of the vulnerable peripheries of the Judaic territory and the firm and all-inclusive circumscription of Jehovah's world, not to speak of the possible impact of both on the sense of *I* and the sense of *We.* When describing a group's space-time, then, we must emphasize configurations which seem to enhance all these qualities or, obversely, threaten inactivation, peripherality, discontinuity, and so on.

As we now return to ancient Israel, the reader will wonder with me whether there has ever been a nation more lacking in all such guarantees—except in the form of prophetic promises uttered in the name of a national god—than was Judaea in Jesus' time.

In the Palestinian homeland as a whole, Galilee was then one of the components of a tetrarchy, that is, a dynastic division between the three sons of King Herod the Great, who died around the time of Jesus' birth. Now Galilee was—very relatively speaking—safely in the hands of one son who managed to rule it until A.D. 39 (although he had John the Baptist killed for reasons of personal pique and may have been suspicious of Jesus as a potential successor). The second, the northeastern part, remained in the hands of another son until A.D. 34. Archelaus, however, the son in possession of Judaea, had been deposed by the Romans already, in the year 6; and since then, Jerusalem had been governed by that precarious deal between a Roman procurator (at that time, Pontius Pilate, as you may have heard) and the priestly aristocracy that "owned" the new temple on the site on which Solomon had built the old one almost a thousand years before. I would underline *deal* as one of the disturbing elements in the Jewish national identity of the day, for it was both religiously and politically demeaning—and Jesus, "the King," was of course to be its victim, as an alleged danger to the Pax Romana. Speaking of national identity, it must, incidentally, be assumed that Jesus and the Romans conversed in what was then the official language, namely, Greek.

But then, there are other circumstances as yet to be italicized. All of Palestine was, as it had been for a thousand years, a *buffer nation* between successively contending empires and a geographic *corridor* for great nations—such as Syria, Egypt, and Persia—seeking to "get at" each other. Thus, its very location, which made the small Jewish nation at times conspicuously important, also made it permanently vulnerable, and most of the major events of its history attested to this. A thousand and a half years before, much of the nation had lived in Egypt, from which, thanks to Jehovah and Moses, it had been brought back: the great *Exodus.* There were then again, as there had been more than two millennia earlier, some great kings and great prophets. But there also were incomprehensible interruptions such as the Assyrian and Babylonian *exiles* and *captivities* (in the eighth and sixth centuries), as well as alternating *occupations* by the Persian and Greek empires and their contending dynastic heirs. Now and again the most unthinkable would happen, namely, that a foreign ruler or general would *intrude* upon the temple's holiest of holies, which only the hereditary high priest should enter once a year on the Day of Atonement to express the nation's confessional commitment to Jehovah. But those few times were deeply remembered.

For one century, however, and from the middle of the second to that of the first century B.C., the Jewish nation had lived in independence, and this after Judas Maccabaeus and his brothers had led a revolt against the occupying Syrians whose king had desecrated the temple and attempted to introduce Hellenic cults. The Maccabaeans made the high priest king and restored a joined territory as great as that of David's and Solomon's. A generation later, however, the rule of these Hasmonaeans (that was their family name) appeared to be bogged down in power struggles. Yet the Romans did not take over until 63 B.C., when Pompey—apparently invited by Palestinian factions—conquered Jerusalem, and, in his turn, entered the holy of holies. It was then that Herod became king of Judaea; he was a Jew by religion, flamboyantly Greek in style, Roman in allegiance, and unpredictably cruel in personality. Passionately interested in architecture, he began to renovate the temple in 20 B.C. It was there in Jesus' time, and it was to survive until A.D. 70—which, after one more national uprising, marked the end of the ancient kind of Jewish nationhood and of the religious center.

Even such a sketch of Palestine's history makes it vividly clear that the Hebrew nation had to survive and to learn to live with a number of devastating time-and-space configurations. In spite of a venerable past untiringly celebrated in the holy writings, the living historical memory suggested a territorial condition which had made the nation alternately vulnerable to foreign powers and all their actions—as emphasized above. In spite of a most intensive history of singular heroism there was, all in all, a complete *inactivation* of defense; and the freedom of the one symbol of central locus and inner autonomy, namely, the temple, was granted only by the consent of the empire on whose *periphery* it existed. The enumerated conditions of this existence obviously violate every dimension of that sense of *I* which any collective must provide; and one could conclude that such a nation had no identity with a chance of survival in centuries to come.

It is here, however, that we must, at last, turn to Jehovah, who had remained (and was yet to remain) the guardian of those people who would continue to develop, even beyond their final national defeat, a lasting sense of ethnic and religious identity and, in fact, of some lasting moral mission, nurtured rather than famished by the very fact of their dispersion among other nations.

This brings us to the dimensions of monotheism, the religious heritage in Jesus' upbringing. Here we must consider its ethical power as well as its daily condition at the time. No doubt monotheism provided strength to the Jews because it permitted them to accept even disaster as a genuine aspect of what must be Jehovah's plan—and pact. Speaking of the significance of the sense of *I*, we have quoted "I am that I am" (Exodus 3:14). Leif Boman has noted that the word for "being" ("hayah"), which is used in connection with Jehovah's very name, has a very active quality. There seems to be, in fact, an identity of being, and becoming, and even of acting and speaking: "For he spoke, and it came to be. He commanded, and it stood forth" (Psalms 33:9). And Jehovah's "hayah" is the people's "hayah": "Obey my voice, and I will be your God, and you shall be my people" (Jeremiah 7:23). And Jehovah is "everlasting" as well as everywhere: "the Creator of the ends of the earth" (Isaiah 40:28). Thus, divine reality of being becomes a worldwide actuality in its total effectiveness.

Furthermore, Jehovah, once the first *among* the gods, eventually becomes the *first* and the *last*—"so that men from the rising and the setting sun may know that there is none but I ... I make the light, I create darkness, author alike of prosperity and trouble. I, the Lord, do all these things" (Isaiah 45:6–7).

"Prosperity *and* trouble." Whatever the native word here translated as "trouble," it stands for the price of having been chosen and rooted: " 'I will plant them upon their land, and they shall never again be plucked up out of the land which I have given them,' says the Lord your God" (Amos 9:15); and to be in their own "house," secure in the generational progression: "from the time that I appointed judges over my people Israel; and I will give you rest from all your enemies. Moreover the Lord declares to you that the Lord will make you a house. When your days are fulfilled and you lie down with your fathers, I will raise up your offspring after you, who shall come forth from your body, and I will establish his kingdom. He shall build a house for my name, and I will establish the throne of his kingdom for ever. I will be his father, and he shall be my son. When he commits iniquity, I will chasten him with the rod of men, with the stripes of the sons of men; but I will not take my steadfast love from him, as I took it from Saul, whom I put away from before you" (2 Samuel 7:11–15). For such actuality in eternity, both messianic promises and apocalyptic threats become confirmations both of being chosen and of having actively, knowingly, chosen judgment as well as salvation. It can all be sealed, in prayers and in rituals, with "Amen: so it *is.*"

Here, of course, man's evolutionary capacity for guilt becomes a pointed part of his sense of existence; and, as creation and procreation become one actuality, so the experience of the Father in monotheism recapitulates the experience of the father in ontogeny. In suggesting that here, too, the most obvious must be taken at its word, I do not mean to reduce such faith to its infantile roots. For the literal believer could well respond with the assertion that human childhood, besides being an evolutionary phenomenon, may well have been created so as to plant in the child at the proper time the potentiality for a comprehension of the Creator's existence, and a readiness for his revelations. And, indeed, the way the father can be experienced in childhood can make it almost impossible *not* to believe deep down in (and indeed to fear as well as to hope for) a fatherly spirit in the universe.

And here the eternal covenant goes right to the heart of matters which are central to the physical and emotive existence of the *I*. Certainly any sense of *I* includes a few basic regions of bodily existence which must be centrally "mine" because they guarantee the core and the extension of my existence: one such center in the *I* space is the heart and one, certainly, the genitals. No wonder, then, that Jehovah as God of a patriarchy takes possession of the region of the penis, so that "my covenant be in your flesh an everlasting covenant" (Genesis 17:13). And more specifically: "This is my covenant, which you shall keep, between me and you and your descendants after you: Every male among you shall be circumcised. You shall be circumcised in the flesh of your foreskins, and it shall be a sign of the covenant between me and you. He that is eight days old among you shall be circumcised; every male throughout your generations, whether born in your house, or bought with your money from any foreigner who is not of your offspring" (Genesis 17:10–12). Deuteronomy (10:16), in turn, pronounces the pointed warning, "Circumcise therefore the foreskin of your heart, and be no longer stubborn."

Thus one could say much about the development in childhood of a father-bound conscience—intensified as it is in a patriarchal and monotheistic setting. Our main interest in this context, however, is some clarification regarding Jehovah's integrative power in a post- and pre-catastrophic political time-space. And as we have just seen, Jehovah is in the center of individual existence, even as he is in the religious center: "Then the nations will know that I, the Lord, sanctify Israel, when my sanctuary is in the midst of them for evermore" (Ezekiel 37:28). But this means that he is in the center of a conscience which, within a network of ritual commitments, can feel affirmative and confirmed, choosing and chosen, and, even at the height of Jehovah's wrath, certain of a "kingdom-to-come."

In the scriptures two messianic world images were attached to Jeho-

vah's name which were to play a great role in the evolution of an existential meaning for man: that of God's reign and that of the "son of
man." Both were charged with defining (but by all means abstaining
from overdefining) the boundaries between history and a "transhistorical" reality (when "all the world will rejoice in the knowledge of Jah-
weh"); between David's royal territory and Jehovah's universal empire;
and between godly, royal, and "ordinary" sonhood, that is, God's dynastic covenant with David and his house and his individual covenant with
each Jew. Most nebulous, of course, were the various emphases on the
dramatic form (messianic or apocalyptic, salvational or judgmental) which
such a New Day or Golden Age would take—not to speak of the human
form in which God's servant and messenger would appear: was he to be
a king or an anointed Lord (Chrystos Kyrios)—that is, was he a royal or
a priestly figure—or both? As Isaiah's God puts it: "It is too light a thing
that you should be my servant to raise up the tribes of Jacob and to restore the preserved of Israel; I will give you as a light to the nations, that
my salvation may reach to the end of the earth" (Isaiah 49:6). And who
or what "remnant of Israel" will survive the apocalypse?

As to the "son of man," it has persistent if persistently ambiguous connotations all the way from an almost evolutionary emergence in Daniel's
prophetic dream of a vaguely human shape ("one like a son of man" or
"a man-like figure" [Daniel 7:13]) emerging from a pack of superreal
beastly creatures; or a human being (ben ādām) sitting at God's right; or,
finally, something we cannot afford to omit here, namely, an Aramaic way
of simply saying *I*. All of these meanings seem to converge on a transcendent sense of awareness lodged in an earthly human shape, and we
will find something of all of them projected by the reporters and historians of that time on Jesus' reference to himself as the son of man.

3

But we should now add a few words on the dangers that can befall yearly
and daily ritualizations of such an overwhelming belief in a tough, a
central, cosmic power's benevolence. Here I must introduce a term which
I find indispensable in any attempt to locate in the social process a phenomenon which corresponds to compulsivity in the individual; I call it
"ritualism" *(Toys and Reasons)*. The greatest ritualizations can eventually

become repetitive and the minutest daily rituals compulsive—whereupon devotion to revered images can become idolism, adherence to detailed laws can become legalism, and reliance on dogma can become dogmatism. This is particularly so under conditions felt to be of danger to the very nature of things; and this, in Jesus' time, may well have been the loss of national power and of cultural consistency under the impact of hellenization. Under such conditions, then, creative enrichment through live rituals can give place to a superconscientious preoccupation with ritualistic details dominated by a compulsive scrupulosity apt to deaden the renewal and rejuvenation which is the essence of an inventive ritual life. Here one may want to consider how much of the creative life of a great nation had in Judaism been totally absorbed by the religious system: consider only the fact that Jehovah's very sanctified presence, and with it all ritual themes, were soon to be forbidden subjects for representative art, and this at a time when the arts of other nations flowered exactly in their images of the divine. By the same token, musical performance and poetic as well as fictional literature were restricted to religious subjects. The ritualization of daily or yearly life, then, was mainly concerned with the confirmation of the word as contained in the scriptures and a scrupulous search for their correct interpretation.

The great yearly holidays celebrated at the temple in Jerusalem, when pilgrims doubled the population, were no doubt occasions of ritual self-transcendence and of national renewal, but the services in the synagogues spread over the countryside had turned more to textual preoccupation with the wording of the scriptures, even as the daily and weekly prayers were (as Jesus was to point out) occasions demonstrating one's righteousness: under such conditions "isms" are apt to dominate behavior, and, indeed, there is the word "sabbatism." All of these concerns with strictness in ritual life are, of course, a potential found in all institutions that have outlived the ideological conditions of their origins.

But there was, and is, in the Jewish community a ritualization of everyday life which must have played a great role in the survival of Judaism. I am referring to family life, as embedded in a process significantly formulated by Klausner (in his Hebrew *Jesus of Nazareth*), who speaks of "a unifying tendency which broke down the dividing wall between religion and daily life, making daily life an essential part of religion and religion an essential part of daily life. That which was holy was not thereby profaned but was brought down to earth, while the secular life was transformed into the sacredness of a religious duty." But not even Klausner, at this point, mentions a "phenomenon" in Jewish daily life which both confirmed and compensated for the credal emphasis on a dominating masculinity of Being. How the *Jewish mother,* in daily and weekly life, in Palestine and throughout the Diaspora, continued to play the role of a most down-to-earth goddess of the hearth—that would call for an intimate cultural history which is grounded in some special chapters of the Old Testament and yet also represents one of the most consistent trends in Jewish history. In Christian mythology it was to be glorified in the counterpart to the Passion, namely, the Nativity. In our context, the specific nature of motherhood is really mandatory for any balanced historical account, for the very basis of any sense of *I* originates in the infant's first interplay with that primal, that maternal *Other,* and certainly continues to be nourished by persistent contact with her.

Now, as to the outstanding subgroups in religious life which considered themselves the caretakers of the messianic age to come: temple life and temple politics were dominated by the Sadducees, a party of the priestly aristocracy, who, as we have noted, shared the maintenance of a precarious Pax Romana with the occupying power. The biggest religious "party" was that of the Pharisees, much closer to the people, who cultivated the old ways but were interested in adaptations. For both these reasons they showed a direct and critical interest in Jesus' ministry. On their "left" were the Zealots, who believed in political change by faith-inspired force; one of Jesus' disciples belonged to them. True religious rebirth, however, was cultivated with no concessions by the religious sects who had withdrawn to lonely parts of the country to await the rejuvenation of ancient religiosity: the Essenes and the residents of Qumran. About both we have learned much in recent decades, especially from the Dead Sea Scrolls.

But there was only one man, a carpenter and rabbi baptized by John the Baptist, who, as we had begun to describe, spoke to the crowds of ordinary people with an "authority" that permitted him to *start* with "Amen"; to continue, "but I say unto you . . ."; and then to say it.

"Authentic" sayings, we said. According to the form critics, this means the "earliest form" known of such a saying that can plausibly be traced to Mark (the first gospel, later independently used by Matthew and Luke) and/or to the even earlier collection of sayings called Q (for the German "Quelle," meaning "source")—if, furthermore, the occurrence of such a form can be shown to be "neither possible nor probable" in ancient Judaism or in the early Church. As we will see (our first example will consist of exactly five words), sayings which survive such a scrutiny are of immense simplicity, especially if seen against the background of the spatial and temporal sweep of the world imagery of much of the preceding Judaic religiosity *and* of the gospels to follow. But such simplicity, we will claim, is of their essence. At the same time, however, the gospels' specific art form permits us, as we have already seen, at least to imagine these simple sayings as spoken within the context of a most vivid encounter. Here let me go back to the story of the woman who was cured of a persistent flow of blood. This example, in its healing aspects, can be seen immediately to be as close to our day and work as it seems to have surprised the Galilee of that day. For, to permit myself a professional and even theoretical response, it makes good sense in modern terms that Jesus, in the midst of a thick throng, should have felt the touch of the desperate woman, and felt it as an acute loss of a powerful quantity of something vital. For this is comparable to and, indeed, is a parabolic representation of a certain interplay or mutual "transfer" of energy (Freud called it libido, that is, love-energy) which is assumed to take place and must be understood—as "transference"—in any therapeutic situation. But now, what *did* Jesus say, having been "touched" in this manner? *"Your faith has healed you."* The King James version is "My daughter, thy faith hath made thee whole"— which underlines the loving as well as the holistic character of all healing. At any rate, he acknowledges the woman's aptitude for trust and her determination to reach him as an essential counterpart to his capacity to help her. Nor is this the only time that Jesus specifies this "interpersonal" and active condition. There was a blind beggar (Mark 10:46–52) seated at the roadside, shouting for the "son of David." Jesus first "activated" him by having somebody call to him, thus inducing him to throw off his cloak, spring up, and come to *him*. Then Jesus said, "Your faith has made you well." And there were the four friends, already mentioned (Mark 2:1–5), who were trying to bring a paralyzed man on a stretcher through the door of the house in which Jesus was teaching. Unable to get through, they broke open the roof "over the place where Jesus was" and lowered the stretcher through. This time, Mark says, when Jesus saw *their* faith, he said to the sick man, "My son, your sins are forgiven"—a rabbi's claim to the right of absolution which resulted in a bit of theological argument from some lawyers: "Why does the fellow talk like that?"

But now to the question of authenticity. Here Norman Perrin declares himself not prepared to argue for the total authenticity of any of these healing narratives. He is only ready to claim that "the emphasis upon the faith of the patient, or his friends, in that tradition is authentic." That is, studies have shown that "faith is never demanded" in either the rabbinic tradition or in Hellenistic stories.

This brings us to the definition of two of the criteria on the basis of which the scholars involved are willing to make a decision for or against authenticity. One is the principle of "dissimilarity" which, as we saw, differentiates the sayings quoted from corresponding Judaic and Hellenistic contexts. The other is the principle of "coherence" which connects a number of stories and suggests an authentic element in all of them even if this element could be more definitely specified in only one or the other. Such "coherence" is, of course, most convincing if it illustrates what Bultmann conservatively called a new "disposition of mind."

It will be clear that Jesus' therapeutic formula is only one of many sayings, all cohering in a basic orientation (to be illustrated further) which emphasizes the individual's vital core in the immediate present rather than in dependence on traditional promises and threats of a cosmic nature. If I relate this to the sense of *I,* it will appear to be simplistic, and certainly too "superficial" for a psychoanalyst. Yet, as we have said, to be active (as well as central, continuous, and whole), or at any rate not to feel inactivated (or peripheral and fragmented), is one of the most essential dimensions of a sense of *I.* I would consider Jesus' emphasis on the patient's propensity for an active faith, then, not only a therapeutic "technique" applied to incapacitated individuals but an ethical message for the bystanders as part of a population which at that time must have been weakened in its sense of being the master—or unsure of a faith that could promise to become master—of its collective fate. And as for the enduring meaning of this saying let me here note only that this orientation reasserted itself in the history of psychotherapy with Freud's decision to make the hysterical patient *work* for recovery by letting his or her own inner voice direct "free associations" in search of the underlying conflicts instead of merely submitting to hypnosis.

And—to pursue our second concern—what did Freud say about the human sense of *I?* Certainly, in his search for a scientific psychology he did not wish to be sidetracked into man's age-old claim to a soul—which all too often has seemed to become a "narcissistic" center of human self-illusion. He concentrated on the means by which man's consciousness may be made useful in the process of calling to mind what to mankind's vast detriment had become denied and repressed in ontogeny and phylogeny. And so he emphasized what he called the human *Ich*—the right word for *I* in German, but always (and sometimes questionably) translated into English as "ego." And it is true that the *Ich* as ego to him became a primarily unconscious inner organization of experience on which human adaptation and sanity depend: the "ego gives mental processes an order in time and submits them to reality testing." Therefore, if it is disturbed its control must be restored by insight; but where is insight located? Freud cautiously claims that "On this ego [*an diesem Ich*] hangs consciousness"—a phenomenon, then, "on the periphery of the ego."

But here we face an issue of vast importance in the understanding of Freud's original concepts. If Freud himself in the early days of theory-formation uses the term *Ich* alternately for a conscious surface phenomenon and for a largely unconscious ordering of experience, one cannot blame his translators for refusing to make themselves responsible for a decision as to when the context might suggest *I* rather than ego. Freud himself, however, wonders aloud what right he has to narrow down the importance of a conscious sense of *I*. "At first we are inclined greatly to reduce the value of the criterion of being conscious since it has shown itself so untrustworthy," he claims; and then he must admit, "But we should be doing it an injustice. As may be said of our life, it is not worth much, but it is all we have. Without the illumination thrown by the quality of consciousness, we should be lost in the obscurity of depth-psychology; but we must attempt to find our bearings afresh." Here again, the translator has given in to Freud's usual tendency *not* to overdo the significance of a numinous sense of aliveness. For the word translated as "illumination" is *"die Leuchte,"* a word denoting, indeed, luminosity, and this in the two senses of the Galilean saying, that is, a *"Leuchter"*—a lamp—and a *"Leuchte,"* i.e., a luminous quality, a shining light. This whole "skeptical" remark, then, in which our consciousness, whatever its worth, is compared with life itself, is in all its caution not too far from the psalmist's acknowledgment of a light given by the creator to the apple of the eye.

And while Freud remains, as it were, religiously scientific because he is determined to pursue his mission, which is to find a truly analytical method to study human obsession (whether "evil" or "sick"), he comes, in the statement quoted, as close as he may wish to the saying, "but when thine eye is evil, thy body also is full of darkness" (Luke 11:34, King James version); except that he continues to pursue the darkness behind consciousness, attempting to reveal some structural divisions in man's psyche—that is, besides the ego, the superego, and, finally, the id, an inner caldron of drives and passions.

Here, as far away from the *I* as we can get, another Galilean saying seems to have expressed a "new disposition" most decisive for a self-aware human attitude. When challenged by some Pharisees who saw his disciples sit down to a meal without washing their hands properly and without seeming concerned about "the washing of pots and cups and vessels of bronze," Jesus says tough things, as Mark reports it, about their "teaching as doctrines the precepts of men," thus "making void the word of God through your tradition." Mark continues: "And he called the people to him again, and said to them, 'Hear me, all of you, and understand: there is nothing outside a man which by going into him can defile him; but the things which come out of a man are what defile him' " (Mark 7:14–16). And later, Jesus added for the sake of his questioning disciples: " 'Do you not see that whatever goes into a man from outside cannot defile him, since it enters, not his heart but his stomach, and so passes on?' (Thus he declared all foods clean.) And he said, 'What comes out of a man is what defiles a man. For from within, out of the heart of man, come evil thoughts, fornication, theft, murder, adultery, coveting, wickedness, deceit, licentiousness, envy, slander, pride, foolishness' " (Mark 7:18–22).

Our form critics, I presume, would not underwrite as authentic the exact list of evils emanating from within, although every believer in the id must acknowledge them. But as to Jesus' simple insistence on the fate of what comes in (*"es geht den natuerlichen Gang,"* Luther puts it: it takes the natural course), Perrin declares it most authentic, and, in fact, "the most radical statement in the whole Jesus tradition," "completely without parallel" in rabbinic or sectarian Judaism. It seems to do away with many deeply ingrained distinctions between clean and unclean which serve the phobic avoidances and the compulsive purifications by daily and weekly ritualisms—at the time probably reinforced in Pharisaic circles by their disdain for the intrusion into Jewish life of Hellenic mores. By then, of course, Jesus had publicly demonstrated not only his unorthodox daily habits but also the liberality of his choice of table fellows. In calling the inner caldron the "heart" of man, however, he certainly points to an *inner* seat of passionate conflict from which emerge the multiple temptations by which the sense of *I* is ruefully inactivated and which it therefore can experience as an inner chaos—an id. And yet, the *I* can possibly manage some of them only by that radical awareness which Jesus here demands.

I have now come dangerously close to claiming that the authentic Jesus does, indeed, make sensible sense in terms of our present-day pursuits. So it is time to present a saying which puts exorcism more explicitly into the (literally) widest actuality in which the Galilean Jesus felt he was operating—that is, the Kingdom: "But if it is by the finger of God that I cast out demons, then the kingdom of God has come upon you" (Luke 11:20). Luther renders this *"den Teufel austreiben,"* that is, "to cast out the devil," and continues: *"so kommt je das Reich Gottes zu Euch,"* that is, "and so, every time, the reign of God comes upon you." The saying itself is said to have "high claims on authenticity," even if Matthew speaks of God's "spirit" rather than "finger"—but then the gospel writers often modify what in the original version seems to them to be a bit extreme. I like the finger, however, because it continues the theme of touch which was so prominent in the episode with the woman; except that here, of course, it is the finger of God which is operative through Jesus' action and makes the Kingdom—well, how shall we put it—come? have come? forever coming? For here we seem to have some play with time appearing in special contrast to those grand prophetic predictions of the Kingdom as some final act in history such as decisive redemption. And if the Kingdom is so vague in its temporal boundaries, *where* is it? This question Jesus answers in another context: "Behold, the kingdom of God is in the midst of you" (Luke 17:21). The Greek original, *entos hymōn,* presumably can mean "between you" as well as "within you," for Luther's translation, *"inwendig in Euch,"* claims just that.

In all these forms, the saying is considered "absolutely characteristic of oral tradition." Thomas, in fact, in his Gnostic way, presents an apparently independent parallel: "The kingdom is within you and it is without you. If you will know yourselves, then you will be known and you will know that you are the sons of the Living Father" (Thomas 3). And again, being asked by the Pharisees (to trick him, no doubt) when the kingdom was coming, Jesus answered: "The kingdom of God is not coming with signs to be observed" (Luke 17:20). This could be seen to contradict the first saying we quoted where Jesus, in fact, refers to his own observable act of healing; but Luther, again, seems to be on the right track, for he translates "not coming with signs to be observed" as *"kommt nicht mit ausserlichen Gebaerden"*; it does not "come with extraneous gestures."

If I may say in my own words what I understand all this to mean: these quotations make it clear that Jesus speaks of the Kingdom as an experience of inner as well as interpersonal actualization open to every individual who accepts his mediation. Since Jehovah, as we saw, is a god whose very being is action, such initiative, it seems, is now certified as a property of human existence—if through Jesus' mediation. For to be the voice announcing such an actuality as a potential in the here and now of every individual—that, it seems, is the essence of Jesus' ministry: "if it is by the finger of God that I . . ." We have seen that one of the conditions for the realization of such a potential is faith, which, of course, includes repentance. But, again, it is an individual decision to become aware of universal sin in one's own personal form which, of course, also means to acknowledge these universal potentials in one's neighbor. All of which implies that the "kingdom" is no longer (if it ever was) a static territory or a predictable time span: it is a dominion *(malkuth shamayim)* in motion, a Coming, a Way—a fulfillment in the present which contains an anticipation of a future.

Why do I repeat here what has been said often and better? I wish, of course, to relate it to the concept of an *I*-time, for which I have postulated, among others, the qualities of activity and wholeness, and to which I must now add that of *centrality*, a being present in the center of events. Thus, repentance as an active choice (and the Greek word for it is *metanoia*, translated by Luther as *"Umkehr"*—"turnabout") makes one central to one's life-space. With all the pain of penitence inherent in the word, one need not be inactivated by bad conscience, nor banned by divine judgment; and this seems to be a step toward the alertness of the sense of *I*, which is also implied in that repeated encouragement: "Be aware! Be wakeful! Watch!"

Having related some sayings concerned with the boundaries of adult existence, we turn to one which focuses on the beginnings of human life: childhood. Mark 10 refers to an episode when the disciples rebuked some people who brought their children ("even infants," according to Luke) to Jesus so that they might be touched by him. Indignantly, he said: " 'Let the children come to me, do not hinder them; for to such belongs the kingdom of God. Truly, I say to you, whoever does not receive the kingdom of God like a child shall not enter it.' And he took them in his arms and blessed them, laying his hands upon them" (Mark 10:14–16). A variation of this saying is offered by Matthew (18:3): "Unless you turn and become like children" . . . suggesting a turn like a positive "metanoia." Perrin places this saying among a special dozen which exhibit the radical and total character of the challenge of Jesus, and among these he calls it, *"the* most memorable and most pregnant." We will cite it as the first of a series of intergenerational expositions, the most fully carried through being the parable of the Prodigal Son. But there a father greets his delinquent young son's repentance as a return from death, and thus reminds us of all the maldevelopments that can blight childhood. Here, the saying under consideration is a total affirmation of the radiant potentials of childhood. This is the more astonishing as today we consider ourselves the discoverers of childhood, its defenders against all those history-wide negative attitudes which permitted proud and righteous as well as thoughtless adults to treat children as essentially weak or bad and in dire need of being corrected by stringent methods, or as expendable even to the point of being killed.

A detrimental counterpart of these attitudes is, of course, a more modern sentimentalization of childhood as an utterly innocent condition to be left pampered and unguided. In view of these and other trends, and especially of the Judaic concentration on bookish learning for spiritual improvement, Jesus' saying seems simply revolutionary. But it must be seen that he refers to an adult condition in which childlikeness has not been destroyed, and in which a potential return to childlike trust has not been forestalled. What is suggested, then, is a preservation and reenactment of the wonder of childhood: the "innocent eye" and ear. Consider in this connection the series of sayings commending the "seeing eyes" and "hearing ears" which can comprehend the parables tacitly.

Keeping in mind the patriarchal days in which this was said, one cannot help noticing, on Jesus' part, an unobtrusive integration of maternal and paternal tenderness. And, indeed, if we ask what reassurance for the individual *I* may be hidden in this and the following intergenerational sayings, it is, I think, the confirmation of *continuity* of the stages of development. The adult must not feel that the step of faith expected of him demands his leaving the child or, indeed, his youth behind him: on the contrary, only the continuation into maturity of true childlikeness guarantees his faith. Perrin, in this context, speaks of the child's ready trust and instinctive obedience; and I have held in my own writings that the strength of infancy is basic trust, developed in the interaction of the budding *I* with the "primal Other," namely, the maternal person (or persons). This continues into adulthood as a mutuality between growing perceptiveness and a discernible order in the universe. As to an "instinctive obedience," this, too, calls for a correspondence with the pedagogic instinct in adults. But this is the point, and probably was the point in Jesus' time: the imposition of a merely compelling obedience, with disregard of the child's natural tendency to conform, can almost guarantee inner ambivalence leading either to rebellious negation or to that widespread compulsiveness of adjustment which then is apt to find an expression in personal scrupulosity and shared ritualisms—which Jesus preached against as dangerous to faith.

4

As we now turn from sayings which have served primarily to clarify dimensions of the sense of *I* to some others concerned also with intergenerational matters, we begin with the shortest example of another of Jesus' art forms: the parable. Here, the storyteller gives away the nature of parables by asking what the contemporary generation of adults may be *comparable* to; and then selects a concrete scene that could take place any day in a Galilean town.

"But to what shall I compare this generation? It is like children sitting in the market places and calling to their playmates, 'We piped to you, and you did not dance; we wailed, and you did not mourn.' For John came neither eating nor drinking, and they say, 'He has a demon'; the Son of man came eating and drinking, and they say, 'Behold, a glutton and a drunkard, a friend of tax collectors and sinners!' Yet wisdom is justified by her deeds" (Matthew 11:16–19).

What is here called "calling" obviously means berating, because these children complain that the other children will not "dance to their piping" and in answer to their wailing will not beat their chests in mourning. In other words, they will not play the more demanding complementary parts of the game. This description, then, is meant to bring home to his listeners what Jesus thinks they are doing with him and with John the Baptist,

his mentor and baptismal initiator. It is noteworthy that Jesus, when referring to John, always speaks of him with loving respect as an absolutely
necessary step in his own revelatory mission—a fact played down by the
early church, which rests its whole case on the absolute uniqueness of
Jesus' mission. At any rate, here, in addition, Jesus proclaims John's historical right to emphasize radical asceticism in *his* part of the story, while Jesus
insists on the legitimacy of his own ritual use of a joyous table-fellowship
in which he—so shockingly for his times—includes tax collectors and sinners of all kinds who are not welcome at anybody else's table or, for that
matter, inside anybody else's house. Thus, as it were, he demonstrates the
historical relativity of all forms of daily ritualization, emphasizing that
nobody has a right to compel others to dance to his piping or, indeed, to
make them compulsively mourn—provided, of course, that whatever rituals one does choose reflect one's function in the "coming."

I know that I again repeat the obvious in all its simplicity, and this, as
before, in order to point to its importance for one of the dimensions of
the sense of *I*. Here it is the choice or the sense of one's participation in
whatever ritualization seems to express the meaning of the historical and
transhistorical moment. I have already mentioned the importance for
basic trust of the early feeding situation of the human infant, including
that meeting of eye to eye which, it is increasingly clear, is an important
source of the sense of *I*—and of a primal *We*. This, I believe, adds to the
experience of ritualized meals, besides the shared gratitude for the selection and preparation of the food served, the joy of shared compan-
ionship as expressed in the natural exchange of special glances and smiles.
This, of course, is an age-old Judaic ritualization which finds its most exalted expression in the expectation of a heavenly table-fellowship with
"many from East and West"—and all of them with Abraham, Isaac, and
Jacob. Here, indeed, each *I* finds its immortal place among the dining *We*.

But now, one word about the conclusion of this saying: "Yet wisdom
is justified by her deeds." Maybe this speaks for itself. Luke has it as "justified by all her children"—meaning, maybe, that a wise gamesmanship
will have the approval of all the "children." It will be felt to be the Way.
The saying's tenderness toward children is matched by Jesus' direct appeal
to God as Abba, an Aramaic term comparable to daddy or papa, used only
by very small children and, of course, not to be found in the Old Testament where, in fact, even the use of the appellation "Father" is rare. It is
at Gethsemane, right after Jesus had assured the disciples that he and they

would all go back to Galilee again, that in a prostrate appeal for God's decision regarding his earthly fate Jesus is said to have addressed God as "Abba" (Mark 14:36).

And now, to the most outstanding example of the use of "Father" as a direct appeal, which is, of course, the Lord's Prayer. Its authentic "directness, brevity, and intimacy," in Perrin's words, is all the more convincing in that it is a version of the traditional Kaddish which prays that God "may establish his kingdom . . . speedily." Besides its convincing poetic form, one word seems to vouch for the genuineness in Luke's version of the Lord's Prayer, which goes back to Q: only in Aramaic can the same word *(hoba')* mean "debt" and "sin" (even as the word *Schuld* in German can mean "guilt" and "debt"). To Matthew, however, the word Father does not seem to be sufficient in its intimate immediacy, and he adds "who art in heaven"—a good example of editorial embellishments of the original sayings—and here, in our terms, a certain distantiation instead of a confirmation of the immediacy which seems concordant in the "authentic" sayings. The prayer, of course, contains, in all its brevity, the principle expressed later in the "golden rule"—that is, a promised complementarity of forgiving and being forgiven which makes unnecessary what is typical in the tradition before and after Jesus, namely, the vindictive threat of a negative outcome in the case of a negative attitude.

As to the sense of *I,* "Abba," besides its radical diminution of a patriarchal, punitive threat, seems to add to the many possible meanings of fatherhood a sure dimension of *"my* father." In fact, it has, within a severe patriarchal setting, an implication of a maternal "touch." The "my" in all this also increases the sense of being selected and confirmed in one's sonship, and thus, again, a generational continuity as well as an affirmation of paternal care. This is especially important where the generational links of "biological" paternity are considered to be the earthly condition of "the Way."

To see Abba in fatherly (or, as I shall claim, parental) action, we must finally turn to some of the parables which are lost-and-found stories. As pointed out, no parable can be declared "authentic" in its totality by our form critics; nor can we claim for sure the designation "Galilean," except in the sense that wherever a parable appears in the gospels its essence must have originated in the treasure of Jesus' early talks. Here is a short one (originating in Q) which once more reminds us of the setting in which parables were apt to "happen":

Now the tax collectors and sinners were all drawing near to hear him. And the Pharisees and the scribes murmured, saying, "This man receives sinners and eats with them." So he told them this parable: "What man of you, having a hundred sheep, if he has lost one of them, does not leave the ninety-nine in the wilderness, and go after the one which is lost, until he finds it? And when he has found it, he lays it on his shoulders, rejoicing. And when he comes home, he calls together his friends and his neighbors, saying to them, 'Rejoice with me, for I have found my sheep which was lost.' Just so, I tell you, there will be more joy in heaven over one sinner who repents than over ninety-nine righteous persons who need no repentance." [Luke 15: 1–7]

To illustrate the inventiveness some of the parables can evoke in different gospel writers, let us compare St. Thomas's Gnostic version:

Jesus said: "The Kingdom is like a shepherd who had a hundred sheep. One of them went astray, which was the largest. He left behind ninety-nine, he sought for the one until he found it. Having tired himself out, he said to the sheep: 'I love thee more than ninety-nine.' " [Thomas 107]

Here we see Thomas making sense out of the parable by appointing the lost sheep the largest of the hundred and therefore a logical object both of the shepherd's search and of his love.

There has been much discussion as to the danger the shepherd exposed the vast majority of the *non*-lost sheep to by following that single lost one: or did he, maybe, as Jeremias suggests, pursue it only after the others were safely in their fold? My group-psychological orientation makes me feel that there is *some* safety in mere numbers for animals with *some* herd instinct. But it is obviously difficult not to wonder by what right God or Jesus may pay such exclusive attention to one nearly lost creature—unless, of course, it reminds us of ourselves.

This brings us to the story of the "Prodigal Son," which immediately follows in Luke 15:11. One must have tried to paraphrase such a parable to realize how essential is every detail. So here it is, in full:

And he said, "There was a man who had two sons; and the younger of them said to his father, 'Father, give me the share of property that falls to me.' And he divided his living between them. Not many days later, the younger son gathered all he had and took his journey into a far country, and there he squandered his property in loose living. And when he had spent everything, a great famine arose in that country, and he began to be in want. So he went and joined himself to one of the citizens of that country, who sent him into his fields to feed swine. And he would gladly have fed on the pods that the swine ate; and no one gave him anything. But when he came to himself he said, 'How many of my father's hired servants have bread enough and to spare, but I perish here with hunger! I will arise and go to my father, and I will say to him, "Father, I have sinned against heaven and before you; I am no longer worthy to be called your son; treat me as one of your hired servants." ' And he arose and came to his father. But while he was yet at a distance, his father saw him and had compassion, and ran and embraced him and kissed him. And the son said to him, 'Father, I have sinned against heaven and before you; I am no longer worthy to be called your son.' But the father said to his servants, 'Bring quickly the best robe, and put it on him; and put a ring on his hand, and shoes on his feet; and bring the fatted calf and kill it, and let us eat and make merry; for this my son was dead, and is alive again; he was lost, and is found.' And they began to make merry.

"Now his elder son was in the field; and as he came and drew near to the house, he heard music and dancing. And he called one of the servants and asked what this meant. And he said to him, 'Your brother has come, and your father has killed the fatted calf, because he has received him safe and sound.' But he was angry and refused to go in. His father came out and entreated him, but he answered his father, 'Lo, these many years I have served you, and I never disobeyed your command; yet you never gave me a kid, that I might make merry with my friends. But when this son of yours came, who has devoured your living with harlots, you killed for him the fatted calf!' And he said to him, 'Son, you are always with me, and all that is mine is yours. It was fitting to make merry and be glad, for this your brother was dead, and is alive; he was lost, and is found.' " [Luke 15:11–32]

The two distinct parts of the parable make us alternately sympathize with the lost son and with the older one who was so concerned over all the excessive attention to his younger brother. Yet the parable is so evenly constructed that we can end up only realizing that both brothers are at odds within us, too. Incidentally, the whole setting must have felt quite ordinary to listeners of that day, since it was apparently quite common then (and quite legal) for younger sons to ask their fathers for their share and to seek their fortunes in, say, a Levantine city. So the really outstanding item is the young man's delinquent disposition and the accident of a famine which made it necessary for him to become dependent on a foreign master who forced him to become a swineherd. Strangely, even to be a shepherd in those days would have put him in the category of an outcast or of a "gentile sinner"—the kind of person that Jesus associated with so liberally but was "rightfully" despised by such Pharisee-like personalities as the older brother. Whether or not the father knew of all his younger son's misfortunes, the highly ritualized welcome immediately established the fact that the son's loss of status did not count with the father. Where Luke's text speaks of the approaching boy's "distance" at the moment when his father espied him, incidentally, the King James version makes him as yet "a great way off," which suggests that the father had begun to look out for him and that the immediate welcome he arranged had long been planned, from the kiss of forgiveness to the robe of an honored guest, from the ring of special status to the fatted calf.

Even lengthy parables can be summarized in a brief saying. I think the last dozen words of the Prodigal Son will do: "Your brother was dead, and is alive; he was lost, and is found." Again, then, the "Way" is "within" and "amidst you." And the Abba was steadfast in loving both these sons—so different in familial status and in personality. Almost like a mother, some readers may be tempted to say, and, indeed, as one reviews this parable's theme of the healing of the generational process, one cannot help asking: was there, in this earthly vision of the comparison, no mother, either dead or alive? And if alive, was she not called to say hello, too? But a parable is not a case history or even history; and as to the implied comparison with God, it must be remembered that in all the masculinity dictated by the patriarchal "system" and the rules of language, the dominating quality of the deity was that of a pervasive spirit, out of bounds for any personal characterization: "I am that I am."

And so the parable's meaning, in its patriarchal and monotheistic setting, is the father's overall parental care and above all his forgiveness which permits him to take special chances with the lost ones—that is, to take chances with those who took chances—so as to let them find both themselves and him. The story of the Prodigal Son thus reaffirms generational and existential continuity, confirmed by the joy of table fellowship.

And, too, the parables are apt to deal with the power of potential growth—for example, in the tiny mustard seed:

> And he said, "With what can we compare the kingdom of God, or what parable shall we use for it? It is like a grain of mustard seed, which, when sown upon the ground, is the smallest of all the seeds on earth; yet when it is sown it grows up and becomes the greatest of all shrubs, and puts forth large branches, so that the birds of the air can make nests in its shade." [Mark 4:30–32]

This text speaks entirely for itself; but Perrin provides an image found in the Jewish literature where birds in the branches of a tall tree symbolize nations finding a common nesting ground in the messianic future. Thus, parables can lead from the simplest and most concrete observations to unlimited implications, always restating in an imagery speaking to the least intellectual of minds the promise of the future which begins in the immediate present.

Jesus' sayings and his parables, then, complement each other in their logic and in their imagery. The parable of the Prodigal Son makes it clear that the father and the sons can find themselves and one another only by gaining their own identity in the very fulfillment of their intergenerational tasks within their cultural and economic matrix (is *that* the missing mother?). And this, as I hope to have indicated, is among the dimensions demanded by every listener's sense of *I*—wherefore in listening the audience becomes tuned to the storyteller's peculiar *caring* about these dimensions. And here, a pervasive peculiarity of Jesus' care seems to be his essential nonviolence, and this in spite of an occasional militancy which, in fact, is a necessary trait for the nonviolent. As he seems to advocate a maximum of work and a minimum of "works," so he demands a maximum of strength but a minimum of violence—whether against the self in the form of debilitating guilt or against others as hatefulness. Let us review, in conclusion, some sayings pertinent to this theme.

In Perrin's discussion of authentic sayings, that about children immediately precedes the following one about overcoming violence:

"But if anyone strikes you on the right cheek, turn to him the other also; and if any one would sue you and take your coat, let him have your cloak as well; and if any one forces you to go one mile, go with him two miles." [Matthew 5:39b–41]

Nothing could be more abruptly (one is tempted to say "violently") demanding than this and similar suggestions of responses to violent challenges: interestingly enough, to those in the know the turning of the left cheek adds the invitation of a special insult to the danger of injury; the offer of the cloak implies total nakedness; and the party that can force you to go one mile is the Roman soldiery. Here, even Perrin is somewhat perplexed and concludes that these are intended to be "vivid examples" which "exceed normal and natural" human tendencies in order to "imitate the reality of God." But here, for once, I must disagree, and this on the basis of having studied the nonviolent tactics of one of Jesus' modern followers, Mahatma Gandhi. Nonviolent behavior must often be shocking in order to shake up the violent opponent's seemingly so normal attitude, to make him feel that his apparently undebatable and spotless advantage in aggressive initiative is being taken away from him and that he is being forced to overdo his own action absurdly. For human violence almost never feels all that "natural," even to the aggressor himself—neither the violence toward children nor that against loved persons nor even that evoked by declared enemies. And here what Freud called the human superego—that is, the self-negating part of the human conscience as developed in childhood—is fortified by the experience of moral as well as physical violence from adults, while in adulthood it can become so oppressive that one can maintain one's self-esteem only by turning the very violence of one's superego against an evil in others which one wishes to deny in oneself. This, then, can lead to the designation of whole groups of others to membership in what I have called a not-quite-human (or quite unhuman) *pseudo-species,* the extermination of which then becomes a service to God.

5

I have now counterposed a few examples of the style and the logic of Jesus of Nazareth's original sayings with some of the dimensions of the human sense of *I.* I did so because I share the belief that the elemental sayings that emerged in the millennium "before Christ," and in Jesus' own short life, all deal with dimensions of human consciousness in a new manner nowadays expressed in the terms of *individuality* and *universality,* that is, a more aware *I* related to a more universal *We,* approaching the idea of one mankind. In my chosen context, however, I could not attempt to look back on the roots of these sayings in the Judaic world; nor could I review some of Freud's dramatic conjectures concerning the archaic and infantile origins of the Mosaic religion—and its gradual self-transcendence through spirituality and intellectuality. As to Jesus' ministry, I had to stop short of the Judaean Passion that followed the Galilean period after Jesus' decision to confront militantly but nonviolently the violence latent in the political and spiritual deals between the Roman and the priestly establishments by which mortally endangered Israel had learned to live. Here, so one could extend the parable just reported, the son of man took chances not just with the lost ones but also with those who act out so strenuously the roles they find appropriate for their superior identity.

What followed was the crucifixion and the reported resurrection of him who thus became Christ and whose course of life was then creatively mythologized—from the nativity to the ascension. What was then recorded in writing for the Hellenistic world in the services of the mother churches of Christianity developed another kind of authenticity best illustrated by the then emerging victorious symbolisms—such as that of the cross, which, in its utter simplicity, seems to combine the form of homo erectus with his arms all-inclusively extended and that of the son of man dying a deliberately human death under the most vulnerable conditions, only to be resurrected as the savior. Or think of the maternal Madonna who gradually occupied such a shining ceremonial center. The ensuing history of ritualization, however, with all its wealth of new social, cultural, and artistic forms, eventually could not escape manufacturing its own kind of compulsive ritualism, including a new pseudo-speciation which permitted the saved species to use even the Christian faith as a rationale for crusades—and murderous hate.

All this must make us even more attentive to the study of the origins and eventual evolution of those simplest revelatory formulations. For their very brevity and simplicity of manifest meaning could never be contrived, and could emerge only when their time had come; even as in subsequent periods they were and had to be experienced with a new immediacy in terms of changing human actualities. In this connection (and to return once more to that question of authenticity) it seems that the least authentic of the reported sayings of Jesus are those which are most concrete or descriptive in their predictions of the forms the kingdom may take, such as those offered so definitively in the apocalyptic expectations. Perrin concludes: "Time is thought . . . as opportunity or occasion, as something which is given meaning by that which fills it." This demonstrates, he adds, "the inadequacy of a linear concept of time"—which reminds us once more of Einstein's concept of an *I*-time:

> The experiences of an individual appear to us arranged in a series of events; in this series the single events which we remember appear to be ordered according to the criterion of "earlier" and "later." There exists, therefore, for the individual, an I-time, or subjective time. This in itself is not measurable. [Lincoln Barnett, *The Universe and Dr. Einstein*]

But what would Einstein have thought of our main concern with Jesus' sayings? With the challenging naivete of genius he makes (in his *Ideas and Opinions*) a number of statements which must interest us most of all, because he associates "the Judaism of the Prophets and Christianity as Jesus Christ taught it" as one body of teaching "capable of curing all the social ills of humanity"—and therefore worthy of being purged of all subsequent additions, "especially those of the priests." In this context Einstein muses that the Jewish God is "simply a negation of superstition, an imaginary result of its elimination. It is also an attempt to base the moral law on fear, a regrettable and discreditable attempt [*bedauernswert, unruehmlich*]. Yet it seems to me that the strong moral tradition of the Jewish nation has to a large extent shaken itself free from this fear. It is clear also that 'serving God' was equated with 'serving the living.' " And again: "The best of the Jewish people, especially the Prophets and Jesus, contended tirelessly for this." Finally, Einstein extols as a contrast to the emphasis on fear "something which finds splendid expression in many of the Psalms, namely, a sort of intoxicated joy and amazement at the beauty and grandeur of this world." And here he adds a sentence connecting it all with the modernity of mind: "This joy is the feeling from which true scientific research draws its spiritual sustenance."

Einstein's reference to "joy" in this connection might remind us of the role "wonder" played during his childhood in drawing him toward scientific observation, which, as he said on another occasion, turned him from the *I* and the *We* to the *It*—and its revelatory power. For he perceived the fact that "the world of our sense experience is comprehensible as a miracle" which permits him to share "Spinoza's God," "who reveals himself in the orderly harmony of what exists."

What must especially interest us, however, is Einstein's remark, made in passing, concerning the strong tendency in Judaism to "base the moral law on fear"—a tendency which, as we saw, seems to be transcended in the Galilean sayings. We have, of course, suggested that the adoration of Jehovah as a threatening and vengeful god was part of a monotheistic covenant which would eventually compensate for all earthly terror, for it would make historical disasters part of an overall plan designed by an ultimately benevolent, universally caring power. But in its most primitive manifestations this trend must be viewed as another manifestation of that innate human tendency to internalize the morally threatening figures of parental voices and gestures, a tendency which Freud so tellingly called the superego—that is, an inner voice lording it over the sense of *I* and, so it appears from many biblical passages, apt to be "projected" on the monotheistic world order. Here, no future world image can afford to neglect the insights of psychoanalysis which awakened human awareness to the superego's pathogenic inner tyranny in order to heal some of the unconscious sources of unmanageable self-hate as well as the hate of otherness. To do this, the psychoanalytic procedure had to open up the forgotten recesses of childhood, first uncovering a primal source of neurotic suffering and then revealing a treasure of human potentialities, the knowledge of which, as we saw, adds such explicit meaning to Jesus' sayings about children. And here we can, for the adult stages of life, add the deeply religious belief of Einstein, the "childlike" scientist, in the correspondence of the *I*'s searching for orientation in the world, and in "Spinoza's God." A corresponding complementarity, here applied to the symbolic equation of the *I* with an inner eye full of light, can be seen in sayings throughout the centuries—such as Meister Eckhart's "The eye with which we see God is the same as the eye with which God sees us." Hegel, in turn, seems to suggest some caution in an otherwise equally sweeping promise: "Man knows about God only insofar as God knows about himself in man." We have seen how, finally, Freud decided that on the way to more knowledge man must learn to understand the human unconscious as the source of the most destructive and self-destructive drives—an aspect of human nature which Einstein, like Freud, all too soon found associated with the most sublime scientific and technical inventiveness.

Therefore, a brief concluding word about the lasting implications of the militant nonviolence practiced and recommended by Jesus. In my *Gandhi's Truth* I reported how on a visit to India I found myself a guest in a city (Ahmedabad) and in a circle of individuals among whom were some survivors of the first nonviolent adventure engaged in by Gandhi in India—a circumstance which permitted me to study this event in psychoanalytical terms: whereupon it became quite apparent to what extent this Indian prophet, in establishing new, nonviolent principles of political and economic action in his South African days, had knowingly combined elements of his native religion with Jesus' sayings and actions. While Gandhi's personal conflicts seem to have included quite a struggle with a somewhat Western superego, his principles included, besides a readiness for martyrdom, the taking of that daring chance already alluded to in these pages, namely, a conscious and determined projection of the *best* in us, on the (seemingly) *worst* enemy, and a willingness to face him nonviolently. (In British terms of understatement, this was expressed in Gandhi's rather regularly having afternoon tea with the very mill owner against whom he was leading a nonviolent strike.) The setting of this strike may now seem to some of us to be as far removed from our worldwide scene as were the Galilean hills of Jesus' time. And, indeed, any possible solution in human terms of today's biggest threats to humanity would have to come to grips with the danger that human beings will become impotent manipulators in a technically perfect system of destruction and thus participate in the killing of millions of individuals without feeling mortally angry even at one.

In this overwhelming technological context, I must now conclude that we can hardly ignore—for whatever denominational reasons—what as yet can be learned about the basic sayings of our religious tradition and thus about the evolution of human consciousness and conscience. Here, the Galilean sayings must count as an event central to our Judaeo-Christian heritage—a step in human comprehension and self-awareness which is by no means fully expressed in, or restricted to, its ecclesiastic fate.

NOTES

I. ON CHILDREN: NEARBY AND FAR AWAY

"Hunters Across the Prairie"

1. Carl Sandburg, *The People, Yes.* New York: Harcourt, Brace, 1936.

2. P. I. Wellman, *Death on the Prairie.* New York: Macmillan, 1934.

3. C. Wissler, "Depression and Revolt," *Natural History,* 41:2, 1938.

4. Wellman, *op. cit.*

5. G. MacGregor, *Warriors without Weapons.* University of Chicago Press, 1946.

6. H. S. Mekeel, *The Economy of a Modern Teton-Dakota Community.* Yale Publications in Anthropology, Nos. 1–7. New Haven: Yale University Press, 1936.

7. C. Wissler, *Societies and Ceremonial Associations in the Oglala Division of the Teton-Dakota.* Anthropological Papers of the American Museum of Natural History, Vol. XI, Part 1. New York, 1912.

8. *Ibid.*

9. T. S. Lincoln, *The Dream in Primitive Cultures.* London: Cresset Press, 1935.

10. G. MacGregor, *op.cit.*

"Fisherman Along a Salmon River"

1. A. L. Kroeber, "The Yurok," in *Handbook of the Indians of California.* Bureau of American Ethnology, Bulletin 78, 1925.

2. T. T. Waterman, *Yurok Geography.* University of California Press, 1920.

3. For a more detailed analysis of the Yurok world see Erikson, *Observations on the Yurok: Childhood and World Image.* University of California Publications in American Archaeology and Ethnology, Vol. 35, No. 10. University of California Press, 1943.

"Toys and Reasons"

1. Sigmund Freud, *A General Selection,* edited by John Rickman. London: The Hogarth Press and the Institute of Psycho-Analysis, 1937.

2. George Santayana, *The Last Puritan.* New York: Charles Scribner's Sons, 1936.

3. Anna Freud, *Psycho-Analytical Treatment of Children.* London: Imago Publishing Co., 1946.

4. Ruth Benedict, "Continuities and Discontinuities in Cultural Conditioning," *Psychiatry,* I: 161–167, 1938.

5. Members of the Federal Writers' Projects, *Phrases of the People.* New York: The Viking Press, 1937.

I I .   O N   P S Y C H O A N A L Y S I S   A N D   H U M A N   D E V E L O P M E N T

"The First Psychoanalyst"

1. Ernest Jones, *The Life and Work of Sigmund Freud.* New York: Basic Books, 1953.

2. Sigmund Freud, "Fragment of an Analysis of a Case of Hysteria" [1905], *Standard Edition,* 7:3–122. London: Hogarth Press, 1953.

3. Sigmund Freud, *The Origins of Psychoanalysis: Letters to Wilhelm Fliess, Drafts and Notes: 1887–1902,* edited by Marie Bonaparte, Anna Freud and Ernst Kris. New York: Basic Books, 1954.

4. Sigmund Freud, *The Interpretation of Dreams* [1900]. *Standard Edition,* 4, London: Hogarth Press, 1953.

5. David Rapaport, "The Structure of Psychoanalytic Theory: A Systemizing Attempt," in *Psychology: A Study of a Science,* Vol. III, edited by Sigmund Koch. New York: McGraw-Hill, 1959.

The Nature of Clinical Evidence

1. R. G. Collingwood, *The Idea of History.* New York: Oxford University Press, 1956.

2. Erik H. Erikson, "The Dream Specimen of Psychoanalysis," *Journal of the American Psychoanalytic Association,* 2:5–56, 1954.

3. Erik H. Erikson, "Identity and the Lifecycle," Monograph, *Psychological Issues,* Vol. I, No. 1. New York: International Universities Press, 1959.

4. Erik H. Erikson, "Youth: Fidelity and Diversity," *Daedalus,* 91:5–27, 1962.

5. David Rapaport and M. Gill, "The Points of View and Assumptions of Metapsychology," *International Journal of Psycho-analysis,* 40:1–10, 1959.

"Human Strength and the Cycle of Generations"

1. Erik H. Erikson, *Childhood and Society,* second edition. New York: W. W. Norton, 1963.

2. Erik H. Erikson, "The Psychosocial Development of Children" and "The Syndrome of Identity Diffusion in Adolescents and Young Adults," *Discussions in Child Development,* World Health Organization, Vol. III. New York: International Universities Press, 1958.

3. Jean Piaget and B. Inhelder, *The Growth of Logical Thinking from Childhood to Adolescence.* New York: Basic Books, 1958. See also P. H. Wolff, "Piaget's Genetic Psychology and Its Relation to Psychoanalysis," Monograph, *Psychological Issues,* Vol. II, No. 5. New York: International Universities Press, 1960.

4. R. W. White, "Motivation Reconsidered: The Concept of Competence," *Psychological Review,* 66:297–333, 1959.

5. Erik H. Erikson, editor, *Youth: Change and Challenge.* New York: Basic Books, 1963.

6. Erik H. Erikson, "Reflections on Womanhood," *Daedalus,* spring 1964.

7. Therese Benedek, "Parenthood as a Developmental Phase," *Journal of the American Psychoanalytic Association,* VII: 3, 1959.

8. C. Buehler, *Der menschliche Lebenslauf als psychologisches Problem.* Goettingen: Verlag fuer Psychologie, 1959.

9. Jean Piaget, *Le Problème des Stades en Psychologie de L'enfant.* Geneva: Presses Universitaires de France, 1955.

10. Erik H. Erikson, *Childhood and Society, op. cit.*

11. C. H. Waddington, *The Ethical Animal.* London: Allen and Unwin, 1960.

12. Erik H. Erikson, "The Roots of Virtue," in *The Humanist Frame,* edited by Julian Huxley. New York: Harper, 1961.

13. A. Roe and L. Z. Freedman, "Evolution and Human Behavior," in *Behavior and Evolution,* edited by A. Roe and G. C. Simpson. New Haven: Yale University Press, 1958.

14. T. H. Huxley and J. S. Huxley, *Touchstone for Ethics.* New York: Harper, 1947.

15. Sigmund Freud, *The Ego and the Id* [1923]. New York: W. W. Norton, 1961.

16. Anna Freud, *The Ego and the Mechanisms of Defense* [1936]. New York: International Universities Press, 1946.

17. H. Hartmann, *Ego Psychology and the Problem of Adaptation* [1939]. New York: International Universities Press, 1958.

18. *The Letters of William James,* edited by Henry James (his son). Boston: Atlantic Monthly Press, 1920.

III. ON LEADERS

"The Legend of Maxim Gorky's Youth"

1. This chapter developed out of my participation as occasional consultant in the Columbia University Research Project in Contemporary Cultures, sponsored by the Office of Naval Research. For facts and insights I owe thanks to the members of the Russian group in this project, especially to Sula Benet, Nicolas Calas, Geoffrey Gorer, Nathan Leites, and Bertram Schaffner; and above all to their seminar leader, Margaret Mead, who introduced me to the moving picture reviewed here.

2. According to a prospectus in the film library of the Museum of Modern Art in New York, the moving picture discussed here was first shown in Moscow in 1938. The producer was a writer named Mark Donskoi, the firm Soyuztetfilm. I saw the picture in New York in March, 1948.

3. A. Roskin, *From the Banks of the Volga.* New York: Philosophical Library, 1946.

4. Maxim Gorky, *Reminiscences of Tolstoy, Chekhov and Andreyev.* New York: The Viking Press, Inc., 1959.

5. Leon Trotsky, "The Russian in Lenin," *Current History Magazine,* March, 1924.

6. Freud, in his paper "Dostoevski and Patricide," likened *The Brothers Karamazov* to Shakespeare's *Hamlet* and to Sophocles' *King Oedipus,* and this because these three works measure up to a common artistic greatness, while they take father-murder as their central theme.

7. Maxim Gorky, *op. cit.*

8. See the following exchange at the Moscow trials:

Vishinsky: "Did you endorse these negotiations [with the Germans]?"

Bukharin: "Or disavow? I did not disavow, consequently I endorsed."

Vishinsky: "But you say that you learned of this post factum."

Bukharin: "Yes, the one does not contradict the other."

9. Tolstoy once said to Gorky: "It is not easy to believe that you were once a child." Gorky, *op. cit.*

10. Geoffrey Gorer, "Some Aspects of the Psychology of the People of Great Russia," *The American Slavic and Eastern European Review,* 1949. See also Geoffrey Gorer and John Rickman, *The People of Great Russia.* New York: W. W. Norton, 1962.

11. Gorky, *op. cit.*

12. Roskin, *op. cit.*

13. Roskin, *op. cit.*

14. Gorky, *op. cit.*

15. Gorky, *op. cit.*

"The Fit in the Choir"

1. Otto Scheel, *Martin Luther: Vom Katholizismus zur Reformation,* II. Tuebingen: J. C. B. Mohr, 1917, p. 116. Source referred to hereafter as Scheel.

2. Otto Scheel, *Dokumente zu Luthers Entwicklung,* No. 533 Tuebingen: No. 533. J. C. B. Mohr, 1929. Source referred to hereafter as *Dok.*

3. *Dok.,* No. 533.

4. Johannes Cochlaeus, *Commentaria de actis et scriptis Martini Lutheri.* Mainz: 1549).

5. Scheel, II, 117.

6. *Dok.,* No. 533.

7. P. Heinrich Denifle, *Luther in Rationalistischer und Christlicher Beleuchtung.* Mainz: Kirchheim & Co., 1904, p. 31.

8. Paul J. Reiter, *Martin Luthers Umwelt, Charakter und Psychose,* II. Kopenhagen: Leven & Munksgaard, 1937, p. 99. Source referred to hereafter as Reiter.

9. Reiter, II, 556.

10. Reiter, II, 240.

11. Preserved Smith, *The Life and Letters of Martin Luther.* New York: Houghton Mifflin & Co., 1911.

12. Preserved Smith, *Luther's Correspondence.* Philadelphia: The Lutheran Publication Society, 1913.

13. Preserved Smith, "Luther's Early Development in the Light of Psychoanalysis," *American Journal of Psychology,* XXIV, 1913.

14. *Ibid.,* 362.

15. *Dok.,* No. 199.

16. Martin Luther, *Werke,* XXXIII, 507. Weimarer Ausgabe, 1883, Source referred to hereafter as *L.W.W.A.*

17. Scheel, I, 261.

18. Heinrich Boehmer, *Road to Reformation.* Philadelphia: Muhlenberg Press, 1946.

19. Leopold von Ranke, *History of the Reformation in Germany.* London, 1905.

20. Theodosius Harnack, *Luthers Theologie I* (1862); *II* (1886).

21. Hartmann Grisar, *Luther.* Freiburg: Herder Verlag, 1911.

22. Lucien Febvre, *Martin Luther, A Destiny.* London: J. M. Dent & Sons, Ltd., 1930, 18.

23. Denifle, *Luther in Rationalistischer, op. cit.,* p. 77.

24. P. Heinrich Denifle, *Luther und Luthertum in der ersten Entwicklung,* I. Mainz: Kirchheim & Co., 1906, pp. 774–75.

25. *Ibid.*

26. Reiter, II, 121.

27. R. Pascal, *The Social Basis of the German Reformation.* London: Watts & Co., 1933, p. 227.

28. Ernst Troeltsch, *The Social Teaching of the Christian Churches.* London: 1931.

29. Max Weber, *The Protestant Ethic and the Spirit of Capitalism.* London: 1948.

30. R. H. Tawney, *Religion and the Rise of Capitalism.* New York: Harcourt, Brace and Co., 1952.

31. Quoted in Heinrich Bornkamm, *Luther in Spiegel der deutschen Geistesgeschichte.* Heidelberg: Quelle und Meyer, 1955, p. 191.

32. *Dok.,* No. 209.

33. *Dok.,* No. 248.

34. Quoted in Bornkamm, *op. cit.,* 330.

35. William James, *Varieties of Religious Experience.* Longmans, Green and Co., 1935, p. 199.

36. E. H. Erikson, "The Problem of Ego Identity," *Journal of the American Psychoanalytic Association,* 4. 1956, p. 56–121.

37. G. B. Shaw, Preface to *Selected Prose* New York: Dodd, Mead and Co., 1952.

38. E. H. Erikson, "The First Psychoanalyst," *The Yale Review,* XLVI. 1956, p. 43.

39. Sigmund Freud, *The Interpretation of Dreams,* Complete Psychological Works of Sigmund Freud, Volumes IV and V. London: Hogarth Press, 1953.

40. *L.W.W.A.,* VII, 838.

"The Meaning of 'Meaning It'"

1. I Corinthians 14:31.

2. Anne Freemantle, *The Age of Belief.* New York: Mentor, 1954, 26–27.

3. *Ibid.,* 28, 33.

4. I Corinthians 4:7.

5. Huizinga, Ref. 15, Chapter III, 204.

6. *Ibid.,* 205.

7. *Ibid.,* 219.

8. *Ibid.,* 199.

9. Wilhelm Link, *Das Ringen Luthers um die Freiheit der Theologie von der Philosophie.* Muenchen: Chr. Kaiser, 1940, 319–21; 324–25; 340.

10. Giorgio de Santillana, *The Age of Adventure.* Boston: Houghton Mifflin Company, 1957, 13–14.

11. Pico, "On the Dignity of Man," *The Renaissance Philosophy of Man,* edited by E. Crosirer, P. O. Rinsteller and J. H. Randall. Chicago: Phoenix Books, 1956, 225.

12. Santillana, *Age of Adventure.* 83–84.

13. *Ibid.,* 155.

14. *Ibid.,* 69.

15. *Ibid.,* 15.

16. Quoted by Preserved Smith, *Life and Letters, op. cit.,* Chapter II, 206.

17. *L.W.W.A.,* III, 593.

18. Erich Vogelsang, *Die Anfaenge von Luthers Christologie.* Berlin: De Gruyter Co., 1929, O. 89, fn. 1. Source referred to hereafter as Vogelsang. *Cf. L.W.W.A.,* XL, 1, 562.

19. *Dok.,* No. 182. *Cf. L.W.W.A.,* XL, 1, 562.

20. *L.W.W.A.,* III, 531.

21. *L.W.W.A.,* III, 134.

22. *L.W.W.A.,* III, 257; III, 14. *Cf.* Vogelsang, 6, fn. 2.

23. *L.W.W.A.,* IV, 330.

24. Vogelsang, 58, fn. 1.

25. *L.W.W.A.,* III, 12. *Cf.* Vogelsang, 26.

26. Vogelsang, 32.

27. Luther's *Tischreden,* V, No. 5247. Weimarer Ausgaben. Source referred to hereafter as *TR.*

28. Vogelsang, 32–33.

29. *Ibid.,* 33.

30. Psalms 31:4.

31. Psalms 31:6.

32. Matthew 27:43.

33. Vogelsang, 50–51.

34. *Dok.,* No. 238.

35. *TR,* V, No. 5537.

36. *L.W.W.A.,* III, 408.

37. *L.W.W.A.,* IV, 9, 18.

38. *L.W.W.A.,* III, 227, 28.

39. *L.W.W.A.,* II, 28, 13.

40. *L.W.W.A.,* III, 651.

41. Sigmund Freud, *The Origins of Psychoanalysis.* London: Imago Publishing Co. Ltd., 1954, p. 236.

42. Johannes Ficker, *Luthers Vorlesung ueber den Roemerbrief Herausg.* Leipzig: Die Scholien, 1930, p. 206.

43. *L.W.W.A.,* IV, 234.

44. *L.W.W.A.,* V, 149.

45. *L.W.W.A.,* IV, 511.

46. *L.W.W.A.,* IX, 639.

47. I Corinthians 1:22–5.

48. I Corinthians 2:1–3.

49. *L.W.W.A.,* III, 420.

50. *L.W.W.A.,* III, 289.

51. *L.W.W.A.,* XL/1, 537.

52. *L.W.W.A.,* IV, 147.

53. *L.W.W.A.,* IV, 330. *Cf.* Vogelsang, 103, fn. 1; and 108, fn. 1.

54. *L.W.W.A.,* IV, 87.

55. *L.W.W.A.,* III, 529. *Cf.* Vogelsang, 136, fn. 5.

56. *L.W.W.A.,* IV, 365.

57. *L.W.W.A.,* IV, 350.

58. *L.W.W.A.,* XXXII, 390.

59. William James, *Varieties of Religious Experience.* Longmans, Green and Co., 1935, Chapter 10.

60. *L.W.W.A.,* IX, 45.

61. *L.W.W.A.,* III, 289.

62. *L.W.W.A.,* VI, 207.

63. I have mislaid this reference; but no fairminded reader will suspect me of having invented this quotation.

64. *L.W.W.A.,* I, 200–201.

65. *L.W.W.A.,* V, 85.

"Epilogue"

1. *TR,* I, No. 352.

2. *L.W.W.A.,* V, 163.

3. *L.W.W.A.,* XIX, 216–17; translated in Gordon Rupp, *The Righteousness of God.* London: Hodder and Stoughton, 1953, Chapter VIII, 108.

4. *L. W. W.A.*, V, 79; translated in Rupp, *op. cit.*, 107.

5. *L. W. W.A.*, XLIV, 504.

6. *L. W. W.A.*, IV, 602; translated in Rupp, *op. cit.*, 109.

7. E. L. Enders, *Martin Luthers Briefwechsel*, V. Frankfurt: 1884–1907, pp. 278–79.

8. E. H. Erikson, "Integrity," *Childhood and Society.*

9. Seng-ts'an, Hsin-hsin, Ming. Alan W. Watts, *The Way of Zen*. New York: Pantheon Books, 1957.

10. See Ernst Kris' concept of a regression in the service of the ego, *Psychoanalytic Explorations in Art* New York: International Universities Press, 1952.

11. Sigmund Freud, *The Origins of Psychoanalysis.* London: Imago Publishing Co. Ltd., 1954, Chapter I.

"Homo Religiosus"

1. For an elaboration of this distinction, see Erik H. Erikson, "Psychological Reality and Historical Actuality," *Insight and Responsibility*. New York: W. W. Norton, 1964, pp. 159–216.

2. For an approach to the problem of psychological immortality, see Robert Lifton, *Revolutionary Immortality—Mao Tse-tung and the Chinese Cultural Revolution*. New York: Random House, 1968.

3. This is uniquely and impressively developed by Joan Bondurant, *Conquest of Violence— The Gandhian Philosophy of Conflict,* revised edition. Berkeley: University of California Press, 1965.

4. A German biographic-psychiatric dictionary spends one of a total of eight lines devoted to the Mahatma on the intelligence that Gandhi "slept with his women servants in one bed"—not specifying the time and duration of such a habit. Similarly, Arthur Koestler in *The Lotus and The Robot,* London: Hutchinson, 1966, relates in a footnote that the aged Gandhi had been found by the British police in bed with a naked young girl, but that they wisely abstained from publishing their discovery. This gossip ignores the fact that the British police at the time of the alleged incident no longer visited Gandhi by surprise at nighttime, that there were neither beds nor doors in the sleeping arrangements, that nakedness is a relative matter in the tropics, and that the whole matter never was a secret.

5. Nirmal Kumar Bose, *My Days With Gandhi*. Calcutta: Nishana, 1953, esp. pp. 131–137, 154–160.

6. Manubehn Gandhi, *Bapu—My Mother.* Ahmedabad: Navajivan, 1949.

7. L. and M. Milne, *The Ages of Life*. New York: Harcourt, Brace & World, 1968, p. 265.

8. Bose, *op. cit.,* p. 183.

9. As detailed for some in Part Three, III.

"The Instrument"

1. *The Collected Works of Mahatma Gandhi.* Delhi: Government of India, Ministry of Information and Broadcasting, The Publications Division, 1958 and following, XV, 4. Source referred to hereafter as *CWMG.*

2. Joan Bondurant, Conquest of Violence—The Ghandian Philosophy of Conflict, revised edition. Berkeley: University of California Press. p. 25.

3. Erikson, *Insight and Responsibility, op. cit.,* pp. 219–243.

4. Bondurant, *op. cit.,* p. 111.

5. Pyarelal, "The Right and Wrong Uses of Fasting: How Gandhiji's Standards Apply Today," *The Statesman,* January 3, 1967, p. 6.

6. *The Statesman,* February 15, 1967, p. 7.

7. Quoted in Fischer, *The Life of Mahatma Gandhi.* p. 238.

8. *Ibid.,* pp. 282, 283.

9. Sigmund Freud, "Why War?" Freud's letter to Einstein dated September 1932, in *Collected Papers,* V, edited by James Strachey. London: Hogarth Press, 1950, p. 274.

10. Konrad Lorenz, *On Aggression,* M. K. Wilson, trans. New York: Harcourt, Brace & World, 1966.

11. See, for example, Konrad Lorenz' vivid description in *King Solomon's Ring.* New York: Thomas Crowell Co., 1952.

12. See my "Psychoanalysis and Ongoing History: Problems of Identity, Hatred and Non-violence," *American Journal of Psychiatry,* CXXII, September, 1965, pp. 241–250; "Ontogeny of Ritualization in Man," and "Concluding Remarks," Discussion on Ritualization of Behavior in Animals and Man, in *Philosophical Transactions of the Royal Society of London,* Series B, vol. 251, 1966, pp. 523, 524.

13. Erikson, "Insight and Freedom," *Insight and responsibility, op. cit.*

14. See Erik H. Erikson, *Young Man Luther, A Study in Psychoanalysis and History.* New York: W. W. Norton, 1958.

15. For an extensive bibliography on the history and recent use of Gandhi's methods, see *Nonviolent Direct Action,* edited by A. Paul Hare and Herbert H. Blumberg. Washington and Cleveland: Corpus Books, 1968.

16. See my review of *Thomas Woodrow Wilson* by Sigmund Freud and William C. Bullitt in *The New York Review of Books,* vol. VIII, no. 2, 1967.

17. *CWMG,* XV, 142.

18. Nikita S. Khrushchev, *The Crimes of the Stalin Era.* New York: The New Leader, 1962.

"March to the Sea"

1. Quoted in Louis Fischer, *The Life of Mahatma Gandhi.* p. 266.

2. M. K. Gandhi, *Satyagraha.* Ahmedabad: Navajivan, 1951, p. 233.

3. *Ibid.,* p. 234.

4. *Young India,* March 20, 1930. Quoted *ibid.,* pp. 236, 237.

5. Fischer, p. 273.

6. *Ibid.,* p. 274.

7. For a review of the statesman's period in Gandhi's life I suggest, in addition to the biographies cited, Penderel Moon, *Gandhi and Modern India.* New York: W. W. Norton, 1969.

IV. ON MORAL MATTERS

"The Golden Rule in the Light of New Insight"

1. C. H. Waddington, *The Ethical Animal.* London: Allen and Unwin, 1960.

2. H. F. Harlow and M. K. Harlow, "A Study of Animal Affection," *The Journal of the American Museum of Natural History,* 70:10, 1961.

3. Sigmund Freud, *The Origins of Psychoanalysis: Letters to Wilhelm Fliess, Drafts and Notes: 1887–1902,* edited by Marie Bonaparte, Anna Freud, and Ernst Kris. New York: Basic Books, 1954.

4. Erik H. Erikson, "Sex Differences in the Play Constructions of Pre-Adolescents," in *Discussions in Child Development,* World Health Organization, Vol. III, New York: International Universities Press, 1958. See also "Reflections on Womanhood," *Daedalus,* spring 1964.

5. Mahadev Haribhai Desai, *A Righteous Struggle.* Ahmedabad: Navajivan Publishing House, 1951.

INDEX